To our families,
who endured

MARKETING
AN ENVIRONMENTAL
PERSPECTIVE

MARKETING
AN ENVIRONMENTAL PERSPECTIVE

ROBERT F. GWINNER
Arizona State University

STEPHEN W. BROWN
Arizona State University

ALFRED J. HAGAN
The University of Texas at the Permian Basin

LONNIE L. OSTROM
Arizona State University

KENNETH L. ROWE
Arizona State University

JOHN L. SCHLACTER
Arizona State University

ALFRED H. SCHMIDT
Arizona State University

DAVID L. SHROCK
Arizona State University

West Publishing Company

St. Paul ▪ New York ▪ Boston ▪ Los Angeles ▪ San Francisco

COPYRIGHT © 1977 By WEST PUBLISHING CO.
All rights reserved
Printed in the United States of America

Library of Congress Cataloging in Publication Data
Main entry under title:

Marketing: an environmental perspective.

  Includes index.
  1. Marketing. I. Gwinner, Robert F.
HF5415.M295   658.8   76-29351
ISBN 0-8299-0119-1

PREFACE

Jim Warrick

Since 1960, the field of marketing has been dominated by a prevailing managerial philosophy. For well over a decade, this philosophy has served to produce scores of textbooks and scholarly articles that focus on the problems of managing marketing activities. Consequently, the study of marketing has concentrated on the decision making process and the efforts of the firm in the development of an integrated marketing program. Popularized as the managerial approach, this emphasis has provided a common framework for marketing textbooks for over fifteen years.

After nearly two decades, many marketing educators are now expressing some discontent with the managerial approach, particularly at the introductory level in those colleges and universities with advanced courses in marketing management and marketing decision making. In those schools, marketing educators have been faced with the difficult task of offering a relevant introductory course for a wide number of audiences, and at the same time, providing a sound conceptual base for students pursuing a major in the field of marketing. The net result has been a relatively unsatisfactory offering of two or more overlapping undergraduate marketing management type courses. The problem has been compounded in those schools providing a decision making orientation at the beginning graduate level.

Faced with the frustrations of dealing with the problem of overlap and duplication at the various levels of undergratuate and graduate education, the authors of this text have attempted to develop a book that can be used to satisfy the needs of the many audiences that seek a knowledge and understanding of marketing. The contention in this text is that these needs can best be met by asking the beginning student in marketing to explore the changing "world" that influences marketing activities. Consequently, the approach used here is heavily oriented to the environment that affects the marketing behavior of firms.

The environmental approach, of course, is not unique to this textbook. Over the past several years, a number of authors have attempted to produce a marketing text with an environmental framework. For the most part, however, these texts have been written in a micro context with a heavy managerial orientation. The end result has been a collection of fairly conventional marketing management textbooks with a limited environmental overview.

As a departure from traditional marketing management textbooks, this text does not use the marketing mix as a framework for analysis. Therefore, the traditional discussion of product, promotion, distribution, and pricing is presented here in a micro structure that focuses on marketing strategy planning. Instead of treating the mix elements in the depth that they are normally covered, the strategic dimensions of marketing are analyzed in a broader framework that recognizes the total marketing environment. This approach, in the authors' view, provides a more meaningful explanation of the "why" of marketing behavior in preference to the "what" of executive action.

In contrast to previous attempts to produce a marketing textbook with an environmental approach, this text provides a total environmental framework. The environment for marketing behavior and executive action is presented as two broad layers of influence. The first layer is the *micro environment,* where marketing activities must be performed in the business system under conditions of constraint imposed by other functional areas such as research and development, engineering, production, and finance. The second layer is the *macro environment,* external to the business system, where marketing institutions, legal forces, sociocultural changes, competition, technology, economic conditions, and the marketplace present both threats and opportunities for marketing.

Although this book presents marketing in an environmental setting, it is the impact of the changing environment on marketing strategy that is the dominant theme. Part I of the text presents an analysis of the marketing process and a detailed view of the environmental framework of the book. Part II explores the micro marketing environment from a strategic point of view, and Part III analyzes the macro marketing environment and the forces in constant change that influence marketing decision making. Part IV deals with contemporary issues in marketing through an in-depth discussion of important topics that are current and relevant to the efficient and effective operation of the marketing system.

As with all books, the errors of omission and commission are the responsibility of the authors. We do, however, wish to recognize the imprint of our colleagues in the Department of Marketing at Arizona State University who influenced the development of our ideas. These colleagues helped formulate the environmental approach used in the beginning course in marketing at ASU and played an important role in the final outcome of this volume.

Beyond our own little micro environment, we are indebted to a number of people who contributed in many ways to the culmination of this work. To Robert C. Boozer of West Publishing Company who served as a catalyst and friend, we owe special thanks. To Chris Gwinner for her tireless efforts in typing the many drafts of the manuscript and attending to thousands of details, we express our sincere appreciation.

For reviewing the manuscript and providing helpful and insightful suggestions, we would like to thank Professors Donald H. Granbois (Indiana University), Richard W. Hansen (Southern Methodist University), Douglas K. Hawes (University of Wyoming), Harold H. Kassarjian (University of California, Los Angeles), Fred L. Myrick, Jr.

(University of Alabama in Birmingham), and Arch G. Woodside, Jr. (University of South Carolina).

Finally, we would like to gratefully acknowledge those who edited our writings: Alice S. Keller from Austin, Texas, provided some "early on" assistance, and June Beeson and Jill Beeson from Tempe, Arizona, skillfully and painstakingly performed the monumental task of editing the final draft.

Robert F. Gwinner
Tempe, Arizona
December, 1976

CONTENTS

MARKETING
AN ENVIRONMENTAL PERSPECTIVE

ONE

MARKETING AND
ITS ENVIRONMENTS

Based on the presentation in Part I, the reader should be able to:

■ discuss the evolution of marketing in the United States and explain why change is the very essence of business

■ define marketing and understand its various dimensions in contemporary society

■ apply the concept of ecology to an understanding of the environmental approach to marketing

■ identify the role of marketing in a modern economic system and discuss both the micro and the macro process of marketing

■ describe the micro and the macro environments and identify the relationships that exist in the total marketing environment

■ discuss marketing in the changing environment as the basis for an analysis of environmental threat and marketing opportunity

1

THE MARKETING PROCESS

1

THE MARKETING PROCESS

This is a book about marketing. More importantly, however, it is a book about change, for success in marketing is dependent on management's ability to recognize and react to the rapidly changing environments that impact on marketing decision making. Therefore, the focus here is on the environments where forces in flux are confronting marketing management with a challenge that is growing at an ever expanding pace. This challenge was posed for all by Alvin Toffler when he wrote *Future Shock,* an extraordinary book about change and how we adapt to it. To be sure, Toffler did not write a marketing book, but he did provide a prophetic environmental clue for marketing when he stated that "between now and the twenty-first century, millions of ordinary, psychologically normal people will face an abrupt collision with the future."[1]

EVOLUTION OF MARKETING

The subject of change, of course, is a critically important one for the field of marketing. Change is the very essence of business, and it has occurred at an accelerated pace fueled by expanding technology and the growing demands of the consumer. While certainly revolutionary in many industries, such as electronics and communications, the impact of change has been more evolutionary in the overall development of marketing in the United States. This evolution may be identified through three rather distinct business eras that serve to characterize American industry since the end of the Civil War:

1. Production Era

2. Sales Era

3. Marketing Era

PRODUCTION ERA   With the advent of the industrial revolution in the United States about 1865, American industry entered an important production era that lasted through the first two decades of the twentieth century.[2] During this period, home handicraft operations were replaced by centralized manufacturing processes. Concurrently, there was a growth in urban centers and a decline in rural areas as large numbers of specialized workers were employed in urban factories. Spurred by industrial tycoons and a rapidly growing technology, great emphasis was placed on large-scale output and efficiency in production. The net result was the development of a mass production system that would one day be capable of producing an output that could exceed demand.

The overall impact of this important period of industrial development in the United States can be seen in some of the early innovations that distinguish the production era.[3] For example, the first consumer appliance became a reality during the middle of the nineteenth century in the form of a sewing machine developed and marketed by I. M. Singer and Company. Under the able leadership of Edward Clark, Singer soon dominated the market through a franchised agency system and later a unique and innovative branch sales office method of distribution. During this same production era, Procter and Gamble became a prominent consumer goods manufacturer with the introduction of Ivory Soap. Other great names such as General Mills, American Tobacco, Kellogg, Post, Pillsbury, and Ford became well known in America as the production era spawned the early industrial growth of the United States.

Henry Ford, of course, has been symbolized as the classic entrepreneur of the production era. As often noted, Ford wanted to make a relatively inexpensive automobile that could be produced in volume for the masses. To accomplish this objective, he concentrated on a single-chassis product in order to cut production costs and final selling prices. Through standardization, Ford implemented mass production methods and was successful in offering his famous Model T for $295. It is important to note, however, that Henry Ford was first and foremost a production specialist. He cared little for the individual interests and desires of the American consumer, and he never personally concerned himself with the cultivation of their favors. This fact has been highlighted in the frequently quoted statement from Ford that "any customer can have a car painted any color he wants so long as it's black."

Henry Ford's apparent lack of interest in the special needs of the consumer was a common characteristic among industrialists during the production era. The emphasis was clearly on production and the ultimate efficiency of the production system. Demand generally exceeded supply, and there was a prevailing "sellers market" as manufacturers were able to sell all that they could produce. With a concentration on the development of manufacturing facilities and an increase in productive output, marketing remained in its infancy until after World War I when the American economy began to shift to a "buyers market."

SALES ERA   Beginning about 1920, the need for a method of mass marketing to complement a flourishing mass production system was quickly recognized by American industry. The terms surplus and overproduction came into common use in industry as America's ability to produce exceeded the ability of her people to consume the bounties of mass production. The supply of many products began to catch up with the demand, and the need for a greater selling effort was apparent. With these developments, the United States economy moved into a sales era that lasted for nearly thirty years.

Covering the period from roughly 1920 through 1950, the sales era was dominated by an emphasis on sales management, advertising, and sales promotion. "Nothing happens until somebody sells something" became the theme for industry as sales management and supporting sales departments rose to prominence in the organization structure. When personal selling methods proved to be insufficient to completely handle the selling effort, advertising grew in importance and scope along with a new stature for the advertising department. The ultimate stress on selling came with the advent of the sales promotion department that was organized to bridge the gap between personal selling and advertising.

Thus, the sales era may be characterized as a period when American industry shifted from an emphasis on making things to an emphasis on selling things. The great prosperity of the 1920s brought selling into focus, and this activity of business continued to enjoy the spotlight in industry during the Great Depression of the 1930s. Business conditions changed dramatically in the 1940s, however, as the United States engaged in World War II, and consumers faced shortages in most goods and services. At the end of the war in 1945, there was a huge pent-up demand for all types of goods, and American industry once again enjoyed a sellers market throughout the remainder of the decade while building up the supply of goods and services that were unavailable during the war years.

1960 according to Prof Bessom

MARKETING ERA   By 1950, the American production system was producing an output unparalleled in economic history. Correspondingly, a strong element of competition served to provide the American consumer with a wide choice of goods and services. Very rapidly, therefore, the sellers market of the late 1940s gave way to a buyers market as supply began to exceed demand. With the dramatic change that materialized in the marketplace over the next few years, a parallel change occurred in industry's view of marketing.

From a dominant emphasis on selling and the corresponding stress on sales management, advertising, and sales promotion, industry began to recognize the broader scope of marketing that extends beyond the sales effort to customer and public relations, marketing research, distribution management, pricing policy, and product development. This recognition was further highlighted by the elevation of marketing to the top of the organization structure, on a level with production and finance, and the creation of a corporate vice-president in charge of the broader marketing function. These developments proved to be a significant move in terms of better coordination for marketing activities that had previously been performed in isolation by departments that operated as independent entities.

As the change in viewpoint regarding marketing has become more prevalent in American industry, it is now clear that marketing is a powerful and pervasive force in society; a force that influences and is influenced by many of our most basic social institutions. To even the casual observer, America is in a marketing era that has made it possible for marketing to come of age. It is clear that marketing is no longer in its infancy; this fact is evidenced by the role it now plays in society.

ROLE OF MARKETING

In today's modern world, marketing is both an adaptive and a formative agent of change. It is adaptive in that it must be responsive to environmental forces that are constantly changing, and it is a powerful formative influence through aggregate product development and marketing communications. As an agent of change in society, marketing is intimately involved in the creation and delivery of the goods and services necessary to provide the standard of living desired by the people. In an economic sense, this involvement centers around the allocation of goods and services, the creation of satisfaction, and the exchange of values.

ALLOCATION PROCESS

As painfully demonstrated by periods of shortages and scarcities in economic goods and services, mankind is faced with a problem of limited resources to satisfy almost insatiable desires. Society, in such a situation, attempts to solve this problem through an orderly allocation process that involves four basic stages (Figure 1.1). The first stage is concerned with extractive and agricultural activities where the produce of the earth is extracted and cultivated for further processing. The second is the fabrication and manufacturing stage that converts raw materials into processed and finished goods. The third stage involves distribution when the output of production is distributed to the market. Finally, the fourth stage is concerned with consumption as the end result of the allocation process.

As the interface between production and consumption, marketing is responsible for efficiently performing the distribution task and for making consumption dynamic. Marketing, therefore, is integrally involved in the allocation and use of society's scarce resources. Furthermore, as an influential link in the allocation process, marketing is vitally concerned with the determination of what is produced. Thus,

FIGURE 1.1.
THE ALLOCATION PROCESS

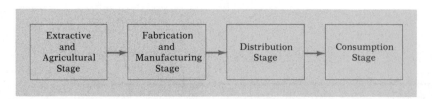

| Extractive and Agricultural Stage | Fabrication and Manufacturing Stage | Distribution Stage | Consumption Stage |

FIGURE 1.2.
UTILITY CREATION

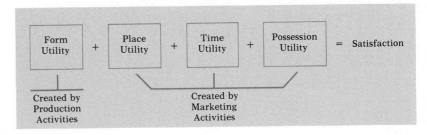

marketing plays a significant role in determining the type of products and services we buy, the kinds of places where we buy, and the time dimensions in which we buy. For the most part, this is an orderly process that results in a high level of consumer satisfaction. There are examples, however, that suggest that this is not always the case.

Many consumers, for instance, strongly feel that the American automobile industry has failed, at times, to meet the needs of the domestic car buyer. In the late 1950s, for example, Detroit built bigger and bigger automobiles with longer tailfins and more horsepower at a time when the car buyer was looking for an economical small car. It took a tremendous increase in foreign import sales for Detroit to finally react to consumer demand. This same phenomenon occurred in the late 1960s as Detroit again placed major emphasis on the production of large, high-powered automobiles. Rapidly declining sales and a significant fuel crisis in the early 1970s eventually forced the American automobile industry to think small cars once again.[4]

UTILITY CREATION

If these criticisms of the automobile industry are valid, even the casual observer could contend that the industry has failed to provide maximum satisfaction for the American car buyer. To the economist, this means that the industry has not created maximum utility in the process of producing and distributing American automobiles. Stated another way, the industry has failed somewhere along the way to get the right product, to the right buyer, at the right place, at the right time.

Defined as the want-satisfaction power of a product or service, *utility* has four distinct dimensions. These are: form, place, time, and possession (Figure 1.2). *Form* utility is created through production activities when the physical form of a raw material or a fabricated part is changed. For example, a tree growing in the forest may eventually become a piece of fine furniture as the form of the raw material is processed and changed. *Time, place,* and *possession* utility are created through marketing activities. When the furniture is produced, additional satisfaction can be derived if it is available where the consumer wishes to buy it (place utility), when he wants to buy it (time utility), and if he can secure title or ownership of the furniture (possession utility).

FIGURE 1.3.
THE EXCHANGE PROCESS

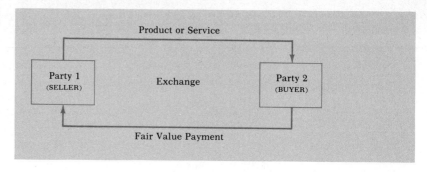

EXCHANGE PROCESS   For utility creation to be maximized, of course, there must be an exchange process. Consequently, a relevant condition of supply and demand coupled with the ability and willingness to buy must prevail in the marketplace. Suppliers, on the one hand, must offer products and services that meet the needs of their prospective buyers. In turn, these prospective buyers must view the product and service offerings as want-satisfiers. Finally, the prospective buyers must have the ability to pay for and the willingness to buy the goods and services that are offered. If all of these conditions prevail, a basis for exchange exists.

When an actual exchange takes place, there are two parties to the exchange. The first party gives up something that the second party wants in exchange for something that the first party wants and the second party is willing to give up. Thus, a buyer-seller relationship is established where the seller offers a product or service to a buyer in exchange for a payment in fair value (Figure 1.3).

The nature and extent of the exchange process, of course, vary considerably depending on the technological and cultural bases of society. Under the most primitive conditions where a money economy is nonexistent, exchange is limited generally to simple barter. For example, one party may own a pig, but no chickens. A second party who owns chickens is willing to give up five of these chickens for one of the neighbor's pigs. If the first party is agreeable, an exchange takes place; a trade of one commodity for a fair value payment in the form of another commodity. Under more advanced conditions where there is a money economy, exchange entails the trade of a product or service for a fair value payment in money. A college student, for example, is willing to exchange twenty hours of his week for wages (money) when he is offered and accepts a part-time job as a waiter at the local steakhouse.

PROCESS OF MARKETING

In an organized, well-developed economic system, a dynamic exchange process is facilitated by marketing activities that are designed to effectively and efficiently match supply and demand. It should be noted, however, that the marketing task must be evaluated at two rather distinct levels. The first level involves the aggregate matching of an economy's total supply of goods and services with total demand. Marketing activities at this level are *macro* in scope, and involve all suppliers and all demanders in the economic system. The second level is confined to the matching of small segments of supply and demand through marketing activities performed by individual productive units. This is the *micro* level of marketing that involves individual suppliers and a small number of demanders.

An appropriate distinction between the macro and micro levels of marketing is made in the analysis of gross national product (GNP). As the measure of aggregate economic activity in an economic system, GNP represents the total market value of all goods and services produced in a given year. The GNP component, of course, is derived from the productive output of literally thousands of individual production units operating at the micro level.

Given the above distinction, it is appropriate to analyze marketing as both a macro and a micro process. As noted, marketing in a macro context focuses on aggregate marketing activity in the economic system, whereas the marketing activity of the individual production unit is examined in a micro context. To provide a conceptual base for the analysis of marketing throughout this text, these two approaches to the study of the marketing process are discussed below.

MACRO PROCESS

As a macro process, marketing in the economic system has the responsibility of providing society with a desired assortment of goods and services when and where they are needed. The accomplishment of this task includes marketing activities on a wide scale as goods and services are sold to farmers, fabricators, manufacturers, wholesalers, retailers, governments, and final consumers. In the aggregate, therefore, a great deal of buying, selling, and physical movement takes place during the production and distribution process. In fact, the marketing activity at the consumer level is only a small part of the total. Far more goods and services are bought and sold by raw materials producers, manufacturers, wholesalers, and retailers than are bought by ultimate consumers.

As an example of the many exchanges that take place prior to final consumption, consider the purchase of a pair of top quality golf shoes. A dedicated golfer would most likely buy this item through his pro shop (a retail store) where the purchase represents one exchange. In all probability, the shoes are manufactured by a small producer. The steel, rubber, leather, dye, and other components that go into a pair of golf shoes, however, are most likely mined, fabricated, and produced by other production units. Each of these items is bought and sold by a number of raw materials producers, fabricators, manufacturers, and wholesale intermediaries throughout the production process prior to the final production and distribution of the shoes. Thus, many transactions precede the final transaction that is effected when the ultimate consumer of the golf shoes buys them from his favorite pro shop.

The really interesting aspect of the above example is that all of the production and marketing activities described take place as the result of the want or desire for golf shoes on the part of a large number of ultimate consumers. In a free enterprise economy, no one decrees or plans the allocation of the resources that are used in the production of golf shoes. Rather, the market directs the allocation of those resources. Through the self-regulating mechanism of a "free market," productive units compete with each other for the favor of the market. If golf shoes are in demand, the resources that go into that product are appropriately allocated and a profit opportunity exists for those business firms involved. In this manner, through aggregate resource utilization, the needs of society are met, resources are appropriately allocated, and industry profits by supplying a desired assortment of goods and services.

On balance, the macro marketing process appears to be a relatively simple procedure that results in the effective matching of supply and demand. There is, however, a radical heterogeneity among suppliers and demanders; heterogeneous is used here to identify the fact that dissimilarities exist between the two sides of the matching process. These dissimilarities create two major discrepancies that must be adjusted through marketing activities. First, there is a discrepancy in quantity when suppliers produce in very large quantities, and demanders buy in very small quantities. Second, there is a discrepancy in assortment when suppliers tend to specialize and produce in very narrow assortments, and demanders buy wide assortments to meet their needs for a variety of goods and services. A manufacturer of golf shoes, for example, may specialize in that one item and produce literally thousands of pairs of shoes. The golfer, on the other hand, generally buys only one pair of shoes at a time (discrepancy in quantity). Further, the golfer also demands a limited portion of the output of a number of different golfing equipment manufacturers in order to meet his need for a wide assortment of golfing gear (discrepancy in assortment).

Stated another way, macro marketing activity may be thought of as an orderly economic process that begins with a conglomeration of goods and services and ends with a desired assortment of goods and services. Through an organized process, marketing brings together heterogeneous supply on the one hand with heterogeneous demand on the other. This organized effort, which involves the use of marketing intermediaries, is referred to as the *sorting process.*[5] In total, the process entails four rather distinct operations. These are *sorting out,* which breaks heterogeneous conglomerations into specific types of goods; *accumulation,* which is concerned with the building-up of large quantities of homogeneous goods; *allocation,* which involves the breaking down of the large quantities into smaller quantities to more

FIGURE 1.4.
SIMPLIFIED DIAGRAM OF THE
SORTING PROCESS

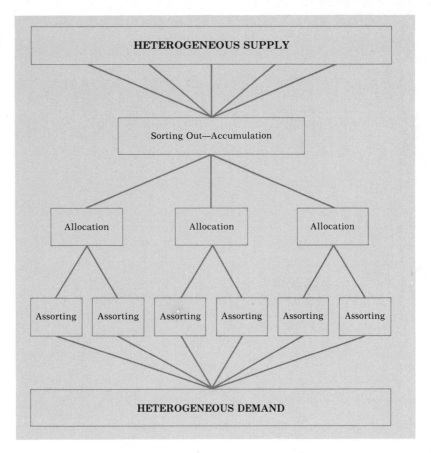

appropriately match demand; and *assorting,* which is the task of putting together unlike goods in desired assortments. A simplified diagram of the sorting process is presented in Figure 1.4.

Sorting out.   As a solution to the discrepancy in assortment that exists between supply and demand, the sorting out operation handles the task of bringing together the output of a number of specialized producers. A large wholesaler of food and grocery items, for example, performs this operation when he buys and "sorts out" the output of several different processors specializing in the processing of different kinds of food. Based on accepted standards and grades that are uniformly established, the wholesaler separates his inventory into homogeneous lots of like quality and brand for further distribution. Those wholesalers and retailers specializing in certain types of food, specific quality, and even specified brands can then have one single source of supply in preference to having to purchase from the larger number of individual food processors. The sorting out operation is simplified, of course, where standards, grades, and accepted brands are common. The operation is far more complex in the absence of some degree of uniformity. Sorting out meat, which is graded prime, choice, good, utility, and commercial, is a much simpler operation than the sorting out of many agricultural products, which vary in quality due to the whims of nature. Complications often arise because of the difficulty in maintaining established standards. Plywood grades, for instance, are set by an industry association, but the variable quality of peeler logs makes it most difficult to maintain accepted standards.

Accumulation.   Once goods have been sorted out into homogeneous lots, the accumulation operation begins as accumulators build up substantial supplies for market requirements. The large wholesaler used in the example above performs this operation when he buys the output of a number of processors and collects large quantities for further distribution. In this case the wholesaler, or the accumulator, effects definite economies in storage, transportation, and procurement. Specialized warehouse operations, such as grain elevators and cold storage facilities, can be utilized to gain economies of scale; lower cost carload shipments can be made; and procurement that takes advantage of quantity discounts and a ready source of supply can be realized.

Allocation.   When economical quantities have been accumulated, they are ready for movement closer to the final user or consumer. This occurs through the allocation operation; that is, the breaking down of the large accumulations into smaller quantities that more appropriately match demand. Thus, allocation is often referred to as breaking bulk. The large wholesaler used in previous examples allocates, or breaks bulk, when he sells to smaller wholesalers. Correspondingly, the smaller wholesaler breaks bulk when he sells to retailers, and the retailer breaks bulk when he sells to final consumers. Throughout the allocation operation, the discrepancy in quantity between supply and demand is solved as each successive demand unit buys in desired quantities.

Assorting.   The final phase of the sorting process is the assorting operation, which involves the task of putting together a line of heterogeneous products that match demand. The assorting operation, therefore, provides a solution to the discrepancy in assortment that exists between supply and demand. Although this operation is performed at both the wholesale and retail levels of distribution, it is normally done by those closest to the final user or consumer. A department store is an excellent illustration of a retailer that carries a highly heterogeneous line of merchandise. The customers of the department store can and do find a wide array of merchandise to meet their needs. Conversely, the manufacturers and wholesalers supplying the department store tend to be more specialized in their merchandise offerings.

MICRO PROCESS   As discussed above, the macro process of marketing involves the aggregate flow of goods and services in the economic system. The efficient operation of the total system, however, is dependent on the effectiveness of individual productive units in the system. A more finite evaluation of marketing must focus on the micro level where individual firms and organizations vie for the expenditures for goods and services by members of society. The micro process of marketing, therefore, involves the strategic and tactical moves of firms and organizations. In the individual productive unit, these tasks are assigned normally to a marketing department or a marketing function that is responsible for the formulation of a general marketing plan, the execution of the plan, and the control of the marketing operation. That is, marketing at the *micro* level is concerned with planning, execution, and control.

Marketing planning. The development of a marketing plan is the very cornerstone of the micro marketing process, for marketing planning entails the selection of a specific market and the development of a marketing mix that will meet the needs of that market. Each of these tasks is distinct in nature, but they are closely related in actual practice. While markets are selected on the basis of potential customers, selection must be tempered by the ability to provide appropriate marketing mixes. Furthermore, as will be discussed later, marketing planning is constrained by both micro and macro environmental forces.

Marketing execution. Whereas marketing planning involves the selection of markets and the development of marketing mixes, marketing execution is concerned with getting the right product or service to the right place at the right price at the right time. In this phase of the micro marketing process, the marketing mix becomes a reality in the form of four basic components. These are product, price, promotion, and distribution. The execution of the marketing plan, therefore, can be viewed as a process that involves the matching of an organization's marketing output with market requirements. When a product offering is appropriately priced, properly promoted, and effectively distributed, a successful market match is realized if that total mix meets the needs of the market and the objectives of the individual marketing unit.

Marketing control. To ensure successful market matches, marketing control must be exercised. This phase of the micro marketing process is devoted to a continuing evaluation and analysis of the marketing plan. Like a thermostat on a furnace, marketing control is designed to react to deviations from the plan and make corrective adjustments. Marketing control, therefore, operates as a feedback mechanism that influences marketing planning. When the marketing program is functioning according to plan, the control mechanism monitors feedback that suggests no need for corrective adjustments. If, however, the program is out of balance, feedback will so indicate and corrections in the program can be made.

A practical illustration of the micro marketing process can be seen in Ford Motor Company's introduction of the now famous Mustang automobile. Introduced in the spring of 1964, this product offering enjoyed phenomenal success under the leadership of Ford's President Lee A. Iacocca, who was then a vice-president in one of Ford's major divisions. A hindsight review of the 1964 market reveals that Ford correctly identified a market that was not being satisfied by American automobile manufacturers. The company offered the Mustang to fill that need, priced it very competitively, promoted it excellently, and distributed it through readily available Ford dealerships. Over time, adjustments were made in design, price, and promotion to meet changing market requirements, and the Mustang continued as a viable product offering in a highly competitive industry.

While success stories such as the Mustang abound in American marketing history, there are numerous examples of colossal failures to attest to the fact that marketing planning is not infallible; it can produce disasters.

Ironically, one of the classic marketing failures of all times was produced by Ford Motor Company less than a decade before the introduction of the Mustang. That disaster, of course, was the Edsel. In the mid-1950s, Ford assessed the market and determined that the company was losing out to General Motors in the big and medium-sized market where GM was dominant with its "BOP" lines—Buick, Oldsmobile, and Pontiac. In an effort to compete in this market, Ford offered the Edsel in the fall of 1957. Three years later, in 1960, the company withdrew the Edsel after a loss of millions of dollars and a great deal of prestige. Many factors were involved in the demise of the Edsel, but poor marketing planning on the part of Ford was a significant part of the overall problem that faced the Edsel automobile from the very beginning.[6]

APPROACHES TO THE STUDY OF MARKETING

From the above discussion of the marketing process, it should be apparent that the study of marketing can be approached from two distinct levels. There are a number of ways to view most things, and marketing is no exception. Consider, for example, the football fan: some prefer to watch the game through the eyes of a television camera, where instant replays and expert commentary chart the flow of the game. The purist, on the other hand, must attend the game in order to savor in person the action, the players, and the other fans. That is, there are differences of opinion about the best way to enjoy the game of football. And there are differences of opinion about how students can best be taught in order to learn and understand the subject of marketing. The primary differences can be grouped into two large classes designated as macro approaches and micro approaches.

MACRO APPROACHES

Those favoring the study of marketing as a broad economic activity have adopted the macro approach. As in the case of the macro process of marketing, the study of marketing in these approaches concentrates on aggregate marketing activities. The most commonly accepted macro approaches emphasize commodities, functions, and institutions.

Commodity approach. In its pure form, this approach to the study of marketing concentrates on the movement of individual commodities or goods from points of production to final users or consumers. Special attention is given to sources of supply, the nature of demand, common channels of distribution, and the special problems that are associated with the marketing of a specific commodity. Because of its repetitive nature in covering many of the same concepts that apply to a variety of commodities, this approach has been modified to deal with broad classes of commodities or goods, such as minerals, agricultural produce, or processed goods. For the most part, it is used only in highly specialized programs, such as those offered in schools and colleges of agriculture. Seldom, if ever, is it used in the more broadly based schools of business administration.

Functional approach. The second macro approach to the study of marketing is *physiological* in nature in that it concentrates on the activities performed in marketing.[7] In this approach, emphasis is given to the functioning or physiology of the total marketing system as it engages in the transfer of ownership and the movement of goods from production to consumption or final use. A description of the commonly accepted marketing functions by type of function and utility created is presented in Table 1.1.

TABLE 1.1.
MARKETING FUNCTIONS

Functions	Type of Function	Utility Created
Buying	Exchange	Possession
Selling	Exchange	Possession
Transportation	Physical Supply	Place
Storage	Physical Supply	Time
Standardization and Grading	Facilitating	None
Market Information	Facilitating	None
Market Risk	Facilitating	None
Market Finance	Facilitating	None

NOTE: Buying and selling are functions of exchange, while transportation and storage are functions of physical supply. The remaining four functions facilitate the performance of the first four and no utility is created through their performance.

Institutional approach.   The final macro approach to the study of marketing—the institutional approach—focuses on the institutional structure of the total marketing system.[8] In this approach, the marketing activities of retailers, wholesalers, manufacturers, and other institutions such as transportation companies are analyzed in great detail. Special attention is given to type of operation, economic importance, the competitive environment, institutional trends, and cost of operation. Valuable institutional data are published regularly by the United States Bureau of the Census on manufacturing, wholesale trade, retail trade, and service industries in recognition of the importance of the institutions that engage in marketing activities. A more detailed view of the institutional structure is presented in Chapter 7 on the macro marketing system, and in Chapter 8 on the institutional environment.

MICRO APPROACHES   In contrast to the broader macro approaches to the study of marketing, the micro approaches concentrate on the marketing activities of individual firms or organizations in the economic system. Marketing is viewed from the perspective of management in preference to the perspective offered by the economic system. Special attention is given to the micro process of marketing with a stress on the strategic dimensions of marketing activities. The micro approaches have been popularly designated the "managerial approach" and the "systems approach."

Managerial approach.   In viewing marketing through the eyes of the marketing manager, the managerial approach to the subject area focuses on the decisions that must be made by management. As popularized by McCarthy and others, these decisions center around the four marketing strategy variables of product, pricing, promotion, and distribution.[9] These variables are considered to be within the control of the marketing manager, who makes decisions in each of the four areas while being constrained by a set of uncontrollable variables, such as competition, technology, and demand. This approach is a useful one, and it did provide a fresh departure from the macro approaches to the study of marketing that were dominant until the early 1960s.

Systems approach.   In an effort to extend the managerial approach, some marketing scholars have attempted to draw on the work of management scientists and electrical engineers to develop a systems approach to the study of marketing.[10] For the most part, these attempts have been made in a micro context wherein the individual firm or organization is viewed as an operating system. The results, however, have been somewhat disappointing as most writers employing the systems approach have failed to adequately develop a total systems framework that is specifically different from the generally accepted managerial approach. Consequently, the systems approach in marketing leaves something to be desired in contemporary marketing literature.

APPROACH USED IN THIS BOOK   In an effort to overcome some of the problems inherent in both the macro and the micro approaches to the study of marketing, this book focuses on marketing and its environments. The basic reason for approaching the subject area in this manner is that an environmental analysis is essential to an understanding of the marketing process. Such an analysis recognizes the fact that marketing activities are not performed in a vacuum, apart from surrounding forces that are in a constant state of change. Clearly, marketing is influenced by its environments and must operate within the constraints imposed by those environments. But in addition, as noted earlier, marketing exerts its own influence in effecting change in the environments. Consequently, the environments define the very nature of marketing's existence and an environmental framework is a most logical one for analyzing the subject area of marketing.

Interest in the environment, of course, is not new. The study of ecology—the relationship between organisms and their environments—has been popular in the biological sciences for a number of years. The study has received increased attention in recent years as man has become concerned over the problems associated with the pollution of land, air, and water.

As used in this book, the term environment has much broader connotations that include all of the forces that surround the activities of marketing. The analysis is expanded to the *total environment,* which contains both the micro and macro forces that influence and are influenced by marketing. The environmental approach, therefore, incorporates the managerial and the societal dimensions of marketing in recognition of the fact that the field is concerned with more than the mere supply of a better and greater quantity of goods and services. As an agent of change in society, marketing also is heavily involved in the quality of life. The major advantage of the environmental approach is that it provides an opportunity to analyze marketing's influence on both the *quantitative* and the *qualitative* factors associated with man's standard of living. This will be discussed in greater detail in Chapter 2, but it should be noted here that the study of marketing using the environmental approach provides an opportunity for the student to look outside the firm and thereby become more keenly aware of marketing's role in society.

DEFINITIONS OF MARKETING

From the preceding discussion of marketing, it is now possible to offer a more precise definition of the term. As in the case of any subject matter, however, definitions are not always easy to formulate. This is certainly true in the field of marketing, for there are as many definitions of marketing as there are marketing textbooks. Before presenting the definition of marketing used in this text, therefore, a brief review of several commonly offered definitions is presented below following the macro and the micro frameworks established in this chapter.

MACRO DEFINITIONS

One of the broadest and most expressive statements of marketing was written a number of years ago by Paul Mazur. He viewed marketing as *the delivery of a standard of living to society.*[11] This notion was later amended by Professor Malcolm McNair of Harvard University when he defined marketing as *the creation and delivery of a standard of living to society.*

A somewhat narrower definition was proposed by the American Marketing Association's Committee on Definitions when it said that *"marketing is the performance of business activities that direct the flow of goods and services from producer to consumer or users."*[12] Unfortunately, this view of marketing reflects a strong production orientation that suggests that marketing begins at the end of the production line and ends with the final sale.

In an effort to broaden the above definition, McCarthy proposed the idea that *"marketing is concerned with designing an efficient (in terms of use of resources) and fair (in terms of distribution of output to all parties involved) system which will direct an economy's flow of goods and services from producers to consumers and accomplish the objectives of the society."*[13] In this definition, it may be noted that McCarthy stresses the objectives of society.

MICRO DEFINITIONS

For the micro level, McCarthy refined his macro definition with the view that *"marketing is the performance of business activities which direct the flow of goods and services from producer to consumer or user in order to satisfy customers and accomplish the company's objectives."*[14] In contrast to his macro definition, McCarthy emphasizes company objectives in his micro view of marketing.

As a more finite micro definition of marketing, Stanton proposed the notion that *"marketing is a total system of interacting business activities designed to plan, price, promote, and distribute want-satisfying products and services to present and potential customers."*[15] This, of course, is a pure managerial definition of marketing stressing the management tasks associated with the micro marketing process.

DEFINITIONS USED IN THIS BOOK

A detailed analysis of the above definitions of marketing reveals a number of commonalities and at least one glaring omission. First, the notion of exchange appears to be a dominant theme. Second, society is the main focal point in the macro definitions. Third, the concept of customer satisfaction is especially significant in the micro definitions. The glaring omission in all of the definitions is the absence of any mention of the significance of the environment in the marketing process. In an effort to overcome this weakness in all of the widely offered definitions of marketing, the following definitions will be used in this text:

environmental

> From a macro standpoint, marketing is concerned with the creation and delivery of a desired standard of living for society through the effective and efficient distribution of an economy's goods and services under conditions of constraint imposed by the marketing environments.
>
> From a micro standpoint, marketing is concerned with the satisfaction of customer needs and the accomplishment of an organization's marketing objectives through the efficient and effective distribution of that organization's goods and services under conditions of constraint imposed by the marketing environments.

When carefully examined, these definitions suggest several important implications. First, they are environmental in scope, emphasizing the idea that marketing activities are conducted under conditions of environmental constraint. Second, they provide a clear distinction between the macro and the micro levels of marketing. Third, they define the role of marketing in society and in the individual organization from the standpoint of the objectives established for each.

MARKETING IN CONTEMPORARY SOCIETY

From the preceding definitions it should be apparent that marketing is a most pervasive force. There are several key dimensions of the term marketing that should be expanded, however, to provide a more meaningful picture of the role of marketing in a modern economy. The remainder of this chapter, therefore, is devoted to a brief discussion of the economic, managerial, environmental, and societal dimensions of marketing as they relate to the marketing process in contemporary society.

ECONOMIC DIMENSIONS

From an economic standpoint, marketing is a highly significant form of human activity in a modern economy. In the United States, for example, the gross national product rose from slightly less than $300 billion in 1950 to over $1 trillion by the early 1970s. Marketing, of course, played a vital role in this growth since it had the responsibility of moving the output of goods and services produced over that period.

By any measure of economic activity, the results were no less than phenomenal. It should be noted, however, that the high level of economic activity enjoyed by the United States would not have been possible without a correspondingly high level of marketing activity.

The economic significance of marketing can be seen in the number of institutions involved in marketing activities. By the early 1970s in the United States, for example, there were over four million organizations of all types engaged to some degree in marketing. A large majority of these were involved solely in marketing, while the others facilitated the marketing process. Over 1.7 million retailers, 380,000 wholesalers, and 42,000 transportation companies were in operation in 1971. These organizations, of course, do not include supporting operations such as advertising agencies, public warehouses, and communication firms that provide support to the economy's marketing function.

In terms of economic value, it is estimated that between 40 and 60 percent of the final selling price of all tangible goods goes toward the creation of time, place, and possession utility. This means that marketing accounts for approximately 50 cents of every dollar spent on tangible goods. To critics, this represents an intolerably high cost for marketing activities. On the other hand, the question of whether marketing costs enough becomes a viable issue when marketing is examined from the standpoint of creating want-satisfying products for society. To be sure, the American consumer continues to enjoy the greatest selection of goods available in the world.

MANAGERIAL DIMENSIONS

The scope and importance of marketing in contemporary society can be further highlighted when examined from the viewpoint of modern management. From a rather low position in the managerial hierarchy, marketing has been elevated to the very top of the modern, progressive business organization. As management philosophy evolved from a production-oriented through a sales-oriented to a marketing-oriented view of business, the marketing manager emerged as a key figure in the organization. As a result, the role of marketing as a force in the long-run survival of the firm was expanded far beyond earlier days when marketing was equated with selling. This trend can be seen best in the changes that have occurred in organizational structure as sales departments were redesignated marketing departments and the top marketing man in the organization became a vice-president of marketing instead of a sales manager.

The movement toward a marketing orientation for business has been popularized as the "marketing concept." Rather than being a concept, however, a marketing orientation is really a whole new philosophy of business that replaces production and sales orientations. Firms operating under a production orientation focus on manufacturing and the internal activities of the organization while seeking profits through manufacturing efficiency. Their managerial philosophy is

FIGURE 1.5.
HISTORICAL EVOLUTION OF
THE MARKETING
ORIENTATION

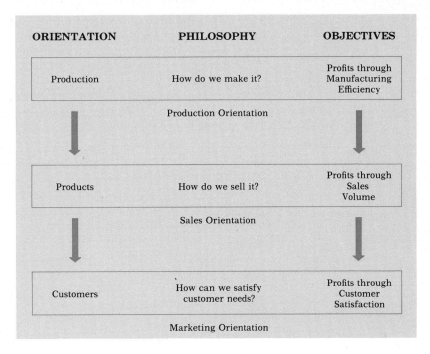

simply "How do we make it?" Sales oriented firms tend to focus on products in order to profit through sales volume. "This is what we make—how do we sell it?" best describes their managerial philosophy. In sharp contrast, marketing oriented firms focus on customers and seek profits through customer satisfaction. Their managerial philosophy is "What are our customers' problems and how can we help solve those problems?" A graphic presentation of the evolutionary movement toward a marketing orientation for business is shown in Figure 1.5.

Although it is somewhat idealistic to assume that all business organizations are marketing oriented, there are countless examples of modern firms that have accepted this philosophy as the "way to conduct the business of business." In describing how a marketing orientation can evolve in an organization, Robert J. Keith of Pillsbury, Inc., preferred to use the term "marketing revolution" when he traced the change in philosophy that took place in one of America's oldest manufacturers of flour, cake mixes, and animal feeds:[16]

Formed in 1869 as a professional flour miller, Pillsbury went through a *production oriented* era that lasted until 1930. Products were relatively scarce during this period, and Pillsbury's most important function was production. From 1930 to about 1950, the company was in a *sales oriented* era as it concentrated on getting customers and preventing dealers from seeking other sources of supply. By 1950, Pillsbury had developed cake mixes and was enjoying great success. At that time, marketing became an integral part of the company as the advertising and sales promotion departments were dissolved into one coordinating policy-making body. With these changes and others, Pillsbury moved into a *marketing oriented* era as marketing began to permeate the entire organization. It was during this period and as a direct result of a new marketing philosophy that Pillsbury began to emerge as a "marketing company."

The above example serves to illustrate how a unified focus can provide a dynamic thrust for an organization. It may be difficult, therefore, to understand why every company does not adopt a marketing orientation. Unfortunately, clear logic does not always prevail as separate and unique entities develop in an organization structure. Production, for example, is concerned with manufacturing efficiency. Finance, on the other hand, is absorbed with the company's financial position. Marketing is interested in getting out want-satisfying products. If the company is successful, no one seems to notice that each group may be engrossed in its own operation. High fences can be erected around each domain, and all may go well until some adversity such as a fall in profits or sales occurs. At that point, there is always a real concern over how it happened. A marketing orientation is not a panacea, or a cure-all, for business ills, but it does provide a systematic approach for the management of an organization. There is a common focus—customers—that serves to bring operational entities together. When this is accomplished, the organization can function as a total system. It should be apparent, therefore, that marketing is a powerful internal force in its influence on management.

ENVIRONMENTAL DIMENSIONS

Even though a marketing orientation is a most logical one for management, it has been pointed out that business does not operate in a vacuum. The study of marketing, therefore, cannot be confined to the organization and the management of the marketing function. It must include the interaction between the organization and its environments; the environmental dimension of marketing is critically important to an understanding of the role of marketing in contemporary society.

As discussed in greater detail in Chapter 2, two separate and distinct broad environments surround and potentially affect the practice of marketing. The first is the *micro environment,* where marketing interacts with other semiautonomous units within the organizational structure, such as production, engineering, research and development, and finance. The micro environment is internal within the organization. The second is the *macro environment* that surrounds the organization externally; it includes all of the various forces and institutions that may impinge on marketing from outside the organization.

Both the macro and the micro environments may be characterized as forces in flux. Consequently, environmental conditions must be constantly monitored to detect changes that may dictate alterations in the marketing program. This is an extremely important dimension of marketing, and it is one that requires the careful attention of marketing management, for even the slightest change in the environments can often make the difference between failure and success.

SOCIETAL DIMENSIONS

In addition to the economic, managerial, and environmental dimensions, marketing also has an important societal dimension that further defines its role. Historically, that role predominantly involved the creation and delivery of a *quantitative* standard of living in the form of more and better goods and services. In contemporary society, however, marketing is being challenged to include the *qualitative* aspects of life. The critics of marketing, for example, contend that marketing must be more responsive to the social needs of society that are over and beyond those needs associated with the consumption of goods and services. This view was expressed by an academician in the field in this way:

> Marketing personnel are at the interface between company and society. In this position they have the responsibility not merely for designing a competitive marketing strategy, but for sensitizing business to the social, as well as the product, demand of society.[17]

The idea that marketing should be concerned with society's social needs is one that contrasts sharply with the more traditional notion that marketing's major responsibility is to provide goods and services to satisfy consumer needs in a profitable and efficient manner. The social view broadens the economic dimensions of marketing to include both economic and social growth. Marketing may be viewed, therefore, as a social discipline with commensurate social responsibilities.

Recent government attention to the areas of product safety, packaging regulations, product warranties, credit practices, truth in advertising, and pricing practices serve to emphasize the broad social nature of marketing. As the referee in the game of business, government has been forced to enact legislation in a number of these areas to protect the consumer. In the absence of socially responsible actions by marketing, it is likely that additional legislation may be enacted. As one writer points out:

> There have been discussions about limiting the amount that can be spent on advertising for a product, about controlling trading stamps, about investigating various promotional devices and marketing activities. Such actions pose serious questions about marketing's social role. If we do not answer them, others will; and perhaps in a manner not too pleasing, or even realistic.[18]

Based on the brief commentary in this section, it should be apparent that the societal dimension of marketing is an important one. Furthermore, current literature suggests that social issues will become even more important as society faces the challenge of the future. This matter will be discussed in greater depth in Chapter 11, but it should be noted here that corporate goals need not be incompatible with the goals of society at large. This view is summarized most effectively in the following statement:

> There need be no wide chasm between the profit motive and social responsibility, between corporate marketing objectives and social goals, between marketing actions and public welfare. What is required is a broader perception and definition of marketing than has hitherto been the case—one that recognizes marketing's societal dimensions and perceives of marketing as more than just a technology of the firm. For the multiple contributions of marketing that are so necessary to meet business challenges, here and abroad, are also necessary to meet the nation's social and cultural problems.[19]

SUMMARY   This chapter places marketing in historical perspective through a discussion of the evolution of marketing during three rather distinct business eras that characterize American industry since the end of the Civil War. In providing an overview of the marketing process, it has been pointed out that marketing is both an adaptive and a formative agent of change in society and that the role of marketing centers around the allocation of goods and services, the creation of satisfaction, and the exchange of values. Thus, marketing plays a significant part in the type of products and services the consumer buys, the kinds of places where the consumer buys, and the time dimensions in which the consumer buys.

The process of marketing at both the macro and the micro levels was discussed as a conceptual base for the analysis of marketing throughout this text. Following this framework, both the macro and the micro approaches to the study of marketing were analyzed as a contrast to the environmental approach that is used in this book. To provide a conceptualization of the field of marketing, common definitions of the subject area were presented in both a macro and a micro context as a comparison to the environmental definitions offered here.

Finally, this chapter analyzed the economic, managerial, environmental, and societal dimensions of marketing as they relate to the marketing process in contemporary society. This analysis was presented in an effort to provide a more meaningful picture of marketing in a modern, affluent economy such as the United States.

QUESTIONS FOR DISCUSSION

1. Explain the meaning and significance of Toffler's view in *Future Shock* that "... between now and the twenty-first century, millions of ordinary, psychologically normal people will face an abrupt collision with the future."

2. Identify and briefly describe the three business eras that characterize American industry since the end of the Civil War. In your discussion, identify the nature and scope of marketing in each era.

3. Marketing has been characterized as both an adaptive and a formative agent of change in society. Explain the meaning of this characterization in an environmental context.

4. Compare and contrast the *macro* process of marketing with the *micro* process.

5. Using the Mustang and the Edsel as examples, explain how one company can experience a dismal failure and enjoy a phenomenal success in the same market within a relatively short period of time.

6. Compare and contrast the *macro* approach to the study of marketing with the *micro* approach. How does the environmental approach differ with these two approaches?

7. Define marketing in both a *macro* and a *micro* context.

8. How do you account for the fact that marketing costs may equal or exceed the costs of production? Does this mean that marketing costs are too high?

9. Explain the managerial philosophy in an organization that has adopted a marketing orientation. How does this philosophy differ with those associated with both a production and a sales orientation?

10. Distinguish between the *micro* and the *macro* environments of marketing. Which one of these two environments would have the greatest impact on the resource support for a new product innovation? Which would have the greatest impact on the ultimate success of the innovation? Explain in both a short-term and a long-term context.

11. How and in what ways is marketing involved in both the quantitative and qualitative aspects of life? In contemporary society, which of these two is the most important? Why?

12. Define and briefly explain each of the following:
    a. Allocation process
    b. Utility
    c. Exchange process
    d. Sorting process
    e. Marketing planning
    f. Marketing execution
    g. Marketing control
    h. Social responsibility

NOTES

[1] Alvin Toffler, *Future Shock* (New York: Random House, Inc., 1970), p. 9.

[2] While the industrial revolution began in England during the latter part of the eighteenth century, industrialization in the United States did not materialize until after the Civil War.

[3] Innovation as used here follows the Schumpeter view that innovation is the

setting up of a new production function. To Schumpeter, invention is the discovery of new products and production processes, while innovation is the commercial utilization of inventions. For a detailed discussion, see the extensive writings of Joseph A. Schumpeter in the economics literature of the 1930s and 1940s.

[4]See "A Beleaguered Detroit Fights Back," *Newsweek* (April 6, 1970), for a good discussion of the general condition of the automobile industry in 1970 and a general review of Detroit's plans to introduce the new sub-compacts of 1970.

[5]See Wroe Alderson, *Marketing Behavior and Executive Action* (Homewood, Illinois: Richard D. Irwin, Inc., 1957), pp. 201–211.

[6]For two excellent articles on the Edsel, see William H. Reynolds, "The Edsel Ten Years Later," *Business Horizons* (Fall, 1967), pp. 39–46; and "Gigantic and Full Meaning: The Rise of the Edsel," in John Brooks, *The Fate of the Edsel and Other Business Adventures* (New York: Harper and Row, Publishers, 1960).

[7]As an example of a traditional marketing textbook using the functional approach see Theodore N. Beckman, William R. Davidson, and W. Wayne Talarzyk, *Marketing* (9th ed.; New York: The Ronald Press Co., 1973).

[8]For an example of a traditional marketing textbook with a heavy emphasis on marketing institutions, see Charles F. Phillips and Delbert J. Duncan, *Marketing Principles and Methods* (6th ed.; Homewood, Illinois: Richard D. Irwin, Inc., 1968).

[9]Three of the best known and most widely adopted textbooks using the managerial approach are E. Jerome McCarthy, *Basic Marketing: A Managerial Approach* (5th ed.; Homewood, Illinois: Richard D. Irwin, Inc., 1976); William J. Stanton, *Fundamentals of Marketing* (4th ed.; New York: McGraw-Hill Book Company, 1975); and Philip Kotler, *Marketing Management—Analysis, Planning, and Control* (3rd ed.; Englewood Cliffs, N.J.: Prentice-Hall, Inc., 1976).

[10]For one of the most comprehensive treatments of the systems approach, see George Fisk, *Marketing Systems: An Introductory Analysis* (New York: Harper and Row, Publishers, 1967).

[11]Paul Mazur, "Does Distribution Cost Enough?," *Fortune* (November, 1947), p. 138.

[12]Committee on Definitions, *Marketing Definitions: A Glossary of Marketing Terms* (Chicago: American Marketing Association, 1960), p. 15.

[13]McCarthy, *Basic Marketing,* pp. 18–19.

[14]*Ibid.,* p. 19

[15]Stanton, *Fundamentals of Marketing,* p. 5.

[16]Robert J. Keith, "The Marketing Revolution," *Journal of Marketing* (January, 1960), pp. 35–38.

[17]Reprinted from Louis L. Stern, "Consumer Protection Via Self Regulation," *Journal of Marketing* (July, 1971), p. 53. Published by the American Marketing Association.

[18]Reprinted from William Lazer, "Marketing's Changing Social Relationships," *Journal of Marketing* (January, 1969), p. 9. Published by the American Marketing Association.

[19]*Ibid.*

SUGGESTED READINGS

Anderson, W. Thomas, Jr., Catherine Carlisle Bentley, and Louis K. Sharpe, *Multidimensional Marketing: Managerial, Societal, Philosophical* (Austin, Texas: Austin Press, 1976).

Bagozzi, Richard P., "Marketing as Exchange," *Journal of Marketing* (October, 1975), pp. 32–39.

Barksdale, Hiram C. and Bill Darden, "Marketers' Attitudes Toward the Marketing Concept," *Journal of Marketing* (October, 1971), pp. 28–36.

Kotler, Philip, *Marketing Management: Analysis Planning and Control* (3rd ed.; Englewood Cliffs, New Jersey: Prentice-Hall, Inc., 1976).

Kotler, Philip, "The Major Tasks of Marketing Management," *Journal of Marketing* (October, 1973), pp. 42–49.

McCarthy, E. Jerome, *Basic Marketing: A Managerial Approach* (5th ed.; Homewood, Illinois: Richard D. Irwin, Inc., 1975).

Stanton, William J., *Fundamentals of Marketing* (4th ed.; New York: McGraw-Hill Book Company, 1975).

Steiner, George A., "Changing Managerial Philosophies," *Business Horizons* (June, 1971), pp. 5–10.

Toffler, Alvin, *Future Shock* (New York: Random House, Inc., 1970).

Webster, Frederick E., Jr., *Social Aspects of Marketing* (Englewood Cliffs, New Jersey: Prentice-Hall, Inc., 1974).

2

THE MARKETING ENVIRONMENTS

THE MARKETING ENVIRONMENTS

In Chapter 1, the process of marketing was described as an economic activity that is intimately involved with the creation and delivery of goods and services needed to maintain a specific standard of living. Marketing, therefore, is an external business function that is conducted primarily outside the confines of the firm as contrasted to production, which is strictly an internal operation. Consequently, the process of marketing is a highly visible and responsible one to society that cannot be performed in a vacuum. To the contrary, it is the one economic activity in the business firm that influences and receives the most influence from the environments that impinge upon its performance. This chapter will focus on the marketing environments and their influence on the effective and efficient creation and delivery of mankind's standard of living.

ENVIRONMENTAL APPROACH TO MARKETING

In today's world, the pressures toward behaving with relevance are being felt on every corner and in every facet of human endeavor. These pressures come from many different sources—from students in the universities, from businessmen, from consumers—and they are providing some very real challenges to both the study and the practice of marketing. Fortunately, there is a positive benefit here in that the cry for greater relevancy is producing more awareness of the expanded role that marketing must play, and an appreciation for the development of new methodologies to deal with marketing problems. This is where the environmental approach enters the picture.

As contrasted to the more traditional approaches to the study of marketing that were discussed in Chapter 1, the environmental approach deals more finitely with the marketing environments that represent the forces in flux that impact on marketing decision making. The focus, therefore, is on environmental change and the manner in which marketers deal with it. First of all, there is the question of how to promote and facilitate change and how to steer it in constructive directions. The second question is how to develop programs that are fully responsive to the many evolutionary, and sometimes revolutionary, changes that are taking place all around us. As a consequence, the marketing environments are the most relevant point of analysis whether the issue is the promotion of change or simply the response to change.

THE CONCEPT OF
ECOLOGY

The study of marketing in an environmental context logically follows the ecological approach that was first developed in the field of biology more than a hundred years ago. Derived from the Greek word *oikos,* which means "place to live," ecology is the study of an organism within its environments. Although originally applied to plants and animals, the ecological framework of analysis is a viable one for the behavioral sciences as evidenced by the developments in human ecology and, more recently, cultural ecology.[1]

In ecology, the main elements are the organism and its environments. The interactions between the two form an interdependent relationship that may be described as an ecological system. In this system, however, there is a very delicate balance between the organism and its environments, for even the slightest disturbance can create a condition of imbalance. For example, nature has developed an intricate ecological system for the wild deer that live in the Rocky Mountain Region of the United States. From time to time, as any deer hunter knows, disturbances in the system, such as a long winter, can materially alter the deer population. In earlier years when man relied on deer as a source of food supply, a significant change in the deer population often produced a major food shortage.

In the commercial world, there are similar types of ecological systems. Consider, for example, the impact of a prolonged strike in the airline industry. In no way could this be viewed as a small disturbance by those individuals and organizations that rely on air travel and air transportation. To the contrary, the strike would pose a major problem for the airline industry and the many ecological relations that have been established over the years through the development of an efficient airline system.

THE ORGANIZED BEHAVIOR SYSTEM

When applied to the field of business, ecological analysis is concerned with the study of the firm in relation to its relevant environments. In this context, the firm is more appropriately defined as a behavior system in preference to the term organism as used in the biological sciences. When provided with structure, or form, the firm becomes an organized behavior system in which people are the interacting components. Through their interactions, the system establishes goals, acquires inputs, and generates outputs.

In addition to people, who provide the organized behavior system with the power to act, the system also contains a set of interacting functions that vary depending on the basic purpose of the firm. In general, these functions may be identified as marketing, research and development, engineering, production, and finance. Collectively, they represent the operational elements within the organized behavior system that employ the input factors of land, labor, capital, and management, and engage in the productive operations that produce the output of the system.

Although input and output relationships vary according to the basic purpose of the firm, every organized behavior system is faced with the problems of survival and growth. For the firm to survive and grow, it must find its place in the ecological system. In effect, this is a position within the environment, or an *ecological niche* wherein an opportunity for survival exists. In recognition of the fact that the balance between the system and the environment may change, Alderson proposed the following "survival theorems" that describe the manner in which a firm can maintain or improve its position in the environment through operative and adaptive activities:[2]

1. An organized behavior system will tend to survive as long as its members achieve their status expectations. Individuals, of course, have a stake in the survival of the behavior system, for it serves them as a ground for status. Further, their income, or gain, from the system can be correlated with status. Thus, collective action oriented toward status can be identified as the main factor in the preservation of the system.

2. An organized behavior system can survive competition if it can hold its position in its own ecological niche. Thus, a well positioned behavior system can fend off competitive attack at the core of its position even though it may lose ground at the fringes where it may lack a differential advantage.

3. An organized behavior system can survive severe functional disturbance resulting from environmental change if it has the ability to adapt to the changed environment. Thus, a behavior system may continue in an entirely new endeavor even though its original function has disappeared. Highly specialized behavior systems, of course, are the most susceptible to functional disturbance, and they must have the ability to remain intact during the period of transition to a new function.

4. An organized behavior system can survive through two distinct forms of growth. It may extend its present activities in its existing ecological niche, or it may diversify into new fields of endeavor. There are distinct advantages, of course, in the second form of growth in that a strong position in a new ecological niche can serve as a protection against functional disturbance in the system's original niche.

THE CONCEPT OF THE ENVIRONMENT

The business environments may be defined as those animate and inanimate forces that surround and potentially affect the process of business. The animate environments are living forces such as customers and competitors; the inanimate environments include nonliving forces such as the law and the economy. It is important to note, however, that the environments that impinge on a specific organized behavior system must be identified with that system and its functions. Each behavior system has its own set of environments and its own unique position in its ecological system.

COMPONENTS OF THE TOTAL MARKETING ENVIRONMENT

The preceding discussions of the ecological system and the corresponding relationships between the firm and its environments provide a basis for the discussion of marketing in an environmental context.

As an important function of the organized behavior system, marketing may be viewed as an operating system. As such, it acquires inputs and generates outputs within the boundaries of a set of environmental forces that impact on the micro process of marketing in the firm and on the aggregation of this activity in the macro process of marketing in the economy.

TWO LEVELS OF THE TOTAL ENVIRONMENT

Micro + Macro components

Defined as the animate and inanimate forces that affect marketing decision making, marketing environments exist at two rather distinct levels. The first level, which may be referred to as the micro marketing environment, is internal within the organized behavior system. The second level consists of all those forces that impinge on marketing from outside the firm; they may be identified as the macro marketing environment. That is, the total marketing environment contains both micro and macro components.

Micro components.   As pointed out earlier in this chapter, the major functions of an organized behavior system are marketing, research and development, engineering, production, and finance. Although a high level of coordination is required to ensure the proper functioning of all of these operational units, it is important to note that each function, in effect, represents an environmental force that affects each of the other functions. For example, marketing can not operate in a vacuum within the organization. Any decisions in the marketing area obviously must be tempered by decisions and programs that are being carried out in the other functional areas.

A diagram of the micro components of the total marketing environment is presented in Figure 2.1. As shown, the micro marketing system is pictured in the center surrounded by research and development, engineering, production, and finance. In this context, marketing represents a function within the organized behavior system that is both an influencee and an influencer in its relationship to the other functional areas within the behavior system. For example, it would be ridiculous for marketing to plan a strategy to meet the needs and wants of a market segment with an innovative new product without considering the ability of research and development to create the product, the capability of engineering and production to design and manufacture the product, and the ability of finance to support the necessary research, engineering, production, and marketing programs that would be required to get the new product on the market. Correspondingly, research and development can not act without looking at the marketing, engineering, production, and financial implications of its decisions. It is essential that each of the functional areas must consider the impact of its decisions on the other operational units in the system.

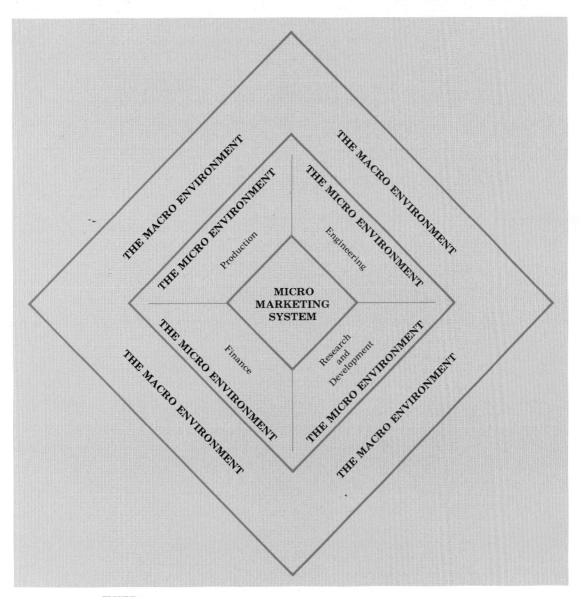

FIGURE 2.1.
THE MICRO MARKETING
ENVIRONMENT

Macro components.   The internal components described above represent environmental forces for marketing that are essentially controllable by the firm's management. The external variables, or the macro components, of the total marketing environment are generally uncontrollable. This is the critical distinction, of course, that identifies the full impact of the macro environment on marketing decision making. In fact, it is this level of the total environment that poses the ultimate challenge for the organized behavior system in search of its own ecological niche and the real acid test for creative management.

As external variables in the total marketing environment, the macro components are largely beyond the control of management in an individual firm. Collectively, of course, it is possible for a number of firms, or a group of persons, to exercise a degree of influence on some aspect of the macro environment. A professional lobbyist, for example, might represent an industry in an effort to effect legislation favorable to that industry. For the most part, however, successful efforts of this nature tend to be long term in scope. It may be argued, therefore, that the macro environment consists of those forces that are largely uncontrollable by the individual firm, and, in the short run, even by the collective efforts of a number of firms.

FIGURE 2.2.
THE MACRO MARKETING
ENVIRONMENT

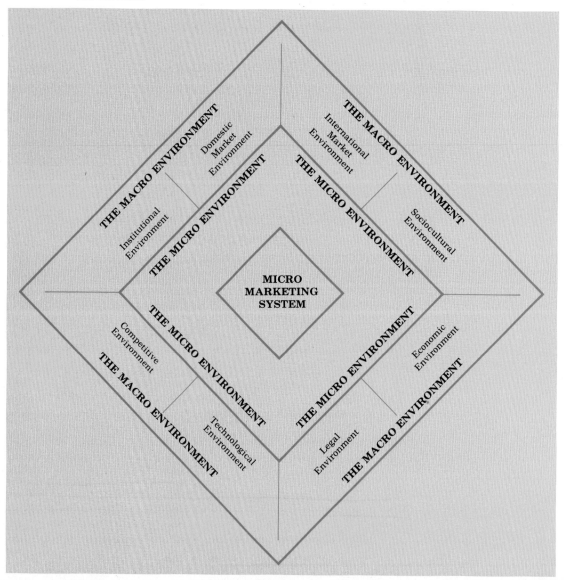

The components of the macro marketing environment are presented in Figure 2.2. As illustrated, each of these external variables represents an uncontrollable force that acts on managerial decision making in the organized behavior system. Even though they represent some environmental influence over all functional areas within the system, the macro forces exercise their greatest influence on the marketing operation. This will be discussed in more detail in the latter part of this chapter. It is important to note here, however, that the institutional, domestic market, international market, sociocultural, economic, competitive, legal, and technological components of the macro marketing environment constitute both a challenge and an

FIGURE 2.3.
THE TOTAL MARKETING
ENVIRONMENT

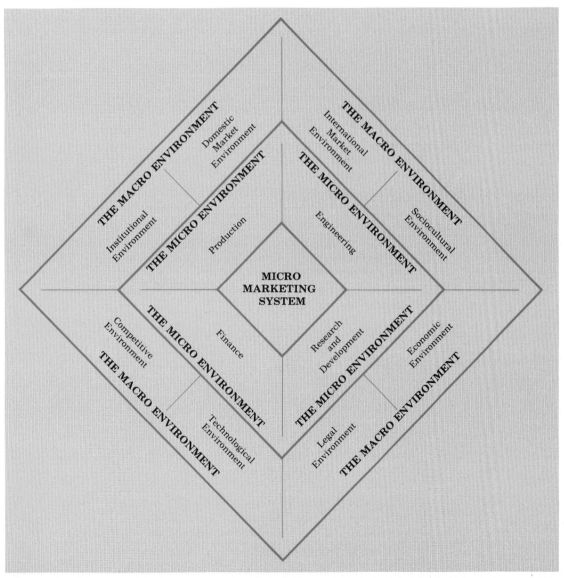

opportunity for marketing. Furthermore, as fluctuating forces, they represent the critical dimensions of the total marketing environment that must be monitored constantly by marketing management.

THE TOTAL MARKETING ENVIRONMENT

When combined in an aggregate framework of analysis, the micro and macro components of the marketing environment form the ecological setting for the performance of the marketing function. As illustrated in Figure 2.3, this setting shows marketing as an operating system in relationship to its *total environment.* As the organism of study, marketing is pictured in the center surrounded by both the internal and external forces that affect its performance and that, in turn, are affected by it. Thus, the total marketing environment concept stresses the adaptive and formative nature of marketing that was described in Chapter 1.

The concept of a total marketing environment also recognizes one other important consideration that is often neglected in the contemporary study of business. Although marketing is certainly the core of its ecological setting, it is only part of a complex network of relationships that involve a large number of forces, entities, and institutions that affect market transactions. Accordingly, as emphasized throughout this textbook, the total marketing environment furnishes a perspective that is vastly more meaningful than the mere examination of the technical and managerial dimensions of the marketing process.

To provide a general view of the relationships that are involved in the total marketing environment, the following two sections are devoted to a discussion of both the micro and the macro forces, entities, and institutions that form the ecological setting for marketing. Since a more detailed analysis of each area is presented in Parts II and III of this text, however, the discussion here will be limited to an introductory examination.

MICRO MARKETING ENVIRONMENT

As an organized behavior system, the business firm develops an internal structure for the purpose of achieving its goals. In this context, the structure, which normally consists of a set of functional entities such as research and development, engineering, production, marketing, and finance, is concerned with the task of utilizing the system's inputs to generate productive outputs. That is, the structure employs resources in the form of labor, managerial talent, raw materials, equipment, and capital to produce a flow of salable products.

Since marketing is the one function that is directly involved with the firm's outputs outside the behavior system, it is appropriate to view the internal organization as a micro marketing environment. Further, it may be argued that marketing considerations should dominate the establishment of business policy that provides the working rules for the functional entities in the system. Employing these concepts, the remainder of this section will be devoted to a discussion of the following internal forces that collectively represent the micro marketing environment:

1. Research and Development

2. Engineering

3. Production

4. Finance

RESEARCH AND DEVELOPMENT

As an operational entity in the business system, research and development (R & D) is concerned primarily with the translation of technology into marketable products. Some industrial research in the form of basic or applied research is devoted to the discovery of new scientific knowledge, but the vast proportion of R & D is commercially oriented. Approximately two-thirds of the money expended in the United States for R & D represents industrial research. From the standpoint of its impact on marketing, R & D is a vital force in the flow of new products. Nearly 80 percent of the money spent on industrial research is spent on new product development. This activity, which is the core of the R & D function, provides the life blood of marketing in that a continuous development of new and improved products is absolutely essential to the survival and growth of the business firm. The shorter life cycles now being experienced by products in all categories are dramatic evidence of the need for an ever increasing transfusion of new blood for the micro marketing system.

The ultimate value of R & D to society is determined largely by the role that it assumes in the business system. In some firms, for example, R & D is technology oriented. In others, it is marketing oriented. Technological R & D departments receive their direction from technological advances, while marketing R & D departments are guided by the needs and wants of the market. Although seemingly a matter of semantics, the distinction between these two orientations is critically significant in determining the nature and scope of R & D as a force in the micro marketing environment. It is important to note, therefore, that management may view industrial research and development as either a technological R & D process or as a marketing R & D process. The former focuses on products, whereas the latter concentrates on the satisfaction of society's needs and wants.

The position here, of course, is that R & D must be performed as a marketing oriented process. It is an important force in the micro environment, and it must be closely integrated with the marketing function. When linked in this manner, R & D and marketing bring all of the firm's scientific and technical knowledge to bear on market oriented problems, such as the selection of corporate goals, the identification of market opportunities, the development of marketing programs, and the formulation of competitive strategies.

ENGINEERING   As the second business entity in the micro marketing environment, engineering is concerned with the application of knowledge from mathematics and the natural sciences to problems dealing with the economic utilization of the materials and forces of nature; engineering functions encompass such areas as design, testing, planning, and service. Additionally, engineering is involved with research, development, production, and sales. Its business function is broad; it acts upon and receives impacts from a wide number of other elements in the organized business system.

While the profession of engineering may be traced to early recorded times when the term engineer was applied to persons who built canals, dams, palaces, temples, and roads, engineering, today is identified with a number of rather specific areas. There are, in fact, at least fifty clearly defined specialties in the field. The more classical branches of engineering are aeronautical, agricultural, bioengineering, ceramics, chemical, civil, electrical, industrial, materials, mechanical, and metallurgical. Each of these areas, of course, exercises its own unique role in the specific industries wherein its functional nature is applicable.

A brief review of one of the above specialties in the field of engineering reveals the position that engineering holds in the micro marketing environment. Industrial engineering, for example, is concerned with the cost and efficient production of goods. This field of engineering employs time and motion studies, psychology, economics, and machine design to personnel, materials, and machinery in an effort to meet the product quality standards set by the business system. Thus, industrial engineering plays an important role in the production of an output that can meet the needs and wants of the market.

Given the scope of the engineering function, it should be apparent that there is a strong need for close coordination between engineering and marketing. Engineering is clearly a part of the internal system environment, and, as such, it influences and is influenced by the marketing function. Through effective coordination, the two functional areas can work harmoniously to effect a system output that meets both the needs of the organization and the requirements of the market. Each set of needs is important and one cannot be stressed at the expense of the other. It makes little sense, for example, to gain production efficiencies for a product that will not sell. Correspondingly, a highly marketable product that cannot be produced economically provides little opportunity for the business system.

PRODUCTION   The ultimate responsibility for the output of the business system, of course, rests with production. This important function is concerned with the problems of plant layout, materials handling, inventory control, quality control, and the administrative organization of the production function. As an entity in the micro marketing environment, it is important, however, that marketing considerations enter the picture when final decisions are made. Take the case of quality control, for example. In setting standards, production must be cognizant of marketing's requirements. A product with too much quality built in may have to be priced at a level that is too high for marketing to provide a competitive offering in the marketplace. On the other hand, quality standards may be so low that marketing is placed in a competitive disadvantage in relation to other products on the market. Both of these examples illustrate the need to begin with market and its needs in designing appropriate quality control procedures.

Quality control

The relationships between marketing and production are best shown where conditions for economies of scale exist. While the benefits of such economies are generally associated with big business, the existence of bigness does not, in itself, ensure economies of scale; it only provides the opportunity. In practice, large scale output is possible when and if there is a corresponding high level of marketing activity. Marketing considerations, of course, must dominate in any decisions concerning the achievement of economies through mass production. The major issue is whether or not large volumes can be used to reduce costs and ultimately prices to provide an opportunity for mass marketing to become a reality.

economies of scale

When economies of scale have been attained, a delicate balance between production and marketing must be maintained. Large plants operating well below capacity can completely destroy the benefits, or economies, that have been achieved. Constant pressure, therefore, is exerted on marketing to maintain the sales volumes that are needed to keep capacity at an acceptable level of economic operation. Rival, or competitive, firms attempt to do the same thing, of course, and the net result is a competitive structure that tends to hold prices and profits down. Thus, under conditions of intense rivalry for share of market, marketing in the final analysis will be the key element that will determine the overall success of the individual firm.

Strategies to secure sales volume:
1. product differentiation
2. market segmentation

In working with the output of production, marketing may employ one or both of two alternate product strategies to secure sales volume. The first, which is called *product differentiation,* is a strategy designed to attract demand through the offering of products with features, quality, style, or images that can be differentiated from rival product offerings. When utilizing this approach, marketing attempts to convince potential buyers that the differentiated product will satisfy their needs and wants better than other products on the market. Branding, as a means of identification, and promotion, as a form of communication, both play an important part in the overall success of this approach. The second strategy, which is called *market segmenta-*

tion, focuses on the offering of special products that will satisfy the particular requirements of specific market segments. In this approach, the total market is viewed as a series of parts, or segments, instead of a broad general market. Product offerings, therefore, tend to be more tailored, or specific in design. Further, product diversification is a natural outgrowth of market segmentation strategy.

In actual practice, product differentiation and market segmentation are not mutually exclusive. In fact, many firms ultimately employ both strategies. Automobile manufactureres, for example, offer a wide number of different kinds of cars to meet the needs and wants of the many separate market segments. Within each market, however, intense rivalry has developed as most of the car builders have attempted to gain a share of the various market segments. In other words, it is rare for one automobile producer to have a market all to itself. Eventually, rivals enter the picture and force product differentiation as a form of competitive strategy. Thus, while market segmentation may be employed for a time, it is likely that some form of product differentiation will be required as the market grows and competitors enter the field.

From the above discussion, it should be apparent that there is a strong need for a close relationship between production and marketing. The two functional areas are clearly interdependent to the extent that one cannot succeed without the other. Today's modern business world stresses economies of production and a volume of output that can be offered at competitive prices. There is, therefore, a need for a delicate balance between production and marketing to ensure that the output goals of the firm are consistent and compatible with the requirements of the market. The contention here, of course, is that a proper balance can be maintained if production is appropriately viewed as a significant part of the micro environment of marketing. With this view, marketing can play both an adaptive and a formative role in influencing the output of the business system.

FINANCE   As the fourth functional entity in the micro marketing environment, finance is concerned with the value of the assets of the organized business system. In this context, finance is involved with the growth aspects of the system. In financial terms, the firm can grow in one of two ways. The first form of growth is through retained earnings generated by operations. The second is through the acquisition of new capital or new assets from the outside. The retention of earnings, of course, is made possible by successful marketing efforts, but new assets from external sources may be acquired from the sale of stocks and bonds, or through merger and acquisition.

As in the case of production, there is a close internal relationship between finance and marketing. On the one hand, the achievement of the financial goals of the business system are directly dependent on marketing. As noted above, retained earnings are generated by marketing. Further, without a recognized marketing program, it would be difficult for a firm to acquire external assets. On the other hand, it should be readily apparent that financial assets are necessary to carry out successful marketing programs. Since finance is viewed as a part of the micro marketing environment, the discussion here will be confined to the latter relationships that exist between finance and marketing.

In order to perform its necessary activities, marketing requires at least two major types of funds. The first is in the form of permanent capital for the purchase of fixed assets such as land, buildings, furniture, and fixtures; the second involves temporary financial requirements to support shorter-term commitments such as promotional efforts and operating needs. Finance is clearly a part of the internal environment for marketing that presents both constraints and opportunities. Since finance can restrain or support the firm's marketing efforts, finance must analyze the marketing implications of all financial decisions that impact on the overall direction of the business system. In this context, it is important to recognize that both finance and marketing are involved with the growth of the system. Marketing is concerned with the task of getting assets to transact a larger volume of business, while finance is interested in expanding market position to support growth through retained earnings and external capital accumulation. Therefore, it is essential that a harmonious relationship be maintained between these two important functional areas.

The giant E. & J. Gallo Winery provides an excellent example of a company that has molded the various functional entities in the business system into a highly successful company. Formed in 1933 by Ernest and Julio Gallo, the firm is by far the largest vintner in the United States with an output of approximately 100 million gallons a year. In research and development, Gallo has the finest technology team in the industry. Its laboratory staff, which includes at least a dozen new product researchers, has kept Gallo well in front of competition. Gallo's production and engineering people have developed a modern "plant" that is literally years ahead of any other in the industry. Financially, the firm has made the Gallos one of America's richest families. Analysts estimate that the Gallo fortune is around $500 million. As a marketer, the Gallo Winery has no equal. The company has dominated the industry for a number of years and is now larger than its next four rivals with approximately 30 percent of the total U.S. wine market. Today, Gallo is a vertically integrated operation that makes its own bottles and caps, employs its own trucking system, and distributes a fair percentage of its output through company owned distributors.[3]

MACRO MARKETING ENVIRONMENT

Based on the above discussion of the micro marketing environment, it should be evident that marketing does not operate in a vacuum. This is certainly the case within the internal organization structure, and it becomes even more apparent when marketing is analyzed outside the business system. In an effort to show how external forces, entities, and institutions affect the practice of marketing, this section will focus on the macro marketing environment. For purposes of introduction, the following areas will be discussed briefly as a prelude to Part III of this book:

1. Institutional Environment

3. Domestic Market Environment

3. International Market Environment

4. Sociocultural Environment

5. Economic Environment

6. Legal Environment

7. Competitive Environment

8. Technological Environment

INSTITUTIONAL ENVIRONMENT

distribution channels

As part of the macro marketing environment, the institutional environment includes all retailing, wholesaling, and service institutions engaged in the physical flow of goods and services and the movement of title between producers and final customers. Although institutional relationships will be developed more fully in Chapters 7 and 8, it should be noted here that concepts pertaining to the institutional environment deal with the institutional structure, types of middlemen, channels of distribution, and channel conflict and control.

The institutional structure of marketing includes all of the persons, establishments, agencies, and companies that are involved in the macro process of marketing. Of significance here is the fact that the structure is constantly undergoing modification in response to changing conditions or to changes in the way customers wish the marketing system to serve them. New types of retailers, innovations in wholesaling, adjustments in transportation services, and new forms of warehousing systems are all examples of the changes that have occurred in the institutional structure in recent years.

Middlemen, representing one of the most significant elements in the institutional environment, are classified as either merchant or agent middlemen. Merchant middlemen buy and sell goods. They, therefore, take title and assume the risks involved in ownership. Agent middlemen, by contrast, negotiate sales for a principal. They usually receive a fee or commission for their services, and they do not take title to the goods they sell.

A channel of distribution begins with a producer, ends with the final customer, and includes all middlemen in the channel who engage in either the physical movement of a good or the transfer of its title. The shortest channel of distribution would entail movement directly from the producer to the final customer without the utilization of middle-men. The longest possible channel would involve the producer, two or more levels of wholesaling, one level of retailing, and the final customer.

Channel conflict and control deal with the issue of competitive conflict within the channel of distribution and the question of who—the producer or a middleman—actually controls distribution. Competitive conflict can occur as the result of both vertical and horizontal relations in the channel. Conflicts between two distinct levels, such as retailing and wholesaling, would be an example of vertical conflict. Clashes between two wholesalers over territorial boundaries would be an example of horizontal conflict. The issue of control in the channel of distribution deals with the ability of one member in the channel to stipulate marketing policies to other channel members. This type of control may be achieved through economic power, by legal means, or through knowledge and experience. By whatever means, however, the channel member in control enjoys a distinct advantage in his relations with other members.

DOMESTIC MARKET ENVIRONMENT

consumer market
non-household market

A second, and a most significant, macro environmental force is the market itself. As treated here, the domestic market is identified as a separate entity from the international market. This distinction is made in recognition of the fact that there is a great variation in the two broad markets in terms of value systems, demographic structures, culture, and buying patterns.

For purposes of analysis, the domestic market includes both household consumers and nonhousehold buyers. The former purchase goods and services for their own personal or household use, whereas the latter purchase goods and services for resale, for use in their own businesses, or for use in the production of other goods and services. A mother, for example, represents her family as a purchasing agent when she buys clothing for her children and food for the family table. In this role, she is clearly a household consumer. A manufacturer, on the other hand, who purchases steel to use in the production of electric fans is a nonhousehold buyer. Thus, the domestic market environment is divided into a "consumer market" and a "non-household market." Since each market buys differently and is motivated by different factors, different, specific marketing programs have to be developed for each.

As an integral part of the domestic market environment, the household consumer market in the United States contains a population in excess of 200 million. People, of course, are only one ingredient in a market. As noted in Chapter 1, exchange requires a relevant demand, an ability to buy, and a willingness to buy. For the domestic market to be viable for a specific product or service, therefore, there must be a group of identifiable people with needs and wants, money to spend, and a desire to spend it. Thus, marketing must be concerned with people and their needs, their purchasing power, and their buying behavior.

The nonhousehold market in the United States consists of more than 10 million buying units that represent a highly diversified group of buyers who purchase raw materials, fabricated parts and materials, installations, accessory equipment, operating supplies, and finished goods. An idea of the broad diversity in this market can be seen in the following industry classifications, which make up the total market.

1. Agriculture, forestry, and fishing

2. Mining and quarrying

3. Construction

4. Manufacturing

5. Transportation, communication, and other public utilities

6. Wholesale trade

7. Retail trade

8. Services

9. Finance, insurance, and real estate

10. Federal, state, and local governments

Collectively, all buyers in the domestic market, whether they be household consumers or nonhousehold buyers, represent a powerful environmental force for marketing. Without question, the ultimate success or failure of a firm's marketing efforts rests with the market. It is essential, therefore, that this dimension of the macro marketing environment be recognized as an external influence on marketing decision making.

INTERNATIONAL
MARKET
ENVIRONMENT

Although American goods and services are produced predominantly for the domestic market, it is important to note that over $50 billion of the U.S. gross national product is exported to foreign countries. The international market is a significant one, therefore, for a rather large number of American firms. For these companies, the economic, political-legal, and cultural components of the international market environment are very real considerations in their ongoing marketing activities.[4]

The economic component of the international market environment should be analyzed from the standpoint of industrial structure and national income. Subsistence economies, for example, are relatively poor markets with their very low family incomes. On the other hand, industrializing and industrial economies produce national incomes that provide a good opportunity for international marketers.

The appropriate economic scene, of course, does not necessarily ensure a viable market situation for American exporters. Political-legal constraints, in fact, often preclude entry in certain foreign markets. A receptivity to international buying, a stable political picture, favorable monetary regulations, and a supportive government bureaucracy are all necessary ingredients in a successful international marketing program. That is, a good political-legal climate must accompany the right economic conditions.

The cultural dimension of the international market environment presents a third hazard for American firms in the international field. Many U.S. marketers, for example, fail because they utilize the same strategies they employ in the domestic market. Businessmen and consumers in foreign countries are a product of their own unique culture. Accordingly, they may think and act differently from their counterparts in the United States.

SOCIOCULTURAL ENVIRONMENT

values, institutions

In a broader context, outside the realm of international marketing, social and cultural factors represent a combined force that is part of the macro marketing environment. Referred to here as the sociocultural environment, this external force includes all of the values and the institutions that shape the patterns of living in a society. In marketing, this is an important area of analysis, for the sociocultural characteristics of society strongly influence the nature and extent of marketing activities.

Sociocultural analysis is concerned with the behavior of people in social groups, social classes, and social institutions. Special attention is devoted to knowledge, values, customs, attitudes, beliefs, and patterns of behavior as they form sociocultural influences on the firm and its marketing activities. These influences, of course, do change over time, and it is important for marketing to be alert to changing conditions so that alterations can be made in marketing programs.

ECONOMIC ENVIRONMENT

As an integral part of the economic system, marketing is greatly affected by the economic environment in which it must operate. The economic structure, policies of the government, general economic conditions, and national resources all have a direct impact on marketing. As every businessman knows, however, the economic environment is a difficult one to monitor. The complex set of institutions and relationships in an economy are constantly changing, and these changes affect the money supply, fiscal policies of the government, economic growth, taxes, interest rates, productivity, and prices.

Although the United States is generally considered to be a "free enterprise" economy, there are many indicators to suggest that the American economic environment is really a blend of many economic systems. For example, the United States is by no means free from the control of tradition that dominates countries like India: Resource allocations in India follow patterns that have been established for years, and to a degree, this is also true in the United States. Likewise, many government decisions in this country are made almost as autocratically as they are in the USSR. Resource commitments to warfare, space programs, and welfare, for example, do not necessarily reflect the sentiments of those who pay the bills through their individual taxes. To be sure, a marketplace economy, wherein the needs and wants of consumers direct the allocation of resources, predominates in the United States. The environment is not a pure marketplace economy, however, in that there are elements that both tradition and government control.

LEGAL ENVIRONMENT

In addition to its impact on marketing through the economic environment, government also greatly influences the activities of marketing in the legal environment. Since the United States has followed a public policy of promoting a competitive market system, the legal environment includes a large number of federal, state, and local regulations. It is interesting to note, however, that government regulation of business is a relatively modern development in the United States. The period from 1776 to 1876 was dominated by a laissez-faire philosophy, which held that competitive market forces would bring about the greatest economic good without the need for government intervention. Conditions changed rapidly during the latter part of the nineteenth century, however, as a limited number of industrialists gained control over large blocks of capital and the large giants waged open warfare against smaller enterprises. When competition failed to adequately regulate itself, both business and the public turned to government for the restoration of competitive order.[5]

Today, the legal environment exercises a strong influence on the field of marketing in the United States. Laws to preserve competition, regulatory measures to control marketing activities, and legislation to protect the consumer are all examples of the forces that establish the legal guidelines and parameters for contemporary marketing practice. From every indication, there is a trend toward more governmental control over business; it is safe to assume that the legal environment will continue to have a major impact on marketing in the future. It will be important, therefore, for marketers to constantly monitor legislation to ensure compliance with the laws.

COMPETITIVE ENVIRONMENT

price Competition
product differentiation
—organiza. service diff.

The seventh external force that will be treated in some detail in Part III of this book is the competitive environment.[6] Competition, of course, is the very essence of business in that firms are rivals for position in the marketplace. In this context, rivalry may take the form of price competition among products that are substitutable one for another, product differentiation on either a physical or psychological basis, organization and enterprise differentiation, and service differentiation. From the viewpoint of marketing, competition includes all of those activities that provide opportunities for the individual firm to gain a competitive position over rivals.

The competitive environment will be presented in depth in Chapter 14, but it should be noted here that an individual firm faces both intraindustry and interindustry competition. Intraindustry competition is rivalry within a given industry between firms producing the same product or service, and interindustry competition comes from firms in other industries offering substitute products and services. The competitive environment within an industry should be analyzed from the standpoint of such factors as industry promotional practices, cost structures, pricing policies, and accepted distribution programs. Since competition between firms in different industries is always a potential threat, it is important for marketing to be constantly alert to this element of the competitive environment.

TECHNOLOGICAL ENVIRONMENT

Although competitive forces are formidable in the American economy, it is interesting to note that competition has served, in part, to create a separate and distinct environment that dramatically affects the field of marketing. This, of course, is the technological environment that is partially an outgrowth of the zealous search for a differential advantage by competitors. In this context, marketing travels a two-way street in its relationship with technology. First of all, marketing influences the direction of technology through a close interface with research and development. Second, as pointed out earlier in this chapter, marketing plays a vital role in the diffusion of technology into society through the development of new want-satisfying products.

In order to place the technological environment in proper perspective, it is important to note that marketing is concerned with existing as well as emerging technology. The former consists of all the accumulated knowledge of society, while the latter is new knowledge. Clearly, marketing is affected by both. In this context, new technology is often the result of existing technology. In the area of medical science, for example, the progress that is now being made in the treatment of cancer is the result of many years of research. This same situation, of course, is true in a wide number of other areas such as aeronautics, electronics, plastics, synthetics, and communications.

MARKETING IN THE CHANGING ENVIRONMENT

From the above discussion of both the micro and the macro environments, it should be apparent that marketing practice is heavily influenced by the total environment in which it must operate and, more especially, by the environmental changes that are so prevalent in contemporary society. It is appropriate, therefore, to end this chapter with a brief look at marketing in the changing environment as a basis for analyzing both the threats and the opportunities posed by the total environment as it impinges on marketing.

ENVIRONMENTAL THREAT

Given the serious and sudden changes that can occur in the environment, it is important to recognize that various components of the total environment often present very real threats for marketing. As defined by Kotler, environmental threat is "a challenge posed by an unfavorable trend or specific disturbance in the environment that would lead, in the absence of purposeful marketing action, to the stagnation or demise of a company, product, or brand."[7] All firms, of course, face a certain amount of environmental threat. Some meet the challenge vigorously; others tend to be more apathetic in their response. The following examples of contemporary environmental threat will provide an insight into this important issue.

Baby food: According to expert demographers, the population explosion has ended in the United States and the "baby boom" has been replaced by a "birth dearth." For firms in the baby food industry, this means that there are only about three million new customers a year as compared to over four million a year during the peak birth period between 1956 and 1962. Although critics of the three major baby food companies—Gerber, Heinz, and Beech-Nut—have faulted the industry for responding too slowly to the birth dearth, there are indications that defensive actions are being taken. Gerber, for example, has moved beyond its traditional food store base by expanding into discount houses, drug chains, and department and specialty stores with a line of nonfood baby products. With over 80 percent of its 1973 sales in baby food, Gerber is now into toiletries, disposable nurser bags and bottles, vaporizers, humidifiers, bottle sterilizers, and a complete line of babywear.[8]

Liquor: Since the early 1970s, radical changes have occurred in the liquor industry that now pose serious problems for many American distillers. Although it was anticipated that demand would grow at the rate of 4 to 6 percent per year during the 1970 decade, actual U.S. liquor consumption has been increasing at a significantly lower rate of less than 3 percent per year. Part of the problem is a keen interindustry competition from the wine industry supported by a wine craze among American consumers. More importantly within the liquor industry, there has been a trend toward lighter liquor, reflecting the shift in tastes of the U.S. drinker. Since the 1960s, when straight bourbons and blended whiskies were the preferred liquor in this country, American drinkers have been gradually shifting to scotch and vodka. *Business Week,* for example, indicates that vodka is rapidly overtaking bourbon as the nation's primary distilled spirit.[9]

Electric typewriters: For many years, the electric typewriter business has been dominated by International Business Machines Corporation, which controls over 80 percent of the market. This dominance was secured, in part, by the development, in 1961, of IBM's selectric typewriter that offered the innovative technology of a speedy, flexible, spinning "golf ball" typing instrument. Ironically, it is this technology that is now posing a serious threat to IBM's position.

Future growth in the electric typewriter business is expected to come from the automatic typewriter that can store information and reproduce it at a very high speed. These typewriters have been made feasible by the golf ball, single element, typing system. Although IBM has been producing an automatic machine for several years, competing products are now being offered by Sperry Rand (Remington), Olympia-Werke (Olympia), and Litton Industries (Royal). Indications are that rival products, which will be competitively priced with IBM, will attempt to secure a differential advantage through special features, such as faster speed, better ribbons, and keyboard memory banks.[10]

Automobiles: In response to a market trend that Ford's president Lee A. Iacocca called "irrevocable," Ford Motor Company introduced two new, and a total of seven, small cars during the 1975 automobile model year. At the same time, Chrysler Corporation chose 1975 as a year to launch a new line of big cars. American Motors continued to place its emphasis on small cars, while General Motors, the industry leader, appeared to straddle the gamut of car sizes without a positive move to small cars. The energy crisis of the 1970s, of course, served to produce a major threat for the automobile industry. Today, the experts contend that the small car trend is massive and irreversible. If they are correct, significant changes in Detroit's marketing strategy can be anticipated for a number of years to come.[11]

Supermarkets: While relatively secure at the present time, the conventional supermarket may well face an environmental threat that could make it completely obsolete. Competition from computerized supermarkets is growing in certain areas of the United States, and many feel that this method of grocery marketing may represent the supermarket of the future. As currently operated, the computerized supermarket offers shoppers the opportunity to consult a weekly updated catalog and order by telephone. Orders are then processed by computer, filled from an automated warehouse, and delivered by truck to the customer's home. The whole system has been designed to appeal to shoppers who are tired of the routine of driving, finding a parking space, and bucking the check-out lines in the conventional supermarket.[12]

The above illustrations of environmental threat serve to emphasize the fact that marketing must operate within the confines of a changing environment. It is important, therefore, for business firms to be aware of change and to recognize the needs for environmental forecasting. Through the use of an accurate monitoring system, threats can be detected early and appropriate actions can be taken. In this manner, potential threats may be ultimately turned into marketing opportunities.

MARKETING OPPORTUNITY   As defined by Martin Bell, "A marketing opportunity is a challenge to purposeful marketing action."[13] According to Bell, marketing opportunities exist in four rather distinct areas. The first is the opportunity to innovate, or introduce something new; the second is the challenge to improve efficiency. The third is the opportunity to create a competitive difference, and the fourth is the chance to carve out a market niche.[14] The following examples of marketing opportunities serve to illustrate Bell's four opportunity areas.

Downtown malls: Until recently, retailers concentrated their investments in new facilities in suburban malls. The mall concept is now being carried back "downtown" in response to a return to the city in many major metropolitan areas. In contrast to the suburban malls, however, the downtown malls are quite innovative in that they are environmentally controlled, integrated shopping centers that are part of a living and working complex. The Broadway Plaza in the heart of downtown Los Angeles, for example, includes a two-level mall with thirty stores, a thirty-two story office building, the Hyatt Regency Hotel, and a collection of good restaurants. This and other innovative mall developments are providing a very strong revitalization of the downtown areas in a number of key American cities.[15]

Transportation: With the advent of the Boeing 747 and the future development of square-bodied all-cargo airplanes, rapid growth in airfreight is optimistically predicted for the remainder of this century. If the optimists are correct, airfreight could serve to greatly improve distribution efficiency and help lower the total cost of physical distribution. Sears, Roebuck and Company provides an excellent illustration of how this could work. Instead of stocking every clothing item in every one of its stores, Sears is considering the idea of a central clothing warehouse, from which items would be air-shipped according to local market demand for styles and colors.[16]

Women's apparel: Historically, women's dress styles changed every year, and everyone knew that the style was either short or long skirts, full or slim lines, high waists or low, or whatever was mandated for that season. In recent years, however, the single look in women's fashions has been replaced by a style that is anything a woman feels like wearing. Many women still want to follow the dictates of the designers and the fashion editors, but a growing segment of the American population is making its own fashion. For this group, concern over wearing the "right thing" is being replaced with an attitude that a woman should wear clothes that please the person. Instead of looking at this trend as a threat, progressive garment manufacturers are viewing it as a real marketing opportunity to create a competitive difference, and they are reducing their risks by offering a broad spectrum of styles to a wide array of markets.

Semiconductors: In the 1970s, a major competitive shakeout occurred in the semiconductor business as overcapacity and a softening market threw business into a turmoil. In an effort to secure profits, many of the companies in the industry are moving beyond components to the manufacture and marketing of finished products that incorporate their components. These companies are now into electronic calculators, digital watches, microcomputers, and other finished products in which semiconductor parts make up a significant portion of the cost. Rockwell International Corporation's entry in the calculator business put that company in a head-on position against Texas Instruments, Inc., the industry leader. Both of these firms have been working on their own electronic watch lines, and it appears that they, along with Bowman Instrument Corporation, will be aggressively competing in an effort to carve a market niche in the finished goods market.[17]

The preceding examples are just four among many that can be used to point out the marketing opportunities that are presented by environmental change. It may be noted, therefore, that there is positive value in change in that it often forces a firm, and even an entire industry, to react in a manner that is in the best interests of society. In the semiconductor business, for example, there is no question that the volatile competitive environment served to provide the market with many excellent, low priced electronic products that would have otherwise been beyond the reach of the average consumer. By the same token, the energy crisis may one day be credited for the development of a national mass-transit system and a return of the automobile industry to the production of a good, inexpensive personal transportation vehicle.

SUMMARY

In this chapter, the marketing environments were the major theme of discussion. As presented, the chapter provides an introductory framework for Parts II and III of this book. The initial section of the chapter focused on the concept of ecology and the ecological framework of analysis as the theoretical basis for the study of marketing in an environmental setting. In this setting, the business firm is viewed as an organized behavior system that establishes goals, acquires inputs, and generates outputs through a set of interacting functions that vary, to some degree, depending on the basic purpose of the firm.

As one of the key functions, or productive operations, in the organized behavior system, marketing is viewed as an operating system that acquires inputs and generates outputs. As such, it must operate within the boundaries of a set of environmental forces. As defined here, the total marketing environment has two rather distinct levels. The first level, which is identified as the micro marketing environment, is internal within the organized behavior system and includes all of the productive operations in the firm that influence and are influenced by marketing decision making. The second level is the macro marketing environment outside the confines of the system.

Following an introductory discussion of both the micro and the macro environments of marketing, the final section of this chapter was devoted to a review of marketing in the changing environment as the basis for a brief analysis of the threats and opportunities posed by the total environment as it impinges on marketing. A series of contemporary examples were used to present various product, company, and industry illustrations that point out the need for a continual environmental audit to detect changes that signal both environmental threats and marketing opportunities.

QUESTIONS FOR DISCUSSION

1. Explain the concept of ecology and show how this concept may be used as a viable framework of analysis in the field of marketing.

2. What is an ecological niche? Explain how a firm can maintain or improve its niche through operative and adaptive activities.

3. Two levels of the total marketing environment have been presented in this chapter. Which of these do you feel is the most significant in terms of the long-run survival of the firm?

4. Identify the components of the micro marketing environment and briefly explain why these internal entities are considered to be within the control of a firm's management.

5. Identify the components of the macro marketing environment and explain why these external forces are generally beyond the control of a firm's management.

6. What is the basic difference between a technological research and development department and a marketing research and development department? What rationale would you use to defend the notion that research and development should always be a marketing oriented process?

7. In working with the output of production, marketing may employ a product differentiation strategy or a market segmentation strategy. Compare and contrast each of these strategies and explain why they are not mutually exclusive.

8. Identify the two broad segments of the domestic market environment and explain why these two segments should be analyzed as separate markets.

9. What is the difference between existing and emerging technology? Can it be assumed that marketing should be more concerned with one than the other? Why?

10. Conduct a brief environmental audit for each of the following industries and identify at least one major environmental threat that may be faced by each: (1) petroleum; (2) drugs; (3) education.

11. Following the same framework of analysis presented in question 10 above, identify at least one major marketing opportunity that may exist for each of the following industries: (1) housing; (2) electronics; (3) aircraft.

NOTES

[1]Wroe Alderson was one of the early scholars in the field of marketing to apply the ecological approach. For two excellent examples of his work, see Wroe Alderson, *Marketing Behavior and Executive Action* (Homewood, Ill.: Richard D. Irwin, Inc., 1957); and Wroe Alderson, *Dynamic Marketing Behavior* (Homewood, Ill.: Richard D. Irwin, Inc., 1965).

[2]Alderson, *Marketing Behavior and Executive Action, Ibid.,* pp. 52–60.

[3]Insights on the wine industry in general and E & J Gallo in particular are provided in "Wine: Selling the New Mass Market," *Business Week* (February 23, 1974), pp. 64–70; and "Their Cup Runneth Over," *Forbes* (October 1, 1975), pp. 24–39.

[4]For a good discussion of the environmental dimensions of international marketing, see Philip Kotler, *Marketing Management: Analysis, Planning, and Control* (3rd ed.; Englewood Cliffs, New Jersey: Prentice-Hall, Inc., 1976), pp. 468–471.

[5]An excellent review of the legal environment is presented in E. T. Grether, *Marketing and Public Policy* (Englewood Cliffs, New Jersey: Prentice-Hall, Inc., 1966).

[6]For a detailed analysis of the competitive environment, see Louis W. Stern and John R. Grabner, Jr., *Competition in the Marketplace* (Glenview, Ill.: Scott, Foresman Company, 1970).

[7]Philip Kotler, *Marketing Management,* p. 34.

[8]"The Lower Birthrate Crimps the Baby-Food Market," *Business Week* (July 13, 1974), pp. 43–50.

[9]"A Barrel of Trouble for the Whiskey Makers," *Business Week* (March 10, 1973), pp. 112–114; and "Liquor Men Feel Like the Morning After," *Business Week* (March 17, 1975), pp. 88–90.

[10]"Tough Competition for IBM's Selectric," *Business Week* (September 28, 1974), pp. 71–74.

[11]"The Small Car Blues at General Motors," *Business Week* (March 16, 1974), pp. 76–83.

[12]"Supermarkets: Dialing for Doughnuts," *Newsweek* (October 22, 1973), pp. 118–120.

[13]Martin L. Bell, Marketing: Concepts and Strategy (2nd ed.; Boston: Houghton Mifflin Company, 1972), p. 18.

[14]*Ibid.,* pp. 19–23.

[15]"Suburban Malls Go Downtown," *Business Week* (November 19, 1973), pp. 90–94.

[16]"Making Money with Air Freight," *Business Week* (November 2, 1974), pp. 105–112.

[17]"The Semiconductor Becomes a New Marketing Force," *Business Week* (August 24, 1974), pp. 34–38; and "Texas Instruments: Pushing Hard into the Consumer Markets," *Business Week* (August 24, 1974), pp. 39–42.

SUGGESTED READINGS

Anderson, W. Thomas, Jr., Louis K. Sharpe, and Robert J. Boewadt, "The Environmental Role of Marketing," *MSU Business Topics* (Summer, 1972), pp. 66–72.

Berry, Leonard L. and James S. Hensel, eds., *Marketing and the Social Environment: A Readings Text* (New York: Petrocelli Books, 1973).

Cooper, Arnold C. and Dan Schendel, "Strategic Responses to Technological Threats," *Business Horizons* (February, 1976), pp. 61–69.

Holloway, Robert J. and Robert S. Hancock, *Marketing in a Changing Environment* (2nd ed.; New York: John Wiley & Sons, Inc., 1973).

Holloway, Robert J. and Robert S. Hancock, *The Environment of Marketing Management: Selections from the Literature* (3rd ed.; New York: John Wiley & Sons, Inc., 1974).

Narver, John C. and Ronald Savitt, *The Marketing Economy* (New York: Holt, Rinehart and Winston, 1971).

Organ, Dennis W., "Linking Pins Between Organizations and Environment," *Business Horizons* (December, 1971), pp. 73–80.

Scott, Richard A. and Norton E. Marks, *Marketing and Its Environment* (Belmont, California: Wadsworth Publishing Co., Inc., 1968).

Sweeney, Daniel J., "Marketing: Management Technology or Social Process?," *Journal of Marketing* (October, 1972), pp. 3–10.

Thompson, Howard A., *The Great Writings in Marketing* (Plymouth, Michigan: The Commerce Press, 1976).

TWO

MARKETING AND THE MICRO ENVIRONMENT

Based on the presentation in Part II, the reader should be able to:

■ understand the systems approach and general systems theory as a basis for business analysis

■ apply general systems theory to an understanding of the firm as a business system

■ discuss marketing strategy from the perspective of marketing management

■ explain the marketing philosophy of management and the role of marketing management in the business system

■ use general systems theory to explain the operation of the micro marketing system within the context of an environmental setting

■ understand the formulation and implementation of product, promotion, distribution, and pricing strategies

3

THE FIRM AS A
BUSINESS SYSTEM

3

THE FIRM AS A BUSINESS SYSTEM

The preceding section examined the process of marketing and established the environmental framework that is used throughout this book. To provide a more detailed view of the micro dimensions of marketing, this section is concerned with the firm and its marketing operation. As the conceptual foundation for analyzing the business organization, Chapter 3 examines the firm as a business system. Chapter 4 is devoted to a discussion of marketing strategy planning. Utilizing the framework established in Chapter 4, the final two chapters of this section present a detailed analysis of the strategic dimensions of marketing. Chapter 5 explores the formulation of product and pricing strategy; Chapter 6 examines the development of promotion and distribution strategy.

THE SYSTEMS CONCEPT

As developed in contemporary literature, a system may be defined as a set of interrelated parts whose actions are coordinated to accomplish a given set of goals.[1] Broad application of the systems concept, however, is relatively new, having been developed during World War II in the field of operations research where teams of scientists were employed to work on complex military problems. Today, the systems concept has been adopted as an analytical tool for evaluating many problems ranging from the management of complex business enterprises to the analysis of ecological balance in the environment.

One of the most comprehensive uses of the systems approach was made in a recent simulation of world economics that was designed to evaluate the world's overall limits to growth. The preliminary results of the study, headed by Professor Dennis L. Meadows and done for The Club of Rome's Project on the Predicament of Mankind, were released in 1972. Based on an analysis of the interrelationships among population, food production, industrialization, pollution, and consumption of renewable natural resources, the study predicted that the limits to growth on this planet would be reached in less than 100 years. The impact of such a pronouncement was understandably great. Even though the results of the study have been less than catastrophic in terms of predicted "doom," they still have made mankind aware of its present predicament. The important thing here is that the results would not have been attainable without application of the systems concept to analyze the interrelationships of pertinent factors.

This chapter presents a general review of the systems concept and provides the framework for Chapters 4 and 7, which are devoted to a more specific analysis of the systems approach in the field of business. The discussion here will concentrate on the development of general systems theory and an identification of the various relationships that are involved in the operation of a system.

SYSTEM STRUCTURE

organization
flow
procedure

The underlying structure of any system consists of three elements: organization, flow, and procedure. First, each system has an underlying physical structure, or *organization,* which forms its basic framework. This framework is made up of a set of interrelated parts whose actions must be coordinated to achieve meaningful output. In fact, if coordination is not achieved, the structure does not constitute a system. Second, coordinated action implies a flow of information through the system that facilitates coordination. In the systems concept, however, the idea of *flows* through the system is broader than this and includes the flow of materials through a manufacturing system or money through a financial system. Third, operating *procedures* must be established to provide the control necessary to ensure coordination and a proper sequence of actions.[2]

An example will help to explain how a system is structured. One of the most common systems found in today's home is the stereophonic high-fidelity sound system made up of individual component parts. A typical system, such as the one shown in Figure 3.1, may include separate speaker subsystems, amplifiers, an AM-FM radio receiver, a phonograph, and a tape deck. If any of the major components are missing, no output will be heard. If the components are not properly matched and tuned, the output may not be recognizable. When properly connected, the components form a system with a definite operating structure. The flow through the system is the set of electrical signals that are transformed, in the speaker system, into a set of sound

FIGURE 3.1.
HIGH FIDELITY COMPONENT
SOUND SYSTEM

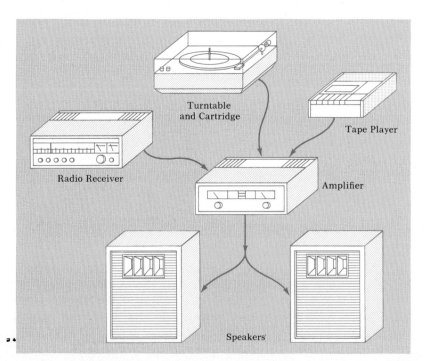

Turntable
and Cartridge

Tape Player

Radio Receiver

Amplifier

Speakers

waves that can be understood by the listener. The procedures that make the system work are both the manual operations, such as tuning the radio to the desired station or placing a record on the phonograph, and the internal design structure of the individual components, which include such things as the mechanics for transforming electrical currents into sound waves in the speaker system.

SYSTEM TYPES

open

closed

Systems are generally categorized as being either open or closed. In a *closed system,* the interactions required for performance never change. An old-fashioned hot water heating system, consisting of pipes and radiators, is an example of a closed system. In an *open system,* interactions are constantly changing, with old variables and system parts leaving the system and new ones continually entering the system.[3] A basketball team is an example of an open system, and the reaction of the team under varying conditions of play illustrates the manner in which a system reacts to change.

In reacting to change, a system is confronted by two sets of environmental forces. The first can be identified as those forces that are internal to the system; the second contains those that are external, or outside of the system. For the most part, the system has control over the internal forces. External forces, however, are largely beyond the control of the system. As developed in Chapters 1 and 2 and used throughout this text, these two sets of forces are the micro and the macro environments respectively. The effect of the environments on the system are described below in a brief discussion of the operation of both a closed and an open system.

2 sets environmental forces:
1) internal (micro)
2) external (macro)

The closed system provides an example of a system that reacts only to the micro environment. In the example of the old-fashioned heating system above, the elements that affect the heat in a building are all internal to the system. Thus, the system produces heat only when it is turned on, the water is hot, and the radiators get warm. All responses in the system are a direct result of internal interactions, and these never change regardless of the temperature in the building. The system is turned on when the building is cold, and it is turned off when the building is too hot.

A more sophisticated heating plant with the capability to react to changes in the outside temperature illustrates the operation of an open system. This plant contains external sensing devices that detect changes in the temperature, and it has an automatic thermostat that adjusts the flow of heat in a building to maintain the internal temperature at an even level. As an open system, this heating plant responds to both the micro and the macro environments, and it has the ability to react to changing environmental conditions.

SYSTEM INPUTS AND OUTPUTS

The basic interrelationships between a system and its environments are the result of system inputs and outputs. *Inputs* to a system may be in the form of information to be acted upon, or materials to be processed. In an open system, the organization's actions will differ, depending upon the nature of the inputs to which it is subjected. No system, however, may operate without a set of inputs to stimulate action. The *outputs* of a system are finished products or sets of behavior produced as a result of the stimulations provided by system inputs. In an information system, for example, raw data is taken as input and processed by the system to produce evaluated information.

INTERACTIONS AMONG SYSTEM COMPONENTS

In order to achieve desired outputs, the various components of the system must operate in a coordinated manner. Without coordinated actions, it is difficult to achieve specified goals. An orchestra without a conductor is capable of producing sound, but it may not produce music that is pleasing to the listener. In this illustration, appropriate interaction among system components (the members of the orchestra) is achieved through the coordination provided by the conductor. The following discussion of the general framework within which a system must operate provides a basis for understanding the required interactions in a system:[4]

1. Because they give a system direction and purpose, the *goals* of a system often dictate required interactions among components. In other words, achieving a stated goal may require that specific courses of coordinated action be followed.

2. The basic *organization* of the system will mold the communications channels through which coordination and control are achieved. These channels will determine how effectively coordination can be accomplished and, therefore, how nearly output will reflect desired objectives.

3. A system is stimulated by *inputs* which in turn create *responses* leading to desired *activity* within the system. The inputs, goals, and organization of the system provide a portion of the internal environment within which the system must operate.

4. The *outputs* of the system may be physical or abstract. They are responses to system inputs and function to help the system achieve its stated goals. How nearly these outputs accomplish stated objectives will be dependent upon the level, from a quality standpoint, at which the system operates.

5. Any open system is subject to *constraints* on its behavior. These may be either internal or external. The *internal constraints,* such as goals, organization, and inputs, inherently limit and guide system operation internally. *External constraints,* such as technology and the law, present limitations inherent in system design over which the designers have little, if any, control.

6. Once the system structure has been designed and constructed, all subsystems must function as a unified whole if the system is to be effective. This is where *interaction* takes place at its most important level. Lack of coordination and cooperation, based quite often on lack of information exchange,

will result in either poor planning, ineffective operation, or both. Correspondingly, effective system operation will result in goal accomplishment.

FEEDBACK AND CONTROL

If a system's performance does not meet desired goals, some mechanism is required to provide information that can be used to modify the behavior of the system so as to facilitate the achievement of goals. This mechanism is called *feedback* and its incorporation as a system function categorizes the system as as information feedback system. For the orchestra, feedback may come during rehearsal as a result of the conductor's critical ear for music. For the business firm, it may be in the form of low sales volume or low profits. In effect, information feedback becomes a new input upon which the system must act. Figure 3.2 presents a schematic diagram of an information feedback system.

The mere existence of information feedback does not, in itself, ensure effective system operation. There must be a set of *controls* that is designed to check the system's performance and make corrective adjustments as necessary. Control implies decisions and actions on the part of the system that are made in light of evaluated information. The decision making relationships that are involved in an information feedback system may be summarized as follows:

An information feedback system exists whenever the environment leads to a decision that results in action which affects the environment and thereby influences future decisions.[5]

Information feedback systems, whether they be mechanical, biological, or social, owe their behavior to three characteristics—structure, delays, and amplification. The structure of a system tells how the parts are related to one another. Delays always exist in the availability of information, in making decisions based on the information, and in taking action on the decisions. Amplification usually exists throughout such systems, especially in the decision policies of our industrial and social systems. Amplification is manifested when an action is more forceful than might at first be implied by the information inputs to the governing decisions. We are only beginning to understand the

FIGURE 3.2.
INFORMATION FEEDBACK
SYSTEM

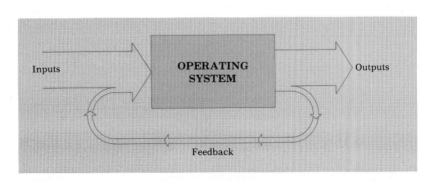

Inputs

OPERATING SYSTEM

Outputs

Feedback

way in which structure, time lags, and amplification combine to determine behavior in our social system.[6]

THE SYSTEMS APPROACH IN BUSINESS

To provide an understanding of the use of the systems approach in the field of business, the remainder of this chapter is devoted to a detailed discussion of the manufacturing enterprise as an organized behavior system. Representing the broadest scope of business activities in one organization, this type of firm will be used to illustrate the functions of the business system, its component parts, and their interrelationships. In the discussion, emphasis will be given only to the basic business functions that are required in the operation of the system. Organizational patterns, which vary from firm to firm, will not be discussed here.

NEED FOR THE SYSTEM APPROACH   In an underdeveloped society, where business has not advanced to the level of complexity that exists throughout most of the industrialized world, it is unnecessary to use the systems approach to understand the intricacies of the business enterprise. In such a society, with small businesses and mostly local trade systems, the complexity of business enterprise is at such a low level that an individual firm does not normally meet the requirements for categorization as a system. The complicated nature of the typical business enterprise in the industrialized world, however, has made adoption of the systems approach a necessity. Some of the problems presented by the modern business enterprise that preclude a simpler analytical approach are described below.[7]

The growing size of the firm.   Modern businesses in industrialized nations are much larger than either their counterparts in underdeveloped nations or those that existed only a few years ago. This growth in size has led to problems of integration, making it difficult to tie together the diverse parts of the organization to achieve the coordinated action required for successful operation.

Corporate complexity.   In addition to growth in the physical size of firms, there has been growth in the number of product lines offered by the typical firm and expansion of operations over wide geographic areas. This has added to the operating complexity of the typical business enterprise. In turn, the complexity of interrelationships between component parts of the firm has precluded simple analysis of cause and effect relationships that may adversely affect the overall operation. Thus, it has been necessary to develop new analytical techniques, such as the systems approach, for the evaluation of business operations.

Management specialization.   There has also been a trend toward specialization of skills within the firm. In a small company, out of necessity, a manager must be a jack-of-all-trades. In a large firm, this may not be possible, or even desirable. Many functional areas have become so involved that a management generalist may not possess the technical skills required to analyze the problems related to the activities of each specific subpart of the firm. Today, the modern organization must employ experts in a wide number of specialized areas to work with specific business problems. With increased diversification, there is an increased need for coordination of activities. No one person can oversee, in detail, the entire set of required business operations.

Diversity of operating objectives.   Modern firms, with a multitude of product lines and specialized production and support units, are faced with various sets of operating objectives that must be coordinated and integrated if the firm's overall operations are to be successful. Since it is necessary to interface the goals of the firm with those of individual components, there is a need for both cooperation among system components and an acceptance of the principle of suboptimization (this concept will be discussed later in this chapter).

Inevitability of change.   It has often been noted that the only thing that is constant in today's world is change. Furthermore, changes can take place very rapidly. When they occur, management must have the ability to react quickly and responsibly. The more complex the scope and nature of change, the more necessary it becomes to adopt a systems approach to describe the workings of a business firm. This is due to the fact that even minor changes can have a dramatic impact on the interrelationships that exist among the various components of the enterprise. For example, a tightening of credit may affect the acquisition of needed new machinery. In this case, application of the systems approach can help to distinguish the interrelationships between the firm's financial function and its production planning department.

Environmental constraints.   Although changes in both the micro and the macro environments present opportunities for business, change also poses a certain level of constraint on operations. These constraints must be understood and their impact on the firm must be met by adaptation or revision of operating procedures. Internally, the failure of engineering to develop a new product design can significantly affect marketing plans for introducing the new product. Externally, changes in the regulations of the Environmental Protection Agency might influence both production and marketing if stringent new requirements are imposed.

BUSINESS SYSTEM ORGANIZATION

If the purpose of a manufacturing firm is to produce and sell products, the primary functions required for daily operation of the firm are production and marketing. Of equal importance, early in the business cycle, are the functions of engineering, finance, and research and development. In addition, a set of support functions are required to facilitate the basic functions. These support functions include accounting (as part of the overall management information system), personnel, and corporate management. A functional organization chart depicting the interrelated components of a business system is shown in Figure 3.3. The basic functions performed by each area are presented below.[8]

MAJOR FUNCTIONAL AREAS

The major functional areas of the business system may be subdivided as activities pertaining to day-to-day operations and activities that facilitate day-to-day operations. The production and marketing functions fall into the former category; engineering, finance, and research and development fall into the latter category.

FIGURE 3.3.
FUNCTIONAL ORGANIZATION
CHART

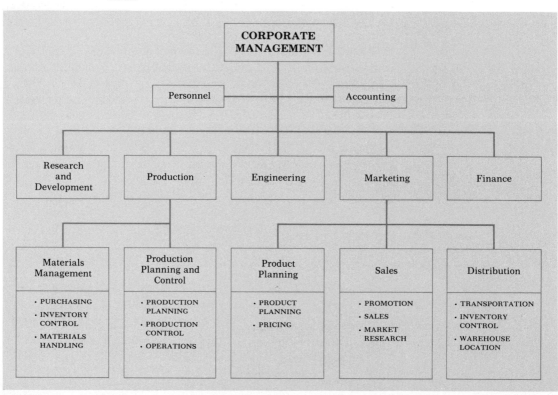

Production.   The production function encompasses the activities required to manufacture goods and services in a timely and cost effective manner. Production related activities fall into two categories. The first includes planning for, controlling, and performing the actual production of goods and services. During production planning, the production process is defined. Production methodologies and assembly line layouts are developed, and the sequencing and length of production runs are determined (how many of one type of product should be built at one time before a second model is introduced). Once production planning has been accomplished, the actual production process is performed. At this point, the function of production control is introduced, which involves direction and supervision of the production process and monitoring of product quality.

The second category of overall production process activities, which are accomplished in three stages, involves acquisition and management of materials needed to facilitate operations. Inventory control mechanisms, including development of ordering procedures and time, are defined during the planning stage. This stage is important in providing needed production materials at the time required. Inventory levels must also be considered so that too much material will not be acquired and held after needed, or acquired too far in advance. The purchasing stage provides the mechanism for material acquisition. Finally, during the materials handling stage, in-plant material movement systems are developed to provide materials to the production line at the time and place needed. Obviously, coordination is required among the parts of the production operation if cost effectiveness is to be achieved.

The basic production process, then, involves the transformation of raw material inputs into useful finished products or sets of services. This transformation process is at the center of the business activity, but cannot stand alone. It is not enough to produce an end product; it is also necessary to place it in the hands of the consumer.

Marketing.   The second major operational activity in a manufacturing firm is marketing. Earlier in this book, marketing was described, in a micro system, as being concerned with:

the satisfaction of customer needs and the accomplishment of an organization's marketing objectives through the efficient and effective distribution of that organization's goods and services to selected market targets under conditions of constraint imposed by the marketing environments.

In performing this task, marketing engages in three sets of activities: product planning, sales, and distribution. Product planning encompasses analysis of consumer needs and the translation of these needs into marketable products that can be produced by the manufacturing firm. It includes market research, development of sales estimates and target markets, recommended pricing strategies, and the timing of product introductions.

The sales function is performed in coordination with the product planning function, and is often referred to as order getting. In this phase of marketing, the product is promoted through advertising or other promotion techniques, and sales contracts are made. At this point, it is also necessary to identify marketing channels; decisions must be made regarding the use of direct selling, wholesalers, retailers, or some combination of these methods.

Once an order has been obtained, it must be filled. Order filling is accomplished through the broad distribution process, which involves the movement of products to customers, but is something larger. Besides purchasing transportation services to facilitate goods movement, the distribution function includes warehouse location and layout, finished goods inventory requirements, and product assortments. In fact, it encompasses all physical requirements and considerations from the end of the production line to the consumer.

Research and development.   The first of the three functional areas involved in the preparation, or planning, for production and marketing activities is research and development. These activities take place on two levels. First, they involve some degree of basic research aimed at the advancement of technologies so that new products may be developed. This type of research may be found in companies such as pharmaceutical firms or chemical companies. The second level deals with product development and applied research. At this level, existing technologies are investigated and present knowledge utilized in an effort to achieve new product designs that will satisfy specific customer needs.

Engineering.   Engineering design of the product is accomplished in three steps. First, product ideas produced through research and development activities are translated into detailed product designs. Second, product designs are "engineered," through the translation of design concepts, into workable product plans and specifications. Third, production methods are defined and equipment and tool designs are completed to permit product manufacture.

Finance.   The third of the interactive preparation functions is concerned with the development of sources of capital for equipment and facility acquisition, and the actual acquisition of required resources. As a result of the need for funds from outside sources during expansion, the financial function also includes long-range planning associated with the acquisition of working capital. This is a critical activity since lack of funds to support expansion efforts may severely limit a manufacturing enterprise's accomplishment of overall objectives.

Support functions.   Although the major functions described above form the mainstream of most business activity, they cannot operate without assistance. Various support functions are required to augment and facilitate the performance of these functions. Services performed by these support areas include coordination of overall firm activities; provision of resources such as personnel; and generation of needed management information. Even though these functions are not directly involved in the manufacturing-distribution mainstream, they are essential to the successful operation of the business system. To illustrate the types of activities performed by support functions, three examples are described below:

1. *Personnel* provides the human resources required to produce goods and services. It is the company's liaison with the labor force and represents an important staff function in the system.

2. The *accounting* function provides the base for the firm's information system. It collects cost data, prepares budgets, pays the bills, and provides financial and cost information to all activity areas within the firm. It also provides the system of checks and balances used to monitor the flow of cash through the system. This information and control base is essential to a firm's operations.

3. *Corporate management,* the executive level of administration, is the coordinating force for a firm's diverse activities. It provides direction through policy formulation and supervision and is also instrumental in solving jurisdictional disputes among operating managers, leading to successful operation of the parts of the firm as a coordinated system. In effect, corporate management provides the master control mechanism for the system's operations. (Figure 3.3).

BUSINESS SYSTEMS NETWORKS

The components described above form the basic structure of the business system. Overlaying this structure is a set of six networks that define the operations of the system and the various functional area relationships. As in the case of the basic components of the business system, these networks are closely interconnected; each crosses several functional area boundaries. A discussion of these interconnections is presented later in this chapter, but the functions of each of the six basic networks are described below.[9]

Materials. The materials network encompasses the flow of goods through the manufacturing process. It also includes stocks of physical goods within the overall production system, such as raw materials, work-in-process, and finished goods inventories.

Orders. The orders network operates at two levels. The first is the short run order cycle for product manufacture, from acceptance of customer orders to delivery of finished goods. This portion of the network is primarily concerned with the external interface between the system and its customers. At the second level, for both short and long time horizons, are internal actions resulting from existing or expected customer orders, and the requisition stream for ordering materials, personnel, or facilities required for production.

Money.   The money network encompasses all actual cash flows required for, or generated by, system operations.

Personnel.   The personnel network is concerned with the availability of people within the system and includes all factors affecting their availability, including company policies, such as overtime policies, and union contracts. It is the personnel network that breathes life into the system's organization chart.

Capital equipment.   The capital equipment network encompasses the physical facilities required for operation of the system, including buildings, tools, and equipment necessary for production operations. This network forms the tangible structure of the system and is the physical foundation for its organizational structure.

Interconnecting information.   The information network ties together the diverse operations of the business system. In Forrester's words, "... it is raised to a position superior to the other networks because it is the interconnecting tissue between all of them."[10] For example, the information network provides the interconnection between customer orders and material requisitions, and between production schedules and sales forecasts. Without an effective information network, system coordination could not be achieved.

OPERATION OF THE BUSINESS SYSTEM

In the preceding section, the organization of a business system was identified through a discussion of the functional areas and the interconnecting networks that are required in system design. This section focuses on the operation of the business system, with an emphasis on the firm's input-output relationships and the operational dimensions of the production and marketing functions.

INPUT-OUTPUT RELATIONSHIPS

As an input-output system, the business organization interfaces with the macro environment. Input-output relationships may be used to define the role of the business organization as a system processor. To illustrate, the firm receives inputs from the macro environment. These inputs are processed internally. When processing is complete, the output flows back to the macro environment in the form of marketable goods. The input-output relationships involved in this process are presented in Figure 3.4.

In the example shown in Figure 3.4, the system's interface with the macro environment has been identified by sets of connecting flows between the system and its suppliers and customers. These flows include system inputs, outputs, and implicit feedback responses generated through interactions. A more detailed analysis of each connecting flow is presented below.

Inputs. The business system receives inputs from the macro environment that may stimulate or constrain its actions, depending upon the specific nature of the inputs. A steady flow of men, materials, money, and machines provides a positive stimulant for the system; a shortage in the supply of these inputs can restrain the system's operation. In 1973 a significantly large number of business organizations were severely hampered by material shortages caused by the energy crisis. Likewise, the recession that followed greatly affected the flow of money as capital became more difficult to obtain.

Information flow is another important input for the business system. A favorable economic forecast, for example, can positively influence the decision making process if estimates indicate the need for an increase in the level of planned production output for an upcoming business period. Alternatively, bad economic forecasts can materially alter expansion plans and force management to reduce output. Other information inputs that stimulate or constrain the business system may flow from the market, sociocultural, legal, competitive, institutional, and technological environments.

Outputs. The outputs of a business system fall into three categories. First, the firm outputs goods and services to meet the needs of its target market. Second, in the case of a business for profit, it outputs a flow of financial returns for its stockholders, workers, and materials suppliers. Finally, the firm outputs information to its potential customers, in the form of advertising and other promotional information, and financial data to stockholders and various government agencies, such as the Internal Revenue Service and the Securities Exchange Commission.

FIGURE 3.4.
INPUT-OUTPUT FLOWS

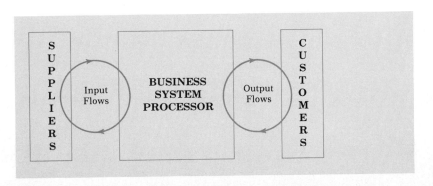

Feedback.   Since the operation of the business organization is best represented as an open system, it is necessary to consider feedback loops, which notify the firm of changes in its environments, which result from actions of the system, or from reactions by customers to the system's market offerings. The lack of this type of information precludes the firm from responding either to unfavorable reactions to its output, or to system movement•in directions that do not lead to achievement of desired objectives. The purpose of the feedback loop, then, is to provide the firm with the needed information to facilitate efforts and alter its behavior. With proper feedback, the system is in a better position to successfully adapt to change in its environments, react to unfavorable changes in its competitive position, and intelligently attempt to alter its environment. Efficient feedback loops shorten the adjustment process, dampening the effects of business fluctuations to which the system may be subjected.

INTERNAL OPERATING RELATIONSHIPS

Based on the general discussion of the functions of a business system that was presented earlier in this chapter, this section will focus on the internal operating relationships in the system. Special attention will be given to the production and marketing components in recognition of their primary role in the creation and delivery of the system's outputs. The marketing and production operations involved in order getting, goods processing, materials management, and order filling form the basis for the discussion. The relationships involved in these primary business system operations are shown in Figure 3.5, followed by a brief analysis of each and an identification of the role of the facilitating components and support functions.

Order-getting.   To be profitable, a business system must be able to sell its output. This is accomplished in the order-getting phase of the system's total operation. During this phase, the system's initial direct interface with its macro environment is formed through the marketing component. Internally, the actions required for order getting are interfaced with the production component in the order-filling operation. The relationships between marketing and production in the order-getting phase are described below.

The marketing component interfaces with the production component during day-to-day operations, providing estimates of production requirements and output timing to meet estimated demands for goods and services. Once an order has been received, either in advance of production or afterward, when goods are in inventory, marketing again interfaces with production in the order-filling operation by initiating requests for product shipments. Completion of the order-filling process closes the external, consumer environment loop.

The key purposes of the order-getting phase are to obtain orders for the system's products and to provide the remainder of the organization with required product demand information. The order-getting opera-

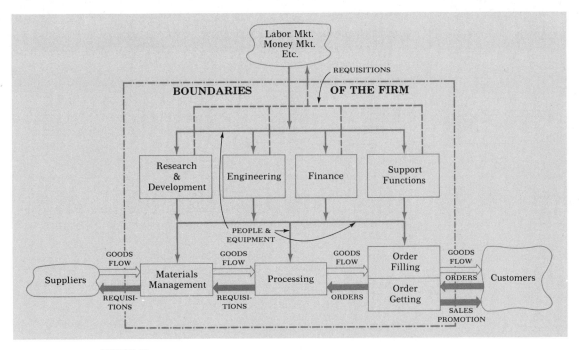

FIGURE 3.5.
INTERACTIONS AMONG
SYSTEM COMPONENTS

tion fits into the firm's information flow network through provision of information on required product flows, and by provision of interfaces, as a part of product planning, with engineering and other facilitating components. In this manner, product design inputs concerning target prices, technical requirements, and financial needs are generated. The order-getting operation also directly influences the money network by generating revenues through sales.

Processing. The production component, encompassing production planning and control, is charged with transforming material and labor inputs into desired goods and services. It stands at the center of the overall business system, yet it does not directly interface with the macro environment. Even though production operations are influenced by the macro environment, the effect of this influence is buffered by actions of the other system components. For example, raw materials inventories, provided through materials management activities, buffer product flows from fluctuations in material availability. Thus, the production component primarily reacts to external demands from the environment that are translated by other system components. The production component performs as a service center for the remainder of the system.

Materials management. Reacting to information received from both the marketing and production components, the materials management operation acquires the inputs needed for production. This operation performs in the role of a customer rather than a seller by purchasing inputs that can be used in the production process. Materials management, therefore, is concerned with the physical flow of required production materials into and through the production system, which requires interface most directly with the production component. This operation also interfaces with the financial component when the demand for outward cash flow is created through material purchases.

Order filling.   The order-filling operation is the last contact between the system and its customers, and provides for the physical distribution of the system's output. The distribution process, of course, is critical to the ultimate success or failure of the system, for it is the key to customer service and resultant customer satisfaction. The order-filling operation interfaces with production and fills a coordinating role between the marketing and production components in the reconciliation of production scheduling and inventory cost tradeoffs.

Facilitating components.   Research and development, engineering, and finance establish important relationships with marketing and production as facilitating components in the system. These relationships are described below.

1. The research and development component must interface with the marketing component to effect product developments that will satisfy market requirements. Likewise, research and development must work closely with both engineering and production to ensure practical product designs and manufacturing feasibility for developed products.

2. The engineering component serves as a liaison between marketing and production by translating marketing information relating to customer requirements into product designs that can be effectively and efficiently produced. Engineering is also involved in both product and packaging modifications that are required as the result of changing market conditions.

3. The finance component is charged with the task of obtaining funds required in the production and distribution of the system's output. In effect, this component interfaces with all of the system's components since all are involved in operations that require funding. Financial operations result from requests from other parts of the system, and the finance component serves as an important interface with the macro environment in the acquisition of funds from investors and in the payment of billings from suppliers.

Support functions.   As noted earlier, three support functions are required to effectively operate the business system. These are personnel, accounting, and corporate management. Each of these and their relationships in the business system are discussed briefly below:

1. The personnel function secures the required people for system operations. Utilizing this function, the system acts on personnel requests from operating components and interfaces with the macro environment through the labor market.

2. The accounting function is the center of the system's information network. From the operating components, this function acquires data input and processes it into useful financial information that can be used to evaluate and control the system's performance.

3. The corporate management function is the executive level of administration in the business system. Through policy formulation and direction, this function provides for the coordination and general supervision of the overall system; it is the guidance and control mechanism that helps the system function properly.

AN INTEGRATIVE EXAMPLE

As an integrative example of the internal operating relationships discussed above, Figure 3.6 presents a diagram of the production-distribution activity chain. The interactions required to complete the chain involve the order cycle and the relationships between the flows of orders and materials. As shown, the interrelated activities demon-

FIGURE 3.6.
PRODUCTION-DISTRIBUTION
ACTIVITY CHAIN

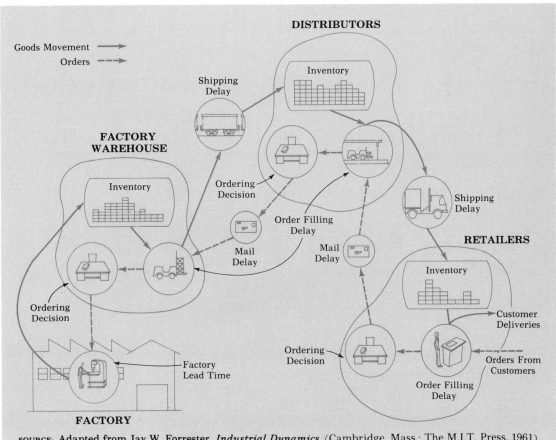

SOURCE: Adapted from Jay W. Forrester, *Industrial Dynamics* (Cambridge, Mass.: The M.I.T. Press, 1961), p. 139.

strate the complexities involved in integrating the operations of system components. Furthermore, this illustration shows that business system operations are in reality far more complex than previous descriptions of system structure have tended to imply. It also points out that system operations do not consist of instantaneous reactions to external stimuli. The delays required for decision making and reaction will increase both the complexity of operations and the difficulty in analyzing system operations.

CONTROL OF THE BUSINESS SYSTEM

In order to avoid unnecessary complications in business system operations, control is a mandatory requirement in system design. The control process is the nervous system of the business organization, for it controls the movements of the system's various components. The process moves from planning, in a broad context, to operations, and on to evaluation. Figure 3.7 presents a diagram of the planning cycle, showing the importance of control.

APPLICATION OF
THE CONTROL
PROCESS

In using the planning cycle as a tool of analysis in the business system, it is important to recognize that there are many interrelated steps in the control process, all of which are needed if successful operation is to be achieved. Three separate phases of the control process are presented here: product planning, resource utilization, and information flow.

Product planning cycle.   As viewed here, product planning is something larger than just planning for products. The planning cycle includes strategic planning, management control, and operational control.[11] It encompasses all of the general business planning cycle extending from the establishment of long-range objectives for the system to the ultimate sale of a product in the course of day-to-day operations.

Strategic planning involves long-term planning for the system over a five-, ten-, or twenty-year period. In this stage, the basic purpose of the business system is defined, and the basic system goals are identified and translated into more specific objectives. Since long-range efforts are being defined, the chief financial, production, and marketing officers in the system must be involved.

Management control spans a three- to five-year planning horizon. In this phase, the long-range goals and objectives of the system are turned into comprehensive plans with supporting programs detailing time schedules and control processes for their implementation.

During the operational control phase, more detailed analyses are conducted and near-term plans are formulated for one year in ad-

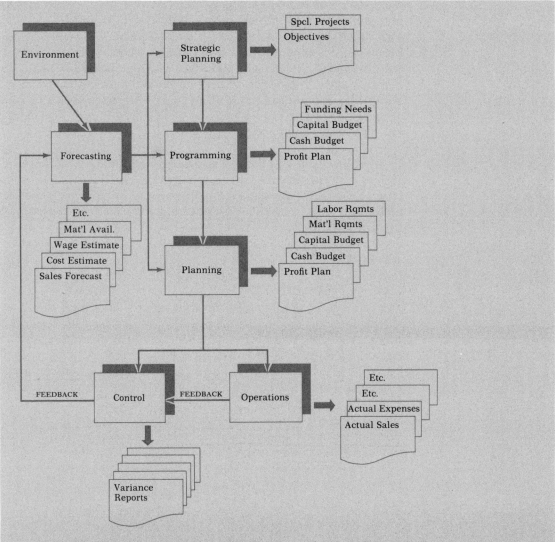

SOURCE: Adapted from Robert N. Anthony, John Deardon, and Richard F. Vancil, *Management Control Systems: Text, Cases, and Readings* (rev. ed.; Homewood, Ill.: Richard D. Irwin, Inc., 1972), Chapter 1.

FIGURE 3.7.
THE PLANNING CYCLE

vance. The plans are translated into established procedures and operations, and from this point forward, they are used to guide operations and to act as bases for evaluating results. Plans must be effectively translated into procedures and communicated to the operating levels if their control value is to be realized.

Resource utilization.   The second phase of the control process revolves around the utilization of resources—personnel, financial, or material—in a timely, effective, and efficient manner. This requires that procedures developed in the latter stages of the planning process be carried out as designed. In addition, resource utilization will require some degree of planning, perhaps at a low level, to ensure that procedures truly reflect operating needs.

During day-to-day operations it may be necessary to revise operating procedures by acting upon the best information available, if operations are to remain efficient. Revisions may be required to facilitate actions needed to correct problems encountered in implementing or performing operations, or to facilitate modifications in operating procedures that will reflect the impact of changes in any part of the system's macro environment.

Information flow.   William G. Ryan once said that "the process of creating information and putting it in the hands of the proper persons seems needlessly complicated, inefficient, and costly. It is incredibly difficult to create, transmit, recover, and use information."[12] Nevertheless, the key to the successful operation of any system is the transference of meaningful information among the separate parts of the overall system. Effective flow of information is needed to guarantee that the system, as a whole, will move in the desired direction. Indeed, most of the interactions among system parts occur through communication of information, not the physical movement of materials.

When developed in the business system, an information system can provide the framework for system operation by transmitting implementation procedures, reporting on environmental inputs that affect system operation, and providing feedback concerning system output in the marketplace. Since late information is often as bad as no information at all, the information system must be structured so that all information is transmitted in a timely manner. It is essential also, that only pertinent information is transmitted. One paradox encountered in today's "age of information" is a tendency to create more information than is actually needed, thus making it difficult to determine what information is most relevant.

THE ROLE OF SUBOPTIMIZATION   In operating the business system, it is necessary to coordinate activities in a manner that will maximize overall output within the context of the system's goals. This can be best understood by considering two important concepts. First, a common set of outputs is required for the system. Second, to obtain these outputs, three separate analytical steps must be performed and their results integrated. These steps are presented below:[13]

1. To obtain direction, it is necessary to develop unified sets of objectives and goals for the system. To be useful, this set of objectives relating to the needs, uses, and purposes of the system must be clearly defined.

2. Internal system constraints, and those external environmental forces that may limit system performance, must be clearly defined.

3. Basic system operating parameters must be identified and analyzed, includ-

ing system inputs, outputs, and component interactions, and operating tradeoffs.

In integrating the results of the analyses described above, it is often necessary to apply the principle of _suboptimization_ if desired system output is to be achieved. In effect, this entails a "tuning" of the system; it may be necessary for the components of the system to operate at individually suboptimal levels in order to accomplish a desired optimal output for the system as a whole.

Examination of a model for determining economic order quantities will demonstrate this principle. Given constant purchase prices and transportation charges (i.e., no quantity discounts), a purchasing department would try to minimize the number of orders placed in a given time period if it sought to minimize costs. Ordering costs, such as clerical costs for paperwork, are minimized when the number of orders placed is minimized. If this is done, however, inventory carrying costs are maximized, since average inventories would be at a high level. To minimize carrying costs, no unit would be ordered until needed for production or sale, in effect eliminating inventory carrying costs. Unfortunately, this would maximize the number of orders needed, thus maximizing ordering costs. Obviously, neither solution will minimize the firm's costs for raw material acquisition or product distribution. Tradeoffs must be made between ordering and carrying costs if total costs are to be optimized. These tradeoffs, as shown in Figure 3.8, produce a result that is best for the firm, but one that is suboptimal for each of the two components.

The concept of suboptimization explains why the systems concept is so important and why it is necessary to consider the operations of complex organizations in a total systems context. Fisk clearly states the need for suboptimization:

However many goals an organization seeks, its managers are ordinarily forced to choose from several combinations offering less than maximum attainment

FIGURE 3.8.
ECONOMIC ORDER QUANTITY
COST TRADEOFFS

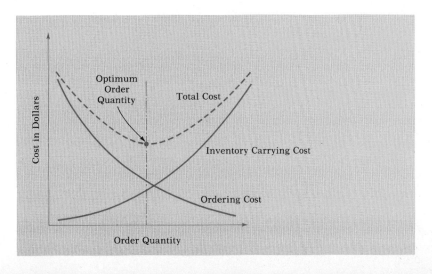

of any one goal in order to secure a satisfactory degree of attainment of others. Known as suboptimization, this procedure permits organizations to resolve their conflicts. Without it, organizations linked together ... would have great difficulty in achieving common goals. ...

Suboptimization requires that each individual perform the "office" assigned to him sufficiently well to enable the organization to move toward its purposes without an undue amount of conflict.[14]

CONCLUDING OBSERVATION

The successful operation of a business system involves the performance of a large number of business functions. Each is important in its own right and is necessary in the overall operation of the system. It is observed here and throughout this book, however, that the marketing function is the very heart of business activity; its role in the operation of the business system is analogous to the role that a horseshoe nail played in the loss of a kingdom long ago.

For want of a nail, the horse could not be shod; for want of a shoe, the horse could not be ridden; for want of his horse, the general could not lead; for want of the general's leadership, the battle was lost; and for want of the victory, the kingdom was lost.

Without an effective marketing program, sales will lag; as sales lag, profits will fall; and, as profits fall, the business system may fail. Marketing plays the crucial role in the generation of profitable sales. To this extent, marketing may be viewed as the "horseshoe nail that holds the kingdom together." Indeed, as shown in Figure 3.9, marketing forms the keystone of business activity in the business system.

FIGURE 3.9.
THE MARKETING KEYSTONE

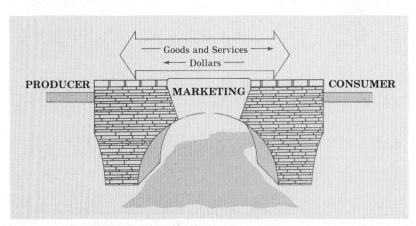

SUMMARY

In this chapter, the systems concept and a broad view of the operation of a business system have been developed. Because of the complexity of the modern business entity, the systems concept has been proposed as the appropriate analytic framework for the business firm. A system was defined as a set of parts whose actions must be coordinated to accomplish a given set of goals.

In applying the systems concept to the business firm, it was shown that the firm is made up of five basic operating components—marketing, production, finance, engineering, and research and development —and a set of supportive functions that include accounting, personnel, and corporate management. The production and marketing components were identified as the primary functional areas in the system; finance, engineering, and research and development were identified as facilitating functions. Production operations include production planning and control and materials management; marketing is involved in order getting and order filling. The research and development function deals with product development; the engineering function deals with turning product designs into workable sets of production specifications; and the financial function deals with obtaining the capital required to operate.

This chapter also discussed the necessity of applying the principle of suboptimization to the operations of the individual parts of a business system. In this manner, some parts are forced to operate at what would be suboptimal levels when considered in isolation. When integrated with the operation of other system components, however, the suboptimized component serves the best interests of the total system in the achievement of maximum output.

The specific operations of the marketing component were not considered in detail in this chapter. These operations will be covered in the following chapters of this section. Rather, emphasis here has been given to the overall operation of the business system. The component relationships within the system were stressed to provide an understanding of the impact of the macro marketing environment on business activity. As noted throughout this chapter, a stimulus to one part of the business system may have a dramatic impact on the operation of another part. The systems concept, of course, is designed to provide a total view of the entire firm that is not clouded by an analysis of isolated parts.

Prod. & Marketing— primary functional areas in system

QUESTIONS FOR DISCUSSION

1. What is the systems concept?

2. Why is it necessary to apply the systems concept to many current problems?

3. Contrast the operations of open and closed systems.

4. Analysis of the business firm requires use of the systems concept as an aid to the understanding of the interrelationships among the functional areas required for operations. Why is application of the systems concept necessary?

5. The operation of a typical manufacturing firm requires the establishment of activities in several functional areas. Describe these areas and explain the reasons why they are necessary.

6. Discuss the role of suboptimization in the operation of the business system.

7. Describe the purposes of the order-getting function and the order-filling function.

8. What interactions take place between the marketing and production components? In an integrated discussion, fully explain the internal relationships that exist between marketing and production.

9. Describe the control process as applied to the activities of the business system. Why is control of the business system necessary?

10. Why is marketing considered the keystone of business activity? Do you agree with this proposition?

NOTES

[1]C. West Churchman, *The Systems Approach* (New York: Dell Publishing Co., Inc., 1968), p. 29.

[2]David B. Smith, "Systems Engineering-Implications for Management," *Financial Analysts Journal* (May–June, 1965), p. 120.

[3]George Fisk, *Marketing Systems: An Introductory Analysis* (New York: Harper Row, Publishers, Incorporated, 1967), p. 12.

[4]*Ibid.,* p. 70.

[5]Jay W. Forrester, *Industrial Dynamics* (Cambridge, Mass.: The M.I.T. Press, 1961), p. 14.

[6]*Ibid.,* pp. 15–16.

[7]Richard A. Johnson, Fremont E. Kast, and James E. Rosenzweig, *The Theory and Management of Systems* (3rd ed.; New York: McGraw-Hill, Inc., 1973), pp. 29–32.

[8]A general discussion of the business enterprise, in more depth than is presented here, may be found in Keith Davis, ed., *The Challenge of Business* (New York: McGraw-Hill, Inc., 1975), among others.

[9]Forrester, *Industrial Dynamics*, pp. 70–72.

[10]*Ibid.,* p. 71.

[11]Robert N. Anthony, John Dearden, and Richard F. Vancil, *Management Control Systems: Text, Cases, and Readings* (rev. ed.; Homewood, Ill.: Richard D. Irwin, Inc., 1972), pp. 4–16.

[12]William G. Ryan, "Six Technologies in Search of a Manager," *Business Horizons* (Winter, 1966), p. 16.

[13]Smith, *Systems Engineering,* p. 120.

[14]Fisk, *Marketing Systems,* pp. 75–76.

SUGGESTED READINGS

Churchman, C. West, *The Systems Approach* (New York: Dell Publishing Co., Inc., 1968).

Davis, Keith, ed., *The Challenge of Business* (New York: McGraw-Hill, Inc., 1975).

Fisk, George, *Marketing Systems: An Introductory Analysis* (New York: Harper & Row, Publishers, Inc., 1967).

Forrester, Jay W., *Industrial Dynamics* (Cambridge, Mass.: The M.I.T. Press, 1961).

Henry, Porter, "Manage Your Sales Force as a System," *Harvard Business Review* (March–April, 1975), pp. 85–94.

Johnson, Richard A., Fremont E. Kast, and James E. Rosenzweig, *The Theory and Management of Systems* (3rd ed.; New York: McGraw-Hill, Inc., 1973).

King, William R. and David I. Cleland, "A New Method for Strategic Systems Planning," *Business Horizons* (August, 1975), pp. 55–64.

Small, John T. and William B. Lee, "In Search of an MIS," *MSU Business Topics* (Autumn, 1975), pp. 47–55.

Stasch, Stanley F., *Systems Analysis for Marketing Planning and Control* (Glenview, Illinois: Scott, Foresman and Company, 1972).

MARKETING
STRATEGY PLANNING

MARKETING STRATEGY PLANNING

The preceding chapter identified marketing as the keystone of business activity. With this concept in mind, it is appropriate to view the firm as a marketing system. The focus of this chapter is on marketing strategy planning and the nature and scope of marketing in the individual firm. Emphasis will be placed on the marketing philosophy of management, the role of marketing management, and the operation of the micro marketing system.

firm = marketing system

MARKETING PHILOSOPHY OF MANAGEMENT

As pointed out in Chapter 1, modern business systems have adopted a marketing oriented managerial philosophy that stresses profits through customer satisfaction. The emphasis is on customers rather than products or production. As shown in Figure 4.1 four major elements may be found in this philosophy of management: a customer orientation, a defined profit motivation, the need for an integrated marketing effort, and a sense of social responsibility. The philosophy embraces top level management and flows throughout the business system where it serves as a guide for the marketing department and all other operations, or functional areas, within the system.

CUSTOMER ORIENTATION

Customer orientation is the cornerstone of a marketing philosophy of management. Essentially, the customer orientation concept requires that a company first define the needs and wants of its customers and

**FIGURE 4.1.
THE FOUR PILLARS OF THE
MARKETING PHILOSOPHY OF
MANAGEMENT**

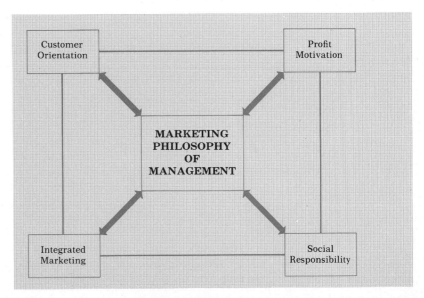

then direct effort toward the satisfaction of these needs and wants. It is a concept that defines marketing as a process that begins prior to the production of a good or service. The marketing process first discovers the needs of customer and marketplace; activity in the firm then revolves around the development of products and services to satisfy the needs of the particular marketing segment defined. This idea can be expressed in a number of ways:

—We're not the boss, the consumer is. What the consumer wants, the consumer gets.

—Under the marketing concept the customer is at the top of the organization chart.

—A company should prefer a franchise over a market to a franchise over a plant.

—Look at the company through the customer's eyes.

—Instead of trying to market what is easiest for us to make, we must find out much more about what the consumer is willing to buy. In other words, we must apply our creativeness more intelligently to people and their wants and needs rather than to products.[1]

PROFIT MOTIVATION

Profit motivation is also an integral part of a marketing philosophy of management. The logic that relates profit motivation to customer orientation is inescapable. Naturally, a firm must make a profit in order to survive; the question is, in what way may the firm best be managed in order to ensure a profit? The answer: by satisfying customers' needs. This does not mean that marketing should be all things to all people. The organization incurs costs, which it must recover. Therefore, the firm can only afford to satisfy those customer needs that will generate a residual profit after the costs of producing and marketing the product have been met. The role of the firm is to *selectively* satisfy customer needs, recognizing, too, that the firm has a responsibility to satisfy the needs of the owners of the business, as well as employees suppliers, and creditors.

INTEGRATED EFFORT

If the objective of the organization is to generate a profit through the satisfaction of customer needs and desires, it is necessary that all elements within the organization be coordinated and activities be integrated toward meeting a common goal. As noted in Chapter 3, certain functions in the organization may have to be suboptimized in order that the overall corporate goal can be reached. For example, production may be forced to operate at less than optimally efficient levels if greater costs would be incurred by producing excess products and maintaining them in inventory when no market exists. Likewise,

FIGURE 4.2.
THE CONCEPT OF
INTEGRATED MARKETING

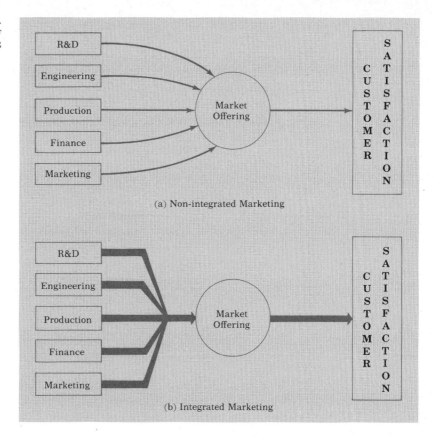

(a) Non-integrated Marketing

(b) Integrated Marketing

a less than optimally efficient distribution system might be necessary in order to reach all profitable segments of the market.

The achievement of an integrated effort within the firm requires a commitment to a marketing philosophy at all levels and throughout all functions. It is unfortunate, perhaps, that this concept has become known as a marketing orientation. Because of this particular term, those functional areas outside of marketing often regard the philosophy as an attempt by marketing to control activity in the firm. As shown in Figure 4.2, such is not the case. Integrated marketing simply provides the firm with an orientation that serves as the basis for a *philosophy of doing business* that is appropriate in a highly developed economy. In such an economy, the dictates of the marketplace will prevail, and all activities and functions of the firm must be attuned to its message through a coordinated and integrated effort.

SOCIAL RESPONSIBILITY   The last element of a marketing philosophy is social responsibility. Today, it is felt by many that the responsibility of business transcends the marketplace and extends to all of society; that business is an institution in society that has a responsibility to conduct itself in a way that will maximize not just the good of the individual consumer and the firm but the good of society as a whole.

In an increasingly complex environment, it is almost impossible for the impact of business activity to be confined solely to the market-place. Critics question whether business is truly serving the public good when it produces products at a cost to the broader environment. No longer can water, air, and land be treated as free goods. Business must be concerned as much with what it takes out of the environment as with what it puts in.

Recently marketers have suggested that marketing has a growing responsibility to deal with such problems as discrimination, a deterio-rating urban environment, crime in the streets, problems of the poor, and the like. The idea that a sense of social responsibility is in the long-run in the best interests of business is gaining wide acceptance; if business neglects the social, cultural, and ecological conditions that affect the nature of the surrounding community, the results will be ultimately disadvantageous to the firm. It may no longer be enough to consider only the short-term benefits of a given management philoso-phy.[2]

The response of the major oil companies to the gasoline shortage provides an excellent illustration of responsible industry-wide action. Instead of urging car owners to consume more fuel, the oil producers promoted ways to economize. This was a rather dramatic turnabout from earlier advertising messages that had encouraged drivers to travel more, hence, consume more. The petroleum companies wisely recognized that they could hardly market a product, gaso-line, that was not available. The response in this industry was obviously in the interest of both the companies themselves and the consuming public.

To summarize, a marketing philosophy of management suggests that a firm can profit best by satisfying customer needs, and that it should do so as efficiently as possible by integrating all functional activities within the firm. In addition, the long-run interests of the community in which the firm operates should become an integral part of strategic marketing-management planning.

THE ROLE OF MARKETING MANAGEMENT

1. planning
2. execution
3. control

Following the philosophy outlined above, marketing management is responsible for matching the firm's output of goods and services with customer requirements. The distinguishing feature of marketing management is its responsibility to create and maintain demand for the firm's goods. One author has suggested that it is the job of the marketing manager to "interpret conditions in the market place."[3] Another has chosen to define marketing management as, "the process of increasing the effectiveness and/or efficiency by which marketing activities are performed by individuals or organizations."[4] Most authors agree that all marketing managers practice certain common functions. In Chapter 1, these functions were defined as: (1) planning, (2) execution, and (3) control.

MARKETING PLANNING

Planning is deciding in the present what to do in the future; it is the method by which the course of the firm is charted; it involves the establishment of goals and objectives along with the steps necessary to accomplish them. Much marketing planning has to do with the creation or selection of markets that offer potentially profitable opportunities and the development of appropriate marketing strategies to exploit those opportunities. As such, the process involves both long- and short-run considerations.

Long-range planning ordinarily encompasses periods of at least five years and perhaps as many as twenty years. In the past, the long-range planning process often began with attention to facilities and financing. Today, however, more companies, recognizing the increasing pressures of competition and technological obsolescence, begin the process with a statement of the company's basic marketing missions and the selection of related opportunities. Financial and facilities planning follows.

Short-range planning, involving periods of one to two years, is a reflection of the long-range plan. It is designed to keep the company headed in a direction that will lead to the accomplishment of the long-range goals and objectives. The short-range plan, though, is not simply one element of the long-range plan. In fact, it may deviate significantly depending on such factors as recent experience, current outlook, or particular interest group expectations. The short-range plan, at the minimum, will provide overall goals and budgets for each marketing strategy area.

MARKETING EXECUTION

Marketing execution involves, as the term suggests, the execution of the marketing plans; it is concerned with getting the right product or service to the right place at the right time at the right price. Essentially, such an approach views the marketing mix as a combination of four basic components: product, promotion, distribution, and price. The execution of the marketing plan can, therefore, be viewed as a process that involves the matching of an organization's marketing output with market requirements.

There are a number of decisions that must be made related to each of the mix components. Product decisions concern the introduction of new products, product modifications, and product deletions. Promotion decisions consider the use and relative emphasis to be given to advertising, personal selling, and other tools, such as sales promotion, public relations, publicity, and packaging and branding. Distribution decisions include creation of the channel network, selection of channel intermediaries, and the determination of the means by which the actual distribution of goods and services will take place. Finally, pricing decisions consider the goals of pricing strategies and methods by which firms can arrive at appropriate prices. Each of the mix elements is discussed in more detail in Chapters 5 and 6 in a strategy context.

MARKETING CONTROL

Marketing control is concerned with continuous evaluation and analysis of the marketing plan. It was described in Chapter 1 as being analogous to a thermostat on a furnace. The marketing control mechanism is designed to react to deviations from the marketing plan and to make corrective adjustments. Marketing control, therefore, operates as a feedback process that influences marketing planning.

The four dimensions of marketing control are: (1) setting the standards of performance, (2) determining the level of actual performance, (3) measuring actual performance against performance standards, and (4) making decisions concerning future marketing operations. Standards, if they are to be meaningful in the control sense, must be measurable. Marketing standards may be established in terms of *results achieved,* such as sales volume or market share, *effort expended,* such as promotional expenses incurred, or *productivity levels,* such as gross margin return on inventory investment.

Once standards are established, two other questions must be answered before actual performance can be measured. They are: When should measurement occur, and how should measurement occur?

Measurement may take place on an almost continuous basis in some cases. Salesperson call reports, for example, are routinely supplied every week; quarterly reporting in other areas is fairly common. Usually, measurement coincides with the time periods for which standards have been set. Basically, the objective of the marketing manager must be to monitor performance often enough that operations never have the chance to get seriously out of control. Measurement may take place through means as straightforward as direct observation and the perusal of operational reports. More sophisticated techniques include customer surveys and statistical analysis.

Once actual performance has been measured, comparison can take place with the standards previously established. This comparison can be made quite simply. If performance is found to significantly deviate from standards, it then becomes the job of the marketing administrator to determine the reason or reasons for the deviation and to take corrective action. Very often this action will be in the form of further study and analysis, since the original data may have revealed only the existence, but not the cause, of a serious problem. At the least, the marketing administrator will want to review the market situation, the reasonableness of objectives and goals, organizational resources, and marketing strategies.

In summary, the fundamental job of the marketing manager is to plan, execute, and control marketing activities in the firm. In order to

fulfill this role properly, the manager must have complete understanding of the marketing system of the firm. The next section looks
at the operation of this system.

OPERATION OF THE MICRO MARKETING SYSTEM

In Chapter 3, the concept of the firm as a business system was introduced. At this point, the systems concept will be reintroduced but with
emphasis on the micro marketing system and the activities involved
in marketing strategy planning. In this context, a system may be
viewed as "an <u>organized whole consisting of a number of identifiable</u>,
<u>relatively independent parts that interact and have some relation</u>ship
<u>to one another</u>. It has a built-in control mechanism that maintains the
relationship by releasing counter forces to any disturbance that could
upset the balance."[5] In this sense, micro marketing is the

process by which the firm keeps surveillance of its markets, detects and evalu-
ates forces for change, and feeds this back as inputs into the firm, thus generating throughout all the strategic decision points in the firm new strategies and
actions with the new or adjusted output behavior designed to defend against
goal obstacles or to exploit opportunities. ....[6]

FIGURE 4.3.
THE MICROMARKETING
SYSTEM

The micro marketing system is depicted in Figure 4.3. In the model,

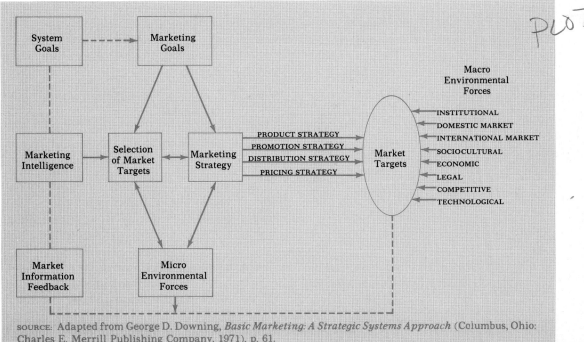

SOURCE: Adapted from George D. Downing, *Basic Marketing: A Strategic Systems Approach* (Columbus, Ohio:
Charles E. Merrill Publishing Company, 1971), p. 61.

the focus of the firm is on market targets and the macro environmental forces that impact on selected markets. An "intelligence system" acquires information from these macro environments that is critical to the formulation of specific firm and marketing goals. These objectives, in turn, influence the selection of markets and products, as well as strategies involving promotion, distribution, and pricing.

Several authors distinguish between the firm's total marketing system and the various components of the marketing system. William Lazer, for example, says that there may be several marketing subsystems within the firm, such as the physical distribution system, the marketing communication system, and the product development system.[7] Lazer further states that there are certain characteristics inherent in marketing systems. First, they are variable and complex, both in terms of the elements employed in them and the physical and spatial dimensions of them. Second, marketing systems are open rather than closed. They respond to environmental forces. Third, marketing systems are adaptive; they must constantly respond to changes in the marketplace. Fourth, marketing systems are externally oriented. The response of the firm is dictated primarily by the market and not other secondary considerations. Fifth, systems are competitive. In the free enterprise system that operates in the United States, the inherent philosophy of conduct is one of competition. Sixth, marketing systems contain discordant or disfunctional elements; the seeds of conflict, strain, and tension are inherent in marketing systems.[8]

Given the earlier discussion of the marketing philosophy of management, it is more appropriate to view the micro marketing system as an entity rather than to adopt the narrow perspective of marketing subsystems. An analysis of the firm's total marketing system provides a view of the operation of the system and an identification of the interrelated marketing strategy planning stages that are required in the generation of profitable customer satisfactions. As operationalized in Figure 4.3, these are:

1. Recognizing Environmental Forces

2. Gathering Marketing Intelligence

3. Developing System Goals

4. Selecting Market Targets

5. Formulating Marketing Strategy

RECOGNIZING ENVIRONMENTAL FORCES

As illustrated in Figure 4.3, the marketing system must react to environmental forces that are both external and internal to the firm. The external elements of the system include the macro forces that impact on the firm in its efforts to attract the market. The internal elements are those micro forces that include the other functional areas of the firm, such as research and development, engineering, production, and finance.

The macro environment. The macro environment of marketing, which was introduced in Chapter 2, contains a number of powerful forces that are constantly changing. Each of these forces may be viewed as a separate marketing environment that is external to the firm and beyond the immediate control of management. It is important to note again that each, in its own way, can dramatically affect the firm. This affect occurs in the marketplace where the firm interacts with selected market targets.

The marketplace, of course, is where the firm must attract customers, cultivate the loyalty of suppliers and distributors, withstand the attacks of competitors, and deal with a host of changing environmental conditions. Since each of the macro environments receives extensive attention in Part III, they will not be discussed here. It is enough to say now that macro environmental forces play a significant role in limiting the scope of the firm's marketing activity in a complex world.

The micro environment. Although marketing activities are essential to the success of the firm, it is important to recognize that marketing must operate within the framework of a micro environment. The business firm develops an internal structure for the purpose of achieving its goals. This structure includes such elements as research and development, engineering, production, finance, and marketing. Its purpose is to efficiently utilize inputs into the system in order to generate productive outputs. These inputs include labor, materials, equipment, and capital.

Just as the marketing activity is influenced by factors in the macro environment, so, too, does the micro environment affect the firm's marketing operations. To a large extent, research and development, engineering, production, and finance function as constraints in the micro marketing system. The exploitation of market opportunities is dependent upon the ability of research and development to create the necessary material, compound, or process, the ability of engineering to take the output of research and development and design a product that can be produced at a reasonable cost, the ability of production to actually produce the product as designed within the cost constraints imposed and at the necessary quality levels, and the ability of finance to provide the necessary capital.

GATHERING MARKETING INTELLIGENCE

From the above discussion, it should be apparent that marketing must be attuned to both the macro and the micro environments if it is to function efficiently. The macro environment provides the firm's opportunities while, at the same time, imposing constraints. Likewise, the micro environment within the firm dramatically influences the ability of the marketing administrator to manage effectively. It is imperative, therefore, that these environments be constantly monitored. As presented earlier in Figure 4.3, this is the function of a marketing intelligence system. Although it is recognized that both external and internal forces must be analyzed in the intelligence system, emphasis here will be given to the monitoring of the external forces, since the macro environment effectively represents the "marketing arena" of the firm.

The firm collects raw data (market information) from the macro environment. This information becomes *marketing intelligence* only when it is evaluated and when a meaning or interpretation is assigned to it. Information, of course, must be generated before it can be evaluated. Marketing information may be primary or secondary in nature

P.L.O.T.

TABLE 4.1.
BASIC SECONDARY SOURCES OF MARKETING INFORMATION

Title	Publisher	Title	Publisher
Statistical Abstract of the U.S.	Dept. of Commerce	World Almanac and Book of Facts	Doubleday Co.
County and City Data Book	Bureau of the Census	Census of Manufacturers	Bureau of the Census
Annual Survey of Manufacturers	Bureau of the Census	U.S. Industrial Outlook	Dept. of Commerce
Current Industrial Reports	Bureau of the Census	Marketing Information Guide	Dept. of Commerce
Business Service Checklist	Dept. of Commerce	Monthly Catalog of U.S. Government Publications	G.P.O.
Guide to Marketing	Printers Ink, Inc.	Survey of Buying Power	Sales Management
Predicasts (Looseleaf)	Predicasts, Inc.	Thomas' Register of Manufacturers	Thomas Pub. Co.
Million Dollar Direc ory	Dun & Bradstreet	Middle Market Directory	Dun & Bradstreet
Directory of Post Offices	P.O. Dept.	Zip Code Directory	U.S. Postal Service
Survey of Current Business	Dept. of Bus. Economics	Financial Executive's Handbook	Dow Jones
American Marketing Association Definitions	AMA	American Marketing Association Directory	AMA
American Marketing Association Bibliography	AMA	Statistical Services of the U.S. Government	G.P.O.
Standard Industrial Classification Manual	G.P.O.	Market Analysis	Frank Scereerow Press

and can be gathered through formal or informal methods. Table 4.1 lists some of the more important secondary sources of marketing information available in the United States.

Primary information is derived from firsthand sources. The marketing organization actively solicits information from primary sources through (1) the use of marketing research techniques; (2) input from the field sales force; (3) observation; and (4) the development of mathematical models.

Marketing research is basically a technique for gathering, analyzing, and interpreting marketing data. A problem is identified, hypotheses about the problem are proposed, and the hypotheses are tested by generating data through some research design. Research of this kind recently caused Holiday Inns to revamp its entire corporate strategy, at which time Clyde H. Dickson, executive vice-president, declared, "Now it's marketing, marketing, marketing all the way. We have to identify our markets and go after them with a rifle instead of a shotgun."[9]

The *field sales force* is also very useful as an information source. Salespersons are particularly valuable because of their every day, face-to-face contact with customers and the immediate problems of the marketplace. In a sense, salespersons act as an interface between the firm and its external environment. Properly utilized, the salesperson can be a useful information conduit to provide active flow of intelligence to the organization. Even though such information lacks the rigor of data provided by marketing research techniques, it is usually intuitively accurate and timely.

If the salesperson is to effectively provide information to the firm, however, the significance of that function must be made clear to the salesperson. Research has indicated that the salesperson often resists this particular aspect of the job. The salesperson sees management's request for information as a drain upon productive time. Instead of selling, the salesperson is forced to fill out what are viewed as endless forms. Furthermore, if the salesperson is provided no feedback as to the use to which the information is put, feelings about the unimportance of the information-gathering task are confirmed. For the salesperson to be an effective information conduit, that person first must see the value of the information that is generated. Second, some incentive must be given to generate the information. Finally, feedback must be received as to the use to which the information is put.[10]

Observation is yet another relatively inexpensive technique for gathering information. Observation involves the firm's executives, managers, and professional specialists in the day-to-day observation of their immediate environments. A sense of the environment may be derived from trade journals, the daily papers, community involvement in clubs and organizations, or any other activities that somehow relate, however broadly, to the behavior of the firm.

Beckman Instruments, Inc., of Fullerton, California, has developed a rather original way of observing a relevant environment. This firm has been able to have customers help design its product. Beckman employs focus groups in which specially invited guests attend lunch or cocktails to talk about process control equipment. The guests, in this case, are engineers and users of this type of equipment. Their input has been instrumental in causing Beckman to record some major changes in equipment design.[11]

Mathematical models have become popular as a means of generating marketing data. The term "model" may be defined as "a simplified representation, often in terms of a mathematical, statistical or logical set of relationships, of some aspect or aspects of human behavior or of a physical system."[12] Models may be either descriptive or decision models. Decision models include: allocation models, which help allocate scarce resources optimally; and game-theory models, which consider moves by rivals in the investigation of alternative actions in decision making. Descriptive models include, among others, waiting line models that help to balance the cost of lost sales against the cost of additional facilities, and simulation models used to introduce to a system different sets of input conditions in order to predict various alternative phenomena that could result.[13]

It was stated earlier that marketing intelligence is evaluated marketing information. There is an important distinction that must be made between marketing information and marketing intelligence. When information comes into the firm, the volume is likely to be overwhelming. It would be impossible for any single executive to comprehend the mass of data that could conceivably cross that person's desk during any given day. Therefore, specialists within the firm must collect this information, digest it, and distill from it those relevant bits of data upon which decisions will be made and plans will be forthcoming. In short, a system must be devised for funneling information into the firm in a logical and ordered sequence so that such information can be brought together for evaluation. This is the essence of a marketing intelligence system. Figure 4.4 illustrates the structure of an ongoing and highly developed system at Mead Johnson.

DEVELOPING SYSTEM GOALS

Again referring to Figure 4.3, the information generated by the intelligence system provides necessary input for the establishment of corporate and marketing goals. Goals may be defined as "plans expressed as quantitative results to be achieved at the end of the planning period. In this broad sense, goals include objectives, missions, deadlines, standards, targets and quotas."[14]

To the extent that a marketing orientation reflects the overall managerial philosophy of the firm, there is no real distinction to be made between the goals of marketing and the goals of the firm itself. It is an essential premise of this book that a firm's success depends upon its marketing success. Likewise, the real success that a firm's management enjoys depends significantly upon the effectiveness of the competitive strategies that it creates or causes to be created. These two

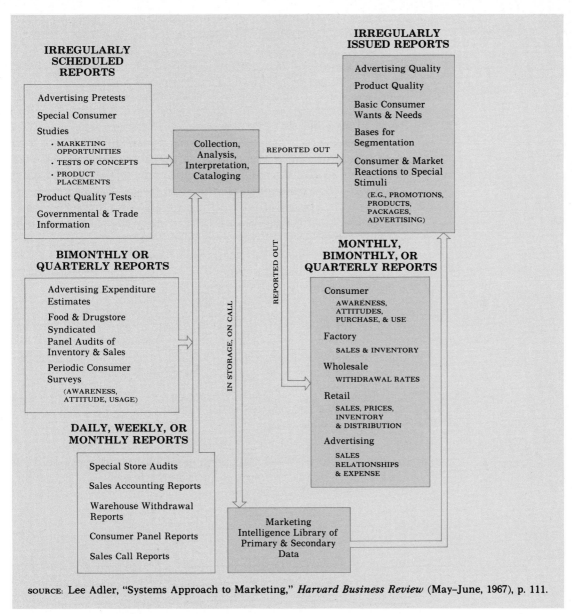

**IRREGULARLY
SCHEDULED
REPORTS**

Advertising Pretests

Special Consumer

Studies
- MARKETING OPPORTUNITIES
- TESTS OF CONCEPTS
- PRODUCT PLACEMENTS

Product Quality Tests

Governmental & Trade
Information

**IRREGULARLY
ISSUED REPORTS**

Advertising Quality

Product Quality

Basic Consumer
Wants & Needs

Bases for
Segmentation

Consumer & Market
Reactions to Special
Stimuli
(E.G., PROMOTIONS, PRODUCTS, PACKAGES, ADVERTISING)

Collection,
Analysis,
Interpretation,
Cataloging

REPORTED OUT

REPORTED OUT

IN STORAGE, ON CALL

**BIMONTHLY OR
QUARTERLY REPORTS**

Advertising Expenditure
Estimates

Food & Drugstore
Syndicated
Panel Audits of
Inventory & Sales

Periodic Consumer
Surveys
(AWARENESS, ATTITUDE, USAGE)

**MONTHLY,
BIMONTHLY, OR
QUARTERLY REPORTS**

Consumer
AWARENESS, ATTITUDES, PURCHASE, & USE

Factory
SALES & INVENTORY

Wholesale
WITHDRAWAL RATES

Retail
SALES, PRICES, INVENTORY & DISTRIBUTION

Advertising
SALES RELATIONSHIPS & EXPENSE

**DAILY, WEEKLY, OR
MONTHLY REPORTS**

Special Store Audits

Sales Accounting Reports

Warehouse Withdrawal
Reports

Consumer Panel Reports

Sales Call Reports

Marketing
Intelligence Library of
Primary & Secondary
Data

SOURCE: Lee Adler, "Systems Approach to Marketing," *Harvard Business Review* (May–June, 1967), p. 111.

FIGURE 4.4.
MEAD JOHNSON'S MARKETING
INTELLIGENCE SYSTEM

basic premises specifically tie marketing to the hierarchy of corporate goals.

It has been suggested that goals should be stated in both economic terms and time periods. A goal might be to realize an average return of 15 percent on invested capital over the next five years; the economic term would be 15 percent on invested capital, and the time period would be the next five years. Other kinds of goals are often labeled missions or charters. For example, General Electric states that its mission is "to carry on a diversified, growing, and profitable worldwide manufacturing business in electrical apparatus, appliances, and supplies and in related materials, products, systems, and services for industry, commerce, agriculture, government, the community, and the home."[15] Basically, however, a firm has three goals. They are profit, growth, and survival.[16]

Profit.   Business exists to serve customers at a profit. One measure of profit is the difference between revenue and cost. This difference is not an effective measure of business performance, however. Profit takes on meaning *as a measure of performance* only at the point at which it is compared to the inputs into the organization that generated the desired result. The result is a return-on-investment measure. The inputs against which profits generally are compared are sales, assets, or equity in the business. A return-on-sales figure

$$\text{return on sales} = \frac{\text{profit dollars}}{\text{sales dollars}}$$

measures the relationship of profit to the total sales of the business. As such, it reflects how well management managed "margins"—the difference between sales, cost of goods sold, and operating expenses—to generate a profit. A return-on-assets figure

$$\text{return on assets} = \frac{\text{profit dollars}}{\text{assets}}$$

in turn, reflects how well management managed both its current and fixed assets. The last measure, return-on-net worth

$$\text{return on net worth} = \frac{\text{net profit}}{\text{net worth}}$$

reflects the return to the owners on their invested capital. To summarize, the return-on-investment approach enables management to establish performance standards by relating desired levels of profit to sales, assets, and owner's investment in the business.

Growth.   A company will almost certainly name "growth" as one of its primary goals. However, "growth" per se, is a meaningless term; its nature must be defined. Growth may be described in terms of physical expansion; that is, growth of resources, plant, and facilities. A specific objective might be to open three branches in the Southwest in the next eighteen months.

Or, growth may be stated in terms of market share, which is the percentage of the total sales of a product or group of products that a firm gains. Many manufacturing firms consider the acquisition of market share to be as important as profit and sales volume objectives, since growth in market share is usually a reasonably good indicator of corporate competitive health.

A large percentage of firms consider growth in sales revenue, or simply growth in sales volume, to be a primary objective. The assumption is that growth in profit parallels growth in sales volume. Other growth objectives of the firm might be the creation and promotion of a favorable corporate image, the introduction of technologically advanced or innovative products, or the establishment of a leadership role in the area of corporate social responsibility.

Survival. Survival may be considered unconsciously or inferentially without ever being verbalized, but survival is the ultimate goal of every organization.

Basically, recognition of survival as the primary goal represents the distinction between short-run and long-run planning. Many firms have been destroyed by a narrow view of their markets. Others have barely survived. In the short run, for example, the film industry perceived its role as that of movie producer. In order to survive in the long run, however, it was necessary to broaden its outlook to include recognition of its role as a provider of entertainment in general. This, in turn, resulted in an awareness of a whole new set of competitors and market opportunities. Likewise, the petroleum industry at one time was content to view itself as a producer of fossil fuels. In order to survive in the long run, it has had to recognize that it is only one part of the total energy-producing industry; competition, such as solar energy and thermal energy, must be considered.

To summarize, in a firm that accepts a marketing philosophy of management, no real distinction needs to be made between corporate and marketing goals. Meaning is added to marketing goals by stating them in economic terms and by placing them within specific time frames. Basic goals of most organizations include a desire for profit and adequate return on investment; growth as measured by physical expansion, increase in market share, and increase in sales volume; and survival in the long run. The following example serves to illustrate these basic goals:

In the early 1970s, the digital display field was a relatively small market that was poised on the edge of rapid growth that came with the introduction of the hand calculator and the digital watch. Prior to the introduction of these two products, however, the digital display market was dominated by one firm that had been successful in maintaining relatively high prices and a good return on investment. New technology in the form of LED's (Light Emitting Diodes) and quartz crystals brought prices down. The resulting "shake-up" forced the leader to reevaluate profit goals as the smaller producers stressed "market share" in their struggle to survive and grow.

SELECTING MARKET TARGETS

Once marketing information has been provided to the firm and goals have been established, the firm undertakes the critically important task of selecting the markets that it chooses to attract or develop. This

4 segmentation bases
1) state-of-being
2) state-of-mind
3) product usage
4) benefit

task was identified in Figure 4.3. Before selection of markets can take place, however, these markets must be defined, or segmented. The process of market segmentation is the division of the total heterogeneous marketplace into smaller homogeneous wholes. Once the segmentation process has been completed, these identifiable wholes may be selected for prospecting by the firm. There are essentially four segmentation bases. They are: (1) state-of-being, (2) state-of-mind, (3) product usage, and (4) benefit.[17]

State-of-being segmentation refers to the physical or demographic characteristics of individuals or organizations. This approach recognizes that markets may be segmented according to geographic and demographic characteristics, such as Northeast, East Coast, South, or race, religion, sex, age.

State-of-mind segmentation deals with the psychological characteristics of potential customer groups. The relationship of attitude to behavior, for example, has been studied rather extensively. Occasionally, state-of-being and state-of-mind bases may be used simultaneously to uncover a new potential market for a product or a service. The recent dramatic success of *Playgirl Magazine* highlights the potential of a heretofore untapped market. The readership for this magazine represents an audience that is 82 percent female, 62 percent college educated, and 66 percent in the $10,000 and above wage bracket.[18]

Product usage segmentation looks at the way in which a product is used, the characteristics of the user, and then attempts to relate certain other factors to use. An organization might choose to try to relate media habits of a particular audience to the use of the firm's product. Another approach is to examine the user's sensitivity to particular marketing mix factors. Perhaps, for example, there may be a price-conscious segment for a particular product.

Benefit segmentation strategies focus upon the benefits that consumers derive from products. Once these benefits are known, marketing programs can be developed to emphasize these product benefits to the relevant market segment. As an example, cigarette smokers might be divided into two distinct market segments—those segments that are concerned primarily with with taste, and those segments that are concerned primarily with tar and nicotine ratings. In the first case, the obvious product benefit is good taste; in the second, a "healthier" smoke.

Once segments have been appropriately defined, management is in a position to select particular segments for attention by the firm. Prior to selection, the segments should be ranked in the order of greatest potential payoff. Although it is quite possible that no definitive quantitative ranking may be possible, at least some qualitative ranking should be attempted.

Certain criteria will influence management in this ranking process. For instance, the firm will undoubtedly want to consider the total revenue potential of any given market. As a corollary, the firm also will want to consider the potential share of the total market that it could attract. The demand characteristics of the various markets should be considered. That is, one segment may appear to have a lesser immediate payoff potential, although its potential for growth, in the long run, might be much greater than an apparently more attractive segment. The nature of competition for any given segment also will receive attention. It may be in the interest of the firm to try to attract a smaller market segment that is relatively competition-free than to try to lock horns with an entrenched competitor in a potentially more profitable market. Compatibility with the firm's total objectives and resources is a relevant issue for marketing management. Finally, some intuitive judgments by management may be in order concerning the feasibility of exploiting specific markets and the nature of the business into which the firm hopes to evolve.

FORMULATING MARKETING STRATEGY

plan of action

If the accomplishment of the firm's goals is the desired end of marketing activity, then strategies are the means for achieving this end. A strategy may be defined as "a long-term commitment of resources to achieve a specified goal in a competitive environment"[19] A strategy, then, is a plan of action or a statement of how objectives will be realized.

Basic elements of marketing strategy. Given selected market targets, marketing strategy is concerned with the development of a marketing mix. In this final stage of the marketing strategy planning process, the firm is concerned with successfully matching its market offerings with market requirements. As identified earlier in this chapter, the marketing mix is composed of four basic elements: product, promotion, distribution, and price. As presented in a strategic context in Figure 4.3, these basic elements represent the controllable strategy variables that are formulated and implemented by marketing management.

Although Henry Ford has been acknowledged as a production genius, he was also an interesting marketing strategist. It was Ford who first saw the potential profitability involved in creating a low-priced automobile for the mass market. Before that time, automobile manufacturers had produced cars primarily for such buyers as the wealthy, the elite, or the sports car driver. Until Ford's vision, the market was viewed as small and very specialized.

It is ironic that Ford's very success should have proved his undoing. In the 1920s Henry Ford was still following his very successful strategy, introduced many years earlier, of offering the public a mass-produced automobile in "any color you want as long as it's black." Alfred P. Sloan, Jr., the man who helped develop and guide General Motors Corporation to its position of dominance, decided at that point that there were opportunities for new strategies in the automobile market. The decision at General Motors, therefore, was to add new colors and styling, even if this necessitated raising prices. To reach this decision, General Motors had to view the marketplace as having several distinct segments based upon price and model types. The goal of General Motors was to offer a full line of cars with entries at the top of each of these price ranges. The appeal was to a quality-conscious consumer.

General Motors, although not immediately successful, persisted with its plan through the 1920s and slowly caught up with the unyielding Ford. Finally, in May 1927, Ford closed down his assembly line in order to switch his own strategy to meet the new competition. He stopped producing the long-successful Model T and introduced the Model A, but General Motors was already well on its way to the commanding market position it now holds.[20]

Marketing strategy criteria.   If it is importnat to establish marketing strategies in order to accomplish corporate goals and objectives, then it is equally important to monitor and evaluate these marketing strategies once they are established. Seymour Tilles has suggested appropriate criteria against which to measure the logic of the strategies that have been established.[21] The criteria that Tilles defined include: (1) internal consistency, (2) external consistency, (3) resource capability, (4) time, and (5) degree of risk.

Internal consistency refers to the compatibility that must exist between marketing objectives and marketing strategies. It would be unrealistic, for example, to determine a basic goal as penetration of a mass market, and then produce exclusively for upper social class segments. Likewise, it would be inconsistent to try to attack a mass market through exclusive and limited distribution channels.

External consistency refers to the need for marketing management to recognize the relationship of marketing strategy to variables outside, and beyond the control of, the firm. A desire to penetrate a foreign market, for example, must recognize potential sociocultural and political-legal barriers to success. Marketing strategies that are successful in the domestic environment may prove totally unsuccessful in a foreign environment.

Marketing strategy, too, must recognize the *resource limitations* of the firm. Marketing strategy must be consistent with the capability of the firm to finance the appropriate product-service mix, and it must be consistent with the manpower resources of the firm. It would be folly for an industrial marketer to try to generate immediate penetration of a highly technical and complex market without a competent and trained sales force or substitute sales force in the form of agents or manufacturers' representatives. Marketing strategy must reflect the production capability of the organization. It would be unwise to launch a promotional campaign if the product advertised were unavailable because of production limitations.

Marketing objectives and marketing strategy must be placed within *a time frame*. Association of a planning horizon with a specific objective has the virtue of being quantitatively measurable. It forces management to consciously consider and document the effort required to undertake new marketing programs.

The *degree of risk* to which the firm will be subjected is perhaps the least measurable of the criteria used to assess marketing strategy. Nevertheless, assessment of risk can be a potentially valuable activity.

Risk can be considered on the basis of the absolute resources that have to be committed, and the proportion of the firm's resources that must be allocated to the marketing program. IBM's commitment of $5 billion for the development of the 360 computer has been called "the $5 billion gamble."[22] Conversely, Montgomery Ward's failure to commit substantial cash resources to store expansion in the period following World War II provided the necessary market opportunity for Sears to assume a leadership position in the industry. Risk strategies must also be considered in terms of the time necessary to accomplish the given task. Obviously the longer the time period required, the greater the potential risk.

SUMMARY

marketing phil. of mgmt
1) customer orientation
2) profit motivation
3) integrated marketing
4) sense social respon

This chapter has dealt with the micro marketing system and the activities in marketing strategy planning. It was suggested that a marketing orientation is appropriate for the business firm. The marketing philosophy of management is built upon the elements of customer orientation, profit motivation, integrated marketing, and a sense of social responsibility.

It is the job of the marketing manager, who must plan, execute, and control the marketing activities of the firm, to make this philosophy work. This requires that the firm adjust not only to environments within the firm, but to those significant macro forces that also impact upon the firm in the external environment.

A firm requires information if it is to be able to adjust to relevant environments. This is the purpose of a marketing intelligence system. This system generates raw marketing data in order to provide "evaluated information." The better the intelligence system the better the data and management's ability to make interpretations, particularly in the development of marketing goals.

Marketing goals are often stated as corporate goals. At the least, they are directly and closely related to the corporate goals of profit, growth, and survival. More specifically, marketing goals may be stated in terms of sales, return on investment, market share, and dollar profits.

Once goals have been identified, market segmentation and selection may take place. This step is necessary before a product or service that can satisfy a specific market need can be designed by the firm.

marketing mgmt creates goals + strategy for implementation

Finally, marketing strategy must be created to accomplish marketing goals. In this sense, marketing strategy goes hand-in-hand with marketing goals and objectives. In short, it is the role of marketing management to establish goals and to create the strategy necessary to accomplish those goals.

QUESTIONS FOR DISCUSSION

1. What is the marketing philosophy of management? What are the elements of this philosophy? In what way might you consider this to be a philosophy of doing business?

2. What is the role of the marketing manager? What functions does the marketing manager perform?

3. What environments impact upon the firm? Explain the difference between the macro and the micro environments.

4. What is an intelligence system? How does it function and why is it necessary?

5. Discuss what you feel are appropriate goals for the marketing oriented firm.

6. What is the distinction between market segmentation and market selection?

7. What is involved in the development of marketing strategy?

8. Explain the systems concept. Identify the firm's marketing system, and through an integrated discussion, show how the system functions in a marketing oriented firm.

NOTES

[1]Reprinted from Charles G. Mortimer, "The Creative Factor in Marketing," 15th Annual Parlin Memorial Lecture, Philadelphia Chapter, American Marketing Association, May 13, 1959. Published by the American Marketing Association.

[2]For a good discussion of current social issues, see the entire issue of *Journal of Marketing* (July, 1971).

[3]Kenneth R. Davis, *Marketing Management* (3rd ed.; New York: The Ronald Press Co., 1972), p. 6.

[4]Ben M. Enis, *Marketing Principles: The Management Process* (Pacific Palisades, California: Goodyear Publishing Co., Inc., 1974), p. 30.

[5]George D. Downing, *Basic Marketing: A Strategic Systems Approach* (Columbus, Ohio: Charles E. Merrill Publishing Company, 1971), p. 20.

[6]*Ibid.,* p. 21.

[7]William Lazer, *A Marketing Management Systems Perspective* (New York: John Wiley and Sons, Inc., 1971), p. 12.

[8]*Ibid.,* pp. 9–11.

[9]"Holiday Inn Takes a New Road to Profits," *Business Week* (September 7, 1974), p. 88.

[10]Dan H. Robertson, "Salesforce Feedback on Competitors' Activities," *Journal of Marketing* (April, 1974), pp. 69–71.

[11]"Beckman Gets Customers to Design Its Products," *Business Week* (August 17, 1974), pp. 53–54.

[12]Ronald E. Frank and Paul E. Green, *Quantitative Methods in Marketing* (Englewood Cliffs, N.J.: Prentice-Hall, Inc., 1967), p. 2.

[13]Phillip Kotler, *Marketing Management* (3rd ed.; Englewood Cliffs, N.J.: Prentice-Hall, Inc., 1976), pp. 434–443.

[14]William H. Newman, *Administrative Action* (2nd ed.; Englewood Cliffs, N.J.: Prentice-Hall, Inc., 1963), p. 18.

[15]General Electric Company, *Professional Management in General Electric:*

General Electric's Organization, Book 2 (New York: General Electric Company, 1955), p. 94.

[16]The discussion of marketing goals is adapted from Downing, *op. cit.,* pp. 24–29.

[17]Enis, *Marketing Principles,* p. 280.

[18]"The girls' magazines claw at each other," *Business Week* (May 11, 1974), p. 36.

[19]Davis, *Marketing Management,* p. 23.

[20]Alfred P. Sloan, Jr., *My Years with General Motors* (New York: MacFadden Books, 1965), Introduction, Chapter 4, and Chapter 9.

[21]Seymour Tilles, "How to Evaluate Corporate Strategy," *Harvard Business Review,* XLI, No. 4 (July-August, 1963), pp. 111–121.

[22]"IBM's $5 Billion Gamble," *Fortune,* LXXIV, No. 4 (September, 1966), p. 118.

SUGGESTED READINGS

Cox, Keith K., James B. Higginbotham, and John Burton, "Applications of Focus Group Interviews in Marketing," *Journal of Marketing* (January, 1976), pp. 77–80.

Dhalla, Nariman K. and Winston H. Mahatoo, "Expanding the Scope of Segmentation Research," *Journal of Marketing* (April, 1976), pp. 34–41.

Hill, Richard M. and James D. Hlavacek, "The Venture Team: A New Concept in Marketing Organization," *Journal of Marketing* (July, 1972), pp. 44–50.

King, William R. and David I. Cleland, "Environmental Information Systems for Strategic Marketing Planning," *Journal of Marketing* (October, 1974), pp. 35–40.

Kotler, Philip, "A Generic Concept of Marketing," *Journal of Marketing* (April, 1972), pp. 46–54.

Levitt, Theodore, "Marketing Myopia," *Harvard Business Review* (July-August, 1960), pp. 45–56.

"Sears Identity Crisis," *Business Week* (December 8, 1975), pp. 52–58.

Shuptrine, F. Kelly and Frank A. Osmanski, "Marketing's Changing Role: Expanding or Contracting," *Journal of Marketing* (April, 1975), pp. 58–66.

Staudt, Thomas A., Donald A. Taylor, and Donald J. Bowersox, *A Managerial Introduction to Marketing* (3rd ed.; Englewood Cliffs, New Jersey: Prentice-Hall, Inc., 1976).

Stidsen, Bent and Thomas F. Schutte, "Marketing as a Communication System: The Marketing Concept Revisited," *Journal of Marketing* (October, 1972), pp. 22–27.

5
PRODUCT AND PRICING STRATEGY

PRODUCT AND PRICING STRATEGY

In the preceding chapter, an overview of the micro marketing system and the activities involved in marketing strategy planning were presented to show how the firm's output of goods and services is matched with market requirements. Since the marketing mix represents the very essence of the firm's offering to the market, this chapter and the following chapter will focus on the marketing strategy variables as they are formulated, implemented, and controlled by marketing management. This chapter will concentrate on the product and pricing areas, while Chapter 6 will be devoted to the promotion and distribution variables.

PRODUCT STRATEGY

1. tangible item
2. need satisfaction
(consumer)

A product (or service) may be defined in at least two ways. From the perspective of the firm, the product is a tangible item that the firm has to sell. From the perspective of the ultimate consumer, however, the product represents need satisfaction. From the consumer's perspective, therefore, the product transcends physical dimensions and is viewed as a means for accomplishing a specific goal. The results of a failure to recognize this important concept are illustrated below.

> Several years ago, DuPont introduced a new synthetic material called Corfam as a substitute for shoe leather. From a technological standpoint, Corfam had several significant advantages, including durability and the ability to snap back into shape. The promotion of these attributes, however, overlooked the fact that the customer is more interested in comfort and style. Leather has the advantage of conforming to the foot after wear, thereby providing comfort. This was something that Corfam could not do. More importantly, the modern consumer of footwear products is *not* primarily interested in durability. Rather, the emphasis is on style. Essentially this means that there is little interest in a shoe that will last a long time if, in fact, at the end of that period the style of the shoe is out of date.[1]

The ability to recognize consumer needs, of course, is an absolute necessity in a successful product-market matching process. Business firms must develop their products with the consumers' needs in mind, and they must make every effort to provide products that will receive market acceptance. The following example provides an illustration of a company that was highly sensitive to the needs of the marketplace.

> AMF Voit, a subsidiary of giant AMF, Inc., developed a new durable baseball bat made out of glass-reinforced nylon. In contrast to aluminum and magnesium bats, this new bat has the advantage of feeling, sounding, and looking like wood. The new product is being marketed particularly to little leaguers. Research has indicated that a little league team can expect to break 50 percent of its wood bats in a season. Voit is responding to an obvious market need by providing a comparable product at a significant long-run cost savings.[2]

APPROACHES TO CLASSIFYING PRODUCTS

Various classification schemes have evolved in an attempt to answer the difficult question "what is a product?" Basically, products may be classified as either consumer goods or industrial goods.[3] *Consumer goods* may be further broken down into convenience goods, shopping goods, and specialty goods.

Convenience goods are those products that the consumer purchases frequently with a minimum amount of search effort. In buying these goods, the consumer rarely visits competing stores, nor is he generally concerned with comparing price and quality. Examples would be chewing gum, milk, bread, butter, and eggs.

Shopping goods are purchased by the consumer after he has made comparisons of competing goods on such bases as price, quality, and style. Typically, shopping goods are more expensive than convenience goods and are products upon which the consumer will expend some effort in shopping before making purchases. Examples may include a new car, a television set, or furniture.

Specialty goods possess a special characteristic or characteristics, which cause the buyer to favor a particular brand or identified item. Specialty goods are typically high-priced and frequently require considerable search effort on the part of the consumer. Outboard motors, object d'art, fine wines, and gourmet restaurants may be examples of specialty goods.

Industrial goods are classified as installations, accessory equipment, fabricated parts and materials, raw materials, and industrial supplies. Installations represent complete products or services installed into a firm's organization, such as computers, heavy machinery, or a diesel locomotive for Amtrak. Such installations are obviously expensive and involve the outlay of large sums of money; moreover, they represent long-run expenditures for the firm.

Accessory equipment bears some resemblance to installations, yet may be contrasted to installations by the fact that it is ordinarily less expensive and has a shorter life. In addition, the purchasing firm is apt to be more price conscious in the purchase of accessory equipment. Examples include typewriters, adding machines, and small machinery.

Fabricated parts and materials represent items that ordinarily become a part of the final product. Digital display readouts on machine tool equipment, tires on automobiles, and flour in bread represent examples of fabricated parts and materials.

Raw materials are typically farm products such as corn, cotton, soy beans, cattle, pigs, eggs, and extracted elements such as copper, iron ore, coal, lumber, and other basic resources. Supplies are regular expense items in the business. They are maintenance items, repair items, and other operating supplies. Purchase of supplies is ordinarily routine and is given low priority in a decision making hierarchy.

THE PRODUCT LIFE CYCLE

Products, whether consumer goods or industrial goods, experience a product life cycle of four stages. These stages ordinarily represent a

Product Life
1. entry
2. retrenchment
3. maturity
4. decline

period of market entry, a period of retrenchment or establishment, a period of entrenchment or market maturity, and finally a period of market decline. Different marketing objectives and strategies are applicable at each stage in the life cycle. Figure 5.1 illustrates these stages.

In reviewing Figure 5.1, it should be noted that while the various stages in the life cycle appear to be divided fairly evenly, the time involved in each stage, and for that matter, the overall life cycle, may vary significantly for individual products and product lines. For example, the life cycle of the original hula hoop was only a matter of months, while the life cycle for the color television receiver continues after nearly thirty years.

An examination of this concept reveals that packages, brands, and even businesses also have life cycles. For example, the automobile, as a means of transportation, is probably now in the maturity stage of its development, having already enjoyed a life cycle of over seventy years. Certain automobile manufacturers, however, have been considerably less fortunate. How many people today can recall the Studebaker, the Packard, and the Stutz-Bearcat? Conversely, some companies continue to prosper, but experience difficulty with certain products in the product line. The owner of an Edsel can consider himself fortunate. It is now a collector's item! Economy cars are in the growth stage of the life cycle; convertibles are in the decline stage.

STRATEGIC CONSIDERATIONS OVER THE LIFE CYCLE

Although the product life cycle concept presents a broad generalization of the birth, growth, and death of products, it provides a useful framework for analyzing competitive conditions in the marketplace. When a marketer can accurately pinpoint the stage of his product in the life cycle, he is in a good position to evaluate his current position and intelligently forecast the future competitive environment. From this information, he can anticipate required marketing effort and adjust to changing market conditions. To provide a relevant picture of the life cycle over time, the remainder of this section is devoted to a

FIGURE 5.1.
STAGES IN THE PRODUCT LIFE CYCLE

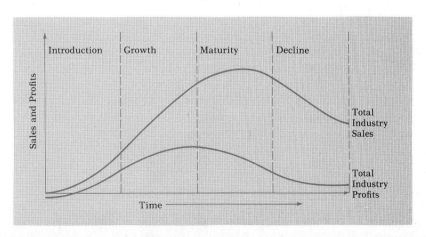

brief examination of the general characteristics of the market, the degree of competition, and the changes that occur in marketing strategy.

Introduction.   This stage of the product life cycle may be characterized as a pioneering stage. The product is new on the market, and awareness of it and acceptance among potential customers is minimal. Although the time frame for this stage varies considerably among products, sales generally rise very slowly over most of the period. Due to the relatively small sales volume and accompanying low level of profits, there are few direct competitors. For the most part, the innovator, or product originator, is the dominant seller in the market. Because of high production costs and extensive marketing costs required for market development, prices tend also to be high. During this stage, emphasis is on primary demand stimulation (promotion of the product) rather than selective demand stimulation (brand promotion). From this review, the following characteristics of the introduction stage may be summarized as:

slow sales

1. Minimal product awareness and acceptance

2. Small sales volume

3. Low levels of profit

4. Few direct competitors

5. High production and marketing costs

6. High prices

7. Emphasis on primary demand stimulation

Growth.   The second stage of the product life cycle may be identified as a market acceptance period. During this stage, product awareness among potential customers increases significantly, and customer acceptance is strong. Sales rise dramatically, and the size of the market expands rapidly. There is a sharp increase in the number of competitors as rivals seek the profit opportunity offered by the product. Production economies are realized, distribution is expanded, and the marketing effort shifts to a stronger emphasis on brand promotion in an effort to stimulate selective demand through individual product improvements. In summary, this stage of the product life cycle may be characterized as:

growth

1. High product awareness

2. Good potential customer acceptance

3. Sharp increase in sales

4. Strong profit picture

5. Rapid increase in competition

6. Production economies are realized

7. Move to selective demand stimulation

8. Expanded distribution

9. Improvements in product design

Maturity. As the product reaches maturity, it enters a period of development that is identified as the turbulence stage. During this period, competitive rivalry is intense, and there is a "survival of the fittest" in the marketplace as marginal producers leave the market. The significant growth in sales that was realized in the growth stage tends to level off. Because of the intense rivalry that exists, competitors stress brand promotion and concentrate on product differentiation through changes in both product and service. Prices begin to decline, and there is a significant shrinkage in profit margins for producers and distributors. Since the product is well diffused (distributed) throughout the market, the securing of new dealers and the retention of old ones becomes difficult. As the result of turbulent market conditions, there is some significant reduction in the number of competitors. From this review, the following characteristics of the maturity stage may be summarized:

1. Intense competitive rivalry

2. Leveling off in sales

3. Selective demand stimulation is stressed *brand promotion*

4. Emphasis on product differentiation

5. Decline in prices

6. Profits tend to decline

7. Product well diffused in the market

8. Some decline in the number of competitors

Decline. In this last stage of the life cycle, the product reaches a saturation point in the market and sales begin to decline. The magnitude of the decline and the final death of the product depend to a large degree on the market strength of substitute products. With declining sales, however, there is a sharp reduction in the number of competitors in the market. Those rivals that remain tend to return to primary demand stimulation (product promotion) in an effort to maintain sales. Although prices may continue to fall during the period, there may be an actual price increase that is supported by the hard core market. Thus, it is possible for price to be revised upward or downward, depending upon what the market will accept. For some competitors, profit opportunities may, in fact, be quite good. A review of conditions during the decline period provides the following summary:

1. Sales reach a saturation point and decline

2. Substitute products affect sales decline

3. Sharp reduction in the number of competitors

4. Emphasis shifts back to primary demand stimulation *product promotion*

5. Prices may move upward or downward

6. Good profit opportunities can still exist

The color television industry provides an excellent illustration of the product life cycle. From its early discovery in the 1930s, the color television receiver has experienced an interesting pattern of development. The product became a reality in the late 1940s and entered the introduction stage of the life cycle at that time. In the absence of color programming, however, sales were quite small until the mid 1960s when the major networks went to all color. The product entered the growth stage about 1965 and enjoyed a phenomenal success for the remainder of the 1960s and into the early 1970s.

An historical review of the industry reveals that RCA was the leader and early pioneer in the field. That company created the primary demand for the product by "selling the color concept." As the product moved into the growth stage, RCA, Zenith, Magnovox, General Electric, Motorola, a few other domestic firms, and a host of foreign manufacturers aggressively competed for a share of the growing market with a heavy emphasis on selective demand stimulation. By the early 1970s, competition was so intense that a number of firms dropped out of the field. Motorola was one of the largest companies to take this action when it sold out to a Japanese manufacturer.

Although the color television receiver has not reached a saturation point in the market, a significantly large percentage of American homes now have color sets. Evidence suggests, therefore, that the product is well into the maturity stage of the life cycle. Based on futuristic projections of new technologies, it is probable that the existing color television set will be replaced by some new device such as a wall hanging unit or a built-in large screen. In such an event, the basic television box that has served as a piece of hard-to-place furniture will no longer exist in the home.

PRODUCT POSITIONING

As indicated in the previous discussion of the product life cycle concept, a firm's product offering is ordinarily only one of many vying for the attention of the consumer at any one point in time. Whether its product will be chosen depends on many market and product factors, not the least of which is how distinct and positively differentiated the product is in the customer's mind. A successful product, then, is one that has some unique or distinguishing characteristics in the view of a profitably significant number of buyers and potential buyers. The astute marketer attempts to endow his product with such attributes.

In a strategic context, product positioning is concerned with the task of finding a distinct position in the competitive field for a company's product. The accomplishment of this task, however, is not as simple as it may appear. First, the marketer must determine the relevant attributes to which customers will respond. Second, the product must be evaluated to determine if those attributes can be introduced. Third, competition must be analyzed as the basis for an overall evaluation of the relative strength of competitive product offerings. Finally, the marketer must determine the correct position for his product in the competitive field.

Positioning strategy.   From the above discussion, it should be obvious that product positioning strategy must be based on a thorough analysis of the market. Unfortunately, this important concept is often ignored in the development of new products. The introduction of the large number of "me too" products that enter the market each year is ample evidence to support this fact. On the other hand, there are some excellent illustrations of highly successful product positioning strategies that lend credibility to the approach. Consider, for example, the recent introduction of Lite beer by the Miller Brewing Company.

Based on a thorough market research study, Miller discovered an important market segment interested in low calorie beer. The product and market analysis also revealed certain other important facts. First, a lower calorie beer is as simple and even less expensive to produce than regular beer. Two, the beer-drinking market is not interested in a "sissy" diet drink. Finally, at the time of the study, there were no competitors producing a low calorie beer. As a result, Miller introduced Lite beer, containing over one-third fewer calories, with the advertising theme "everything you always wanted in a beer—and less." Another theme was directed to "he-men who want to drink all night and not get filled up." Individuals such as Dick Butkus, the former Chicago Bear football player, were used to communicate the message to the market.[4]

Repositioning strategy.   Once a product is positioned in the competitive field, it must be monitored continuously to ensure that it is effectively positioned. As the result of changes in the macro environment, a product can lose its position, or its position can be altered, within a short period of time. For example, new competition can enter the field to rival a successfully established position. This happened to Miller when Schlitz brought out its own light beer under the brand name "Light." Customer preferences may also shift, causing a decline in demand. That is, a firm may find that its product position is no longer a sound one. When this occurs, repositioning strategy may be required.

The Christian Brothers vintners provide an excellent illustration of a highly successful repositioning strategy. In the mid-1960s, Christian Brothers wines were appealing to elderly, blue collar, and low-income groups with only modest success. Fromm & Sichel, Inc., the Christian Brothers sole distributor, decided that the winery's labels, bottles and general packaging were the major cause of the problem. Through a major repositioning program, The Christian Brothers changed all of their packages and labels and more than doubled their advertising budget. This effort completely altered the image of Christian Brothers wines from the low end of the market to an image of high quality. As the result of this change, sales increased from $40 million in 1965 to around $80 million in 1973.[5]

THE STRATEGIC
PRODUCT
DECISIONS

Given the volatile nature of the marketplace, the marketer must constantly evaluate his product mix in order to maintain an optimal product-market match. This evaluation provides inputs for three decision making areas in product management. First, decisions must be made in the realm of new product development. Second, the marketer must determine when it is strategically necessary to modify existing products. Finally, decisions must be made regarding the elimination of products in the line. This section is devoted to a detailed discussion of each one of these critically important decisions.

1. new product
2. modify existing prod
3. eliminate prod.

New product development decisions.   A recurring strategy for the progressive marketing oriented firm is the development of new products to meet new market needs. Whereas some firms choose to be followers, others assume a position of leadership by virtue of the innovative stance they take in the area of product management. When these more progressive firms are examined, a unique type of organizational unit, called a venture group, is often found. This group enjoys more latitude than other planning groups within the corporation, since its charge is to create totally new products and services. A venture group is ordinarily comprised of experts from the various functional areas of the organization.[6]   It works closely with the development arm of the company and at the same time stays attuned to the nuances of the marketplace.

Regardless of the pattern of organization adopted, the introduction of new products represents significant risk, particularly in markets that are increasingly viewed as unpredictable at best. Most firms must be innovative if for no other reason than to be prepared to respond to competition. Conversely, to attempt to be innovative and to fail is extremely costly and may hasten the demise of the organization. Therefore, the new product development decision is a critically important one.

From a strategic standpoint, decision making in the area of new product development involves a series of "go, no-go" managerial determinations, each of which may abort a product idea before it becomes a viable market offering. Therefore, the infusion of new products in a company's product mix may be viewed as an orderly process that guides management from the inception of a new product idea to the final commercialization of the idea in the form of a marketable product. As presented in Figure 5.2, the sequential steps in the process are:[7]

1. Exploration

2. Screening

3. Business analysis

4. Product development

5. Test marketing

6. Commercialization

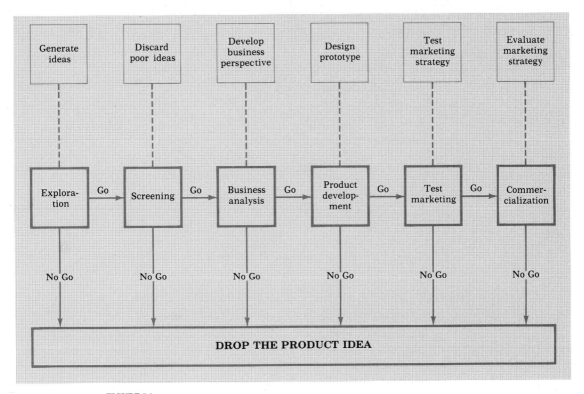

FIGURE 5.2.
THE NEW PRODUCT
DEVELOPMENT DECISION
PROCESS

Exploration is the idea creation stage of the new product development process. Ideas from both the micro and macro environments are collected for further evaluation. Since a large number of ideas must be considered to find one good one, the firm should monitor all available sources and create an organizational atmosphere that is receptive to new ideas. From practical experience, most firms have found that customers, company salesmen, dealers, competitors, scientists, and company management are the best sources of new product ideas.

Screening is used to discard those ideas that are not worth further consideration. At this point, no investment has been made, and little effort has been expended. Care, of course, must be taken to ensure that good ideas are not lost in the screening stage for lack of vision on the part of management. At the same time, wasted energy on poor ideas must also be avoided.

Business analysis is the stage that results in the first real resource commitment on the part of the firm. In this stage, the idea is subjected to rigorous examination from a business perspective; an analysis is made of potential market demand, estimated costs, anticipated revenues, breakeven analysis, and projected profits.

Product development begins on a preliminary scale if all of the indicators in the business analysis point to a potentially successful product. At this stage, the idea begins to take a physical form as a product as it is developed into a prototype by engineering and production. If a "go" decision is indicated from a technical standpoint, the prototype is further subjected to use tests and preliminary market refinements such as branding and packaging.

Test marketing may now be implemented in the new product development process to establish market feasibility. If used, this step is designed to test the proposed marketing program and determine customer and competitive reactions. Normally, test marketing is conducted in one or more selected markets as a small-scale trial of total market commercialization. Test marketing, of course, is an optional step, and it should be noted that many firms choose to skip this stage because of competitive or other reasons.

Commercialization entails full-scale launching of the product to the selected market targets. This may be accomplished through national distribution, or through regional distribution depending on the objectives and resources of the firm. At this time, the firm is fully committed to the idea, and the product is on the market. If successful, plans are formulated to keep the product on the market. If expectations are not realized, a drop decision may have to be exercised.

The Procter & Gamble corporation is one of America's finest examples of a company that is dedicated to the use of an orderly new product development process. Although the company has introduced a limited number of new products since 1970, it has achieved a high degree of success with a revolutionary new potato chip product called Pringle's. P & G's development of this product is a classic case of recognizing a consumer need and marketing an offering to meet it.

Through an analysis of the potato chip market, P & G discovered that Americans spend about $1 billion on this tasty little meal and snack item. Historically, however, there has always been a problem with potato chips because of breakage in shipment. Consequently, the industry has tended to be somewhat localized in scope with shipments less than 200 miles.

Beginning with an idea to solve the breakage problem, P & G developed a process of using dehydrated potatoes, making a potato mash, and then pressing it into a precise shape for frying. When everything seemed to work from a technical standpoint, P & G prototyped its new product and test marketed it with great success. Full commercialization followed on a regional basis, and the product is now reaching national distribution. To date, one new competitor has entered the field in the form of Laura Scudder's "Dittos" brand.

Product modification decisions. As indicated earlier in this chapter, some products, after enjoying initial market success, begin to lose position in the market. Others never achieve the level of success predicted. Short of the decision to remove the product from the market, a modification of the product is possible. It is important to recognize, however, that to be a candidate for a "repair job," a product should suffer from no more than one significant flaw. Moreover, the defect should be clearly definable and easy to correct. Consider, for example, the following situation:

A small company in Minnesota determined that it would produce a superior mouse trap. The result was a trap that was practically fail-safe, could be produced and sold at a price only slightly above that of existing traps, and could be used repeatedly, so that only one purchase was necessary. This was in contrast to the existing 10¢ trap, the wooden variety that would ordinarily be thrown away.

The manner in which a trap is used by the customer is the key to the marketing of the product. Ordinarily it is the woman who disposes of a trapped mouse. She emerges in the morning only to be confronted with the unpleasant prospect of disposing of a small corpse lying in a trap in a corner of the room. Deciding that the issue cannot be avoided, she gingerly picks up the trap, holds it at arms length, walks through the back door to the garbage can and drops it in. Her unpleasant task completed, she promptly forgets the incident.

But what of our company that produced the technologically superior product? To the woman, the trap looks considerably more expensive than the wooden variety, although it is not. Therefore, she is now faced with a rather delicate problem. On the one hand she does not care to handle the mouse; conversely, she cannot bring herself to throw the trap away. She avoids the unpleasant situation by simply not purchasing the trap at all.[8]

In the above illustration, it is obvious that some modification of the product must take place before the product can enjoy any degree of market acceptance. The company is faced with a dilemma. On the one hand, it can alter the technical characteristics of the product so as to make it possible to release the dead mouse from the trap without touching it, while still retaining the trap. On the other hand, it can cosmetically alter the appearance of the trap so that the purchaser will not be reluctant to throw it away. While the solution to this problem is not an easy one, there are three product modification options available to the firm. These are shown in Figure 5.3.

Quality changes in products are often required when the amount of quality built into a product is either too high or too low to meet competition and satisfy market requirements. In such cases, management should give serious consideration to modifying the product accordingly. A review of the mouse trap example presented above suggests

FIGURE 5.3.
THE PRODUCT MODIFICATION
DECISION

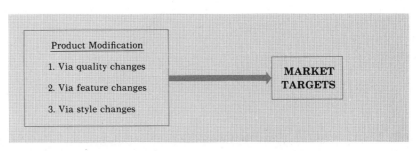

Product Modification

1. Via quality changes

2. Via feature changes

3. Via style changes

MARKET
TARGETS

that perceived quality of the new mouse trap might be reduced to encourage the user to dispose of the trap without feeling that an expensive item is being needlessly discarded.

Feature changes are made in products to gain a differential advantage over competition by increasing user benefits. Feature changes can be implemented throughout the product life cycle, but this form of modification strategy is most often used in the maturity stage when competitive rivalry is at a high level of intensity. The addition of a knife sharpener to the electric can opener is a good example of such a strategy.

Style changes are designed to increase the aesthetic appeal of products. This can be an extremely effective modification strategy for many kinds of products, for it does enable a firm to achieve a distinctiveness and an identification for its products. There is a high risk in styling competition, however, in that it is not always easy to predict what styles will be accepted. This problem was confronted by the automobile industry during the tail fin era and by the fashion industry in the introduction of the maxi-length skirt.

Product elimination decisions.   At some point, it is no longer feasible to continue to offer a product to the market, and a decision must be made to delete the product from the product line. Product elimination decisions are often difficult, however. Frequently, hard data on the profitability of products is lacking. Arguments, in many cases valid, can be made that the product is important to the company's image or enhances the sales of other products in the line. Executives become protective of products that they have championed. Yet, if waste is to be avoided, products should be pruned.

The Monsanto Company produced the world's first low sudsing detergent in the early 1950s in response to requirements of the new automatic washing machines. Marketed under the brand name ALL, this product enjoyed limited success under Monsanto's direction. Since the company's sales force was primarily involved in marketing chemicals to large-scale industrial buyers, Monsanto was forced to create a second sales force to handle the demand for ALL at the retail level. When Proctor and Gamble introduced Dash shortly thereafter through its established nationwide network of salesmen, it became uneconomical for Monsanto to compete. As a result, Monsanto sold ALL to Lever Brothers in 1958.[9]

In recognition of the high cost of carrying weak products, management must objectively evaluate the product elimination decision and subject the product mix to a periodic review. Through a formal review process, the following questions can be answered as the basis for a final elimination decision:

Do existing and projected sales support elimination?
What are present and projected profits?
Can the product be saved through modification?
Will elimination affect the sale of other products?

How will elimination affect company personnel?
What will be the impact of the elimination on suppliers?
How will the elimination affect customer relations?
What are the alternative uses for committed resources?

PRODUCT STRATEGY AND THE MARKETING ENVIRONMENTS

In making strategic product decisions, marketers must consider their actions in terms of the environmental setting. As stressed throughout this book, marketing does not operate in a vacuum. This concept is especially significant in the field of product management. Like all marketing mix decisions, those made in the product area are highly visible and subject to tremendous environmental influence. Consider, for example, the case of a major corporation when it attempted to enter a new product field.

In 1970, the Sperry Rand Corporation decided to form an information display division to produce digital readouts for use in calculators, process control equipment, and other new applications that it hoped would develop. The division was organized and a plant was opened in 1970 in Scottsdale, Arizona. From the beginning, however, a number of key environmental factors impinged on management's decisions.

Internally, top-level Sperry management had to commit heavy financial resources to the new venture. Production, engineering, and research and development were critically important because of the high technology dimensions of the new product. An effective marketing effort was viewed as the key to success in the field. To operationalize the division, Sperry transferred key personnel within the company and employed additional skilled people from the outside.

Externally, several forces in the macro environment significantly influenced the company's operations. The market for digital displays was small, but it was expected to grow tremendously as product use expanded. Technology was changing rapidly with new and improved product types and manufacturing techniques. Competition was very intense, and the price of digital displays began to decline.

Although Sperry successfully operated the new division for approximately three years, management made a major decision to get out of the information display business at the end of that time. In 1973, the entire operation was sold to Beckman Instruments of Fullerton, California. Today, the original Sperry venture is called Beckman Information Displays.

PRICING STRATEGY

Like product, pricing is a form of output behavior for the firm. Furthermore, price is a highly visible element in the marketing mix, and

FIGURE 5.4.
THE PRICE MAKING DECISION
FRAMEWORK

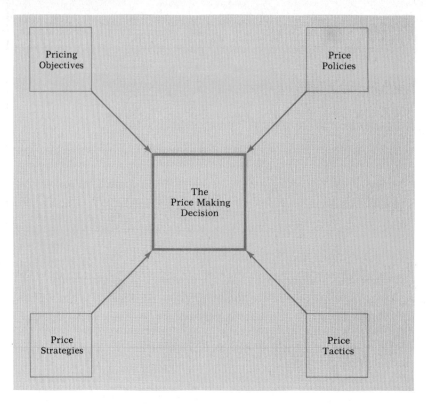

it is a powerful strategic weapon for the marketer. In making price decisions, marketing management is concerned with price determination, its implementation, and its strategic adjustment. As shown in Figure 5.4, this requires the development of pricing objectives, the establishment of price policies, the formulation of price strategy, and the implementation of price tactics. Therefore, the remainder of this broad section will be devoted to the following topic areas:

1. Pricing Objectives

2. Price Policies

3. Price Strategies

4. Price Tactics

**PRICING
OBJECTIVES**

4 goals

Since price is a powerful strategic weapon in the marketplace, it should be used to accomplish specified firm objectives. In one of the most comprehensive studies ever completed on pricing objectives, Robert F. Lanzillotti found that large industrial corporations use price to accomplish four main goals.[10] These have been identified as the achievement of a target return on investment, the maintenance or improvement of market share, meeting competition, and the stabilization of industry prices.

PLOT

GM set ROI at 20%

Target return.   In the Lanzillotti study, a specified target return on investment or sales was the most often mentioned goal of pricing. In actual practice, this objective may be stated in terms of a short-run target return (normally one year) or a long-run basis of more than one year. Most companies that establish this objective think in long-run terms since it is very difficult to reach a planned goal every year. In actuality, returns may vary considerably from year to year. Lanzillotti's results indicate that common return goals may range from a low of 8 percent on investment (after taxes) to a high of 20 percent on investment (after taxes).

plot

Market share.   Many companies use price aggressively to maintain or improve their market share. Since most firms usually have some idea of their share of the market, this is a reasonably easy objective to monitor. In establishing market share goals, management argues that market share is really a better indicator of how well the company is doing than return on investment or sales. In a relative sense, this is a valid argument, especially during periods of volatile sales caused by inflation and recession.

Price stability.   In many industries, there is a strong desire to avoid price wars. Although price leadership is normally found in these industries, stable prices are not uncommon in the absence of price leadership. By the same token, price stability should not imply that all sellers in the market must price at exactly the same level. In the petroleum industry, for example, there has been a long standing practice for major brand distributors to price at about the same level, while independents usually price a few cents below the market. In the absence of price wars, this may be considered a "stable price" situation.

Meeting competition.   As might be expected, many firms conscientiously price to meet competition. For these companies, the objective is to simply follow accepted pricing practices. Highly competitive supermarkets, major brand gasoline distributors, and fast food franchises are all good examples of firms that employ this objective. In addition to using price to meet competition, other firms establish price objectives to prevent competition. The use of this objective is frequently found in the introduction of new products when an innovator prices at a relatively low level to keep profits down and discourage the entry of rivals in the market.

PRICE POLICIES   After identifying what it wishes to accomplish with price in terms of broad objectives, management must establish price policies as a guide to price strategy and tactics. A price policy may be viewed as a prescribed course of pricing action that is predetermined to ensure uniformity of procedure by those in management responsible for the administration of prices. Although price policies vary in degree and scope among business firms, the most common in use may be identified in the following categories:

Price Policies

1. Price Variation Policies

2. Price Discount Policies

3. Geographic Price Policies

4. Objectives Oriented Price Policies

5. Competition Oriented Price Policies

Price variation policies.   In setting prices, firms may follow either a one-price policy or a variable price policy. The one-price policy stipulates that the same price must be quoted and charged to all customers who purchase under similar conditions. Although different prices may be charged, these differences are the result of variations in the conditions of purchase such as quantities, distance, and timing. A variable price policy permits price concessions, and the actual prices charged are a function of negotiation. The one-price policy is common among retailers; the variable price policy is used by manufacturers and wholesalers.

Because of legal restrictions, there has been a trend away from variable price policies to a more uniform use of one-price policies. Price discrimination is expressly prohibited by law, and firms charging variable prices under similar conditions of sale must justify differences on the basis of cost savings or meeting competition in good faith. Since the burden of proof is on the seller, most firms prefer not to become entangled in this legal web. (For a complete discussion of this area, refer to the Robinson-Patman Act in Chapter 13.)

Price discount policies.   To allow for legitimate and legal adjustments from listed prices, firms establish discount policies. These reductions may be given in cash or in the form of other concessions such as free merchandise. Although the customers of retail establishments do occasionally receive discounts, price discount policies normally apply to sales made by manufacturers and wholesalers. These policies cover quantity, trade, cash, and seasonal discounts, plus certain types of promotional allowances.

When customers buy in large volumes, they may be given quantity discounts as a buying inducement. Trade discounts, also referred to as functional discounts, are granted to middlemen in payment for the functions that they perform. Cash discounts are given to customers for paying their bills on time. This is the common 2/10, net 30, which means a 2 percent discount for paying within ten days of billing or total payment in thirty days. Seasonal discounts are used to encourage off-season buying. Promotional allowances are given to customers as a payment for performing part or all of the promotion function. These allowances are common between manufacturers and middlemen and may be in the form of either cash or merchandise.

Geographic price policies.   For all practical purposes, the cost of freight is an actual part of the price that a customer pays. In order to clearly establish who pays the transportation charges, firms use geographic price policies to define when the buyer pays the freight, when the seller pays, and when the expenses are shared. Although the complexities of geographic price policies are beyond the scope of this book, it should be noted that transportation costs play an important role in establishing the geographic limits of the market for an individual firm. Under the circumstances, established price policy is essential to cover this important area.[11]

Objectives oriented price policies.   As indicated previously, objectives should be a primary consideration in every pricing decision. Two specific price policies relate directly to this concept. First, a skimming price policy may be used by a firm when there is a desire to maximize profits in the short run. For example, this policy might be adopted to quickly recoup investment in a new product. It calls for a high price and may be implemented if there is a segment of the market that is not price sensitive, and when there are few competitors. Second, a penetration price policy may be used if the firm has a strong growth objective. Implementation of this policy requires a low price and an emphasis on volume. Thus, a penetration policy is designed to appeal to the price sensitive segment of the market.

Skimming, penetration [handwritten marginal note]

Skimming pricing.   The Polaroid Corporation is an interesting example of a company that has used a skimming pricing policy most effectively. As the innovator and long-term developer of a camera that processes its own picture, Polaroid has offered the market a number of different products. Historically, however, each new generation of the Polaroid camera has always entered the market at a high price. Although scaled down models appear after a time at lower prices, Polaroid has consistently maintained a premium price structure on all of its new innovations.

Penetration pricing.   The McDonald's Corporation has made a science out of penetration pricing in the manner in which it has captured a sizable share of the fast food market. McDonald's is the dominant leader in this field, and it has achieved that leadership, in part, through a very delicate pricing strategy designed to appeal to the mass market. Every item that goes into a McDonald's product is carefully measured and precisely costed. With this type of precision, profits can be monitored and relative prices can be maintained to ensure a strong competitive position.

Competition oriented price polices.   Since competition significantly influences all pricing decisions, firms consciously develop price policies to deal with competitive conditions in the marketplace. Some *price discounters* (handwritten margin note)

firms intentionally engage in price competition, and others stress non-price competition. Policies dealing with price competition encourage the aggressive use of price as a competitive weapon in the marketing mix. Discounters represent one of the prime examples of firms that employ price in this manner. Firms with a policy of nonprice competition use other elements in the marketing mix in an attempt to gain a differential advantage. These firms emphasize their products, their distribution system, strong service programs, and the promotional effort. Accordingly, they attempt to down play price in the mix.

nonprice — stress service etc (handwritten margin note)

The convenience food store is one of the most successful retailers to employ nonprice competition in recent years. Through distribution, with a large number of excellently located outlets, and through service, in the form of long store hours, these outlets have achieved phenomenal growth with a price structure that ranges well above that of conventional supermarkets. For customers who frequently patronize the convenience market, price is not a factor in the buying decision.

PRICE STRATEGIES

Having established pricing objectives and price policies, marketers must consider three major factors in determining the prices that they charge for their products and services. These are costs, demand, and competition. Thus, pricing strategy tends to be either cost oriented, demand oriented, or competition oriented. To show how these key elements influence pricing practices, the following price strategies are discussed below:

Price Strategies (handwritten note)

1. Life Cycle Price Strategies

2. Price Level Strategies

3. Price Lining Strategies

4. Target Return Price Strategies

Life cycle price strategies.   As discussed earlier in the product section of this chapter, it is important to anticipate price changes as products move through the various stages of the life cycle. As a general pattern, prices tend to be high early in the cycle and fail as demand increases. If demand can be stabilized for a hard core market in the decline stage, however, it is possible to increase price. Knowing when to adjust price is the key to strategic pricing over the life cycle. Costs, demand, and competitive factors, of course, must be considered.

One popular solution to the problem of pricing over the life cycle has been developed by the Boston Consulting Group and exploited by several companies in the semiconductor field. Known as "experience curve pricing," this approach establishes the price of a new product in relation to costs that are expected when the product is in the maturity stage of the life cycle. Initial prices are lower and market dominance can be achieved through volume sales.

As the product matures, prices are in line with costs that have decreased as the result of manufacturing cost reductions.[12]

Price level strategies. In an effort to adapt to the competitive environment, firms review the pricing structure of the industry to determine if various price levels exist. Although there may be a generally accepted price level, some firms may be pricing above that level and others below it. Therefore, prices tend to be either at the market, above the market, or below the market. In pricing strategy, an individual firm must choose a course of action that it plans to follow. At-the-market pricing would be best for those firms with little or no differential advantage. For those with a differential disadvantage, below-the-market pricing is more appropriate. If a firm can gain distinctiveness in the market and strong brand preference among buyers, it may be able to price above the market.

The independent gasoline service station must use below-the-market pricing to compete. Most independent stations are poorly located relative to major brand rivals, and they do not have the product recognition, nor the promotional backing of the majors. Consequently, price is the one thing that they really have to sell. Although most customers realize that the independents purchase their gasoline from the major petroleum companies, they have no reason to buy from the independents. Price, therefore, becomes the significant patronage motive.

Price lining strategies. When a firm wants to compete in all levels of the market, it may develop a full line of products to offer at various price levels. This has been a common practice in the retailing field where the merchant may carry a good, better, and best assortment of merchandise. In so doing, the retailer can appeal to different buyers who are interested in different priced merchandise. Department stores have used this strategy effectively in the development of fashion boutiques and bargain basement shops to complement their regular lines.

In the manufacturing field, automobile producers effectively employ this pricing strategy by providing car buyers an opportunity to "package" their own cars. Through a wide range of options, the buyer can purchase a "stripped down" model or go all the way to a "fully loaded" deluxe model with every extra cost option imaginable. Likewise, the major automobile manufacturers provide a wide selection of offerings ranging from a low end compact to a high end luxury sedan. In using this pricing strategy, they feel that they can appeal to every possible potential customer.

Target return price strategies. Those firms with clearly established return-on-investment objectives employ target return price strategies. Costs, of course, are a major factor in the determination of price for these firms. Since costs are different at each level of output, however, it is necessary to develop accurate estimates of both costs and demand. From this data, appropriate prices can be developed to correspond with desired return on investment. As noted earlier, however, this price strategy is most effective in the accomplishment of long-run return on investment goals.

Hewlett-Packard is a classic example of a company that has a clearly established target return objective in lieu of market share goals. Instead of fighting it out with competition in the minicalculator market by lowering price, Hewlett-Packard has remained the price leader in the industry. As late as 1973, for example, its HP-35 hand-held scientific calculator was selling for $395. A new generation HP-21 was introduced in 1975 at a price of $125 and a comparable profit level. Although these units are the most sophisticated on the market, they are also the most expensive. Hewlett-Packard's strategy, however, is geared to a concentration on profitability, and management steadfastly refuses to enter the mass market race for the sake of market share.[13]

PRICE TACTICS   Following the price making decision framework presented in Figure 5.4, this final section on pricing strategy is devoted to a discussion of the price tactics followed by management in setting specific prices. In the presentation, the following tactical decisions are discussed to illustrate managerial price tactics:

1. Unit Pricing Tactics

2. Price Discrimination Tactics

3. Psychological Price Tactics

4. Price Leader Tactics

Unit pricing tactics.   In response to consumer protests over the confusing number of package sizes offered by the food industry, a number of supermarket chains are now using a unit price system. When this tactic is employed, every product and package size is identified with a shelf label showing the price of the package and a breakdown of the price expressed in dollars and cents per ounce, pound, pint, or other unit of measure.

Although this tactic is relatively new, having been introduced first in the 1970s, it is gaining in popularity among both merchants and consumers. From the supermarket operations standpoint, successful users indicate that pricing is greatly simplified with the system. For the consumer, there is more information and less confusion in deciding which package size is the best buy. On the manufacturing side, however, more attention must be given to packaging and labeling so that complete information is available to the consumer.

Price discrimination tactics.   Although price discrimination is illegal, as noted earlier in this chapter, firms do practice discriminatory tactics that are perfectly within the scope of the law. From a pricing standpoint, these tactics would be attempted when demand conditions permit. In all probability, cost factors do not influence the decision. To clarify this point, consider the following examples of discriminatory pricing:

1. The use of different prices at different times (for example, a lower price for a matinee and a higher price for an evening performance of a movie).

2. The use of different final prices for the same product based on the bargaining ability of the buyer (for example, when two buyers purchase an identical automobile from the same dealer).

3. The use of different prices for the same product in two locations (for example, a higher price for a cocktail in a restaurant than the price charged for the same cocktail in the restaurant's lounge).

4. The use of different prices for two almost identical products (for example, a higher price for essentially the same fashion item in a junior department that can be found for a lower price in the children's department).

Psychological price tactics. The use of odd pricing is a common price tactic that has been employed for a number of years in the retail field. When used, prices end in odd amounts such as 29 cents, 49 cents, $1.49, and $21.95. More recently, it is interesting to note that marketers of higher priced items are now using this tactic. For example, automobiles are priced at $3,195 and homes are listed at $39,950. These pricing decisions are made in the belief that odd prices are psychologically better than even prices. Recent studies, however, indicate that there appears to be no real psychological value in odd prices.[14]

Price leader tactics. In an effort to build traffic and attract customers, some retail firms use leader pricing tactics. Linked with promotion strategy, this tactic is simply the offering of a well known, frequently purchased item at a price well below normally expected price. Bread, sugar, milk, and coffee are all common examples of products that are sold as price leaders. Backed by heavy promotion, these items are used to bring customers into the store in the hope that they will purchase other items to offset profit losses from the price leaders.

PRICINGS STRATEGY AND THE MARKETING ENVIRONMENTS

In concluding this section on pricing strategy, it is important to note that pricing decisions are heavily constrained by the total marketing environment. For this reason, pricing must be viewed from a very broad perspective. As a first step, management should start with an examination of those forces in the macro environment that may influ-

FIGURE 5.5.
A CONSTRAINT APPROACH TO
PRICING STRATEGY

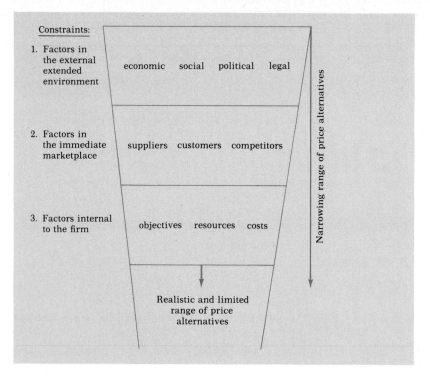

Constraints:

1. Factors in the external extended environment — economic   social   political   legal

2. Factors in the immediate marketplace — suppliers   customers   competitors

3. Factors internal to the firm — objectives   resources   costs

Narrowing range of price alternatives

Realistic and limited range of price alternatives

ence a specific pricing decision. Special attention should be given to the economic, sociocultural, and legal environments.

Within the firm's immediate marketplace, pricing freedom will be constrained by suppliers, the activities of competitors, and the general mood of the customer. Consider, for example, the impact that the energy crisis of the early 1970s had on the supply of petroleum based products. The prices of supplies were rising so rapidly that it was almost impossible for finished goods manufacturers to price their products in an orderly manner.

Beyond the marketplace, factors internal to the firm within the micro environment pose serious constraints for the pricing decision. The firm's objectives, its resources, and its cost structure all play an important part in determining final prices. These factors coupled with those highlighted above dictate the use of a high degree of constraint in the pricing decision. By applying a constraint approach in pricing, the marketing strategist can arrive at a narrow range of potential prices that can be realistically charged for the firm's offering of product or service. Although such an approach will not allow the decision-maker to arrive at the precise price at which a product should be sold, it will help the marketer focus upon a set of reasonable alternatives. A framework for using a constraint approach is summarized in Figure 5.5.

SUMMARY

This chapter has examined the key marketing strategy areas of product and pricing. The product is the firm's direct response to a perceived market need. It is the result of a combination of market opportunity and the organization's ability to respond. New products are introduced, mature, and decline. Furthermore, they find a position in the competitive field that may or may not be the most desirable one.

For management, there are three major decision-making areas in the field of product management. These are new product development decisions, product modification decisions, and product elimination decisions. All are essential in the maintenance of an effective product mix. This chapter provided a discussion of the steps that are involved in new product development, the different ways in which products can be modified, and an identification of the problems associated with product elimination.

In the area of pricing strategy, this chapter presented a price decision-making framework that includes the development of pricing objectives, the establishment of price policies, the formulation of price strategy, and the implementation of price tactics. Pricing objectives were explored to show how a firm can use price to accomplish specified company and marketing goals. Price policies were examined as a guide to the formulation and implementation of price strategy and tactics. The discussion of price strategies focused on management's use of cost, demand, and competitive information in establishing prices. Finally, the section on price tactics provided a discussion of the tactics followed by management in setting specific prices.

QUESTIONS FOR DISCUSSION

1. Explain the meaning of the term product from the viewpoint of the firm and from the viewpoint of the ultimate users of products.

2. How may products be classified? What is the purpose of identifying products into meaningful categories?

3. Identify the stages in the product life cycle and present an integrated discussion of the changes that take place over the life cycle in the market, competition, and the elements of marketing strategy.

4. In an integrated discussion, explain the meaning and significance of the concept of product positioning.

5. Identify and briefly discuss the three key decision-making areas in product management.

6. In an integrated discussion, present the price decision making framework and explain the interrelationships that are involved in price determination.

7. From your readings, present several specific examples of each of the following:
   a. pricing objectives

    b. price policies

    c. price strategies

    d. price tactics

NOTES

[1]"Corfam Turns Out To Be DuPont's Edsel," *Arizona Republic and Gazette* (April 10, 1971), p. 44.

[2]"A Synthetic Takes a Swing at the Market," *Business Week* (November 10, 1973), p. 180.

[3]E. Jerome McCarthy, *Basic Marketing: A Managerial Approach* (5th ed.; Homewood, Illinois: Richard D. Irwin, Inc., 1975), Chapters 14 and 15.

[4]"The Light Beer Game," *Forbes* (January 15, 1976), pp. 30–31.

[5]"Wine: Selling the New Mass Market," *Business Week* (February 23, 1974), p. 68.

[6]Richard M. Hill and James D. Hlevacek, "The Venture Team: A New Concept in Marketing Organization," *Journal of Marketing,* XXXVI (July, 1972), pp. 44–50.

[7]The framework for this process is presented in *Management of New Products* (4th ed.; New York: Booz, Allen and Hamilton, Inc., 1968).

[8]"So We Made a Better Mousetrap," *The Presidents' Forum* (Fall, 1962), pp. 26–27.

[9]Spencer Klaw, "The Soap Wars: A Strategic Analysis," *Fortune,* Vol. 68 (June, 1963), pp. 122ff.

[10]Robert F. Lanzillotti, "Pricing Objectives in Large Companies," *American Economic Review* (December, 1958), pp. 921–940.

[11]For an excellent discussion of geographic price policies, see William J. Stanton, *Fundamentals of Marketing* (4th ed.; New York: McGraw-Hill, Inc., 1975), pp. 295–301.

[12]"Hewlett-Packard: Where Slower Growth Is Smarter Management," *Business Week* (June 9, 1975), p. 51.

[13]*Ibid.,* p. 58.

[14]David M. Georgoff, "Price Illusion and the Effect of Odd-Even Retail Pricing," *Southern Journal of Business* (April, 1969), pp. 95–103.

SUGGESTED READINGS

Alpert, Mark I., *Pricing Decisions* (Glenview, Illinois: Scott, Foresman and Company, 1971).

Cravens, David W., Gerald E. Hills, and Robert B. Woodruff, *Marketing Decision Making: Concepts and Strategy* (Homewood, Illinois: Richard D. Irwin, Inc., 1976).

Kotler, Philip, *Marketing Management: Analysis, Planning, and Control* (3rd ed.; Englewood Cliffs, New Jersey: Prentice-Hall, Inc., 1976).

Rothberg, Robert R., ed., *Corporate Strategy and Product Innovation* (New York: The Free Press, 1976).

Smallwood, John E., "The Product Life Cycle: A Key to Strategic Marketing," *MSU Business Topics* (Winter, 1973), pp. 29–35.

Staudt, Thomas A., "Higher Management Risks in Product Strategy," *Journal of Marketing* (January, 1973), pp. 4–9.

Tauber, Edward M., "Reduce New Product Failures: Measure Needs as Well as Purchase Interest," *Journal of Marketing* (July, 1973), pp. 61–64.

Varble, Dale L., "Social and Environmental Considerations in New Product Development," *Journal of Marketing* (October, 1972), pp. 11–15.

Wind, Yoram and Henry J. Claycamp, "Planning Product Line Strategy: A Matrix Approach," *Journal of Marketing* (January, 1976), pp. 2–9.

6

PROMOTION AND
DISTRIBUTION STRATEGY

PROMOTION AND DISTRIBUTION STRATEGY

Following the format established in Chapter 5, this final chapter on the micro marketing environment is devoted to the promotion and distribution elements of the marketing mix. Strategic considerations in formulating, implementing, and controlling these two elements provide the focus of the chapter. In the discussion, special attention is devoted to the various forms of promotion, the development of channels of distribution, and the tasks involved in physical distribution management.

PROMOTION STRATEGY

Promotion is essentially an exercise in *communications*. MacDonald's may have the most tasty, low-priced hamburger in town, but unless they can communicate this information to the public, their success will be limited. MacDonald's has, of course, recognized the importance of effective communication, and this has been one of the major keys to their success.

All communication involves a source, channel, and receiver. The *source* may be a person, a group, or an institution, such as a business. In marketing, the source may take on a number of forms, such as an advertising message or a salesman. The *channel* is the medium or carrier of the communication. In the case of an advertising message, the channel could be a billboard, a TV commercial, or a magazine ad. The *receiver* is the object for whom the source has intended the message. An individual consumer, groups of people, or an institution may be recipients of marketing communications.

As an exercise in communication, promotion is any means of informing, persuading, and reminding consumers about all aspects of the firm and its products and services. The promotion may be designed to generate an immediate or deferred response from consumers. When Sears holds their "After Christmas Sale," their goal is to have people flock to the store immediately. On the other hand, energy conservation advertising by the petroleum companies is designed, in part, to build long-term good will on the public's part toward the company.

The marketer has at his disposal a number of promotional tools. The job becomes one of selecting the most strategic combination of these tools. To be more specific, various combinations of *advertising, personal selling, sales promotion, packaging, branding, public relations,* and *publicity* may be chosen. Although each of these promotional elements communicates to the buyer, the following pages will show that each has different characteristics.

Generally, the two most significant elements in promotion strategy are advertising and personal selling. In terms of communication, advertising enables a single source to reach numerous receivers. The receivers of the message may, however, either "tune-in" or "tune-out" the advertisement. Personal selling, on the other hand, consists of a

145

one-to-one relationship between the source and the receiver. Even though fewer consumers are reached, the effectiveness of the communication typically exceeds the results of advertising to a large anonymous audience because personal selling provides for a two-way communication flow between the seller and buyer. The impersonal nature of advertising prohibits this type of direct interaction. Figure 6.1 illustrates these basic differences between the two major promotional elements.

ADVERTISING

copy strategy
media strategy

Advertising may be defined as "the impersonal communication of ideas, goods, or services, to a mass audience by an identified paying sponsor."[1] Broad advertising objectives might include an increase in sales volume, or an increase in market share. Looked at differently, the objectives of advertising are to increase awareness of, increase interest in, generate a trial of, or hasten adoption of the product or service. Rather specific advertising objectives might also exist. For example, a campaign might be aimed at increasing attendance at an upcoming rock concert, improving the flow of goods in the channel of distribution, or simply generating inquiries about a product.

Given a set of advertising objectives, strategies for achieving them must then be formulated. These strategic decisions are made in two basic areas: copy strategy and media strategy.

Copy strategy is the actual message, but includes more than just what is said; that is, how the message is conveyed, its style, its design. The effectiveness of the advertising message is highly dependent on copy strategy. The writing and artistic skills involved suggest that technical expertise and creativity are required to develop quality copy.

Media strategy involves the choice of channels through which ad-

FIGURE 6.1.
BASIC COMMUNICATION DIFFERENCES BETWEEN ADVERTISING AND PERSONAL SELLING

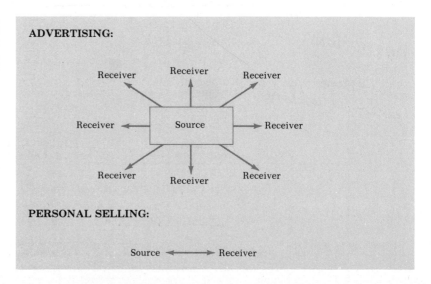

FIGURE 6.2.
TYPES OF ADVERTISING MEDIA

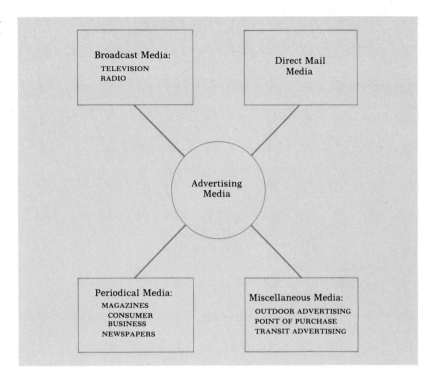

vertising messages flow. Many types of media are available as Figure 6.2 illustrates. Despite the prominence of television advertising, the major medium for advertising expenditures is newspapers. Approximately one-third of all expenditures go to newspapers, followed in order by television, direct mail, radio, and magazines (see Table 6.1).

Strategic decisions. Determining the appropriate copy and media are important advertising decisions. The following factors should be considered in making these decisions: *market characteristics, product attributes,* and *cost.*

Market characteristics should be uppermost in the advertiser's mind when making copy and media decisions. The objective should be to match the copy and media to the targeted consumer group.

The toothpaste industry is led by Crest, which claims close to 40 percent of the market. Procter and Gamble, the marketer of Crest, has successfully tailored its copy and media selection to the market, which consists of people primarily interested in decay prevention. Since this market is characterized by families with children, advertising copy has made good use of the "look mom, no cavities" appeal. Furthermore, media emphasis is devoted to family oriented television shows and magazines such as *Good Housekeeping* and *Better Homes and Gardens.*

Close-Up toothpaste, on the other hand, uses a different copy and media strategy because its market is composed of relatively young adults interested

TABLE 6.1.
DISTRIBUTION OF
ADVERTISING EXPENDITURES
BY MEDIA—1972

Media	Percent of Total	Dollar Expenditures (Millions of $)
Newpapers	30.2	$ 6,960
Television	17.9	4,110
Direct Mail	14.5	3,350
Radio	6.6	1,530
Magazines	6.4	1,480
Business Papers	3.3	770
Outdoor	1.3	290
Miscellaneous*	19.7	4,541
	99.9	$23,031

*Miscellaneous includes costs of company advertising departments, signs, advertising novelties, motion pictures, art work, and mechanical costs not counted elsewhere.
SOURCE: *Advertising Age* (November 21, 1973), p. 62.

in both white teeth and clean-smelling breath. Copy shows young couples in "various degrees of affection," while media emphasis is on television shows like American Bandstand, magazines such as *Seventeen* and *Rolling Stone,* and rock radio stations.

Product attributes may also dictate particular decisions. Copy illustrating how the camera functions has been necessary for most Polaroid advertisements. The company has also found that television and selected magazines are the best media for communicating their messages. Women's cosmetics make use of a similar media combination because of the necessity of conveying a multicolored, visual message.

Cost is obviously an important determinant in copy and media selection. No firm has unlimited advertising dollars, and this element of promotion can be expensive. A full page ad in *Cosmopolitan* magazine, for example, costs over $8,000 for one issue; the same size ad in the *Wall Street Journal* costs over $22,000. Interestingly enough, the two publications have similar circulations.[2] In assessing cost, a firm should look at both absolute and relative figures. Actual dollar outlays would show, for instance, that television is considerably more expensive than having the same copy communicated in several newspapers. But is this all that should be considered? Obviously, the relative cost —the comparison between the absolute cost and the number of customers reached by the message—is also important. The significance of relative costs indicates why marketers are often willing to spend more on a particular media. Table 6.2 shows the advertising budgets of some of America's leading businesses.

Use of agencies.   Because of the specialized nature of advertising, many firms use the services of advertising agencies. These experts often assist companies in the creative and technical aspects of adver-

TABLE 6.2.   1972 BUDGETS OF SELECTED LEADING ADVERTISERS

Rank and Company	Advertising	Sales	Adv. as % of Sales
Cars			
4 General Motors Corp.	$146,000,000	$30,435,231,414	0.5
6 Ford Motor Co.	132,500,000	20,194,400,000	0.7
10 Chrysler Corp.	95,415,400	7,300,000,000	1.3
47 Volkswagen of America	43,850,000	4,998,750,000	0.9
88 Toyota Motor Sales U.S.A.	22,700,000	4,789,288,000	0.5
92 American Motors Corp.	20,007,000	1,403,803,000	1.4
Food			
3 General Foods Corp.	170,000,000	1,966,200,000	8.6
20 General Mills	67,100,000	1,593,167,000	4.2
25 Nabisco	65,000,000	863,000,000	7.5
26 Kraftco	64,500,000	2,735,472,000	2.4
35 Standard Brands Inc.	54,000,000	958,292,008	5.6
Soaps, cleansers (and allied)			
1 Procter & Gamble	275,000,000	3,906,744,000	7.0
9 Colgate-Palmolive Co.	105,000,000	865,000,000	12.1
24 Lever Brothers	65,000,000	527,100,000	12.3
49 S. C. Johnson & Son	43,000,000	240,000,000	17.9
90 Clorox Corp.	21,000,000	188,203,000	11.2
Tobacco			
15 R. J. Reynolds Tobacco Co.	78,200,000	2,957,630,000	2.6
28 Philip Morris Co.	61,000,000	2,131,224,000	2.9
31 American Brands	57,000,000	2,998,869,000	1.9
40 Brown & Williamson Tobacco	52,200,000	876,267,795	6.0
57 Liggett & Myers Tobacco Corp.	37,000,000	753,627,611	4.9
Drugs and cosmetics			
5 Warner-Lambert Pharmaceutical	134,000,000	915,321,000	14.6
7 American Home Products	116,000,000	1,238,528,000	9.4
8 Bristol-Myers Co.	115,000,000	954,979,000	12.0
13 Sterling Drug Inc.	83,933,600	490,630,000	17.1
17 Gillette Co.	72,000,000	870,532,000	8.3
Retail chains			
2 Sears, Roebuck & Co.†	215,000,000	9,798,192,000	2.2
36 J. C. Penney Co. Inc.	53,000,000	5,529,600,000	1.0
75 Great Atlantic & Pacific Tea Co.	27,150,000	6,347,818,000	0.4
97 F. W. Woolworth Co.	16,300,000	3,148,108,000	0.5
Chemicals			
32 American Cyanamid Co.	56,000,000	973,038,000	5.8
38 Du Pont	52,752,000	4,366,000,000	1.2
89 Union Carbide Corp.	22,600,000	3,261,000,000	0.7
Photographic equipment			
37 Eastman-Kodak Co.	52,800,000	2,124,100,000	2.5
83 Polaroid Corp.	23,800,000	434,079,320	5.5

†Does not include local advertising.
SOURCE: Advertising Age, (August 27, 1973), p. 28.

tising, including idea creation, copy and art work, media evaluation, and production. To a lesser extent, a firm's agency may also offer services in marketing research, sales promotion, merchandising, and public relations. Although many activities may be "farmed out" to an agency, all firms should have someone within the organization to oversee and give direction to this important element of promotion strategy.

PERSONAL SELLING

The virtue of advertising is that it is a very economical form of communication in terms of the number of people reached per dollar spent. Personal selling, on the other hand, is quite costly per individual or firm contacted. The advantage of personal selling is that it can approach the market on a much more selective basis and benefit from the one-to-one interaction.

Personal selling may be defined as "oral presentation in a conversation with one or more prospective purchasers for the purpose of making a sale."[3] It has often been said about business that nothing happens until someone sells something to someone else. That statement is as true today as it ever was. The United States Census Bureau statistics show that almost 10 percent of the total U.S. labor force is involved in sales. When it is understood that the Bureau is likely to put many persons who are primarily personal sellers into other classifications, it is quite possible that more than 10 percent of the nation's labor force, or over 7 million people, are engaged in personal selling.

The role of the salesperson may be described in many ways. One of the most appropriate involves a classification of selling situations. The classification includes:

1. Situations in which the salesperson's job is primarily to deliver a product; e.g., driver salesperson for soft drinks, milk, bread, fuel oil.

2. Situations in which the salesperson is primarily an inside order taker; e.g., the retail clerk.

3. Situations in which the salesperson is primarily an outside order taker going to the customer in the field; e.g., a packing house, soap, or spice salesperson.

4. Situations in which the salesperson is not expected or permitted to solicit an order—the job is to build goodwill, perform promotional activities, or provide services for the customer. This type of salesperson is often called the missionary salesperson, and may represent a distiller, an ethical pharmaceutical manufacturer, or similar occupations.

5. Situations in which the major emphasis is placed upon the salesperson's technical knowledge; e.g., a salesperson with an engineering background who is primarily consultant to the customer.

6. Situations in which there is a demand for creative selling of tangible products, such as vacuum cleaners, airplanes, encyclopedias, or oil well drilling equipment.

7. Situations in which intangibles such as insurance, advertising, services, or communications systems are sold.[4]

These situations have been arranged in a hierarchy (from first to last) of increasing complexity. A perusal of the list indicates that the talents required of the sellers vary dramatically with the nature of the selling job.

A situation not included in the above classification has recently emerged. Since 1974 economic conditions have created significant shortages in major portions of the economy. The obvious question is, what does a salesperson do when there is nothing to sell? The answer would appear to be "drum up supplies" for favored customers whether they are products of the seller's own company or not.

A drilling rig company in Texas needed a huge quantity of steel plate and went to Ducommun, Inc., the big Los Angeles-based metals distributor. Ducommun could not fill the order from normal sources, but rather than leave a customer in the lurch, a Ducommun salesperson went to work as a temporary purchasing agent and finally lined up a Rumanian source. "If our customer had not gotten that steel plate," said Charles K. Preston, Ducommun Executive Vice-President, "he would have been unable to make production schedules. We figure customers will remember this kind of extra service once it's not quite such a sellers' market."[5]

Unfortunately, the public's view of sellers is often colored by the behavior of the state-fair huckster and the used car salesman. Most of today's sellers, particularly those marketing nonhousehold goods, are professionals. They are attuned to their customers' needs and familiar with the intricate attributes of their products and services. Salespersons working for companies such as IBM and Procter and Gamble serve their customers almost as quasi-consultants. They recognize that their own success as sales professionals is intimately tied to the satisfaction their customers derive from their products and services.

In combination with advertising, personal selling forms the core of promotion strategy. It is primarily through these two techniques that the prospect is initially made aware of a product and service and later sold. After examining the other elements of promotional strategy, the coordination of advertising and personal selling will be discussed.

OTHER FORMS OF PROMOTION

There are several other promotion elements in addition to advertising and personal selling. As indicated previously, these are sales promotion, branding and packaging, public relations, and publicity.

Sales promotion. These activities are designed to complement advertising and personal selling. Sales promotion can be defined as "those marketing activities other than personal selling, advertising, and publicity that stimulate consumer purchasing and dealer effectiveness, such as displays, shows and exhibitions, demonstrations, and various non-recurring selling efforts not in the ordinary routine."[6]

While sales promotion is ordinarily viewed as a complementary type of promotional activity, its importance should not be underestimated. Sales promotion expenditures in industrialized economies have been variously estimated at between 20 and 35 percent of total promotional budgets.[7] Consider, for example, the impact of coupons.

The shopping public is being deluged with coupons as never before. A. C. Nielson, the biggest of the coupon clearing houses, notes that in 1966 manufacturers issued 12.8 billion coupons. That figure more than doubled by 1973 to 27.6 billion and Nielson predicts another 15 percent rise atop this in 1974—to 31.5 billion. The big surge of late has come in retailers' own in-ad coupons. No one knows how many will be printed this year, but estimates range from a conservative 20 billion to 40 billion and up.

Far-fetched? Consider the possibilities. One chain running six in-ad coupons a week in the Philadelphia Inquirer (press run 212,000 copies) would publish 66,174,000 coupons a year. Direct mail flyers and shopper newspapers would add millions more. Result: between manufacturers and retailers 50 billion of the little money saving certificates will be printed by year's end—more than 15 for every man, woman, and child on the globe.[8]

Branding and packaging.   These elements are a part of the promotional mix in that both brand and package communicate information and images about the product to the public. A brand is a "word, mark, symbol, design, term, or a combination of these, both visual and oral, used for the purpose of identification of some product or service."[9] The communication functions of packaging are several. For instance, the package attracts attention, provides distinctiveness, influences attitudes by its design and physical attributes, facilitates display through its shape, and informs.[10] Brands perform certain functions for the promotional strategist. Specifically, the brand permits product identification, differentiation, and distinctiveness.[11]

Promote A New Product Without National Advertising And Pass Savings On To The Consumer? That's what New York-based Witco Chemical Corp. is trying with its new detergent, Active. The box, not TV commercials, sells, Witco says. Box copy reads: "Active cleans as well as leading nationally advertised all-purpose laundry detergents. Active can be sold for less than most nationally advertised detergents because Active is not nationally advertised." To induce consumers to look for the box, Witco and its agency, Ries Cappiello Colwell, New York, hired spokeswomen to appear on TV and radio talk shows and before consumerist groups and will furnish material for columns in newspapers and women's magazines. Maybe today's consumer is so fed up with the volume of repetitive advertising in a product category like laundry detergents (at a time when Tide is spending $10 million and Cheer $8 million) that she (or he) is ready to buy a non-advertised brand.[12]

Public relations.   An important part of a successful promotion is public relations strategy. This term may be defined as: "the activities of a corporation, union, government, or other organization in building and maintaining sound productive relations with special publics, such as customers, employees, or stockholders, and with the public at large so as to adapt itself to its environment, and interpret itself to society."[13] The field of public relations is today maturing and assuming new dimensions. Following the marketing philosophy of management, the public relations function must be tuned to the marketplace, must be responsive to needs, and must communicate its response to an interested public(s).

Publicity.   This final, but by no means least important, element of promotion strategy is the "non-personal stimulation of demand for a product, service, or business unit by planting commercially significant news about it in a published medium or obtaining favorable presentation of it on radio, television, or stage, that is not paid for by the sponsor."[14] Publicity *can* be managed and it is a valuable supplement to advertising and personal selling. Since a newsworthy item is not identified with a sponsor, it has the aura of objectivity that is often missing in advertising. Furthermore, there is generally no direct cost to the firm in that the communication is accepted by the medium as a news item as opposed to an advertisement.

COORDINATING THE PROMOTIONAL ELEMENTS

While each of the previously discussed promotional techniques is separate and distinct, an effective promotional strategy orchestrates the elements into a coordinated communications effort (see Figure 6.3). Potential disaster may exist, for example, when the sales force is unfamiliar with the firm's advertising messages.

A major bank in the South constructed a beautiful new headquarters building in the mid-1970s. While under construction, the structure was surrounded by an ugly construction fence. Since the evolving structure and fence were somewhat of an eyesore, the advertising people at the bank decided to do something about it. A campaign was introduced, primarily through newspaper ads, to encourage interested individuals to paint a portion of the fence. The only requirements to participate were that (a) what was painted had to have a bicentennial theme, and (b) a person had to fill out a short form "available at any branch" prior to beginning work on the fence. It was here that the coordination between advertising and personal selling broke down.

One person interested in participating in the painting project went to a nearby branch and asked a teller for the appropriate form to paint the fence. The teller's reaction was essentially, "What fence? I don't know what you're talking about; you'll have to see Ms. Ziede, our customer service representative." Ms. Ziede was vaguely familiar with the fence painting, but knew nothing about "any form to fill out." Furthermore, she bad-mouthed the whole campaign as some "dumb gimmick dreamed up by the main office."

The lady who was interested in painting a portion of the fence was *not* a customer of the bank. Prior to the aforementioned incident, she was seriously

FIGURE 6.3.
ORCHESTRATING THE
ELEMENTS OF PROMOTIONAL
STRATEGY

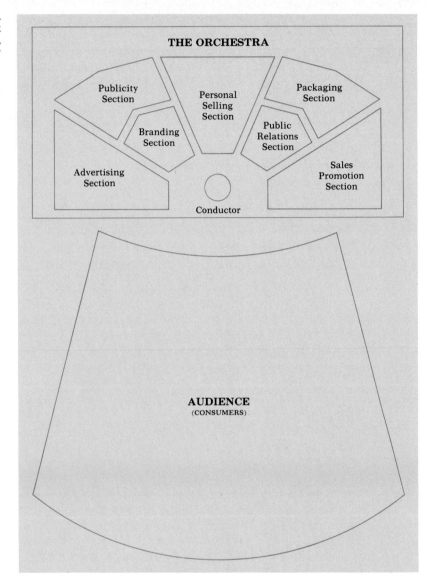

considering a change, but this experience totally turned her against the bank in question, and all because of an absence of coordination between advertising and personal selling.

All promotion elements utilized should be communicating a consistent message to the marketplace.

In considering promotion as a whole, the firm must determine the relative usage of each of the available elements. This is not easy, but some obvious rules of thumb are apparent. In marketing Crest, Procter and Gamble places primary emphasis on advertising. Honeywell's computer division, on the other hand, allocates most of its promotional dollars to personal selling. Factors such as the nature of the market, funds available, nature of the product, and its stage in the life cycle should be considered in determining the relative usage of the various elements. Advertising is generally considered the primary promotional tool in marketing consumer goods, whereas personal selling occupies the most important position in nonhousehold (e.g., industrial) goods. This practice should not imply, however, that advertising is unimportant in nonhousehold marketing and personal selling is unimportant in household marketing. The Honeywell computer salesman would be in a vulnerable position if a prospective client responded, "Honeywell sells computers? I didn't know that." The salesman depends on advertising to create an awareness among prospects that Honeywell does indeed market computers.

THE MACRO ENVIRONMENT AND PROMOTION STRATEGY

Many forces *outside* the firm influence the formulation of promotion strategy. The macro environment establishes constraints as well as opportunities for a company. The ability of the firm to adapt its communications to the changing institutional, international, sociocultural, economic, legal, competitive, and technological environments will help determine the results of its marketing effort. For this reason, the astute organization will continually monitor the macro environment, noting the changes that suggest adjustments in promotional strategy.

Marketers of feminine hygiene products have substantially altered their marketing communications after careful investigation of the *sociocultural* environment. Changing life styles and a new "openness" in society have broadened the acceptable promotional alternatives for these companies. Once limited to a select number of women's magazines, feminine hygiene products are now advertised on television and in campus newspapers.

Economic, competitive, and *international* forces necessitated major adjustments by American automotive companies in recent years. Public concern over fuel economy and competitive inroads by foreign producers led the Chevrolet Division of General Motors to introduce the Chevette a year ahead of schedule. While Ford, Chrysler, and AMC would have liked to have had a new 1976 subcompact available, it should be noted that Chevrolet's "one-upsmanship" occurred in part because the Chevette had been marketed in South America prior to its domestic introduction. The introductory promotion of the Chevette stressed its excellent fuel economy and positioned the product head-to-head with the major economy imports.

DISTRIBUTION STRATEGY

Once the product has been created, priced, and promoted, means must be found to place the product in the hands of the ultimate consumer.

[handwritten margin notes: Distribution / 1. Qy of channel / 2. physical movement of products]

Distribution strategy involves getting the product to the customer *when* he wants it and *where* he wants it.

Distribution strategy can be divided into two areas of investigation. The first area involves the development of a channel through which the product will flow, and the second area involves the physical movement of products through the channel.

CHANNEL STRATEGY

A channel of distribution may be defined as "the structure of intra-company organization units and extra-company agents and dealers, wholesale and retail, through which a commodity, product or service is marketed."[15] The typical channel is made up of the manufacturing organization and one or more intermediaries. Possible channel structures are shown in Figures 6.4 and 6.5 for consumer and industrial products, respectively. The second consumer products channel (manufacturer-retailer-household) has experienced the greatest growth in the past decade. In the industrial products channel, the manufacturer to industrial user alternative is the most significant.

In an advanced economy such as the United States, middlemen exist to *concentrate, sort,* and *disperse* products between manufacturers and ultimate consumers.

Assume for a moment that no middleman exist. A housewife is preparing a shopping list that includes Crest toothpaste, Coca-cola, Fritos corn chips, and

FIGURE 6.4.
SELECTED CHANNELS FOR
CONSUMER PRODUCTS

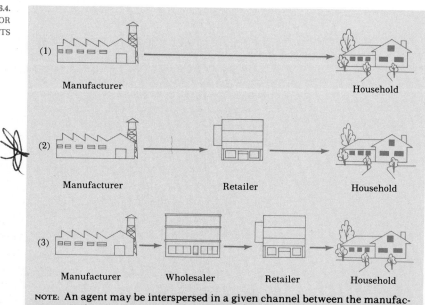

(1) Manufacturer			Household
(2) Manufacturer		Retailer	Household
(3) Manufacturer	Wholesaler	Retailer	Household

NOTE: An agent may be interspersed in a given channel between the manufacturer-retailer, manufacturer-wholesaler, or wholesaler-retailer. An agent's job is to facilitate the flows in the channel.

FIGURE 6.5.
SELECTED CHANNELS FOR
INDUSTRIAL PRODUCTS

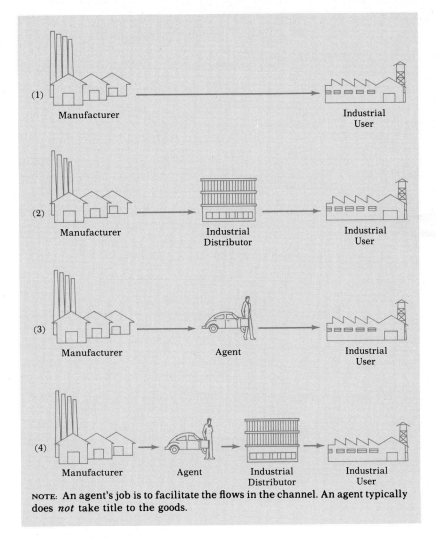

NOTE: **An agent's job is to facilitate the flows in the channel. An agent typically does *not* take title to the goods.**

a six pack of Schlitz. How is she going to purchase these products without middlemen? If she is in a hurry, it may be best for her to get airline reservations that would route her to Cincinnati (Crest) and then on to Atlanta (Coke), Dallas (Fritos), and Milwaukee (Schlitz).

The middleman, be it a wholesaler, retailer, or agent, *concentrates* products from geographically dispersed manufacturers; *sorts* the merchandise into salable units; and subsequently *disperses* the products to the ultimate consumer. One or more middlemen may be eliminated from the channel, but these three functions still have to be performed. In Sears' channels of distribution, the wholesaler has essentially been eliminated, but Sears has assumed the functions of concentrating, sorting, and dispersing. Regardless of the intermediaries involved, the following concepts hold true for distribution channels:

1. Exchange involves negotiation of terms of trade between parties.

2. Middlemen interposed between the producer and the ultimate consumer can improve the efficiency of the economic system.

3. In an industrial economy, producers and ultimate consumers seldom confront each other directly. Most products are handled by one or more middlemen.

4. In addition to products themselves, channels accommodate flows of use rights, payment, and information.

5. The flow between a producer and a buyer must occur if exchange transactions are to be consummated. Channel length and complexity, therefore, depend upon the effectiveness and the efficiency of the middlemen who manage the various flows.[16]

Channel organization.   A basic decision faced by the marketing manager is how to organize vertical relationships in the channel in such a way that the return to the organization will be greatest. Note that this is a decision that takes place at every channel level. Note, too, that in some cases the channel member may have no opportunity to make this decision, but rather must respond to the dictates of a more powerful member.

The ability to create, control, or influence other members in the channel is a function of many factors.[17] These factors are largely economic and have to do with the impact of the effect of participating in the channel versus some other alternative.

Until the energy shortage, the major petroleum companies sold excess gasoline to the small independents at a price that would allow the independents to offer the gasoline for sale several cents per gallon below the price charged by their larger competitors. As oil became scarce, however, this source of supply dried up, and many independents were forced into bankruptcy.

In the above example, power in the channel was a direct result of the ability of the major oil producers to control supply. Similar control can emanate from the demand side. Several of the major retail chains have such great buying power that they can virtually dictate terms to manufacturing organizations. The manufacturer can, of course, refuse to deal with the retail organization, but the potential loss of market share makes this a difficult decision to implement.

Although few relish the thought of being "controlled," certain advantages may accrue to those channel members who submit to the leadership of a more powerful channel member. Members of the channel can often reduce their risk by association with a large supplier or buyer, thus assuring a steady supply of, or demand for, the product. Such a relationship can generate economies of scale for participants, further providing a competitive advantage.

In addition, the channel leader is often in a position to provide expertise and to share promotional expenses. A positive "halo effect" might accrue from association with a firm that has a very favorable public image. Often smaller participants in the channel are happy to have the responsibility of burdensome management decisions assumed by more knowledgeable members. There is a danger, of course, in "putting all your eggs in one basket." Should the major source of supply or demand be lost, the channel member with no alternatives is in an extremely vulnerable position.

Often the channel leader is found at the manufacturing level of the channel. This is true usually for two reasons. First, he knows his product best and has control of the manufacturing process. Second, he frequently, though not always, has greater economic power.

manufacturing

It can also be argued that the logical seat of power in the channel does, or at least should, reside at the retail level. Again, two reasons exist. First, since the retailer represents the interface with the buying public, he should be in the best position to control market information and access to markets. As logical and consistent with the marketing philosophy of management as this idea might sound, however, it usually holds true only when the second source of power, economic power, is present. Sears, Penney's, Safeway, and other retailing giants can and do provide channel leadership.

The channel leader is found far less frequently at the wholesale level. This is interesting in that traditionally wholesalers dominated distribution channels. When manufacturers and retailers are both relatively small, the wholesaler often provides a critical integrative function. In the grocery industry, wholesalers such as Associated Grocers and IGA (Independent Grocers' Association) help small food retailers remain competitive with the Safeway's and A & P's.

In nonhousehold markets the manufacturer is almost always the channel leader. This is the case in part because the major channel in these markets contains no middlemen. However, even when middlemen are involved, the economic power of the manufacturers results in their assuming leadership.

Vertical channel systems.   In the previous section, the basic dilemma faced by the marketing manager of whether to attempt to lead the channel or submit to the direction of others was presented. As noted, this decision is a product of a variety of economic considerations. The strategy of channel integration is really an extension of the idea of channel leadership and control. By integrating individual channel members into an organized whole, channel conflicts are ideally reduced and a common set of goals is obtained.

Vertical systems are created in three distinct ways. The most obvious way is through *direct ownership of channel members.* Companies that produce and market their products and services directly to the consumer include the Singer Corporation and Goodyear, to name but two. With ownership, of course, comes complete control.

A second form of vertical channel system is the *administered sys-*

1. *direct ownership*
2. *adminis. system*
3. *contractual system*
   franchising

tem. This is simply a formalized extension of the <u>channel leadership</u> idea. Simply, when a firm can control the channel through some form of economic power, it becomes a natural next step to begin to plan integrated programs for channel members. Kraftco, for example, markets its products aggressively to consumers, and also provides display and merchandising advice to retail stores.

The third method of achieving vertical integration is through *con-* *tractual systems*. This arrangement represents the most rapid growth of the three systems and is illustrated by such organizations as Mac-Donald's, Ramada Inn, Midas Muffler shops, automobile corporations and their dealerships, McKesson and Robbins, and many others. Franchising is a form of contractual system. Note that in each of the three systems, leadership may come from any level of the channel.[18]

Channel trends.   Several significant changes have occurred in distribution channels in the past ten to fifteen years.[19] In the past, once a manufacturer sold a product to a wholesaler, the latter pushed the product forward to the retailer, who in turn pushed the product to the ultimate consumer. This *push* philosophy has changed to a marked degree as a result of the channel leader being attuned to the ultimate consumers' needs and wants. Today, most channel leaders have adopted a *pull* philosophy, which suggests that the leader has the responsibility of preselling the product to the household. A schematic of the change in philosophies is shown in Figure 6.6. The cereal and automobile industries are good examples of pull philosophies in operation.

Channel amalgamation is a second significant trend. Amalgamation is associated with the emergence of large manufacturers and retailers in many industries. This emergence has brought about the decline of selected wholesalers and other intermediaries operating between the manufacturer and the retailer.

The home furnishing industry has been traditionally composed of many

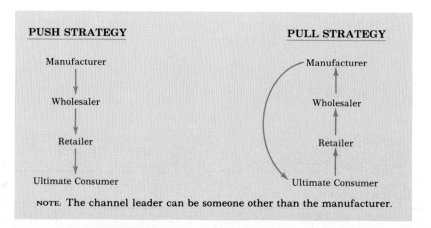

FIGURE 6.6.
CHANGE IN CHANNEL
PHILOSOPHY

PUSH STRATEGY

Manufacturer

Wholesaler

Retailer

Ultimate Consumer

PULL STRATEGY

Manufacturer

Wholesaler

Retailer

Ultimate Consumer

NOTE: The channel leader can be someone other than the manufacturer.

small furniture producers and thousands of small retailers. Given this channel composition, highly profitable intermediaries performed many significant functions. Recently, however, giant firms like Armstrong Cork and Weyerhauser have extended their product lines into home furnishings. On the retail side, national and regional firms, such as Levitz and RB Furniture, have assumed growing prominence. Where does this put the intermediary? Since the industry is changing, all channel members must adjust. The intermediaries must redefine the services they render to both the manufacturers and the retailers.[20]

Low margin retailing is a trend that has been going on for some time now. Firms such as K-Mart have adopted a strategy of accepting a lower price per item sold in order to gain profits through higher volume sales. The advent of self-service has helped lower costs and hence kept prices attractive. Low margin retailing has forced most small independents to stress their nonprice competitive advantages and stimulated the growth of retailer- and wholesaler-dominated associations.

Stock philosophy has completed a full cycle from the general store to retailer specialization to *scrambled merchandising.* The latter term describes competition between different *types* of retail outlets marketing similar goods. A food store such as Safeway or A & P is now marketing housewares, nonprescription drugs, and clothing, as well as food. The variety of products marketed suggests that the food store is competing with retailers within and outside the food business. Interestingly enough, a most recent retailing phenomenon is the emergence of the boutique. This may seem to represent a movement back to specialization, but it should be noted that the boutiques prosper best when surrounded by a variety of other retailers, such as the situation found in major shopping malls. All members of the distribution channel need to continually monitor the strategic implications of these retailing changes.

The *location* of retailing establishments has changed drastically in the last decade. The decline of downtown shopping areas and the growth of shopping centers is obvious, but other trends are also in various stages of development. More and more outlets are moving into or near the larger office buildings, industrial parks, and apartment complexes. This development is a response to people who want to spend less time and effort shopping for certain items—particularly convenience goods. Furthermore, an increasing percentage of retail volume is done outside the store. The popularity of catalog shopping may be the prelude to buying through means of a minicomputer in the home.

Leasing and *credit* availability have also facilitated channel trends. Tax and capital advantages have led many industrial firms to leasing on a massive scale. Many airlines, in fact, lease their aircraft from commercial banks. Although leasing in nonhousehold markets is well developed, observers also anticipate substantial growth in consumer leasing in the years ahead.[21] Credit availability and arrangements have stimulated all institutions in the channel by making it easier for buyers to engage in consumption activities.

In summary, channel strategy involves the goal of attaining an optimal distributive structure through which products and services may flow. A channel may have any number of members, and control will usually reside with the firm possessing the greatest economic power. Given this background, the next section will examine the actual physical movement of products from the manufacturer to the consumer.

PHYSICAL DISTRIBUTION STRATEGY   Given a specified level of customer service and an existing channel structure, the goal of physical distribution strategy is to minimize the cost involved in physically moving and storing the product from its production point to the point where it is ultimately purchased.

The task of physical distribution may be divided into three areas:

1. Determining inventory dispersion

2. Determining the level of inventory

3. Selecting a mode(s) of transportation

Unfortunately, these tasks have often been viewed as a group of unrelated activities. Managerial responsibility for them has often been assigned to areas in the firm that may have incongruent goals. The ultimate result of this fragmented approach is the suboptimization of overall physical distribution goals. It is irrational, for instance, to focus on reducing transportation costs when to do so has the effect of increasing the cost of carrying inventory by an increment greater than the amount saved.[22]

Inventory dispersion.   The strategic decision here is to what extent does the firm want to centralize its inventory or disperse it throughout the market. If the firm is the marketer of Winston cigarettes, it may want its product available within an arm's length of consumption. On the other hand, if the firm is marketing steamshovels, it would be ludicrous for it to have the product available on every corner. As a matter of fact, for some products, it is advisable to maintain *no* inventory and simply produce the item when an order is received. The no inventory policy is particularly appropriate when the product is customized to the needs of the customer.

What are the factors that should be considered in determining inventory dispersion? First, and foremost, is demand or market considerations coupled with what competitors are doing. These factors, in turn, must be balanced against cost variables. Various mathematical models are available to help guide this strategic decision.

Inventory size.   Determining optimal inventory size is a natural extention of the dispersion decision. Inventory control represents a tradeoff between the cost of carrying inventory versus the cost of being out of stock. If a firm could afford to be solely concerned with serving customers, it would make sure that it always had ample inventory available to satisfy potential customers' orders. Higher service levels, however, require larger inventories, which in turn lead to high storage costs, capital costs, taxes and insurance, possible deterioration and obsolescence, and losses if prices decline. Conversely, smaller inventory levels can lead to frequent order processing, high handling charges, loss of quantity discounts, losses if prices increase, and possible out of stock, with resulting customer dissatisfaction. The basic tradeoff is illustrated in Figure. 6.7.

Every student has probably experienced something like the following situation. The semester begins and you go over to the bookstore to purchase your texts. Unfortunately, you discover that *Marketing: An Environmental Perspective* has been sold out and another shipment will not be in for three weeks. After exhibiting various levels of disgust toward the bookstore (and maybe even toward the authors of the text), you resign yourself to being without the book for the beginning of the course. Where did the bookstore go wrong? Obviously, they underestimated the demand for your marketing book, and there are costs to them as a result. On the other hand, if they had over-estimated demand, they would be left with an excess inventory and its associated costs. Thus, the bookstore tries to correctly guess the correct number of texts to order to minimize the aforementioned costs.

These tradeoffs make the timing of inventory purchases critical. Guidelines must be established so that reordering of stock automatically takes place when prescribed inventory levels are reached. Most companies maintain a basic inventory at all times, along with a "safety stock" as a hedge against variability of lead order time. Quantitative relationships can ordinarily be developed to provide insight as to appropriate reorder points and economic order quantities.

Transportation modes. In addition to inventory strategy, physical distribution also involves selecting modes of transportation.[23] Basi-

FIGURE 6.7.
BASIC INVENTORY
MANAGEMENT TRADE-OFFS

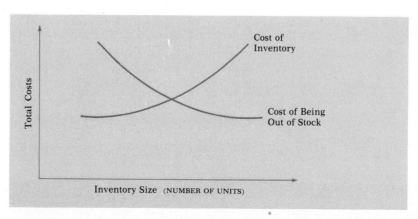

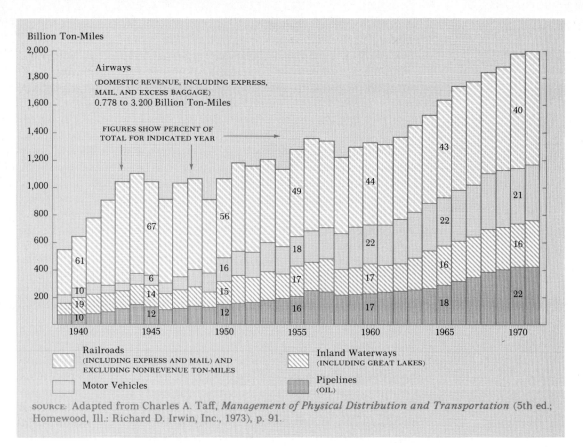

Billion Ton-Miles

Airways
(DOMESTIC REVENUE, INCLUDING EXPRESS, MAIL, AND EXCESS BAGGAGE)
0.778 to 3.200 Billion Ton-Miles

FIGURES SHOW PERCENT OF TOTAL FOR INDICATED YEAR

Railroads
(INCLUDING EXPRESS AND MAIL) AND EXCLUDING NONREVENUE TON-MILES

Motor Vehicles

Inland Waterways
(INCLUDING GREAT LAKES)

Pipelines
(OIL)

SOURCE: Adapted from Charles A. Taff, *Management of Physical Distribution and Transportation* (5th ed.; Homewood, Ill.: Richard D. Irwin, Inc., 1973), p. 91.

FIGURE 6.8.
INTERCITY TON-MILES BY THE VARIOUS TRANSPORT MODES: 1940–1971

cally, there are five alternatives that can be used: railroads, motor carriers, water carriers, pipelines, and airlines. Excluding air freight which accounts for less than 1 percent of all shipments, Figure 6.8 shows the relative importance of the four major modes of transportation in terms of intercity ton-miles hauled by each during the period 1940–1971.

Railroads are the leading mode, followed by pipelines, motor carriers, and water carriers. The attractiveness of the railroads is their ability to haul bulk products and raw materials relatively inexpensively and quickly to almost any point in the United States.

The motor carrier industry, which has shown dramatic growth in the past ten years, provides fast and consistent service for both large and small shipments. Although it cannot ordinarily haul bulk products as inexpensively as the railroads, it frequently can provide a cost advantage for manufactured products. As a result, in the early 1970s truckers received revenue of five times the cents per ton-mile than the railroads.

Water carriers, particularly barge lines that operate on the inland waterways, concentrate on bulk commodities. Ocean-going ships operate on the Great Lakes and international waters. In 1971 domestic water billings amounted to $1.37 billion, and the international freight bill was more than $4.3 billion.[24]

Many people overlook pipelines as a major means of transportation, but they are second only to railroads in number of ton-miles transported. Pipelines are the most efficient conveyors of oil products and natural gas with average revenue per ton-mile being less than 3 cents.[25] Basically, oil pipelines haul two types of commodities—crude oil and refined products such as gasoline and kerosene. A third area of increasing importance is slurry pipelines. They transport ground-up products, such as coal, in a water suspension.

The last mode of transportation is air freight. Growth has been dramatic, as evidenced by an increase of almost 2.5 billion ton-miles flown in the last decade. Yet, air freight still only accounts for less than 1 percent of total ton-miles transported. Air freight, because of its relatively high cost, is used primarily for the shipment of very valuable or highly perishable products.

The complex decisions involved in selecting a given mode have made transportation a specialized field in itself. Strategically, the firm should select the mode(s) that best matches transport costs and services with customer requirements. If speed, for example, is the essential need of the buyer, then air freight is the appropriate mode, assuming the buyer is willing to bear the cost. Table 6.3 compares selected modes in terms of their strategic strengths and limitations.

Organization.   The area of physical distribution is receiving great attention today. This interest is a direct result of the increasing complexity and importance of the activity.

Organizationally, physical distribution is positioned in various departments, such as marketing, production, and traffic. The fact that physical distribution has no common home reinforces our knowledge that it is a multifaceted activity. The importance of the activity to many firms has resulted in the creation of a separate physical distribution department at the same level as marketing, production, and other departments. If a high level of customer service is required and physical flows are an important element in the firm's overall success, a separate unit may be justifiable.

THE MACRO ENVIRONMENT AND DISTRIBUTION STRATEGY

As with the other three elements of the marketing mix, distribution strategy is influenced by forces *outside* the firm. A company must continually monitor changes in the macro environment and assess their impact on distribution strategy.

A dictate from the *legal* environment in the spring of 1976 required changes in the distribution strategy of the Gallo winery. The Federal Trade Commission ordered the nation's largest wine seller *not* to require its distributors to sell all of its more than forty brands. Furthermore, Gallo is now prohibited from pun-

Mode	Service Level	Cost	Pickup	Delivery	Additional Characteristics
REA Express	Good	Economical on mid-sizes	Yes	Yes	
Freight Forwarder	Good	Moderate	Yes	Yes	Possible surcharge to smaller communities
Less-than-carload rail	Slow	Economical	Varies	Varies	
Motor	Good	Moderate	Yes	Yes	Variable costs among different carriers
Greyhound	Good	Economical on small packages	Extra	Extra	
Water	Slow	Inexpensive	No	No	Limited areas served
Air parcel post	Fast	Expensive	No	Yes	Cheaper than air express on small packages
REA Air Express	Very Fast	Expensive	Yes	Yes	Cheaper than air freight on small packages
Air freight forwarder	Fast	Expensive	Generally	Generally	Limited areas served
Air freight	Fast	Expensive	Extra	Extra	Limited areas served

TABLE 6.3.
A STRATEGIC COMPARISON OF
TRANSPORTATION MODES

ishing wholesalers who also distribute wine from other producers. The FTC order curtails the power and control of Gallo over its distribution channels and suggests needed strategic adjustments on the company's part.

Sociocultural, legal, and *competitive* forces are relevant in the distribution of Coors beer in the eastern half of the United States. Coors is the nation's fourth largest selling beer, despite being widely distributed in only eleven western states. The beer's light, smooth taste, coupled with its limited geographical distribution, have created a "Coors mystique" among beer drinkers outside the west. Coors' ability to totally control its distribution channels is slipping as a result of a Supreme Court ruling that the company could not prohibit sales to the other 39 states. As a consequence, wholesalers and retailers are now buying the beer in western states and transporting it eastward. The "Coors mystique" and the few places it is available outside the west have allowed selected retailers to charge astronomical prices for the beer. Philadelphia distributor Paul Lipschutz, for example, began importing the beer and lines formed even though the price was $12.50 a case. Coors, distributors, and retailers will be carefully monitoring the public to see if the increased availability of the beer will hurt the "Coors mystique."

COORDINATING THE MARKETING MIX

Chapters 5 and 6 have investigated the strategic use of the product, promotion, distribution, and price elements of the marketing mix. An organization must be able to adjust these elements for existing and new products periodically if it wants to have a successful marketing effort.

While each of the four mix elements requires a specific strategy, each depends on and affects the others. Changes in a product, for example, are likely to suggest adjustments in promotion strategy. A good illustration of the interaction of the mix elements was shown in the discussion of the product life cycle in Chapter 5. As the product passes through the introductory, growth, maturity, and decline stages, the marketing mix should change.

SUMMARY

This chapter has examined promotion and distribution strategy—two of the four elements of the marketing mix.

Promotion strategy is the means by which the organization communicates with the marketplace. Marketing communications flow from a source through a channel to a receiver. The goal of promotion is to inform, persuade, and remind consumers about all relevant aspects of the firm's offering.

The marketer has a number of promotional tools to select from. The marketer may choose various combinations of advertising, personal selling, sales promotion, packaging, branding, public relations, and publicity. Generally, the two most significant elements in promotion strategy are advertising and personal selling.

Advertising is the impersonal communication of ideas, goods, or services to a mass audience by an identified paying sponsor. The ultimate objective of most advertising is to hasten the adoption or ensure repeat purchases of a product or service. Determining the appropriate copy and media are strategic advertising decisions. Market characteristics, product attributes, and cost are important considerations in making these decisions. The creative and technical aspects of advertising often result in firms using the services of advertising agencies.

Personal selling, in contrast to advertising, enables the firm to approach the market on a more selective basis and benefit from one-to-one interaction. Various estimates suggest that 10 percent of the nation's labor force may be engaged in this activity. Today's professional salespersons are attuned to their customers' needs and familiar with the intricate attributes of their products and services.

Although each of the promotion techniques is separate and distinct, an effective promotion strategy orchestrates the elements into a coordinated communications effort. The macro environment establishes constraints as well as opportunities in formulating promotion strategy.

Distribution strategy consists of getting the product to the customer when and where he or she wants it. The broad strategic decisions can be divided into (a) the channels through which products flow, and (b) the physical movement of products through the channel.

Distribution channels encompass all of the institutions involved in product flow from point of manufacture to point of final purchase. Middlemen such as wholesalers, retailers, and agents help facilitate the flow. Generally, one of the institutions in the channel assumes the leadership in influencing channel decisions. Although channels represent an aggregation of separate firms, the movement toward vertical channel systems has reduced interfirm conflicts and often led to goal congruence among the participants. Significant channel trends in recent years include the adoption of the pull philosophy, channel amalgamation, low margin retailing, variable stock philosophy, location changes, and the popularity of leasing and credit.

The strategic task of physical distribution may be divided into three areas: (1) determining inventory dispersion; (2) determining the level of inventory; and (3) selecting a mode(s) of transportation. Inventory dispersion is to what extent a firm wants to centralize its inventory or disperse it throughout the market. Inventory level decisions represent a tradeoff between the cost of carrying inventory versus the cost of being out of stock. Transportation modes may be selected from rail, motor, water, pipeline, and air carriers. The complexity and importance of physical distribution has led to debates on where in the organization this activity should be located.

A successful distribution strategy coordinates all of the relevant elements into a systematized effort. As with promotion strategy, decisions concerning this mix element are influenced by the macro environment.

The chapter closed with an integrative look at the material presented in Chapters 5 and 6. Strategic decisions within each marketing mix element of product, price, promotion, and distribution have effects on the other elements.

QUESTIONS FOR DISCUSSION

1. Why is promotion strategy often described as an "exercise in communication"?

2. Identify and discuss the advantages and disadvantages of the six elements of promotion.

3. Discuss the basic considerations involved in formulating copy and media strategy.

4. Advertising and personal selling are the primary promotion elements for most firms. Discuss the interrelationships and coordination between the two elements.

5. Why do many firms turn to advertising agencies to assist their advertising efforts?

6. What is a channel of distribution? Describe some of the different channel arrangements that are available.

7. Generally one member of the distribution channel assumes a leadership role. Discuss situations in which the manufacturer, wholesaler, and retailer may occupy the position of leadership.

8. The dynamic nature of distribution channels is evidenced by the significant trends occurring in this area. Discuss the marketing implications of any three of these trends.

9. Physical distribution strategy includes decisions concerning the level of inventory. Discuss the tradeoffs involved in determining inventory size.

10. Discuss the strengths and limitations of each of the five alternative modes of transportation.

NOTES

[1] Ronald R. Gist, *Marketing and Society—A Conceptual Introduction* (2nd ed.; New York: Holt, Rinehart, Winston, Inc., 1974), p. 385.

[2] For more detailed information on rates and circulation for advertising in selected media, see James L. Heskett, *Marketing* (New York: Macmillan Publishing Co., Inc., 1976), pp. 194–195.

[3] The American Marketing Association, Committee on Definitions, *Marketing Definitions: A Glossary of Marketing Terms* (Chicago: The American Marketing Association, 1960), p. 9.

[4] Robert N. McMurray, "The Mystic of Supersalesmanship," *Harvard Business Review* (May-April, 1961), p. 114.

[5] "The Salesman's New Job: Drumming Up Supplies," *Business Week* (October 26, 1974), pp. 54–55.

[6] The American Marketing Association, *Marketing Definitions,* p. 20.

[7] Ben M. Enis, *Marketing Principles* (Pacific Palisades, California: Goodyear Publishing Company, Inc., 1974), p. 403.

[8] "Coupons—Everybody's Problem," *Progressive Grocer* (October, 1974), p. 1.

[9] Albert Wesley Fry, ed., *Marketing Handbook* (2nd ed.; New York: Ronald Press Company, 1965), section 6, by Robert I. Goldberg, "Packaging," p. 36.

[10] Frederick E. Webster, Jr., *Marketing Communication: Modern Promotional Strategy* (New York: Holt, Rinehart, Winston, Inc., 1971), pp. 589–593.

[11] *Ibid.,* p. 595.

[12] Reprinted from "Promote a New Product Without National Advertising," *Marketing News* (November 1, 1974), p. 2. Published by the American Marketing Association.

[13] Webster, *Marketing Communication,* p. 625.

[14] The American Marketing Association, *Marketing Definitions,* p. 19.

[15] *Ibid.,* p. 10.

[16] Adapted from Enis, *Marketing Principles,* p. 448.

[17] For two insightful looks at power and control in distribution channels see Louis P. Bucklin, "A Theory of Channel Control," *Journal of Marketing,* Vol.

37 (January, 1973), pp. 39–47 and Adel I. El-Ansary and Robert A. Robicheaux, "A Theory of Channel Control: Revisited," *Journal of Marketing,* Vol. 38 (January, 1974), pp. 2–7.

[18]For further discussion on vertical marketing systems see Louis P. Bucklin, ed., *Vertical Marketing Systems* (Glenview, Illinois: Scott Foresman, Company, 1970).

[19]Portions of this section are derived from Don L. James, Bruce J. Walker, and Michael J. Etzel, *Retailing Today* (New York: Harcourt Brace Jovanovich, Inc., 1975), pp. 584–602, 612–624 and Philip Kotler, *Marketing Management* (3rd ed.; Englewood Cliffs, New Jersey: Prentice-Hall, Inc., 1976), pp. 281–282.

[20]Louis H. Grossman and Roger Dickinson, *Changes in Homefurnishing Retailing* (Chicago: International Homefurnishing Representatives Association, 1969).

[21]Leonard L. Berry and Kenneth E. Maricle, "Consumption Without Ownership: Marketing Opportunity for Today and Tomorrow," *MSU Business Topics,* Vol. 21 (Spring, 1973), pp. 33–41 and Robert Obenberger and Parks B. Dimsdale, Jr., "Changing Consumer Attitudes Toward Ownership: Implications for Marketing Strategy" (paper presented at the Southern Marketing Association's Annual Meeting, Washington, D.C., November, 1972).

[22]Grant M. Davis and Stephen W. Brown, *Logistics Management* (Lexington, Massachusetts: D. C. Heath and Company, Lexington Series, 1974), pp. 218–219.

[23]For a detailed look at the alternative transportation modes see Roy J. Sampson and Martin T. Farris, *Domestic Transportation* (3rd ed.; Boston: Houghton Mifflin Company, 1975), pp. 53–87.

[24]"Water Transportation," *Handling and Shipping* (January, 1972), p. 74.

[25]Charles A. Taff, *Management of Physical Distribution and Transportation* (5th ed.; Homewood, Illinois: Richard D. Irwin, 1972), p. 103.

SUGGESTED READINGS

Davis, Grant M. and Stephen W. Brown, *Logistics Management* (Lexington, Massachusetts: D. C. Heath and Company, Lexington Series, 1974).

Downing, George D., *Sales Management* (New York: John Wiley and Sons, Inc., 1969).

Kotler, Philip, *Marketing Management* (3rd ed.; Englewood Cliffs, New Jersey: Prentice-Hall, Inc., 1976).

Kurtz, David L. and Charles W. Hubbard, eds., *The Sales Force and Its Management* (Morristown, New Jersey: General Learning Press, 1971).

Littlefield, James E. and C. A. Kirkpatrick, *Advertising* (3rd ed.; Boston: Houghton Mifflin Company, 1970).

Sampson, Roy J. and Martin T. Farris, *Domestic Transportation* (3rd ed.; Boston: Houghton Mifflin Company, 1975).

Stanton, William J. and Richard H. Buskirk, *Management of the Sales Force* (3rd ed.; Homewood, Illinois: Richard D. Irwin, Inc., 1969).

Still, Richard R. and Edward W. Cundiff, *Sales Management* (3rd ed.; Englewood Cliffs, New Jersey: Prentice-Hall, Inc., 1969).

Webster, Frederick E., *Marketing Communications* (New York: The Ronald Press Company, 1971).

THREE

MARKETING AND THE MACRO ENVIRONMENT

Based on the presentation in Part III, the reader should be able to:

■ discuss the macro marketing system and objectively evaluate its performance in the United States

■ recognize the importance of the domestic market environment and identify the household and non-household sectors of the market

■ recognize the importance of the international market environment and discuss international marketing strategy

■ explain the institutional environment and identify the marketing middlemen and facilitating agencies that operate in the macro marketing system

■ identify the various dimensions of the sociocultural environment and understand its impact on marketing

■ see the role of government in society and analyze the impact of the legal environment on marketing

■ discuss the scope and importance of the economic environment in both a macro and a micro context

■ understand the technological environment and discuss the impact of man's changing technological world on marketing

■ explain the significance of the competitive environment and recognize the nature of competition in the marketplace

7

THE MACRO MARKETING SYSTEM

7

THE MACRO MARKETING SYSTEM

In the previous section, the *micro marketing environment* was examined through a discussion that focused on the individual firm. To provide an introduction for the *macro marketing environment,* this chapter is devoted to an analysis of the *macro marketing system* in the American economy. The discussion here will deemphasize the individual firm and concentrate on the total complex of marketing organizations that serve the economy in the translation of the resources of society into the more than one trillion dollars of goods and services that are consumed annually in the United States. Emphasis, therefore, will be given to both the function and the structure of the system as the basis for an analytical description of how the macro marketing system operates.

FUNCTIONS OF THE MACRO MARKETING SYSTEM

Although marketing is performed by individual business firms, it is the aggregate marketing activity of all suppliers in an economy that determines how well society's total needs and wants are satisfied. The achievement of a high level of satisfaction, however, is not an easy task, for a number of key decisions have to be made. Someone, for instance, must decide what and how much to produce, when to produce, and who should produce for whom. In a state-run economy, these issues are settled with varying degrees of success by central planners in government. This is a command form of resource allocation that exists in the USSR, Yugoslavia, and Communist China. In contrast, the United States employs a self-regulating mechanism that relies on a free market that allows individual business firms to make their own decisions regarding what to produce and sell.

Regardless of the basic differences in the organization of economic systems, it should be apparent that all modern economies must perform certain necessary functions associated with the acquisition and utilization of scarce resources. These functions are performed in the macro marketing system, which may be defined as the total network of individuals, organizations, and customer groups that engage in marketing activities. Collectively, they represent the component parts of the system's structure and are directly involved in the following macro marketing system functions:

IMPORTANT:→

1. Resource allocation
2. Supply-demand adjustment
3. Need satisfaction
4. Physical distribution

RESOURCE ALLOCATION

As discussed in Chapter 1, every economic society is faced with the problem of limited resources and insatiable desires. Therefore, important economic decisions must be made as to how and in what ways scarce resources are to be allocated to the members of society. As noted earlier, there are two approaches to the problem: allocation through a command system and allocation by means of a market system.

COMMAND System →

The command system. In theory, the command system is supposed to provide for enlightened leadership that can decide what products and services will best satisfy the needs and wants of the members of society. Given centralized decisions of this nature, however, there are obvious tradeoffs that must be considered. In Communist China, for example, the emphasis on building up the industrial sector of the economy has taken precedent over the provision of consumer goods and services. Consequently, few Chinese Communist citizens enjoy the basic consumer items that are almost necessities in the United States today.

efficiency & productivity

In practice, therefore, the command system of resource allocation leaves something to be desired. Under even the best conditions of planning, there is the problem of political conflict over what should be produced. People have different needs and wants. Accordingly, what may be satisfactory to one segment of society may be totally unsatisfactory to another. Furthermore, there is no assurance that central planning can meet the needs of the total society. Russia, for example, has committed significant resources in the last few years to the manufacture of automobiles and the construction of new roads. Many experts contend, however, that even the huge increases that are projected will serve only city dwellers and government leaders. It is expected that rank and file Russians will remain unsatisfied in private transportation for many years to come.

An evaluation of the command system of resource allocation suggests that little attention has been devoted to the task of marketing. Efficiency in physical distribution and overall productivity have received the greatest attention, while promotion, display techniques, and personal selling generally have been ignored. The concentration on capital goods has resulted in the imposition of rationing and price controls. Furthermore, a deemphasis on consumer goods has produced a relatively low standard of consumer life, and the general quality of available consumer goods and services has been well below the quality that is acceptable in the United States. In general, therefore, it may be argued that while the command system may be an appealing one in theory, its implementation in reality is below standards expected by Americans.

MARKET SYSTEM →

The market system. Characterized by the absence of structured planning, the market system of resource allocation relies on the operation of a free market to provide for the needs and wants of the members of society. As noted in an earlier chapter, this system is based on the fundamental assumption that competition by business for market acceptance will result in the best allocation of resources. Adam Smith in his *Wealth of Nations* described the operation of the market mechanism as an *invisible hand* that leads the economy toward maximum satisfaction of the needs and wants of all members of society. Even though Smith's theory may be considered somewhat idealistic today, the relative abundance of goods and services offered in the United States is a strong indicator of the general success of the system.

Three key principles of economic behavior provide for the effectiveness of the market system. These are the right to private property, a strong profit incentive, and freedom of choice. Owners of private property can make independent decisions as to the disposition of their wealth, and they are motivated by profit to search out the highest rewards available. Furthermore, they can enter or exit the marketplace with complete freedom. That is, businessmen can produce and sell what they choose to offer in the market, and the consumer is free to accept or reject any product or service. In this manner, resources are channeled in the direction that best meets the needs of society.

An evaluation of the market system, of course, does reveal short-run imbalances. The energy crisis of the early 1970s is an example of what can happen in a free market. Past experience, however, indicates that the system does have the capability to adjust to imbalances. In the case of the energy crisis, it is now apparent that more resources are being allocated to meet increased demand for fuel and related products. Thus, while the market system is not a perfect one, especially in the short run, its advantages tend to outweigh its disadvantages over the long term.

SUPPLY-DEMAND ADJUSTMENT

As illustrated by the shortages in energy related products and services, the macro marketing system is constantly confronted with the task of adjusting supply to meet the demands of society. To demonstrate how the market mechanism operates in the adjustment of supply and demand, this section presents a brief summary of supply-demand relationships and a discussion of their interaction in the establishment of market size and price level.

On the supply side, there are a number of suppliers who freely enter a market with a product or service offering. The quantity that they are willing to supply, of course, is dependent on the price that they can reasonably expect to receive for their offering. Figure 7.1 presents a hypothetical situation showing, other things being equal, the potential supply of widgets at various prices. As price increases, the quantity supplied increases; conversely, as price decreases, the quantity supplied decreases.

On the demand side, there are a number of demanders who feel that widgets can satisfy a portion of their needs and wants. Accordingly, they are willing to give up their dollars for widgets. The actual quan-

FIGURE 7.1.
HYPOTHETICAL SUPPLY CURVE
FOR WIDGETS

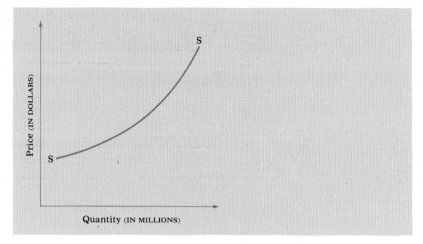

FIGURE 7.2.
HYPOTHETICAL DEMAND
CURVE FOR WIDGETS

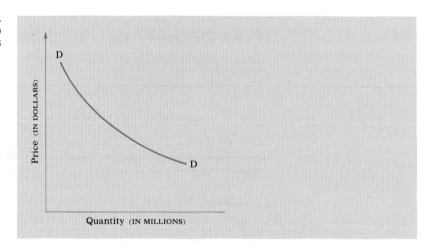

FIGURE 7.3.
HYPOTHETICAL EQUILIBRIUM
OF SUPPLY AND DEMAND

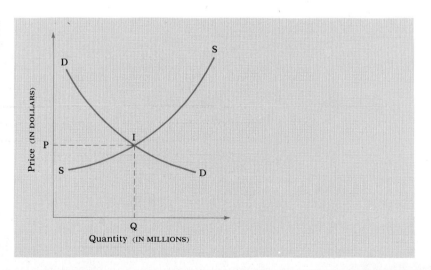

(AS PRICE INCREASES
SO DOES SUPPLY)

PRICE GOES ↓

AS DEMAND ↑

tity that they will purchase is dependent on the price that they have to pay. Figure 7.2 presents a hypothetical situation showing, other things being equal, the potential demand for widgets at various prices. As price increases, the quantity demanded decreases; conversely, as price decreases, the quantity demanded increases.

The macro marketing system provides a structure for bringing suppliers and demanders together in the marketplace. Here, of course, is where supply and demand interact to establish the size of the market and a price for the product or service. As shown in Figure 7.3, supply and demand intersect at point I. At that point, suppliers are willing to sell quantity Q at a price of P. Likewise, at point I, demanders are willing to purchase quantity Q at a price of P, and the market is in equilibrium. Other things being equal, the market will remain in equilibrium as long as the same relationships between supply and demand exist. Any change in either the actual quantity supplied or the actual quantity demanded will force a new equilibrium point and correspondingly a new P and Q.

While the above demonstration is grossly oversimplified and purposely excludes many of the important economic concepts in supply and demand analysis that are covered later in Chapter 12, it serves to illustrate the basic relationships that exist in the establishment of equilibrium. It is this intersection of supply and demand that is of primary importance for the macro marketing system. Imbalances in supply and demand must be adjusted by the system in order to avoid shortages in·demand and excesses in supply. When shortages occur, the system is encouraged to supply more to meet the increased demand. Likewise, a cutback in supply is effected when supplies are greater than demand. All of this is made possible, of course, through the operation of the market mechanism that serves to alert the macro marketing system to imbalances as they occur.

NEED SATISFACTION

The ability of the macro marketing system to keep supply and demand in equilibrium is largely a function of how well the system creates customer satisfactions. In economic terms, this refers to the capability of the system to deliver utility to the various members of society. Nonhousehold customers, for example, will seek those products and services that can solve their specific problems and earn them a profit. Household customers, on the other hand, will buy goods and services that they believe will best satisfy their wide variety of needs and wants. When the system fails to provide these forms of satisfactions through its market offerings, the net result is a misallocation of resources. Continued production of high energy consumption automobiles at a time when the market was clamoring for more economical private transportation is a perfect example of what can happen.

While need satisfaction may appear to be an obvious function of the macro marketing system, there is a subtle factor that often escapes

TABLE 7.1.
SOME PRODUCT AND UTILITY
RELATIONSHIPS

Product	Primary Utility	Secondary Utility
Automobiles	Transportation	Safety Status Economy
Toothpaste	Decay prevention	Fresh breath Whiteness
Convenience foods	Nutrition	Fast preparation Variety
Stereo equipment	Entertainment	Status Relaxation
Houses	Shelter	Prestige Recognition

many well intentioned businessmen. This factor relates to the issue of the basic purpose of the system. Some would argue, for example, that the macro marketing system in the United States has been developed to provide society with an abundance of goods and services. Up to a point, this is a valid argument. The key factor, however, is that the members of society do not buy goods and services. As noted above, they buy solutions to their problems and satisfactions of their needs. In this context, products and services intrinsically are relatively unimportant. The satisfaction (utility) that they render is far more basic. Table 7.1 illustrates this point with several product examples and the primary and secondary utility that they provide.

PHYSICAL DISTRIBUTION

The actual delivery of utility to the members of society is a function of the macro marketing system that is performed through physical distribution; the system is responsible for getting the national output of more than one trillion dollars to the right place at the right time. The physical flow of goods and services produced in the United States originates with agriculture, the extractive industries, imports, public utilities, transportation, and the service industries. From there, it continues to manufacturing and construction, then to the trade sector, and finally to the consumption and use sector where the flow terminates.

Without an orderly system of physical distribution, it would be impossible to properly direct the complex flows described above. Fortunately, the macro marketing system has solved the problem through the development of marketing intermediaries that specialize in distribution. These intermediaries will be identified in the next section of this chapter and discussed in complete detail in Chapter 8. It is important to recognize here, however, that specialized wholesalers and retailers serve an important role in the physical distribution function of the macro marketing system. This is shown in Figure 7.4, which illustrates the number of transactions required in a simplified distribution system containing four producers and six customers. Without intermediaries, a total of twenty-four transactions are necessary to distribute the output of the four producers. With one intermediary, the number of transactions is reduced to ten.

CHARACTERISTICS OF THE
MACRO MARKETING SYSTEM

From the above discussion of the functions of the macro marketing system, it should be apparent that the aggregate process of marketing generates billions of transactions and requires the efforts of a large number of individuals and organizations. To provide a clearer picture

FIGURE 7.4.
THE USE OF INTERMEDIARIES IN PHYSICAL DISTRIBUTION

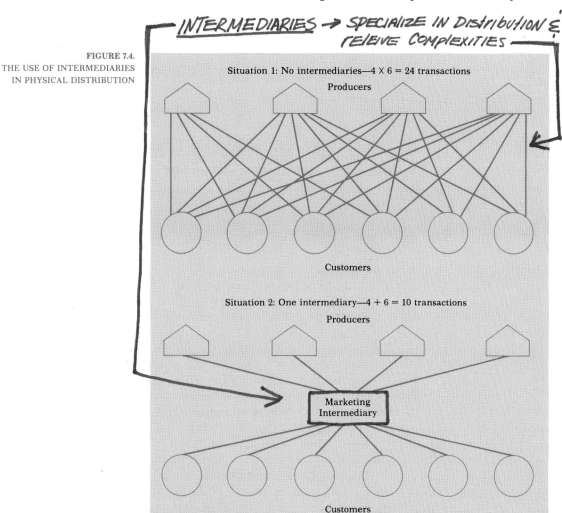

INTERMEDIARIES → SPECIALIZE IN DISTRIBUTION & relieve COMPLEXITIES

Situation 1: No intermediaries—4 X 6 = 24 transactions

Producers

Customers

Situation 2: One intermediary—4 + 6 = 10 transactions

Producers

Marketing Intermediary

Customers

FIGURE 7.5.
THE MACRO MARKETING
SYSTEM

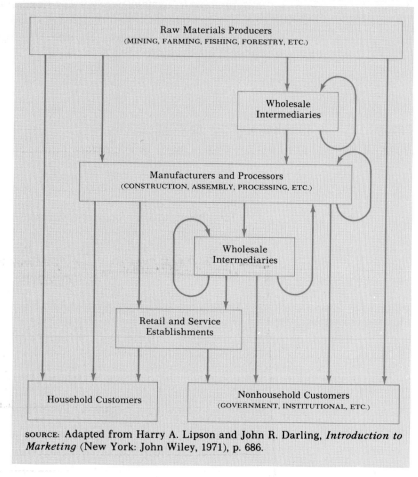

SOURCE: Adapted from Harry A. Lipson and John R. Darling, *Introduction to Marketing* (New York: John Wiley, 1971), p. 686.

of the complex process, this section is devoted to a discussion of the characteristics of the macro marketing system and its operation.

COMPONENTS OF THE SYSTEM

As defined earlier, the macro marketing system includes all individuals, organizations, and customer groups that engage in marketing activities. The components of the system and their relationships are shown in Figure 7.5. As presented, the system contains two levels of production, two levels of distribution, and two distinct customer groups. Specifically, these sectors may be separated into the following categories: raw materials producers, manufacturers and processors, wholesale intermediaries, retail establishments, service establishments, household customers, and nonhousehold customers.

Raw materials producers.   With the exclusion of imports, the billions of dollars of goods that are distributed annually in the United States

#1 RAW MATERIAL
#2 MANUFACTURERS
#3 Wholesale
     INTERMEDIARIES

#4 RETAIL
#5 SERVICE
#6 HouseHold
    CustoMers

#7 Non Household
    Customers

begin as raw materials, unprocessed items such as farm produce, logs, fish, and minerals. Raw materials producers are those individuals and organizations that operate in the field of agriculture, forestry, commercial fishing, and mining. In total, the more than three million establishments in this category employ nearly four million people and produce a volume of sales in excess of $100 billion.

Manufacturers and processors. After the produce of the earth and sea has been harvested, extracted, and mined, it flows to manufacturers and processors who produce finished goods and components for use in further production. More than one million establishments of this type operate in the United States. They employ over one-third of the labor force and generate sales receipts totaling nearly one trillion dollars.

Wholesale intermediaries. As an important link in the flow of goods, wholesale intermediaries are middlemen who perform marketing functions and facilitate exchange on the wholesale level of distribution. Wholesalers buy and resell goods to other wholesale intermediaries, retailers, and nonhousehold customers such as business, institutional, and government users. As a group, they do about $500 billion worth of business annually and employ close to four million persons. Although many have predicted the demise of the wholesaler for a number of years, wholesaling is a large, growing industry today with over 300,000 establishments in operation throughout the United States. The wholesaling sector is examined in detail in Chapter 8.

Retail establishments. Organized to serve the household consumer, the retailer is a type of middleman who buys and resells goods for final consumption. Thus, the distinguishing characteristic of a retail transaction is that goods are not resold. With approximately two million retail establishments in the United States, the American consumer enjoys a wide variety of retail operations ranging from small specialty stores to full line department stores. In total, these establishments produce in excess of $400 billion in annual sales and employ over one million persons. A detailed discussion of the retailing sector will be found in Chapter 8.

Service establishments. As one of the fastest growing areas of business in the American economy, service establishments are a significant industrial category. Expenditures for services now represent more than one-fourth of the gross national product and nearly half of all personal consumption expenditures. Furthermore, over one-third of all businesses in the United States are service establishments, and they collectively employ approximately one-half of the nation's labor force. A total list of all service establishments is too lengthy to enumerate here, but it includes all commercial operations that provide services for both household and nonhousehold customers.

Household customers. With a population in excess of 200 million persons and 65 million households, the market for consumer goods in the United States is a formidable one. This market, of course, is made up of household customers who buy products and services for their own personal or household use. Buyers in this segment of the domestic market purchase to satisfy nonbusiness needs and wants, and they constitute what is called the "household consumer market." A detailed analysis of this market is presented in Chapter 9.

Nonhousehold customers. The second group of buyers in the domestic market are those who purchase goods and services to use in their own operations or for the purpose of making other products; that is, all business, industrial, institutional, and governmental organizations are classified as nonhousehold customers. The nonhousehold market is discussed in detail in Chapter 9.

STRUCTURAL
DIMENSIONS OF THE
SYSTEM

In addition to its basic components, the macro marketing system contains a number of key structural dimensions. These dimensions identify the complex relationships that exist among the components of the system and show how its various parts are linked together to form an integrated macro marketing system. These linkages exist along spatial, horizontal, vertical, parallel, and convergent lines.

[STORES THAT ARE LINKED TOGETHER]

Spatial dimensions. With few, if any, exceptions, marketing components tend to be linked together in physical space. The stores in a shopping center, for example, are geographically linked; individual stores in the same city block are joined together in a psychological context. They serve the same market area and may even appeal to the same customers. To this extent, they are in the same spatial environment. This structural dimension of the macro system serves to define the geographical configuration of those components that are closely related in a spatial context.

[CHAINS OF THE SAME STORE]

Horizontal dimensions. When marketing components perform essentially the same type of marketing activities on a common level of the macro marketing process, they may be joined horizontally. They may be aligned formally through ownership, or more informally through trade associations, cooperative marketing associations, and voluntary groups. Sears, Roebuck and Company, with several hundred retail stores, is a good example of horizontal linkage through ownership. The National Wholesale Druggists' Association links its members together in a trade association, while Sunkist Growers, Inc., has formed Arizona and California fruit growers into a cooperative. The Independent Grocerymens' Association (IGA) and Associated Grocers (AG) are both examples of voluntary groups that join their members horizontally.

CONTROLS or OWNS all Aspects of the Marketing process from the raw Material to the point it reaches the customer

Vertical dimensions. Marketing components operating on different levels of the macro marketing process may be linked together along vertical lines. The conventional channel of distribution involving independent manufacturer, wholesaler, retailer, and consumer provides one of the most common forms of vertical linkage. This alignment produces an integrated distribution structure, and it works for the benefit of the various members of the channel. Another form of vertical linkage can be effected by one principal who owns and controls the various marketing components at all levels of the macro marketing process. The Goodyear Tire and Rubber Company is a good example of this since Goodyear manufactures its own tires and distributes them through company owned stores to the household consumer market.

Parallel dimensions. This dimension of the macro marketing system is the parallel, or duplicate, structures that develop as the system expands. In a given industry where there are a number of competitors, each rival develops his own distribution channel with exclusive wholesale and retail outlets. Each of these channels parallels, or duplicates, those of competitors. This is an example of vertical parallelism. In some industries, there is also horizontal parallelism. In the drug industry, for instance, strong trade associations operate at both the wholesale and retail levels of distribution. The National Wholesale Druggists' Association represents the wholesalers interests, while the National Retail Druggists' Association is the emissary for the retailers.

An outlet carrying different Brand names

Convergent dimensions. As illustrated by the convergent dimensions of the macro marketing system, there are many examples of nonparallelism in the structure. Supermarket operations, for example, have evolved to handle the retail distribution of a large number of food manufacturers and processors. In most instances, a given outlet will stock many competing brands; the output of soap manufacturers "converges" as it moves to the wholesale and finally to the retail level of distribution. There are no exclusive wholesalers or retailers, and rival products compete in the same outlets.

MARKETING FLOWS IN THE SYSTEM

Earlier in this chapter, the concept of flow in the macro marketing system was introduced; the components of the system are linked by structural relationships and by those marketing flows that bring the components together in the system. Although that discussion emphasized the flow of goods and services, it should be noted that their successful movement through the system necessitates additional flows such as transactions, money, title, information, and risk. The remainder of this section will briefly discuss each of these flows that are a necessary and integral part of the macro marketing process.

Goods and services flow. As noted in Chapter 5, goods and services may be broadly classified according to the markets that they serve. The aggregate flow of goods and services includes those intended for household consumption as well as those designed for use by business, government, and other institutions. As discussed previously, goods and services flow in the macro marketing system through the various marketing components that have been structured to serve the consumption and use sectors of the market.

Transactions flow. Goods and services, of course, do not flow aimlessly through the system; further, their movement begins only when negotiations occur and transactions are consummated. Transactions flow, therefore, entails the buying and selling activity that takes place in the macro marketing process. Buying and selling were identified as functions of exchange in Chapter 1, and it is the performance of these functions that makes transactions flow possible.

Money flow. In a modern economy, the flow of transactions is greatly facilitated by the flow of money. As readily apparent in primitive societies that rely on the barter system of exchange, it would be impossible to achieve a high level of marketing activity without money. In advanced societies, of course, the flow of money involves more than cash. Credit, which is based on the principal of borrowing from future income, provides an additional flow of money that is essential in the exchange process.

Title flow. As goods and services flow through the system, their movement is ordinarily followed by a concurrent flow of title; that is, the transfer of ownership that occurs when transactions are consummated and money changes hands. Through the exchange process, a seller gives up his right of ownership and transfers it to a buyer for a payment in fair value that is agreed upon through negotiation. While most transactions are effected in this manner, it should be noted that all negotiations do not involve title flow between the parties involved in the negotiation. As will be discussed in Chapter 8, certain types of marketing intermediaries, such as agents and brokers, negotiate sales for a principal without assuming title to the goods and services they sell. Title, in these cases, flows to the buyer from a seller who is not involved in the negotiation.

Information flow. The movement of goods and services would be impossible without a concurrent flow of information. This flow serves as a further linkage that joins the components of the system together in both a formal and informal context. Formal information flow may take the form of advertising, personal selling, and other types of organized marketing communication. It also may be in the form of marketing information that is generated through the marketing intelligence system. Informal information flow occurs through word-of-mouth communication among members within various groups in the system, such as consumers, suppliers, channel members, and competitors.

Risk flow.   Throughout the macro marketing system, the components in the system continually assume risk in the performance of the marketing process. Without risks, there would be little opportunity for profit. Producers, therefore, are willing to face the uncertainty of demand, changes in price levels, and the threat of competition. By the same token, marketing intermediaries take on the risk of ownership and the possibility that they will not be able to sell their accumulated inventories. At the consumer and use level, there is always the risk that a purchased good or service will not result in expected satisfaction. Some risk, of course, can be shifted as in the case of an owner insuring his property against loss through fire or destruction. Risk also can be minimized as illustrated by the manufacturer who produces to order, thus virtually eliminating risk associated with unsold inventories. In any event, risk flow is an inherent part of the macro marketing system.

POWER AND CONTROL IN THE SYSTEM

Given the diverse components, the complex structural relationships, and the many flows that exist in the macro marketing system, it follows that the system requires some form of control in order to operate effectively as an integrated whole. Control may be defined as the ability of one component in the system to exercise the power necessary to stipulate marketing policies and practices to the other components. This power may be gained through sheer economic strength, political or legal means, superior knowledge, and coercion. The manufacturer, the wholesaler, and the retailer represent the various components in the system that potentially can control the system.

A review of power and control in the macro marketing system is really a study in history, for significant changes in the control of the system have occurred throughout the development of the United States. In fact, the shifts in power among the various components in the system provide an interesting study in the business annals of America. As the basis for a brief discussion of power and control, the remainder of this section will focus on the historical evolution of the American marketing system from the colonial period through the modern era.

During colonial times, the United States was totally dependent on foreign manufactured goods. Little or no domestic manufacturing existed, and retailing was performed by importers and small-scale retailers. Consequently, control of the marketing system rested with the wholesaler who was in a position to be the dominant component. It was during this period that the full-service wholesaler developed in both size and strength. Retailers relied almost exclusively on the wholesalers' judgment in the selection of the goods that were offered to the market, and the wholesaler literally directed the total marketing system well into the nineteenth century.

Following the Civil War, the Industrial Revolution spread to America, and the country experienced a rapid growth in domestic manufacturing during the latter part of the nineteenth century and the early part of the twentieth century. By 1920, the United States was a flourishing industrial nation, and the existence of a strong manufacturing base served to shift power from the wholesaler to the manufacturer. The economic strength of the manufacturer, a growing population hungry for new products, the development of the transcontinental railroad, and the rapid growth in formal communication techniques that provided media for advertising all served to give the control of the marketing system to the manufacturer.

In the modern era since 1920, the manufacturer has continued to dominate the American marketing system. There are indications, however, that the retailer has been gaining more power in the last decade or so. Small-scale retailing is being replaced by large-scale retailing, and the "mom and pop" stores of another era have given way to the chains and the super stores. With the concentration of buying power now enjoyed by many retail operations, retailing as a sector in the system enjoys more power than the wholesaling sector. Whether giant retailing will ever assume complete control over the total system is somewhat doubtful, but there are many examples of retailer control where retail brands are as dominant as manufacturers' brands.

While no mention has been made of the consumer or use sector in this discussion, it should be apparent that this sector has never had enough power to control the marketing system. In the absence of such power, marketing decisions are made by marketers and not by consumers. It should be noted, however, that the rise of consumerism and a sharp increase in consumer legislation have given the consumer a stronger voice in the marketplace. Consequently, there is a growing recognition on the part of those in control of the marketing system that marketing decisions must be made with the consumer or user in the forefront of the decision-making process. This, of course, is the essence of the marketing philosophy that has been discussed in earlier chapters.

EVALUATION OF THE MACRO MARKETING SYSTEM

Although the emphasis in this chapter has been on the function and structure of the macro marketing system, the discussion would be incomplete without an assessment of its effectiveness. In an effort to appraise the overall performance of the system, this section will focus on several important questions that may be used as the basis for an evaluation of macro marketing in the United States. Special attention, therefore, will be devoted to the following issues: What are the major criticisms of the macro marketing system? How valid are these criticisms? Does macro marketing cost too much? How efficient is the macro marketing system?

CRITICISMS OF THE MACRO SYSTEM

Because of its immense power to shape social values, the marketing system in the United States has received and will continue to receive a great deal of criticism. Many of the areas of concern are valid ones that do need correction, but others are simply based on misinformation and a lack of understanding of how the macro marketing system operates. It seems reasonable, therefore, to judge the system in the light of a reality that ignores emotionalism, crusading, and selective individual value judgments. Following this approach, this section will present the major criticisms of the system and attempt to provide an objective analysis of each.

Marketing creates unnecessary wants. According to the critics, the marketing system has the power to create wants through mass selling techniques, large-scale retailing, and easily obtained installment credit. They argue further that many of these wants are unnecessary and that the system unfairly capitalizes on the vulnerability of the consumer. The major charge, in other words, is that marketing has emphasized materialism over other values that should be just as important to society.

Comment: This criticism is not without some degree of validity. Marketing does create wants by offering products and services and showing how these products and services can provide need satisfaction. This is the very essence of the marketing process. The claim that marketing creates unnecessary wants, however, is open to question. What is necessary? What is unnecessary? The answer is not an easy one, for value judgments enter the picture. What is necessary for one person may be unnecessary for another. Since buyers are free to make their own choices in the marketplace, dollar votes in the form of expressed demand ultimately determine the issue. It seems logical to assume, therefore, that those products and services that succeed in the market are necessary, while those that fail are unnecessary.

Marketing manipulates people. Popularized by Vance Packard in *The Hidden Persuaders,* this criticism charges that marketing brainwashes gullible consumers and forces them to buy. In later years following Packard's original presentation in 1957, the critics have expanded this criticism by crediting marketers with the power to form the tastes of the nation, dictate the content of radio and television programs, determine the life and death of mass-circulation magazines, and control the economic destiny of mankind. The marketer is pictured as a puppeteer with the public at the end of the strings in the role of a manipulated puppet.

Comment: The assumptions in this attack on marketing are not well grounded. First, the consumer is not as naïve and directable as the critics imply. Today's American consumer is relatively sophisticated and generally quite knowledgeable in the marketplace. Second, freedom of choice is the very cornerstone of the market system that prevails in the United States. People are not forced to act against their wishes, and would be quite resistant to any efforts to make them do so. Finally, forces in the legal environment in the form of the Federal Trade Commission, the Federal Communications Commission, and other regulatory agencies governing the field of marketing provide strong checks against attempted manipulations.

Marketing engages in false, misleading, and deceptive practices.   For the most part, this criticism is directed at the field of advertising for the use of exaggerations, conflicting claims, and fear appeals. In other areas, however, the critics cite exposed cases of price fixing, faulty products, deceptive packaging, and worthless guarantees as prima facie evidence of shady dealings in marketing. Practices of this nature are a major social concern, and they call attention to weaknesses in the system.

Comment: The charge of false, misleading, and deceptive practices in marketing is a valid one, but such practices are the exception rather than the rule. The principal offenders are in the household consumer goods field, where a relatively small number of aggressive competitors attempt to use deception to gain market position. Their actions, of course, cannot be defended, and the fact that there are only occasional cases of this nature does not invalidate the claims. To the contrary, this criticism exposes the deficiencies in the system that must be corrected internally. Without corrective action on the part of component members, the alternative solution is government legislation. Recent truth-in-lending, truth-in-labeling, and truth-in-packaging laws are examples of the latter alternative.

Marketing contributes to a misallocation of resources.   Led by John K. Galbraith and others, the critics contend that marketing encourages the consumption of private goods at the expense of public goods. As an example, they cite the promotion of frills on automobiles at a time when there should be a concern over slum clearance, school improvement, road maintenance, and the elimination of air and water pollution. These critics maintain that more of the nation's output should be diverted from the private to the public sector.

Comment: To a degree, this criticism of marketing deserves attention in the system. In those instances where the production and consumption of private goods creates social costs, both private and social costs should be absorbed by the private sector. The process of production of many items for private consumption, for example, results in air and water pollution. It may be argued, therefore, that the costs of cleaning up the air and water should be built into the price of the private goods. If people are willing to pay higher prices, then the resource allocation is appropriate. If not, those resources will move to other uses. In this manner, it should be possible to achieve a degree of balance in production and proper support for both public and private goods.

Marketing contributes to a waste of resources. In addition to the concern over the misallocation of resources, many critics of marketing are distressed by the apparent waste generated by the system. This criticism is directed at the many brands that are offered in the marketplace and the imaginary brand differentials that are promoted through advertising. Additionally, the critics point to the multitude of new products that never succeed and are withdrawn from the market because of a lack of acceptance or poor profit performance.

Comment: Again, there is an element of validity in this criticism. New product failure rates have been estimated conservatively at 50 percent and as high as 80 percent in some studies. When eight out of ten new products fail, the question of waste is an obvious one. On the other hand, it may be argued that successful competing brands and competing alternatives help to maintain a healthy competitive environment and hold prices to a level that is in the best interest of the consumer. Furthermore, multiple offerings provide a wide range of choice for the consumer. Thus, while waste is repugnant to everyone, there is positive benefit in our system of resource utilization.

MACRO MARKETING COSTS

Beyond the specific criticisms of marketing, the American public is now expressing grave concern over the cost of marketing in the United States. The high rate of inflation in recent years has made the public price conscious, and many complaints about the cost of marketing have been raised by both producers and consumers. While the complaints often come from people who do not understand the magnitude of the marketing task, it is true that marketing costs have risen substantially in both absolute and relative terms during the past one hundred years. Today, it is estimated that approximately half of the average retail dollar is absorbed by marketing costs. The basic question, of course, is why does marketing cost so much? A second important question is does marketing cost too much?

For the uninformed, a logical assumption is that marketing costs are high because of gross inefficiencies in the performance of marketing activities. It would be a mistake to jump to this conclusion, however, for there is evidence to support the fact that a number of internal and external environmental factors have influenced the rise in marketing expenses. It is important to understand the reasons for the increases that have occurred over the past century.

Part of the rise in marketing costs is the direct result of the need to develop a mass marketing system to correspond to the mass production system. Furthermore, automation and other labor-saving devices have greatly reduced the number of workers in production, while there has been a significant increase in the employment of people in the distribution trades. A mass marketing system requires a large work force, and employment statistics show that more people are now employed in the trade sector than in the extraction and production sectors.

The demand for more services and refinements in market offerings is another reason why marketing costs have increased. Credit, delivery, attractive stores, and free parking are all examples of services that are essential in today's marketplace. Further, merchandise variety, better packaging, higher quality, and more style represent costly refinements that are demanded by the modern consumer. Although it would be possible to reduce marketing costs by eliminating many of the service and product refinements that are offered today, it is probable that the market would not accept such changes.

Another important point to consider is that reductions in production costs often result in an increase in marketing costs. Thus, while production costs have declined relatively, marketing costs have increased. As an example, economies in production may be realized by locating a plant near sources of raw materials. Marketing costs, such as transportation, may have to be increased, however, when the finished product is moved to a distant market. By the same token, unit cost reductions resulting from an increase in production may be offset by corresponding increases in advertising and selling expenditures required to market a large volume of output.

Obviously, questions regarding marketing costs are not easy ones to answer. First, there are no absolute measures of marketing costs, for it is difficult to neatly separate marketing cost data from other costs of doing business. Second, absolute measures of marketing costs tend to be meaningless because cost is only one input in the determination of overall efficiency. Marketing "costs too much" only if costs can be reduced without diminishing the productivity (satisfactions) provided by the macro marketing system.

EFFICIENCY OF THE MACRO SYSTEM

The question, "Does marketing cost too much?" can only be answered through an objective evaluation of the efficiency of the macro system. Since the system has been established to accomplish specified goals, however, efficiency must be measured in terms of productivity. Goal achievement in both the customer sector and the business sector pro-

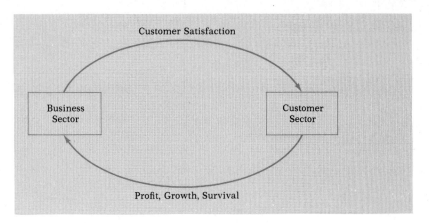

FIGURE 7.6.
GOALS OF THE MACRO
MARKETING SYSTEM

vides the appropriate frame of analysis for evaluating the efficiency of the macro marketing system. An identification of the system's broad goals and their interaction is presented in Figure 7.6.

Customer sector.   To even the casual observer, the American marketing system is a highly productive one in terms of its capability to provide customer satisfactions. In the aggregate, the American household consumer enjoys the highest standard of living in the world. Likewise, business customers realize solutions to their problems and satisfactions of their needs in a manner clearly superior to that accorded business counterparts in other industialized nations. It may be argued, therefore, that the macro marketing system is successfully accomplishing its assigned goals in the customer sector.

While there are "pockets" of unsatisfied demand in both the household and the nonhousehold segments of the customer sector, it should be noted that these conditions are an economic fact of life. No society will ever totally satisfy every single one of its members. Utopia exists only in the minds of the idealists. It is important, therefore, to evaluate the marketing system in aggregate terms relative to the systems of other nations in the world. When this is done, the macro marketing system in the United States stands alone as a model of efficiency in terms of customer satisfactions.

Business Sector.   The system's ability to produce customer satisfactions is a direct function of the efficiency of the business sector. In order to provide customer satisfactions, therefore, the business sector must be able to achieve its own goals. Clearly, business would be unable to satisfy the needs of its customers without making a profit. Gains in the form of profits allow business to grow and survive. Thus, the efficiency of the macro marketing system may also be measured in terms of the achievement of the profit, growth, and survival goals of the business sector.

While gross inefficiencies can be cited using specific examples of selected individual business firms in the United States, the total business sector in this country must be evaluated as a highly efficient one, especially in comparison with other industrialized nations. Even more significant is the fact that America's business sector is relatively young, having evolved over a period of less than two hundred years. Given the spectacular development that has occurred during this period, it may be argued that the macro marketing system has been quite successful in meeting the profit, growth, and survival goals of business.

In the above discussion of both the customer and business sectors, this section has concluded that the macro marketing system in the United States is relatively efficient when compared to the marketing systems of other industrialized nations throughout the world. For those who might take issue with this basic proposition, it should be noted again that the focus here is on the macro rather than the micro dimension of marketing. The conclusions apply only to the aggregate process of marketing. A more finite evaluation of marketing efficiency and productivity in the individual firm is reserved for Chapter 16.

SUMMARY

To provide a better understanding of the aggregate process of marketing in the United States, this chapter has been devoted to an analysis of the macro marketing system. Special attention was given to both the function and the structure of the system as the basis for an analytical description of how the macro marketing system operates in a high-level economy.

In the first major section of this chapter, the macro marketing system was defined as the total network of individuals, organizations, and customer groups that engage in marketing activities. The macro marketing system functions performed by these components of the system were identified as resource allocation, supply-demand adjustment, need satisfaction, and physical distribution.

Following a discussion of each one of the above functions, the second section of this chapter presented the framework of the macro marketing system and more specifically defined its components as raw materials producers, manufacturers and processors, wholesale intermediaries, retail establishments, service establishments, household customers, and nonhousehold customers. The remainder of the section was devoted to the structural dimensions of the system, marketing flows in the system, and the concept of power in the system.

The final section of this chapter provided an evaluation of the macro marketing system in terms of several basic questions relating to the major criticisms of the system, the costs of the system, and the general efficiency of the system. From this evaluation, it was concluded that the macro marketing system in the United States does not cost too much and that the system is relatively efficient when compared to the marketing systems of other industrialized nations.

QUESTIONS FOR DISCUSSION

1. Identify and explain the macro functions of marketing. Through an integrated discussion, show how these functions are performed in the macro marketing system.

2. Explain how resources are allocated in both the command system and the market system. What are the distinguishing features of each system?

3. Identify and briefly define each of the components in the macro marketing system. Explain the economic importance of each in the total system.

4. What is the structural dimension of the macro marketing system? Identify and define each of the structural dimensions discussed in this chapter.

5. What are marketing flows? Identify and explain each of the marketing flows that are discussed in this chapter.

6. Explain the concept of power in the system. Through a review of the historical evolution of the macro marketing system in the United States, discuss the shift in power that has occurred in the system.

7. What are the major criticisms of the macro marketing system? In an integrated discussion, explain each of these criticisms and comment on their validity.

8. Consider the question, "Does marketing cost too much?" Based on your understanding of the macro marketing system, defend the position that marketing does not cost too much.

9. Evaluate the efficiency of the macro marketing system. Based on your evaluation, what improvements and/or changes would you recommend for the system?

SUGGESTED READINGS

Bucklin, Louis P., *Competition and Evolution in the Distributive Trades* (Englewood Cliffs, New Jersey: Prentice-Hall, Inc., 1972).

Davis, Keith and Robert L. Blomstrom, *Business and Society* (3rd ed.; New York: McGraw-Hill Book Co., 1975).

Dommermuth, William P. and R. Clifton Andersen, "Distribution Systems: Firms, Functions, and Efficiencies," *MSU Business Topics* (Spring, 1969), pp. 51–56.

Gist, Ronald R., *Marketing and Society* (2nd ed.; Hinsdale, Illinois: The Dryden Press, 1974).

Grashof, John F. and Alan P. Kelman, *Introduction to Macro-Marketing* (Columbus, Ohio: Grid, Inc., 1973).

Greenland, Leo, "Advertisers Must Stop Conning Consumers," *Harvard Business Review* (July–August, 1974), p. 18.

Moyer, Reed, *Macro Marketing: A Social Perspective* (New York: John Wiley & Sons, Inc., 1972).

Walker, Bruce J. and Joel B. Haynes, *Marketing Channels and Institutions* (Columbus, Ohio: Grid, Inc., 1973).

8
THE INSTITUTIONAL
ENVIRONMENT

THE INSTITUTIONAL ENVIRONMENT

Following the introduction presented in Chapter 7, this chapter provides a detailed examination of the various institutions that comprise the macro marketing system. The organization and relationship of these institutions constitute the network that develops assortments of goods and services and brings them from points of origin to the individuals and organizations that consume them directly, or use them in the performance of their mission.

INTRODUCTION

Most accepted definitions of an institution usually include reference to an organization having a social, business, or educational purpose, or the building housing such an establishment. In this book, the term marketing institution is used *to include all of the individuals, groups, or organizations that carry on the work of marketing both directly and indirectly*. This concept of a marketing institution also includes the working relationships of the various independent firms working together that comprise the channels of distribution. Marketing channels will be considered later in this chapter.

CLASSIFICATION OF MARKETING INSTITUTIONS

Marketing institutions may be classified broadly into two categories: (1) marketing middlemen (retailers and wholesalers), and (2) facilitating marketing agencies (transportation, promotion, marketing research, and warehousing agencies). These are shown in Figure 8.1. It should also be noted that numerous other business institutions such as manufacturers, processors, financial institutions, professional sports, the theater, and even individuals perform marketing functions. The marketing activities of this last group are not the subject matter of this chapter.

The two major categories of marketing institutions listed above are the basic subject matter of this chapter and will be discussed in some detail. These institutions do not operate in a vacuum, however. As noted in Chapter 7, efficient and economical performance of these marketing institutions requires interaction with other parts of the total macro system. Marketing institutions need the facilities and expertise of such institutions as banks, factors, insurance companies, public accountants, legal firms, trade associations, and government bureaus.

 Marketing middlemen. These business firms are marketing institutions in the fullest sense. Their basic purpose is to identify, develop, and serve markets. A market is people or organizations with needs to satisfy, the resources with which to satisfy them, and the willingness to use their resources. Retailers and wholesalers are marketing mid-

FIGURE 8.1.
CLASSIFYING MARKETING
INSTITUTIONS

IMPORTANT

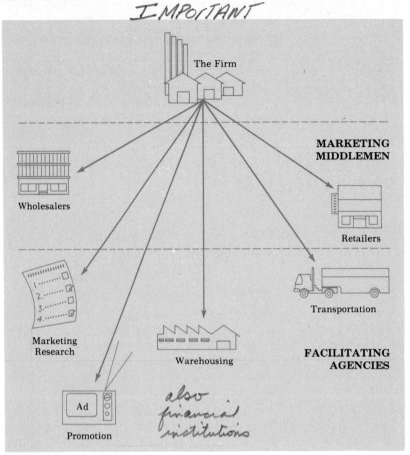

The Firm

**MARKETING
MIDDLEMEN**

Wholesalers

Retailers

Marketing
Research

Transportation

Warehousing

**FACILITATING
AGENCIES**

Ad

Promotion

*also
financial
institutions*

dlemen, for they neither create nor consume the goods or services that they provide to their markets. Retailers gather and build assortments of goods and services for resale to household consumers for personal or family consumption. Wholesalers gather and build assortments of goods and services for resale to retailers, other wholesalers, manufacturers, governments, and other organizations such as schools and churches. As marketing institutions, both wholesalers and retailers are concerned with the ownership and resale of the goods they handle. Yet, ownership for the purpose of holding the goods they buy is not the primary reason for their existence.

*MARKETING RESEARCH
PROMOTION
WAREHOUSING
TRANSPORTATION*

Facilitating marketing agencies.   In order to complete the marketing process, marketing middlemen normally require assistance or support from other institutions whose functions are highly specialized and supportive to the total process. Some of the larger middlemen organizations do integrate some of the facilitating functions into their own organizations, but even these must normally use other agencies, such as transportation. The institutions or agencies whose functions are necessary to the total marketing process are transportation, promotion, marketing research, and warehousing.

MARKETING MIDDLEMEN

Classified into the two broad categories of retailers and wholesalers, marketing middlemen are the dominant force in the movement of goods and services in the macro marketing system. As noted in Chapter 7, these intermediaries play an important role in the system's physical distribution function, and their activities greatly simplify the giant task of getting the national output of more than one trillion dollars to the right place at the right time. This section provides a detailed discussion of the marketing middlemen through an analysis of their operation and function in the distribution structure.

RETAILERS   *Retailing* is a productive human activity and is a necessary and important part of the macro marketing system. Through the sale of goods and services to household consumers, this activity creates time, place, and possession utilities that add value to the things purchased. Retailing establishments, therefore, are marketing institutions whose principle activity is selling goods or services to individuals who buy for personal or family consumption. The basic concept of this definition is the motive of the purchaser—personal or family consumption.

PLOT

History of retailing.   The history of retailing in the United States is a story of adaptation to meet the needs of an expanding population in a dynamic environment. The first retailers in the United States were the trading posts, where products from Europe were bartered for animal furs and other goods brought in by Indians and early white settlers. These were located along the travel and trading routes that led to the frontiers. As settlements developed, trading posts became the general store, which was the backbone of retailing in the midwest and west into the early years of the twentieth century. Another early retailer was the Yankee peddler who brought his goods in horse-drawn wagons to those living in the more remote areas of rural America.

As the economy expanded and cities grew larger, the retail store grew in size and complexity to meet the changing needs of the population. In the larger cities, single-line and specialty stores and department stores took the place of the general store to serve the increasing demand. From these early beginnings, retail institutions have grown in size, and new types have developed as major social forces in the environment. Mail-order retailing became a force in the United States in the late 1800s, and stores like Montgomery Ward and Sears Roebuck were highly viable in meeting the needs of the agricultural midwest through the 1930s. The modern supermarket had its beginning in the mid-1930s, while the discounter was a post World War II institution which grew rapidly after 1950. The planned shopping center is also a product of this later period.

The tremendous changes that have taken place in the environment

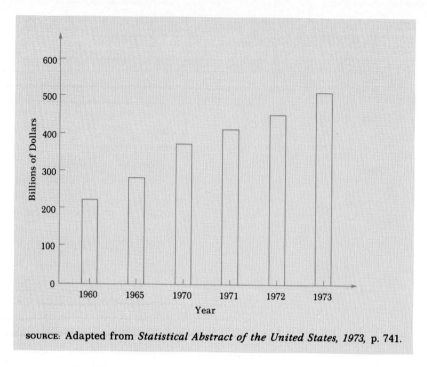

SOURCE: Adapted from *Statistical Abstract of the United States, 1973*, p. 741.

account for the dynamics of retail institutional change. The several environments, discussed in other chapters of this book, all have affected the growth and development of the retail structure. Social forces, for example, have had a significant influence on the conduct of retail enterprises. Among these are general population growth, population growth in certain age groups, population mobility, suburban living, better educated and informed buyers, increased leisure time, and a noticeable change in ethical and moral standards.

Although the number of retail establishments has remained relatively stable at approximately 1.75 million since 1939, the total volume of retail sales, and the number of people employed in retailing has increased substantially. Figures 8.2 and 8.3 show the growth of this industry in recent years.

Classification of retail stores.   Because retail institutions vary substantially in size, in the merchandise assortments they offer, and in the strategies they employ in serving their markets, it is of little value to generalize about retailers as a homogeneous group. For meaningful analysis, these establishments must be grouped according to the physical and operational characteristics that identify their mode of operation. While each retail establishment is unique, there are common characteristics among those retailers serving similar or identical market segments.

Low-margin/high-turnover vs. high-margin/low-turnover.   This is a broad classification that identifies opposites in regard to (a) the store's

FIGURE 8.3.
PERSONS IN DISTRIBUTION
AND SERVICE INDUSTRIES—
RETAIL TRADE

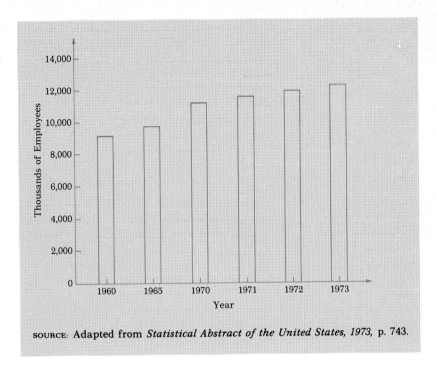

SOURCE: Adapted from *Statistical Abstract of the United States, 1973,* p. 743.

merchandise assortment, (b) the pricing strategy of the retailer, (c) the amount and kind of promotional effort, and (d) the types and quality of services the store provides. The term "margin" means the difference between the delivered net cost to the retailer and the asking price to the store's customers. Turnover is the rate at which a store's average inventory is sold and replaced, normally in a twelve-month period. Turnover may be calculated on the retail value of the inventory, its cost value, or on the number of units. Considering the modern type retail stores, the discounter can be identified as a low-margin/high-turnover type, and the exclusive specialty store as an example of the high-margin/low-turnover type. Obviously, there are many retail units that operate somewhere between these two extremes.

MARGIN

Convenience, shopping, and specialty stores.   This classification was originally used by Copeland to describe different types of consumer goods, based on product characteristics, consumer buying habits, and manufacturers' promotional and channel strategy.[1] In 1963, Bucklin proposed that the system of classifying consumer goods could be extended to retailing and used as a basis for retail store classification.[2] He suggested that the extension of the goods concept to retailing could be made through the notion of patronage motives which are derived from consumer attitudes about specific retail establishments. Examples of patronage motives are location, merchandise assortment, services, and price. These factors are basically retailer controlled and are sometimes referred to as the elements of the retailing mix.

CONVENIENCE STORES

Convenience stores are defined as "those stores for which the consumer, before his need for some product arises, possesses a preference map that indicates a willingness to buy from the most accessible store."[3] Merchandise assortments in these stores are normally composed of frequently purchased items about which the customer is generally knowledgeable. Specific brand preference is not a primary factor in the decision to buy. Easy access to the store's location is important, although the normal range of retail services is not important. Familiar stores that fit this classification are the "Circle K," "U-Tote-M," and "7-11" convenience markets, and neighborhood drug stores.

SHOPPING STORES

Shopping stores are defined as "those stores for which the consumer has not developed a complete preference map relative to the product he wishes to buy, requiring him to undertake a search to construct such a map before purchase."[4] Shopping stores provide a range of goods and prices that enable buyers to compare quality, style, brand, or other product features. Customers who visit shopping stores normally lack complete knowledge of a product's features or price, and want to make comparisons (shop) before a definite decision to purchase is made. The location of a shopping store is an important marketing consideration, but in a different sense than the ready accessibility that is of prime importance to the convenience store.

The concept of "cumulative attraction" should be considered by the shopping goods retailer. This concept recognizes that the shopping goods customer prefers the opportunity to shop or compare the offerings of several shopping stores located in close proximity to each other. The downtown core of the central city and planned shopping centers are ideally suited for shopping stores, because cumulatively they attract more people. Retailers of men's and women's apparel, furniture and home furnishings, and home appliances are typical examples of shopping stores. Department stores, such as the May Company and Marshall Field and Company, are also classified as shopping stores.

SPECIALTY STORES

Specialty stores are defined as, "those stores for which the consumer, before his need for some product arises, possesses a preference map that indicates a willingness to buy the item from a particular establishment even though it may not be the most accessible."[5] While this definition focuses on the retail store as a total entity, it should be noted that its particular characteristics give it the specialty classification. The specialty store is considered a high-price retailer, but this is not always the case. The willingness of the buyer to make a special effort to obtain the precise item he wants is really the key concept that distinguishes the specialty store. Among the characteristics that differentiate the specialty store from other type stores are special brands or labels, broader assortments of special classes of merchandise, and a comprehensive service mix. It is really the customer who perceives a particular store as a specialty store, and it is the retailer's job to identify the characteristics viewed as special by certain cus-

TABLE 8.1.
TYPES OF CONSUMER BUYING
BEHAVIOR

1. *Convenience Store-Convenience Good:* The consumer represented by this category prefers to buy the most readily available brand of product at the most accessible store.
2. *Convenience Store-Shopping Good:* The consumer selects his purchase from among the assortment carried by the most accessible store.
3. *Convenience Store-Specialty Good:* The consumer purchases his favored brand from the most accessible store which has the item in stock.
4. *Shopping Store-Convenience Good:* The consumer is indifferent to the brand of product he buys, but shops among different stores in order to secure better retail services and/or lower retail price.
5. *Shopping Store-Shopping Good:* The consumer makes comparisons among both retail-controlled factors and factors associated with the product (brand).
6. *Shopping Store-Specialty Good:* The consumer has a strong preference with respect to the brand of the product, but shops among a number of stores in order to secure the best retail service and/or price for this brand.
7. *Specialty Store-Convenience Good:* The consumer prefers to trade at a specific store, but is indifferent to the brand of product purchased.
8. *Specialty Store-Shopping Good:* The consumer prefers to trade at a specific store, but is uncertain as to which product he wishes to buy and examines the store's assortment for the best purchase.
9. *Specialty Store-Specialty Good:* The consumer has both a preference for a particular store and a specific brand.

SOURCE: Reprinted from Louis P. Bucklin, "Retail Strategy and the Classification of Consumer Goods," *Journal of Marketing*, Vol. 27, (January, 1963), pp. 53-54. Published by the American Marketing Association.

tomer groups and integrate these features to develop the specialty image he wishes to create.

As proposed by Bucklin, the classification of stores by convenience, shopping, and specialty types affords the retailer a means to consider alternative strategies. Bucklin further suggests that a finer classification system may be obtained by relating consumer product motives to consumer patronage motives. Table 8.1 presents a nine-cell matrix obtained by cross-classifying each product motive with each patronage motive, and represents nine possible types of consumer buying behavior.

Other methods of classifying retail stores. The general public commonly identifies stores by their generic names, such as department stores, supermarkets, discount stores, and mailorder retailers. Because of the substantial variation in size, type of organization, and other characteristics, however, this identification lacks the detail necessary for comparison, analysis, and evaluation needed by other retailers,

A. By Ownership of Establishment:
   1. Single-unit independent stores
   2. Multiunit retail organizations:
      a) chain stores
      b) branch stores
   3. Manufacturer-owned retail outlets
   4. Consumers' cooperative stores
   5. Farmer-owned establishments
   6. Company-owned stores (industrial stores) or commissaries
   7. Government operated stores (post exchanges, state liquor stores)
   8. Public utility company stores (for sale of major appliances)
B. By Kind of Business (Merchandise Handled)
   1. General merchandise group:
      a) department stores
      b) dry goods, general merchandise stores
      c) general stores
      d) variety stores
   2. Single-line stores (e.g., grocery, apparel, furniture)
   3. Specialty stores (e.g., meat markets, lingerie shops, floor coverings stores)
C. By Size of Establishment:
   1. By number of employees
   2. By annual sales volume

D. By Degree of Vertical Integration:
   1. Nonintegrated (retailing functions only)
   2. Integrated with wholesaling functions
   3. Integrated with manufacturing or other form-utility creation
E. By Type of Relationship with Other Business Organizations:
   1. Unaffiliated
   2. Voluntarily affiliated with other retailers:
      a) through wholesaler-sponsored voluntary chains
      b) through retailer cooperation
   3. Affiliated with manufacturers by dealer franchises
F. By method of Consumer Contact:
   1. Regular store:
      a) leased department
   2. Mail order:
      a) by catalog selling
      b) by advertising in regular media
      c) by membership club plans
   3. Household contacts:
      a) by house-to-house canvassing
      b) by regular delivery route service
      c) by party plan selling

G. By Type of Location:
   1. Urban:
      a) central business district
      b) secondary business district
      c) string street location
      d) neighborhood location
      e) controlled (planned) shopping center
      f) public market stalls
   2. Small city:
      a) downtown
      b) neighborhood
   3. Rural stores
   4. Roadside stands
H. By Type of Service Rendered:
   1. Full service
   2. Limited service (cash-and-carry)
   3. Self-service
I. By Legal Form of Organization:
   1. Proprietorship
   2. Partnership
   3. Corporation
   4. Special types
J. By Management Organization or Operational Technique:
   1. Undifferentiated
   2. Departmentized

SOURCE: Theodore N. Beckman, William R. Davidson, and W. Wayne Talarzyk, *Marketing* (9th ed.; New York: The Ronald Press Co., Copyright © 1973), p. 239.

TABLE 8.2.
OUTLINE OF SELECTED ALTERNATIVE BASES USED FOR CLASSIFYING RETAIL ESTABLISHMENTS

trade groups, and scholars who are interested in comparing the efficiency of similar type institutions.

The system of classification presented in Table 8.2 provides a number of alternative bases for classifying retail stores. While no single one of these classifications is totally adequate for analysis, it is possible to use several of these classes for purposes of comparative analysis. For example, in comparing the results of department store operations, it would be necessary to consider at least the annual sales volume, the type of ownership, and the type of location if useful comparisons are to be made.

WHOLESALERS   A simple definition of wholesalers might describe these institutions as marketing middlemen who are not retailers simply because they do not sell their goods or services to household consumers. This definition, however, does not adequately describe the role of this type of marketing institution. Any definition of wholesaling as a marketing activity must distinguish wholesale transactions from those of retailing, since all business transactions are either wholesale or retail. Most retail transactions are made at retail establishments, but it is the status or motive of the purchaser—personal or family consumption—that identifies a retail sale. Wholesale transactions include all business transactions where the motive is other than personal or family consumption.

Several bases have been used to define the wholesale transaction. Among these are the price of the goods sold, the quantity involved in the transaction, and the method of operation of the selling concern. Although each of these bases are useful, none of them completely describe wholesaling from either a theoretical or practical basis. More precisely, therefore, wholesaling may be identified as those "marketing transactions in which the purchaser is actuated by a profit or business motive in making the purchase, whether the goods are purchased for resale in the same form or for use in the business or industrial process."[6] Although theoretically sound, this definition does pose some practical problems in classifying certain kinds of transactions as either wholesale or retail. For example, a small retail establishment frequently purchases its cleaning supplies, such as soap and scouring powder, from a local supermarket at the regular retail price. A transaction of this nature is technically a wholesale transaction, but for practical purposes it is counted as a retail sale by the supermarket. For purposes of identifying wholesale and retail establishments, the U. S. Bureau of Census analyzes the nature of transactions. If a merchant sells more than half of his goods to ultimate consumers, he is classified as a retailer. Conversely, if he sells more than half of his goods to buyers for business or institutional use, he is classified as a wholesaler. Thus, the following types of sales generally fall within the province of wholesaling:

1. Sales by manufacturers or their sales branches to wholesalers and other types of wholesale middlemen.

2. Sales to retailers of all kinds.

3. Sales to restaurants and hotels.

4. Sales to manufacturers, mines, oil well companies, fisheries, railroads, public utilities, and government departments.

5. Sales to barbers in the form of supplies and equipment; all sales of equipment and supplies by all so-called supply houses, so long as such equipment and supplies are not purchased by ultimate consumers for their own personal use.

6. Sales of laboratory or office equipment and supplies to professional men such as doctors and dentists.

7. Sales of building materials to contractors, except when they act as agents of home owners.

8. All operations and activities of middlemen who in some way aid in the

transfer of title to goods when such goods are not sold to ultimate or individual consumers; in this group are included brokers, resident buyers, purchasing agents, selling agents, manufacturers agents, and the like.

9. All purchases of farm products for resale to other than individual consumers, irrespective of whether such purchases are made directly from farmers or from middlemen.[7]

The role of wholesalers.   As marketing middlemen, wholesalers are part of the macro marketing structure and are justified economically as members of a channel of distribution to the extent that they perform certain marketing functions, such as selling, storage, and transportation, more efficiently and economically than other channel members. Wholesalers may perform marketing functions for either suppliers or their own customers. The role of wholesalers in the marketing system can be seen best by looking at some of the functions they may perform for these groups. As a marketing specialist, they may perform the following functions for *suppliers*:

1. Establish contacts with a selected customer group. Depending on their product specialty, wholesalers develop market contacts with retailers and institutional groups, thereby providing a sales force and market for a producer's products.

2. Provide advice on marketing problems. The wholesalers' contacts and relationships with user markets enable them to advise suppliers on such items as product lines, prices, and promotional methods.

3. Store inventories for manufacturers. The storage function performed by wholesalers helps manufacturers to reduce their cost of physical distribution and capital requirements needed for the storage of larger inventories.

4. Reduce accounting and credit costs. A producer who uses wholesalers rather than selling direct to retailers or other small buyers has fewer large customers (the wholesaler) who normally pay promptly within the discount period.

The wholesaler may also perform the following functions for retailers, manufacturers, or institutional buyers in their capacity as wholesale *customers*:

1. Anticipate customers' demand and rate of use including items, quantity, and timing.

2. Assemble assortments to meet customers' needs from a wide range of suppliers, making it unnecessary for the customer to buy direct, normally at higher prices, from many manufacturers. Retailers with very broad product lines, such as drug stores and food retailers, benefit greatly from this service.

3. Provide inventories of customers' goods nearer the point of ultimate demand with prompt delivery service. This permits smaller inventories to be carried by the customer, which results in a higher turnover and less inventory investment.

4. Provide assistance on merchandising and operating problems for his customers based on wide market contacts and special marketing skills.

5. Provide financial assistance and credit that may not be available to his customers if they buy direct from producers.

Classification of wholesalers. The *Census of Business*, published by the U. S. Department of Commerce, classifies wholesale trade into five broad categories by type of operation. Figure 8.4 identifies these categories and the number of establishments in each category. As developed for the Bureau of Census, this five-way classification system does not distinguish wholesalers by ownership or type of operation. The following descriptions are presented as a more detailed review of these five important dimensions of the wholesale structure.

 1. *Merchant Wholesalers.* These are marketing intermediaries that purchase their inventories from manufacturers in large quantities, and take title to the goods they buy. They normally store and physically handle the goods before reselling them in smaller quantities to retailers, smaller wholesalers, and industrial and business users.

FIGURE 8.4.
WHOLESALE TRADE BY TYPE
OF OPERATIONS, 1963–1967

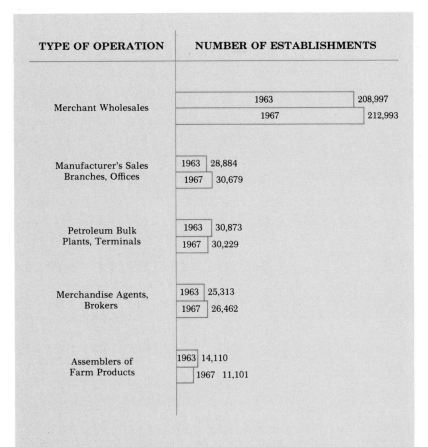

TYPE OF OPERATION	NUMBER OF ESTABLISHMENTS	
Merchant Wholesales	1963	208,997
	1967	212,993
Manufacturer's Sales Branches, Offices	1963	28,884
	1967	30,679
Petroleum Bulk Plants, Terminals	1963	30,873
	1967	30,229
Merchandise Agents, Brokers	1963	25,313
	1967	26,462
Assemblers of Farm Products	1963	14,110
	1967	11,101

SOURCE: Adapted from U.S., Department of Commerce, Bureau of the Census, *1967 Census of Business, Wholesale Trade,* p. 5.

2. *Manufacturer's Sales Branches*. These establishments are separate, but integrated businesses operated by large manufacturers for the sale of their products and services at wholesale. These branches are usually geographically separated from the manufacturing facility and may either maintain inventories closer to their customers or may be operated as sales offices without inventories. In some cases they may carry allied, but noncompeting products of other manufacturers.

3. *Petroleum Bulk Stations*. These are specialized merchant wholesalers that handle a wide range of liquid petroleum products in bulk. The importance of petroleum products to the economy and the specialized equipment required in petroleum distribution justify this separate classification. They may operate as part of the integrated structure of petroleum refining companies, or as independent wholesalers serving smaller chains of gasoline service stations.

4. *Agents and Brokers*. These wholesalers are called functional middlemen because they do not perform the complete range of functions carried out by merchant wholesalers. For the most part, they neither take title to nor possession of the goods in which they deal. Their role in marketing is to negotiate sales or purchases for the clients they represent, and they are compensated in the form of commissions based on the dollar value of sales or purchases.

5. *Assemblers*. These are marketing institutions that operate primarily in agricultural growing areas, or in port areas where fishing fleets bring in their catches. Assemblers purchase relatively small quantities from numerous producers and concentrate large quantities for economical shipments to major market centers. Some assemblers operate as adjuncts to large retail food chains; others serve large wholesale distributors in major metropolitan areas.

FACILITATING MARKETING AGENCIES

As mentioned earlier in this chapter, retailers and wholesalers require the specialized services of other institutions that assist them in defining and communicating with their markets, physically moving products, and storing goods in strategic locations until needed by the appropriate institution. Certain of the larger retailers and wholesalers may integrate some of these functions into their own structure, but the functions performed by the facilitating agencies are an integral part of the macro marketing system. This section provides a review of the facilitating agencies through a brief discussion of four types of agencies: transportation, warehousing, promotion, and marketing research.

TRANSPORTATION AGENCIES   The movement of products through space and time must be coordinated as an integral part of the total marketing process in order to

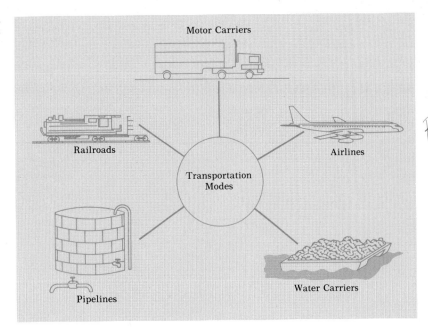

make goods available to buyers and users in places where they are demanded and at times when they are needed. The costs of these movements account for a portion of the price paid by the final buyer and may be a significant part of the final price. Consequently, the marketer's decision concerning the choice of a particular mode of transportation has a direct bearing on the price of the product to intermediate and final users.

While the total cost of moving products is important, factors other than cost must be considered; that is, weight, value, bulk, and perishability have a bearing on the method of transportation that is selected. In addition, depending on the location of the shipper and the buyer, an ideal carrier may not be available; it may be necessary to utilize a combination of transportation methods. As discussed in Chapter 6, the major modes of transportation in the United States are railroad, truck, water, pipeline, and air. These are shown in Figure 8.5. A brief discussion of the transportation agencies operating in each of these areas is presented below.

Railroads.   In spite of current financial problems, railroads are still the dominant carrier for moving large quantities of heavy or bulky merchandise. To the extent that the seller can ship in carload quantities, rail is usually the least costly method of inland transportation available. Railroads do handle less-than-carload shipments, but long delivery times cause shippers to use other means. In order to increase the productivity of large capital investments, railroads offer a number of special services to shippers such as pool cars, in-transit rates, unitized trains, "piggy-back" service, and containerization.

Water carriers. Inland waterways provide an important transportation network for raw materials such as petroleum, coal, grain, and chemicals. The total inland waterway system in the United States includes the following subsystems: the Great Lakes, the Mississippi River, the Gulf Coast rivers, the Atlantic Coast rivers, and the Pacific Coast rivers. While a slow mode, the low cost of water transportation provides substantial savings when time is not a relatively important factor.

Motor carriers. Utilizing the nation's highways, motor carriers provide an important service for less-than-carload shippers. Today, the majority of these shipments are carried by motor trucks, which are commonly classified into three types: common carriers, contract or "for-hire" carriers, and private carriers. Trucks are used for the transportation of nearly all kinds of goods, especially manufactured products such as food, textiles, rubber, and plastics. They also dominate in the movement of household goods.

Pipelines. Although pipelines are used primarily in the transportation of liquid petroleum products and natural gas, any product that can be put into a fluid state can be carried by pipelines. Among the solid products moved by pipelines are coal, minerals, sulphite pulp, and wood chips.[8]

Airlines. Still the smallest of the transportation agencies in terms of volume of goods carried, airlines represent an important carrier of certain types of goods. The high relative cost of this mode, however, has restricted its use to items of high unit value, such as drugs and electronic components, and to perishable products, such as cut flowers and fresh seafood.

Other transportation agencies. For infrequent shippers of small sized packages, there are a number of private and semi-government transportation agencies. The more important of these are Parcel Post, United Parcel Service, freight forwarders, and passenger bus lines. It should also be noted that many firms shipping substantial quantities of their own products find it economically feasible to buy or rent their own trucks, rather than utilize common or contract carriers. Perishability of goods and the quality of service required are common reasons for this choice.

WAREHOUSING AGENCIES

In addition to transportation agencies, specialized warehousing agencies operate in the macro marketing system to facilitate the storage function. Storage is the holding of inventories (raw materials, parts, semifinished goods, and finished goods) in proper condition until they are needed by the next institution in the channel of distribution. This section presents a brief discussion of the major warehousing agencies in recognition of the important role that they play in the institutional structure.

Private warehouses.   Wholesalers and retailers hold inventories in the day-to-day conduct of their business operations. Independent single-unit retail stores and merchant wholesalers normally hold their entire inventory in their place of business. Large retailers with branch stores, and large retail chains typically operate their own warehouses (a wholesaling operation) to hold inventories in order to service the units of their retail organization. In addition, many manufacturers, especially those who produce heavy or bulky products, such as appliances and carpets, operate their own warehouses in strategic market areas in order to serve their customers more economically and efficiently. Storage in all of these facilities is referred to as private warehousing.

Public warehouses.   These institutions are privately-owned storage facilities that profit by renting space and performing certain related services for others. Warehouses of this type usually specialize in a particular line of merchandise and provide facilities for handling that particular line of products, such as cold storage or freezer warehouses. A special type of public warehouse is the "bonded" warehouse. This agency is used to store products on which a federal tax must be paid before they can be sold. For example, alcoholic beverages and tobacco products are typically stored in bonded warehouses.

Transportation economies provide a principal reason for using public warehouses. Another benefit is that inventories are made conveniently available to customers in strategic market areas. A third benefit is flexibility. All major cities throughout the United States have public warehouses that can be used as economical substitutes for private warehouses. Further, their use can be expanded or contracted in line with market demand. Additionally, public warehouses may assist the owner of stored goods in a financial manner by issuing a warehouse receipt and providing a custodial service. The warehouse receipt may then be used as collateral by the owner to obtain a loan. When the goods are sold and the loan paid off, the ownership receipt is redeemed and the goods are released from the warehouse.

PROMOTION AGENCIES

As the third major category of facilitating agencies in the institutional structure of marketing, promotion agencies facilitate the flow of goods and services in the macro marketing system through their role in the marketing communication process. To provide a better understanding of how the system uses promotion agencies, this section focuses on the activities of promotion specialists in the fields of advertising and public relations. In addition this section will present a brief review of the promotion support provided by trade associations.

Advertising firms.   As a communication medium, advertising is concerned with the task of "communicating information pertaining to products, services, or ideas by other than direct personal contact and on an openly paid basis with intent to sell or otherwise obtain favorable consideration."[9] The accomplishment of this task in the macro marketing system is greatly facilitated through the activities performed by three major groups in the field of advertising. These are:[10]

1. Advertising agencies—specialized agencies that assist advertisers in carrying on the advertising function.

2. Advertising media—organizations providing facilities for the dissemination of advertising messages.

3. Facilitating organizations—suppliers of such items as art, photoengraving, TV production, or research services necessary in an advertising program.

An advertising agency is an organization of specialists in the communication-promotion field whose principal product is a service that entails the planning and execution of advertising programs for its clients. The services provided by an agency include the development of campaign strategy, the selection of media, the preparation of copy, layouts, or commercial scripts for broadcast media, and the production of printed or broadcast advertising. The advertising agency works closely with its client, usually through an account executive in the provision of its services.

Advertising media are the vehicles that provide the means by which the advertising message is carried to its designated publics. These include: (1) periodical media—newspapers and magazines; (2) position media—outdoor, transportation, and point-of-purchase advertising; (3) broadcast media—television and radio; and (4) advertising disseminated directly—direct mail, flyers, and remembrance advertising such as pens and matchbooks.[11]

The facilitating organizations in the field of advertising supply their specialized services direct to companies preparing their own advertising, to advertising agencies, and to the media. For the most part, the services of the facilitating organizations may be classified into three categories. They are: (1) services dealing with the production of advertising, (2) services dealing with sales of space or time, and (3) research services.[12]

Public relations firms.   Public relations is a broad concept that refers to the total impressions conveyed by a firm to a given segment(s) of the public. Advertising, publicity, public speeches by executives, and company publications all work in concert to create and develop favorable public relations for a company. This function gets little formal attention in the small organization. The very large firms, however, typically have their own public relations staffs. In addition, there are over 1,600 public relations counseling firms in the United States that range widely in size and scope of service. It is these firms that provide specialized talents in the field of promotion. As facilitating promotion agencies, they provide direct services for smaller firms and supplement the activities of the public relations staffs of larger firms. Events where public relations consultants may be needed to assist in promotion are the introduction of a new product or product line, opening of a new branch or division, and publicizing a firm's contribution to some segment of society.

Trade associations. These associations are voluntary organizations of firms in a specific industry or trade group. Examples of well known trade associations are The National Association of Manufacturers, The National Retail Merchants Association, The American Iron and Steel Institute, and The National Plywood Distributors Association. Such associations play an important role in gathering information for their members, other businessmen, government agencies, and the general public. Of special interest and value to marketers is the information they gather and disseminate on prices, cost, and volume. They also lobby for their members to appropriate government agencies and legislatures (state and federal), and they provide information on their industries to the public. Some associations develop codes of conduct and ethical behavior for their industry and encourage members to conduct their businesses according to prescribed standards.

MARKETING
RESEARCH
AGENCIES

Marketing research agencies represent the final category of facilitating institutions in the macro marketing system that are discussed here. Although marketing research is clearly recognized in larger organizations and is a viable internal staff function in many of these firms, the need for expertise in a wide number of problem areas in the field has created a demand for private research organizations. These firms generate research data for their clients and sell their specialized services for a fee.

There are hundreds of research agencies in operation through the United States; some offer a fairly broad range of services, whereas others are highly specialized. A. C. Nielsen Company, the largest and probably the best-known marketing research firm, provides a variety of continuous services such as their *Retail Index* and *Television Index*. Marketing Research Corporation of America is another large independent firm; it maintains a consumer panel of over 7,500 families. Data on consumer sales by brands and types of stores based on demographic characteristics are sold to clients.

In addition to these private research agencies, a number of federal, state, and local government agencies provide valuable data for marketers that can be obtained at little or no cost. Most state universities, for instance, operate specialized bureaus and research units that conduct studies in a variety of disciplines, and many are available for contract research on a fee basis.

CHANNEL CONCEPTS

Up to this point, this chapter has examined the various institutions that, together with the manufacturers, comprise the macro marketing system. Since these institutions are independent entities, however, the consummation of the marketing task cannot be finalized unless coordination and cooperation among these separate entities takes place in an efficient and economical manner. Together, all the interactions among these separate institutions form channels of distribution. A general model of a set of marketing channels is presented in Figure 8.6.

In describing the relationships that exist in a channel of distribution, one author has suggested: "A manufacturer, together with his distributors and dealers, may be said to constitute a loose coalition engaged in exploiting joint opportunity in the market."[13] When channels are organized in this manner, they form fragmented networks of loosely aligned manufacturers, wholesalers, and retailers that tend to behave somewhat autonomously. Representing the historical pattern of distribution in the United States, these arrangements are often referred to as individualistic channel systems.

Given a loose alignment in channels, competitive conflict within channels of distribution is a natural fact of economic life. Conflict between middlemen of the same type, between different types of middlemen, and between manufacturers and middlemen has occurred throughout the history of distribution in the United States. Furthermore, institutional change and shifts in the nature of market demand have perpetuated the problem. These changes have produced severe

not static

FIGURE 8.6.
MARKETING CHANNELS

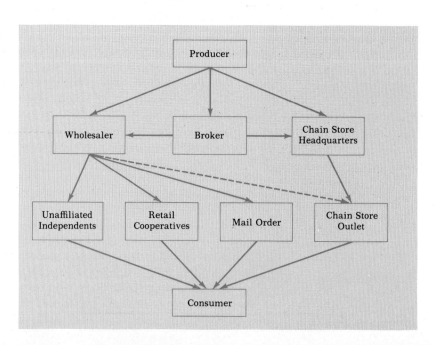

conflict in the vertical dimensions of the channel; competitive struggles exist between retailers and wholesalers, between manufacturers and retailers, and between manufacturers and wholesalers.

In recent years, efforts to improve the efficiencies of loosely aligned channel systems have resulted in the development of vertical channel systems. This concept emphasizes the idea that a channel is a total system of distribution and not a fragmented assortment of independent institutions operating in an uncoordinated manner. As noted in Chapter 6, the integration of channel members is designed to reduce conflicts and establish a common set of goals. A review of that presentation reveals that vertical channel systems may be created through ownership, administration, and contracts.

Regardless of the form of alignment that exists in the channel, it should be noted that a given channel of distribution is not a permanent arrangement. Although channels may represent continuous and ongoing relationships, the dynamics of the market may call for changes as market conditions change. Furthermore, the institutional structure is not static, and alterations in its composition frequently necessitate the establishment of new relationships in the channel. Consequently, a continual monitoring of the institutional environment is mandatory in today's changing world.

INSTITUTIONAL CHANGE

The discussion throughout this chapter may imply that the various institutions and their relationships form a relatively static arrangement in the macro marketing system, but nothing could be further from the truth. The underlying thesis of this chapter is the necessity for adaptation by middlemen to changing conditions. The brief history of retailing earlier in the chapter revealed how retailing and retail institutions have adapted to changes in the macro environment. The dominant general merchandise wholesaler of the first quarter of this century basically disappeared with the changing economic environment of the 1930s. The preceding section indicated how firms have adjusted to change by developing new types of institutional arrangements to serve their markets more efficiently and economically through vertical channel systems.

Change, of course, provides a major challenge to individuals and institutions in the macro marketing system to perceive new opportunities in the environment and to develop new institutions and institutional arrangements that can serve buyers more efficiently and economically. Fortunately, the system has responded in a positive manner. The wide adoption of the private automobile and improved transportation networks prompted the development of planned shopping centers and the shift of retailing from the central business district to neighborhoods and the suburbs. Increases in personal income brought about better products and merchandise assortments. More leisure produced whole new industries in spectator and participative sports. Other examples of adjustment by marketing to changes in the market, institutional, social, legal, economic, competitive, and technological environments are almost endless. Detailed discussions of these areas are reserved for the following chapters in this section.

As a final note, it may be observed that change is occurring in all of the macro environments of marketing. This is especially true in the institutional environment, where current social problems such as consumerism, shortages, and inflation are forcing structural realignments and the need to develop new marketing institutions. Thus, while marketing functions necessary to close the gap between production and consumption remain basic, the institutions that perform them must change and adjust in a dynamic environment.

SUMMARY

This chapter has considered the business firms that comprise the institutional environment of marketing. Two classes of institutions were identified. These are marketing middlemen and facilitating marketing agencies.

Retailers and wholesalers are classified as marketing middlemen because they handle the goods produced by manufacturers and make them available to business and institutional buyers and to ultimate consumers. Retailing was defined and a brief history of retailing was provided. Different methods of classifying retail stores were suggested based on margin, turnover, and the way buyers perceive stores. Wholesaling was defined, and the role of wholesalers in the economy was discussed. This was followed by a classification of wholesaling institutions and a discussion of the various types of wholesalers.

In recognition of the fact that retailers and wholesalers use the services of specialized institutions, this chapter also presented a brief discussion of facilitating marketing agencies. These include transportation agencies, warehousing agencies, promotion agencies, and marketing research agencies.

Channel concepts were discussed, followed by a brief analysis of the institutional arrangements that form channels of distribution. This discussion identified both individualistic and vertical systems.

The final section examined institutional change and the adaptation of institutions and institutional arrangements to meet changing environmental conditions in recognition of the fact that change is continuously occurring in the field of marketing.

QUESTIONS FOR DISCUSSION

1. Define retailing and wholesaling and fully discuss their roles in the macro marketing system.

2. What are facilitating marketing agencies and how do their activities relate to the functions of marketing performed by manufacturers, wholesalers, and retailers?

3. What is the role of marketing institutions in providing goods and services to ultimate consumers?

4. Discuss the changing role of retailing in the two hundred-year history of the United States.

5. How are retail stores classified and what is the value of classifying stores as discussed in this chapter?

6. Define wholesaling and list a number of the types of transactions that fall within the province of wholesaling.

7. What are some of the functions that a wholesaler performs for his supplier, for his customers?

8. Identify and briefly define the five types of wholesalers as listed in the *Census of Business.*

9. Identify and discuss the four types of facilitating marketing agencies considered in this chapter. What role do they play in the macro marketing system?

10. What are channels of distribution? What is the basic difference between an individualistic system and a vertical system?

11. Discuss the meaning and importance of institutional change to society and the economy.

MARKETING MIDDLEMEN:
1. Wholesalers
2. Retailers

FACILITATING AGENCIES
1. TRANSPORTATION
2. PROMOTION
3. WAREHOUSING
4. MARKET RESEARCH
5. FINANCIAL INSTITUTIONS

NOTES

[1] Melvin T. Copeland, "Relation of Consumers' Buying Habits to Marketing Methods," *Harvard Business Review,* Vol. 1 (April, 1923), pp. 282–289.

[2] Louis P. Bucklin, "Retail Strategy and the Classification of Consumer Goods," *Journal of Marketing* (January, 1963), pp. 50–55.

[3] *Ibid.,* p. 53.

[4] *Ibid.*

[5] *Ibid.*

[6] Theodore N. Beckman, William R. Davidson, and W. Wayne Talarzyk, *Marketing* (9th ed.; New York: The Ronald Press, Co., Copyright © 1973), p. 288.

[7] *Ibid.,* pp. 288–289.

[8] D. L. Shrock and M. T. Farris, "Transportation Innovations in Arizona," *Arizona Business* (August-September, 1974), pp. 11–15.

[9] R. V. Zacher, *Advertising Techniques and Management* (rev. ed.; Homewood, Illinois: Richard D. Irwin, Inc., 1967), p. 4.

[10] *Ibid.,* p. 28.

[11] *Ibid.,* pp. 50–52.

[12] *Ibid.,* p. 52.

[13] Wroe Alderson, "Factors Governing the Development of Marketing Channels," in R. M. Clewett, ed., *Marketing Channels* (Homewood, Illinois: Richard D. Irwin, Inc., 1954), p. 30.

SUGGESTED READINGS

Bessom, R. M., "New Challenges for Marketing," *Arizona Business* (November, 1975), pp. 11–17.

Cooper, P. D., "Will Success Produce Problems for the Convenience Store?," *MSU Business Topics* (Winter, 1972), pp. 39–43.

Dickinson, R. A., *Retail Management: A Channels Approach* (Belmont, California: Wadsworth Publishing Co., Inc., 1974).

Dommermuth, William P. and R. Clifton Andersen, "Distribution Systems: Firms, Functions, and Efficiencies," *MSU Business Topics* (Spring, 1969), pp. 51–56.

Donnelly, J. H., Jr., "Marketing Intermediaries in Channels of Distribution," *Journal of Marketing* (January, 1976), pp. 55–57.

Harrell, G. D. and M. D. Hutt, "Crowding in Retail Stores," *MSU Business Topics* (Winter, 1976), pp. 33–39.

James, Don L., Bruce J. Walker, and Michael J. Etzel, *Retailing Today: An Introduction* (New York: Harcourt Brace Jovanovich, Inc., 1975).

McCarthy, E. Jerome, *Basic Marketing: A Managerial Approach* (5th ed.; Homewood, Illinois: Richard D. Irwin, Inc., 1975).

Weigand, R. E. and H. C. Wasson, "Arbitration in the Marketing Channel," *Business Horizons* (October, 1974), pp. 39–47.

THE DOMESTIC
MARKET ENVIRONMENT

THE DOMESTIC MARKET ENVIRONMENT

Following the macro presentation of the American marketing system and its institutional structure, this chapter examines the United States' domestic market. This broad market comprises all individuals and organizations residing in the fifty states with the desire and means to exchange their dollars for something of value. How large is the domestic market? The most widely used measure of size is Gross National Product, which consists of the total of goods and services produced by a nation, calculated at market prices. The GNP in the United States is currently in excess of $1 trillion; stated another way, the nation has a $1 trillion market.

DOMESTIC MARKET CONCEPTS

Individual firms are not concerned with the total dollar value of the market, except in the sense that its magnitude and movement tells them something about the state of the total economy and society. Most firms would subscribe to the truism that no one can satisfy everybody all of the time. What, then, is a market? The answer to this question is not simple and clear-cut; the meaning depends on who defines it. An economist would define the market as a price-making mechanism, the businessman would view a market as a geographic area, and the marketing manager might see the market as the potential demand for a firm's product. To develop an acceptable, broad definition of a market, its basic elements must be identified. They are commonly stated as people, money, and a willingness to buy; in this book, using these elements, a market is defined as people or organizations with needs and with both the ability and willingness to buy.

MARKET DIMENSIONS   In order to make a definition of the domestic market more meaningful, this section will elaborate on some of its dimensions. That people have needs is clearly understood, but organizations also have needs that must be filled in order to carry out objectives that are associated with serving people or other organizations. A need may be defined as a lack of something requisite, desirable, or useful. The ability to buy requires purchasing power, which means personal income for people and capital for organizations. Willingness to buy refers to buying behavior, or the underlying motives and the buying methods of people and organizations. Since needs also apply to business firms, the concept of a need extends beyond the basic physiological needs of people for food, clothing, and shelter. People also have psychological and social needs as they pursue a chosen lifestyle; specifically, they need education, work satisfaction, recreation, social intercourse, and transportation, to name a few. The satisfaction of these needs requires the

Consumer & Organization Markets

availability of goods and services, and, hence, leads to the creation of markets.

In the balance of this chapter, the domestic market will be examined in two broad dimensions, namely consumer markets, and nonhousehold, or organization markets. The latter will be further examined according to reseller, industrial, institutional, and government organizations. The final sections of the chapter will present some environmental considerations about the markets, will look briefly at the buying process, and finally consider some implications for marketing that flow from these considerations. At this point, however, it is necessary to reconsider the concept of market segmentation that was presented in earlier chapters.

MARKET SEGMENTATION

Product & Service Markets are Heterogeneous

The basic concept of market segmentation recognizes that product and service markets are heterogeneous rather than homogeneous. The early economic growth of this nation was based on a manufacturing production oriented philosophy. During this period, management typically developed one product and one marketing program to reach as many customers as possible. This approach to markets, sometimes called *market aggregation,* enabled a company to pursue economies of scale in production, promotion, and physical distribution. This philosophy was effective as long as competition was minimal in many product categories. Longer production runs at lower unit costs, and minimized inventory costs, made this method of production and marketing very profitable.

As population and personal income increased, and new technologies in production and marketing developed, former views of substantial homogeneous markets became blurred. Along with these changes in the environment came increased competition and the concomitant efforts of firms to deal with this problem. One early response to the new competition was to reduce prices, but in the long run this meant lower profits as others met the new lower prices. An alternative approach involved an attempt to differentiate a firm's product from those of its competitors. Frequently these changes were more cosmetic than real or functional and involved such features as a new package, color, size, or flavor. In both of these responses, it should be noted that the firm follows a production oriented philosophy of serving a single homogeneous market.

Modern marketers now generally recognize the fact that whenever a market for a product or service consists of two or more buyers it is capable of being segmented, which means that it can be divided into meaningful buyer groups. This strategy is known as *market segmentation* and basically views broad product and service markets as heterogeneous rather than homogeneous. Market segmentation, therefore, is a process of taking a large heterogeneous market for a product and dividing it into a number of submarkets or segments, each of which tends to be homogeneous in a number of important characteristics. With this approach to markets, the firm develops a demand schedule,

FIGURE 9.1.
MODERN AUTOMOBILE
MARKET SEGMENTATION

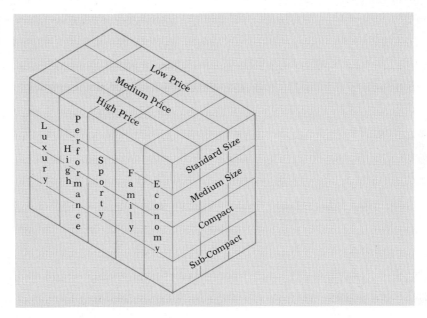

or market forecast, for each segment rather than a single forecast for one homogeneous market. Henry Ford's "Model T" is an example of the former, whereas the full line of cars offered by the Ford Motor Company today is an example of market segmentation. The implications of this can be seen from an analysis of automobile market segmentation, as shown in Figure 9.1.

Market segmentation is a consumer oriented philosophy and is consistent with a major premise of the marketing philosophy of management, which says that firms should be customer oriented rather than product oriented. Although some writers suggest that this concept is little more than a play on words, there is evidence that successful products must satisfy customer's needs and expectations. The managerial approach to developing and implementing segmentation strategies was discussed in Chapter 4.

The next two sections of this chapter examine the domestic market in two broad categories—the consumer markets and the nonhousehold markets. As these are considered, the reader is asked to think of the various ways in which the broader segments may be even further segmented.

HOUSEHOLD CONSUMER MARKETS

This section examines the consumer markets in the United States and includes all markets other than business, institutional, and government markets. Stated another way, it is an examination of retail markets, or those markets in which ultimate consumers purchase the goods and services required for the maintenance of their standard of living. There are numerous environmental factors that influence the size and shape of these markets. Among the factors that will be considered here are population, education, employment, income, leisure, and lifestyle. As marketers identify the particular segments they choose to serve, they must consider the above-mentioned environmental factors in order to develop a marketing program that will communicate the availability and suitability of the products they desire to produce and sell.

POPULATION

As stated earlier, one element of a market is people. It follows, therefore, that in any consideration of consumer markets, marketers must know the number of people that comprise the segment of the market they intend to serve, as well as certain relevant characteristics of the markets. As the domestic population has increased over the years, so have the markets increased in both size and complexity. The nation's population has increased continually since its founding and today exceeds two hundred million. Figure 9.2 shows the size of the United States population for selected years, and indicates that the population increased over four times from 1800 to 1850, three times from 1850 to 1900, and twice from 1900 to 1950.

Even though the rate of growth is declining, it seems certain that the United States population will continue to grow well into the next century. The most pessimistic population projection for the year 2000 is over 250 million.[1] Changes in the social and economic environments impact on the birth rate, and it is expected that these could reverse the future population projections. Currently, much is being written about "zero population growth," although demographers predict that this will not occur for at least fifty years. New attitudes toward marriage, family size, and family planning could, of course, change present projections. Significant changes in the population size present numerous implications for marketing. Consider, for example, the effect of a stable or declining population on the demand for housing and home furnishings and appliances.

The distribution of the population, in addition to size, is also of great concern to marketers. The U.S. population is not only distributed unevenly, it is also constantly changing. The theoretical "center of population" has moved from south central Ohio in 1860 to south central Illinois in 1960 and has continued to move westward. As a result of population shifts, the size and shape of regional markets is constantly changing. Therefore, marketers must regularly monitor and change their product lines and marketing programs in order to continue to serve their markets profitably. Table 9.1 shows, on a percentage basis, the population changes by region.

Regional shifts in the United States population are of concern to marketers because of different "lifestyles" in various geographic areas, and, hence, differences in the type of products demanded. Of

FIGURE 9.2.
UNITED STATES POPULATION

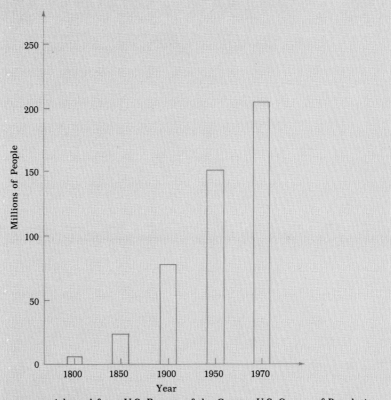

SOURCE: Adapted from U.S. Bureau of the Census, U.S. Census of Population: 1970, Number of Inhabitants, Final Report PC(1)–A1 (December, 1972), pp. 1–46 and 1–47.

TABLE 9.1.
POPULATION CHANGE BY
REGIONS, 1960–1970 AND
1970–1973

Region	Percentage Change 1960-1970	Percentage Change 1970-1973
Total United States	13.3	3.3
New England States (ME, NH, VT, MA, RI, CT)	12.7	2.6
Middle Atlantic (NY, NJ, PA)	8.9	.9
East North Central (OH, IN, IL, MI, WI)	11.1	1.6
West North Central (MN, IA, MO, ND, SD, NB, KS)	6.0	2.3
South Atlantic (DE, MD, DC, VA, WV, NC, SC, GA, FL)	18.1	5.8
East South Central (KY, TN, AL, MS)	6.3	3.8
West South Central (AR, LA, OK, TX)	14.0	4.8
Mountain (MT, ID, WY, CO, NM, AZ, UT, NV)	20.8	10.5
Pacific (WA, OR, CA, AK, HI)	25.1	3.4

SOURCE: *Statistical Abstract of the United States*, 1974, p. 13.

concern also is the movement from rural to urban areas. In 1920, about half the population lived in rural areas. Only fifty years later, the proportion had declined to about 5 percent. Within urban areas, there has been a sizeable shift from the central city to the suburbs since the end of World War II. All of these movements affect the nature of firm and industry markets. Any long-run projection of these population shifts is pure speculation, however, as many families, disenchanted with suburban problems, are returning to the central cities and numerous young families are moving to rural areas.

As a result of urban growth and the continuing movements to and from urban and suburban areas, population data based on traditional geographic boundaries of cities and counties lacked the preciseness required for meaningful market analysis. To remedy this problem, the U.S. Bureau of the Census developed a separate population classification called the Standard Metropolitan Statistical Area (SMSA) and now collects data based on characteristics of people in these areas.

An SMSA is an integrated economic and social unit with a total population of at least one hundred thousand people including a central city or "twin cities" with a minimum population of fifty thousand each. In 1974, the Bureau of the Census had identified 264 SMSA's that accounted for over two-thirds of the nation's population. Since virtually all employment in these areas is nonagricultural, marketers can use SMSA data to identify fairly homogeneous market segments. For detailed market analysis, marketers are also concerned with population breakdowns by age, sex, and race, and the Census of Population provides these data, which are valuable in formulating marketing programs.

EDUCATION   The educational level of the population has numerous implications for marketers, both directly and indirectly. A significant relationship exists between education and income. The mean lifetime income of persons from ages eighteen to sixty-five varies from $305,000 for persons completing eight years of elementary education to $421,000 for those completing four years of high school, and $655,000 for those completing four years of college.[2] An increase in income of an increasing number of people quite naturally increases the dollar size of markets. Table 9.2 shows the increase in the level of education of the population for selected years.

Reinforced by the fact that more education means a higher level of personal income, the increase in the number of more educated people has other implications for marketing. A greater variety of products and higher quality products are demanded as people tend to develop life styles they deem appropriate for their educational level. The shift in demand from goods to services seems to be related, in part, to a more educated society. The level of education also fosters new technologies that are applied to products and marketing methods, and increases the willingness of people to try what is new. Overall, it can be seen that

TABLE 9.2.
HIGH SCHOOL AND COLLEGE
GRADUATES (SELECTED
YEARS)

Year of Graduation	High School Percent of Persons 17 Years Old	College Percent of High School Graduates
1900	6.4	28.4
1940	50.8	15.3
1960	65.1	21.0
1965	74.0	19.9
1970	75.7	28.6
1972	75.1	30.5

NOTE: Beginning in 1962, data are based on persons 18 years of age.
SOURCE: *Statistical Abstract of the United States*, 1974, p. 132.

the level of education has a positive impact on product preference, promotional methods, and the type, size, and strategy of retail institutions that serve the more highly educated market segments.

EMPLOYMENT

Employment is an important aspect of the consumer market that must be understood by firms in relation to the products they produce and the marketing programs they employ. Information needed by marketers concerning employment includes (1) the level of employment and unemployment, (2) the occupations in which people are employed, (3) the age distribution of the work force, (4) the sex and marital status of the work force, (5) the ethnic and nationality composition of the work force, and (6) the major industries in which the work force is employed. These factors singly and collectively aid marketers in determining the types and quantities of goods and services that will be demanded, since income and expenditure patterns are influenced by the factors listed above.

Before considering some of the marketing implications of the above aspects of employment, it would be helpful to review Table 9.3, which summarizes employment data by occupational classes for selected years from 1957 to 1973.

Levels of employment and unemployment, both nationally and regionally, are important to marketers because employment, together with income (including transfer payments and retirement income) determine the level of personal income, which is the basis of personal consumption expenditures. For precise estimates of the size of markets, consideration must also include the differences between disposable income and discretionary income. This detail, however, is beyond the scope of this book.

The occupations in which the work force are employed are also of major concern to marketers. The clothes people wear, the amount and type of food people eat, and the types of recreation they enjoy are

Occupation	White					Negro and Other				
	1957[a]	1960	1970	1972	1973	1957[a]	1960	1970	1972	1973
Total employed (000's)	57,513	58,850	70,182	73,074	75,278	6,647	6,927	8,445	8,628	9,131
Percent	100.0	100.0	100.0	100.0	100.0	100.0	100.0	100.0	100.0	100.0
White-collar workers	44.2	46.6	50.8	50.0	49.9	12.8	16.1	27.9	29.8	31.1
Professional, technical, and kindred	10.8	12.1	14.8	14.6	14.4	3.7	4.8	9.1	9.5	9.9
Medical and other health	1.9	2.1	2.3	2.4	2.3	0.6	0.8	1.6	1.8	2.0
Teachers, except college	2.2	2.6	3.2	3.5	3.5	1.3	1.7	2.9	3.0	3.0
Managers, administrators, except farm	11.4	11.7	11.4	10.6	11.0	2.1	2.6	3.5	3.7	4.1
Salaried workers	5.2	5.9	8.4	8.3	8.7	0.5	0.9	2.1	2.6	2.9
Self-employed	6.2	5.8	3.0	2.2	2.3	1.6	1.7	1.4	1.1	1.2
Salesworkers	6.7	7.0	6.7	7.1	6.9	1.0	1.5	2.1	2.2	2.3
Retail trade	4.0	4.1	4.0	4.1	3.9	0.8	1.0	1.6	1.7	1.7
Clerical workers	15.2	15.7	18.0	17.8	17.5	6.0	7.3	13.2	14.4	14.9
Stenographers, typists, and secretaries	3.6	3.9	4.7	5.2	5.2	1.2	1.4	2.3	3.3	3.6
Blue-collar workers	38.2	36.2	34.5	34.4	34.7	41.8	40.1	42.2	39.9	40.8
Craftsmen and kindred workers	14.4	13.8	13.5	13.8	13.9	5.7	6.0	8.2	8.7	8.9
Carpenters	1.5	1.4	1.1	1.3	1.4	0.5	0.4	0.7	0.7	0.7
Constr. craftworkers, exc. carpenters	2.7	2.7	2.5	2.8	2.9	1.4	1.6	1.8	2.3	2.2
Mechanics and repairers	3.3	3.2	3.7	3.5	3.6	1.8	1.7	2.6	2.1	2.2
Metalcraft workers, except mechanics	2.0	1.8	1.6	1.4	1.4	0.5	0.6	0.8	0.7	0.8
Blue-collar supervisors, n.e.c.	2.0	1.9	2.0	1.8	1.8	0.3	0.4	0.9	1.0	1.1
Operatives	19.3	17.9	17.0	16.0	16.3	21.2	20.4	23.7	21.3	22.2
Operatives, except transport	(NA)	(NA)	(NA)	12.3	12.5	(NA)	(NA)	(NA)	15.8	16.9
Transport equipment operatives	(NA)	(NA)	(NA)	3.7	3.7	(NA)	(NA)	(NA)	5.5	5.3
Drivers, motor vehicles	3.5	3.5	3.1	3.2	3.2	4.7	4.4	4.1	4.4	4.2
Nonfarm laborers	4.5	4.4	4.1	4.6	4.6	14.9	13.7	10.3	9.9	9.7
Service industries	9.1	9.9	10.7	11.8	11.7	32.0	31.7	26.0	27.2	25.3
Private household workers	1.5	1.7	1.3	1.2	1.1	14.9	14.2	7.7	6.8	5.7
Service workers, exc. priv. household	7.5	8.2	9.4	10.6	10.6	17.1	17.5	18.3	20.5	19.6
Protective service workers	1.2	1.2	1.3	1.4	1.4	0.5	0.5	0.9	1.4	1.4
Farmworkers	8.6	7.4	4.0	3.8	3.7	13.5	12.1	3.9	3.0	2.8
Farmers and farm managers	5.3	4.3	2.4	2.2	2.1	4.2	3.2	1.0	0.6	0.7
Farm laborers and supervisors	3.3	3.0	1.6	1.6	1.6	9.3	9.0	2.9	2.4	2.1
Paid workers	1.6	1.7	1.0	1.0	1.0	6.6	6.6	2.6	2.3	2.0
Unpaid family workers	1.6	1.3	0.7	0.6	0.5	2.7	2.4	0.3	0.1	0.1

NA   Not available.

[a] Based on figures for Jan., Apr., July, and Oct.

(Percent distribution, 1957 excludes Alaska and Hawaii. Covers persons 16 years old and over. Annual figures are monthly averages, except as noted. 1972–1973 not comparable with prior years due to reclassification of census occupations. "N.e.c." means not elsewhere classified.)

SOURCE: *Statistical Abstract of the United States*, 1974, p. 351.

TABLE 9.3.
EMPLOYED PERSONS, BY
OCCUPATION AND RACE: 1957
TO 1973

strongly influenced by the type of work that individuals do. A review of Table 9.3 will show the changes that have taken place in the occupational mix in the period from 1957 to 1973. For example, 8.6 percent of the white population were farm workers in 1957. By 1973, only 3.8 percent of the population was employed in this category.

INCOME AND INCOME DISTRIBUTION

People alone do not make a market. Most definitions of a market include money and a willingness to spend in addition to the number of people. The amount of money in a market is derived from the value of a nation's output of goods and services. This aggregate amount is known as the Gross National Product (GNP) and is defined as the dollar value of all the products and services exchanged in one year's time. To the economist, GNP indicates a nation's economic standing and capability. As noted earlier, GNP in the United States presently exceeds $1 trillion.

GNP #1 Trillion

A detailed study of income, its distribution, and how it is spent, is a necessary input for the marketer in estimating the quantitative dimensions of the market opportunity the firm intends to serve. A single definition of income lacks precision, however, as there are several concepts of income, each of which may have a special meaning to the marketer. The following definitions of income are based on those used in the national income and product accounts of the Department of Commerce. The largest income figure is *National Income,* which is GNP minus depreciation and other capital consumption, indirect business taxes, and the nontax liabilities of government. National income minus corporate profits and social security contributions, plus dividends, government transfer payments to individuals, and net interest paid by government equals *Personal Income,* which includes money and imputed income received by individuals, unincorporated business, and nonprofit institutions. Imputed income is the estimated value of goods or services used without a direct payment, for example, the rental value assigned to owner-occupied houses. *Disposable Personal Income* is personal income minus taxes to all levels of government. This is the amount available for personal consumption expenditures and savings. *Discretionary Income* is the balance of disposable income remaining after spending units have provided for the basic necessities of their standard of living, normally food, clothing, shelter, and medical care. This income figure is of special interest to marketers because it is the amount of money available for so-called luxuries, recreation, and entertainment.[3]

Disposable & Discretionary Income

In estimating market potential, individual firms will be interested in specific classes of income data. Two examples of income data are shown in Figure 9.3 and Table 9.4. Marketers must make careful analyses of variations and trends in the distribution of income among regions and population groups in order to obtain the best possible estimate of potential sales. Additionally, marketers may require income data by cities or sections within metropolitan areas to indicate

FIGURE 9.3.
UNITED STATES PERSONAL
INCOME

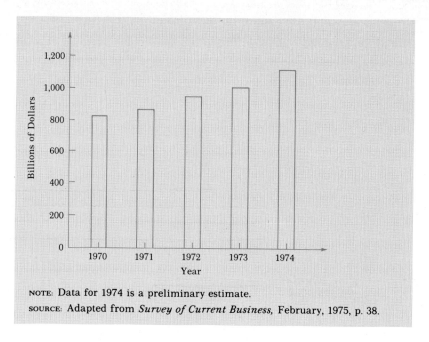

NOTE: Data for 1974 is a preliminary estimate.

SOURCE: Adapted from *Survey of Current Business*, February, 1975, p. 38.

potential profitable locations for shopping centers and outlying branches of downtown stores.

The various classes of income data made available by the U.S. government and private groups has significant marketing implications. A smaller percentage of families in the poverty bracket together with the increase in upper-income groups results in increasing levels of discretionary purchasing power. This change alters substantially the demand patterns of various market segments. Today, the middle-income market is a large and growing market. This has brought about many changes in marketing strategy for both manufacturers and retailers as they adjust their market offerings to the greater numbers in the higher income groups.

In adjusting to these environmental changes, many stores have "traded-up" in the quality of their merchandise and service mix, a strategy change that was generally successful in the early 1970s. Some firms, however, have encountered problems in their volume and market shares due to the changing economic environment (inflation and unemployment) that began in 1973. The dynamics of the marketplace have revived an old cliché that firms "cannot be all things to all people." This is causing business firms to segment their markets more carefully and design product and marketing strategies tailored to smaller, but more profitable segments.

EXPENDITURE PATTERNS

What are the underlying reasons that explain an increase in spending by consumers? The initial response to this question is an obvious one

Characteristics	Current Dollars				1967 Dollars			
	1970	1971	1972	1973	1970	1971	1972	1973
All workers	$130	$138	$144	$159	$112	$114	$115	$119
Male	151	162	168	188	131	134	135	141
16-24 years old	112	114	119	136	97	94	95	102
25 years and over	160	172	178	203	138	142	143	153
Female	94	100	106	117	81	83	85	88
16-24 years old	88	91	96	103	76	75	77	77
25 years and over	96	103	110	121	83	85	88	91
White	134	142	149	163	116	118	119	122
Male	157	168	172	194	136	139	138	146
Female	95	102	108	118	82	84	87	89
Negro and other races	99	107	115	129	86	89	92	97
Male	113	123	129	149	98	102	103	112
Female	81	87	99	108	70	72	79	81
Occupation:								
Professional and technical workers	181	189	192	213	156	156	154	160
Managers, administrators, exc. farm	190	[a]200+	214	238	164	[a]165+	172	179
Saleworkers	133	141	151	163	115	117	121	122
Clerical workers	109	115	121	131	94	95	97	98
Craftsmen and kindred workers	157	167	172	195	136	138	138	147
Operatives	115	120	126	140	99	99	101	105
Operatives, except transport	(NA)	(NA)	119	132	(NA)	(NA)	95	99
Transport equip. operatives	(NA)	(NA)	152	169	(NA)	(NA)	122	127
Nonfarm laborers	110	117	123	138	95	97	99	104
Private household workers	38	38	40	40	33	31	32	30
Other service workers	87	96	104	111	75	79	83	83
Farmworkers	71	74	80	97	61	61	64	73

NA   Not Available.
[a] Exact medians could not be computed.
U.S. Bureau of Labor Statistics, *Special Labor Force Report*, No. 143, *Usual Weekly Earnings of American Workers, 1971*, and unpublished data.
SOURCE: *Statistical Abstract of the United States*. 1974. p. 351.

TABLE 9.4.
WEEKLY EARNINGS OF
FULL-TIME WAGE AND SALARY
WORKERS IN CURRENT AND
1967 DOLLARS: 1970 TO 1973

—income has increased. In general, of course, this is true. As consumer's income increases, so do their expenditures. Naturally, increased income brings about increased personal expenditures, but income explains only the total amount the consumer spends. Marketers must be concerned with not only the total amount that is spent, but also the types of goods the consumer buys.

Before examining some of the factors that impinge upon consumer expenditure patterns, it will be helpful to look at the aggregate figures for total consumer expenditures and a breakdown by major classes of purchases. Figure 9.4 shows this data for selected years from 1960.

An examination of this data shows some interesting changes in these aggregate figures. Although personal consumption expenditures (PCE) increased less than two and a half times, durable goods expenditures increased almost three times, nondurable goods expenditures only slightly over two times, and expenditures for service increased

FIGURE 9.4.
PERSONAL CONSUMPTION
EXPENDITURES

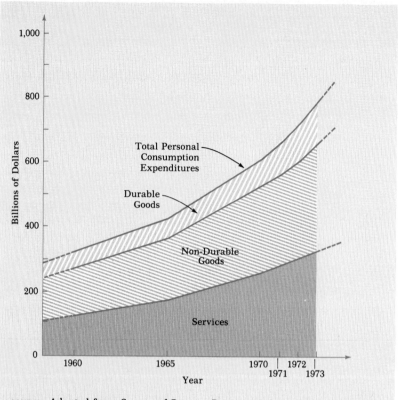

SOURCE: Adapted from *Survey of Current Business,* July issues and February, 1975.

almost three times. This data is useful to marketers in planning their product mix and strategy. It also suggests that some generalizations related to consumer expenditure patterns are helpful in explaining what happens when household income increases.

Ernst Engel, a German statistician, published the first study of consumer spending patterns in 1857. Later, students of consumer spending expanded on Engel's work to provide a concept that is now generally known as Engel's laws of consumption. These laws, or generalizations, show that as family income increases:

ENGELS LAWS

1. A smaller percentage of income is spent on food.

2. The percentage spent on clothing remains approximately the same.

3. The percentage spent on housing, fuel, and light does not change.

4. A larger percentage of total income is allotted to miscellaneous items, such as education, recreation, and religion.

Because Engel's laws were based on working-class families who spent all their income, their application by modern marketers is somewhat limited. They provide insights for marketers, however, when family income moves to higher levels, or when per capita income increases in a seller's market. More recent studies, adopted to modern times to include new categories of consumer goods, such as automobiles, show that Engel's first and third laws still hold true, whereas the fourth law is valid with the exception of the higher cost of medical care.

An important contemporary study was conducted in 1956 by Alfred Politz Research, Inc., under the sponsorship of LIFE magazine. One aspect of this study is shown in Table 9.5. It is interesting to compare some parts of this table with Engel's laws.

As indicated earlier in this chapter, personal income is the prime determinant of how much is spent by spending units and when income increases change the pattern of spending. Marketers, however, must monitor the environmental factors, which exert significant influences on how income is spent and saved. The following paragraphs comment briefly on some of these factors.

It was noted earlier that the educational level of consumers influ-

TABLE 9.5.
PERCENTAGE DIVISION OF
TOTAL SPENDING AMONG
MAJOR GOODS AND SERVICES

BBCE

	All House-holds		Household Income Before Taxes					
		Under $2,000	$2,000 to $3,000	$3,000 to $4,000	$4,000 to $5,000	$5,000 to $7,000	$7,000 to $10,000	$10,000 or over
Total annual expenditures per household	$4,110	$1,933	$2,924	$3,839	$4,363	$5,016	$ 6,063	$ 7,946
Percent of total expenditures	100	100	100	100	100	100	100	100
Food, Beverages, Tobacco	29	36	33	30	29	28	26	24
Clothing, Accessories	12	11	11	13	12	11	13	14
Home Operation, Improvement	19	17	20	18	19	19	18	18
Home Furnishings, Equipment, Appliances	9	7	8	8	8	9	9	10
Medical, Personal Care	5	7	5	5	5	5	5	6
Automotive[a]	14	11	13	15	14	16	15	15
Recreation	5	5	5	5	6	5	5	6
Other[b]	7	6	5	6	7	7	9	7
Total U.S. Households (000's)	49,140	8,610	7,080	7,510	9,250	9,680	4,680	2,330
Sample base	10,243	1,940	1,546	1,544	1,882	1,934	913	484
Average number of persons per household	3.3	2.7	3.2	3.4	3.4	3.6	3.7	3.8

[a]Expenditures on automobiles in this category refer to net outlays after trade-in allowances.
[b]Includes life insurance premiums and non-medical professional services.
SOURCE: Reprinted from R. H. Ostheimer, "Who Buys What," *Journal of Marketing* (January, 1958), p. 265. Published by the American Marketing Association.

ences the level of income, but it also influences the ways in which consumers spend their income. The type and location of homes, as well as furniture and home furnishings, are clearly influenced by educational levels. The growth of suburban areas and shifts among the types of residence (single family unit, apartment, town house, condominium) are examples of educational influence. Because people in higher educational levels tend to have more discretionary income, they offer greater market opportunities for objects of art, literature, music, and various participative and spectator sports. Likewise, the importance of current fashion trends in clothing and home furnishings is related to higher educational levels.

As noted earlier in this chapter, the occupation of the head of the family also influences the type of goods and services purchased by the family unit. Work that requires considerable physical labor influences the amount and type of food consumed by workers in these occupations. The type of clothing worn by physical workers is different from that worn by those employed in white collar industries. It follows, therefore, that the clothing industry must provide products that meet the requirements of various occupational classes. Recreational and entertainment products and services are also influenced by a person's occupation, a matter of concern to marketers who supply this type of product.

The age of the family and its stage in the "life cycle" also influence expenditure patterns. Young families with no children spend differently than those with children. Young couples without children seem to be more receptive to new products and tend to accumulate durable products, such as furniture, home furnishings, and automobiles. With the arrival of children, spending typically shifts to soft goods and services to meet the needs of the new members of the family. Marketers must monitor the movement of children through the life cycle, since the type of products demanded changes as children move through the school years into young adulthood. After children leave home, a new market develops for what has come to be called "empty-nesters." This typically comprises the age group from fifty to sixty-five. The demand pattern of this group varies widely. Travel and entertainment markets for "empty-nesters" become important and the products demanded vary widely according to all the factors previously mentioned. The final stage of the family life cycle, the "senior citizen" market, should not be ignored by marketers. Older singles, as well as retired couples, now constitute about 10 percent of the population. Demand patterns of this group are influenced substantially not only by age but also by health and income, which may vary widely within this group.

Nationality, race, and religion also influence the expenditure patterns in the market. Traditional views concerning spending tend to suggest that these factors influence the purchase of certain products or services, such as food, automobiles, and entertainment. Marketers should not accept these historical beliefs blindly. Some original marketing research may be helpful in segmenting markets according to these influences.

Finally, marketers must recognize that changing life styles exert various influences on spending patterns. An individual's life style is, of course, influenced by the basic factors already considered, namely, income, education, and occupation. Other factors also influence life style. These include working wives, unmarried households at both ends of the adult life cycle, welfare payments, and retirement income, as well as changes in ethical and moral traditional norms.[4]

NONHOUSEHOLD MARKETS

The preceding section discussed consumer markets, which, although large and important, do not equal the volume sold in nonhousehold, or intermediate markets. Even though there are great numbers of individual markets in this broad category when specific product or service markets are identified, this chapter will consider only four broad categories. Specifically, the discussion will focus on reseller, industrial, institutional, and government markets.

RESELLER MARKETS Retailers and wholesalers together comprise the marketing institutions in the reseller domestic markets. The preceding chapter on the institutional environment examined in some detail the nature and type of these institutions. At this point, consideration is given to these institutions as a segment of the total domestic market environment. The basic distinguishing characteristic of these institutions is that they do not create form utility. This means that, with rare exceptions, they sell the items they buy in the same form in which they receive them. Their contribution to society and the economy is the creation of time, place, and possession utilities.

Before considering the primary functions of these institutions, it should be noted that they do not resell all of the items they buy. The operation of reseller institutions requires many products in order to conduct their businesses in the competitive markets they supply. Their demand for these items create special markets that are supplied by the industrial marketer. Because reseller institutions operate from a fixed place of business, they provide substantial markets for building materials and supplies, such as concrete, lumber, and electrical supplies. Retailers are an important market for store fixture producers, including elevators and escalators. Wholesalers typically require various kinds of material handling equipment, such as conveyors and lift trucks. Both wholesalers and retailers are important markets for suppliers of office equipment and supplies that are needed in the conduct of their businesses. The current concern with the efficient management of inventories has created important markets for computers, including point of sale (POS) terminals now being put into operation in many retail stores.

Although the products of consumer goods manufacturers go to the household markets, the immediate customer of these firms are wholesalers and retailers. For this reason, the manufacturer of consumer goods must be knowledgeable about the marketing requirements of retailers, as well as the needs of the ultimate consumer of the product. Among the factors to be considered in selling retailers are timing, or when purchases are made, the quantities in which the retailer buys (a packaging consideration), and the operation of the retail buyer, or how purchases are made. Retail buyers, quite naturally, have the ultimate consumer in mind before and during purchase considerations. Their buying process, however, reflects a more careful and professional approach than that of the consumer buyer. Because profit is a motive, the retail buyer must be viewed as a true professional, and suppliers must be cognizant of this in developing their marketing and selling strategies.

At the risk of oversimplification, wholesale markets can be divided into two major segments: those that supply primarily retail markets, and those that supply other nonhousehold markets. A careful examination of individual wholesalers will reveal, however, that considerable overlap exists. Wholesalers are true intermediate types of marketing institutions because they bring producers' goods closer to the point of their use and consumption and hold them in storage until required by their customers. Consequently, in the conduct of their operations, they are important elements of the domestic market environment.

The modern wholesaler typically specializes along product lines and, therefore, becomes an important part of the customer's environment as well as the environment of suppliers. The typical modern wholesaler does not handle perishable products, including fashion goods, although exceptions may be noted in the assembly function of produce wholesalers. The most dominant wholesalers selling to retail markets are found in foods, drugs, cosmetics, carpets, appliances, and certain hardware and glassware lines. The customers of these institutions include a wide range of medium to large retail outlets. A smaller type of wholesaler, the wagon distributor, supplies candy, tobacco, and other items to roadside restaurants, gasoline service stations, and other small retail businesses that buy in smaller quantities.

INDUSTRIAL MARKETS

As presented here, industrial markets may be defined as manufacturing markets. Industrial goods are goods sold primarily to the manufacturing industry rather than to ultimate consumers. The goods purchased are for use in the production of goods and services, or for the operation of a business rather than for resale in the same form.

In order to understand the dimensions of the industrial market, it must first be observed that it is not a single uniform market, but a number of different markets. Again, at the risk of oversimplification, this section identifies three types of manufacturers in the industrial market: (1) the manufacturer who processes raw materials into basic industrial products, such as the steel mill that uses iron ore, coal, and limestone to produce a variety of steel products; (2) the manufacturer who buys basic raw materials from the steel mill and other markets to produce machinery and other products needed by manufacturers of consumer goods and other industrial goods; and (3) the manufacturer who buys machinery, agricultural products, and parts and assemblies to produce the products that enter other manufacturing firms, reseller markets, institutional markets, and government markets. A complete classification of industrial markets is presented in Table 9.6.

Because the pattern of demand in industrial markets differs substantially from that in consumer domestic markets, the following paragraphs will examine some of the important characteristics of industrial markets. These characteristics are important from a marketing point of view because they impinge upon market planning as well as on strategic and tactical marketing considerations.

TABLE 9.6.
CLASSIFICATION OF
INDUSTRIAL MARKETS

I. By Nature or Type of Good
    A. Direct Industrial Products (those which enter the product)
        1. Raw Materials
        2. Semi-Finished or Processed Materials
        3. Parts and Sub-Assemblies
    B. Indirect Goods (do not enter the product but are necessary for its production or sale)
        1. Capital Goods (subject to depreciation, installations and major equipment)
        2. Accessory or Minor Equipment (hand tools)
        3. Operating Supplies (non-durables used in the operation of the business, e.g., fuel, stationery, light bulbs)

II. By Type of Buyer
    A. Extractive Industries (lumber, mining, fishing)
    B. Agriculture
    C. Construction Contractors
    D. Manufacturers
    E. Commercial Buyers (wholesalers, retailers, service traders)
    F. Institutions (schools, hotels, prisons)
    G. Government (federal, state, local)

SOURCE: Based on Paul D. Converse, Harvey W. Huegy, and Robert V. Mitchell, *Elements of Marketing* (7th ed.; Englewood Cliffs, New Jersey: Prentice-Hall, Inc., 1965), pp. 364-365.

c<i
i

Size of purchase by customers.   Household consumers normally buy one unit of an item, or perhaps a few units at a time. Normally, the maximum dollar outlay by ultimate consumers for tangible goods, other than real estate, is for an automobile. In contrast, industrial goods sales are for a substantial number of units and the dollar value of a single purchase contract may exceed a million dollars.

Number of customers.   The number of customers for a consumer goods product, especially a convenience item, may well be in the millions. On the other hand, the possible number of customers for an industrial product may be very small. When an industrial product is used by only one, or a small number of industry or trade groups, this product is said to have a *vertical* market. This type of market is narrow but deep, in that most prospective customers in the industry may need the product. (Machinery for a specialized industry, such as shoe manufacturing or textile weaving, is a good example.) Other industrial markets may be described as *horizontal* in nature. This description applies when a product is bought by many different kinds of firms in different industries. (Most supplies fall into this category, as well as office machinery and materials handling equipment.) Horizontal markets may actually be rather broad as compared to vertical markets, but the total number of customers is still small when compared with the numbers in consumer goods markets.

Diffused buying responsibility.   Marketers of consumer goods normally have little difficulty in identifying the purchaser of consumer items. One individual, or a couple, typically fill the role of buyer. The industrial goods salesman, on the other hand, may have considerable difficulty in identifying the decision maker in connection with the sale of his product. The industrial purchasing manager occupies a role that has no real counterpart in consumer goods markets. Frequently, this individual has little influence on items or quantities purchased other than for routine supplies or other items purchased on a specification or bid basis. Major installations and highly technical products, such as computers, may involve plant engineers, plant managers, or even the company president. In connection with this type of product, the industrial salesman must be able to identify and reach the key individuals who will make the purchase decision.

Derived demand.   The most basic characteristic of industrial goods markets is the concept of derived demand. This means that the demand for these goods is derived from, or depends upon, the demand for the final consumer goods. Although many examples of derived demand may be offered, the steel industry provides the best illustration. Without the ultimate consumer, there would be little or no demand for steel. The automobile industry is a major purchaser of steel, but the amount purchased is based on the number of automobiles sold in the consumer market. This is shown in Figure 9.5. Other buyers of

FIGURE 9.5.
EXAMPLE OF DERIVED
DEMAND

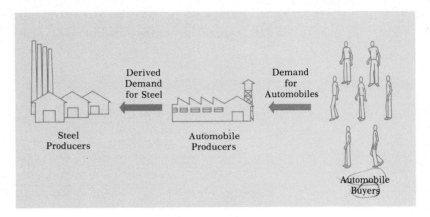

steel are the many factories that produce other consumer goods and require steel for the construction of plants and the machinery required in further production. It is easy to see, therefore, that the demand for steel is influenced by the consumer demand for such items as food, clothing, and recreational items.

Inelastic short-run demand.   This characteristic is related to derived demand, but is also significant in its own right. The concept of short-run inelasticity is that the demand for some industrial products responds very little to changes in price, especially if the cost of the item is small compared to the price of the final product. The demand for final products in the clothing industry will probably not vary significantly with an increase in the price of material, even if the increase in cost is passed on to the consumer. Likewise, the demand for toys is not likely to be influenced by an increase in the price of paint or enamel.

Widely fluctuating demand.   A third aspect of demand in industrial markets is that it exhibits substantial swings in its pattern over time. Except for normal seasonal patterns in the demand for consumer products, the demand for these items can be predicted with a relatively high degree of certainty. On the other hand, demand patterns in industrial markets is influenced substantially by changes in the economic and technological environments. Major installations, plant equipment, machinery, and materials handling equipment, for example, frequently exhibit substantial swings in demand due to environmental impacts.

Purchase on a performance basis.   Because of the nature of the items purchased in this market, contracts are normally based on specifications related to quality and performance. In other words, rational buying motives typically govern the purchase decision. Emotional motives and reciprocity considerations, however, are occasionally a purchase consideration. The impact of style and fashion, which are very important in the purchase of consumer goods, is seldom an important consideration in industrial markets.

INSTITUTIONAL MARKETS

The organizations comprising this type of market segment are occasionally either lightly considered or not considered at all in the body of marketing literature. This is due to their lack of homogeneity and their government, or quasi government nature. Institutional markets, like industrial markets, are not a single type of market, but rather a complex of markets, each with a demand for some special type of product they require in the performance of their mission.

In this book, institutional markets are defined to include educational institutions, penal institutions, religious institutions, hospitals, and the vast number of nonprofit institutions such as the Red Cross and various other charitable institutions. Public institutions, such as museums and zoos, which rely substantially on donations for their operation, are also included in this category. Goods purchased by these institutions come principally from industrial producers, although many purchases are made from firms in reseller markets, especially wholesalers. The single major identifying characteristic of these institutions is that they are not basically business organizations that provide goods or services with the objective of profit. Fees to cover part of their cost of operation, as in the case of educational institutions or hospitals, may be charged.

The substantial number and size of these institutions create important markets for large numbers of business firms. The larger-sized institutions require separate physical plants, creating markets for the building trades and the manufacturers of furniture and equipment. In many cases, the items produced are made especially for a specific type of institution, such as furniture for schools.

GOVERNMENT MARKETS

Many marketing texts include educational and penal institutions in the category of government markets. These were treated as part of the institutional market in the preceding section because of the special characteristics of their operation and the types of goods and services they demand. As defined here, government markets comprise the federal government, including all its agencies and bureaus, state and county governments, township and city governments, and miscellaneous agencies related to many of the above major units.

The tremendously large government market as defined above deserves special attention from marketers of all types of goods and services. Expenditures for goods and services (including manpower costs) by the federal government alone was estimated at $111.5 billion for 1974.[5] Although national defense expenditures account for almost 75 percent of the above amount, the balance, excluding manpower costs, is substantial and goes for an extremely wide variety of items too numerous to mention here. The diversity of purchasing units among governmental agencies at all levels presents special problems and challenges to marketers desirous of serving these markets.

Any attempt to identify government markets by type of product purchased is beyond the scope of this book. When one considers that governments operate police and fire departments, public utilities, research laboratories, and offices of all kinds, to list just a few, however, the importance of this segment of demand can readily be seen. Furthermore, an examination of recent trends shows that expenditures by government units has been growing constantly and can be expected to continue to grow in the foreseeable future.

Facing this fantastically large market, business firms desiring to serve it should view marketing to the government as the performance of those activities necessary to find, develop, and maintain contractual relationships with government institutions and agencies.[6] The key point to this definition is that business firms must identify specific government markets and learn how to do business with them. Although there are certain common characteristics among government markets and industrial markets, such as the size of the order, there are also many differences. Differences in detail also exist among the different governmental levels, although this discussion will focus only on the common characteristics among the government markets.

One of the major responsibilities of government procurement agencies is to describe in detail the specifications of the items to be purchased, including delivery schedules and any penalties for late delivery of needed items. Most government agencies go to great lengths to attract sellers, advise them of needs, and show how formal relationships can be established. Many agencies of the government, such as the Department of Defense and the Department of Commerce, provide publications to prospective suppliers, which tell them how to contact and do business with specific government agencies.

The most common procedure used by government agencies is a prescribed method of mandatory bidding that is open to public scrutiny. Under this method, the government buyer is normally required to accept the lowest bid. This procedure requires procurement agencies to detail their needs with great care. Likewise, the procedure requires suppliers to be certain that they estimate carefully their ability to perform according to the bids they make. Under the law, a government agency cannot detail specifications that only a single firm can meet (although this probably is done). Many common items that governments buy, such as gasoline and construction materials, do not create problems in detailing specifications, but firms bidding on these items must be certain that their product meets the minimum specifications and delivery requirements.

Many items required by governments, especially the federal government, cannot logically be handled by open bidding. This is especially true in the case of research and development contracts and the majority of military material required by the Department of Defense. In cases like this, especially where no effective competition may exist, contracts are individually negotiated with suppliers deemed qualified to develop the required items. Although the negotiated contract is clearly necessary, it should be noted that it does permit favoritism and "influence" to exist, and anyone who follows the daily press knows that this is not uncommon in city, county, and state governments. In spite of this weakness, the negotiated contract is certain to continue, and marketers seeking this type of contract must develop appropriate broad strategies to serve the government market.

ENVIRONMENTAL CONSIDERATIONS

Chapters 8 through 15 in this book examine in detail the macro environments of marketing. This section will point out some of the influence that selected environments have on segments of the domestic markets. As noted earlier, both household and nonhousehold markets must be viewed as dynamic rather than static. In other words, if the marketer is to serve them effectively and economically, he must recognize change as a continuing characteristic and adjust the dimensions of his marketing program in light of the changes brought about by dynamic environments.

ECONOMIC CONSIDERATIONS

The impact of the economic environment on markets of all kinds must be obvious to even the casual observer of the business scene. Per capita personal income in constant dollars rose from $1,810 in 1950 to $3,390 in 1973, and personal consumption expenditures on the same base rose from $1,520 to $2,632 during the same period.[7] The impact of this growth on consumer markets and through derived demand on industrial markets can be readily seen. The modest rate of inflation along with rising income was hardly an issue during the period 1950–1970. The more recent double-digit inflation and increased unemployment rates brought about new problems. Higher interest rates of the 1970s have created problems for both consumers and marketers. Increased taxes by all levels of government affect consumer purchase decisions and create special problems for business firms interested in increasing their productivity. These few examples illustrate the necessity of a continuous monitoring of the economic environment in order to keep marketing programs effective.

COMPETITIVE CONSIDERATIONS

Any attempt by marketers to assess the number and size of competitors in the markets they serve is at best a difficult task. Chapter 14 examines in detail the dimensions of the competitive environment. At this point, the reader is asked only to view competition as rivalry among two or more firms, each of which tries to capture and serve part of a specific market. Even though competition is generally considered to be the foundation of the economic process, various groups perceive it differently. Economists, lawyers, government officials, and businessmen all tend to see it from different perspectives. In fact, individuals within the same professional group often disagree on some aspects of the meaning of competition.

No attempt will be made here to reconcile the differences among these groups, since that discussion is reserved for Chapter 14. It is important to note, however, that businesses must understand and anticipate the behavior of their rivals and develop their own strategies accordingly. The intelligent businessman should not worry about competitors, but rather, must recognize them and understand them. In addition, it must be understood that there are many competitive tools available other than price. Product quality, packaging, service, and promotion are among the competitive tools, and these must be blended effectively to differentiate the "total product" from that of competitors in order to carve a market niche for each firm. To sustain an individual firm in its chosen markets, the firm must monitor the competitive environment on a continuing basis.

LEGAL CONSIDERATIONS

Marketing decision making, especially in connection with strategic planning and implementation cannot be undertaken without careful consideration of all dimensions of the legal environment. Product planning and development must consider, among other things, product safety, and guarantees. Pricing decisions can not be made in ignorance of legal constraints concerning market sharing and the impact of prices on competitors. Decisions in connection with channel development must consider the legal constraints on vertical and conglomerate integration. Finally, promotional programs and strategies must be made only after legal constraints are considered. Consider, for example, the law that denies the cigarette industry the opportunity to use the television medium.

It is important to note that many of the laws that regulate business have been enacted, not in the face of business opposition, but at the urgent request of business itself. Tarriffs and patent laws have had the support of business, as have state fair trade laws. The latter were given support by federal legislation, which exempted these laws from certain provisions of the antitrust laws until fair trade laws were repealed by Congress in 1976. Marketers must also recognize that legislation relating to taxes and the social welfare all have marketing implications.

TECHNOLOGICAL CONSIDERATIONS

In Chapter 15 the various aspects of the technological environment and their impact on marketing will be considered. At this point, the reader is asked to recognize that new technologies are always present and heavily influence marketing plans and strategies. It is commonly thought that technology is related only to the physical products that business firms produce and offer to the market. Technology, however, is much broader than this to the marketer. Some examples of new technologies of importance to marketers include medicine as it affects fertility control and the prolonging of life, the electronics industry and its impact on the communications media, physical handling and transportation systems that present new opportunities for better inventory control, and the more efficient operation of consumer credit.

SOCIAL AND CULTURAL CONSIDERATIONS

It has often been said that marketing is a social as well as an economic institution. This is true because people's living habits, their aspirations, how they perceive things, and the nature of their consumption behavior are all related in part to the impact of culture and man's social heritage. Chapter 11 will examine some of the major affects of culture on human behavior and the need for marketers to monitor this important dynamic environment. Marketers must be aware of the fact that although culture tends to be fairly uniform and integrated within a particular society, it must not be thought of as being imposed. Sociologists say that in order to survive, culture needs to be both gratifying and adaptive. For these reasons, a knowledge of cultural change must be a major concern of marketing.

ETHICAL CONSIDERATIONS

Westing points out that, "Business is having trouble with its ethics today. But, then business has always had trouble with its ethics."[8] Marketing ethics and social responsibility is the subject matter of Chapter 17, but it is important to recognize here that business behavior in these areas affects the domestic market environment.

It may seem illogical that the subject of business ethics is receiving so much attention today when the real strength of the market system is based on mutual trust. That is, millions of transactions are consummated daily by consumers using a wide variety of credit cards as well as personal checks. Product warranties and guarantees are normally honored by manufacturers and retailers. Surely it is a fact that an effective exchange system demands honest behavior and the fulfillment of promises by both parties to a market transaction. The wide acceptance and practice of the marketing philosophy of management, with its focus on serving the consumer, suggests that ethics should not create problems in the marketplace. Unfortunately, however, modern societies still have their share of crooks, swindlers, and fraudulent operators, and the nation's efficient mass communication media tells about this behavior with glaring headlines. The honest businessman is hurt by dishonest competitors, and some consumers tend to equate all business behavior as suspect. The point made here is that the honest businessman must monitor the behavior of all business in order to survive and help maintain a viable, honest market system.

SUMMARY

This chapter began by recognizing that markets were comprised of people, businesses, and institutions with needs to satisfy and the resources and willingness to buy. The need for both producers and resellers to segment their markets was discussed. Having considered the characteristics of both consumer and nonhousehold markets and identified the various environments that impinge on marketing planning and strategy, summary consideration was given to the major concerns of marketers in the domestic markets. In order to serve a chosen market profitably, the marketer must be able to answer three basic questions: (1) what does the market buy?; (2) why does the market buy?; and (3) how does the market buy?

A basic premise about markets is the fact that they are heterogeneous rather than homogeneous. Therefore, the first objective of the marketer is to identify a homogeneous segment that can be served well and profitably. In consumer or household markets, a commonly used basis of classification of consumer purchases is the tangibility of what is purchased and its rate of consumption. Based on these factors, consumers buy durable goods, nondurable goods, and services. Another classification of consumer goods is based on the shopping habits of the consumer. On this basis the consumer sees and buys convenience, shopping, or specialty goods.

Any attempt to classify in detail the items bought in nonhousehold markets would be a monumental task. Fortunately, this task is made easier by the Standard Industrial Classification (S.I.C.) system, a publication of the federal government. A shorthand classification is the same as that used for consumer markets, namely, durable goods, nondurable goods, and services.

To answer the question of why the market buys is difficult and, surely, in some cases impossible. Without reasonably correct answers to this question, however, the marketer, at best, can only guess what marketing strategy should be employed. Chapters 11 and 12 discuss many of the factors that impinge on the forces that underlie this important question facing the marketer.

The marketer's concern in finding an answer to the question of how the market buys should be clear. Without knowing how the market buys, there really is no way for the marketers to communicate with potential buyers. This task is generally an easy one in the case of consumer markets, where an individual, usually the head of the household, is the decision maker. The firm's promotional effort, including both advertising and personal selling, is directed to the potential buyer, and the "how," once the decision to buy is made, frequently concerns the choice between paying cash and using some form of available credit.

The answer to "how" in the case of nonhousehold markets is usually more complex in industrial, government, and institutional markets. Generally, for routine items, the purchasing manager is the buyer. In the case of more costly and complex items, the actual buying decision may be made by engineers, or top level managers. In some cases, especially in government purchases, bidding to product and delivery specifications are required. In these cases, the answer to "how" is frequently difficult, but is extremely necessary as a part of the seller's strategy.

QUESTIONS FOR DISCUSSION

1. What are the basic elements of a market, and why is it important for the marketer to be knowledgeable of these elements?

2. What is the meaning of market segmentation, and why is this concept important to the marketer?

3. What are the important population characteristics that are significant to the marketer? Identify and explain.

4. Why are educational levels and types of employment important to marketers of consumer goods?

5. Discuss income and income distribution as significant market characteristics.

6. What are Engel's Laws of Consumption, and why are these important to marketers?

7. What are the four major categories of nonhousehold markets?

8. How are industrial markets classified? Why is a classification important to the marketer?

9. What are the major differences between household and nonhousehold markets as they affect marketing strategy?

10. What are the major environmental considerations affecting the domestic market?

NOTES

[1] U.S. Bureau of the Census, *Current Population Reports,* Series P-25; Nos. 310, 483, 490, and 493.

[2] Based on 1972 dollars of actual reported amounts. *Statistical Abstract of the United States,* 1974, p. 120.

[3] These definitions are adapted from Paul D. Converse, Harvey W. Huegy, and Robert V. Mitchell, *Elements of Marketing* (7th ed.; Englewood Cliffs, New Jersey: Prentice-Hall, Inc., 1965), pp. 63–64.

[4]W. T. Anderson, Jr., and L. K. Sharpe, "The New Marketplace: Life Style in Revolution," *Business Horizons* (August, 1971), pp. 43–50.

[5]Federal Receipts and Expenditures in the National Income Accounts, 1950 – 1974, *Statistical Abstract of the United States,* 1974, p. 222.

[6]Based on C. N. Hynes and N. Zabriskie, *Marketing to Governments* (Columbus, Ohio: Grid, Inc., 1974), p. 1.

[7]*Statistical Abstract of the United States,* 1974, p. 376.

[8]John H. Westing, "Some Thoughts on the Nature of Ethics in Marketing," in *Changing Marketing Systems* (Chicago: American Marketing Association, 1967), p. 161.

SUGGESTED READINGS

Beik, L. L. and S. L. Buzby, "Profitability Analysis by Market Segments," *Journal of Marketing* (July, 1973), pp. 48–53.

Bell, M. L., *Marketing: Concepts and Strategy* (2nd ed.; Boston: Houghton Mifflin Co., 1972).

Dawson, L. M., "The Human Concept: New Philosophy for Business," *Business Horizons* (December, 1969), pp. 29–38.

Johnson, R. M., "Market Segmentation: A Strategic Management Tool," *Journal of Marketing Research* (February, 1971), pp. 13–18.

Sheth, J. N., "A Model of Industrial Buyer Behavior," *Journal of Marketing* (October, 1973), pp. 50–56.

Walker, O. C., Jr., G. A. Churchill, Jr., and N. M. Ford, "Organizational Determinants of the Industrial Salesman's Role Conflict and Ambiguity," *Journal of Marketing* (January, 1975), pp. 32–39.

Webster, Frederick E., Jr., "Informal Communication in Industrial Markets," *Journal of Marketing Research* (May, 1970), pp. 186–189.

Webster, Frederick E., Jr. and Yoram Wind, "A General Model for Understanding Organizational Buying Behavior," *Journal of Marketing* (April, 1972), pp. 12–19.

10

THE INTERNATIONAL MARKET ENVIRONMENT

10

THE INTERNATIONAL MARKET ENVIRONMENT

Although marketing efforts in the domestic market environment produce over 90 percent of the gross national product in the United States, the international marketing activity of firms engaged in the export of American goods and services and in investments in foreign countries is quite significant. Many of these firms are involved exclusively in the international market; others are seeking international marketing opportunities to offset slow rates of growth in the United States. To provide an insight into the scope and importance of international marketing, this chapter is devoted to a discussion of the international market environment and the special problems associated with the development of international marketing programs by United States firms.

INTERNATIONAL MARKETING TRENDS

As shown in Figure 10.1, the increase in world trade has been substantial over the past two decades. This data illustrates that there has been a significant shift in trade among the world's major exporting regions. Although these shifts are the result of a number of factors, effective marketing efforts have played an important role. Consider, for example, a comparison between Communist China and Japan. In 1950, both shared the same percentage of world exports. By 1970, however, Japan had captured nearly seven times the Chinese portion of world exports. This is an especially significant development, since China has an overwhelming abundance of resources in the form of labor, land, and materials. On the other hand, Japan lacks both land and materials and has considerably less available labor. In this comparison, successful marketing has been the key factor that has enabled Japan to acquire such a commanding lead over China.

In the United States, many people have long believed that world trade is relatively unimportant to the well-being of the American economy. Apart from merely looking about in the United States at the various foreign goods that are in common use throughout the country, the U.S. foreign trade statistics demonstrate the ever-increasing importance of foreign trade to the economy and its business firms. Figure 10.2 presents the foreign trade position of the United States from 1953 through 1975. As noted, the dollar value of exports in 1974 was 3.6 times that in 1965. As can be seen, however, the import record has increased even more rapidly, producing a very small trade surplus. This means, in part, that American consumers have found foreign goods more attractive than foreigners have found American goods over the period presented. Alternatively, the declining position of American goods in world markets can be interpreted as the inability, or unwillingness, of American firms to properly market their goods in competition with foreigners.

In evaluating the international marketing performance of American firms, C. Tait Ratcliffe indicates that in a U.S.-Japan comparison of marketing ability, the Japanese clearly emerge the winners. Part of his explanation is the fact that Japan needs to export to a greater degree than does the United States. Both nations must import to feed their heavy industries, but Japan is without national petroleum, bauxite, and many of its needed raw materials. In order to be able to import these materials, it must export. Therefore, it must invest and innovate.[1] The degree to which Japan has been successful can be seen in the number of Japanese cars in the United States and elsewhere.

In addition to the exports that it generates from domestic produc-

FIGURE 10.1.
THE CHANGING COMPOSITION
OF WORLD EXPORTS, 1950–1970

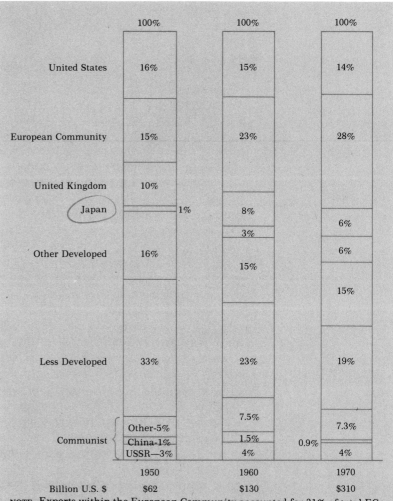

NOTE: Exports within the European Community accounted for 31% of total EC exports in 1950; 35% in 1960; 48% in 1970. In 1970, Soviet exports to Communist countries accounted for 65% of total exports.

SOURCE: *The United States in a Changing World Economy*, Vol. II (Washington, D.C.: U.S. Government Printing Office, 1971), Chart 12.

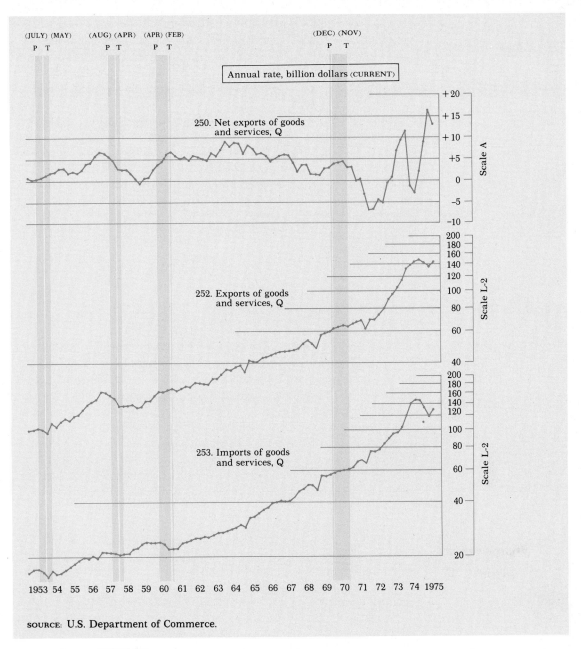

(JULY) (MAY)   (AUG) (APR)   (APR) (FEB)   (DEC) (NOV)
P   T   P   T   P   T   P   T

Annual rate, billion dollars (CURRENT)

250. Net exports of goods
     and services, Q

Scale A

252. Exports of goods
     and services, Q

Scale L-2

253. Imports of goods
     and services, Q

Scale L-2

1953 54 55 56 57 58 59 60 61 62 63 64 65 66 67 68 69 70 71 72 73 74 1975

SOURCE: U.S. Department of Commerce.

FIGURE 10.2.
UNITED STATES FOREIGN
TRADE, 1953–1975

tion, American firms have been investing, producing, and marketing abroad for over a hundred years. In 1970, U.S. private direct investment abroad amounted to $78 billion, and it produced about $156 billion of international production. This is especially noteworthy given the fact that U.S. origin exports that year were less than $43 billion— only about 28 percent of U.S. controlled international production. Since U.S. controlled international production is growing more rapidly than domestically produced exports, this discrepancy can be expected to grow. Increasing international production means that U.S. firms will be receiving more of their growth in sales and profits from abroad in the future.

The 1970 U.S. private overseas investment figure of $78 billion yielded earnings of $8.7 billion.[2] Much of these earnings are being returned to the U.S. parent firm for domestic use and for further foreign investment. More and more U.S. firms, both large and small, are reaching the point where more than 50 percent of their sales and profits are derived from foreign activities. To understand how all of this foreign investment came about and how and why nations can benefit from foreign trade, it is appropriate to briefly review the rationale for international trade.

RATIONALE FOR INTERNATIONAL TRADE

In a comparison between Norway and Ecuador, most people would agree that Ecuador is best suited to the production of bananas. Because of natural factor endowments, Ecuador has an absolute advantage over Norway in the production of bananas. If Norway wants bananas, it will have to trade with Ecuador as the cost of producing that crop in Norway is infinite. What if both countries each produced the same goods? Would there be opportunities for trade? This is the issue that David Ricardo treated when he wrote his "doctrine of comparative advantage" in the early nineteenth Century. He observed that there are relative differences in cost as well as absolute differences.

COMPARATIVE
ADVANTAGE

Following Ricardo's example, two countries and two products will be used to illustrate the concept of comparative advantage. Figure 10.3 shows the production possibility curves for two countries that each produce bread and wine. The explanation of these curves is as follows:

Country "A" can produce both bread and wine. If it produces only bread and no wine and allocates all of its factors of production to the production of bread, it will be able to produce three hundred units of bread. If, however, it decides to withdraw all of its factors of production from the production of bread and transfers these factors to the production of wine, then it can produce one hundred units of wine and no bread. Line A shows the production possibilities for bread and wine production in country "A." That is, country "A" can produce three hundred units of bread, or one hundred units of wine. What happens if "A" wants some bread and some wine? Clearly, it will have to give

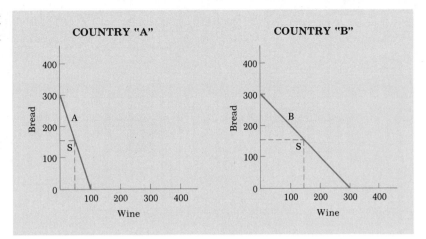

FIGURE 10.3.
THE CONCEPT OF
COMPARATIVE ADVANTAGE

up some of one in order to get some of the other. The points at maximum production of each provide the ratio of exchange between these goods in country "A." That ratio is three hundred to one hundred, or 3/1. Therefore, to get some wine, say fifty units, it will have to give up 150 units of bread. This means that the country can produce a satisfaction level (S) of 150 units of bread and fifty units of wine at the same time. Since bread is easier to produce in this country and wine is relatively scarce, the price relationship between the two will be one in which wine is higher priced than bread.

Country "B" can also produce just two commodities, bread and wine. If country "B" allocates all of its factors of production to the production of bread, it will be able to produce three hundred units of bread. If it withdraws all of its factors of production from bread and allocates them only to the production of wine, it will be able to produce three hundred units of wine. Line B shows the production possibilities for bread and wine in country "B." That is, it can produce three hundred units of bread, or three hundred units of wine. What if the people in country "B" decide they want some of both? The points at maximum production of each provide the exchange ratio between these goods. This exchange ratio for country "B" is three hundred to three hundred or 3/3, or 1/1. Therefore, to get some wine with their bread, the people in country "B" only have to give up one unit of bread for each unit of wine that they desire. Should they decide that they want 150 units of wine, they can produce a satisfaction level (S) of 150 units of wine and 150 units of bread.

If these countries begin to trade, "A" will produce only bread and "B" will produce only wine. Country "A" will keep the 150 units of bread it normally consumes and will trade the remainder to "B." Country "B" should be willing to give up seventy-five units of its wine for 150 units of country "A's" bread, since it would normally have to

FIGURE 10.4.
CONSUMPTION AFTER TRADE

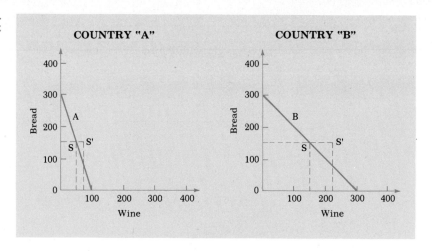

give up 150 units of wine at home to obtain the same amount of bread. If this exchange ratio is accepted by both countries, the result will be as indicated in Figure 10.4. For country "A," the satisfaction level without trade (S) was 150 units of bread and fifty units of wine. With trade, the new satisfaction level (S') is 150 bread and seventy-five wine. For country "B," the satisfaction level without trade (S) was 150 units of bread and 150 units of wine. With trade, the new satisfaction level (S') is 150 bread and 225 wine. As can be seen, the new satisfaction levels (S') for both countries are beyond the production possibility lines that produced the satisfaction levels (S) that existed before trade was begun.

DIVISION OF THE GAINS FROM TRADE

In the example above, someone will begin to ponder the issue of which country is getting the most benefit from the trade. Despite the fact that both have improved beyond their individual abilities, the question of the division of the gains will arise. Both countries will probably waste considerable resources arguing over who got the most of the newly expanded pie. As a result, restrictions to free trade will probably appear.

LIMITS TO FREE TRADE

Five reasons for restricting trade are usually offered: national security, infant industry development, economic diversification, job protection, and wage protection. The first three reasons are generally accepted. First, trade or no trade, war seems always possible. If one nation is dependent upon another for vital goods or services, war between those nations would be especially disastrous for the dependent nation. Therefore, nations prefer to set up trade barriers, even at higher cost to citizen consumers, rather than become so dependent upon another nation that no war could be fought on their part, let alone, won.

The second two reasons are so close in objective that they can be treated together as one. Nations that are raw materials and food producers have long claimed that the terms of trade go against them in the long run. What they mean by this is that as incomes rise, a smaller percentage of these higher incomes will go for food and raw materials, and more will go into higher-order consumption. Therefore, nations want to get in on the industrial revolution as quickly as possible. To do this they need to diversify their economies from agricultural, or raw materials production, to include larger proportions of industrial production. When these "infant" industries "grow up," they require protection from trade with foreigners who have mature industrial experience. One of the problems here is that protection inevitably brings higher prices for domestic consumers; some of the "infants" get to be over two hundred years old and still have protection.

The last two reasons are frequently tossed aside by those who feel that any jobs or wages that are not internationally competitive ought to be lost, and the people in those jobs retrained to some other job that is internationally competitive. There is much to be said for this point of view from a strictly economic standpoint (so long as it is not your job or your wage they want to do away with); but it is usually political disaster to let market forces weigh heavily on workers in a declining industry.

TRADE AND ECONOMIC DEVELOPMENT

With all of the sense and nonsense that surrounds the arguments for free trade versus protection from free trade, there is fairly clear evidence that freer trade is beneficial. Much of this evidence comes from such sources as the European Economic Community (EEC) and the Central American Common Market (CACM). In both cases, there has been a significant increase in regional and individual national economic growth through expanded trade opportunities due to lower trade barriers. The conclusion seems to be that increased internationally competitive trade is a clear force for development.

DEVELOPING INTERNATIONAL MARKETING PROGRAMS

The approach of the individual firm to entry in the international marketing field has tended to be rather hit or miss. The firm may have decided to enter the field as a result of a vacation trip made by one of the top managers to some area of the world where the firm's product wasn't known. Deciding that the firm was missing a market, the manager may have returned excited about the possibilities of marketing the product abroad. Alternatively, a French vacationer in the United States may have come to the U.S. producer's plant excited about the possibilities of importing the product for sale in Europe. In brief, the average U.S. firm has not been aggressive in the international marketing area until fairly recently.

THE INTERNATIONAL MARKETING FIRM

The giants of U.S. industry, however, have long been active in the field of international marketing. For example, a British author in 1901 noted that, "The most serious aspect of the American industrial invasion lies in the fact that these incomers have acquired control of almost every new industry created during the past fifteen years."[3] Writing of the British, he made a now familiar statement often employed by the lesser developed countries of the world against the multinational firm: "We are becoming the hewers of wood and the drawers of water while the most skilled, most profitable, and the easiest trades are becoming American."[4] Nearly seventy years later, *The American Challenge,* by Jean-Jacques Servan-Schreiber, warned Europe that U.S. industry in Europe would become the third largest industrial power in the world (just after the U.S. itself and Russia) in fifteen years.[5]

Not all American ventures overseas have been successful. It is generally accepted that there are three reasons for going overseas: (1) as a raw materials seeker, (2) as a production efficiency seeker, and (3) as a market seeker. It is the last reason that is treated here.

Firms that want to go international can do so by several methods. For many firms, as previously indicated, export has been the means of entry. Export, for the right reasons, can be a sound base for international marketing activity, but there are a number of pitfalls. For instance, the use of exports as a technique for getting rid of excess U.S. production that cannot be sold domestically is not likely to sustain the firm interested in international marketing.

Another often used means for going international has been licensing. In licensing, the firm sells the use of patents, trademarks, or other technology to foreign firms. This method is often employed by the small- and medium-sized firm that feels it cannot spare the firm's resources for international entry at the particular time. This technique provides revenue for the technology-owning firm, but is seldom used alone. Frequently, it is a supplement to other techniques, such as export. Naturally, licensing is less expensive and less risky than full-scale entry, and relatively easy to accomplish.

A third method is the joint venture. In the joint venture, a U.S. firm may decide to enter a foreign market only to discover that exporting is too difficult due to high tariff barriers, quotas, or other nontariff barriers to trade. Joining with a local firm in manufacturing and marketing in the foreign country may be the only solution. This technique can have many positive aspects. Using the specialized knowledge of the foreign partner is likely to improve the chance of success in the region. The required investment is reduced for the U.S. firm as the investment is shared between the two partners.

A fourth method is manufacturing. The statistics on foreign investment by U.S. and other multinational firms would indicate that this method is a major means of going international. Trade barriers set up by foreign governments, the emergence of Common Markets, reluctance to share technology—either industrial or commercial—with foreign competitors, capital availability in the United States, and the general lack of easily available investment capital abroad are some of the reasons for selecting manufacturing as a mode of entrance to international marketing.

One model designed to explain this international expansion may shed some light on this phenomenon. The Product Cycle Model developed by Ramond Vernon at Harvard University leans heavily on the product cycle model used in general marketing theory. There are three stages described in the life cycle of an internationally marketed product: (1) the new product stage, (2) the mature product stage, and (3) the standardized product stage. In the first stage, the product is developed and manufactured in the United States because of its high level of technology and its highly experimental character. Quick reaction is required in manufacturing, product design, pricing, promotion, channel placement, and so forth. The product at this stage is essentially a U.S. product and is introduced to foreign markets through exports. Profit margins are likely to be large enough to cover the need for correcting the marketing effort after receiving feedback from the market. Cost considerations, therefore, are not as important as they will become at a later stage. In the second stage, technology is sufficiently routine to be transferred. The firm's export position may become threatened, and foreign demand is likely to be sufficiently strong to warrant foreign manufacture in a technologically sophisticated country. Finally, in the third stage the technology is so standardized that production can be transferred to low-cost locations and exported back to the United States and U.S.-originated foreign markets.

Clearly, there is a powerful motivating force that draws firms into the international market environment. The international marketing firm that successfully establishes products abroad must pay at least as much attention to the foreign market environment as it does to its home market environment. The reasons behind the willingness of firms to accept this extra workload and extra risk are profit and growth.

U.S. population increases seem to be diminishing with each year, and population levels elsewhere in the world are growing at rates never experienced in the United States. The U.S. economy, although the largest in money terms of any in the world, is not growing at nearly the rate of some countries, such as Japan, Brazil, and West Germany, whose combined population far exceeds that of the United States.

Opportunity still exists in the United States, but American firms have discovered that great opportunity also exists outside of the United States for many of their products and processes.

An example of the impact of the international environment on a firm may be taken from the experience of IBM. This internationally oriented firm has grown over the past two decades at an average rate of approximately 20 percent a year. In 1969, IBM reported sales of $7.2 billion, of which $2.5 billion were foreign sales. IBM's foreign sales are handled by its World Trade Corporation, which has operations in 108 nations of the world, employs 108,000 people in eighteen plants, 336 branch offices, 248 data centers, seven development laboratories, and six regional and area headquarters. Only a part of the 1969 reported foreign sales of $2.5 billion were shipped from the United States. Most of these foreign sales were derived from foreign production and sales efforts.

Even though IBM's foreign sales made up nearly 35 percent of total sales in 1969, that figure increased to over 39 percent in 1970. What may be more important, the company's net foreign income was 17.4 percent of foreign sales, whereas net U.S. income was only 11.1 percent of U.S. sales, and the firm derived 50 percent of its total net income from foreign sources.[6]

Admittedly, IBM is a rather spectacular firm to use as an example, but, in this case, its experience has been enjoyed by many smaller firms that have adopted a global approach to their marketing strategy. Black and Decker, for example, had net sales in 1970 of only $225 million, just 3 percent of IBM's sales that year. Its net foreign income was 9.4 percent of net foreign sales and net U.S. income was only 6.8 percent of net U.S. sales. Black and Decker's return on foreign sales showed a bigger improvement over the return on U.S. sales than did IBM. Black and Decker also earned 50 percent of its net income from foreign operations.[7]

Large or small, firms with a global attitude toward the development of markets tend to do better abroad than they do at home. Increasingly, the successful international firm is finding that more than a third of its assets are overseas, and more than 40 percent of its profits are derived from overseas operations.

INTERNATIONAL MARKETING AND GOVERNMENT

Many of the problems that firms encounter in doing business have to do with the firm-government relationships that are necessary at home or anywhere in the world. As discussed in Chapter 13, the legal environment is a significant force in any economy. Government taxes and regulates industry and commerce within its borders, and most governments try to influence firms outside of their borders. Tariffs provide a significant source of government revenue in many countries. Firms that go overseas cannot ignore either their home government or their host government. In some cases, these governments can be in conflict over what the firm should be doing. Recently, the Argentine government decided that the Ford Motor Company's Argentina plant should sell cars to Cuba. Argentina, as a country, needed more trade. Cuba was willing to buy cars. The Ford Motor Company wanted to sell cars. Despite the fact that the Ford plant that was to sell the cars was located in Argentina, the U.S. government refused to allow Ford to sell cars to Cuba. What could Ford do? If it acted according to the wishes of the host government, Argentina, it would violate the laws of its home government, the United States, and could expect penalties. If it acted according to the wishes of the U.S. government, it would violate Argentine law and could expect penalties. Fortunately, the issue was finally resolved by the U.S. government's decision to let Ford, Argentina, do what the Argentine government wanted it to do—sell cars to Cuba.

Governments are not always restrictive toward business. They can be and often are promoters of business. In the Argentine case, Ford has a plant in that country because Argentina decided to have an industrialization program and was willing to offer protection to those firms that would put a manufacturing facility in the country. Among other forms of protection for this new or "infant" industry, the Argentine government put up prohibitive import duties against foreign produced automobiles. This meant that anyone in Argentina who wanted a car would have to buy one made in Argentina no matter what the local cost, since import duties against imported cars were over 100 percent. Therefore, even though it might have been cheaper to acquire a car in the U.S. or Europe, the foreign made cars with import duties were considerably more expensive than the same car made in Argentina. In this example, Ford had to decide whether it wanted to lose the Argentine market because export sales to that country would disappear, or keep the Argentine market by taking advantage of the government's assistance in setting up a production facility. Obviously, Ford chose the latter alternative.

Why do governments worry about controlling or sponsoring business? In the international market environment, the answer often lies in the same sort of considerations that were treated under the reasons for restricting trade. Countries are concerned about becoming too dependent upon other countries, or other countries' business firms for vital goods or services. Countries are also concerned about economic development, especially if they are currently only suppliers of agricultural or raw material goods. These countries need to import many things, but imports cost money and that money leaves the importing country. Therefore, exporters must be aware of government goals, or they will lose their markets. The techniques that governments use to hinder imports can be grouped under tariff and nontariff barriers to trade.

Tariff barriers. In effect, tariffs are a form of tax on imports. There are two general types of tariffs: (1) ad valorem tariffs, which are taxes expressed as a percentage of the landed value of the goods being imported; and (2) specific tariffs, which are fixed taxes per unit. That is, a 10 percent tax on the value of an imported automobile would be an ad valorem tariff, while a flat $1,000 tax per automobile, regardless of value, would be a specific tariff.

Nontariff barriers.   Other barriers to trade are nontariff in nature. For the most part, these are quotas and restrictions. Quotas establish numerical limits on an imported item. For example, a country might impose a limit on the number of automobiles that can be imported. Restrictions may be established for a number of reasons, such as health, national security, or simply general harassment. Through restrictions, a nation can totally restrain, or restrict, imports. This may be done for political reasons, when a country does not want to put tariffs and quotas on another nation's goods. Whatever the reasons, restrictions are a very flexible technique for stopping unwanted imports.

A major reason for wanting to restrict imports is the effect of these imports, and their cost, on the balance of payments of the nation. A nation's balance of payments includes the payments a nation makes to all other nations of the world and all the payments that other nations in the world make to that nation. A part of the balance of payments is the balance of trade, which is the algebraic sum of the value of total exports and total imports. For some nations, the balance of trade is a significant part of the balance of payments, for other nations it is relatively small compared to the other accounts that make up the total balance of payments.

The balance of trade tells a nation how well exports pay for imports. If the residents of a country are importing far more than they are exporting, they will have to dip into other accounts to be able to continue paying for these foreign goods. These other accounts may dry up and serious consequences will ensue regarding the value of that nation's currency in terms of other nations' currencies. Continued poor export performance and high import purchases can "bankrupt" a nation. The international marketer must be aware of this and take this into consideration in global market planning. Markets must either be given up, as, for example, General Motors decided to give up markets in Pakistan, India, and Peru; or the global marketer must find ways to keep that market through investment in local manufacturing. This means that at least the same level of effort must be placed on identifying international markets as is expended on identifying national and regional markets at home.

IDENTIFYING INTERNATIONAL MARKETS

Market research is especially important in international marketing. In domestic marketing, a great deal of information is readily available to the potential marketer. Furthermore, the marketer is familiar with many of the attributes of the potential market since it is the marketer's home country and the lifestyle is understood. Through market research, reassurance can be obtained that judgments about the viability of the potential market are correct, and the exact size of the potential market can be defined. In international marketing efforts, however, this home knowledge is absent. In fact, the actual market conditions may be the reverse of what the potential marketer might have expected at home.

Serious mistakes can be made by the American marketer even in a common language country like England. One recent study of American versus British television commercials in Britain indicated that, "despite a common language, the social, cultural, and marketing differences between the two countries are so great that a commercial that is successful in one country is unlikely to be very successful in the other. . . ."[8] As an example, an American advertisement in England had to be dropped, for it had been built on the slogan, "Don't spend a penny until you've tried _____." What the Americans didn't realize was that the phrase "to spend a penny" in Britain is a euphemism for going to the bathroom. Other examples of outstanding and innovative companies from various countries around the world making incredible mistakes in other countries have prompted the writing of a popular book that describes a number of interesting international marketing blunders.[9] To avoid these kinds of mistakes, it is essential that marketers develop appropriate market research information. The various sources of international data are described below.

Supranational data sources.   The United Nations and its various suborganizations provide a remarkable number of publications specifically directed to those wishing to know more about markets in developed and developing countries. The Food and Agriculture Organization of the United Nations (FAO), for example, publishes a *Bibliography of Food and Agricultural Marketing* that lists thousands of books, articles, and pamphlets on this subject from all over the world. The International Labor Organization of the United Nations (ILO) also publishes detailed information regarding labor law and practice in countries around the world and reliable income figures for various levels of wage earners. Other supranational organizations with significant output that is of interest and necessary to the international marketer are: (1) the Organization for Economic Cooperation and Development (OECD); (2) the European Economic Community (EEC); (3) the European Free Trade Association (EFTA); (4) the Latin American Free Trade Association (LAFTA); (5) the Central American Common Market (CACM); and (6) various supranational banks.

National data sources.   Because of the rise of economic planning requirements as an input to the development efforts of nations the world over, most governments do everything in their power to acquire and update facts and figures regarding the level of economic activity within their boundaries. Therefore, apart from the efforts of supranational agencies, the national governments produce a significant amount of data that can be valuable to the international marketing firm. All of the major trading nations also try to develop data banks of information for those nations with whom they trade.

Individual foreign nations that maintain embassies in the United States provide information on business opportunities in their respective countries. In addition, the U.S. government is a vital source of data for the international marketer. The U.S. Department of Commerce has regional offices throughout the country that maintain library facilities and staff specifically for the purpose of assisting firms interested in international marketing. Major publications such as the *World Trade Directory Reports, Marketing Handbooks, Overseas Business Reports,* and *International Commerce,* all provide American firms with updated information on foreign business opportunities.

Business, banking, and professional data sources.   All of the major banks and investment houses gather and provide information on international trade opportunities. The Chambers of Commerce through the U.S. Chamber of Commerce are quite active in stimulating foreign trade. Their publication, *Foreign Commerce Handbook,* is one of the most complete guides to information sources available. Major accounting firms provide constantly updated studies on foreign tax laws and business practices in developed and major developing countries. Newsletters are available at a fee from many international marketing research organizations within the United States. Furthermore, marketing research and consulting firms overseas are continually improving their output as they augment their staff with local nationals who have significant training in U.S. and European schools of business. As one international researcher put it:

The greatest diversity of overseas market research facilities is found in the countries of Europe, followed closely by Canada, Japan, and Australia. Particularly affected by the stimulus of American exports and investments have been the countries of Latin America, so that today it is possible to conduct full-scale professional-quality research throughout this continent. More sparse are the facilities in Asia and Africa, but even there the leading countries, in terms of economic development, all have sound and effective local research agencies that are capable of providing a wide range and scope of market research.[10]

Since the above article came out, ten years of experience and improvements have significantly increased the quality of America's international market research capability. There are still special requirements in international market research, however. For example, a skilled interpreter of international data is needed to successfully employ much of the data that is available, since definitions and data gathering techniques vary considerably between nations and, more especially, between global regions.

SERVING INTERNATIONAL MARKETS   Once international marketing opportunities are identified, the special problems associated with serving international markets must be considered. Beyond the task of dealing with regional economic integration, the international marketer must also organize for international trade and carefully analyze the environmental forces that are unique to the international market. Each of these areas is briefly discussed below.

Regional economic integration.   The advent of the European Economic Community (EEC), commonly known in the United States as the European Common Market, brought about major changes in international marketing. Since the success of the EEC, several such common market arrangements have been developed. All of these common markets have severely restricted old-style exporting and have brought about a new era in international marketing. Despite this impact, there are few people in the United States who really understand just what a common market is.

The EEC provides an excellent example of what member countries attempt to achieve through regional economic integration. The EEC was established under the Treaty of Rome in 1958, after much prior discussion and organization. Politically, it hoped to finally achieve a United States of Europe. Economically, it hoped to achieve an economic entity like the United States of America. Its founders recognized that the United States is really a common market. The different states of the United States agree to a single tariff system against all others, and further agree to free trade within the boundaries of the member states. In ten and a half years, a year and a half ahead of schedule, the EEC achieved that economic goal, thereby fulfilling one of the major requirements of a common market—no tariffs between members and a unified tariff schedule against all outsiders.

Needless to say, the EEC has not achieved its political goal, although it has moved much closer than many observers thought was possible in the beginning. Free movement of labor between countries has been virtually achieved, and the free mobility of capital will soon be achieved. All of this has been made possible through the many executive, quasi-legislative, and judicial agencies of the EEC, but the cornerstone of the success it has achieved has been the ability to reach virtually complete agreement on trade policy. Severely restrictive trade practices against all outsiders stimulated a great deal of foreign investment by those who feared losing valuable markets to high tariffs. This investment added to the rapid recovery of the area after the destruction of World War II.

The Treaty of Rome makes association with the Community open to all countries, but does not spell out the format for association. As a result, the Community has dealt with each application pragmatically. At the present time, there are some sixty-two countries that hold membership of one classification or another in the EEC. This presents a formidable market opportunity for any firm.

[handwritten margin note:] Partially Responsible For SOME FREE TRADE

It is precisely this market opportunity that attracts firms to common markets. Whereas Belgium alone may not provide enough of a market for a U.S. manufacturer's goods, all nine full members of the EEC, to which Belgium belongs, provide a market that includes 255 million people, has gold reserves equal to twice those of the United States, and annual production that amounts to nearly two-thirds that of the United States.

Many other regions have attempted such regional economic integration, but not with the same degree of success as the EEC. The Central American Common Market (CACM) managed to increase intraregional trade by over 500 percent from 1961 to 1967. It eliminated tariffs between member nations and established a common external tariff, but political problems and the small size of the combined five nations has hindered further significant development. Nevertheless, the combining of markets allowed for better utilization of productive capacity, generated many new industries, and permitted expansion into more complex production capability.

Organizing for international marketing. Organization for domestic marketing is vital in the United States because there is significant diversity between regions of the country, between cities and rural areas, and between income classes. To adequately manage this diversity, organization is required. Such organization, however, is perhaps even more necessary in global international marketing.

The organizational structure of European firms seems to differ greatly from that adopted by U.S. firms that go international. European firms seem to prefer a global structure giving all regions of the world, including their own, more or less equal emphasis. The U.S. firm tends to separate out international activities from the main activity of the firm. These different approaches emerge as a result of the differing experiences of firms in the two base areas. The U.S. firm is typically a late comer to international marketing and considers that its home market is far more important. Many U.S. firms with major proportions of their sales and profits coming from international activities still employ organizational techniques similar to those used when they were just beginning to enter the international field.

There are other reasons for the separate international division, or departments, in U.S. firms. Principal among these is the lack of people skilled in international activities within the corporate structure. The history of university education in international business and marketing is a brief one. Furthermore, few Americans are bilingual, much less bicultural. Therefore, the U.S. international firm tends to keep its scarce resources in international expertise and experience concentrated in divisions and departments specifically concerned with international activity.

European firms, on the other hand, find that they have an abundance of bilingual and bicultural manpower within their entire structure. They further find that their home market is such a small

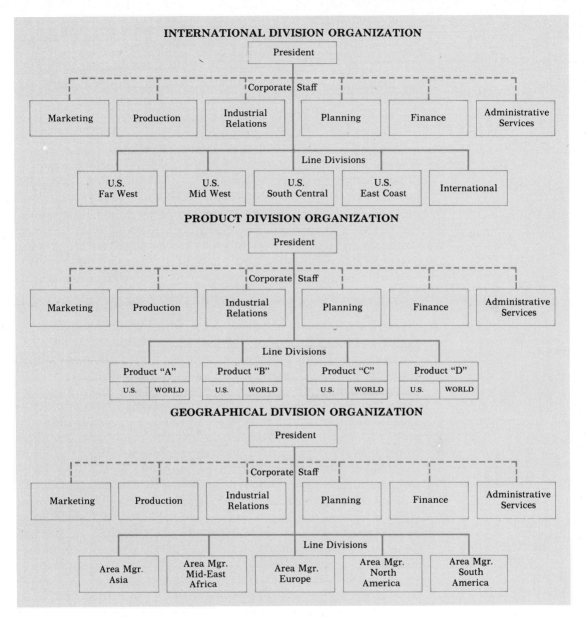

INTERNATIONAL DIVISION ORGANIZATION

President

Corporate Staff

| Marketing | Production | Industrial Relations | Planning | Finance | Administrative Services |

Line Divisions

| U.S. Far West | U.S. Mid West | U.S. South Central | U.S. East Coast | International |

PRODUCT DIVISION ORGANIZATION

President

Corporate Staff

| Marketing | Production | Industrial Relations | Planning | Finance | Administrative Services |

Line Divisions

| Product "A" | | Product "B" | | Product "C" | | Product "D" | |
| U.S. | WORLD | U.S. | WORLD | U.S. | WORLD | U.S. | WORLD |

GEOGRAPHICAL DIVISION ORGANIZATION

President

Corporate Staff

| Marketing | Production | Industrial Relations | Planning | Finance | Administrative Services |

Line Divisions

| Area Mgr. Asia | Area Mgr. Mid-East Africa | Area Mgr. Europe | Area Mgr. North America | Area Mgr. South America |

FIGURE 10.5.
ORGANIZING FOR
INTERNATIONAL MARKETING

percentage of the total market they serve that it pays them to organize the entire firm for the international market environment. The major European firms began as international firms, and their organization charts demonstrate that orientation.

The standard approaches to organization for international marketing by U.S. firms are presented in Figure 10.5. Three elements are especially important in designing the organization for international marketing. These are: (1) the product area; (2) the size of international activities relative to total activities of the firm; and (3) the attitude of the top executive staff toward the future of the firm in the international arena. There are many benefits and penalties associated with each form of organization. The serious student of corporate organization should refer to Arvind V. Phatak's analysis of this issue.[11]

The cultural environment of international marketing.   While there is a great body of knowledge regarding the price and income effects on demand for a good once that good has been accepted by society, there is very little information about whether, or to what extent, a product will be accepted in the first place. Acceptance in one culture and society does not necessarily mean acceptance in another. The diffusion of certain goods, such as fried chicken and other such convenience foods, automobiles, and television, throughout Europe, Japan, and other areas of the world, tend to indicate that there is emerging a certain internationalization of culture at income levels that can support these goods. This experience leads marketers to seek out cultural universals that enable firms to market the same goods the world over.

Very early in the development of U.S. international marketing, research by George P. Murdock led to the identification and classification of many cultural universals. Some of these identified were: ethics, etiquette, education, folklore, food taboos, sexual restrictions, decorative art, religious rituals, status differentiation, dancing, and music.[12] Nevertheless, great care must be used in applying these cultural universals. Although music may be a cultural universal and the tango may be a Latin American form of music, the tango more specifically is Argentine. If tango music is used as part of a promotional effort in countries in Latin America that have traditionally feuded with Argentina, the effort may result in disaster for the product being promoted.

Many decision criteria have been put forward to assist the international marketing manager in adapting cultural universals. Even these rather broad criteria must be used with caution, however. Nothing changes quite so rapidly, or dramatically, as the international environment. Decision criteria that worked for a high growth period in Japan almost certainly will not work for a declining growth, or negative growth period in that same country.

The social environment of international marketing.   In all societies of the world, there are clear social classes. Mankind seems always to find some means to rank individuals and groups, whether by birthright, money, or dedication to party ideology. Also, there are few, if any, countries in the world where the businessman, as a businessman, enjoys the country's highest status. Nevertheless, there are countries wherein the owners of major business enterprises have very high status within their society. This anomaly can usually be traced to the fact that the businessman as an individual has high status aside from participation in the business world. Such status derives from birthright, and a good education that often reflects family position. Higher education is often reserved for those with high social status, and the type of education tends to be in liberal arts, medicine, and law, even if the latter two are not practiced. This is the traditional notion of education for living the good life. As a result, the percentage of the population with higher education is small and generally not trained in fields directly applicable to business.

In the United States, ethnic barriers to entry to the higher positions of a business firm are breaking down rapidly, but this is not the case in many foreign nations. The emerging middle class in the developing areas of the world typically is not gaining access to the upper classes and is struggling to define what the outward manifestations of its newly emerging middleclass level should be. This has decided implications for marketing abroad. Just as markets can be segmented by income, geography, and so forth, in most foreign markets it is clearly necessary to segment markets by social class. Of course, as in the United States, income will not always decide the issue.

INTERNATIONAL MARKETING STRATEGY

Given appropriate organization and market identification with full recognition of the cultural and social norms that exist, firms interested in the international arena must next formulate and implement marketing strategy. As in the case of domestic marketing, this involves key decisions in the product, pricing, promotion, and distribution areas. Each of these decision areas is discussed below in the context of international marketing.

Product decisions. A marketing firm cannot make the assumption that it can sell as many, say, carpet cleaners in France per capita as it can in the United States. For one major reason, the French tend not to use carpets as floor coverings, nor do the Italians for that matter. The Dutch do make heavy use of carpeting and there the U.S. carpet cleaner manufacturer may well sell more carpet cleaners per capita than in the United States. Similarly, a coffee percolator manufacturer in America cannot assume that the per capita use of percolators in Great Britain can be developed on the level that the per capita use of coffee there would indicate. The reason is that the British are mostly tea drinkers, and those who have adopted coffee make it like tea and favor instant coffee. Furthermore, British coffee drinkers tend to use as much sugar and milk in their coffee as they use in their tea. This hides the flavor of coffee to the point where the difference between percolator coffee flavor and instant coffee flavor is undetectable.

The Campbell Soup Company's mistakes in the transfer of its products to overseas markets have drawn considerable comment. Believing that Britain would be an easy market to enter, Campbell discovered that similar language did not mean similar usage of common products. A competitor, Heinz, had been there earlier and sold its soups in the British-preferred, ready-to-eat form. Campbell failed to inform the British housewife how to prepare its condensed soup; repeat sales were not spectacular. Fortunately, Campbell was persistent and made the necessary changes in its British marketing plans.[13]

Other adaptation problems have been encountered. General Foods found that while "there's always room for Jell-O" in the United States, no one in England seemed to have room for it. After an unprofitable introduction, market research attempted to discover what went wrong. It was determined that the British prefer gelatine in solid wafers or cakes. Jell-O's powdered form was so unfamiliar that it was unacceptable. After significant losses and unsuccessful remedial promotion, Jell-O gave up the British market.[14]

Apart from the increasing tendency to halt or restrict imports through the establishment of common markets or other forms of regional integration, there seems to be a pattern of changing location of production facilities as a product moves from the new product to standardized product stage. Figure 10.6 sheds some additional light on Vernon's Product Cycle Model described earlier in this chapter.

Just as factor allocations and the resulting factor cost differentials have their place in international trade theory, so do they also affect product design and acceptance. An example from the design of competing commercial aircraft may serve as an illustration. When the British were designing their Comet jet airplane, labor cost and fuel cost were major considerations. The British placed their jet engines inside the wing. The effect was lowered wind resistance, which required less fuel, but more labor in repair as the engines were less accessible than externally mounted engines. The American design incorporated externally slung engines with poorer fuel economy, but much-reduced time expense in maintenance and repair. Fuel costs were much higher in the United States, but labor cost was much lower.[15]

Apart from the normal nontariff requirements placed on foreign products, some of which are strictly enforced regarding size and shape, there are serious compatibility problems that can emerge as a result of product design. Some European cars, for example, have notorious problems with the severe road heat in American summers and subzero temperatures in midwinter. One problem that has already hindered U.S. exports and will become an even greater problem in the near future is compatibility of measurement systems. With most of the world on the metric system, the inches-and-pounds system (derived originally from the British) puts American exports at a considerable disadvantage.

Pricing decisions.   A recent article, based on a doctoral dissertation study of intracorporate pricing, concluded:

Two opposing trends appear on a definite collision course. As a multinational firm's size and percentage of international operations increase, there is an increasing preference for, and use of, cost-oriented systems. As government

FIGURE 10.6.
A TRADE CYCLE MODEL

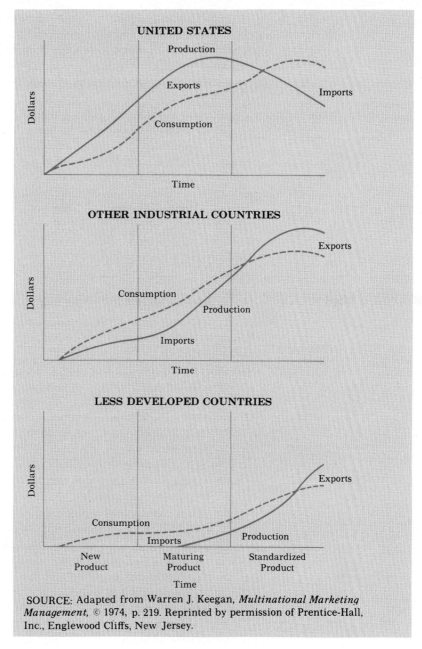

UNITED STATES

OTHER INDUSTRIAL COUNTRIES

LESS DEVELOPED COUNTRIES

SOURCE: Adapted from Warren J. Keegan, *Multinational Marketing Management,* © 1974, p. 219. Reprinted by permission of Prentice-Hall, Inc., Englewood Cliffs, New Jersey.

awareness and concern over transfer pricing increase, there is an increasing preference for (and often laws requiring) market-oriented systems. Thus it appears that in still another area a head-on collision is inevitable between the big multinational firms and sovereign state governments.[16]

Although the above comments do not cover all aspects of the pricing of goods in international marketing, they do point out the complexity of the issue and the concern host governments have over pricing policies of foreign firms. Foreign governments even become concerned over the U.S. government's attitudes toward pricing activities of U.S. firms that have international sales. When IBM, in response to U.S. government pressure, offered its equipment on a purchase basis as well as through leasing, and raised its lease prices as part of developing a purchase price schedule, the British government stepped in. British calculations indicated that the price increases would cost the U.K. several millions of dollars per year. The British government then forced IBM to roll back its price increase for the U.K. market.

Since prices affect so many of the publics that the firm faces—its local and international customers, the customers of competitors, its employees, its stockholders, and the various governments with which it deals—pricing becomes a critical area of international marketing. Of course, there is the same standard list of considerations in international pricing as there is in pricing for domestic markets. Cost considerations, which are usually a floor in all price determinations, are important, but have the added factors indicated in Table 10.1 This price escalation situation is by no means uncommon. There are many examples that would be much worse in terms of price escalation. In this example, the duty was only 20 percent. In the case of an American import of cotton goods, the tariff is 40 percent.

Perhaps because of the heavy cost element in many goods in international marketing, there is a tendency for firms to use a cost-plus method of pricing. This system, while simple to calculate and manage, has one severe disadvantage; it gives no consideration to the workings of the market. There is no consideration of the possibility of pricing at a lower level and taking advantage of price elasticity of demand to increase revenues. Nor is there any consideration of the possibility of inelastic demand, which would enable the firm to increase prices without generating a proportional reduction in quantity demanded.

Other issues emerge in pricing for international marketing. There is considerable interest in the workings of "transfer pricing," which is the pricing of goods sold from one plant of a corporation to another. There are many opportunities to avoid taxes and high duties through the use of careful transfer pricing. If, for example, a firm has to ship some parts for assembly to a subsidiary in a country with a corporate income tax that is very low, say 10 percent, and its home tax rate is 50 percent, headquarters would benefit if it sold to its subsidiary at a price below cost at home. It would thereby incur a loss at home, which would reduce its taxes at home, and it would generate very high profit abroad where the tax rate is low.

For finished goods there is the possibility of selling abroad at a lower price than the firm uses at home so as to take advantage of an opportunity to get rid of surplus production at any price. This practice is relatively common. It is known as "dumping," and is illegal. Even though this may benefit the consumer of such goods, through lower

TABLE 10.1.
PRICE ESCALATION IN
INTERNATIONAL MARKETING

Item			As Percent of F.O.B. Price
F.O.B. Kansas City		$10,090	100.0
Freight to New Orleans	$ 110		
Freight to Encarnación, Paraguay	1,897		
Counselor Invoices	21		
Port Toulaye	6		
Forwarding Fee	8		
Insurance ($19,000 value)	383		
Port Charge	434		
Documentation	3		
Total Shipping Charges		2,859	28.0
C.I.F. Value		$12,949	
Duty (20.0% on C.I.F. value)		2,590	26.0
Distributor Markup (10.0%)		1,553	15.0
Dealer Markup (25.0%)		4,295	43.0
Total Retail Price		$21,387	214.0

NOTE: This is an example of a shipment of 1,908 cases of assorted household chemicals, weighing 35,000 pounds and measuring 40 cubic feet. The shipment was sent by truck to New Orleans, by ocean freighter to Buenos Aires, Argentina, and by river steamer to Encarnación, Paraguay. Total transit time from Kansas City to distributor was six to ten weeks.

SOURCE: Cook Chemical Company, Kansas City, Missouri, as presented in: Warren J. Keegan, *Multinational Marketing Management* © 1974, p. 261. Prentice-Hall, Inc., Englewood Cliffs, New Jersey.

prices, it is certainly injurious to local competitors who sell such goods.

The recent emergence of inflation and fluctuating currencies has added significantly to the problems of those who must decide on prices for goods in international markets. Differential rates of inflation in each of the various countries with which a firm may trade can cause errors in pricing. These errors may either make goods unacceptable due to high prices, or cause the home firm to lose all of its profit or more, through pricing at a level that does not cover the changing relationships in the value of each country's currency.

It is for this reason perhaps, among others, that oil nations talk of not accepting either British pounds or U.S. dollars for their oil. Both countries have experienced high rates of inflation with lagging devaluation. Therefore, an oil nation that receives a payment of $1,000 a year now may find that this $1,000 will only buy $850 worth of goods from some third country, say Germany.

These situations are indicative of the problems in international pricing. They illustrate why it is that foreign governments are so very interested in what international firms are using as a price setting mechanism and why firms must be aware of possible home and foreign government reactions to price setting.

Promotional decisions.   Probably more errors are made in attempting to promote a product in a foreign country than in all the other marketing strategy variables combined. The amount of promotional effort that is required is clearly a function of the stage of economic development. In many developing countries, very little advertising is employed simply because there is such a scarcity of many goods and such a scarcity of buying power that a sellers market exists. Surely, there is not much benefit to be gained from promoting a product that is sold out the first day the month's allocation arrives.

Media selection is a problem that must be worked out country by country. There are still many countries where large percentages of the populations cannot read. Some countries have no television, and, in some countries with television, advertising is prohibited, or severely constrained. According to a United Nations study, in twenty-one of fifty-eight major countries in the world, no television advertising is permitted. Still other countries have no national language and may have over forty languages in use in various areas. Thus, in some areas of the world, effective promotion for mass markets may be restricted to the message on the label or package.

There is some evidence to indicate that advertising expenditures as a percentage of GNP grows as GNP per capita grows. When GNP per capita exceeds about $4,000, however, advertising expenditures as a percentage of GNP declines. This has been the case in the United States. The United States has always had the highest advertising expenditure in the world in both absolute dollars and as a proportion of GNP. By the late 1960s, the rate of expenditures on advertising declined. Countries such as West Germany, Jamaica, and Switzerland now spend more per capita than the United States. Still, the United States and Canada spent 61 percent of the world's advertising expenditures, and all of Europe spent only 28 percent. These three, therefore, accounted for nearly 90 percent of the world advertising expenditures.[17]

Even though the principles of effective communication may be the same the world over, the specific message and media strategy must be carefully reviewed even from region to region within a country. The prevailing opinion in the 1950s was that these strategies were best left to individuals within the region or country in question. Since that time there has been considerable interest and some success in generating universal ads. Pepsi and Coca Cola, for example, have found fairly general acceptance of their slogans "Come alive with Pepsi," and "Coke refreshes you best." Pepsi had a problem in Germany, however, as the slogan translated to "come alive out of the grave."[18]

Insistence on retention of a given trademark can cause problems also. Colgate-Palmolive maintained its trademark "CUE" for toothpaste in France where "cue" is a pornographic word.[19] Even the highly successful Esso campaign, "Put a tiger in your tank," caused problems of translation in France. The French word for "tank" is *reservoir,* which, when placed in context was so highly suggestive that "motor" or *moteur* was substituted. Esso also missed a cultural identification issue when it took its campaign to Thailand. There the tiger has no connotation of power, and the ad was not effective.[20] A fashion model may add allure to women's make-up products in the United States, but such an appeal would have negative connotations in Belgium, where there are few fashion models and their profession is not considered honorable.

The issue of universal advertising versus narrow specific treatment of this important communication device for the international marketing firm has not been settled. All that is clear is that there are many universal opportunities, but that they need to be rigorously reviewed by nationals first.

Channel decisions. Many times the channel decision is left to the discretion of the local marketing manager. Nevertheless, this highly important part of the marketing mix can never be treated as a poor relative to the other strategy variables. The major international firm is at a clear advantage in the area of channel decision making over the smaller firm, since it can bring much more talent to bear on the issue. It is often said that the major reason that small firms do not enter into international marketing is their inability to establish effective channels of distribution for their goods. It is also often said that most of the competition a firm faces is encountered in the channel. Therefore, this aspect of the marketing mix is extremely important to the success of the firm.

Incorrectly identifying the motivational characteristics of consumers can bring about the same sort of problems in channel use as was previously described in the promotion of a product. One company operating abroad found that its pride in rapid delivery of parts via radio-equipped vans was of little consequence to buyers whose principal motivation was price. The U.S. firm's competitors made no deliveries at all, but were careful to pass the cost savings along to their customers. The U.S. firm found that they were giving too much service. They were treating their foreign customers as they would treat their U.S. customers.

Even though it is usually more cost effective to seek a channel or create a channel to reach the largest number of potential customers possible, such an attempt in a country with long and well-established channels that are held together by close personal relationships may spell disaster.

For example, this is the situation in Spain. One major U.S. producer of mixed feed and poultry decided to enter the Spanish market. Despite advice to the contrary from local businessmen, the firm insisted on establishing a wholly-owned subsidiary. Operating independently, the production facilities were readied and began producing. Unfortunately, no sales were made. The local producers of grains and poultry were a closely knit group, and the group feeling was reinforced through generations of contact and cooperation. Still trying to "go it alone," the subsidiary bought chicken farms. The firm then had a market for its feed, but no market for its chickens. Last reports indicate that the firm was busy buying restaurants in Spain.[21]

It is generally conceded in the United States that the variables of the marketing mix can, to a degree, substitute one for another. That is, holding price constant and increasing advertising may produce the same results at the same cost as reducing price and holding advertising expense constant. Often, this sort of decision can be left to the discretion of the channel leader. Experimentation is conducted in the United States on the varying efficacy of such manipulations. Many firms, after reaching a decision as to what is the best course of action for them, however, simply stay with a given mix. Furthermore, they will often force this U.S. mix on their foreign channel leaders.

One German subsidiary of a major U.S. firm was ordered by its parent firm to spend the same percentage of sales on advertising as the parent, and furthermore, to spend it in the same way. Not only was there general disagreement with funding the advertising budget as a percentage of sales, but this subsidiary was attempting to break into a new market dominated by a national competitor. Its sales were small and, therefore, the dollar amount it could spend was correspondingly small. Channel leaders might have reacted to price concessions. They did not, however, react to small advertising budgets.

What all this points out is that perhaps those who feel that most of the competition is met in the channels are correct, and that the firm engaging in international marketing must consider the local channel leaders and the possible effects on the retailer or final consumer of trying to "buck the system."

Channel credit is becoming an increasingly important competitive variable in international marketing. U.S. manufacturers are finding that to get into the appropriate channel for their goods, they may have to compensate for their middlemen's lack of capital by putting merchandise on consignment, providing floorplan financing, or even providing long-term credit. Foreign suppliers are accustomed to this and have often displaced or kept out U.S. goods by their provision of such credit to middlemen. In addition to the need for providing credit to middlemen, more and more U.S. firms are learning that they have to provide credit to consumers overseas as well as at home. This is, of course, a risky business. No manufacturer wants to lose his profits through uncollectable debts, but there are offsetting benefits apart from increased sales. In many countries, consumer credit may carry interest rates in excess of 3 percent per month. U.S. firms are masters at credit management at home. The indications are that credit management principles are universal. The firm should investigate the possibility of a separate organization to provide credit to middlemen and consumers as a necessary marketing tool.

SUMMARY

To provide a better understanding of the scope and importance of international marketing, this chapter has been devoted to a discussion of the international market environment and the special problems associated with the development of international marketing programs by United States business firms. In the chapter, special attention was given to international marketing trends, the rationale for international trade, and the task of developing international programs.

To summarize the major ideas presented in this chapter, American firms have been negligent in taking advantage of existing international opportunities. This is evident in spite of the fact that population increases and rates of economic growth overseas far exceed the increases in the United States. To illustrate this important point, the U.S. Department of Commerce has estimated that over 90 percent of American firms with products that have international trade potential do nothing to capitalize on that potential.

Yet, there are numerous examples of major firms in the United States that are becoming truly multinational in their sales, production, financing, and general outlook. Rising incomes and increasing population elsewhere in the world mean rising demand. This increased demand will be felt by firms in the United States whether or not they engage in international marketing themselves. Raw material inputs will become scarcer as foreign firms compete for scarce inputs. The United States will need to import more goods and will therefore need to export more goods in order to pay for these increased imports. In the face of such opportunities and critical needs, the American firm will find itself increasingly involved in international marketing.

QUESTIONS FOR DISCUSSION

1. Briefly analyze the major international trade trends that have evolved over the past two or three decades. How do you account for the shifts in trade that have occurred?

2. What is the rationale for international trade? Explain in detail.

3. Compare and contrast export entry in the international area with the investment method of entry. Are these modes of entry really alternatives? In the future, which of these two will be the most important? Explain.

4. What special problems does the international marketing firm encounter in its relationships with foreign governments? What special problems does it encounter with its own government? Explain.

5. Explain the differences between tariff and nontariff barriers to trade. Which of these two is most commonly used? Why?

6. Discuss the role of marketing research in the international arena. How does marketing research differ in the international environment from the research conducted in the domestic environment?

7. Identify and describe three methods of organization that may be used by firms interested in entering the international arena. Which one of these

appears to be best for a company manufacturing a wide line of consumer goods? Which would be best for an industrial goods manufacturer?

8. What is the importance of the cultural environment in the field of international marketing? Compare and contrast the cultural environment in the United States with the cultural environment in a country like England.

9. Compare and contrast international marketing strategy with domestic marketing strategy for each of the four major marketing strategy variables.

10. What does the future hold for American firms entering the international arena? Do world conditions suggest that American firms must engage in international marketing in order to survive?

NOTES

[1] C. Tait Ratcliffe, "Approaches to Distribution in Japan," in *The Japanese Economy in International Perspective,* ed. by Isaiah Frank (Baltimore: The Johns Hopkins University Press, 1975), pp. 101–133.

[2] David Belli and Julius Freidlin, "U.S. Direct Investment Abroad in 1970," *Survey of Current Business* (Washington, D.C.: U.S. Department of Commerce, October, 1971), p. 28.

[3] Fred A. McKenzie, *The American Invaders* (New York: Street and Smith, 1901), p. 31.

[4] *Ibid.,* p. 157.

[5] J. J. Servan-Schreiber, *The American Challenge* (New York: Atheneum, 1968).

[6] U.S., Congress, Senate, Committee on Finance, *The Multinational Corporation and the World Economy,* February 26, 1973, p. 14.

[7] *Ibid.,* p. 15.

[8] John Caffyn and Nigel Rogers, "British Reactions to T.V. Commercials," *Journal of Advertising Research,* Vol. X, No. 3 (June, 1970), p. 27.

[9] David Ricks, *et al., International Business Blunders* (Columbus, Ohio: Grid, Inc., 1974).

[10] Elmo C. Wilson, "Sizing Up Overseas Markets," *Printer's Ink* (June 5, 1964), p. 35.

[11] Arvind V. Phatak, *Managing Multinational Corporations* (New York: Praeger, 1974), pp. 170–188.

[12] George P. Murdock, "The Common Denominator of Culture," in *The Science of Man in World Crisis,* ed. by Ralph Linton (New York: Columbia University Press, 1945), p. 145.

[13] "The Thirty Million Dollar Lesson," *Sales Management* (March 1, 1967), pp. 31–38.

[14] Ricks, *et al., International Business Blunders,* p. 17.

[15] Warren J. Keegan, *Multinational Marketing Management* (Englewood Cliffs, New Jersey: Prentice-Hall, Inc., 1974), pp. 273–274.

[16]Jeffrey S. Arpan, "International Intracorporate Pricing: Non-American Systems and Views," *Journal of International Business Studies* (Spring, 1972), p. 18.

[17]*World Advertising Expenditures (1968)* (New York: International Advertising Association, 1970).

[18]Ricks, *et al., International Business Blunders,* p. 11.

[19]*Ibid.,* p. 12.

[20]John K. Ryans, "Is It Too Soon to Put a Tiger in Every Tank?", *Columbia Journal of World Business* (March-April, 1969), pp. 69–75.

[21]"The Spanish-American Business Wars," *Worldwide P & I Planning* (May-June, 1971), pp. 30–40, as cited in Ricks, *et al., International Business Blunders,* pp. 24–25.

SUGGESTED READINGS

Baker, James C. and John K. Ryans, Jr., *Multinational Marketing* (Columbus, Ohio: Grid, Inc., 1975).

Kacker, M. P., "Export-Oriented Product Adaptation," *Management International Review,* Vol. 15 (1975), pp. 61–70.

Kacker, M. P., "SMM's Multinational Marketing Guide," *Sales and Marketing Management* (December 8, 1975), pp. 49–57.

Keegan, Warren J., "Multinational Marketing: The Headquarters Role," *Columbia Journal of World Business* (January-February, 1971), pp. 85–90.

Leff, Nathaniel H., "Multinational Corporate Pricing Strategy in the Developing Countries," *Journal of International Business Studies* (Fall, 1975), pp. 55–64.

McIntyre, David, "Multinational Positioning Strategy," *Columbia Journal of World Business* (Fall, 1975), pp. 106–110.

McNown, R., "Impact of Currency Depreciation and International Markets on U.S. Inflation," *Quarterly Review of Economics and Business* (Winter, 1975), pp. 7–14.

Ricks, David, *et al., International Business Blunders (Columbus, Ohio: Grid, Inc., 1974).*

Wright, Richard W. and Colin S. Russell, "Joint Ventures in Developing Countries," *Columbia Journal of World Business* (Summer, 1975), pp. 74–80.

11

THE SOCIOCULTURAL ENVIRONMENT

11

THE SOCIOCULTURAL ENVIRONMENT

The consumer along with marketing institutions interfaces with the sociocultural environment. The consumer is a member of a family; he may belong to various social, religious, and community organizations; he has associates at his place of work, as well as a circle of friends and neighbors; he also has one or more reference groups, is a part of a social class, perhaps a subculture, and lives in a society with a variety of cultural features. This chapter focuses on the sociocultural environment as it affects people in their roles as buyers.

DIMENSIONS OF THE SOCIOCULTURAL ENVIRONMENT

From the above introduction, it should be apparent that the various dimensions of the sociocultural environment are extremely important to an understanding of marketing. Because of the prominence of the consumer in contemporary marketing practice, this environment significantly influences the scope and direction of marketing programs and strategies that are executed in the marketplace. As noted in earlier chapters, the adoption of the marketing philosophy of management requires the acceptance of a consumer orientation. In implementing this philosophy, forward looking managers must commit themselves to the task of discovering consumer needs and matching those needs with an appropriate offering of goods and services.

A second factor, the rise of consumerism, has also increased the interest of businessmen and public officials in understanding the consumer. Since the mid-1960s, there has been a continuously growing concern for the welfare of the buying public. To make intelligent suggestions for changes in nutritional labeling practices and laws, for example, it is necessary to determine what consumers believe to be the weaknesses of existing practices and laws.

Since the behavior of consumers is shaped and adjusted by their sociocultural environment, this chapter is devoted to an investigation of this environment and its impact on buying behavior. Figure 11.1 illustrates the more specific dimensions of the sociocultural environment. The top half of the figure presents the broader dimensions, *culture* and *social class;* the balance of the exhibit shows more explicit groups, *reference groups* and the *family.* Each of these dimensions will be discussed in this chapter in the order presented in Figure 11.1.

Before examining these four groups, it is important to note that understanding of the sociocultural environment has been developed in the fields of anthropology, sociology, and psychology—aggregately referred to as the behavioral sciences. *Anthropology* is the study of whole societies, or major segments of a society, such as culture, sub-

FIGURE 11.1.
DIMENSIONS OF THE
SOCIOCULTURAL
ENVIRONMENT

Culture
Social Class
Reference Groups
The family

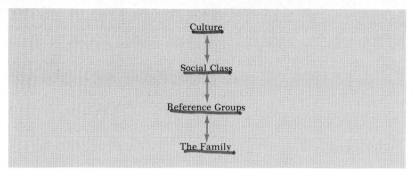

culture, and symbolism. *Sociology,* on the other hand, concentrates on somewhat smaller societal groupings such as social class, reference groups, and the family. *Psychology* focuses on the individual, and his learning, perception, personality, attitudes, and motivation. Since the broad subject of individual buyer behavior is beyond the scope of this chapter, the discussion here will draw most heavily on the contributions of anthropology and sociology in the analysis of the sociocultural environment.

CULTURES AND SUBCULTURES

Culture may be defined as the aggregate of values, norms, and customs that are imparted to individuals in a given society. This definition connotes a relatively nebulous, but very pervasive force in a society. Since much of man's behavior is prescribed by culture, its study is particularly significant to understanding consumer behavior. Marketing managers must assess whether their new product, adjusted advertising, and other decisions fit the existing boundaries of the customs of the market they are trying to reach. Consequently, in attempting to discern the actions of a buyer, it is logical to begin by scrutinizing the culture that has been absorbed by him.

GENERAL
CULTURAL
CHARACTERISTICS

The significance of culture as a determinant of behavior warrants a look at the general characteristics of the phenomenon. These are discussed below in the context of learned behavior, value inculcation, need satisfiers, and cultural change.

Learned behavior. Culture consists of learned responses to various stimuli. The process of learning one's culture is termed *socialization.* When a person learns a new or second culture, the process is called *acculturation.* An individual's social class, reference group(s), and family all contribute to that person's socialization and acculturation.

Cultural lessons are given to a small child by his parents and older siblings. They provide models of what is "right" or "wrong" for each of the sexes. Young boys, for example, may be taught that playing with dolls is frowned upon, even though the little girl next door is encouraged to act out this motherly role. On the other hand, the aspiring man may be rewarded for masculine behavior, such as playing ball, or role-playing a traditionally male position in society. It should be noted, however, that sex roles and the role training that develops them are changing.

The learning of culturally appropriate behavior continues throughout an individual's life. Research findings suggest that the cultural elements learned early in life are more difficult to change than those acquired in later years. This tendency has substantial implications for marketing; product and promotional efforts designed to alter deeply ingrained cultural values may be worthless. Despite this barrier, various marketing efforts, particularly advertising, can occupy a significant position in the socialization process.

Value inculcation. Implicit in the recognition of culture as a learned phenomenon is the knowledge that it is imparted from one generation to the next by parents, various groups, and institutions. The traditions associated with holidays such as Christmas and Thanksgiving, for example, are passed on to children from their family as well as other sources.

This imparting of values, however, is not as effortless as it might appear on the surface. It is a recognizable fact that the younger generation is prone to question the values of their elders. Although this is a natural inclination, it is also a function of different lifetime experiences. People born since 1940 in the United States did not experience the Depression or World War II, and, therefore, have a tendency to be less materialistic and patriotic than older Americans. Their exposure to events such as the civil rights movement, nuclear power, and the importance of ecology tends to make the nation's youth place more emphasis on understanding, disarmament, and environmental quality.

The marketing significance of value inculcation is demonstrated in a variety of ways. Depending upon the market they wish to reach, firms may formulate marketing strategy variables harmonious with a particular generation, or they may attempt to bridge the generation gap. Advertisements, for example, highlighting love, humanity, and communication ("You've got a lot to live") are intended to communicate product information to younger consumers.

Need satisfiers. Specific features of a culture cease to exist when they fail to be gratifying to at least a portion of society. Social fraternities, by way of illustration, experienced severe membership declines until recent years because of their failure to meet basic secondary needs of college men. Through adjustments in the nature and image of these social institutions, many young men now perceive the fraternity as a group with which they would like to identify.

In a more traditional marketing sense, it is easy to identify products that are already, or likely to become, extinct—buggy whips, wringer washing machines, and gas-guzzling automobiles. In the case of the latter product, automobile marketers recognize that many consumer needs would be best satisfied through offering more economical forms of transportation.

Cultural change.   Historically, culture has been thought to change in an evolutionary fashion. As noted in Chapter 1, however, Toffler and others have suggested that accelerated technological change in today's developed nations is producing reverberations throughout these societies in terms of altered values and customs.[1] Table 11.1 highlights a few of the traditional American values that are adjusting to new positions. A number of these values will be examined in greater detail in a later section of this chapter.

While certainly contributing to changes in culture, marketers should be primarily concerned with the adjustments in their efforts suggested by these changes. They must be in a position to develop new promotional appeals, recommend new products, and propose other modifications in marketing strategy to better satisfy the changing cultural values.

FEATURES OF THE AMERICAN CULTURE

Given the base provided by the previously discussed cultural characteristics, some of the major features of the American culture can now be examined. Since this culture is a "melting pot," it is composed of the many subcultures, which will be discussed later in this chapter. Nevertheless, a number of universals hold true for a wide spectrum of the society. Some of the features presented in succeeding paragraphs are permanent, deep-seated elements, whereas others are of a more recent vintage.

Religiosity.   Attitudes toward interpersonal relations, work, and morality are encompassed under the term religiosity. The major faiths in this country incorporate the Puritan ethic and its belief in the worth

TABLE 11.1.
SELECTED AMERICAN VALUES
UNDERGOING CHANGE

Traditional Value	Adjusted Value
Husband-dominated family	Family partnership
Institutionalized religious beliefs	Individualized religious beliefs
Saving	Spending
Sexual chastity	Sexual freedom
Risk taking	Security

of the individual, hard work, thriftiness in savings and purchasing, and wealth accumulation. Religiosity has also given rise to the belief that other people and societal institutions can be trusted. The rise in consumerism can be partially attributed to the failure of businesses to live up to this ideal of trustworthiness in areas such as implied warrantees, product performance, and advertising content.

The impact of religiosity is not limited to those who are members of a church. In fact, many of the beliefs growing out of our Judaic-Christian heritage are now so much a part of American society that they are accepted by nonreligious people. In addition, various beliefs with a religious base are now protected by legal statutes. Examples of these laws include ceilings on interest rates, prohibition of liquor purchases at certain times and in certain geographical sectors of the nation, and restrictions on the opening of certain business establishments, including a variety of retail outlets, on the sabbath.

There is evidence, however, that indicates religion's influence on the American culture is waning. According to one group of respected marketing scholars, the Puritan ethic is being replaced with a "theology of pleasure." The desire for play is compatible with societal affluence, but has been curbed until recently by the Puritan ethic. Bright colors, sensuous packaging, availability of credit, and sexually based products are all examples of the recognition among marketers of the changing religious emphasis in society.[2]

Achievement.   The socialization of achievement begins at a very early age in the United States. A casual review of storybooks and observations of childhood games indicate that competitiveness and winning is generally ingrained into American children during their early years. "Keeping up with the Jones" and the desire for "more" are the adult manifestations of achievement. Products acquired by the individual are symbols to the rest of the world that the person has a certain status, or has reached a given level of achievement. For example, top executives wear Brooks Brothers suits, and successful professional athletes own multiroom mansions. Marketers, as one would expect, have long recognized the economic implications of the achievement value. The desire to wear fashionable clothing, drive a status-enhancing automobile, and own a home have been stimulated by marketing efforts.

The achievement orientation of America is by no means a cultural universal. Through content analysis of children's stories, David C. McClelland has identified nations of the world where competitiveness and aggression are virtually unknown, or at least relatively unimportant.[3] Today, there is evidence that the achievement orientation in the United States is gradually declining.

Leisure.   The typical American of today has more leisure time, and the individual's use of that time is of major significance to marketing. Not only do people have more free time, but they are also demonstrating a shift in values toward recreational leisure-time activities as opposed to the more traditional value attached to work. One implication of the preference for leisure pursuits is the consumers' demand for time-related products. The success of a number of fast-food franchisors, such as McDonald's can be in part attributed to their ability to feed people quickly and enable them to have more free time for discretionary pursuits. Food manufacturers and retailers have also responded to the demand for time saving alternatives by producing convenience and frozen foods, offering "express lane" checkout service, night hours, and ample parking.

The expansion in the time available for leisure pursuits has also stimulated the demand for goods and services that are consumed during these free hours. The growth in the market for recreational and sporting equipment are obvious examples of this phenomenon. Americans play more tennis, do more camping, and patronize health clubs in greater numbers than ever before.

Youthfulness.   Although the cultural value associated with youthfulness cannot be arbitrarily attached to a particular age group, the set of attitudes related to this value can be correlated with age. Youthfulness suggests that many of the values considered highly desirable by our society are most readily seen in young people. Physical attractiveness, intellectual talent, and athletic ability, for example, are characteristics desired by the whole society, but are most strongly exhibited in youth.

The pervasiveness of the value placed on youthfulness suggests that many older people may want to be perceived as youthful. Automobiles, clothing, personal care products, and other items have been promoted with a youthful approach, even though the average consumer could be considered middle aged. When the Ford Mustang was first introduced, for example, it was promoted as a sporty, racy, young person's automobile. The introduction of the Mustang was a true marketing success, since many of these cars were purchased. The average buyer, however, was in his forties. Although young people can provide a sizable market themselves, their larger impact on marketing is the substantial influence they have on other age groups.[4]

America's preoccupation with youthfulness is somewhat atypical in relation to other cultures of the world. Most societies value age and experience. In this country, the respect accorded to longevity has been shifted to a great extent to respect for education. Although education and the expertise that it generates is not restricted to the young, the lower age groups have more chance than their elders to develop intellectually because they have had a greater opportunity to gain a higher education.

Other features.   The above features do not exhaust the principal cultural values of the United States. Noted marketing researcher Daniel Yankelovich has conducted a major study of American values with particular attention to their influence on the buying public. These values are noted in Table 11.2.

Our ability to measure cultural features has advanced substantially in recent decades, but the marketing researcher has not fully refined his skills in this area. Nevertheless, the projection of values and their impact on society is certain to become an important requirement for the marketer of the future.

CROSSCULTURAL ANALYSIS

Crosscultural analysis is the assessment of the similarities and differences in the customs, values, and behavior among two or more societies. For firms engaged in international marketing, an appreciation of these potential differences is crucial. This need was examined in the previous chapter on the international marketing environment. As noted, a marketing effort that is well received in one country might fail in another because of different cultural values. Unfortunately, the experience of most marketing managers is limited to one culture. This suggests the importance of skilled consumer research in foreign markets, and the importance of acquiring business associates native to the country in question.

SUBCULTURES

To fully comprehend a culture as complex as that of the United States, it is essential to be familiar with its subcultures. In addition to their role in molding the total culture, subcultures may also represent significant markets for certain products. Nationality groups, geographic areas, and racial groups are probably the three major subcultural classifications in this country.

Nationality groups. Virtually every population center includes identifiable nationality groups. Irish, Italian, Mexican, and Polish people are examples. Over time, many of these groups have become acculturated through the great "melting pot" process that occurs in the United States. Others, however, have maintained many of the characteristics of their native culture. These relatively isolated nationality groups often live in a certain sector of a city and interact essentially only with other members of their group. These areas of a community become known as Chinatown or Little Italy, and provide the vehicle for cultural maintenance.

Firms interested in marketing their products to one or more of these nationalities must adapt their efforts to the special values and customs of each subculture. The success of a number of tobacco companies among certain nationalities, for example, is based upon the incorporation of subcultural realities into their marketing programs.

European subcultures are losing their identity, but other groups will probably remain distinguishable; particularly, nonwhite nationality

TABLE 11.2.
TRENDS IN AMERICAN
CULTURAL VALUES

(1) Psychology of Affluence

Trend toward physical self-enhancement: Spending more time, effort, and money on improving one's physical appearance; the things people do to enhance their looks.

Trend toward personalization: Expressing one's individuality through products, possessions, and new life styles; the need to be "a little bit different" from other people.

Trend toward physical health and well-being: The level of concern with one's health, diet, and what people do to take better care of themselves.

Trend toward new forms of materialism: The new status symbols and the extent of deemphasis on money and material possessions.

Trend toward social and cultural self-expression: The "culture explosion" and what it means to various segments of the population.

Trend toward personal creativity: The growing conviction that being "creative" is not confined to the artist. Each man can be creative in his own way, as expressed through a wide variety of activities, hobbies, and new uses of leisure time.

Trend toward meaningful work: The spread of the demand for work that is challenging and meaningful over and above how well it pays.

(2) Antifunctional Trends

Trend toward the "new romanticism": The desire to restore romance, mystery, and adventure to modern life.

Trend toward novelty and change: The search for constant change, novelty, new experience, reaction against sameness, and habit.

Trend toward adding beauty to one's daily surroundings: The stress on beauty in the home and the things people do and buy to achieve it.

Trend toward sensuousness: Placing greater emphasis on a total sensory experience—touching, feeling, smelling, and psychedelic phenomena; a moving away from the purely linear, logical, and visual.

Trend toward mysticism: The search for new modes of spiritual experience and beliefs, as typified by the growing interest in astrology.

Trend toward Introspection: An enhanced need for self-understanding and life experiences in contrast to automatic conformity to external pressures and expectations.

(3) Reaction against Complexity Trends

Trend toward life simplification: The turning away from complicated products, services and ways of life.

Trend toward return to nature: Rejection of the artificial, the "chemical," the man-made improvements on nature; the adoption of more "natural" ways of dressing, eating, and living.

Trend toward increased ethnicity: Finding new satisfactions and identifications in foods, dress, customs, and life styles of various ethnic groups such as Black, Italian, Irish, Polish, Jewish, German.

SOURCE: *Marketing News* (Mid-May, 1971), pp. 7–8.

Trend toward increased community involvement: Increasing affiliation with local, community, and neighborhood activities; greater involvement in local groups.

Trend toward greater reliance on technology versus tradition: Distrust of tradition and reputation that is based on age and experience, due to the swift tempo of change; greater confidence in science and technology.

Trend away from bigness: The departure from the belief that "big" necessarily means "good," beginning to manifest itself with respect to "big" brands, "big" stores.

(4) Trends That Move Away from Puritan Values

Trend toward pleasure for its own sake: Putting pleasure before duty; changing life styles and what that means for product usage and communication.

Trend toward blurring of the sexes: Moving away from traditional distinctions between men and women and the role each should play in marriage, work, and other walks of life.

Trend toward living in the present: Straying from traditional beliefs in planning, saving, and living for the future.

Trend toward more liberal sexual attitudes: The relaxation of sexual prohibitions and the devaluation of "virtue" in the traditional sense, among women.

Trend toward acceptance of stimulants and drugs: Greater acceptance of artificial agents (legal and illegal) for mood change, stimulation, and relaxation as opposed to the view that these should be accomplished by strength of character alone.

Trend toward relaxation of self-improvement standards: The inclination to stop working as hard at self-improvement, letting yourself be whatever you are.

Trend toward individual religions: Rejection of institutionalized religions and the substitution of more personalized forms of religious experience, characterized by the emergence of numerous small and more intimate religious sects and cults.

(5) Trends Related to Child Centeredness

Trend toward greater tolerance of chaos and disorder: Less need for schedules, routines, plans, regular shopping, and purchasing; tolerance of less order and cleanliness in the home, less regular eating and entertaining patterns.

Trend toward challenge to authority: Less automatic acceptance of the authority and "correctness" of public figures, institutions and established brands.

Trend toward rejection of hypocrisy: Less acceptance of sham, exaggeration, indirection, and misleading language.

Trends toward female careerism: Belief that homemaking is not sufficient as the sole source of fulfillment and that more challenging and productive work for the woman is needed.

Trend toward familism: Renewed faith in the belief that the essential life satisfactions stem from activities centering on the immediate family unit rather than on "outside" sources such as work and community affairs.

groups and, to a lesser extent, non-English speaking peoples. These groups will continue to exert influence on the buying behavior of their members.

Geographic areas. For a variety of reasons, various sections of the country also develop subcultural identities. Because of its history, climate, and wide-open spaces, the Southwest has a characteristic life style that emphasizes informality, newness, outdoor recreation, and hospitality. Southern Louisiana, on the other hand, has a rich heritage based on a historical background of political rule under five different countries, a number of identifiable ethnic groups, and a strong Catholic religious tradition. These characteristics have combined to build a relatively free-spirited life style marked by numerous festivals and a distinctive cuisine. On a larger geographic scale, various studies have shown that the Eastern and Western parts of the United States are more innovative and receptive toward new products than the more conservative Midwest and South. Although the mobility of Americans tends to diminish geographic differences, marketers still need to recognize their significance for specific products in specific areas.

Racial groups. Another subculture affecting consumers is racial influences. Although people with Oriental backgrounds are important in certain Western cities and Hawaii, the black subculture predominates among the nonwhite races.

Over 10 percent of the population of the United States is black. This racial group has long suffered from educational and income deprivation, but in recent years meaningful improvement has occurred in both of these areas. Nevertheless, the effects of discrimination on black Americans are so imbedded in our social fabric that the topic cannot be ignored in the analysis of black buying behavior. Since blacks have traditionally accepted white middle class values, many of the differences between black and white consumers can be traced to various restrictions placed on the former's activities. Although formal restrictions on housing purchases are now illegal, various quasi-legal and psychological means are still utilized to narrow the housing alternatives of blacks. As a result of these kinds of restrictions, as well as their cultural traditions, blacks tend to underspend in several consumption categories in comparison to whites of equal income. By the same token, blacks spend a greater proportion of their income on other categories. In comparison to whites, for example, blacks spend less on housing, food, and medical care; more on clothing and transportation, and equal amounts for home furnishings and leisure activities. Blacks also tend to be more loyal to particular brands than whites.[5]

The size and growing affluence of blacks coupled with their sociocultural differences have led many marketers to recognize this racial group as a distinct market segment. As early as the late 1960s, for example, Pepsi Cola established a "Special Markets Department" whose primary mission was the formulation of marketing strategies tailored to minority (essentially black) markets. One overt result of this development was the use of advertisements in media oriented to blacks, and the use of black models in these promotions of Pepsi.

As mentioned earlier, this racial group has traditionally accepted white middle class values—at least implicitly. In recent years, however, a proud consciousness of a black cultural heritage among America's black people has developed. A feeling of "black pride" is particularly pronounced among younger age groups. This trend suggests the possibility of an even greater degree of future distinctiveness among the black segment of the total market.

SOCIAL CLASS

What is the cause of the great similarity of thinking and behavior among students, businessmen, and retired people? It is the result of the fact that behavior, to a great extent, is a product of group membership. All individuals belong to a variety of groups, one of which is their social class.

Social classes are groupings of people whose socioeconomic status is objectively similar. An individual member of a particular class is given a certain amount of esteem based upon the degree of esteem accorded to that social class. Social classes help determine the expectations of society for groups of people. For example, the cultural values influenced by social class may determine the amount and type of education an individual receives, the recreational pursuits engaged in, and the nature of the individual's personal interactions.

Implicit in the discussion of social classes is the recognition that groups occupy inferior or superior positions in the society. To some, the idea of class systems is unpalatable. Nevertheless, class hierarchies are characteristic of all societies, including the Union of Soviet Socialist Republics, a business organization, the university, and student groups. Marketers must study social classes because they help understand the behavior of consumers.

MEASUREMENT

Various approaches have been used in an effort to define the social classes. All of these measurement methods incorporate a number of variables. The most well known approach is Warner's *Index of Status Characteristics* (ISC).[6] This index consists of four variables: *occupation, source of income, residential area,* and *type of dwelling.* Under the ISC method, ratings are obtained for each variable for an individual, the person's rating is multiplied by a weighting factor associated with each variable, the four scores are summed, and a social class is

FIGURE 11.2.
ALLOCATION OF SOCIAL
CLASSES IN THE UNITED
STATES

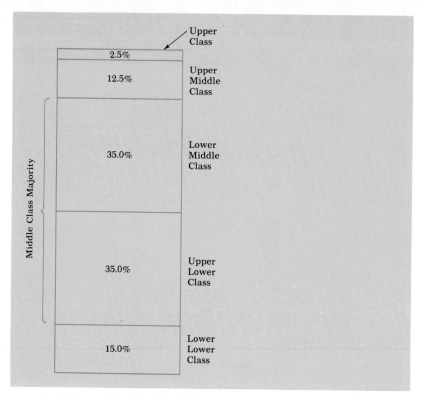

assigned to the individual. In Warner's and other indices, occupation receives more weight than other variables.

Particular note should be made of the absence of income as a variable in class determination. Often people make the casual remark that "someone" is in the upper class because that person makes a lot of money. This is not automatically true, for another individual making far less money may actually be in the upper class, and the person with the higher income a member of the middle class, because of differences in the four variables listed above. Assignment of class membership based on these variables typically places the high school teacher in a higher social class than the truck driver, even though the latter commands a higher salary.

The distribution of people in class categories depends upon the definitions used for each category. Most research has used a five or six category approach; a majority of Americans fall in the middle or lower classes, as shown in Figure 11.2. Each of these classes may be briefly characterized in the following manner:

Upper Upper:	Individuals with old wealth and family status
Lower Upper:	Very wealthy new rich
Upper Middle:	Professionals and managers
Lower Middle:	White-collar workers

Upper Lower: Blue-collar workers

Lower Lower: Unskilled laborers

IMPORTANCE TO MARKETING

Most major marketing decisions are made by individuals in the top two classes, but the primary market for most goods and services is the middle and upper lower classes. This suggests that research is necessary to uncover the differences in class behavior. Pierre Martineau in some early research described the differences in attitudes and values of the two largest classes; these are shown in Table 11.3.[7]

Varying life styles may be associated with social classes in a number of important ways. The manner in which a family spends its money, for example, often suggests both the individual emotions of family members and what they implicitly think would be appropriate for their class. The "right" clothes, house, and furniture are all symbols determined in part by class-sanctioned behavior.

Market Segments. Since there is a tendency for social classes to match class attitudes and value orientations with product market offerings that project congruent characteristics, identified social classes may be used for purposes of market segmentation. Research studies, for example, have shown that the social class concept is a useful one in the analysis of certain marketing strategies. To date, however, the potential of class segmentation is greater than its proven value. Consequently, the marketer should not expect to be able to apply social class perspectives to every situation, but instead should

TABLE 11.3.
CLASS DIFFERENCES IN ATTITUDES AND VALUES

Middle Class	Lower Class
1. Pointed to the future	Pointed to the present and past
2. Viewpoint embraces a long expanse of time	Lives and thinks in a short expanse of time
3. More urban identification	More rural identification
4. Stresses rationality	Nonrational essentially
5. Has a well-structured sense of the universe	Vague and unclear structuring of the world
6. Horizons vastly extended or not limited	Horizons sharply defined and limited
7. Greater sense of choice making	Limited sense of choice making
8. Self-confident, willing to take risks	Very much concerned with security and insecurity
9. Immaterial and abstract in thinking	Concrete and perceptive in thinking
10. Sees himself tied to national happenings	World revolves around his family and his body

use them when they will obviously aid in a particular segmentation problem.

Evaluative criteria.   The term "evaluative criteria" refers to specifications used by an individual to compare alternatives.[8] It is important to note, however, that these criteria are often related to social class in that they are shaped by an individual's basic attitudes, past experience, and interaction with that person's social environment.

Clothing, for example, offers an immediate visual symbol to the class standing of people. Various studies have shown relationships between social class and clothing. The relationship of credit card acceptance and use has also been related to social class. One study, for example, found more positive attitudes toward the use of credit among higher classes. It also found that the higher classes preferred to use bank credit cards for items such as gasoline and restaurants, whereas the lower classes were more inclined to charge durable goods and necessity items.[9] Leisure time activities are also influenced by social class. Attending a boxing match is predominantly lower class, while professional football is middle class. Bridge is a game of the upper middle and higher classes. Bingo and bowling are lower class. Even participant sports show certain class tendencies. Evaluative criteria are also used in the purchases of automobiles, home furnishings, and appliances.

Continuing controversy.   As empirical research has replaced intuition, the relationship between social class and buying behavior has become more controversial. Some experts have argued that recent changes in education, leisure time, income, and other factors have diminished the usefulness of social class analysis. Researchers and practitioners, nevertheless, continue to be fascinated with the concept of social class. The problems of using class categories as predictors of consumer behavior may arise from the fact that this is one of the most complex variables in marketing. The very existence of social classes and their impact on consumption, however, necessitates continuing examination of this phenomenon.

REFERENCE GROUPS

The third major dimension of the sociocultural environment is reference groups. This dimension represents a more direct influence on the individual than either culture or social class. Virtually all consumer attitudes and actions in selecting a product, service, or retailer are influenced to a great degree by their assessment of how other people they relate to would act in a similar situation. It follows that those individuals or groups to which a person looks for shaping personal

FIGURE 11.3.
REFERENCE GROUP
INFLUENCES ON CONSUMER
BEHAVIOR

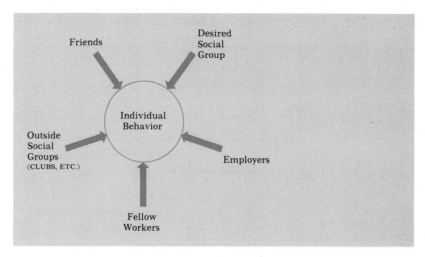

attitudes or actions are called reference groups. The consumer identifies with the thinking and norms of these groups, shown in Figure 11.3, in order to be a "member in good standing."

The typical person belongs to more than one reference group, and these groups may be of two forms. One group is *contractual* in nature; it consists of those individuals with whom a person has direct contact or group membership. An *aspiration* group is one in which an individual aspires to acquire membership. Examples of contractual groups include social friends, neighbors, and coworkers. Examples of aspirational groups are: a junior high school boy admires the high school football team and aspires to be a member of their reference group; a university accounting major aspires to be a future member of his chosen profession. In these situations, the groups may exert either a positive influence, as when an individual attempts to emulate behavior, or a negative influence, as when an individual avoids certain behavior.

IMPACT ON BEHAVIOR

Reference groups exert significant influence on individual behavior in the following forms: (1) they provide comparison points in making self-judgments; (2) they provide a frame of reference for the individual's actions; and (3) they influence the individual's aspiration levels.[10] In a classic study of reference group influence, for example, Kurt Lewin found that consumers were more inclined to alter their attitudes and behavior concerning unusual meat dishes (such as tongue, kidney, and heart) through group discussions about these items, than they were when such information was presented as a lecture.[11] The "we" feeling associated with such group interaction is a powerful change agent. In another study, Venkatesan demonstrated that consumers accept information offered by reference or peer groups and that these groups focus the attention of their members on new products and styles.[12]

IMPORTANCE TO MARKETING

Although the research on reference group influences in marketing is limited, most studies can be categorized into two types: (1) research to determine whether reference groups do in fact affect buying behavior and (2) research to isolate the consuming situations most affected by group influence.

Existence of influence.   As suggested, early studies by Lewin and Venkatesan indicate that reference groups can exert pressure on their members. Lending support to these studies is an experiment conducted by James E. Stafford. Identical brands of bread labeled M, N, O . . . were presented to people randomly selected from pre-existing reference groups. Results indicated that the groups had a definite impact on the brands of bread preferred by their members.[13] Assuming that these studies establish the reality of reference group influence, marketers will then want to identify the situations where the influence occurs.

Relevant consumption situations.   The product involved and the characteristics of the group determine the nature of group influence on buying decisions.[14] Each of these conditions will be briefly discussed.

The product category or brand type affect the amount of reference group influence. A widely cited study identified products subject to strong and weak influences.[15] Table 11.4 illustrates these products. Products with strong product or brand specifications appear to be those that people discuss with one another and have norms about. In addition, the *conspicuousness* of the product determines whether the item will be heavily influenced by reference groups. That is, inconspicuous products, like salt or canned goods have weak influences, but cigarettes and beer have high influences.

Group characteristics also determine the degree of group influence. The loyalty of the group's opinion leader toward a particular brand is likely to affect the members' opinion regarding the brand. For example, four neighbors are having coffee, and the informal leader of the group stresses the wonderful brand of ice cream recently purchased. In this situation, the brand chosen by the opinion leader is likely to be a seriously considered alternative by other group members. In addition, it has been shown that group cohesiveness affects individual choices. The fact that the four neighbors are good friends and meet daily for coffee enhances the probability that other group members will purchase the same brand of ice cream.

As was the case with social classes, the potential value to marketing of reference group analysis exceeds the realized value. Although the

TABLE 11.4.
REFERENCE GROUP
INFLUENCE ON SELECTED
PRODUCTS

	Strong Product Influence	Weak Product Influence
Strong Brand Influence	Cars Cigarettes Beer (premium or regular) Drugs	Clothing Furniture Magazines Refrigerator (type) Toilet soap
Weak Brand Influence	Air conditioners Instant coffee TV (black and white)	Soap Canned peaches Laundry soap Refrigerator (brand) Radios

SOURCE: Adapted from Foundation for Research on Human Behavior, *Group Influence in Marketing and Public Relations* (Ann Arbor, Michigan: The Foundation, 1956), p. 8.

concept is crucial to understanding consumer behavior, its practical use among marketers has been limited. Further and more extensive research is obviously needed on this topic.

THE FAMILY

The family is an institution that exists in various forms throughout the world. The *nuclear family* is characterized by face-to-face interaction on a regular basis. It serves as an earning as well as a consuming unit; the buying desires of both the individual and the family must be met from a common pool of economic resources.

In addition to its economic role, the family is the primary group in a person's acquisition of information and social norms. The social class and reference groups of the individual are in large part determined by the family. Many attitudes and values, particularly those formed in younger years, about products and consumption in general are shaped by this basic societal unit.

FUNCTIONS AND STRUCTURE

Role specialization characterizes the American family. Members of the family look upon each other as "specialists" possessing different functions, talents, and interests. Six of the basic functions of the family in the United States are:

1. to provide love and affection for family members

2. to provide security for family members, particularly younger children

3. to transmit cultural values to family members

4. to allocate economic resources to family members

5. to serve as a source of recreation for the family

6. to act as a source of knowledge, reference, and satisfaction for a diverse number of other needs.[16]

A substantial amount of interaction occurs between the individuals within a family. Husband-wife, parent-child, and child-child relationships are seen in typical families. Furthermore, two other families, those of the husband and the wife, often play a significant role in the nuclear family's behavior.

Several recent trends suggest that the American family is going through a period of momentous transition. First, as more women enter the work environment, parent-child interaction declines and pre-schools transmit many values to small children. Second, the increasing divorce rate has placed many youngsters in one-parent households, and this family instability leads to relatively more values being learned from the media and peers. Third, the geographic mobility of society has diminished the influence of the husband's and wife's family on the socialization of members of the nuclear family. Fourth, the sexual revolution, women's liberation movement, and the orientation of the youth culture has resulted in profound changes in family functions and structures. Although some authorities have argued that the family is a dying institution, environmentalists would argue that the family is simply adjusting to cultural, social, technological, and economic changes.

IMPORTANCE TO MARKETING

How important are various family members in influencing the buying decisions of the unit? Should a furniture marketer direct his promotional efforts to the wife, husband and wife, or to all family members? Should a cereal marketer advertise to small children, or to the mother? Questions such as these suggest that the marketing manager should carefully monitor the relative influence of members of the household.[17]

Husband-wife decision making.   Among spouses, consumer decision making may be wife-dominated, husband-dominated, or joint (spouses sharing equally). Traditionally, marketers have often viewed the housewife as the family purchasing agent. Today, such a view is myopic in that it presumes that since the woman of the house buys, she also decides for the family. This is not necessarily the case because all family members are consumers, and most have an influence on family buying.

Various authorities suggest that a family member's weight in decision making is determined by the relative resources (income, wealth) that he or she contributes to the unit. With this theory, it may be assumed that the husband is usually the dominant member of the household. Families with working wives, however, would be more inclined to have relatively equal power between spouses. The growth in the number of families with both spouses working indicates that the relative dominance of the husband has declined.

Race, social class, and stage in the family life cycle also affect husband-wife decision making in the United States. Wife domination is most prevalent among black families, but husband control is most prevalent among oriental-American households. White families exhibit the greatest tendency toward joint decision making.

Among social classes, joint dominance is most pronounced among the middle social class levels. The wife's decision making responsibilities are far greater at the lower, than at the upper class levels. Additional research indicates that joint decision making tends to decline as a family proceeds through its life cycle. This occurs because each spouse becomes more familiar with each other's tastes and preferences, which leads to the evolvement of greater role specialization. A later section of this chapter examines the family life cycle in greater detail. A simple example of husband-wife decision making is shown in Figure 11.4.

Role of children. As soon as they begin to master the basic rudiments of communication, children become contributors to family decision making. At an early age, children say to their parents, "I want to eat a McDonald's," or "Let's buy a new Mattell race car set." Actions of other family members, interactions with playmates, and exposure to television advertising serve as consumption stimuli. One writer has even characterized the molding of youth by television advertising as follows:

FIGURE 11.4.
HUSBAND-WIFE DECISION
MAKING

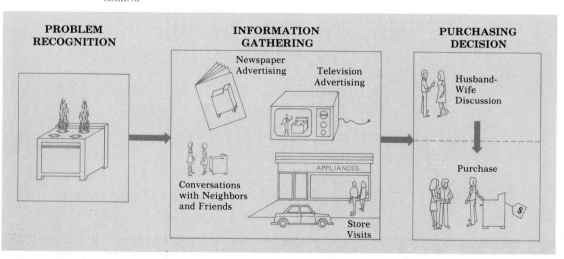

As toddlers they were handed over to the Box and were propagandized by merchandisers who, speaking directly to them, encourage them to believe in their own importance and the importance of Something Else (Something New, Improved) and in the obligation to acquire status through possession.[18]

The child centeredness of many American families often results in the parents allowing the youngster to choose a product or brand from a parental list of approved possibilities. In-store studies have shown that children, when present, influence adult purchases particularly on candy and cereal.[19] Furthermore, many authorities believe the influence of children in family decision making is underestimated. A growing number of marketing practitioners, however, appear to recognize the weight of young people. A savings institution in the Southwest, for example, recently initiated a savings club for children. The club is promoted through two television personalities who have a popular regional "kiddie" show. Although the strategy of this firm includes securing the savings accounts of young people, they are primarily planning on the ability of the kids to implicitly influence mom and dad to open an account as well.

In addition to influencing family decision making, young people are a major market by themselves for many goods. Teen-agers, for example, account for over half of the sales of records, tape recorders, soft drinks, and movie tickets in the Unites States. The parental value of wanting their children to "enjoy the good life" contributes to the power of children in many markets.

The family life cycle.   Just as human beings pass through various stages of life from infanthood to old age, so do families pass through a life cycle. Even though it does not include all possible stages, the family life cycle model of Wells and Gubar is useful to marketers:

1. Bachelor: young, single people

2. Newly married couples: young, no children

3. Full nest 1: young married couples with youngest child under six

4. Full nest 2: young married couples with youngest child six or over

5. Full next 3: older married couples with dependent children

6. Empty nest 1: older married couples with no children living at home, head of household in labor force

7. Empty nest 2: older married couples with no children living at home, head of household retired

8. Solitary survivor 1: older single person in labor force

9. Solitary survivor 2: older single person retired.[20]

The utility of the family life cycle to marketing managers stems from its ability to pinpoint probable consumption patterns of families in the various stages. By way of illustration, newly married couples can be compared with full nest 1 families (at least one child under six). Even though they have limited purchasing experience, the newlyweds would be likely to have more discretionary income because both spouses probably work. The full nest family, on the other hand, would be less likely to have both partners working and would therefore be expected to have less discretionary income. Furthermore, the existence of children will alter consumption patterns and plans. Table 11.5 gives an overview of the financial characteristics and purchasing patterns of each stage of the life cycle.

TABLE 11.5
OVERVIEW OF THE LIFE CYCLE

Life-Cycle Stage	Financial Characteristics	Purchasing Patterns
Bachelor	Few financial burdens; fashion opinion leaders; recreation-oriented	Basic kitchen equipment; basic furniture; cars; equipment for the mating game; vacations
Newly married couples	Better off financially than they will be in the near future; highest purchase rate; highest average purchasers of durables	Cars; refrigerators; stoves; sensible and durable furniture; vacations
Full nest 1	Home purchasing at peak; liquid assets low; dissatisfied with financial position and amount of money saved; interested in new products; like advertised products	Washers; dryers; TVs; baby food; chest rubs and cough medicines; vitamins; dolls; wagons; sleds; skates
Full nest 2	Financial position better; some wives work; less influenced by advertising; buy larger-sized packages and multiple-unit "deals"	Many foods; cleaning materials; bicycles; music lessons; pianos
Full nest 3	Financial position even more improved; more wives work; some children get jobs; hard to influence with advertising; high average purchase of durables	New, more expensive furniture; automobile travel; nonnecessary appliances; boats; dental services; magazines
Empty nest 1	Home ownership at peak; most satisfied with financial position and money saved; interested in travel, recreation, self-education; make gifts and contributions; not interested in new products	Vacations; luxuries; home improvements
Empty nest 2	Drastic cut in income; keep home	Medical appliances; medical care; products that aid health, sleep, digestion
Solitary survivor, working	Income still good, but likely to sell home	
Solitary survivor, retired	Same medical and product needs as other solitary-survivor group; drastic cut in income; special need for attention, affection, security	

SOURCE: William D. Wells and George Gubar, "Life Cycle Concept in Marketing Research," *Journal of Marketing Research*, Vol. 3 (November, 1966), pp. 355–363.

SUMMARY

This chapter has concentrated on one of the major macro environments of marketing—the sociocultural environment. This dimension of the environment recognizes that the cornerstone of marketing is an understanding of buyer behavior. This behavior is influenced by the four components of the sociocultural environment: culture and subculture, social class, reference groups, and the family.

Culture, the broadest and most nebulous category of group behavior, refers to learned patterns of behavior shared by members of a society. America's culture is characterized by change in basic values and institutions. Within this culture are subcultures that can be identified on a nationality, geographic, and racial basis. These groupings help mold the total culture and also represent distinct markets in themselves.

Controversy surrounds the degree of significance of social classes to marketing. Representing the summation of a number of separate variables, social class analysis has potential usefulness to marketers in market segmentation and selected evaluative situations (for example, choice of recreational pursuits). Reference groups are generally smaller than social classes and represent a more direct input to an individual's buying patterns. In their role of setting norms and customs for members, reference groups are particularly relevant to marketing in selected consumption situations.

The most basic and influencial group in society is the family. This small but complex unit filters many of the group influences on the individual. Over time, family consumption decisions have become more jointly based, with children exercising increased power.

QUESTIONS FOR DISCUSSION

1. List the four major groups that compose the sociocultural environment. What are the essential differences between each of these groups in terms of their influence on the consumer?

2. Explain what is meant by the fact that culture is learned.

3. Traditionally, culture has been thought to change in an evolutionary fashion. Some authorities, however, argue that this is no longer true in this country as we are now experiencing accelerated cultural change. Comment.

4. What are the marketing implications of our society's (a) achievement and (b) leisure orientations?

5. Blacks probably represent the most important subculture in America. Holding the income variable constant, how do the buying patterns of blacks differ from those of their white counterparts?

6. Discuss the "evaluative criteria" related to social class that are used by individuals to compare consumption alternatives.

7. Does an individual have to be a member of a group to have it serve as a referent for his behavior? Explain.

8. Discuss some of the major trends that are affecting the American family. What do you foresee as the implications of these trends for marketing?

9. Within the American family, what partner dominates consumption decisions? What role do children typically play?

10. What is the family life cycle? What is the value of this concept to marketing?

NOTES

[1] See Alvin Toffler, *Future Shock* (New York: Random House, 1970).

[2] James F. Engel, David T. Kollat, and Roger D. Blackwell, *Consumer Behavior* (2nd ed.; New York: Holt, Rinehart and Winston, Inc., 1973), pp. 103–104.

[3] David C. McClelland, *The Achieving Society* (Princeton, New Jersey: Van Nostrand, 1961).

[4] For additional information on the significance of youthfulness to marketing see "Youth Market: Are They Mini-Adults or Maxi Mysteries?" *Marketing/Communications* (December, 1970), pp. 54–57; Lee Adler, "Cashing-In on the Cop-Out," *Business Horizons,* Vol. 13 (February, 1970), pp. 19–30; and William Lazer, *et al.,* "Consumer Environments and Life Styles of the Seventies," *MSU Business Topics,* Vol. 20, No. 2 (Spring, 1972), pp. 5–17.

[5] James Stafford, Keith Cox, and James Higginbotham, "Some Consumption

Pattern Differences Between Urban Whites and Negroes," *Social Science Quarterly* (December, 1968), pp. 619–630; and Marcus Alexis, "Some Negro-White Differences in Consumption," *American Journal of Economics and Sociology,* Vol. 21 (January, 1962).

[6]W. Lloyd Warner, Marchia Meeker, and Kenneth Eels, *Social Class in America: A Manual of Procedure for the Measurement of Social Status* (Chicago: Science Research Associates, 1949).

[7]Reprinted from Pierre Martineau, "Social Classes and Spending Behavior," *Journal of Marketing,* Vol. 23 (October, 1958), pp. 121–130. Published by the American Marketing Association.

[8]Engel, Kollat, and Blackwell, *Consumer Behavior,* p. 151.

[9]H. Lee Mathews and John W. Slocum, Jr., "Social Class and Commercial Bank Credit Card Usage," *Journal of Marketing,* Vol. 33 (January, 1969), pp. 71–78.

[10]Elizabeth Bott, "The Concept of Class as a Reference Group," *Human Relations,* Vol. 7, No. 3 (1954), p. 265.

[11]Kurt Lewin, "Group Decision and Social Change," in *Readings in Social Psychology,* Eleanor E. Maccoby, Theodore M. Newcomb, and Eugene L. Hartley, eds. (3rd ed.; New York: Holt, Rinehart, and Winston, Inc., 1958), pp. 197–211.

[12]M. Venkatesan, "Experimental Study of Consumer Behavior, Conformity and Independence," *Journal of Marketing Research,* Vol. 3 (November, 1966), pp. 384–387.

[13]James E. Stafford, "Effects of Group Influence on Consumer Brand Preferences," *Journal of Marketing Research,* Vol. 3 (February, 1966), pp. 68–75.

[14]Engel, Kollat, and Blackwell, *Consumer Behavior,* pp. 173–176.

[15]Foundation for Research on Human Behavior, *Group Influence in Marketing and Public Relations* (Ann Arbor, Michigan: The Foundation, 1956).

[16]Burton Marcus, *et al., Modern Marketing* (New York: Random House, Inc., 1975), p. 70.

[17]For an excellent review of research on household decision making, see Harry L. Davis, "Decision Making Within the Household," *Journal of Consumer Research,* Vol. 2, No. 4 (March, 1976), pp. 241–260.

[18]Roger Price, *The Great Roob Revolution* (New York: Random House, Inc., 1970), p. 88.

[19]William D. Wells and Leonard A. Losciuto, "Direct Observation of Purchasing Behavior," *Journal of Marketing Research,* Vol. 3 (August, 1966), pp. 227–233.

[20]Reprinted from William D. Wells and George Gubar, "Life Cycle Concept in Marketing Research," *Journal of Marketing Research,* Vol. 3 (November, 1966), pp. 355–363. Published by the American Marketing Association.

SUGGESTED READINGS

Davis, Harry L., "Decision Making Within the Household," *Journal of Consumer Research* (March, 1976), pp. 241–260.

Day, George S. and David A. Aaker, "A Guide to Consumerism," *Journal of Marketing* (July, 1970), pp. 12–19.

Engel, James F., David T. Kollat, and Roger D. Blackwell, *Consumer Behavior* (2nd ed.; New York: Holt, Rinehart, and Winston, 1973).

Markin, Rom J., Jr., *Consumer Behavior: A Cognitive Orientation* (New York: Macmillan Publishing Co., Inc., 1974).

Plummer, Joseph T., "The Concept and Application of Life Style Segmentation," *Journal of Marketing* (January, 1974), pp. 33–37.

Ward, Scott, "Consumer Socialization," *Journal of Consumer Research* (September, 1974), pp. 1–14.

Ward, Scott and Thomas S. Robertson, eds., *Consumer Behavior: Theoretical Sources* (Englewood Cliffs, New Jersey: Prentice-Hall, Inc., 1973).

Warner, W. L., *et al., Social Class in America* (New York: Harper and Row Publishers, 1960).

12

THE ECONOMIC ENVIRONMENT

12

THE ECONOMIC ENVIRONMENT

In Chapter 7, the function and structure of the macro marketing system were discussed in the context of the market system that operates in the American economy. As noted throughout that chapter, economic forces significantly influence the macro process of marketing. Further, the importance of this influence on the micro process of marketing was briefly identified in Chapter 4 in the discussion of the micro marketing system. To provide a broader working knowledge of the economic forces that influence marketing, this chapter is devoted to a detailed analysis of the economic environment. In the discussion, emphasis will be given to both micro and macro economic factors as they impact on the marketing process of the firm and the nation.

SCOPE AND IMPORTANCE OF THE ECONOMIC ENVIRONMENT

Perhaps at no other time since World War II has the economic environment had such an impact on marketing. Inflation and recession have become harsh economic realities in the United States, making it extremely difficult for those firms that actively review the state of the economy as an input to their marketing decision making to properly evaluate the changes that are taking place. Acceptance of the social costs of manufacturing and marketing also has added to the problem. Furthermore, foreign economic trends in general, and individual foreign economies in particular, are affecting the American economy in ways that few firms or consumers could have anticipated only a few years ago.

In April, 1973, Dr. Henry Kissinger indicated in his "Year of Europe" speech that coordination of economic policies between the United States and Europe was essential. At the time, however, Europe was enjoying a boom economy and had little interest in further discussions on the issue. More recently, with worldwide recession and double digit inflation, American and European leaders have recognized that individual national policies are totally inadequate for dealing with current economic problems.[1] It should be noted, of course, that Europe is not the only area of the world that is of concern to the United States. Newly rich Arab oil states are having a serious impact on the world economy, and efforts of third world nations to gain independence and equal participation in world affairs are dramatically impinging on industrialized countries that depend on third world nations for food and raw material imports.

For too long, firms and consumers in the United States have taken constant growth in the American economy for granted. Gross National Product (GNP) was expected to increase steadily year after year. It was assumed that the United States was entirely independent of forces at work in other economies and in other parts of the world. American products were world leaders, our workers were more productive, and our lifestyles were the best. Inflation and recession were misunderstood, and they were always small enough to be of little importance. Furthermore, the euphoria of becoming the world's first trillion dollar economy was prevalent among both business and government leaders.

For some time, however, the whole issue of growth has been questioned by environmentalists. Pressures of pollution, an awareness of missing elements in prevailing lifestyles, and a desire on the part of a growing number of people to preserve the natural environment give impetus to a vague uneasiness that has developed into a growing movement against unbridled growth. Today, this philosophy is becoming more pervasive in the United States. In other areas of the world, rapid growth is seen as desperately needed to ward off starvation, disease, and death for teeming millions.

Of course, there are those in the United States who still believe in the need for continued growth. These proponents of growth question the effect of zero growth. With zero growth they fear that young managers will have to wait for older managers to die, or retire, before the young can move up the executive ladder. They also feel that there will be fewer jobs at all levels in comparison to the employment opportunities that existed in earlier growth periods. The issue is not likely to be settled soon. Ideas will have to change dramatically regarding new lifestyles with fewer material goods, smaller living accommodations, and less international and national long distance travel.

POPULATION AND DEMOGRAPHICS

The importance of the general size of an economy to marketers was pointed out in Chapter 9. In an economic context, however, population and demographic data must be matched with collateral information about the people in an economy. Clearly, additional detail regarding the population of a nation is extremely important as an input to the marketing information system. Is the population growing? Where do the people live? How old are they? How many are married and have children? How much education do they have? How much money do they earn? The answers to these questions are extremely important in marketing, for they yield data that are essential to the formulation and implementation of marketing strategies. To provide an insight into their implications for marketing, this section is devoted to a brief review of population and demographic forces in the economic environment.

As indicated in Chapter 9, total population is constantly changing. Although it is increasing in the United States as a whole, it is decreasing in some states and rising in others. Generally speaking, the increase in any population comes from the difference between the crude

	1900	1950	1970	1973
Crude Birth Rate	32.3	24.1	18.4	15.0
Less Crude Death Rate	17.2	9.6	9.5	9.4
Equal Net Natural Increase	15.1	14.5	8.9	5.6

SOURCE: 1900 and 1950 figures are from U.S. Department of Commerce, *Historial Statistics of the United States, Colonial Times to 1957* (Washington, D.C.: Government Printing Office, 1960), pp. 23, 27. 1970 figures are from U.S. Bureau of the Census, *Statistical Abstract of the United States: 1974* (Washington, D.C.: Government Printing Office, 1974), pp. 53, 60. 1973 figures are from *United Nations Demographic Yearbook, Special Topic, Population Census Statistics III* (New York: United Nations, 1974), p. 96.

birth rate (CBR) and the crude death rate (CDR). This difference yields the net natural increase (NNI). To this figure must be added in-migration and out-migration figures to arrive at the increase in the total population. The CBR, CDR, and resulting NNI figures for the United States for the years 1900, 1950, 1970, and 1973 are presented in Table 12.1. As shown, there has been a substantial diminution in the growth of the American population through natural increase over the period indicated. This decrease in NNI resulted from a decrease in the birth rate, despite the decrease that has occurred in the death rate.

While the rates presented in Table 12.1 are measures of the numbers of births, deaths, and natural increase per thousand population, the important thing to notice is that even with the relatively low NNI figure, America is still a growing nation. Since there is no such thing as a negative birth rate (all birth rates are positive or zero), the only way for population to decline through natural causes is for the birth rate to be lower than the death rate, so that NNI figures are negative. This does occasionally happen. United Nations' data, for example reveal that there is a naturally declining population in the Channel Islands (between England and France), West Germany, East Germany, the Isle of Man (between England and Ireland), Luxembourg and Monaco. Since half of these countries have lower crude death rates than the United States, the major source of the natural decline in their population is through significantly lower birth rates.[2]

For most nations in the world, however, there is still a significant increase in population. The highest NNI figure in the world actually lies within the United States. The U.S. Virgin Islands has an NNI of 41.6, meaning that the population could double in only 17 years and 4 months.[3] Fortunately, the population is quite small. If the People's Republic of China had such an incredible NNI figure, the world would have serious problems indeed. The implications of these figures for marketing are discussed later in this chapter and also in the chapter on the international market environment.

As discussed in Chapter 9, other elements of the U.S. population that are of interest to the marketer include: (1) distribution, (2) mobility, (3) age, and (4) income. Future projections for these elements of the population will be presented in Chapter 20 in a section dealing with shifting population and income patterns that are expected to develop over the last quarter of this century.

MACRO ECONOMIC DIMENSIONS

While population and demographic information is important to marketers, the macro and micro economic forces that emanate from the interactions of people in an economy are also significant in shaping marketing strategy. This section briefly reviews the macro dimensions of the economic environment, and the next section presents an analysis of the micro dimensions.

GROSS NATIONAL PRODUCT

For marketers, the most often used measure of Gross National Product (GNP) is that which measures expenditures on final products. Table 12.2 illustrates the major accounts of this tabulation. Given these data, the marketer can get a fairly clear view of how Americans spend their incomes. To what extent do they buy durable goods such as automobiles, washing machines, television sets? To what extent do they buy nondurables such as food, clothing, gasoline? To what extent do they buy services? How big a consumer is the government? How large is America's foreign trade? These questions can be answered relatively easily by referring to data such as that presented in Table 12.2, which are available from a number of sources. These data illustrate just what GNP really is. As can be seen, it is simply the sum of the final purchase prices paid for all goods and services produced in the country, including net exports.

GNP is also presented in another form, which is the sum of all of the prices received by the producers of goods and services. In that context, the presentation is in the form of the wages, salaries, interest earned, dividends received, taxes received by government for its services, and so on.

Both figures for GNP are the same amount. This is because of the well known "circular flow" that occurs in any economy. The simplest representation of this circular flow is the family. The family unit is at once a consumer and a producer of goods and services. Those members of the family unit who work are producing goods and services for which they receive payment. The family then takes its earnings and spreads them over the purchases they must make to satisfy their needs. By making these purchases, the family is simply paying other producers of goods and services. When growth is occurring, this circular flow expands, indicating that someone in the circle has made an

Gross National Product	$1,397.4
Personal Consumption Expenditures, total	876.7
Durable goods, total	127.5
Automobiles and parts	49.7
Furniture and household equipment	58.8
Other	19.0
Nondurable goods, total	380.2
Clothing and shoes	74.1
Food and beverages	187.7
Gasoline and oil	35.9
Other	82.5
Services, total	369.0
Household operation	52.9
Housing	126.4
Transportation	26.1
Other	163.6
Gross Private Domestic Investment, total	209.4
Fixed investment	195.2
Nonresidential	149.2
Structures	52.2
Producers' durable equipment	97.1
Residential structures	46.0
Nonfarm	45.2
Other	.8
Change in business inventories	14.2
Nonfarm	11.9
Other	2.3
Net Exports of Goods and Services	2.1
Exports	140.2
Imports	138.1
Government Purchases of Goods and Services, total	209.2
Federal	116.9
National defense	78.7
Other federal	38.2
State and local	192.3

SOURCE: U.S. Department of Commerce, *Survey of Current Business* (Washington, D.C.: Government Printing Office, December 1975), p. S-1.

"investment" that has produced an increase in the amount of goods and services that can be derived from the original system. The system, then, has become more productive.

The increases that occur in the circular flow are extremely important to marketers, for it is from these increases that firms derive their growth. Although Table 12.2 does not provide data on growth, past and current data reveal some clues as to what will probably happen in the future. Figure 12.1 presents some of the more important data of interest to the marketer. Of special note are the personal consumption expenditure graphs. These two graphs tell the same story, but in different dollars. Line 230 shows the growth of personal consumption

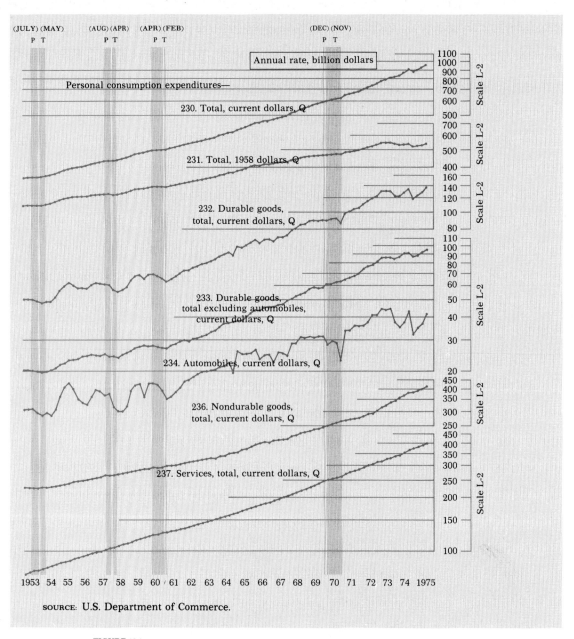

SOURCE: U.S. Department of Commerce.

FIGURE 12.1.
PERSONAL CONSUMPTION
EXPENDITURES IN THE
UNITED STATES, 1953–1975

expenditures (PCE) in current dollars. Line 231 shows PCE after eliminating the effects of the inflation that has occurred since 1958. Put another way, if a consumer in June, 1974 bought $1,000 worth of goods, the chart indicates that he would have gotten those same goods for about $600 in 1958. This means that the purchasing power of the dollar in 1974 was only about $.60 of the 1958 dollar.

Figure 12.1 also presents the relative growth of durable, nondurable, and services purchases made by American consumers. Clearly the most rapidly growing sector is services. This is to be expected since Americans have acquired large inventories of durable and nondurable goods over the years since World War II. Today, more and more consumer dollars are being spent on more and better service items. In this trend, it is interesting to note that 49.9 percent of the dollars spent for services in 1973 was for housing and household operation. Table 12.3 illustrates the dollar and index growth in GNP and goods and services using 1965 as a base period.

All of these goods and services, of course, are paid for out of consumer incomes. What has happened to consumer incomes recently? How do consumers handle their increased income? In part, the question of how they handle new found incomes is answered by analyzing the income elasticity of demand treated later in this chapter. As discussed in Chapter 9, it is important to recognize that as incomes rise, consumers tend to spend a smaller percentage of their income on food items, and approximately the same percentage of their incomes on clothing, housing, fuel, and light. On the other hand, as incomes rise, the percentage spent on recreation, education, health care, and religion tends to increase. Americans may experience a change in these patterns, however, as the prices of certain goods such as food, fuel, and light rise faster than other goods. What this could mean is that, despite rising incomes, the amount that must be spent on higher cost food items will cause the percentage of the family budget that is allocated to food to rise. The same may be true of fuel expenditures if lower cost per-passenger-mile transportation is not made available.

Not all of any increase in earnings is likely to go to pure consumption, of course. Consumers also save part of their incomes. This saving may be a long-term feature, or it may reflect a short-term saving effort

TABLE 12.3.
GNP AND GOODS AND
SERVICES, 1965–1974 (IN
MILLIONS OF DOLLARS)

Year	GNP	Total Goods	Index	Durable Goods	Index	Nondurable Goods	Index	Services	Index
1965	$ 684.9	$337.6	100	$133.0	100	$204.7	100	$262.9	100
1966	749.9	368.5	109	146.2	110	222.3	109	289.1	110
1967	793.9	390.7	116	156.5	118	234.2	114	316.5	120
1968	864.2	422.4	125	169.6	128	252.9	124	346.6	132
1969	930.3	449.7	133	182.3	137	267.4	131	377.9	144
1970	976.4	467.0	138	183.0	138	284.0	139	409.2	156
1971	1,050.4	491.8	146	194.5	146	297.3	145	443.9	169
1972	1,158.0	535.2	159	214.3	161	321.0	157	488.1	186
1973	1,294.9	607.3	180	240.9	181	366.5	180	534.4	203
1974	1,397.4	656.1	194	249.2	187	406.9	198	590.3	224

NOTE: Structures and changes in business inventories omitted in Total Goods column.
SOURCE: U.S. Department of Commerce, *Survey of Current Business* (Washington, D.C.: Government Printing Office, July, 1966–1975).

Personal Income		$1,150.5
Wage and Salary Disbursements		751.2
Other Labor Income		51.4
Proprietors' Income		93.0
Rental Income of Persons		26.5
Dividends		32.7
Personal Interest Income		103.8
Transfer Payments		139.8
Less:	Personal Contributions for Social Security	47.9
	Personal Tax and Nontax Payments	170.8
Equals:	Disposable Personal Income	979.7
Less:	Personal Outlays	902.7
	Personal Consumption Expenditures	876.7
	Interest Paid by Consumers	25.0
	Personal Transfer Payments to Foreigners	1.0
Equals:	Personal Saving	77.0

SOURCE: U.S. Department of Commerce, *Survey of Current Business* (Washington, D.C.: Government Printing Office, December, 1975), p. 5.

that will soon be spent as a down payment on some new consumer good. Table 12.4 illustrates that for 1973, consumers saved only a little over 7.0 percent of their personal incomes. After taxes, however, this saving represented over 8.0 percent of their disposable personal incomes. Furthermore, consumers borrow, which is, in effect, the reverse of saving. As illustrated in Table 12.4, the interest paid by consumers in 1973 amounted to 2.5 percent of disposable personal income. This indicates a much larger amount of borrowing for current consumption.

Keeping track of these changes for the whole economy is obviously important to the nationally based firms. What about the regional or local firm? These firms may also make use of such data, but they are perhaps less concerned with the entire nation's trends than they are with their region or city. Fortunately, smaller breakdowns of GNP, personal income, disposable personal income, and credit are available on a more localized level and can be used to analyze important local and regional trends.

MICRO ECONOMIC DIMENSIONS

In addition to the macro dimensions of the economic environment, there are two significant micro dimensions that affect marketing. These are the force of demand and the force of supply as they interact in the marketplace. To provide a review of these important basic economics concepts, this section is devoted to a discussion of demand analysis and supply analysis, presented in a marketing context.

DEMAND ANALYSIS   An estimate of potential demand for a company's product is highly valuable to managerial decision making. Yet, demand curve estimation is a difficult and costly operation in the business world. Still, many firms make such estimates and recheck these demand curves when prices are altered. For these firms, demand curve estimation is not merely an academic exercise. Nevertheless, there are still many firms that are quite proud of the fact that they make no such estimates, relying instead on their "high quality products" and "fair prices" to ensure a good market. Although this may be true, knowledge of the forces that affect demand is extremely valuable to the marketing effort.

The demand schedule.   Marketers measure demand in terms of the quantity of a good that consumers will purchase at given prices; that is, they use a demand schedule. As an illustration, Table 12.5 shows the demand schedule for 8-track stereo tapes. The example shows that consumers will buy 60,000 tapes per month at a price of $4.00 per tape, but only 3,333 tapes per month at a price of $20.00.

Price, of course, is not the only consideration. Additional factors such as income, distribution of income, population, the prices of substitutes and complementary goods, and taste all enter into the buying decision. What the demand schedule shows is the quantity that will be purchased at various prices once all of the other factors that enter into the decision are known or assumed to be true.

The demand curve.   The demand curve shown in Figure 12.2 is simply a graphic reproduction of the demand schedule in Table 12.5. Each of the quantities at the various prices is plotted and then connected by a curve. This is a better representation of the demand data in that the analyst now has a view of the price environment for tapes and can generate information about what is likely to happen at any point along the curve. It is assumed here that the manufacturer of 8-track tapes compiled these price-quantity relationships from experience and that they are, in fact, responses obtained from the marketplace. If it is further assumed that the seller is currently selling his tapes at the $10.00 per unit price, but that he is interested in increasing his total revenue, what should he do with his price? He can change price, and he knows that demand will vary inversely with his price movements. In other words, he can increase sales by lowering price. Alternatively,

TABLE 12.5.
DEMAND SCHEDULE FOR
8-TRACK STEREO TAPES

Price per Tape	Tapes per Month
$20.00	3,333
10.00	5,000
7.50	6,667
5.00	20,000
4.00	60,000

FIGURE 12.2.
DEMAND CURVE FOR 8-TRACK
STEREO TAPES

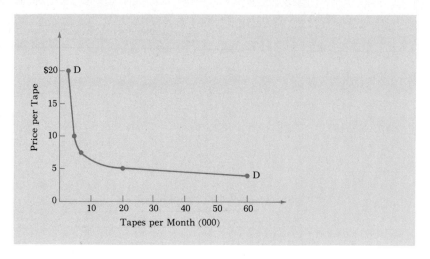

he can try to change demand by using nonprice variables to influence demand, in which case he attempts to shift the demand curve to the right. The impact of these two alternatives on total revenue is described below.

Changing demand.   If, by changing price, the seller can influence the quantity that will be purchased, the really important question is "by how much?" Using the experience of many other sellers, he should know that price changes cause movements along the demand curve, but they do not cause the entire curve to shift. Therefore, when the seller considers changing price, he knows that he will only be moving along the current demand curve. A quick review of that curve will show that price changes can produce drastically different results, depending on the elasticity of the curve. (This effect is discussed in the next section.)

In an effort to shift the demand curve, the seller may decide to advertise (a nonprice variable) to convince potential buyers to purchase more tapes. If this advertising campaign is successful, he will experience an increase in demand. This increase would be the result of a change in consumer attitudes, which were influenced by the advertising, regarding the ownership of tapes.

It should be noted that the same result, a change in demand or shift in the demand curve, could have been brought about by increasing population, increasing income, improved income distribution, an increase in the price of substitutes, or a decrease in the price of complementary goods. Since the seller has little or no control over these aspects of the economic environment, he must rely on a nonprice variable such as advertising to make tape ownership more appealing.

When the seller is successful in the use of nonprice elements, the demand curve shifts to the right indicating that consumers are demanding more of that product at every price. Figure 12.3 illustrates

FIGURE 12.3.
SHIFTING THE DEMAND FOR
8-TRACK STEREO TAPES

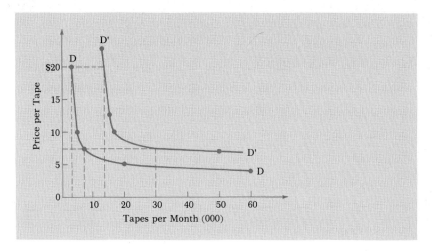

this total movement of the demand curve. An additional point to be considered in the new curve DD' is the great difference in the increase in quantity demanded at low prices versus the quantity demanded at some higher prices on the same curve. In this illustration, demand tends to be more elastic at lower prices. This concept is discussed below.

Elasticities. Marketers are interested in both price elasticities and income elasticities of demand. These forms of elasticity provide information regarding the changes in demand that will occur, given changes in either income or price.

The price elasticity of demand is most easily determined by the following formula:

$$E_p = \frac{\text{percentage change in quantity}}{\text{percentage change in price}}$$

When, after application of this formula, the price elasticity of demand for a good is determined to be 1.0, a reduction in price of 10.0 percent, for example, will produce a corresponding 10.0 percent increase in the quantity demanded. This means that, despite the drop in price, the total revenue from the sale of this item will not have changed. If the number for the price elasticity of demand for a good is less than 1.0, say 0.6, the 10.0 percent reduction in price will effect only a 6.0 percent increase in the quantity demanded. In this case, total revenue will decrease. Should the price elasticity be a number greater than 1.0, say 4.0, then the price reduction of 10.0 percent will produce a 40.0 percent increase in the quantity demanded, and total revenue will increase. The first case is known as unitary demand, the second case is known as price inelastic demand, and the last case is known as price elastic demand. The usual shapes of curves that describe these variations in

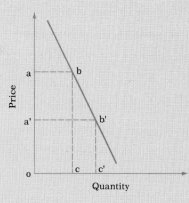

INELASTIC DEMAND

Here the percentage increase in quantity demanded is not sufficient to overcome the percentage decrease in price. The area of oa'b'c' is less than the area of oabc, indicating lower total revenue than before price reduction.

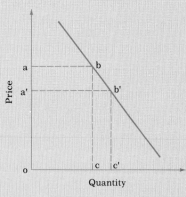

UNITARY DEMAND

Here the percentage increase in quantity demanded is just equal to the percentage decrease in price. The area of oa'b'c' is equal to the area of oabc, indicating equal total revenue at either price.

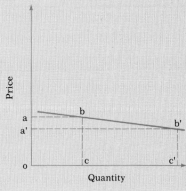

ELASTIC DEMAND

Here the percentage increase in quantity demanded is greater than the percentage decrease in price. The area of oa'b'c' is greater than the area of oabc, indicating greater total revenue at the lower price.

FIGURE 12.4.
THREE CASES OF PRICE
ELASTICITY OF DEMAND

price elasticity of demand are presented in Figure 12.4. Great care should be exercised, however, in reading a curve's elasticity by its shape. The scale selected for the axes can make an inelastic good appear quite elastic.

Table 12.6 presents the monthly revenue potential of the demand schedule that was provided in Table 12.5. Table 12.7 shows the derivations of the price elasticity coefficients for movements between the prices of the demand schedule. Drawing from all these inputs, it can be seen that the seller will have to sell at some price below $7.50 each in order to reach that part of the demand schedule that will bring about an increase in quantity demanded that is significant enough to increase total revenue. Also, it should be noted that if he is successful in bringing about a shift in the whole demand curve, perhaps through the advertising mentioned earlier, he could significantly increase his total revenue. This, of course, is one reason why firms advertise.

TABLE 12.6.
MONTHLY REVENUE
POTENTIAL FOR 8-TRACK
STEREO TAPES

Price	Tapes per Month	Revenue
$20.00	3,333	$ 66,660
10.00	5,000	50,000
7.50	6,667	50,000
5.00	20,000	100,000
4.00	60,000	240,000

TABLE 12.7.
PRICE ELASTICITY OF DEMAND
COEFFICIENTS COMPUTED FOR
8-TRACK STEREO TAPES

Old Amount	New Amount	Difference	Average Amount	Percent Change	Elasticity Coefficient
Q 3,333	5,000	1,667	4,167	$\frac{1,667}{4,167}(100) = 40.0$	
					$\frac{40.0}{66.7} = .6$
P $20.00	$10.00	$10.00	$15.00	$\frac{10.00}{15.00}(100) = 66.7$	
Q 5,000	6,667	1,667	5,834	$\frac{1,667}{5,834}(100) = 28.6$	
					$\frac{28.6}{28.6} = 1.0$
P $10.00	$7.50	$2.50	$8.75	$\frac{2.50}{8.75}(100) = 28.6$	
Q 6,667	20,000	13,333	13,333	$\frac{13,333}{13,333}(100) = 100.0$	
					$\frac{100.0}{40.0} = 2.5$
P $7.50	$5.00	$2.50	$6.25	$\frac{2.50}{6.25}(100) = 40.0$	
Q 20,000	60,000	40,000	40,000	$\frac{40,000}{40,000}(100) = 100.0$	
					$\frac{100.0}{22.2} = 4.5$
P $5.00	$4.00	$1.00	$4.50	$\frac{1.00}{4.50}(100) = 22.2$	

* These computations were derived from the use of a slightly more sophisticated formula:

$$\frac{\frac{\Delta Q}{(Q_1 + Q_2)/2}}{\frac{\Delta P}{(P_1 + P_2)/2}}$$

The income elasticity of demand measures the amount by which demand varies as income varies. It can be determined by the following formula:

$$E_i = \frac{\text{percentage change in quantity}}{\text{percentage change in income}}$$

Should income rise by 10.0 percent followed by an increase in demand for the good in question of 10.0 percent, the product would have a coefficiency of 1.0 (unitary elasticity). If income rises by 10.0 percent, but demand increases by some lesser figure, such as 2.0 percent, the good in question would be income inelastic, indicating that as income rises, demand also rises, but not as rapidly. An income elastic product would be one where, when income rises by 10.0 percent, demand increases by more than 10.0 percent.

SUPPLY ANALYSIS   In addition to demand, supply is of critical importance to the firm, since it reflects what the firm is willing to offer consumers at various prices. Decisions regarding supply influence the success or failure of the firm, especially in times of declining economic activity and during periods of uncertainty in the minds of consumers and suppliers as to what the future holds.

The supply schedule.   The supply schedule records the quantities of a good that a supplier is willing to offer at given prices. Unlike the demand schedule, the supply schedule demonstrates a direct relationship between price and quantity. This means that as prices rise, a supplier will be willing to supply more goods at the higher prices. When prices fall, the supplier will offer fewer goods in the marketplace. There are very sound reasons for this reaction on the part of manufacturers and holders of goods. These reasons are known as the determinants of supply. As should be obvious from previous discussion, price is a key factor in determining the quantity of a good that will be offered to the market. Three other factors are also important: (1) attitudes of businessmen, (2) factor cost and technology, and (3) relative prices.

In describing the attitudes of businessmen, there is the temptation to reduce all the possible attitudes down to one: profit maximization. All things being equal, this may serve as a satisfactory model of businessmen's attitudes. All things are seldom equal, however. A businessman may decide to take more leisure in lieu of more profits. He may opt for more consumption rather than increasing his investment. In short, profit maximization may be severely curtailed by elements that are controllable by the manager, such as his choosing more leisure rather than more profit, and by the elements outside of his control,

[handwritten margin note: FACTORS DETERMINING QUANTITY OF a good — PRICE, ATTITUDES OF BUSINESSMEN, FACTOR COST & TECHNOLOGY, RELATIVE PRICES]

such as increased competition and lower prices. Other goals for the firm, given that the firm generates at least some satisfactory profit level, may be sales maximization, or producing "morally superior" goods, such as orange juice rather than whiskey.

Factor cost and technology are closely related. In modern manufacturing, agriculture, and services, there are many options as to how much land, labor, and capital are required for production. Still, if one or more of these factor inputs rises in price beyond the ability of a manufacturer to pay, then, for all intents and purposes, the input ceases to exist. With no close substitutes, the manufacturer ceases production. If the price of factor inputs rises only slightly, the manufacturer may be able to pass along this price rise to consumers. Of course, there is always the risk that consumers may refuse his offering at the higher price. Here, relative prices become significant.

Relative prices are important because, in a sense, all goods compete with other goods. Clearly, in the example of stereo tapes, competition exists between tapes, records, and cassettes. If the spread in prices between records and tapes were to grow to the point that tapes were four times as expensive as records, demand for tapes would decline as consumers switch to records. In response, some tape manufacturers might move to the manufacture of records. This movement of consumers and firms between substitute goods could cause a movement in relative prices of factor inputs. These changes in factor inputs could produce a change in manufacturing technology. A change in manufacturing technology might bring about a new process that would lower tape production costs and make tapes once again competitive.

Table 12.8 illustrates a supply schedule for tapes. At a very low price, say $2.00, the manufacturer may be uninterested in gathering together all of the factors of production that go into the manufacture of these tapes. Or, it may be that the cost of gathering together the factor inputs, producing the tapes, and distributing them, exceeds the price obtainable, or provides an unacceptable profit to the manufacturer. From this schedule, it may be noted that as price rises, the manufacturer is willing to offer more and more tapes. The general assumption here is that there is more profit at higher prices than at lower.

The supply curve.   Following the presentation in demand analysis, Figure 12.5 provides a graphic display of the supply curve. An analysis of this curve indicates that any point on the curve may be traced back to both the price axis and the quantity axis to determine the relationship of price to quantity supplied.

Once again, as was the case in the analysis of demand, there is a difference between a price-caused change in supply, and a shift in the supply curve. Figure 12.6 illustrates an outward movement of the supply curve for 8-track tapes. This sort of a movement can be caused by a change in the attitudes of the businessman, such as an orientation toward sales maximization, a reduction in the cost of factor inputs, an

FIGURE 12.5.
SUPPLY CURVE FOR 8-TRACK
STEREO TAPES

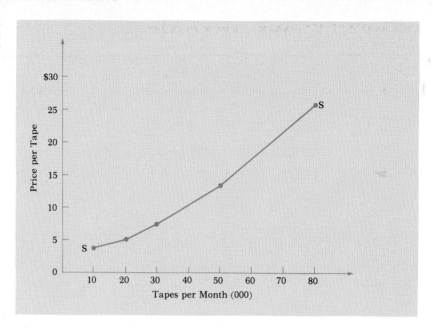

FIGURE 12.5.
SUPPLY CURVE FOR 8-TRACK
STEREO TAPES

FIGURE 12.6.
SHIFTING THE SUPPLY CURVE
FOR 8-TRACK STEREO TAPES

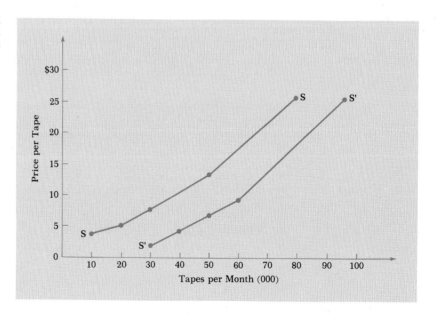

FIGURE 12.6.
SHIFTING THE SUPPLY CURVE
FOR 8-TRACK STEREO TAPES

improvement in technology, or competition from the record industry manifested by a reduction of prices for records. A movement in the opposite direction—inward toward the origin—would be caused by actions in reverse of the outward movement.

MARKETPLACE INTERACTION

Given the review of the micro dimensions of the economic environment presented above in the discussion of demand and supply analysis, it is now appropriate to discuss marketplace interaction between the buyer and the seller. Using the 8-track stereo tape example, this section focuses on the manner in which equilibrium prices are established. Finally, the section presents a brief discussion of breakeven analysis as an important concept used in the evaluation of the relationships that exist between costs and profits.

EQUILIBRIUM ANALYSIS

In Figure 12.7, the supply curve for 8-track tapes derived from the supply schedule presented in Table 12.8 is superimposed over the demand curve for these tapes as developed from the demand schedule in Table 12.5. As shown, Figure 12.7 may be viewed as a graphic representation of buyer-seller interaction in the marketplace. The de-

TABLE 12.8.
SUPPLY SCHEDULE FOR
8-TRACK STEREO TAPES

Price per Tape	Tapes per Month
$ 4.00	10,000
5.00	20,000
7.50	30,000
13.20	50,000
25.50	80,000

FIGURE 12.7.
EQUILIBRIUM IN THE
MARKETPLACE FOR 8-TRACK
STEREO TAPES

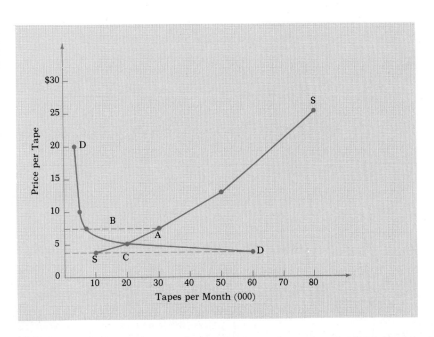

mand curve represents the number of tapes per month that buyers are willing to purchase at various prices. The supply curve represents the number of tapes per month that the seller is willing to supply at various prices. Clearly, there is very little agreement between the participants in the marketplace. In fact, there is only one point on the curves that expresses agreement, and that is point A. At point A, both buyers and sellers agree on a price of $5.00 per tape. At that price, the seller will offer 20,000 tapes per month and buyers will purchase 20,000 tapes per month. There will be no surplus on the market at a price of $5.00, and there will be no buyers seeking tapes that have been offered at a $5.00 price. Therefore, this is the *equilibrium,* or *market clearing price.*

Line B presents a situation in which there is disagreement. Although at the line B price, $7.50 each, there are buyers who would take 6,667 tapes per month, the seller refuses this market demand and insists on producing 30,000 tapes per month. This leaves a surplus of unsold tapes amounting to 23,333 tapes per month. Since this is a case of excess supply, or supply exceeding demand, there is considerable pressure for the supplier to reduce price because at any higher price there would clearly be an even greater surplus of supply over demand. Any price lower than $7.50 would bring buyers and the seller closer together, but it is not until a price of $5.00 per tape is reached that there is agreement between both the seller and the buyers.

Having won that argument, buyers might be willing to push for an even greater reduction in price. Line C indicates the result of buyers refusing the $5.00 price and pushing for a $4.00 price per tape. At the $4.00 price, buyers would be willing to take 60,000 tapes per month from the market, a considerable increase over the $7.50 price or the $5.00 price, indicating as proved in Table 12.7 that the price elasticity of demand for 8-track tapes is extremely price elastic in this price range. The seller, however, is not impressed with this increase in quantity demanded at this low price and still offers only 10,000 tapes per month at a price of $4.00 each, which leaves a surplus of demand in the marketplace amounting to 50,000 tapes per month. Given such a dramatic excess of demand over supply, there is considerable pressure for consumers to bid the price back up to some higher level. Once again, at any price greater than $4.00 per tape, buyers and the seller will be closer to agreement, but it is not until a price of $5.00 per tape is reached that complete agreement is reached.

Why does the marketplace work this way? The answer lies in the excesses of demand and supply. When there is an excess of demand over supply present in the marketplace, there is always a chance that some of the buyers who wish to acquire the goods in question will be able to do so at the price that led to the excess of demand. In the illustration, that price is $4.00 per tape. At this price, one buyer could acquire 10,000 tapes per month. Other buyers, having no opportunity to acquire any tapes at that price, but still desiring to acquire tapes, will bid the price up until some producer will be willing to accept that higher price and offer additional tapes. Eventually a price will be

FIGURE 12.8.
SHIFTING DEMAND AND
SUPPLY CURVES FOR 8-TRACK
STEREO TAPES, AFTER
EQUILIBRIUM

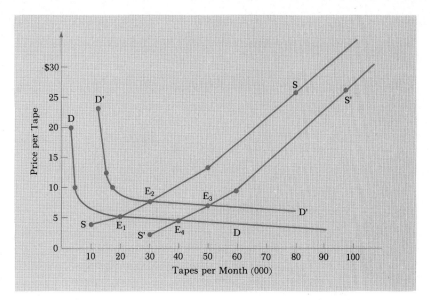

reached at which both suppliers and purchasers are satisfied. In the example, that price is $5.00 per tape.

In the situation described by Line B, there is an excess of supply over demand. The supplier, discovering that he has unsold tapes at a price of $7.50 per tape and having money invested in these tapes will try to recover as much of his investment as possible. If he can not sell all of the tapes at $7.50 each, he may decide to reduce the price until they are all sold. This price will level out at $5.00 per tape. The manufacturer will no longer manufacture 30,000 tapes per month, but rather will offer only 20,000 tapes per month. He will not be concerned then with what to do with unsold tapes.

What will happen if there is a change in some of the factors that have been held constant? These nonprice effects on demand and supply, as discussed above, will cause a shift in the demand or supply curve. Figure 12.8 illustrates the shifts that can occur in both curves.

Demand curve DD and supply curve SS illustrate the now familiar demand and supply curves that have been used in this discussion. Equilibrium point E_1 is the familiar market clearing price of $5.00 per unit with buyers purchasing 20,000 tapes per month. The other equilibrium points are the result of movements in the supply and demand curves. A review of the changes of events that can bring about such movements should explain these new equilibrium points.

The elements of supply and demand discussed so far treat the basic marketplace as though producers and consumers were the only actors involved. It is now time to introduce government as another of the actors in the marketplace.

What is the effect of a tax placed on the sale of tapes? Figure 12.9 shows the demand and supply curves DD and SS, and the effect of a tax upon the previous equilibrium position E_1. Since a tax immedi-

FIGURE 12.9.
THE POST-EQUILIBRIUM
EFFECT OF A TAX ON 8-TRACK
STEREO TAPES

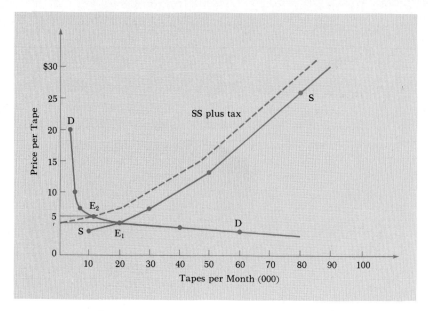

ately raises the selling price of a good, at all levels of output, its effect is to shift the supply curve to the left bringing about a new equilibrium point at a higher price and, therefore, a lower quantity sold. In the case presented in Figure 12.9, a $2.00 tax is imposed by the government, which brings about a market clearing price of $6.38 and a monthly quantity purchased of 12,500 units. It should be noted that the price has not increased by the full amount of the tax. The consumer is not paying the full burden of the tax; he is sharing it with the manufacturer. The consumer pays $6.38, which is $1.38 more than the original price—but, the tax was $2.00. What happened to the rest of the $2.00? The manufacturer absorbed it. How was it decided who would pay what percentage of the tax? In the absence of some forced requirement, the market mechanism will handle this matter. The shape of the demand curve between the points E_1 and E_2 takes care of this allocation problem neatly without any interference. The more elastic the demand curve, the more of the tax the manufacturer will have to pay. The more inelastic the demand curve, the more the consumer will have to pay. Price-inelastic demand is very strong demand. If price rises, quantity demanded drops, to be sure, but not by as great a percentage as the percentage price increase. Elastic demand is not as strong, for demand drops by a larger percentage than the percentage price increases. Therefore, the market forces, when they go to work in adjusting the burden of the tax, will tend to favor the supplier in the case of inelastic demand and will favor the buyer in the case of elastic demand.

In addition to taxes, subsidies, rationing, and price controls also may affect equilibrium. Consider, for example, the recent impact of the price controls and rationing that occurred in the petroleum industry.

Although beyond the scope of this chapter, these issues pose serious concerns for the consumer.

BREAKEVEN = (REVENUE = CoST)

BREAKEVEN ANALYSIS

To this point, this section has focused on the basic interaction of supply and demand in the marketplace. One of the elements that influences this interaction is cost. Breakeven analysis attempts to look at cost and its effect on profit at different levels of output. Figure 12.10 shows the simplest form of breakeven chart. Price per unit (P), variable cost per unit (V), and total fixed cost (FC) are all assumed to remain constant over the entire range of output and sales. Based on these assumptions, Figure 12.10 was constructed from the following data:

Profit = Total Revenue – Total Cost
Total Revenue = (Price per Unit) (Units Sold)
Total Cost = [(Variable Cost per Unit) (Units Produced)] + Total Fixed Cost
Price per Unit (P) = $0.75
Variable Cost per Unit (V) = $0.50
Total Fixed Cost (FC) = $50,000.

Since the breakeven point (BEP) is defined as that volume of sales (in dollars or units) where revenue equals costs, the above data may be used to compute breakeven by employing the following formulas:

FIGURE 12.10.
BREAKEVEN ANALYSIS I

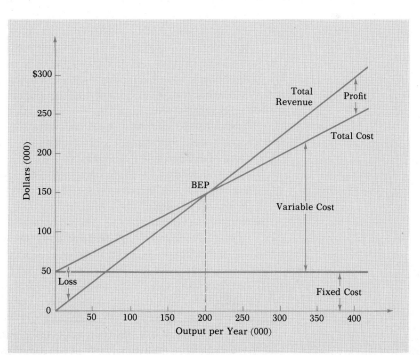

$$\text{BEP (in units)} \quad = \quad \frac{FC}{P - V}$$

$$= \quad \frac{50,000}{.75 - .50}$$

$$= \quad 200,000 \text{ units}$$

$$\text{BEP (in dollars)} \quad = \quad \frac{FC}{1 - \dfrac{V}{P}}$$

$$= \quad \frac{50,000}{1 - \dfrac{.50}{.75}}$$

$$= \quad \$150,000$$

A review of Figure 12.10 shows that the above calculations are correct. At the breakeven point, the unit volume is 200,000. This is further verified by the fact that a selling price of $0.75 times 200,000 units will produce a dollar volume of $150,000. The same data, of course, can be used to determine profits at any given sales level. For example, the firm in this illustration would make $25,000 profit on a sales volume of 300,000 units. This may be calculated as follows:

Profit = Total Revenue – [Total Fixed Cost + (Variable Cost per Unit) (Units Produced)]
   = $0.75 (300,000) – [$50,000 + $0.50 (300,000)]
   = $225,000 – ($50,000 + $150,000)
   = $225,000 – $200,000
   = $25,000

Although this is a relatively simple graphic concept, it does not tell the whole story. It should be clear that the fixed cost of operating a plant at an output of 10,000 units ought to be less than the fixed cost of operating a plant at an output of 300,000 units. At the higher level of production, more factory floor space would be required, more machines would be required, more management would be required, and so on. Still this type of straight line graphic analysis can be a valuable tool to the marketer in analyzing the economic environment in which he operates.

Another example that is still simplified, but much improved over the previous straight line chart, is presented in Figure 12.11. There are two obvious changes. First, fixed cost is higher. This is because the example only considers a range of production possibilities from 150,-000 units per year to 500,000 units per year. Variable cost is also substantially different. Working with a reduced range of outputs, it is possible to construct a curve that more accurately represents variable cost per unit at various output levels. Variable cost per unit rises slowly at lower levels of output. It should be noted, however, that once

FIGURE 12.11.
BREAKEVEN ANALYSIS II

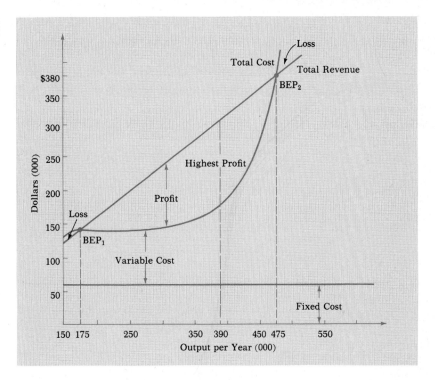

the firm reaches an optimum utilization of plant and facilities, variable costs rise dramatically.

A review of Figure 12.11 reveals two breakeven points, not just one. Furthermore, there is one optimum point of sales and production that generates the most profit for the firm. Continuing to produce and sell beyond the breakeven point as suggested in Figure 12.10 will not lead to higher and higher profits, but will eventually lead to losses.

Since it is recognized that there are two breakeven points, the decision to increase fixed investment in plant and facilities can be more sensibly made. Obviously, given the structure of the breakeven chart in Figure 12.11, the best sales objective is 390,000 units. This is so because at 390,000 units the firm is gaining the largest possible profit on its operations. If sales either drop or rise slightly from this highest profit point, there will still be significant profit for the firm. The idea presented in the two-breakeven point chart, however, is that the profit will not continually increase as sales increase. Plant capacity is designed for sales volume defined within certain boundaries. Above and below these boundaries, plant size must be changed to operate with profit. If sales should drop significantly below the planned volume, then fixed costs will weigh heavily in the total cost structure, and profit potential will be greatly reduced. If sales volume rises significantly above the planned volume, then the increasing variable cost per unit will eat into profit. Thus, as indicated in Figure 12.11, it is possible for a firm to experience losses at both low and high volume levels.

SUMMARY

In this chapter, the macro and micro dimensions of the economic environment provided the basis for a discussion of the economic forces that affect marketing. The initial section of the chapter focused on the scope and importance of the economic environment. In this section, attention was devoted to the significance of the world economic environment and the issue of growth in the American economy.

The second section of this chapter explored the economic aspects of population and demographics. Following a brief discussion of net natural increase (NNI) in population, other elements of population of interest to marketers were identified as distribution, mobility, age, and income.

The last three sections of this chapter were devoted to a review of the macro and micro dimensions of the economic environment. The macro section provided a discussion of gross national product (GNP), while the micro section focused on the forces of supply and demand. A detailed analysis of each one of these areas was presented as the base for a final section devoted to the interaction of buyers and sellers in the marketplace. Here, the discussion presented a review of equilibrium analysis and breakeven analysis.

QUESTIONS FOR DISCUSSION

1. Today, what is the basic issue in the concept of economic growth? Compare and contrast the views of the proponents of growth with those views presented by the opponents to growth.

2. Explain the term net natural increase (NNI) in population. Based on your understanding of this idea, would you classify the United States as a growing nation? Why?

3. What is gross national product (GNP)? Why is this macro area of economic analysis important to marketers? Explain.

4. In an integrated discussion, fully explain the forces of demand. In your discussion, show why this concept is important to marketers.

5. In an integrated discussion, fully explain the forces of supply. In your discussion, show why this concept is important to marketers.

6. In a discussion of equilibrium analysis, identify and explain marketplace interaction.

7. What is breakeven analysis? How and in what ways can this concept be used by marketers?

NOTES

[1]"Kissinger on Oil, Food, and Trade," *Business Week,* (January 13, 1975), p. 66.

[2]*United Nations Demographic Yearbook, Special Topic, Population Census Statistics III* (New York: United Nations, 1974), p. 97.

[3]*Ibid.*

SUGGESTED READINGS

Adler, Lee, "How Marketing Research Helps Sales," *Sales Management* (November 3, 1975), pp. 105–107.

Bagozzi, Richard P., "Marketing as Exchange," *Journal of Marketing* (October, 1975), pp. 32–39.

Burck, Gilbert, "The Myths and Realities of Corporate Pricing," *Fortune* (April, 1972), p. 85.

Corr, Arthur V., "A Cost Effectiveness Approach to Marketing Outlays," *Management Accounting* (January, 1976), pp. 33–36.

Guiltinan, Joseph P., "Risk-aversive Pricing Policies: Problems and Alternatives," *Journal of Marketing* (January, 1976), pp. 10–15.

Hatchford, Brian T., "The New Economic Theory of Consumer Behavior: An Interpretive Essay," *Journal of Consumer Research* (September, 1975), pp. 65–75.

Linden, Fabian, "The Second Half of the Seventies," *Conference Board Record* (December, 1975), pp. 13–16.

Morris, D., "Some Economic Aspects of Large-scale Advertising," *Journal of Industrial Economics* (December, 1975), pp. 119–130.

Weiss, E. B., "New Era of Shortages Complicates Marketing," *Advertising Age* (December 16, 1974), p. 56.

White, Gary E. and Philip F. Ostwald, "Life Cycle Costing," *Management Accounting* (January, 1976), pp. 39–40.

13
THE LEGAL ENVIRONMENT

13

THE LEGAL ENVIRONMENT

Due to the widening scope of the role of government in business, the study of marketing would be incomplete without a working knowledge of the legal environment. To provide a better understanding of the relevant laws that affect marketing, this chapter is devoted to a review of the major federal statutes that affect marketing practice in the domestic market. Special attention will be devoted to antitrust and consumer protection legislation with an emphasis on relationships, interpretation, and enforcement. In addition, legal controversies and trends of current importance to marketing will be highlighted.

RATIONALE FOR GOVERNMENT REGULATION

The maintenance of competition was a major goal in the United States long before the passage of the Sherman Act in 1890. Although the relationship between business and government was dominated by a laissez-faire philosophy, the threat to the free enterprise system from monopoly had been recognized for some time. Practices that were considered monopolistic in nature were not in the public interest and were regulated by common law. Common law represents "the body of unwritten law based on custom, usage, and the decisions of the courts."[1] These court decisions were made without the benefit of legislative policy guides. In the early history of the United States, as in England, judge-made rules were established that outlawed the following practices:

1. Contracts in restraint of trade;

2. Agreements to fix prices;

3. Agreements to control markets;

4. Agreements to abstain from engaging in the same kind of business for an unreasonable time after selling out to a competitor;

5. Trust agreements and holding company devices.[2]

Common law, however, did not prove to be an effective instrument for maintaining competition and protecting the interests of the public. Its major deficiencies became apparent after the Civil War, when the changes brought about by the Industrial Revolution began to operate at full force. With the development of improved transportation, large-scale production, and the corporate form of business organization, local markets were transformed overnight into national markets. Competition became intense; businessmen searched for ways to insulate themselves from competitors. Richard Caves summarized a number of devices found and used by businessmen:

Some took the form of agreements among sellers to fix prices, divide up markets, share industry profits among themselves in some pre-set proportions, and the like. Others involved combining independent firms in an industry by various legal devices to raise the degree of seller concentration. One of these was the outright merger, often in those days a spectacular affair sweeping together dozens of firms into the one giant combine. Another was the trust, a legal device for putting independent firms under a common control. To form a trust, majority stockholders of a number of independent companies turned over their shares, carrying voting control over the affairs of their companies, to a single group of "trustees." They received in return trust certificates entitling them to share in the profits of the companies operated by the trustees as a group. The trustees could then run the formerly competing firms as a single enterprise, extracting whatever monopoly profits might be available. The trust device waned by the turn of the century, but not before giving its name to a whole branch of public policy. Similar to the trust was the holding company. It likewise centralized voting control over a number of operating companies in the hands of a newly-formed "holding company." But the holding company was simpler than the trust. It could be formed simply by buying up the operating companies' common stock and did not require complex negotiations and agreements with their stockholders.[3]

The growth of these combinations became so extensive that the late nineteenth century became known as the "Era of the Trusts."[4] During this period, trusts were established in the whiskey, sugar, petroleum, meat packing, coal, and tobacco industries, to name only a few. The market tactics employed by these trusts were so flagrant and their market power so great that criticism arose from many sources. Those most vocal in their criticism were the small businessmen and the farmers, since they were the most vulnerable to the pressure applied by the giant corporate monopolies. Other critics, including many consumers and labor unions, soon joined to express their dissatisfaction. The first to legislate acts against these powerful combines and their tactics were the states. State laws, however, were ineffective in dealing with the problem, and their failure emphasized the need for federal response.

ANTITRUST LEGISLATION

In dealing with the problem at the federal level, the government had available to it a number of alternatives with which to respond to the monopoly threat of the trusts.

1. It could take no action, trusting the public interest to be saved by the voluntary choice of the monopolist.

2. It could break up existing monopolies and prevent the formulation of new monopolies, protecting the public interest by restoring and preserving the force of competition.

3. It could acquiesce to the existence of monopoly and safeguard the public

interest by regulating the services rendered and the prices charged by the monopolist.

4. It could take monopoly into public ownership.[5]

SHERMAN
ANTI TRUST

The public's resentment of the abuses by the trusts resulted in the passage of the Sherman Antitrust Act in 1890. With its passage, Congress determined national policy by providing for the statutory control of monopoly and by expressing its faith in competition and the market system. The Sherman Antitrust Act was the first of a network of laws designed to preserve competition. These trade laws, or antitrust laws as they are more commonly known, are the foundation of the legal framework of marketing. Three major statutes and their amendments form the basis of antitrust at the federal level. The specific statutes and their relationships are presented in Figure 13.1. A summary of their major provisions is provided in Table 13.1.

SHERMAN ANTITRUST ACT

The Sherman Act is the cornerstone of federal antitrust legislation. When passed in 1890, it was surprisingly brief with only two main provisions:

Section 1.   Every contract, combination in the form of trust or otherwise, or conspiracy, in restraint of trade or commerce ... is hereby declared to be illegal. ...

Section 2.   Every person who shall monopolize, or attempt to monopolize, or

FIGURE 13.1.
MAJOR FEDERAL ANTITRUST
LEGISLATION AFFECTING
MARKETING

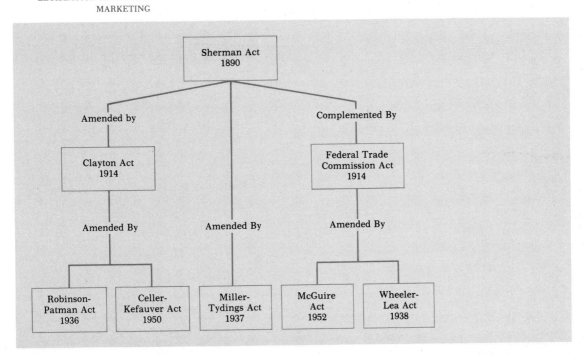

TABLE 13.1.
SUMMARY OF MAJOR FEDERAL
ANTITRUST LEGISLATION
AFFECTING MARKETING

Year	Legislation	Major Provisions
1890	Sherman Act (as amended)	A. Prohibits: 1. Contracts, combinations, conspiracies in restraint of trade (Section 1). 2. Monopolizing; attempting to monopolize, combinations or conspiracies to monopolize (Section 2). B. Exempts: 1. Resale price maintenance contracts, including those binding on third party non-signers (Miller-Tydings Act of 1937; McGuire-Keogh Act of 1952).
1914	Clayton Act (as amended)	A. Prohibits: 1. Brokerage *per se*, non-proportional advertising and sales allowances, and price discriminations, except where cost justified or where in good faith to meet equally low price of competitor, where effect is substantially to lessen competition or to tend to create a monopoly (Section 2, as amended by the Robinson-Patman Act of 1936). 2. Tying agreements (Section 3) under same conditions. 3. Mergers either as result of acquisition of stock or of assets, where the effect may be substantially to lessen competition in any line of commerce in any section of the country (Section 7, as amended by the Celler-Kefauver Act of 1950). B. Exempts: 1. Labor from antitrust laws (Sections 6 and 20). 2. Agriculture from antitrust laws (Section 6).
1914	Federal Trade Commission Act (as amended)	A. Creates Commission whose orders are binding if not appealed to court by the defendant. B. Prohibits: 1. Unfair methods of competition (Section 5). 2. Unfair or deceptive practices in commerce (Section 5, as amended by the Wheeler-Lea Act of 1938).
1936	Robinson-Patman Act	A. Prohibits: 1. Price discriminations which have effect of lessening competition or tending to create a monopoly in any line of commerce. 2. Brokerage payments to buyers outright. 3. Advertising or sales allowances not made on "proportionately equal terms" to all purchasers.

SOURCE: Adapted from H. H. Liebhafsky, *American Government and Business* (New York: John Wiley & Sons, Inc., 1971), pp. 223–224.

Year	Legislation	Major Provisions
		4. Buyers from "knowingly receiving" or "knowingly inducing such discriminations in price."
		B. Exempts:
		1. Allows price discrimination to be made "in good faith to meet the equally low price of a competitor or where the differences in price reflect differences in costs incurred."
1937	Miller-Tydings Act	A. Permits:
		1. Contracts between manufacturers and retailers to fix resale prices (fair-trade law) where state laws permit such contracts to be made.
		B. Prohibits:
		1. Intermediate buyer (retailer or wholesaler) will not willfully or knowingly advertise or offer to sell manufacturer's products below stipulated price.
		2. Non-signers from violating law (if one retailer in state agrees to manufacturer's price, all other retailers in state are bound by his action when they are notified of the agreement).
1938	Wheeler-Lea Act	A. Prohibits:
		1. "Unfair methods of competition in commerce" (original prohibition in FTC Act) but also prohibits "unfair or deceptive acts or practices in commerce.
		2. Necessity of FTC court action for enforcement of FTC orders. FTC order becomes final unless appealed.
1950	Celler-Kefauver Act (Anti-Merger Act)	A. Prohibits:
		1. Acquisition by a corporation of the "whole or any part of the stock—and the whole or any part of the assets" where "in any line of commerce in any section of the country, the effect of such acquisition may be substantially to lessen competition or to tend to create a monopoly."
1952	McGuire-Keough Act	A. Permits:
		1. Non-signer's clause in interstate resale-price-maintenance contracts (exempting from antitrust laws such provisions).

combine or conspire with any other person or persons, to monopolize ... trade or commerce ... shall be deemed guilty of a misde-
meanor. ...

Violations of the Act were made punishable by fines and/or imprison-
ment, and persons injured by violators could sue for recovery of three
times the amount of damages sustained. Although the Act seemed to
provide the basis for positive government action against monopolies
and trusts, its language was found to be so vague that the courts were
given wide latitude in its interpretation. This controversy over the
meaning of the Act led to numerous government defeats by the courts
in their attempts to break up trusts. For example, it was unclear
whether the Sherman Act prohibited all restraints of trade, or only
those unreasonable combinations in restraint of trade.

Early Sherman enforcement.   Under Theodore Roosevelt, the government pursued a more vigorous enforcement policy by arguing that the
Act applied to all combinations and conspiracies in restraint of trade.
Nevertheless, in 1911, the Supreme Court, in deciding the Standard Oil
Company and American Tobacco Company cases, established the interpretation of the Sherman Act through its formulation of the "rule
of reason."[6] Even though both firms were found guilty under Sections
1 and 2 of the Sherman Act and dissolved into several independent
firms, the basis of the decision in both cases was that the firms had
"unreasonably" restrained trade. Even though Standard Oil refined,
distributed, and sold approximately 75 percent of the petroleum products in the country and American Tobacco controlled the manufacturing of approximately 75 percent of the tobacco in the country, size was
not the determining factor. The "rule of reason" thus limited the scope
of the Sherman Act, for it allowed large trusts or monopolies to exist
as long as their intent or conduct was deemed reasonable.

Refusal by the courts to consider the size of a firm as a deterrent to
effective competition was felt by the trust busters to be a serious blow.
This interpretation was to persist until 1945. In 1945, a new interpretation was established by a Federal Court of Appeals in the Aluminum
Company of America (Alcoa) case. In the Alcoa case, the mere fact
that the firm manufactured approximately 90 percent of the new aluminum ingots produced in the country was sufficient to declare it a
monopoly even though its conduct was not offensive.[7] This interpretation was reinforced in the second American Tobacco case in 1946. In
upholding a lower court decision which found American Tobacco,
Liggett and Myers, and Reynolds Tobacco guilty of monopoly, Justice
Burton of the Supreme Court stated that "the material consideration
in determining whether a monopoly exists is not that prices are raised
and that competition actually is excluded but that power exists to raise
prices or to exclude competition when it is desired to do so."[8] Exceptions to this interpretation may exist, but certainly both the size of the
firm and its conduct are significant factors affecting court decisions in
regard to monopoly.

Modern Sherman enforcement. Early enforcement of the Sherman Act focused on Section 2, which concerns monopolization; the majority of present antitrust violations are based on Section 1, which concerns contracts, combinations, and conspiracies in restraint of trade. In fact, Section 1 has become one of the most effective federal statutes. A major area of today's antitrust violations is concerned with collusive price-fixing. The seriousness of this anticompetitive action was highlighted as early as 1898 in the Addyston Pipe and Steel Company case.[9] In this case, the court ruled that the mere proof of existence of price fixing was sufficient to find guilty the firms, which had agreed to fix prices in dividing the market for sales of pipe to gas and water works companies. The ruling in this case was reaffirmed in the Trenton Potteries Company and Socony Vacuum Oil Company cases.[10] These cases established that price fixing is inherently unreasonable and that such agreements are per se in violation of the Sherman Act.

In recent years, price-fixing has received a great deal of attention by the federal government. The majority of the cases, however, have been settled by agreement between the government and the defendants, with the defendants pleading nolo contendere (no contest) to price-fixing charges. Recent cases involving DuPont, Armco Steel, International Paper, Pepsi Company, Pet, Sunshine Biscuit, and Genesco were settled in this manner. Others, such as the famous 1961 electrical industry case, have involved extensive litigation.[11] In this case, 29 electrical companies, including General Electric and Westinghouse, were fined nearly $2 million and several top executives were given jail sentences. To date, defrauded customers have sued for damages totaling more than $25 million, and the amount is expected to go higher before the case is completely settled.

CLAYTON ACT   From the above comments on the enforcement of the Sherman Act, it should be apparent that the Act continues to be an effective piece of legislation in certain types of major antitrust and conspiracy cases. Its vagueness in specifying what actions are prohibited, and the narrow interpretations of the courts, however, forced Congress to enact more specific legislation in 1914. At that time the Clayton Act was passed as an amendment to the Sherman Act to deal with specific business practices that "substantially lessen competition or tend to create a monopoly." The more important provisions of the Clayton Act are identified in the following sections:

Section 2.   Forbids sellers to discriminate in price between purchasers of commodities unless there were differences in the grade, quality or quantity of the commodity sold, where the lower prices made only due allowance for differences in the cost of selling or transportation and where they were offered in good faith to meet competition.

Section 3.   Forbids sellers from leasing or making a sale or contract for the sale of commodities on the conditions that the lessee or purchaser shall not deal in the commodity of a competitor.

Section 7.   Forbids any corporation engaged in commerce from acquiring the shares of a competing corporation or from purchasing the stocks of two or more corporations that were competitors.

Section 8.   Forbids the same man or men from serving on the boards of directors of two or more competing corporations where one of the corporations has assets of more than one million dollars and where the elimination of competition between them would violate any of the provisions of the antitrust laws.

From the above, it may be noted that the Clayton Act deals most directly with price discrimination, certain distribution restrictions, and mergers. As shown in Figure 13.1, however, the Clayton Act was later amended by the Robinson-Patman Act in 1936 to strengthen the control of price discrimination and by the Celler-Kefauver Act in 1950 to more effectively deal with mergers. The remainder of this section presents a discussion of distribution restrictions and mergers; and the subject of price discrimination is discussed in the next section of this chapter under the Robinson-Patman Act.

Distribution restrictions. In an attempt to compete or develop a differential advantage, many firms establish distribution restriction arrangements. These arrangements result through agreements between supplier and reseller-buyers of products in which one of the parties, or both of them, accept(s) limitations on the scope of their managerial discretion with respect to certain marketing practices. These restrictions vary from enterprise to enterprise in terms of form, substance, and the particular marketing contexts in which they are applied. The two most commonly disputed distribution restrictions are:

1. _Customer-territorial restrictions_ which limit distributors in their choice of customers or sales areas; they thus reduce the direct competition between distributors of the same line of products, although they may be used not only to extend market coverage to customers to whom the products would not otherwise be made available but also to provide competitive support for the entry of a new firm or the introduction of a new product in the market.

2. _Product restrictions_ which either compel distributors to carry certain of the supplier's other products (tying) or prohibit them from carrying the products of competitors (exclusive dealing) as a condition of their being allowed to purchase certain items for resale. Product restrictions foreclose particular distributors as routes of market access for competitive products and weaken competition among suppliers by limiting the market choices of distributors and customers by creating barriers to the appearance of new products in the market.[12]

These restrictions can be attacked as substantially lessening competition under Section 3 of the Clayton Act, or as restraints of trade under

Section 1 of the Sherman Act, or, as shall be discussed later, as unfair methods of competition under Section 5 of the Federal Trade Commission Act.

The complexities of these distribution restriction arrangements have created an atmosphere of legal uncertainty for the businessman. Due to the diversity of opinions and interpretations of the laws by the courts concerning distribution restrictions, the only discernible trend in evidence is that antitrust limitations are becoming more stringent. For example, the trend of Supreme Court decisions concerning vertical territorial restrictions (those imposed unilaterally by a supplier upon its dealers) is characteristic of the Court's present attitude toward distribution restrictions. In the first specific case involving such restrictions to reach the Supreme Court, White Motor Company versus the United States, the Court stated that:

We do not know enough of the economic and business stuff out of which these arrangements emerge to be certain. . . . We need to know more than we do about the actual impact of these arrangements on competition to decide whether they have such a pernicious effect on competition and lack any redeeming virtue . . . and therefore should be classified as *per se* violations of the Sherman Act.[13]

In this case, the Court ruled that vertical territorial restrictions might be legal if: (1) the company was failing, (2) the company was small and was attempting to break into the market, or (3) the company adopted vertical territorial restrictions to protect itself against aggressive competitors. This ruling was considered significant in that it was the first case that recognized that vertical arrangements may not only be different from the inherently illegal horizontal arrangements, but also acceptable under certain conditions.

In 1967, only four years later, in the United States versus Arnold, Schwinn & Co. case, the Supreme Court took a much different stand concerning the vertical restrictions placed by Schwinn on its distributors.[14] The Court found that Schwinn's vertical territorial and customer restrictions were per se violations since they were unilaterally imposed upon distributors who purchased products from Schwinn. Here the Court ruled that the passage of title precluded Schwinn from imposing restrictions on independent distributors who own the goods they distribute. The Court did state, however, that such restrictions "may be permissible in an appropriate and impelling competitive setting," but only in the "unusual" not in the "ordinary" distribution of products.

Nevertheless, the decision established a ruling that has far-reaching implications on many firms, especially small ones. This ruling strongly suggests that vertical territorial restrictions imposed upon distributors by suppliers are legal only if the supplier owns the distributors. Also, any belief that a firm's unique position, as described above, may provide a defense was laid to rest by the Court in the 1972 Topco Associates case when it ruled that all territorial allocations among distributors are unlawful, even if they might foster competition against others.[15] Certainly these rulings give an inherent advantage to the large, financially strong firm. In addition, they establish a powerful precedent and indicate a trend of what may develop legally in regard to other well accepted and necessary marketing practices used by firms to protect their image, sales, and service when distributing their products.

Mergers.   The acquisition by a corporation of another's stock or assets wherein the acquired firm is controlled by the acquiring firm is called a "merger." Today, as in the past, mergers remain popular for numerous reasons. These include the desire to:

1. Increase overall corporate profits,

2. Obtain diversified holdings for stockholders,

3. Reduce risk, especially with regard to shifts in market demand for present products,

4. Enhance long-term corporate growth,

5. Broaden product bases, and

6. Invest relatively idle funds.[16]

Whatever the reason for mergers, they can certainly affect the structure of American industry and even the nature of competition. In the early part of this century, the inability of the Sherman Act to prevent firms from combining to the extent they injured competition led to the passage of the Clayton Act. In fact, the stated purpose of the Act was "to arrest the creation of trusts, conspiracies and monopolies in their incipiency and before consummation."[17] The most important provision of the Act was Section 7, which forbids the acquisition of the stock of a corporation by another where the effect would substantially lessen competition, or tend to create a monopoly. Unfortunately, the merger provision of the Clayton Act did not prove to be a success. The law, as worded, prevented firms from acquiring the stock of another firm, but it said nothing about the acquisition of assets. Moreover, in numerous decisions, the Supreme Court held that mergers effected through the acquisition of assets were not illegal.[18]

Alarmed by the Supreme Court's merger decisions, Congress enacted the Celler-Kefauver Act in 1950 amending Section 7 of the Clayton Act. The Celler-Kefauver Act (also known as the Antimerger Act) broadened considerably the prohibition against mergers. Specifically, it states:

No corporation engaged in commerce shall acquire, directly or indirectly, the whole or any part of the stock or other share capital and no corporation . . . shall acquire the whole or any part of the assets of another corporation engaged also in commerce, where in any line of commerce in any section of the country, the effect of such acquisition may be substantially to lessen competition or tend to create a monopoly.

Horizontal
MERGER

VERTICAL
MERGER

The Act not only plugged the asset acquisition loophole in the Clayton Act, it also expanded coverage of the Act to include mergers that take place outside a particular industry. Therefore, in addition to horizontal mergers (those between direct competitors), the Act forbids vertical mergers (those between firms at different levels in a distribution channel) and conglomerate mergers (those between all other firms) provided that it can be shown that the effects may substantially lessen competition, or tend toward a monopoly.

The first major case testing the strengthened Section 7 of the Clayton Act was Brown Shoe Co. versus the United States in 1962, which included both horizontal and vertical implications.[19] The merger of Brown Shoe Company, the fourth largest shoe manufacturer, with G. R. Kinney, the twelfth largest, was denied by the courts, even though Brown accounted for 4 percent and Kinney only 0.5 percent of the national output of shoes. With both firms vertically integrated into shoe retailing, Brown was directly responsible for approximately 3.0 percent and Kinney 1.6 percent of the nation's total shoe sales. Although the share of market of these firms was small, the court was concerned with both the concentration of the industry and the opportunity for Brown to require Kinney to carry only its shoes, thus foreclosing a substantial share of the market to competitors. Here the merger was denied on the grounds that its probable effect would be to substantially lessen competition both horizontally and vertically.

In 1966, the Supreme Court denied a merger between Pabst Brewing Company and Blatz Brewing Company on the grounds that the relevant market was Wisconsin, where the two companies controlled 24.0 percent of the state's beer sales.[20] Also, in 1966, the Court denied the merger between Von's Grocery Company and Shopping Bag.[21] Again, the basis for this denial was that these two grocery chains account for 7.5 percent of all grocery sales in the relevant market area of Los Angeles. To the businessman, decisions such as these preclude firms from growing and becoming more competitive. They believe it represents protection for competitors, rather than the protection of competition. In regard to horizontal and vertical mergers, it appears that federal agencies and the Supreme Court believe that more firms provide more competition.

Conglomerate
MERGERS

The conglomerate merger, on the other hand, poses a more complex set of circumstances for the enforcement agencies and courts. The conglomerate merger is a merger among firms that operate in separate and distinct markets. More specifically, conglomerate mergers are classified as follows:

1. *Market extension*—merger between companies in the same product line but located in different geographic markets (i.e., Federated Department Stores acquiring controlling interest in the Bullocks Department Stores in Los Angeles).

2. *Product extension*—merger between firms functionally related in production or distribution (i.e., Procter & Gamble acquiring Clorox).

3. *Pure conglomerate*—merger between firms with unrelated products or product technology (i.e., Phillip Morris Tobacco and American Safety Razor Company).[22]

Of the large mergers that took place in the late 1960s and early 1970s, the majority were conglomerate. The unique facets of the conglomerate merger have required the enforcement agencies and the courts to develop other criteria in addition to the traditional market share analysis for determining the probability of anticompetitive effects. An analysis of the conglomerate court cases reveals the criteria established:

1. The acquisition may lessen "potential" competition because one of the merger partners, although not an actual competitor of the other, may be a potential market entrant.

2. Normal competition might be prevented by reciprocal buying practices because companies that would like to sell Product A to the conglomerate might decide to reciprocate and purchase their requirements of Product B from the conglomerate.

3. Entry barriers may be raised by the substitution of the acquiring company for the acquired company, which will dissuade smaller firms from vigorous competition, or precipitate additional mergers. In addition, a large conglomerate might charge abnormally low prices for its new product line with expectation of driving smaller competing firms out of the business.[23]

Probably one of the most well known of the product extension conglomerate merger cases was the 1967 FTC versus Proctor and Gamble Company.[24] In this case, the Supreme Court forced dissolution of the 1957 merger between Proctor and Gamble and the Clorox Company on the following grounds: (1) Proctor and Gamble was a potential entrant in the chlorine bleach market; (2) ownership of Clorox made available financial resources that could support predatory pricing; and (3) the merger would raise entry barriers by increasing advertising expenditures by Clorox.

Although a number of the conglomerate cases have been settled by the Supreme Court, the enforcement agencies in their aggressiveness have also been successful in obtaining the dissolution of mergers through consent decrees. In a pure conglomerate merger case in 1970 between International Telephone (ITT) and Canteen Corporation, the Department of Justice entered into an agreement with ITT that required ITT to divest itself within two years of its interests in the food service field. This was based primarily on the grounds that the relationship between the two firms might preclude Canteen's competitors from providing food service to ITT-owned firms.[25]

Although the conglomerate merger wave of the 1960s caused major concern over its supposedly disastrous impact on concentration, this concern has never really been borne out. In fact, the FTC in 1972 in a report on nine large conglomerates concluded that "from a competitive standpoint, the effects of conglomerate diversification appear to be largely neutral."[26] Even though this finding cannot be generalized to all conglomerate mergers, the experience of firms such as Litton, Gulf and Western, LTV, and others is applicable. Because of mergers, these firms have found themselves spread so thin both in product and in management that survival has been difficult.

ROBINSON-PATMAN ACT

In 1936, Congress amended Section 2 of the Clayton Act by passing the Robinson-Patman Act. Section 2 of the Clayton Act was the first statutory pronouncement against price discrimination. Price discrimination is said to occur when an individual pays a price that is different from the price paid by another individual for an identical product or service. Many prefer the term "differential pricing" to "price discrimination" since the practice is legal in many instances, and is also a common pricing practice of marketing managers. Some of the more common legal examples include theaters charging lower admission fees for children than for adults, professional journals charging lower subscription rates to students than to nonstudents, and state universities charging higher tuition rates to out-of-state students than to residents.

Initially, Section 2 forbade price discrimination between different buyers where the effect "may be to substantially lessen competition or tend to create a monopoly." Due to the courts' interpretation and two major loopholes, the law was never really enforced. In fact, of the 43 complaints filed in this area between 1914 and 1936, only eight were upheld by the courts.[27] The courts, by limiting application of the law to sellers, prevented buyers injured by the practice from coverage by the law. In addition, the law condoned the practice of price discrimination when justified on a basis of "quantity discounts" or "necessary to meet competition." Consequently, the effectiveness of the law was eliminated for all practical purposes.

Whereas the initial section of the Clayton Act was designed to prevent large manufacturers from instituting temporary price cuts in selected parts of the country to drive small firms out of business, the Robinson-Patman Act grew out of a somewhat different situation. In the 1930s, chain stores like A&P began to significantly effect the structure of retail distribution in the United States. As pointed out in a 1934 Federal Trade Commission study, chain store growth was due in major part to their ability to exact large and unjustified price reductions from suppliers. By passing these reductions on to consumers, the chains were able to place the independent businessman at a competitive disadvantage and, thus, drive many out of business.[28]

Major provisions. In response to the need for additional legislation to strengthen the price discrimination section of the Clayton Act, Congress passed the Robinson-Patman Act. A number of practices not considered in the Clayton Act were included in the law. The major provisions of this amending act are as follows:[29]

1. *Sections 2a and 2b*—prohibit charging different prices to different purchasers of "goods of like grade and quality" where the effect may be substantially to lessen competition or tend to create a monopoly in any line of commerce, or to injure, destroy, or prevent competition with any person who either grants or knowingly receives the benefit of such discrimination or with customers of either of them. The amendment expanded the application of the law to now include injury to customers as well as competitors. Even though for defense purposes it is necessary for quantity discount schedules to accurately reflect cost differences, there can be instances where cost justification *per se* is not acceptable. For example, where the quantity discount would be "unjustly discriminatory or promotive of monopoly in any line of commerce," the Commission has been granted the authority to establish quantity discount limits. In addition, three potential defenses for justifying price discrimination were identified including: (1) it was carried out to dispose of perishable or obsolescent goods, or under a close-out or bankruptcy sale; (2) it merely makes due allowance for differences in the cost of manufacture, sale or delivery resulting from the differing methods or quantities in which the product is sold or delivered; or (3) it is effected "in good faith to meet an equally low price of a competitor."

2. *Section 2c*—prohibits the payment of brokerage fees of any type except to middlemen actually performing services as independent brokers. This was intended to eliminate the practice of some chains from demanding the regular brokerage fee as a discount when they purchased direct from manufacturers.

3. *Sections 2d and 2e*—prohibit sellers from granting allowances (such as advertising) and services (such as special display racks) to a buyer unless such assistance is made available to other competing buyers "on proportionally equal terms." Proportionally equal terms, according to the FTC, means that sellers should give the same percentage of the cost of promotion and other services for both large and small buyers. This provision was designed to prevent promotional allowances and services from being granted to large-scale buyers without being made available to competitors on a proportionally equal basis.

4. *Section 2f*—makes it unlawful for a buyer "knowingly to induce or receive a discrimination in price" prohibited by other parts of the law. This provision reflects the belief that large chain store buyers generated the need for the Robinson-Patman Act.

ROBINSON PATMAN ACT

Critical issues. The Robinson-Patman Act is more specific than the Clayton Act in identifying price discrimination prohibitions, but it is also much more controversial. Although legal controversies are found to exist in each section, the critical issues of present-day price discrimination law are embodied in Sections 2a and 2b. More specifically, in relation to marketing, there is a need for answers to the following questions:

1. What is meant by "like grade and quality"?

2. What are acceptable price discrimination defenses?

First, a clear understanding of "like grade and quality" is of major significance to marketers because illegal price discrimination can be implied only if products sold at different prices are of "like grade and quality." In the Borden Company case in 1966, for example, the Supreme Court ruled that products with similar physical and chemical compositions are of like grade and quality.[30] The Court found Borden guilty of price discrimination for selling unbranded condensed milk at a lower price than that sold under the Borden label, when, in fact, the chemical composition of the milk was identical. On a remand from the Supreme Court, however, an appellate court ruled that there was not sufficient evidence to show injury to competition; therefore, the cease and desist order against Borden was set aside. Even though a number of lower court decisions have supported the "market acceptability test" for determining like grade and quality, the law is not clear on this issue. Until clarifying legislation is provided, firms producing and selling private brands at prices below their primary brand are encouraged to build tangible differences into these products.

Regarding price discrimination defenses, a firm is required to prove that differences in price are: (1) implemented to dispose of perishable or obsolete goods; (2) the result of differences in costs incurred; or (3) given in good faith to meet an equally low price of a competitor. In actual practice, the courts have accepted few defenses that were justified on the basis of differences in costs or as the result of competitive pressures. This is one of the reasons why the Robinson-Patman Act is the most controversial of the antitrust statutes.

Many critics of the Act believe it to be anticompetitive and inconsistent with the objectives of a competitive economy. The enforcing agencies in their zeal to administer the Act have been more concerned with the protection of competitors than with the protection of competition. The end result is that the Act has not protected the small independent retailer from the chain. Instead, it has limited the marketing manager's discretion in emphasizing price in the marketing mix, thus forcing the consumer to pay higher prices.

In recent years, the lower courts have recognized these inequities and have been more willing to accept "cost" and "good faith" defenses.[31] Even representatives of the enforcing agencies have attacked the Act for its negative effect on legitimate price competition.[32] These agencies are also recommending to Congress that it is time to reexamine this law that was written in a depression economy. Nevertheless, until the Supreme Court provides a new set of guidelines, or Congress legislates changes, the marketer must heed the present interpretation of the Act in developing and administering price policies.

FEDERAL TRADE COMMISSION ACT

The Federal Trade Commission Act was passed in 1914 as companion legislation to the Clayton Act. The reasoning behind the passage of this Act was basically the same as that used to pass the Clayton Act. Businessmen were demanding a statute that provided much broader protection by prohibiting all business practices that injured competition but did not necessarily tend toward monopoly or restraint of trade. In addition, there was increasing criticism of the intensity and skill of the Department of Justice in its enforcement of the Sherman Act. Congress, in its attempt to meet these demands, passed an act which stated simply that "unfair methods of competition in commerce are hereby declared unlawful," and established the Federal Trade Commission (FTC) to enforce it.

Early interpretation.   The vagueness of the law and the Supreme Court's skepticism as to the Commission's role made early enforcement of the Federal Trade Commission Act nonexistent. In 1920, the Supreme Court ruled in the Gratz case that the courts and not the Commission would determine the meaning of the words "unfair method of competition."[33] In fact, the ruling by the Court limited the Commission's authority to business practices that had been declared illegal under Common Law and the Sherman Act.[34] In 1931, in the Raladam case, the Commission's authority was again limited.[35] In this case, the Supreme Court suppressed a cease and desist order issued by the FTC to the Raladam Company for advertising that their patent medicine would easily and safely remove excess weight, when, in fact, it had been found that the product contained ingredients that could be harmful. The Court ruled that even though the product could be harmful to health, the Commission did not provide sufficient evidence to prove that injury to a competitor had resulted.

The first opportunity for a more general and positive application of the statute took place in the 1934 Keppel case.[36] The FTC brought proceedings against Keppel for using a lottery scheme in the selling of penny candy, primarily to children. In upholding the FTC's charge that this practice was an unfair method of competition, the Court stated that "new or different practices must be considered in the light of the circumstances in which they are employed."[37] This decision tentatively broadened the Commission's authority, and Congress took steps to make it permanent.

After Wheeler-Lea.   In 1938, Congress passed the Wheeler-Lea Act amending Section 5 of the Federal Trade Commission Act by declaring illegal "unfair or deceptive acts or practices in commerce." This amendment expanded the Commission's power in many areas, but of more importance, it enabled the Commission to protect consumers as well as competitors. This amendment is of great consequence in the Commission's attack on deceptive advertising in that both misrepresentation of the facts and omission of relevant facts can be construed as unlawful. In fact, it allows the Commission to bring proceedings against unfair or deceptive acts that injure consumers without reference to any competitive effect.

In one of the initial tests of its newly established authority, the

Supreme Court upheld the Commission in the second Raladam case by finding that Raladam's claims for curing obesity deceived the public.[38] Following this in 1944, in the Hertzfeld case, the Court determined that a "fair probability" of having been deceived, not fraudulent intent, is sufficient to be illegal.[39] In 1965, the Supreme Court delivered a significant decision in the Colgate-Palmolive case, affirming the broad discretionary power of the FTC to prohibit deceptive advertising on television.[40] In this commercial, the advertiser attempted to provide proof of the moistening quality of their shaving cream by using it to soften sandpaper. In fact, however, the material used was not sandpaper, but rather a simulated prop made of plexiglass that had been covered with sand. In reversing a Court of Appeals decision and finding in favor of the FTC, the Supreme Court stated that "as an administrative agency which deals continually with cases in this area, the Commission is often in a better position than are courts to determine when a practice is 'deceptive' within the meaning of the Act."

In recent years, the Commission, even with its broadened power, has been under increasing criticism from consumers for its failure to deal effectively with deceptive advertising. In 1971, the FTC responded by introducing its advertising substantiation program. The two major objectives of the program were to: (1) improve consumer decision making by requiring advertisers to provide substantiating data, and (2) deter firms by publicly exposing those that cannot be substantiated.[41] In those instances where the Commission has determined that an advertisement contains inaccurate or inadequate information, a firm can be required to provide Commission-approved additional information in future advertisements, or approved corrective advertisements to reduce the effect of previous misleading or inaccurate advertisements, or both. Due to the recent application of these remedies, there is no clear consensus as to their effectiveness.

In addition to challenging those advertisements that could not be adequately supported, the Commission broadened its program focus to include advertisements that may only imply a product uniqueness that cannot be supported. For example, the Commission accused ITT Continental Baking Company of implying in their Wonder Bread advertisements that its bread was more nutritious than other similarly produced enriched white breads. Similar charges were brought by the Commission against Coca Cola in its advertising of Hi-C, Proctor & Gamble in its advertising of Crisco, and Standard Oil of California in its advertising of Chevron.

Even though the Commission has experienced success in general with its substantiation program, its expanded focus has so far had mixed results. In fact, the Commission has not been able to sustain its charges in the Hi-C and Wonder Bread cases.[42] These defeats have brought criticism from consumerists who believe that these case reversals were the result of weak case preparation. Businessmen, on the other hand, are critical of the Commission for acting without sufficient evidence and for failing to provide adequate guidelines to business in order for it to comply with the program. Most of the vested interest groups do agree, however, that the Commission needs to use more consumer research in determining whether a particular advertisement is deceptive.

Nevertheless, the substantiation program is indicative of the new aggressiveness being exhibited by the Commission not only in relation to deception but also in its other enforcement areas of responsibility. Even though the Commission may modify its direction and emphasis at times during the life of the program, it behooves the marketer now and in the future to test all products to the extent that there exists a "reasonable basis" for product claims. Although there are varying interpretations as to what constitutes a "reasonable basis," this concept will, in all probability, be the marketer's major guidepost for the next few years.

MILLER-TYDINGS ACT

The 1937 Miller-Tydings Act, an amendment to the Sherman Antitrust Act, exempted from the federal antitrust laws contracts fixing resale prices for branded and trademarked goods when such contracts have been approved by the state. More specifically, the Act permitted manufacturers the freedom of establishing the price at which retailers may sell products. This is referred to as fair trade, vertical price fixing, or resale price maintenance. The most neutral term and the one to be used here will be resale price maintenance.

Growth of resale price maintenance.   Manufacturers had for many years prior to the passage of the Miller-Tydings Act recognized the benefits of resale price maintenance. Many manufacturers feared that use by the large retail chains of well known branded products as loss leaders would not only damage their image, but also destroy the loyalty they had developed with the independent wholesalers and retailers. Although a partial solution was provided in the 1919 Colgate case[43] when the Supreme Court upheld the right of a manufacturer to refuse to sell to price-cutting retailers, the Court in subsequent decisions tended to eliminate its effectiveness. The only other alternatives available to the manufacturer to control price was by selling his products through his own stores, door-to-door with his own sales force, or on a consignment basis. These alternatives are for most manufacturers somewhat impractical.

Ultimately, as with the Robinson-Patman Act, it was the conflict between the chains and the independent retailers that led to the passage of resale price maintenance legislation. Recognizing the difficulty of obtaining federal government support for their position, independent retailers turned to the states for help. In support of their position, the retailers argued that resale price maintenance:

1. Protects the margin between retail and wholesale prices from being eroded by cutthroat competition and therefore retailers are better off economically,

2. Prevents the sale of a manufacturer's products as "loss leaders," which not only may injure the manufacturer by detracting from his reputation for quality and by limiting his access to the market but may also endanger the survival of small retailers who specialize in a product that multiproduct, multibrand stores use as a loss leader, and

3. Protects the small, locally-owned retail establishment from the competition of big, more efficient chain stores and discount houses seeking to achieve high volume at low markups.[44]

In 1931, California passed the first statute that exempted from the state antitrust laws resale price maintenance agreements. Coverage by the law was limited in that it applied only to manufacturers and retailers located within the state and to retailers that signed the agreement. To strengthen the law, a "nonsigners" clause was passed in 1933, which provided that once a manufacturer and retailer had signed a resale price maintenance agreement, it was illegal for another retailer to charge a price below the established contract price. In other words, the clause made the contract binding on all other retailers selling that good in the state. Other states using the California statute as a model adopted resale price maintenance legislation. Most of the statutes included a "nonsigner" provision, which made it possible for the manufacturers to more easily establish price setting procedures.

The effectiveness of existing state statutes was enhanced by the federal government's passage of the Miller-Tydings Act in 1937. Even though 46 states were to eventually pass resale price maintenance legislation, it was constantly under attack. The first major test of the amendment came in the 1951 Schwegmann Bros. case.[45] In this case, the Supreme Court ruled that Schwegmann Bros. price cutting tactics in the sale of liquor were legal because they had refused to sign a price maintenance agreement. This precedent-setting decision made the Miller-Tydings Act ineffective by holding the Act inapplicable to "nonsigners." In response to the Supreme Court's decision, Congress, in 1952, passed the McGuire-Keough Act, which made the nonsigners clause effective in those states having such clauses in their statutes.

The decline of resale price maintenance. In the absence of a strong fair trade law at the federal level, resale price maintenance reached its peak in the early 1950s. Following the removal of the "nonsigners" clause from the Miller-Tydings Act, scores of states repealed their own resale price maintenance laws. In 1975, Congress passed Public Law 94–145 entitled the Consumer Goods Pricing Act of 1975. At that time, only thirteen states had retained fair trade laws. The Act went into effect March 11, 1976, and today, resale price maintenance is a dead issue, much to the delight of the critics who have been trying to get rid of these laws since the early 1930s.

ANTITRUST ENFORCEMENT

Primary responsibility for enforcement of the antitrust laws rests with the Department of Justice and the Federal Trade Commission. The

Department of Justice has sole jurisdiction over violations of the Sherman Act, while the Commission is solely responsible for violations of Section 5 of the Federal Trade Commission Act. Both agencies share responsibility for enforcing the Clayton Act and related amendments. In many cases, this flexibility enables the agencies to bring suit against firms charging them with violation of more than one antitrust statute.

The agencies do, however, informally coordinate their efforts in various areas to reduce duplication. The Commission, for example, has taken primary responsibility for enforcing Section 2 of the Clayton Act (as amended by the Robinson-Patman Act). This coordination is even carried into specific industries. For example, the Commission usually investigates problems in the food industry, and the Justice Department is responsible for the steel industry.

Even though these two agencies have been given substantial authority to enforce the antitrust laws, they are limited in their annual budgets for antitrust purposes. Because of this fact, the majority of antitrust cases initiated by these agencies are resolved without formal litigation. In cases involving the Department of Justice, a defendant is allowed to negotiate a consent decree with the Department by which he agrees to certain restrictions, but is technically not guilty of violating the law. Once agreed upon, the decree must be approved by the identified case judge and filed with the court. Approximately three-fourths of the Department of Justice cases are settled by consent decree. The Federal Trade Commission, as an administrative agency, functions more informally. After issuing a formal complaint, the Commission allows firms to cease their present activities by agreeing to a consent order. Over 80 percent of the Commission's cases are disposed of in this manner.

Although limited in the past by the costly and time-consuming litigation, a growing number of suits are being filed by corporations against corporations. These cases are important in that they not only indicate a shift in approach, but also involve, in many instances, a battle between corporate giants such as Control Data versus IBM, Litton versus Xerox, and ITT versus General Telephone. Whether the reasons behind this trend reflect a dispute over technology or an attempt to win a fortune in the courtroom, they do provide another major source of corporate behavior scrutiny. The importance of this factor in antitrust enforcement is shown in the suits failed. Since 1973, over 90 percent of the antitrust suits filed were by private businesses. For example, in 1973, the government filed 45 antitrust suits while businessmen and other private parties filed 1,152.[46]

CONSUMER PROTECTION LEGISLATION

In addition to the impact of antitrust legislation, marketing is significantly influenced by a sizable network of consumer protection laws.

An analysis of consumer legislation reveals that there have been three periods of active consumer legislation in the United States. The first period came after the turn of the century, the second in the 1930s, and the third period began in the 1950s and continues today. These three periods roughly coincide with the three periods of active consumerism in this country. A comprehensive discussion of consumerism and its implications for marketing is found in Chapter 18. Of major significance here is that there has been more consumer legislation enacted in the last two decades than in all prior years taken together. A list of the major consumer protection laws and their provisions is presented in Table 13.2.

A detailed discussion of each act and its implications for marketing are beyond the scope of this text, but a close look at one recent consumer protection law will illustrate the significance of this important legislative area to the marketer. For purposes of the discussion, the Consumer Product Safety Act has been selected for examination.

CONSUMER PRODUCT SAFETY ACT

The Consumer Product Safety Act was enacted in 1972. This Act represents the most precedent-setting legislation in the product liability area to date. Product liability is the legal responsibility of sellers to compensate buyers for damages suffered because of defects in goods purchased. The Act is the result of a number of recommendations made by the National Commission on Product Safety. In its investigation, the Commission found that each year 30,000 Americans are killed, 110,000 permanently disabled, and more than 20 million injured in their homes in connection with the use of consumer products.[47]

The primary purpose of the Consumer Product Safety Act is to protect the consumer against unreasonable risk of injury related to the use of potentially hazardous products. The coverage of the Act includes all products produced or distributed for sale to consumers for use in or around a household, school, or recreation area. Also, this Act extends the liability for unsafe merchandise to all other members of the channel of distribution, as well as the manufacturer. In other words, the manufacturer, wholesaler, and retailer are all liable if they manufacture or sell to a consumer a defective product that causes injury.[48]

Probably a more realistic long-term purpose of the Act lies in its ability to promote the establishment of uniform standards for consumer products. This second objective is indicative of both a positive and preventive orientation, whereas the first deals primarily with after-the-fact situations.

A five-man Consumer Products Safety Commission was created to administer the Act. This body has the authority to force a firm to recall, repair, or replace any product that the Commission believes is hazardous to the consumer. Firms failing to comply with the Commission's orders are subject to civil penalties not to exceed $2,000 for each

TABLE 13.2.
MAJOR FEDERAL CONSUMER
LEGISLATION AFFECTING
MARKETING

Year	Legislation	Provisions
1906	Pure Food and Drug Act	Prohibits adulteration and misbranding of foods and drugs sold in interstate commerce. Places enforcement responsibilities with FDA under the Department of Agriculture.
1906	Meat Inspection Act	Required government inspection and certification of meat to upgrade slaughtering and meat handling practices.
1914	Federal Trade Commission Act	Established the agency that deals with deceptive practices.
1935	Federal Alcohol Administration Act	Prohibits commercial bribery, misleading advertising, and deceptive labeling of alcoholic beverages.
1938	Wheeler-Lea Act (Amendment to FTC Act)	Prohibits unfair or deceptive practices that have been interpreted to include protection for consumers as well as competitors.
1938	Federal Food, Drug and Cosmetic Act (Amended Pure Food and Drug Act)	Added cosmetics and therapeutic devices to the FDA's responsibility. The Act requires specific and informative labeling of foods, drugs, and cosmetics. Broadened the definition of misbranding to include any "false and misleading" label. The FDA was subsequently removed from the Department of Agriculture and is now a part of the Department of Health, Education, and Welfare.
1939	Wool Products Labeling Act	Requires full disclosure of the percentages of new wool, reprocessed wool, and other fibers or fillers used. Such information must be shown on the labels of products containing wool, except carpets, rugs, and some other textile items.
1951	Fur Products Labeling Act	Requires labels that fully disclose the name of the animal and from what part the fur derives, whether the fur is new or used, and whether the fur is bleached or dyed.
1953	Flammable Fabrics Act	Prohibits the shipment in interstate commerce of weaving apparel and fabrics so highly flammable as to be dangerous when worn.
1958	Textile Fiber Products Identification Act	Protects consumers against misbranding and false advertising of the fiber content of textile fiber products not covered by the Wool or Fur Products Labeling Acts.
1958	Automobile Information Disclosure Act	Requires auto manufacturers to affix to the auto the suggested retail price, detailing the price of all extra equipment and transportation charges on all new passenger vehicles.
1960	Federal Hazardous Substances Labeling Act	Requires warning labels on hazardous household chemicals.
1962	Kefauver-Harris Drug Amendments (amended Food and Drug Act)	Requires manufacturers to produce drugs in accordance with accepted standards of safety and purity, to provide substantial evidence of their effectiveness and to accurately label them.
1966	Fair Labeling and Packaging Act	Requires packages to be honestly and informatively labeled and attempts to reduce package size proliferation.

Year	Legislation	Provisions
1966	Cigarette Labeling Act	Requires cigarette manufacturers to label cigarettes: "Caution: Cigarette smoking may be hazardous to your health."
1967	Wholesome Meat Act	Provides the Secretary of Agriculture specific authority to require inspection and authorizes the Secretary to require denaturing and identification of meat not suitable for human consumption.
1968	Consumer Credit Protection Act	Requires all persons extending credit to another to make full disclosure in writing of all finance charges prior to consummation of the transaction.
1969	Child Protection and Toy Safety Act	Allows FDA to ban products that are so dangerous that adequate safety warnings cannot be given.
1970	Public Health Smoking Act	Bans cigarette advertising on radio and television and revised the caution on cigarette package labels to read: "Warning: The Surgeon General has determined that cigarette smoking is dangerous to your health." An amendment in 1973 extended the ban on broadcast advertising to "little cigars."
1970	Poison Prevention Labeling Act	Requires safety packaging for products that may be injurious to children.
1970	Federal Deposit Insurance Act *Amendment*	Prohibits the issuance of unsolicited credit cards, limits a consumer's liability to $50, regulates credit bureaus, and provides consumers with access to their credit files.
1972	Drug Listing Act	Provides FDA with access to wide information on drug manufacturers.
1972	Consumer Product Safety Act	Created the machinery for government-enforced quality control and is designed (1) to protect the public against unreasonable risks of injury from consumer products, (2) to assist consumers in evaluating the safety of consumer products, and (3) to develop uniform safety standards for consumer products and to promote research and investigation into the causes and prevention of product-related injuries and deaths.
1975	Consumer Product Warranty and Federal Trade Commission Improvements Act	Establishes minimum disclosure standards for written consumer product warranties and defines federal content standards for those warranties. In addition, the Act extends the consumer protection authority of the Federal Trade Commission when deceptive consumer warranties and other unfair acts and practices are found to exist.
1975	Fair Billing Credit Act	Permits the consumer to withhold payment from the issuer of a credit card when seeking restitution from a merchant for defective merchandise. The Act also provides greater legal protection against credit practices and billing errors by establishing a procedure with which all merchants must comply or else face legal redress. It also prohibits agreements barring discounts to cash-paying customers.

violation, with a maximum of $500,000 for any related series of violations.[49]

Although deficiency in self-regulation was one of the reasons for the development of the Consumer Product Safety Act, a modified form of this type of policing has been included in the Act. This provision, sometimes referred to as the "sleeper effect" or "tattle tale clause," states that if a firm recognizes a substantial hazard in a product, it has 24 hours in which to report this finding to the Commission without penalty. The Commission is authorized at this point to require the firm to recall the product, replace the product, repair the product, or make refunds, whichever is most appropriate.

Additional responsibilities of the Commission are to develop and maintain an information data base for injury information and to analyze and report this to the public. At present, information is collected daily from 119 hospitals and analyzed by the National Electronic Injury Surveillance System (NEISS—pronounced "nice"). Although an expensive system, agency engineers have been able to use the information to design remedies for product hazards; one example is the determination of "how large a baby pacifier must be to prevent a baby from breathing it in and suffocating."[50]

New consumer climate.   While the possibility of litigation is a risk to which businessmen have long been accustomed, the present volume of suits being brought against firms far outstrips all previous experience. In the product liability area alone, the number of cases on the dockets of the courts increased from fewer than 10,000 in 1953 to 50,000 in 1963 and more than 500,000 in 1973.[51] Five major reasons can be identified for the increase in product liability cases during the past few years:

1. Consumers have become more sophisticated and knowledgeable, and thus able to buy more wisely. Their resulting insistence upon complete satisfaction and fair treatment makes product safety more essential than ever before.

2. Changes in the distribution patterns of many products present the potential for rapid dissemination of defective merchandise over broad geographic areas.

3. Improved communication permits widespread and immediate public awareness of potential product hazards. This awareness encompasses not only knowledge of the potential product hazard but also awareness of the opportunity to bring suit if a defective product causes injury.

4. The unprecedented pace of technological development has provided the impetus for marketing thousands of new and untried products. Products, in turn, are becoming increasingly complex. As more and more of these products are produced, the task of maintaining adequate product safety control becomes increasingly difficult.

5. Expanded governmental concern for consumers has resulted in increased legislation in many areas. The area of product liability, because of the tangi-

ble and demonstrable nature of the complaints, lends itself particularly well to judicial review.

New legal climate.   The evolution of product liability court decisions, beginning in 1916, has eroded many of the defenses formerly available to the businessman.[52] Courts today are less likely than in the past to dismiss cases because a direct contractual relationship does not exist between the user and manufacturer or because a product has been designed and manufactured with reasonable care. This trend by the courts has facilitated recovery by buyers under the traditional claims of "breach of contract" and "negligence."

The most significant change in product liability law, however, has been the increased application by the courts of the concept of strict liability. In effect, this concept makes the seller an insurer of his product for the safety of the user. Under strict liability, a seller is liable for any and all defective or hazardous products that unduly threaten a consumer's personal safety. It makes no material difference under this concept whether warranties were or were not made, or whether negligence was present. As noted previously, the concept applies to all members involved in the manufacturing and selling of any facet of the product: manufacturers, suppliers, contractors, assemblers, and sellers alike.

Marketing implications.   It is apparent from previous discussion that the Act has significant implications for marketing. First, it makes all wholesalers and retailers as legally responsible for defective or hazardous products as the manufacturers. It certainly behooves the manufacturer to develop a product design and quality control system that not only keeps him out of court but also enables him to assure the middleman of consistent product standards.

Second, it requires the development of a channel of distribution that is efficient in moving products both ways. Due to forced recall, many manufacturers have found it much easier to distribute products than to recall them from a consumer. Compounding the problem is that many not only do not know where to look but they have no idea who buys their products. For example, Panasonic Corporation recently had to recall and modify 280,000 television sets because the units in question may emit harmful radiation. The cost of this entire task was estimated to be around $11.2 million.[53]

Third, it requires the development of an advertising program for recall that least effects the product's image. Many firms have learned that it is much easier to ruin an image than to establish one.

Fourth, the mere fact that there is a greater probability of a product liability should force most firms to take a careful look at their new product development process. Before entering the market with a product, they need to be sure not only that the product will perform safely under ordinary circumstances but also under extraordinary circumstances. This may reduce the rate of new products that enter the marketplace.

These are only a few of the implications for marketing. The cost to establish these systems, as well as the cost of liability insurance, has to influence the pricing of the products. The salesmen will need to play an important role in maintaining a two-way channel of communication with other channel members. It may also generate more stringent labeling requirements. The implications for marketers may seem limitless; as a consequence, each firm must give serious consideration to the inferences of this Act, or take the chance of heavy losses.

DOES REGULATION COST TOO MUCH?

As discussed in this chapter, there are numerous trade and consumer protection laws that have a significant effect on the conduct of business. The rate of legislation has not diminished in recent years, but rather has increased at an almost geometric rate, as shown in Figure 13.2. In the past decade, for example, Congress has enacted more than sixty major pieces of legislation affecting business. Much of this legislation was encouraged by Congress and by expressions of concern about the market power of big business. Certainly, the aggressiveness of the consumer activists has helped to foster the belief that additional legislation is necessary. As for the future, a recent public survey by the Commerce Department and the Advertising Council showed that 56.0 percent of Americans want even more government regulation, while 35.0 percent want less.[54]

The growth in legislation, however, is not without its critics. In fact, there has been increasing concern over the effectiveness of not only the laws but also the agencies established to enforce them. Businessmen are critical of the trend toward more laws and more government agencies, for they see themselves spending more time in court than in other firm-related activities. The legal costs for firms have doubled and, in some cases, tripled in the past few years. It is estimated that the legal bill for all United States corporations in 1976 will be in excess

FIGURE 13.2.
GROWTH OF BUSINESS
LEGISLATION

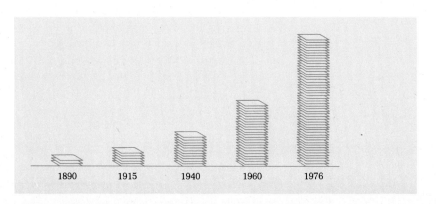

| 1890 | 1915 | 1940 | 1960 | 1976 |

of $3 billion. For many firms, the costs could be staggering. Consider the following:

Mandatory safety standards for power lawnmowers being developed for the Consumer Product Safety Commission could increase the cost of a $100 mower to $186 and might put 25 manufacturers out of business.[55]

A closer look at the implications of these laws reveals that consumers are also paying their share of the bill. At present, the structure necessary to carry out the regulatory functions is massive; over 63,400 federal regulators are employed. It is estimated that "the annual cost to consumers of unnecessary and wasteful regulatory policies is $2,000 per family."[56] For the public, this amounts to approximately $130 billion per year. The majority of consumers are willing to incur these costs if there is improvement in the quality and safety of the products they purchase. In many instances, however, this is not the case. Consider, for example, the following:

A tire-quality grading system being developed by the National Highway Traffic Safety Administration could cost consumers as much as $150 million a year and yet be too confusing to be of use to tire buyers.[57]

The quality of the laws that exist to protect the consumer and the competitor in the marketplace, and the total impact of these laws on business and society must be weighed. In regard to consumer protection legislation, Alan Greenspan, Chairman of the President's Council of Economic Advisers, stated that:

To paraphrase Gresham's Law: bad "protection" drives out good. The attempt to protect the consumer by force undercuts the protection he gets from incentive. First, it undercuts the value of reputation by placing the reputable company on the same basis as the unknown, the newcomer or the fly-by-nighter. Second, it grants an automatic (though, in fact, unachievable) guarantee of safety of products of any company that complies with its arbitrarily set minimum standards. . . .

Protection of the consumer by regulation is thus illusory. Rather than isolating the consumer from the dishonest businessman, it is gradually destroying the only reliable protection the consumer has: competition for reputation.[58]

Although Mr. Greenspan's argument may seem to imply that consumer protection is unnecessary, past experience has shown that for items such as drugs, foodstuffs, household chemicals, and many others, the laws are necessary. They have allowed the consumer, faced with a multitude of complex products and decisions, to place greater reliance on the dependability and safety of products, thus making the buying process easier.

On the other hand, the laws should be written and enforced so that the firms that willingly comply are not penalized. It appears that the pressure for additional legislation has not provided the time for Congress, the enforcement agencies, and consumers to ask the realistic question: Are the benefits received worth the costs presently being incurred? Even though the answer is yes, consider one company's harrowing experience:

Ed Sohmers knows what it's like to run into the federal regulatory buzz saw. Mr. Sohmers is general manager of Marlin Toy Products, Inc., a small manufacturer of a line of toys for infants and preschool children located in Horicon, Wis., a farming community of about 3,500 persons. Two years ago, the company employed 85 persons and was a thriving enterprise. Today, after a bitter encounter with the bureaucracy, it is teetering on the edge of bankruptcy.

The story involves the Consumer Product Safety Commission, once termed "the most powerful independent regulatory agency ever created." In November, 1972, the Food and Drug Administration informed Marlin that the toy plastic balls it manufactured were unsafe because they contained plastic butterflies and colored pellets that could be swallowed by a child if the toys broke open. The company had never received a complaint of any harm being caused by the toys since they were first marketed in 1962. At a cost of $96,000, the company recalled the balls and removed the pellets with the approval of the FDA.

In 1973, anticipating big holiday sales, Marlin produced hundreds of thousands of the toys, hoping to recover losses. In the meantime, however, the Consumer Product Safety Commission, which had taken over regulation of toys, published a banned-products list—including the toys Marlin had redesigned months before. The Commission acknowledged a "printing error," but by that time stores all across the country had canceled orders. Marlin lost a total of 1.2 million dollars, and had to sell its toy lines that had accounted for 85 per cent of its income. Congress passed a resolution to award the company damages, but the amount has yet to be set by a claims court.

Now, Marlin has laid off all but 10 employees. "I feel like the captain of a lifeboat," says Mr. Sohmers. "I don't know who to kick out next. We are just emotionally drained and demoralized by this experience. We're staying afloat through small contract jobs, but if we don't get a court settlement by the middle of July, we'll just collapse. I was just a virgin in the woods in Washington's bureaucracy when this hit us," says Mr. Sohmers. "We have been badgered, intimidated, stonewalled and ignored by Government." "Strangely," he adds, "we aren't bitter. People in Government aren't malicious and they don't have evil motives. We found lots of Government officals sympathetic. But we just got snared in a bureaucratic mistake, and the system just seemed to be rigged against us." Now, says Mr. Sohmers, he's glad the company fought for its rights. "I think we will serve as an example to other businesses not to let big Government beat them down."[59]

SUMMARY

This chapter focused upon the role of legislation in maintaining a healthy and effective competitive market economy. The U.S. experience has shown that government intervention is not only necessary but also demanded by both business competitors and consumers. The legislation affecting marketing can be divided into two broad categories: (1) antitrust legislation, and (2) consumer protection legislation.

The two agencies responsible for enforcing much of the relevant marketing legislation are the Department of Justice and the Federal Trade Commission. The Federal Trade Commission may have the more far-reaching impact on marketing in that it is responsible for enforcing not only many of the antitrust laws but also a significant number of the consumer protection laws. Although the majority of suits brought by these agencies are settled out of court, their recent aggressiveness in enforcement has made the legal implications with respect to marketing decisions of critical importance. The involvement of additional agencies in the regulation of business, such as the Consumer Product Safety Commission, complicates the process even though it provides a necessary service. It cannot be denied that the technologies of business require protection for its participants. Yet, it is also necessary to consider the costs incurred, both tangible and intangible, and the quality of benefits received.

QUESTIONS FOR DISCUSSION

1. What is the rationale for government regulation?

2. Identify and discuss the major antitrust laws, their relationships to each other, and their major provisions.

3. Why is price-fixing still one of the most common antitrust violations that exists today?

4. Describe the differences between horizontal, vertical, and conglomerate mergers. Can the same criterion be applied in judging their legality?

5. The Federal Trade Commission Act has been referred to as the most far-reaching antitrust law. Why is this true?

6. Explain the nature and scope of the FTC's advertising substantiation program.

7. The Robinson-Patman Act was enacted to protect the small retailers from the large retail chains. Describe its principal provisions and the available defenses. Has the law been effective?

8. It was stated that the marketplace will be better for both consumers and businessmen with more consumer protection legislation. Do you agree or disagree? Defend your position.

9. What is the Consumer Product Safety Act? What are its implications for marketers?

10. "Legislation that is designed to protect the consumer can never cost too much." What is your personal reaction to this statement?

NOTES

[1]Robert F. Hartley, *Marketing: Management and Social Change* (San Francisco, California: Intext Educational Publishers, 1972), p. 175.

[2]*Ibid.*

[3]Richard Caves, *American Industry: Structure, Conduct, Performance,* 2nd. ed., © 1967, p. 57. Reprinted by permission of Prentice-Hall, Inc., Englewood Cliffs, New Jersey.

[4]In a strict legal sense, the term "trust" applies only to the trustee form of organization. During this period, however, it was generically used to identify any form of big business.

[5]Clair Wilcox, *Public Policies Toward Business* (4th ed.; Homewood, Illinois: Richard D. Irwin, Inc., 1971), p. 47.

[6]Standard Oil Co. v. U.S., 221 U.S. 1 (1911); United States v. American Tobacco Co., 221 U.S. 106 (1911).

[7]U.S. v. Aluminum Company of America, 148F (2d) 416 (1945).

[8]American Tobacco Company v. U.S., 328 U.S. 781, 811 (1946).

[9]U.S. v. Addyston Pipe & Steel Company, 85 F 271, 29 C.C.A. 141, affirmed 175 U.S. 211, 20 S. Ct. 96, 44 L. Ed. 136 (1899).

[10]U.S. v. Trenton Potteries Company, 273 U.S. 392, 47 S. Ct. 377, 71 L. Ed. 700 (1927); U.S. v. Socony-Vacuum Oil Co., Inc., 310 U.S. 150, 60 S. Ct. 811, 84 L. Ed. 1129 (1940).

[11]United States v. Westinghouse Electric Co., *et al.*; General Electric Co., *et al.*; I-T-E Circuit Breaker Co., *et al.*; Ohio Brass Co., *et al.*; McGraw-Edison Co., *et al.*; A. B. Chance Co., *et al.*; and Lapp Insulator Co., Inc. (D.C. Pa. 1960).

[12]Lee E. Preston, "Restrictive Distribution Arrangements: Economic Analysis and Public Policy Standards," *Law and Contemporary Problems,* Vol. 30 (Summer, 1965), p. 508.

[13]*Ibid.*

[14]U.S. v. Arnold, Schwinn & Co., *et al.*, 383 U.S. 365, 374 (1967).

[15]U.S. v. Topco Associates, 405 U.S. 596 (1972).

[16]Louis W. Stern and John R. Grabner, Jr., *Competition in the Marketplace* (Glenview, Illinois: Scott, Foresman and Company, 1970), pp. 86–87.

[17]Senate Report No. 698, to accompany H. R. 15, 657 (63rd Congress, 2nd Session, 1914), p. 1.

[18]Thatcher Mfg. Co. v. FTC, Swift & Co. v. FTC, 272 U.S. 554 (1926); Arrow-Hart & Hegeman Electric Co. v. FTC, 291 U.S. 587 (1934).

[19]Brown Shoe Co. v. U.S., 370 U.S. 294 (1962).

[20]U.S. v. Pabst Brewing Co., 384 U.S. 546 (1966).

[21]U.S. v. Von's Grocery Co., 384 U.S. 280 (1966).

[22]Arthur J. Marinelli, "Conglomerate Mergers," *American Business Law Journal* (Spring, 1973), pp. 1–2.

[23]*Ibid.*, pp. 6–7.

[24]FTC v. Procter & Gamble, 87 S. Ct. 1224, 1231 (1967).

[25]Theodore N. Beckman, William R. Davidson, and W. Wayne Talarzyk, *Marketing* (9th ed.; New York: The Ronald Press Company, 1973), p. 61.

[26]Lewis Beman, "What We Learned from the Great Merger Frenzy," *Fortune* (April, 1973), p. 71.

[27]F. M. Scherer, *Industrial Market Structure and Economic Performance* (Chicago, Illinois: Rand McNally College Publishing Company, 1970), 496.

[28]Federal Trade Commission, *Chain Stores: Final Report in the Chain Store Investigation* (Washington, D.C.: U.S. Government Printing Office, 1935), p. 90.

[29]Much of this has been adapted from Scherer, *Industrial Market Structure and Economic Performance,* pp. 495–504.

[30]U.S. v. The Borden Company, 383 U.S. 637, 649–50 (1966).

[31]Hansen Paint & Glass Co. v. Pittsburgh Plate, CCH Sec. 74,563 (CA-5, June 1973), *Journal of Marketing,* Vol. 38, No. 1 (January, 1974), pp. 74–75; Cardigan v. Texaco, Inc., CCH Sec. 74,935 (CA-9, March 1974), *Journal of Marketing,* Vol. 38, No. 4 (October, 1974), p. 87; Harbor Banana Distributors, Inc. v. FTC, CCH Sec. 75,216 (CA-5, August 1974), *Journal of Marketing,* Vol. 39, No. 2 (April, 1975), p. 81.

[32]"Robinson-Patman Act under Attack," *CCH Trade Regulation Report Newsletter No. 162* (February 4, 1975).

[33]FTC v. Gratz, 253 U.S. 421, 427 (1920).

[34]Elmer E. Smead, *Governmental Promotion and Regulation of Business* (New York: Meredith Corporation, 1969), pp. 90–91.

[35]FTC v. Raladam Co., 283 U.S. 643 (1931), affirming 42 F. (2d) 430 (1930).

[36]FTC v. Keppel & Bros., 291 U.S. 304, 309–314 (1934).

[37]*Ibid.*

[38]FTC v. Raladam Co., 316 U.S. 149 (1942).

[39]Hertzfeld, *et al.* v. FTC, 140 F (2d) 207 (1944).

[40]FTC v. Colgate-Palmolive Co., *et al.*, 380 U.S. 374 (1965).

[41]Robert E. Wilkes and James B. Wilcox, "Recent FTC Actions: Implications for the Advertising Strategist," *Journal of Marketing,* Vol. 38 (January, 1974), p. 55.

[42]A summarization of these cases are found in the "Legal Developments in Marketing" sections of the *Journal of Marketing* (October, 1973), p. 91; and (July 1973), p. 81.

[43]U.S. v. Colgate & Co., 250 U.S. 300 (1919).

[44]Scherer, *Industrial Market Structure and Economic Performance,* pp. 513–514.

[45]Schwegmann Bros. v. Calvert Distillers Corp., 341 U.S. 384 (1951).

[46]"Is John Sherman's Antitrust Obsolete?" *Business Week* (March 23, 1974), p. 48.

[47]Paul H. Weaver, "The Hazards of Trying to Make Consumer Products Safer," *Fortune* (July, 1975), p. 133.

[48]E. Patrick McGuire, "Consumer Product Safety," *The Conference Board Record* (September, 1973), p. 61.

[49]U.S. Consumer Product Safety Commission, *First Annual Report* (November, 1973), p. 65.

[50]Weaver, "The Hazards . . .," p. 135.

[51]Norman L. Staats, "Coping with Product Liability," *Credit and Finance Management* (October, 1973), p. 11.

[52]First court decision which held that the privity requirement afforded no protection to a negligent manufacturer or seller if the product which caused injury was the type of product that is reasonably certain to be dangerous if negligently manufactured. MacPherson v. Buick Motor, 217 NY 382, 111 NE 1050 (1916).

[53]E. Patrick McGuire, "The High Cost of Recalls," *The New York Times,* Section 3 (Business and Finance), March 30, 1975, p. 1.

[54]"The Regulators," *U.S. News & World Report* (June 30, 1975), p. 26.

[55]*Ibid.*, p. 24.

[56]*Ibid.*

[57]*Ibid.*

[58]Robert M. Bleiberg, "Government and Business," *Barron's* (April 28, 1975), p. 12.

[59]"The Regulators," reprinted from *U.S. News & World Report* (June 30, 1975), p. 28. Copyright 1975, U.S. News & World Report, Inc.

SUGGESTED READINGS

Beman, Lewis, "What We Learned from the Great Merger Frenzy," *Fortune* (April, 1973), pp. 70–73

Brozen, Yale, "Antitrust Out of Hand," *The Conference Board Record* (March, 1974), pp. 14–19.

Burley, James R., "Territorial Restriction in Distribution Systems: Current Legal Developments," *Journal of Marketing* (October, 1975), pp. 52–56.

Cunningham, William H. and Isabella C. M. Cunningham, "Consumer Protection: More Information or More Regulation," *Journal of Marketing* (April, 1976), pp. 63–68.

Hunt, Shelby D. and John R. Nevin, "Tying Agreements in Franchising," *Journal of Marketing* (July, 1975), pp. 20–26.

"Is John Sherman's Antitrust Obsolete?" *Business Week* (March 23, 1974), pp. 46–56.

Kintner, Earl W., *An Antitrust Primer: A Guide to Antitrust and Trade Regulation Laws for Businessmen* (2nd ed.; New York: The Macmillan Co., 1973).

Loudenback, Lynn J. and John W. Goebel, "Marketing in the Age of Strict Liability," *Journal of Marketing* (January, 1974), pp. 62–66.

Marinelli, Arthur J., "Conglomerate Mergers," *American Business Law Journal* (Spring, 1973), pp. 1–14.

Stern, Louis W. and John R. Grabner, Jr., *Competition in the Marketplace* (Glenview, Illinois: Scott, Foresman and Company, 1970).

Stern, Louis W., Orize Agodo, and Fuat A. Firat, "Territorial Restrictions in Distribution: A Case Analysis," *Journal of Marketing* (April, 1976), pp. 69–75.

Wilkes, Robert E. and James B. Wilcox, "Recent FTC Actions: Implications for the Advertising Strategist," *Journal of Marketing* (January, 1974), pp. 55–61.

14
THE COMPETITIVE ENVIRONMENT

THE COMPETITIVE ENVIRONMENT

As emphasized throughout this book, marketing takes place within a competitive environment. In an earlier chapter, it was noted that the rivalry among firms for position in the market creates competition. Chapter 7 pointed out the role of competition in directing resources in a market system economy. The preceding chapter on the legal environment stressed the significance of maintaining a competitive market structure. From a marketing perspective, therefore, competition is an important element in both the macro and the micro process of marketing. In recognition of its scope and importance in business decision making, this chapter examines the competitive environment as it functions in the American economy.

PERSPECTIVES OF COMPETITION

Although the maintenance of competition in the United States is a national economic policy, its interpretation by those who should know the most about it differs significantly. When defining competition, R. C. Bernhard highlighted this problem:

> Neither unity nor consistency is apparent in the various meanings which lawyers, judges, economists, and businessmen give to the term competition. Competition is a standard by which the law judges the legality of many business practices; competition is an abstraction which economists use to pass judgment on economic institutions and policies; competition is a plague upon firms who feel that their share of the market is insecure.[1]

The problem is compounded even further in that the participants find it difficult to agree among themselves. To provide a relevant interpretation, this section focuses on two perspectives of competition from the viewpoints of those who have professionalized it—the economists —and those who have practiced it—the businessmen. This does not mean that those who must determine the extent to which competition exists, those in government, are to be excluded. The government's viewpoint is established by trends developed from public policy decisions. As may be expected, the logic of most public policy decisions tends to be largely a reflection of the dominant economic perspective. For the marketer, an examination of the varying perspectives of competition provides insight into both the government's responsibility to maintain competition as a viable national policy and the firm's discretion in applying the elements of the marketing mix.

THE ECONOMISTS'
PERSPECTIVE

An economist may generally define competition as the existence of a number of sellers and buyers of a specific commodity, acting independently of each other and limited in size so no one participant can influence price.[2] By maintaining these two conditions in the market-place, the economy is better able to achieve maximum economic efficiency. According to the classical economist, the most desirable form is "pure competition."

Dissatisfaction with the use of pure competition as an analytical model of the marketplace, however, forced economists to develop additional market models that were more descriptive of the American economy. Since it would have been almost impossible to examine each and every industry, it was necessary to develop market structure models that were general abstractions. Although few, if any, of these abstractions fit all of the characteristics identified in a specific market structure, they do enable the economist to develop a much more precise meaning of competition.

The economists have identified four relatively distinct market structures: pure competition, pure monopoly, monopolistic competition, and oligopoly. Pure competition represents the economist's "ideal" market structure, and pure monopoly at the other end of the market structure continuum is the least acceptable. In between these two extremes are found monopolistic competition and oligopolistic competition, which are more typical of present-day American industry. These two structures contain elements of both pure competition and pure monopoly. Table 14.1 provides a summary of the four market structures and their characteristics.[3] Although the general characteristics of these market structures are applicable to both the seller and buyer, the discussion here will emphasize the selling side of the market.

Pure competition. The purely competitive market structure, although subject to certain constraints and exceptions, is identified as the structure that will lead to the most efficient allocation of resources. In order for pure competition to exist, the following conditions are essential:

1. A large number of small sellers, so that no one seller's action will have any appreciable effect on supply of the product and consequently its price.

2. A large number of small buyers, so that the action of one buyer will have no appreciable effect on the demand for the product and the resultant price.

3. A homogeneous product, so that it would make no difference whether it was obtained from one seller or another.

4. No artificial barriers that would preclude easy entry to and exit from the market.

5. All sellers must offer to sell and all buyers must buy under exactly the same conditions with regards to price, credit terms, delivery, quantities, etc.[4]

In a purely competitive market, there is no discretion for setting marketing policies. The price for a product is determined by the market, and the firm merely adjusts to market price. With all marketing

Characteristics	Pure Competition	Monopolistic Competition	Oligopoly	Monopoly
Number of Sellers	Infinite	Many	Few	One
Nature of Product	Standardized (Infinite Substitutes)	Differentiated (Many Substitutes)	Differentiated (Few Substitutes)	Unique, No Close Substitutes
Market Entry	Easy, No Obstacles	Relatively Easy	Restricted	Blocked
Price Control	None, Market Determined	Some, but Determined by the Degree of Differentiation	Some, but Limited by Competitor Mutual Interdependence	Considerable
Marketing Mix Discretion	None	Considerable, Emphasizing all Elements of the Marketing Mix	Considerable, Emphasizing the Non-Price Elements of the Marketing Mix	Some, to Reduce Product Elasticity and Expand Demand

SOURCE: Adapted from Robert J. Holloway and Robert S. Hancock, *Marketing in a Changing Environment* (2nd ed.; New York: John Wiley & Sons, Inc., 1973), p. 107 and *Marketing Principles: The Management Process*, by Ben M. Enis, page 102. Copyright © 1974 by Goodyear Publishing Company.

TABLE 14.1.
MARKET STRUCTURE
CONTINUUM AND
CHARACTERISTICS

related elements of the firm standardized, differences in product quality, advertising, packaging, or distribution outlets are nonexistent. No firm, therefore, is able to obtain a quality edge over its rivals.

Although the ascribed major advantage of a purely competitive structure is that it allocates resources efficiently, it does suffer from two very significant deficiencies. First, since it is under the operation of the market system, a firm responds only to those demands of consumers that can be expressed in the marketplace. Thus, the purely competitive market system ignores the importance of certain social goods, such as education, national defense, and welfare for the poor. Second, and what appears to be a far more fundamental deficiency, consumers have no true choice as to what they can buy. This is the result of all products being assumed identical. Because of these rigorous conditions, it is doubtful that pure competition exists in reality.

Pure monopoly. At the opposite end of the continuum is a market structure generally known as pure monopoly. Pure monopoly can be defined as complete control of an economic good for which there is no close substitute. This structure is characterized by a single firm producing the entire output of a given product. In contrast to the firm operating in the purely competitive market structure, the monopolist has complete control over the price of the product. Once a particular price is selected, however, market conditions automatically impose a quantity to be purchased. The primary area of marketing discretion available in a pure monopoly market structure is in pricing, where the task is to determine the best combination of price and quantity to achieve the company's goals.

Due to the lack of close substitutes for the product, the other marketing mix components are not nearly as important. Although monopolists may use other elements of the marketing mix, such as advertising or sales promotion, they do so only to reduce the elasticity of or expand the demand for their particular product or service. Because monopolists are able to control price, they are able to obtain profits significantly above those that would be obtained in a competitive market structure. Continued success of monopolists depends on their ability to prevent competitors from entering their market. This no-substitute product is maintained by developing barriers to entry, such as ownership of raw materials, economies of large-scale production, and patents.

As is true in the purely competitive market, the consumer's freedom of choice is limited in a pure monopoly market structure. There are no close substitutes, and the consumer must pay a higher price. That is, the consumer loses both real income and real choice. The majority of monopolies that exist today are regulated by the government. Two prominent examples in the United States are American Telephone and Telegraph and the various public utility firms that supply power and gas in assigned market areas.

Monopolistic Competition. The monopolistic competition market structure combines some of the features of pure competition and pure monopoly. It is characterized by a significant number of both reasonably large and small competitors offering similar, but not identical products. A large number of individual sellers is necessary in order that each has neither complete freedom from competitive pressures, nor complete servitude to them. The large number of firms tends to limit both the amount of control each has over market price and the concern for the reaction of each to the others. The individual seller can develop some insulation from competitive pressures through product differentiation, which enables the seller to assume the role of a monopolist. This means monopolists exist in a specific market to the extent that they are the only seller of their own identified brand name product. Coca Cola, for example, is a monopolist even though it faces the competition of Pepsi Cola, Seven Up, and other brands of soft drinks; however, the existence of close substitutes limits the seller's monopoly power.

This structure provides the marketer with significant decision making discretion, but it also provides the consumer with a variety of products from which to choose. This particular market structure is responsive to the fact that consumers do not have identical wants and that their preferences for products are dependent upon taste and values developed over time. Although the market price may be somewhat above that established in pure competition, it is not considered excessive because of the existence of a large number of firms and close substitutes, which keep prices down. Monopolistic competition is characteristic of a wide number of industries in the American economy. The women's garment industry, which is made up of a large number of small producers that are concentrated in a few areas, is an excellent example of monopolistic competition. This structure also exists in many cities that have a large number of grocery stores, clothing shops, service stations, and restaurants.

Oligopoly.   Oligopoly is characterized by a small number of firms in an industry where each firm's share of the market is sufficiently large that its actions and policies affect other firms in the industry. Accordingly, mutual interdependence develops among industry members, because the large market share possessed by each forces rivals to anticipate the actions of competing firms. Firms do have some control over price, but price competition is limited by the mutual interdependence of the firms. To clarify, a firm that increased price in an oligopolistic market would find that competitors would not follow, which would cause the firm to lose both customers and revenue. Conversely, if a firm in an oligopolistic market lowered the price of its product, competitors would be required to follow or else lose customers and revenue. This type of action, however, could lead to a price war. Therefore, the nonprice elements of the marketing mix take on increased competitive importance in an oligopolistic structure. This structure differs from the monopolistic competitive market structure in that a firm attempts to insulate itself from competitors by emphasizing marketing mix components other than price; that is, such components as product, promotion, and distribution. In their operations, oligopolies are classified into two types—differentiated and undifferentiated. Differentiated oligopolistic industries are those that sell products that may differ in real or imaginary qualities, such as automobiles, soap, or cereal. Undifferentiated oligopolistic industries are those with products that are homogeneous, such as aluminum, nylon, steel, or bread.

As would be expected, when an industry is dominated by a few large firms, it may be almost impossible to enter that particular industry.

Entry is usually made difficult by the extremely high capital requirements, or high fixed costs associated with the particular industry. Entry can also be hindered by ownership of patents, access to raw materials, and the reputation of the firm and its products that has been developed over time. Since oligopoly tends toward monopoly on the market structure continuum, economic theory contends that the consumer is required to pay higher prices. Yet, the argument can be made that if it were not for the ability of these large firms to obtain economies of scale, the price might be much higher. In addition, it is also argued that firms in oligopolistic industries are able, with their profits, to undertake the expensive task of modern research, which develops new products, lower prices, and enhanced consumer satisfaction for the future.

THE BUSINESSMAN'S PERSPECTIVE

If a businessman were asked if the industry was highly competitive, the answer would likely be yes. In fact, concern may be expressed not only about present competitors, but also about new firms that might enter the industry. Concern may also be expressed about decisions in regard to the number of salespersons that must be employed, the advertising budget that must be met, efforts needed to obtain new business, product improvement, and other efforts that are necessary to maintain old and expand new product lines. In fact, it doesn't really matter which market structure characterizes an industry; the businessman's response would probably not differ substantially. The businessman simply has a different orientation toward competition than the economist. The economist is interested principally with the role of competition as it effects the overall performance of the economic system; that is, the economist examines competition primarily from a macro perspective. The businessman, on the other hand, is interested in rivalry on an individual basis as it affects the particular firm in a micro context. Joel Dean described competition from a businessman's point of view:

> Generally speaking, competition to the businessman is whatever he has to do to get business away from his rivals and whatever they do to take sales away from him. ... the same behavior traits which the businessman sees as hallmarks of competition are viewed by economists as indicia of monopoly.[5]

Most businessmen agree that by economists' standards, business competition is basically imperfect competition. Yet, the businessman believes that business competition is a much more dynamic and active process than that identified by the imperfect market structures. In traditional market structures, competition is viewed as a struggle among companies in the same industry, but this represents only part of the task faced by the businessman. The dynamics of today's marketplace require the businessman to consider two distinct forms of competition: generic competition and enterprise competition.

Generic competition. Generic competition is recognition by the businessman of the necessity to produce a total product that will satisfy a basic need. Although the basic need behind a purchase may be difficult to identify and may be satisfied by a number of different products, the need will continue to exist long after specific products have been withdrawn from the market. Each firm, regardless of its product, represents an alternative way for the consumer to spend income. In this context, Vega not only competes with Pinto, but also Volkswagen, the city transit system, Schwinn, Honda, walking shoes, savings, and any other alternative available to the consumer searching for economical transportation. Since each consumer has a variety of needs to be met, each firm is basically competing with all other firms. Competition viewed from this perspective forces businessmen to consider why their product is purchased and what its role and importance is in relation to other products on the market. Answers to these questions may identify present product line weaknesses, as well as generate opportunities for satisfying similar needs. Generic competition represents a firm's effort to sell a profitable volume of goods in the face of the offerings of all other sellers.

Enterprise competition. Enterprise competition exists among firms selling similar products in an identifiable industry such as General Motors, Ford, Chrysler, and Volkswagen. In enterprise competition, the firm can increase its profitable volume by expanding the total demand for the product, or by taking sales away from competitors. Primary responsibility for achieving a profitable volume rests with marketing. The objective of a marketing strategy is to develop for the firm a marketing mix that will provide a substantial differential advantage, as viewed by the relevant market segments, over the offerings of competitors. By monitoring its consumers and competitors, a firm is better able to vary the marketing mix components in order to develop or maintain its differential advantage. As today's businessman knows, the success of any particular marketing mix is temporary, especially when price is emphasized, because it can be so quickly imitated.

Firms selling similar products may be equally successful even though they are using a different marketing mix. In the cosmetics industry, for example, where Avon and Revlon each use a significantly different marketing mix, both have been very successful. Avon sells their cosmetics door-to-door and employs over 450,000 sales people in carrying out this task. Revlon, on the other hand, sells only through retail outlets and places a much greater emphasis on advertising and sales promotion activities, such as point-of-purchase displays.

Firms may also profit by imitating the marketing mix of the industry leader. Church's Fried Chicken has been successful by copying the basic marketing mix used by Kentucky Fried Chicken. However, not to be outdone, Kentucky Fried Chicken has continued to innovate by modifying its marketing mix to include new product line items, such as crispy chicken, barbecued chicken, barbecued spare ribs, as well as other assorted but related fast food items. In regard to the marketing mix, the contemporary businessman must act and react in order to survive.

No pure competition

COMPETITION IN THE MARKETPLACE

From the above discussion of the perspectives of competition, it should be evident that competition in the American marketplace does not exist in a pure form. The competitive environment in the United States provides a system of "workable competition." According to J. M. Clark, a pioneer of the concept, a "workably competitive" market is more economically advantageous to society than any other achievable alternative.[6] The concept has numerous interpretations, but all include two basic factors:

1. a sufficient number of sellers to offer buyers a reasonable number of competing sources of supply, and

2. sufficient elements of monopoly power to ensure technological progress and economies of scale.[7]

Workable competition as a concept is all-inclusive and attempts to consider the interrelationships of the structure of a market, the behavior of enterprises in the market, and their performance in the market. Market performance is generally accepted as a standard for ascertaining the existence of workable competition. A market is workably competitive when it offers the consumer sufficient choice among products and the ability to influence market characteristics. The difficulty experienced in trying to operationalize the components of this concept, however, has led to a decrease in its importance.

Whatever the current status of workable competition, the efforts of industrial organization economists to apply the concept to imperfectly competitive markets has resulted in useful industry studies and new

(Workable Competition) →

FIGURE 14.1.
THE DIMENSIONS OF A
MARKET STRUCTURE

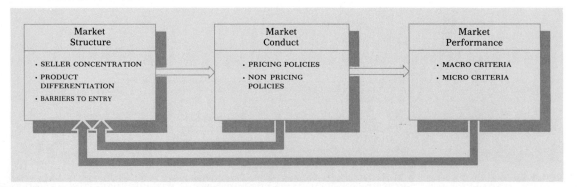

Company Rank Group in Respective Years	Percent of Value Added by Manufacture							
	1970	1967	1966	1963	1962	1958	1954	1947
Largest 50 Companies	24	25	25	25	24	23	23	17
Largest 100 Companies	33	33	33	33	32	30	30	23
Largest 150 Companies	38	38	38	37	36	35	34	27
Largest 200 Companies	43	42	42	41	40	38	37	30

NOTE: 1962, 1966, and 1970 based on the annual survey of manufacturers. Other years based on census of manufacturers.

SOURCE: U.S. Bureau of the Census, Annual Survey of Manufactures: 1970, *Value-of-Shipment Concentration Ratios*, M70(AS)-9 (Washington, D.C.: U.S. Government Printing Office, 1972), p. 3.

TABLE 14.2.
SHARE OF TOTAL VALUE
ADDED BY MANUFACTURE
ACCOUNTED FOR BY LARGEST
MANUFACTURING COMPANIES
IN 1970 COMPARED WITH
SHARE ACCOUNTED FOR BY
LARGEST COMPANIES IN
EARLIER YEARS

techniques for examining competition in the marketplace. Industrial organization economists analyze markets on three dimensions: (1) structure, (2) conduct, and (3) performance.[8] Market structure refers to the organizational characteristics of a market; market conduct refers to the actual commercial behavior of firms in an industry; and market performance refers to the results of market activity and the criteria by which market results are evaluated. The major assumption underlying present public policy is that the structure of an industry determines the conduct of member firms, which, in turn, determines the industry's performance. These relationships are presented in Figure 14.1.

CONCENTRATION, product differentiation, BARRIRS

MARKET STRUCTURE   Identified as the initial determinant of market conduct and performance, market structure is given a significant position in establishing the extensiveness of competition. Any study of market structure begins with an analysis of its elements. The major elements of market structure are seller concentration, product differentiation, and barriers to entry.

MOST IMP →

Concentration.   Of the three major factors of market structure, concentration receives the most attention. It was estimated in 1932 that the two hundred largest firms controlled 49 percent of the nation's total production assets. Today, the two hundred largest firms control two-thirds of these assets.[9] However, many people are skeptical of these figures since the variation in accounting rules make assets difficult to measure. A preferred measure of large firm dominance is the use of "value added," the margin between purchase and sales.[10] Table 14.2 identifies the percent of value added by manufacturers for the largest 50, 100, 150, and 200 firms over a selected number of years.

Even though a general trend toward increased concentration from 1947 to 1970 can be identified, it is not nearly as dramatic as suggested by the total assets approach. A partial explanation for the increased trend lies in the fact that industries composed of larger firms have grown much faster than industries containing smaller firms.[11]

A discussion of growth in aggregate concentration is limited in value, since it does not provide any information on concentration in individual markets. From a marketing standpoint, a more important measure is market concentration, or the number and size distribution of the firms in a particular industry. A widely used method for measuring market concentration is the concentration ratio, which is the relative share of an industry's shipments by an identified number of the largest firms. Table 14.3 presents the concentration ratios for the four, eight, and twenty largest firms in selected industries.

When the percentage of sales accounted for by the largest four firms in an industry exceeds 50 percent, the industry is considered an oligopoly. As noted earlier, sellers in an oligopolistic industry act interdependently to set prices and raise barriers to entry in order to insulate themselves as much as possible from competition. This interdependence of action limits potential entrants, raises consumer prices, and ensures high profits. If this situation truly exists, it does not speak well of the U.S. economic system. This indictment, however, is not accepted by all, especially when the statistics indicate that there has been no significant increase in market concentration since World War II.[12] Neil Jacoby, a noted economist, argues the following:

> Large firms and concentrated industries result from efforts to realize the financial, marketing, research and management economies of multiplant, multidivisional and vertical integration. These are generally ignored by economists who focus on the manufacturing economies in relation to the scale of individual plants.[13]

The major limitation in measuring concentration is the uncertainty that exists in establishing market definitions. Most experts, including marketing academicians, tend to define markets in simplified and outdated terms. Definitions such as the following are representative of both academic and industrial usage:

> A market is an exchange relationship among buyers and sellers. . . . Buyers and sellers communicate to acquaint each other with the products and services available and desired, and with their willingness and ability to trade, which includes prices and quantities.[14]

> The market is a point, place, or sphere in which transfers in the ownership of goods are effected. . . . markets can also be thought of as relatively homogeneous groups or segments of potential customers with similar interests, needs . . .[15]

These definitions may be representative, but they do little to assist the marketing manager in defining the scope of the market. On the other hand, the courts, in deciding antitrust cases, must determine the scope of a market as measured by the product substitutes and the

Industry	Total Number of Companies	Percentage of Value of Shipments Accounted for by:		
		4 Largest	8 Largest	20 Largest
Prepared Meats	2,529	26	38	50
Canned Fruits and Vegetables	930	22	34	52
Cereal	30	88	97	99+
Bread, Cake and Related Products	3,445	26	38	47
Chewing Gum	19	86	96	100
Bottled and Canned Soft Drinks	3,057	13	20	28
Roasted Coffee	206	53	71	87
Cigarettes	8	81	100	—
Women's Hosiery	302	32	44	64
Women's and Misses' Dresses	5,008	7	9	14
Wallpaper	74	39	55	79
Book Publishing	973	20	32	57
Commercial Printing	11,955	14	21	29
Greeting Card Publishing	203	67	79	88
Soaps and Detergents	599	70	78˙	86
Tires	119	70	88	97
Luggage	328	34	45	59
Ready-Mixed Concrete	4,032	6	9	16
Primary Copper	15	77	98	100
Farm Machinery	1,526	44	56	68
Electronic Computing Equipment	134	66	83	92
Typewriters	20	81	99	100
Sewing Machines	83	81	92	97
Motor Vehicles	107	92	98	99+
Motorcycles, Bicycles and Parts	87	57	76	95

NOTE: Concentration ratio information for 1970 did not provide information relating to the number of companies in the industry or concentration ratios above the eight largest companies.
SOURCE: *Census of Manufacturers, 1967*, Vol. 1 (Washington, D.C.: U.S. Department of Commerce, Bureau of the Census, 1967).

TABLE 14.3.
CONCENTRATION RATIOS IN
SELECTED AMERICAN
INDUSTRIES, 1967

geographical area over which the market extends. Yet, the courts have spent little time in developing effective criteria for these important decisions. For example, the government contended that DuPont's production of 75.0 percent of the cellophane sold in the United States was monopolistic in nature. The court found for DuPont, however, defining the market broadly to include all flexible wrapping materials such as aluminum foil, glassine, and waxed paper—a total market in which cellophane constituted less than 20 percent.[16] As can be seen from this case, the breadth with which a market is defined has a significant impact on the importance of a single product or service and the extent of market concentration that exists.

A more appropriate market definition might be developed from the perceptions of the consumer. This means that the measure could include the sale of all competing products as determined by the consumers, not just those that are produced in a like manner. For example, a motorcycle may be an adequate substitute for a small automobile. As a result, the concentration ratio for both motor vehicles and motorcycles could be overstated. It is easy to envision the difficulty in determining product substitutes from the consumer's perspective, but this does point up the limitations of concentration ratios.

Product differentiation. Product differentiation refers to the ability of a seller to develop a product with distinctiveness that will make it preferable to consumers over competitive products. Much of the criticism of product differentiation lies in the fact that the distinctiveness may be more imaginary than real. Willard Mueller, former Chief Economist of the Federal Trade Commission, went so far as to state that "product differentiation poses the greatest single threat to effective competition in our economy."[17] If, as a characteristic of competition in the United States, product differentiation were the exception rather than the rule, there could be some truth in that statement. The marketplace, however, does not perceive all products as being homogeneous. Stern and Grabner respond to the charge by stating:

> This type of reasoning completely overlooks the fact that goods and services have social and psychological as well as functional values, and that the enhancement of "nonfunctional" values may increase total utility for the consumer. In fact, heavily advertised or extensively differentiated goods may yield greater satisfaction than others—simply because people perceive them as more satisfying.[18]

The effectiveness of product differentiation as a concept lies in its relevance to the consumer, not whether the difference is real or imaginary. Even though research findings indicate that, in products such as beer, consumers are not able to identify their preferred brands, it is almost impossible to convince consumers of this. A family-brewed beer from Golden, Colorado, is one of the best examples of this. Coors is the nation's fourth largest selling beer, although it is distributed in only eleven western states. In those states in which it actively competes, Coors commands 41.0 percent of the market. Coors' legend, however, extends beyond the western states. A beer that normally sells at a price similar to the other premium beers at approximately $6.75 a case, Coors is being sold outside of its market area in Philadelphia at $12.50 a case. This price is a dollar per case more than the average imported beer. To many consumers, Coors represents a beer with a distinctive difference.

Price, of course, may be used in a positive way to effect product differentiation. Research has indicated that sellers may employ a low price as a competitive weapon, but there are limitations. First, its use to develop product distinctiveness is more difficult because rivals can more easily respond to price than to other elements in the marketing mix. Second, constant price emphasis can lead to price wars that may force a number of firms out of the market, thereby deteriorating market competition. A classic example of this is now taking place in the calculator market.[19] Most firms, including foreign, have been cutting prices so drastically that even the largest firms find their profits dwindling. One firm, Hewlett-Packard, has concentrated in efforts on premium quality products and has been able to avoid the low price fight for market share; Hewlett-Packard has even raised prices while its competitors are cutting theirs. In addition, Hewlett-Packard has been able to increase spending on research and development to maintain its "quality" differential advantage. Only by being able to establish a distinctiveness and preference for a product in the minds of the consumer can the seller obtain some degree of control over the product in the marketplace. As products and services continue to expand in number and complexity, the role of marketing in establishing a differential advantage for the firm becomes more critical.

Barriers to entry.   The existence and height of barriers are important in determining the ease with which firms are able to enter an existing industry. According to classical economics, when an industry is earning more than normal profits, firms are attracted into the industry and drive down both profits to the firm and prices to the consumer. In moving from the economic model of pure competition to pure monopoly, the barriers to entry become more formidable. Although barriers to entry can take many forms, discussion here will be limited to product differentiation, economies of scale, and government policy. Examples of entry barriers are shown in Figure 14.2.

A major characteristic of market structure, *product differentiation,* may also serve as an effective barrier to entry into an industry. A firm's product that is preferred by a significant number of consumers is partially insulated from existing and potential competitors. This is especially true in the automobile industry where both the initial and continuing investment, coupled with consumer preference, are so great that very few firms have been able to penetrate the market. A potential entrant must not only invest enough to produce and distribute the product, but a substantial number of consumers must be convinced that the new product and new firm can better meet their individual automobile needs. Although a few United States firms have attempted to bring out a unique or different automobile, most have been limited to very small scale. The only successful firms to enter the American automobile market have been the foreign manufacturers, and they are, in most cases, nearly as large as the American firms. The foreign firms, including Volkswagen, Saab, Volvo, Fiat, and Datsun, were able to penetrate the American market by satisfying the American consumers' desire for good mileage. In total, foreign firms captured more than 21 percent of the car market in 1975.[20]

Another structural factor that can inhibit market entry is *economies of scale.* This barrier results from efficiencies in size that enable firms

FIGURE 14.2.
EXAMPLES OF ENTRY
BARRIERS

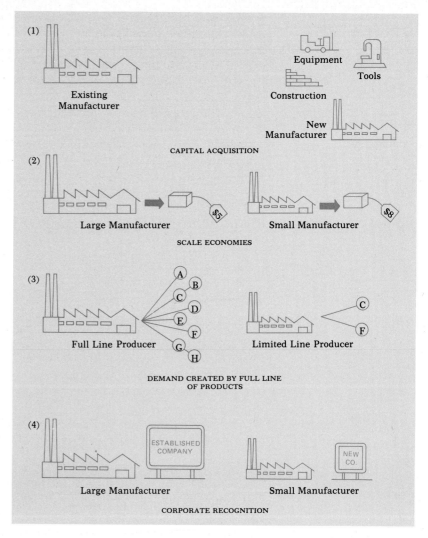

to manufacture and market their products at a lower average cost per unit than the relatively small producers. Although most firms stress factors that provide cost economies, firms can also obtain demand economies; in fact, many of the economies gained from marketing are demand economies. Demand economies are those that enable a firm, because of its size, to increase demand for its products. For example, a large firm may be able to produce and market a full line of products, and attract more customers because of the confidence in product quality generated by a full line and the convenience of being able to purchase from one firm. Also, the large firm may enjoy additional cost and demand economies through its national advertising. Leonard Weiss, in an automobile industry study, pointed out that General Motors and Ford paid less than half on advertising per car as did the other major firms in the industry.[21]

The third major factor that can affect the ease in which firms may enter a particular market is *government policy*; that is, any government legislation, program, or activity on a federal, state, or local level that may contribute to increasing the difficulty of entering an industry. Much emphasis is given to the government's role in promoting entry, but a number of government actions take the form of strengthening entry barriers, including patents, government procurement, and research and development. As an example, patents were designed to reward inventors for their creations; but patent protection fortifies the positions of large companies and insulates them from rival firms that might enter their industry.

When DuPont scientists invented nylon, they did not rest content with patenting the basic superpolymer composition and processes for producing it. They systematically investigated the whole array of molecular variations with properties potentially similar to nylon, blanketing their findings with hundreds of patent applications to prevent other firms from developing an effective substitute. Similar tactics have been pursued by DuPont and many other corporations in such fields as cellophane, plastics, synthetic leather, synthetic rubber, photo supplies, radio, television, shoe machinery, data processing equipment, electric lamps, telephone equipment, copying processes, and can-closing machinery, to name just a few.[22]

MARKET CONDUCT

Market conduct is the second major dimension of a market that identifies competition in the marketplace. As used here, market conduct refers broadly to the patterns of behavior that sellers follow in adapting to the markets in which they sell. More specifically, from a marketing perspective, it is the combination of price and nonprice policies used by the seller in the marketplace. These marketing decision areas represent the link between the market structure and its corresponding quality of performance.

Present public policy is based on the presumption that at least some definable relationship exists between the structure of various industrial markets, the conduct of firms in them, and their ultimate performance. Yet, the existence of such a relationship is based more upon the economic models of perfect and imperfect competition than upon any comprehensive, empirically tested relationships. This is particularly true of the relationship between structure and conduct. As Joel Bain has stated:

On the level of either observation or *a priori* prediction, there does not seem to be any very close association of patterns of intermarket coordination to the character of market structure.[23]

In other words, one cannot predict with certainty the business practices of a firm in the market, even though the structural characteristics of the market are known.

Although market conduct is difficult to define, it is not considered a real limitation by one group of economists, called "structuralists." They believe that market behavior is basically short-term in nature and that the real cause of ineffective competiton is the result of deficiencies in the market structure. They argue, therefore, that all public policy decisions should be based on structure, since market behavior and market performance are a direct function of the existing market structure. The structuralists believe that any departure from the purely competitive standard is a movement toward ineffective competition, especially when there appears to be little seller independence, impeded entry, or few sellers in the marketplace. In any imperfect market, there is the fear that firms may possess sufficient market power to make decisions based soley on self interest rather than on the pressures exerted by consumer demand.

A growing number of economists, however, feel that the purely competitive model is obsolete and that its acceptance may lead to a misdirected public policy. Although the purely competitive model stresses the importance of price competition, innovation of all types is necessary for effective competition. Joseph Schumpeter favored the concept of "dynamic competition" and believed that each firm should possess some monopoly power to ensure innovation and technological progress. Without this monopoly power, firms would lack both the incentive and ability to spend money on research and development. In this regard, one noted economist states:

> Oligopoly is the only realistic and desirable mode of competition in industries marked by important economies of enterprise scale.[24]

Agreement with this philosophy has led to the development of the "behaviorist school" of thought.

According to the behaviorists, no assumption can be made that a concentrated industry structure causes conduct that results in poor market performance. Although conduct may lead to a concentrated structure, it does not necessarily need to result in poor market performance. For example, nonprice methods of competition that do not deliberately mislead consumers are acceptable even though they result in concentration. The behaviorist school accepts the fact that a decision maker's discretion may be constrained by the existing market structure, but it gives much more importance to the role of the firm's organization and its decision making philosophy. In other words, the conduct of each firm, with its own objectives and organizational structure, coupled with its mix of price and nonprice policies, is of great importance in determining its performance in the industry in which it participates.

The present dominance of the structuralist philosophy in public policy decisions has led to increased investigation into the relationship between market structure and market performance to the neglect of market conduct. It should be acknowledged, however, that the emphasis on market structure does not imply that the federal agencies and courts have abandoned enforcement of market conduct statutes.

On the other hand, the behaviorist's philosophy is more consistent with existing public policy, which attacks activities of sellers and buyers that are aimed at preventing or reducing competition through practices such as price-fixing, tying agreements, predatory pricing, and deceptive advertising. More importantly, this philosophy allows for the development of a truer concept of competition—a concept based on a complete market analysis that includes structure, conduct, and performance.

MARKET PERFORMANCE   The importance of analyzing the nature of market structure and market conduct is to determine their impact on market performance. As previously stated, market performance refers to the end results of market activity and the criteria by which market results are evaluated. The major problem in relating market performance to structure and conduct is the difficulty experienced in obtaining agreement on acceptable market performance criteria.[25] The problem exists at both the macro and micro levels of marketing.

Macro performance criteria represent standards against which the performance of aggregate markets in the economy are evaluated. Criteria usually considered include productivity measures, employment figures, and income distribution. A fundamental objective of macro economic policy is to maximize the utility accruing to the economy as a whole, rather than to any single part. A fundamental problem is the difficulty of defining a set of criteria that are measurable and upon which a majority of economic planners agree.

The micro approach to evaluating market performance differs from the macro in that it is taken from the perspective of the individual firm or industry, where the ultimate objective is long-run survival and profitability. Although the issue is by no means clear-cut, there would appear to be a greater concensus as to acceptable performance criteria at the micro level than at the macro. Micro performance criteria include efficiency, profits, costs, and value-added measures.

It is by no means certain that maximizing performance at the micro level will ensure optimal utility in the macro sense. Herein lies the dilemma of economic practice, if not theory, since the assumptions and standards of the classical economists no longer reflect reality. In short, there is a basic question regarding the internal consistency of macro and micro performance criteria. An analysis of the literature reveals that six performance criteria are commonly identified.[26] As shown in Table 14.4, the list includes both macro and micro criteria, as well as the specific type of performance that is valued. The following paragraphs briefly discuss these criteria as they are used and describe their impact on marketing practice.

Efficiency.   To the economist, the primary economic criterion is efficiency. Efficiency takes two major forms—allocative and technical. Allocative efficiency, a macro form, refers to the allocation of resources among industries; technical efficiency, a micro form, refers primarily to the manner in which resources are allocated within an industry or firm. Consistent with the theory of pure competition, the structuralists believe that the existence of high concentration within an industry reduces efficiency, especially in an allocative sense. When high concentration exists in an industry, allocative efficiency is precluded because the highly interdependent decisions of the firms enable them to earn profit at a rate higher than those industries that are less concentrated. Technical efficiency is generally believed to be enhanced in industries with high levels of concentration. Although a number of early studies tended to support the relationship between high concentration and high profits, more recent studies have contradicted those results. In fact, recent studies indicate that there is no difference in the profits earned in concentrated or unconcentrated industries and that earlier findings are the result of study deficiencies.[27] From a marketing perspective, a more cogent criticism of efficiency measurement is that, at present, there is no adequate method for adjusting changes in services or changes in the quality design of a product. Since these factors are an integral part of the total product and tend to change substantially over time, they must be considered along with the physical unit when measuring efficiency.

Profits.   In a market dominated system, profits are the basis for a firm's survival and a measure of its successful performance. In addition, profits should be of sufficient size to reward a firm for its efficiency and promote its continued innovation. Yet, it is also agreed by most that profits should not be excessive, but rather approximate some reasonable return. According to classical economic theory, large profits in industries where extensive marketing programs exist are a strong indicator that product differentiation barriers to entry exist. Robert Buzzell counters this argument by pointing out that since research has shown that profits, as well as expenditures for personal selling and advertising, are much higher for relatively new products than established products, high profits may better reflect the association between both advertising and profits, and product innovation.[28] From a marketing perspective, there should exist a positive relationship between a firm's profit and the degree to which it enhances consumer satisfaction through its market offering. Although profit is only one measure of a firm or industry's performance, it is the prime motivating factor for all. Nevertheless, much more needs to be known about profit and its corresponding relationships before it can be used as a suitable basis for public policy determination.

Innovation.   The importance of innovation to America's economic success is well accepted. In fact, Schumpeter believed that innovation is the very foundation of growth. The more than $25 billion that are presently being spent on research and development indicates that American industry is heavily engaged in innovation. Yet, research and development expenditures may not be an accurate indicator of innovation because such figures indicate nothing about the output of the research. To the marketer, the only true measure of a new innovation's success is the acceptance of the product in the marketplace.

Marketing costs. Although marketing costs are seldom used as a measure of economic performance, this measure is included here because it represents a more appropriate criterion than those often adopted by industrial organization economists, such as the level of selling costs or the level of advertising costs. Economists generally include advertising, personal selling, sales promotion, and product development costs in determining selling costs only to the extent that they represent useful information and quality product features. However, the determination of an acceptable level of marketing costs, or selling costs, or advertising costs, is purely an arbitrary judgment. The important point to be emphasized in using marketing costs is that they represent the total costs generated in the marketing mix. Some examples of the types of expenditures included in marketing costs are shown in Figure 14.3.

Consumer benefits. Marketing, like economics, is concerned with enhancing consumer welfare, or benefits. Thus, a measure of a firm

FIGURE 14.3.
EXAMPLES OF MARKETING
COSTS

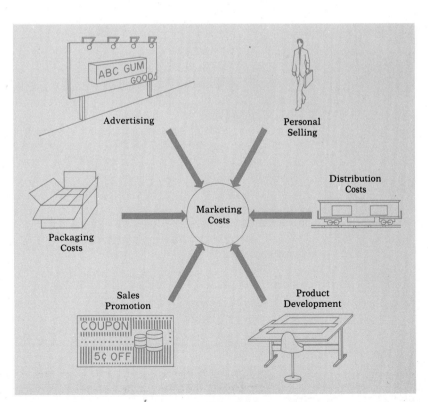

or industry's performance can be determined by the degree to which the individual is provided maximum freedom in the choice of consumer goods. Actually, the achievement of the other valued performance factors listed under the consumer benefits criterion in Table 14.4 enhances freedom of choice.

Consumer choice is of major importance, yet little has been done to develop measures for this performance dimension. Furthermore, critics state that the consumer is not offered any real meaningful choice in the goods and services produced today. Tibor Scitovsky, for example, states that there has been a "...secular increase in the uniformity and a decline in the range of products in most every field."[29] Research in this area is limited, but several contradicting studies indicate that the range of consumer choice is increasing. A study by William Moran, Director of Marketing Research at Lever Brothers, indicates that

TABLE 14.4.
MARKET PERFORMANCE
CRITERIA

Market Criterion	Valued Performance
1. Efficiency	Maximum use of society's resources Plants built to optimal scale Good use of resources and capacity Adoption of modern management techniques Rapid growth of labor productivity
2. Profits	Return adequate to reward investment and efficiency and induce innovation Return on assets relative to "normal" rates
3. Innovation	Adequate and productive R & D Rapid adoption of innovations
4. Marketing Costs	Acceptable level for the market Acceptable level for the firm Low advertising to sales ratio
5. Consumer Benefits	Maximum freedom of choice in which each individual consumer spends his wealth to satisfy his wants Pricing that promotes widespread use of output Quality conforming to consumer interests Lack of deceptive promotional practices
6. National Economy Benefits	Policies promoting full employment Policies promoting equitable income distribution Policies promoting environmental quality

SOURCE: Adapted from William N. Leonard, *Business Size, Market Power, and Public Policy* (New York: Thomas Y. Crowell Company, Inc., 1969), p. 92.

consumers may have a better selection of products today as compared to the choices available ten to twenty years ago:

For durable goods, Moran analyzed the number of models and the range of prices offered in six appliance categories in the Sears, Roebuck catalog in 1950, as compared to 1970. In every case, he found that the 1970 catalog offered a greater variety of models and types than were available in 1950. Moreover, in every case but one (phonographs), a model was available in 1970 at a price equal to or lower than the lowest 1950 price, despite the fact that the prices were not adjusted to constant dollar equivalents.

Comparing 1970 offerings with those of 1960 for a series of non-durable products such as deodorants, toilet soaps, sandwich bags, and margarine, Moran showed that in each case, new product types were introduced; and, in each case, average prices (this time adjusted by the Consumer Price Index) of the new types declined following introduction, while older product types continued to be available.[30]

National economy benefits.   Society today expects a firm to do more than produce and distribute a good or service. It expects, and in certain cases demands, that the firm contribute to the achievement of national economic goals, such as full employment, equitable income distribution, and environmental quality. Although the role of the firm in helping to achieve these goals may be important, accurate measurement of a firm or industry's performance in these areas is almost impossible. Nevertheless, the growth of consumerism and environmentalism leads one to believe that national goals, both economic and social, will be of increasing importance in evaluating a firm's economic performance.

MARKET
PERFORMANCE
IMPROVEMENT

There is today a significant number of critics of the present market performance of business. Agreement among the critics, however, is limited solely to the need for improved market performance. Although much of the criticism is directed toward the antitrust laws, which are the major weapon by which the government attempts to harmonize firm conduct with the public interest, the suggested alternatives are numerous. Two of the more extreme alternatives include the abolishment of laws or the replacement of them with direct government regulation.

Businessmen are extremely dissatisfied with the rapid expansion in legislation, but few would support the total elimination of antitrust laws. Yet, increased legislation has led to a tripling of the law suits filed in the past six years, and many businessmen believe that the recent legal explosion threatens the firm's survival. William May, Chairman of American Can, indicates that he spends approximately 60 percent of his time on legal problems, more than twice as much as five years ago.[31] Many would agree, however, that some legislation is necessary for the betterment of both society and business. In reflecting on a laissez-faire, market-dominated economic system, Karl Polanyi stated in *The Great Transformation*:

no society could stand the effects of such a system of crude fictions even for the shortest stretch of time unless its human and natural substance, as well as its business organization, was protected against the ravages of this satanic mill.[32]

Another group of critics believe that modern firms have grown so large that they are able to dominate and control the markets in which they function. In addition, it is believed that these firms no longer attempt to maximize their economic gains, but rather seek some minimum acceptable level of performance to satisfy their own basic self interests. To these critics, the firms have become the masters rather than the servants of the marketplace, and the only viable alternative available is direct government regulation. The leading proponent of this philosophy is economist John Kenneth Galbraith. Galbraith points a critical finger at the large firm and its advertising, specifically, when he states:

It is true that the consumer may still imagine that his actions respond to his own view of his satisfactions. But this is superficial and proximate, the result of illusions created in connection with the management of his wants. Only those wishing to evade the reality will be satisfied with such a simplistic explanation. All others will note, if an individual's satisfaction is less from an additional expenditure on automobiles than from one on housing, this can as well be corrected by a change in the selling strategy of General Motors as by an increased expenditure on his house.[33]

Galbraith's proposal is not universally accepted. Critics not only disagree with Galbraith on the extent of competition and the power of large firms, they also challenge his belief that government regulation is a better alternative. Opponents point to the government's performance in its regulation of transportation, where there is an almost unanimous cry to loosen the reins of regulation and allow more competition. At the present time, this alternative does not seem to be acceptable to American society.

Another group of critics contend that antitrust laws have not been very effective; they believe that the solution lies in the need for tougher enforcement. As might be expected from the previous discussion, the behaviorists suggest more stringent enforcement of the conduct of firms; the structuralists seek additional legislation and enforcement that attacks the structure of large heavily concentrated industries. The structuralists gained additional support in 1968 when the Neal Report, a White House Task Force study on antitrust policy, concluded:

An impressive body of economic opinion and analysis support the judgment that this (existing) degree of concentration precludes effective market competition and interferes with the optimum use of economic resources.[34]

This conclusion prompted the Neal Committee and numerous other economists and legislators to recommend specific proposals for restructuring industries where firms have excessive monopoly or market power. Even though these proposals vary substantially in many respects, they all have as their primary objective the maintenance of a competitive market economy.

In the Concentrated Industries Act proposed by the Neal Committee in 1968, it was recommended that the goal of court ordered restructuring should be a maximum market share of 12 percent for any firm.[35] The "Industrial Organization Act" introduced by Senator Philip Hart in 1972 declares the existence of monopoly power to be unlawful as well as a presumption of monopoly power whenever:

1. a company's average rate of return is greater than 15 percent of its net worth for each of five consecutive years,

2. there has been no substantial price competition for three consecutive years among two or more corporations within an industry, or

3. four or fewer companies account for half or more of an industry's sales in a single year.[36]

The Hart proposal, however, does not automatically require divesture even though a firm meets any of the three criteria. Nevertheless, the only defenses possibly available before a special industrial reorganization court would be the existence of "legally acquired patents or that divesture would deprive the firm of substantial economies."[37] The effect of this bill on business would be staggering. Senator Hart's staff indicates that the proposal would affect one-quarter to one-third of all U. S. manufacturing firms. This proposal would not only affect a number of the nation's most basic industrial goods industries, such as iron and steel, nonferrous metals, electrical machinery and equipment, and electronic computing and communications equipment, it would also affect numerous highly visible consumer goods industries, including the automobile, cereal, and detergent industries.

Opponents of a deconcentration policy are quick to point out that recent studies indicate that high profits and concentration are due primarily to the efficient performance of these large firms and that breaking them up would do more harm than good. In a published article on the detergent industry, where four firms control over 90 percent of the market, economist Steve Cox suggests that although market competition may appear to be enhanced through deconcentration, there exist two major drawbacks:

First, deconcentrating the industry may not curtail promotional expenditures, which seems to be a major entry barrier for new competition. In fact, non-price competition may be intensified with each new firm trying to differentiate its brand from all others in order to capture or maintain a market share sufficient to realize all production economies of scale. Second, since a minimum efficient size spray tower can produce five percent or more of the total U. S. market for detergents, some real economies of scale may be sacrificed by dissolution. The actual extent of multiplant economies is admittedly unknown, but, unless a number of new firms were formed from the three leading producers, it is unlikely that concentration in household detergents would be altered sufficiently to replace price coordination with price competition.

Restricting advertising and other promotional expenditures may appear to attack the very core of the market power in the detergent industry, but an examination of how such a policy would be implemented raises a number of problems. If applied to all detergent manufacturers, new entrants and current producers alike, would find that advertising restrictions would give a real advantage to established brands. By limiting promotional expenditures, one means by which new entrants could introduce a detergent brand and convince consumers of its distinction and superiority would be eliminated. If advertising of established *brands only* were limited, current producers would likely shift all promotional resources to marketing new brands. Product differentiation barriers to new competition would not be reduced, and the market share of established producers would probably remain unchanged. The only change would be in the names of the leading detergents. Finally, if promotional expenditures of established *firms only* were restricted, their ability to compete with new entrants would be impaired; and so, in the long run, merely the names of the leading firms would likely change.[38]

Cox believes that the consumer can obtain significant cost savings by purchasing private label detergents instead of national brands. He suggests that the reason many consumers pass up these savings is the lack of adequate product knowledge. Cox recommends that the performance testing and grading of household detergents may be more acceptable and more effective in increasing competition, since it gives consumers more information with which to compare detergents, regardless of the brand.[39]

Although most businessmen would find the Cox recommendation more acceptable, it must be pointed out that both the recommendation and implementation of proposals to improve market performance are going to continue. It behooves the marketer to not only understand but also to participate with all parties involved as a more aggressive enforcement policy is applied. Yet, if aggressive enforcement is not effective, then more extreme measures, including those that are presently unacceptable, may be found by society to be more desirable.

SUMMARY

This chapter examined the role and nature of competition in the United States. Although other alternatives are available, competition is the basic regulatory mechanism in the market dominated system and its maintenance has been clearly established as national policy by the U.S. Supreme Court.

Competition is well accepted as a national policy, but its interpretation by the economist and the businessman is significantly different. In order to better define U.S. competition, the economist has developed four market structure models: pure competition, pure monopoly, monopolistic competition, and oligopoly. Although monopolistic competition and oligopoly typify American industry, the economist has established pure competition as the ideal structure or market standard. Pure competition, which is characterized by a large number of sellers, a standardized product, and free entry into the market, is, to the businessman, totally unrealistic. The businessman can more easily relate to monopolistic competition and oligopoly, but believes that generic and enterprise competition more accurately reflect the dynamics of competition in the United States.

In an attempt to develop a more contemporary concept of competition to use as a legal standard, this chapter presented a more appropriate model for examining competition, which analyzes it in markets by structure, conduct, and performance. The major assumption underlying present public policy is that the structure of an industry determines the conduct of the member firms, which in turn determines the industry's performance. Although empirical support for this framework is relatively weak, the framework offers the marketer insight into the economic rationale underlying public policy decisions and a better understanding of the parameters that may limit decision making effectiveness.

As noted in this chapter, the major emphasis in public policy today rests with those that believe that market structure is the primary determinant of the quality of market performance. Structuralists, as they are called, believe market conduct to be totally determined by market structure. The major elements of market structure are seller concentration, product differentiation, and barriers to entry. Disagreement with the structuralist's assumption that a concentrated industry causes conduct that results in poor market performance has led to the development of the behaviorist school of thought. The behaviorist philosophy gives importance to the firm's objectives, organization, policies, and strategies in determining its market performance. Certainly this philosophy gives much more credit to the role of marketing in contributing to a firm's success.

Structure and conduct are important, but only in their impact on market performance. Although defining a set of criteria that is measurable and upon which a majority agree is difficult, this chapter identified a number of criteria that are used to evaluate market performance at both the macro and the micro levels. These include efficiency, profits, innovation, marketing costs, consumer benefits, and national economy benefits.

Finally, this chapter discussed the ways in which market performance may be improved. The solutions for improvement range from abolishment of laws to direct government regulation of business. A more probable course is the present trend toward more aggressive enforcement. If, however, it does not provide the desired quality of performance, business, and especially marketing, may find its role affected by more drastic changes.

QUESTIONS FOR DISCUSSION

1. Under which of the economist's four market structures discussed in the chapter do each of the following most accurately fit: (a) the cereal industry; (b) an Iowa corn farm; (c) a women's dress shop located in your hometown; (d) a ready mix concrete firm in your hometown; (e) the automobile industry? In each case justify your response.

2. Identify and briefly define the three dimensions by which industrial organization economists analyze markets.

3. Identify and define the three major elements of market structure.

4. What are the marketing implications of Willard Mueller's statement that "product differentiation poses the greatest single threat to effective competition in our economy"? Do you agree or disagree? Justify your response.

5. Compare and contrast the structuralist philosophy with the behaviorist philosophy in regard to the relationship among market structure, conduct, and performance.

6. Care must be exercised in making judgments concerning price behavior and the degree of competition existing in a market. Elaborate on this statement.

7. A market can be defined as a "sphere within which price-making forces operate and in which exchanges of title tend to be accompanied by the actual movement of the goods affected." Are definitions such as this useful in assisting the marketing manager to define the scope of his market? If not, why? Are there better approaches to defining a market?

8. Identify and briefly define the six criteria that are used in evaluating market performance. Discuss the problems that may be encountered in attempting to accurately evaluate a particular firm or industry's performance.

9. What would be the marketing implications if each of the following courses of action is taken to improve market performance: (a) abolishment of antitrust laws; (b) direct government regulation of business; (c) passage of a deconcentration act? In each case defend your position.

10. Define and briefly explain each of the following:
    a. Generic competition
    b. Enterprise competition
    c. Workable competition
    d. Allocative efficiency
    e. Technical efficiency
    f. Economies of scale

NOTES

[1] R. C. Bernhard, "Competition in Law and Economics," *Antitrust Bulletin*, Vol. 12 (Winter, 1967), p. 1099.

[2] George J. Stigler, *The Theory of Price* (rev. ed.; New York: The Macmillan Company, 1952), pp. 12–14.

[3] Adapted from a number of sources including: Campbell R. McConnell, *Economics* (3rd ed.; New York: McGraw-Hill Book Company, 1966), p. 407; Robert

J. Holloway and Robert S. Hancock, *Marketing in a Changing Environment* (2nd ed.; New York: John Wiley & Sons, Inc., 1973), p. 107; Ben Enis, *Marketing Principles* (Pacific Palisades, California: Goodyear Publishing Company, Inc., 1974), p. 102.

[4]Adapted from Theodore N. Beckman, William R. Davidson, and W. Wayne Talarzyk, *Marketing* (9th ed.; New York: The Ronald Press, Co., Copyright © 1973), pp. 363–364.

[5]Joel Dean, "Competition as Seen by the Businessman and by the Economist," in *The Role and Nature of Competition in Our Marketing Economy,* ed. by Harvey W. Huegy (University of Illinois: Bureau of Economic and Business Research, 1954), pp. 10–11.

[6]J. M. Clark, "Toward a Concept of Workable Competition," *American Economic Review,* Vol. 30 (1940), pp. 241–256.

[7]For a more detailed discussion, see W. Adams, "The Rule of Reason: Workable Competition or Workable Monopoly," *Yale Law Journal,* Vol. 63 (1954), p. 362; Corwin D. Adams, *Maintaining Competition: Requisites of a Governmental Policy* (New York: McGraw-Hill Book Company, 1949), pp. 9–11; Jesse W. Markham, "An Alternative Approach to the Concept of Workable Competition," *American Economic Review,* Vol. 40 (June, 1950), pp. 349–361.

[8]F. M. Scherer, *Industrial Market Structure and Economic Performance* (Chicago, Illinois: Rand McNally College Publishing Company, 1970), pp. 4–7.

[9]"The New Monopolies," *Consumers Reports* (June, 1975), p. 378.

[10]M. A. Adelman, "The Two Faces of Economic Concentration," *The Public Interest,* No. 21 (Fall, 1970), pp. 122–123.

[11]*Ibid.,* p. 123.

[12]Neil H. Jacoby, "Antitrust or Pro-Competition." © by the Regents of the University of California. Reprinted from California Management Review, volume XVI, number 4, pp. 56–57, by permission of the Regents.

[13]*Ibid.,* p. 57.

[14]Lee E. Preston, *Markets and Marketing: An Orientation* (Glenview, Illinois: Scott, Foresman and Company, 1970), p. 1.

[15]Beckman, *et al, Marketing,* pp. 4–6.

[16]United States v. E. I. DuPont de Nemours & Co., 351 U.S. 377 (1956).

[17]Dr. Willard F. Mueller, statement before Senate Committee on Small Business, March 15, 1967, p. 50.

[18]Louis W. Stern and John R. Grabner, Jr., *Competition in the Marketplace* (Glenview, Illinois: Scott, Foresman and Company, 1970), p. 142.

[19]"Hewlett-Packard: Where Slower Growth Is Smarter Management," *Business Week* (June 9, 1975), pp. 50–58; "The Semiconductor Becomes a New Marketing Force," *Business Week* (August 24, 1974), pp. 34–42; "Calculator Competition Helps Consumer, But Many Manufactures Are Troubled," *The Wall Street Journal* (January 14, 1975), p. 30.

[20]"As U. S. Auto Sales Slip, Imports' Share of the Market Widens," *The Wall Street Journal* (May 5, 1975), p. 1.

[21]Leonard W. Weiss, *Economics and American Industry* (New York: John Wiley & Sons, Inc., 1961), p. 342.

[22]Scherer, *Industrial Market Structure,* p. 391.

[23] Joe S. Bain, *Industrial Organization* (2nd ed.; New York: John Wiley & Sons, Inc., 1968), pp. 12, 329–348.

[24] Jacoby, "Antitrust or Pro-Competition," p. 56.

[25] For a more extensive discussion, see Richard E. Low, *Modern Economic Organization* (Homewood, Illinois: Richard D. Irwin, Inc., 1970), pp. 295–297.

[26] *Ibid.,* pp. 298–323; Scherer, *Industrial Market Structure,* pp. 400–411; Stern and Grabner, *Competition,* pp. 48–68; Richard Caves, *American Industry: Structure, Conduct, Performance* (2nd ed.; Englewood Cliffs, New Jersey: Prentice-Hall, Inc., 1967), pp. 96–114.

[27] Stanley I. Ornstein, "Concentration and Profits," *The Journal of Business,* Vol. 45 (October, 1972), pp. 519–541; Yale Brozen, "Concentration and Profits: Does Concentration Matter?" *The Antitrust Bulletin,* Vol. XIX, No. 2 (Summer, 1974), pp. 381–397.

[28] Robert D. Buzzell, "Marketing and Economic Performance: Meaning and Measurement," *Marketing Science Institute Working Paper* (August, 1972), pp. 14–16.

[29] Tibor Scitovsky, "A Critique of Present and Proposed Standards," *American Economic Review,* Vol. 50 (May, 1960), supplement, p. 15.

[30] Buzzell, *Marketing and Economic Performance,* pp. 20–21.

[31] Eleanore Carruth, "The 'Legal Explosion' Has Left Business Shell-Shocked," *Fortune,* Vol. LXXXVII, No. 4 (April, 1973), p. 65.

[32] Karl Polanyi, *The Great Transformation* (Boston: Beacon Press, 1957), p. 73.

[33] J. K. Galbraith, *The New Industrial State* (Boston: Houghton Mifflin, 1967), pp. 214–215.

[34] "White House Task Force Report on Antitrust Policy," *Antitrust & Trade Regulation Report,* No. 411, Special Supplement, Part II (Washington: Bureau of National Affairs, Inc., May 27, 1969), p. 3.

[35] Lee E. Preston, "Is It Time for Industrial Reorganization?" *California Management Review,* Vol. XVI, No. 4 (Summer, 1974), p. 69.

[36] "Is John Sherman's Antitrust Obsolete?" *Business Week* (March 23, 1974), p. 51.

[37] *Ibid.*

[38] Steven R. Cox, "Consumer Information and Competition in the Synthetic Detergent Industry," *Nebraska Journal of Economics and Business* (Summer, 1976), pp. 55–56.

[39] *Ibid.,* p. 56.

SUGGESTED READINGS

Buzzell, Robert D., "Marketing and Economic Performance: Meaning and Measurement," *Marketing Science Institute Working Paper* (August, 1972).

Cox, Steven R., "Consumer Information and Competition in the Synthetic Detergent Industry," *Nebraska Journal of Economics and Business* (Summer, 1976), pp. 41–58.

Grether, E. T., "Competition Policy in the United States: Looking Ahead," *California Management Review* (Summer, 1974), pp. 60–67.

Grether, E. T., "Marketing and Public Policy: A Contemporary View," *Journal of Marketing* (July, 1974), pp. 2–7.

"Is John Sherman's Antitrust Obsolete?" *Business Week* (March 23, 1974), pp. 46–56.

Jacoby, Neil H., "Antitrust or Pro-Competition?" *California Management Review* (Summer, 1974), pp. 53–59.

Jacoby, Neil H., ed., *The Business-Government Relationship: A Reassessment* (Pacific Palisades, California: Goodyear Publishing Company, 1975).

Preston, Lee E., "Is It Time for Industrial Reorganization?" *California Management Review* (Summer, 1974), pp. 68–80.

Scherer, F. M., *Industrial Market Structure and Economic Performance* (Chicago, Illinois: Rand McNally College Publishing Company, 1970).

Stern, Louis W. and John R. Grabner, Jr., *Competition in the Marketplace* (Glenview, Illinois: Scott, Foresman and Company, 1970).

Market Structure
- Concentration
- Product diff.
- Barriers to Entry

Market Conduct
- Structuralists
- dynamic
- Behaviorist

Market Performance
- Efficiency
- Profits
- Innovation
- Mktng Cost
- Consumer Benefits
- National Economy

15

THE TECHNOLOGICAL ENVIRONMENT

15

THE TECHNOLOGICAL ENVIRONMENT

When the United States celebrated its bicentennial in 1976, few people fully realized that the products of their technical world were created over a relatively short span of time during the most recent period of this nation's two-hundred-year history. Centennial celebrants in 1876, for example, did not know about automobiles, radios, stereos, airplanes, and electric lights. By the same token, those who were around in 1926 at the time of America's 150th anniversary did not know about television, home air conditioning, electric disposals, moon rockets, and antibiotics. Today's average man-on-the-street does not envision a future of food pills, flying automobiles, practical laser beam applications, and drugs that will cure cancer. To provide some insight into how man's world is altered by science, this chapter focuses on the technological environment.

THE RAPIDITY OF CHANGE

Throughout history man has had to adjust to change. His ability to do so has, in large part, dictated the success of the civilization with which he has been associated. Yet, accommodation to change has never been easy. There is security in the present, high risk with the unknown. Today, change is increasingly thrust upon us, and the pace of change is accelerating. J. Robert Oppenheimer put this concept into perspective when he stated that:

In an important sense, this world of ours is a new world in which the unity of knowledge, the nature of human communities, the order of society, the order of ideas, the very notions of society and culture have changed and will not return to what they have been in the past. What is new is not new because it has never been there before, but because it has changed in quality. One thing that is new is the prevalence of newness, the changing scale and scope of change itself so that the world alters as we walk in it, so that the years of man's life measure not some small growth or rearrangement or moderation of what he learned in childhood, but a great upheaval. What is new is that, in one generation, our knowledge of the natural world engulfs, upsets and complements all knowledge of the natural world before. . . .[1]

This comment suggests that change occurs "when there is a shift in pattern, when new relationships emerge, when new standards and goals become shared."[2] The increasing rapidity of technological change is illustrated in Figure 15.1. Although it took over one hundred years to develop the photographic process, it took only six years to develop the atomic bomb, three years to develop transistors, and two years to develop solar batteries.

Casting change in a different perspective, Table 15.1 depicts the average time period between the incubation of a new technological breakthrough and its commercial development and market applica-

414

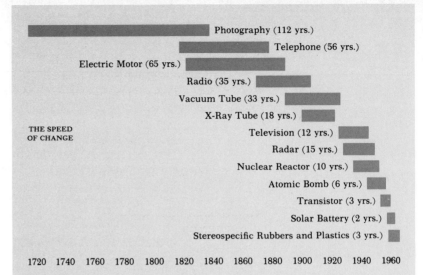

THE SPEED
OF CHANGE

Photography (112 yrs.)

Telephone (56 yrs.)

Electric Motor (65 yrs.)

Radio (35 yrs.)

Vacuum Tube (33 yrs.)

X-Ray Tube (18 yrs.)

Television (12 yrs.)

Radar (15 yrs.)

Nuclear Reactor (10 yrs.)

Atomic Bomb (6 yrs.)

Transistor (3 yrs.)

Solar Battery (2 yrs.)

Stereospecific Rubbers and Plastics (3 yrs.)

1720 1740 1760 1780 1800 1820 1840 1860 1880 1900 1920 1940 1960

FIGURE 15.1.
SELECTIVE ILLUSTRATIONS OF
THE SPEED FOR INTRODUCING
TECHNICAL DEVELOPMENT
INTO SOCIAL USE

SOURCE: State University of New York, Center for Integrative Studies, School of Advanced Technology, "World Facts and Trends" (Binghamton, New York: State University of New York, 1969).

TABLE 15.1.
AVERAGE RATE OF
DEVELOPMENT OF SELECTED
TECHNOLOGICAL
INNOVATIONS[a]

Factors Influencing the Rate of Technological Development	Average Time Interval (years)		
	Incubation Period[b]	Commercial Development[c]	Total
Time Period			
Early twentieth century (1885–1919)	30	7	37
Post-World War I (1920–1944)	16	8	24
Post-World War II (1945–1964)	9	5	14
Type of Market Application			
Consumer	13	7	20
Industrial	28	6	34
Source of Development			
Private industry	24	7	31
Federal government	12	7	19

SOURCE: Frank Lynn, "An Investigation of the Rate of Development and Diffusion of Technology in Our Modern Industrial Society," *Report of the National Commission on Technology, Automation, and Economic Progress*, Washington, D.C., 1966.
[a] Based on study of twenty major innovations whose commercial development started in the period 1885–1950.
[b] Incubation Period—begins with basic discovery and establishment of technological feasibility, and ends when commercial development begins.
[c] Commercial Development—begins with recognition of commercial potential and the commitment of development funds to reach a reasonably well-defined commercial objective, and ends when the innovation is introduced as a commercial product or process.

tion. Again, it is evident that time has been compressed. From this data, it is interesting to note that consumer products are more quickly developed than are industrial products, and that the federal government apparently is somewhat more successful in introducing its products than is private industry.

TECHNOLOGY AND SOCIETY

Even though there appears to be some time lag between incubation and application, many social critics contend that the rapidity of technological change is more than mankind can absorb. Others argue that society's preoccupation with technology is preparation for the future. It must be conceded that technology, per se, is neutral; it is simply a means to an end. Society determines the priorities for the direction technology is to take.

DEFINITION OF
TECHNOLOGY

The question of what technology is presents complex problems of definition, depending largely upon who is doing the defining. To the engineer, technology may be represented by machinery and processes. The anthropologist might view technology as a reflection of a civilization. The sociologist probably interprets technology in terms of its impact on established norms and behavior patterns. Technology may appear to be a threat to the worker. And for most of us, technology is likely something we take for granted, except when it does not work. Therefore:

> While the influence of technology is both widespread and fundamental, the term cannot be defined with precision. In its simplest terms, technology is man's efforts to cope with his physical environment—both that provided by nature and that created by man's own technological deeds such as cities—and his attempts to subdue or control that environment by means of his imagination and ingenuity in the use of available resources. In the popular mind, technology is synonymous with machines of various sorts—the steam engine, the locomotive and the automobile—as well as such developments as printing, photography, radio, and television ...
>
>   Sometimes technology is defined as applied science. Science itself is viewed as an attempt by man to understand the physical world; technology is the attempt by man to control the physical world. This distinction may be briefly put as the difference between the 'know why' and the 'know how' ... Technology, then, is much more than tools and artifacts, machines and processes—it deals with human work, with man's attempts to satisfy his wants by human action on physical objects.[3]

Based on the foregoing, technology may be defined as "the result of the application of knowledge to old products and methods or to new products and methods or to new combinations of products and methods which allow the more efficient performance of an established function or allow the performance of a function not previously achievable."[4]

INVENTION VERSUS INNOVATION

it's intro.

A definition of technology is not, in and of itself, sufficient to explain the process of technological change, however. Two additional concepts, invention and innovation, must be considered. Invention is technological, involving the application of scientific principles to the contrivance of a new device or process. Innovation is related to business, involving the organization of markets, capital, labor, and supplies for the production or use of a new device or process. Technological innovation, then, includes all the actions taken as a consequence of a decision to bring a device or product into commercial use. Among these actions may be scientific and theorized experiments, and the building of working models to develop and perfect an invention.[5]

On the other hand, all inventions need not be directed toward immediate commercial production. They may be inspired by academic curiosity, military urgency, or simply a desire to control patents for encouraging, exploiting, or preventing innovations by others. Thus, the two concepts overlap. Invention includes technical changes made before, during, and after attempts to introduce a new process or product commercially, and innovation may or may not involve technical development as part of other activities.[6]

A broader approach to the concept of innovation suggests that it is an idea perceived as new by the potential user. It makes little difference as far as human behavior is concerned whether an idea is objectively new, as measured by the amount of time elapsed since its first use or discovery; it is the newness of the idea to the individual that determines reaction to it. Such an approach has broad marketing implications, for it suggests that a proper role for marketing in the innovative process is to introduce existing technology to new markets.

In summary, it may be said that an invention is the conceiving of an idea, product, or technology. Innovation is the process by which an invention, idea or technology is translated into the economy.[7]

P.L.D.T.

THE PROCESS OF TECHNOLOGICAL CHANGE

It is clear that the concepts of invention and innovation are fundamental to the understanding of the broader concept of the process of technological change. This process may be broken down into five steps: (1) new technological development creates a new opportunity; (2) people capitalize on the opportunity; (3) changes in social organizations result from the opportunity created by the new technology; (4) new organizational forms replace existing social structures that were

DIFFUSION — SPREADING OF AN INNOVATION throughout society

organized to use earlier technologies; and (5) the gains achieved through the application of new technologies are offset in part by loss in the realization of older goals. Thus, a technological process brings about both a gain and a loss.[8]

It is not enough that new technology creates new opportunities; people must capitalize on an opportunity once it becomes available. Before that is possible, technological capability must be diffused through society as it has been at a steadily increasing pace. During this century, the lag between the initial discovery of an innovation and the recognition of its commercial potential has decreased.

Finally, in order to capitalize on new technology, changes in social structures and organizations may, or, in some cases, must, take place. The result is that new forms replace existing ones. Such changes do not take place rapidly; disruptions in established patterns of behavior are quite frequently met with a considerable amount of resistance by those affected by the change. However, people will more readily accept changes that improve the quality of life in some aspect, or that are perceived as producing an overall benefit for them.

In summary, the process of technological change is unpredictable. A new technology may be viewed as a significant threat, or it may provide a positive motivating force for progress. Unquestionably, losses as well as gains are associated with the process.

THE DIFFUSION OF TECHNOLOGY

Diffusion theory, which is concerned with the spreading of an innovation throughout society, and technological change are inextricably interwoven. One significant aspect of diffusion theory deals with the role of the innovator in the change process. An examination of important technological phenomena indicates that in many cases the source of a new idea or technology is, in fact, an independent inventor-innovator. For example, one study found that out of sixty-one important innovations in the twentieth century, over half originated with independent inventors and small firms.

Another study discovered that during the period 1946–1955 over two-thirds of the major inventions resulted from the work of independent inventors in small companies. In still a further study, an analysis of 194 inventions in aluminum welding fabricating techniques and in aluminum finishing showed that major producers accounted for only one of seven important inventions.[9]

Research in the American steel industry revealed that of thirteen major innovations, four came from inventions in European companies, seven from independent inventors, and none from the American steel companies themselves.[10] Finally, a look at seven major inventions in the refining and cracking of petroleum revealed that all were discovered by independent inventors. Contributions of the large companies were primarily in the area of improvement in existing processes.[11]

INNOVATION

Lg. AMT OF CAPITAL

In analyzing the diffusion of technology, care should be taken in the generalization of the above findings to all product or technology categories. Some innovators exhibit characteristics of creativity that are related more to a specific product than to innovativeness in general; they would probably not be as creative in dealing with another product. Nevertheless, the innovator-entrepreneur is instrumental in the diffusion of new ideas and in the process of technological change.

THE ECONOMIC IMPACT OF TECHNOLOGICAL CHANGE

The evolution of new technologies accounts in large part for the economic growth of a society. At some point, the individual, using ingenuity and the information available, invents and establishes by experiment the feasibility and possible value of the invention. The significance of the new invention than must be communicated to others so that they can make the new process or technology operational. The movement from the invention stage to application is what Joseph Schumpeter has called innovatión. Once the innovation is incorporated or used to undertake a new set of operations, the transfer of technology has occurred. It is only then that an economy is transformed and a more productive level of operations attained. Figure 15.2 indicates the relationship between the transfer of technology and economic growth.

Many contend that the main reason that most technology is adopted is because of the important role it has played in the increases that have been realized in productivity. Electronic monitoring equipment in health care facilities affects productivity in a qualitative sense, while newer, faster machinery in factories influences it in quantitative terms. The impact of technology on productivity is demonstrated by the following examples:

Some of the changes in technology have been striking. Nylon filament is extruded at 4,000 feet a minute, which is one-half million times faster than a silkworm produces silk. A good glassblower with a helper could make some fifteen hundred light bulbs a day, but a single machine can produce 132,000 bulbs an hour. Another dramatic example of productivity increase is the telephone system. It is estimated that if the telephone system of the 1960s depended on manual operation as used in the 1930s, every woman in the United States over eighteen years of age would need to be employed in telephone work to handle the volume of calls being made in the 1960s.[12]

Another way to look at the relationship of technological change to productivity increases is to pose three fundamental questions: (1) how large is the net increase in aggregate output per capita and to what extent has this increase been obtained as a result of greater labor or

FIGURE 15.2.
TECHNOLOGY TRANSFER AND
HUMAN GROWTH

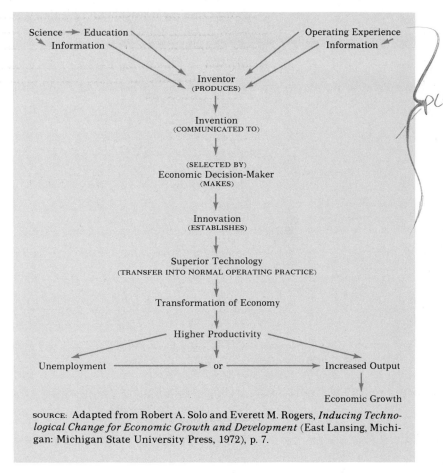

Science → Education
Information

Operating Experience
Information

Inventor
(PRODUCES)

Invention
(COMMUNICATED TO)

(SELECTED BY)
Economic Decision-Maker
(MAKES)

Innovation
(ESTABLISHES)

Superior Technology
(TRANSFER INTO NORMAL OPERATING PRACTICE)

Transformation of Economy

Higher Productivity

Unemployment ← or → Increased Output

Economic Growth

SOURCE: Adapted from Robert A. Solo and Everett M. Rogers, *Inducing Technological Change for Economic Growth and Development* (East Lansing, Michigan: Michigan State University Press, 1972), p. 7.

capital input on the one hand, and of a rise in productivity on the other; (2) is there evidence of retardation or, conceivably, acceleration in the growth of per capita output; and (3) have there been fluctuations in the rate of growth of output apart from the short-term fluctuations in business cycles, and if so, what is the significance of these swings?

THE SOCIETAL IMPACT OF TECHNOLOGICAL CHANGE

Beyond the pure economic realm, technological change has materially affected society in a larger context. It has altered sociocultural norms, influenced ecological movements, and reordered many basic institutions. In order to provide some idea of the broader influence of technological change on society, this section is devoted to its impact on social values, ecology, government, and education.

IMPACT ON SOCIAL VALUES

Technology influences and is, in turn, influenced by social values. Traditional values and ethics are in a state of fluctuation caused by three major developments: (1) the predominance of young people in the culture; (2) the movement from a production to a service economy; and (3) the rejection of quantity and status as values in the search for quality and equality. People are reevaluating their goals and ideals and finding, in quite a few instances, the new norms of behavior, dress, leisure, and lifestyle can be embraced which improve the conditions of living. The important question for marketers is, of course, which values will be retained, and which rejected.

One of the most significant changes in values concerns attitudes toward work and leisure. These attitudes are directly influenced by emerging technologies. Up to the present, American society has been dominated by the Puritan concept of work, that work is unavoidable, it is hard, and it is a duty. Yet, higher productivity, gained through improved technology, has made it possible to produce all the things a society needs with only a fraction of the total labor force. By 1980, it is estimated that less than one-fifth of the labor force will be directly involved in manufacturing products, mining, growing crops, and constructing buildings.[13]

The notion that hard or unpleasant work must be tolerated because it is unavoidable is expected to enjoy less and less acceptability. Institutions are finding that they simply cannot afford to pay the premium demanded for the performance of unpleasant work. And the concept of work as a duty is being questioned. Increasingly, both leisure and work are viewed as equally valid activities. Leisure is seen as a right, not something that has to be earned.

The changing values of American society have been discussed in a previous chapter. Many of the social values that will be undergoing change in the next several decades will be the result of dramatic technological change. These shifts in values will result in future technological change.

IMPACT ON ECOLOGY

As noted in Chapter 2, ecology refers to the study of the interrelationships between organisms and their environments. By its very nature, all ecology is complex, but human ecology is especially so because of the nature of man. Not only must man adapt to the physical and biological environment, man must also adapt to the social environment, including community, family, job, other social structures and the people in them, and the changing technology created by man.

The rapid development of technology has, in part, led to the growing concern with human ecology. New pesticides have been applied to fields to attain greater crop yields. Although these yields have been obtained, other plants and animals are being destroyed. In some instances, the chemicals have been returned to the human system. It is well known that modern convenience appliances have allowed women to greatly increase their freedom from household chores. At the same time, however, some of the new detergents introduced with dishwashers, for example, have proven immune to the antibacterial action that destroys soap.

Automobiles provide transportation, incinerators burn trash, power plants supply society's ever-growing needs for electricity. An undesirable by-product of all of these developments is haze over cities and photochemical smog. A highly visible example of environmental pollution, which technology has helped to create, and which technology will be called upon to solve, is the smoke from incinerators and burning dumps that are used to dispose of the enormous quantities of debris and waste cast off by affluent American society.

As man views the long-run impact of technology on the environment, the inevitable conclusion is that ecologically benign technology must be generated to serve the needs of the future. The problem with introducing this kind of technology in many cases, however, is simply that it is more profitable for businesses and for society to maintain the status quo. In the future, government will undoubtedly play an increasing role; it will be the government's task to make the introduction of ecologically benign technology and corrective technology profitable.

IMPACT ON GOVERNMENT

Because of its immense spending power, government is involved heavily in the diffusion of technology. Furthermore, many government agencies, especially at the federal level, are primary sources of new technology. The Departments of Agriculture, Commerce, Defense, Health, Education and Welfare, Interior, Labor, Post Office, and State, as well as agencies such as the Atomic Energy Commission, National Aeronautics and Space Administration, the National Science Foundation, Tennessee Valley Authority, and others, all have substantial research and development budgets. That is, the government plays a significant role in the advancement of technology in a wide number of different industries.

Society often appears to take for granted the spin-offs from new technology that have emerged directly from government, or through government sponsorship. Benefits from the exploration of space are considerable, yet in many cases unrecognized, and in others almost routinely accepted. Today, the by-products of space technology provided by the National Aeronautics and Space Administration (NASA) are being applied to almost every field of human activity. The rechargeable heart pacemaker and the Telecare emergency medical system and emergency medical kit are examples of such spin-offs. The perfection of the fuel cell is based upon work in the Apollo space program. Computer image enhancement techniques developed by the

Jet Propulsion Laboratory have been adapted to analyze blood vessel x-rays to determine changes in the size of plaques that form on blood vessel walls. NASA also has developed a technique for separating and reclaiming nonferrous metals such as copper, zinc, and aluminum from scrap. Likewise, new NASA management techniques are aiding the offshore oil drilling process. Quality control techniques are helping to make offshore oil operations safer and more efficient.[14]

In the consumer goods field, NASA technology has been applied to packaging materials. The steak purchased in the supermarket is probably wrapped in the same type of transparent polyester film one two-thousandths of an inch thick that was used for America's giant balloon satellites. The aluminum foil used to wrap freezer-dried foods is the same as that used on communications satellites. Soon, laser beam systems may be able to predict major earthquakes by measuring minute surface movements and pinpointing areas of earth's stress.[15]

Both NASA and the Small Business Administration (SBA) provide excellent examples of the important government-business interface that has developed in the area of technology. Through this type of interface, industry has enjoyed a smooth flow of technology from government to business, and the public dollars expended for research and development have been more than justified in the results that have been achieved. The following examples illustrate the roles that NASA and the SBA have assumed in the transfer of technology:

Since its inception in 1958, NASA has amassed 2,594 of its own patents. Patents, however, are only a part of the total NASA package. In addition to patented information, NASA has produced huge amounts of technical information that either were patented by others or were not of a patentable nature. The nonpatented information collected by NASA amounts to 10 million documents collected from NASA, the Pentagon, the Atomic Energy Commission, and other federal agencies. The availability of this material has already led to some significant breakthroughs for individual businesses and industries. A glass manufacturer, for example, saved 200 hours of laboratory research time by screening documented evidence of failures in the application of certain chemical compounds. A marine firm saved $1.5 million in research time by obtaining NASA developed information about biological problems and applications. A chemical manufacturer's design of a large bulk processing system was greatly enhanced by information on techniques that could be used to reduce the acid corrosion of steel.[16]

Through its technology utilization program, the SBA keeps small manufacturers informed about and motivates small businessmen to apply relevant innovations, processes, techniques and materials. Information is communicated through conferences, seminars, workshops, individual counseling, and publication about new products, processes and technical methods. Government contributors to the storehouse of SBA technical information include the Department of Defense, the National Aeronautics and Space Administration, the Atomic Energy Commission, the Department of Agriculture, the Department of Labor, the Department of the Interior, and the Department of Health, Education, and Welfare.[17]

IMPACT ON EDUCATION

The educational system in the United States generates a great deal of technology through its research and development efforts. At the same time, it benefits from technology in the form of new techniques, approaches, designs, and methods. More broadly conceived, education is the key in the process of adaptation to change. In the context of technology, this means that educators have significant influence in altering not only teaching methods, but concepts of what is relevant and what is irrelevant.

Educational institutions, particularly colleges and universities, are important sources of new technology in the United States. These schools generate their own research and development monies as well as capture research funds from other sources. Certain programs have been particularly effective in developing new technologies and entrepreneurs. Massachusetts Institute of Technology, for example, whose previous generations of scientists were responsible for such technological advances as synthetic penicillin, over-the-horizon radar transmission, minicomputers, and the electro-static generator, is intent on pulling fledgling scientists and budding entrepreneurs into its laboratories. In 1973, with the assistance of a $1.2 million National Science Foundation grant, MIT opened its information center to teach basic skills needed for everything from conceiving new product ideas to moving those conceptions into pilot production.[18]

MIT's Donation to Technology

Over the past few years, personnel departing from MIT to establish their own companies have generated a considerable amount of economic activity: more than one hundred new companies have developed out of MIT laboratories; over fifty companies have developed out of MIT academic departments. Another program that attempts to perform essentially the same service as the MIT program was started by Southern Methodist University, which offers courses in entrepreneurship. At least one individual has achieved commercial success based upon the business plan that he developed in that program.[19]

Unquestionably, the university will be a major catalyst for change in the future. Much of the change that will occur will be generated not merely by new technology, but by the thought process that precedes the evolution of that technology. That thought process will, in turn, be assisted by such technology as computer-aided instruction.

"As recently as the early 1950s the United States was spending on education an amount equal to approximately 3 percent of the gross national product. Today that percentage has more than doubled, and so has GNP. Predictably this figure will approach and probably pass the 10 percent mark by the end of the 1970s"[20] Given the trend in expenditures for education, it should be apparent that society is placing an increasing premium on more and better education in recognition of the fact that change demands versatility and flexibility. It may be said that up until now education has been concerned with the transmission of accumulated knowledge and the perpetuation of culture. In the future, the role of education will be to prepare its citizens for change.[21]

TECHNOLOGY AND MARKETING

The economic and societal impact of technological change has significantly influenced the scope and direction of the field of marketing. Technology determines, to a large extent, the products and services offered through marketing, and it has affected the conduct of both the micro and the macro processes of marketing. To provide a better understanding of the relationships between technology and marketing, this section focuses on the impact of the technological environment on the individual firm.

TECHNOLOGY'S IMPACT ON MARKETING PRACTICE

The introduction of new technology into the corporate environment brings with it both problems and opportunities. The farsighted organization will have planned and organized for change in anticipation of the problems, leaving the opportunities to be exploited. This section explores the impact of new technology on marketing practice. Specifically, it considers the product-market match, distribution activity, and the promotion process as they relate to the introduction of new technology.

Product-market matching.   Technology and marketing meet head on in the introduction of new technological products, processes, and services for the marketplace. Marketing almost by definition must be intimately involved in the innovation phase of product development. Many companies develop new technology, yet lack a sense of direction for that technology. Companies as sophisticated as DuPont face this dilemma.

When DuPont originally invented nylon fiber, the applications for the new product were almost unlimited. Yet the product itself has gone through several evolutionary cycles, each as surprising as the one that preceded it. Nylon was first used essentially as a material in parachutes. Later the product established a new trend in women's hosiery. Today the fabric supports automobiles in the form of tires, and feet in the form of carpets. The applications are limited only by the degree of creativity the marketer can bring to the marketplace.

Potential applications of new technology are not always evident. When they are, it is possible to focus technology in the direction of the problem or opportunity. The guiding genius at Polaroid, Edwin Land, has followed such a philosophy in creating and marketing cameras. Recently, Polaroid introduced the SX-70 instant camera, quickly followed by a lower-priced model, the second generation Model II. The rapid introduction of the new product was, in part at least, a response to the competitive threat of Eastman Kodak, a major Polaroid supplier, which itself threatens to become a big competitor in the instant photography market.[22]

The computer market is also being forced to switch from a technical orientation to a marketing orientation. Shortly after IBM had shaken the entire minicomputer systems industry by introducing "the lowest-priced IBM business computer ever," Digital Equipment Corporation announced the "world's lowest-priced, fully programmable computer system."[23] Digital Equipment Corporation seized an opportunity to market a minicomputer system rather than simply a minicomputer. Although many minicomputers are already available in the $1,000 to $2,000 range, Digital Equipment Corporation's system, which sells for $12,000, includes a PDP-8A computer, a TV screen display, a keyboard, a printer, and a "floppy disk" magnetic memory.[24]

The semiconductor industry provides another example of intensive technological competition. The direction of that industry is to integrate downward to the ultimate consumer. Recently, some of the largest companies within the industry have begun to produce such consumer products as electronic calculators, digital watches, and, for business, microcomputers. The electronic calculator market itself is growing at a rate of approximately 50 percent per year in unit sales. The industry is experiencing all of the traditional marketing problems, such as intense price competition, elimination of marginal producers and marketers, shrinking profit margins, product proliferation, and production scheduling-distribution lags.

There is virtually no limit to a discussion of the market for new technologies. The lesson is evident, however. For every new technology to succeed, there must be a market opportunity and a marketing system for delivery.

Physical distribution. The physical distribution system includes both transportation and storage. New technology today is making it possible to view transportation and storage not as separate entities, but as parts of a continuous system of delivery. Technology has made a significant impact on warehousing efficiency. Within the warehouse, computerized inventory systems control inflow and outflow of supplies and products; automated equipment moves material; and packaging machinery wraps, boxes, and bundles products at the outlet point. In addition, computerized systems help to locate optimum warehouse sites.

Modes of transportation are dramatically changing. Customer service has been improved and physical distribution costs have been decreased with faster shipments. Today, Lighter Aboard Ship (LASH) vessels move commodities quickly and efficiently. LASH vessels carry their own "lighter," a smaller ship used to unload larger ships, especially in shallow harbors. The lighters, already loaded, can themselves be unloaded from the LASH. The time necessary to unload the lighter is also considerably less than that required by a conventional vessel. An equally dramatic development in shipping is the supercargo, which was designed to carry bulk products; the Japanese have the largest fleet of these huge ships. The United States has recently launched its first supertanker.

The jet cargo plane has helped to create a revolution in air freight. The advent of the jumbo jet has in some cases reduced altogether the need for warehousing. It has also reduced significantly the level of inventories companies must maintain. And it has dramatically cut the cost of shipment by air freight, which has historically been prohibitively expensive for some companies.

As with ships and planes, innovations have also taken place in the railroad industry. Locomotives have been developed that can travel comfortably at one hundred miles per hour. Prototypes of superhoppers have been built that parallel the introduction of the jet cargo plane and the supertanker. Track-side electric scanners can report instantly on the movement of trains. This is particularly significant since efficient operation of railroad cars requires that the cars be utilized to the greatest extent possible.

All areas of transportation benefit from the integration of different modes of transportation. Examples of such integration are piggy-backing and containerization. Piggy-backing occurs when motor carriers are transported by train. A new term, "fishy-backing," has been coined to indicate a similar procedure when motor carriers are transported by ships. Containerization refers to the placement of movable containers aboard ships, trains, planes, or motor carriers.

The technology discussed above is presently available. As it becomes more commonly used, this technology will play a dominant role in everyday living. Imagine, for example, the following scenario that could become a reality in the not so distant future:

Scene: The large and comfortably furnished two-story, four-bedroom suburban home of Jim and Susan Brown. The sturdy, rustic furniture gives evidence of casual family living. A modern kitchen can be seen through a large entrance upstage. A door to the right opens into the master bedroom. The time is 11:15 p.m. on a Thursday night in the 1970s. Jim is sprawled on the sofa thumbing through a magazine. Susan is seated in an easy chair knitting. Jim drops the magazine to the floor and stretches.

Jim: "I think I'll hit the hay; are you coming?"

Susan: "In a few minutes, just as soon as I do the shopping."

Jim: "Order me another 25-foot length of that flexible, plastic garden hose we got last week, will you?"

As Jim retires to the bedroom, Susan goes into the kitchen and sits at her planning desk. A tiny color television screen is mounted on the wall at eye level from where she is sitting. Settling comfortably into her chair, Susan lifts the protective cover from the direct-shop console on the desk and presses a set of buttons that connect her directly with the Customer Communications Department of City-Wide Distribution Center, Incorporated. For several minutes Susan is busy at her desk placing her order by punching various keys. Images of many kinds of merchandise appear on the screen—some fleetingly, and some held several seconds for her examination. As she continues to push buttons, Susan seems to get impatient, and finally she pushes a tally button on the console. In a second, a recap of her order appears on the screen. It itemizes her purchases and shows a total. She examines the recap, and with a nod of approval, pushes another button to confirm and clear the order, authorizing City-Wide to begin processing the order and clearing payment from her checkless bank account. Susan smiles with the satisfaction of someone who has just completed an irksome task. She yawns as she walks back from the kitchen and into the bedroom. From the bedroom we hear . . .

Jim: "How was the shopping expedition?"

Susan: (Jokingly) "Oh, it was absolutely exhausting—it took ten whole minutes. I'm going to get it down to five or six some night."

Meanwhile, while the Browns sleep, City-Wide goes to work. An elaborate computer-controlled and automated conveyor system moves the itemized order to a central processing point. When it arrives, the order is wrapped by a process which blows a super-strength film over the assorted items. This material insulates the frozen food products, as well as protects the entire package. The order, on a pallet, is then conveyed to the loading dock. At that point, it is consolidated with other shipments. A computerized printout is presented to the driver of the motor carrier, showing him the most efficient route to travel to deliver all the orders in the least amount of time. When Jim and Susan Brown awake the following morning, their order is waiting on the doorstep.[25]

Will such a fantasy ever take place? Perhaps not exactly in the form in which it has been described, though prototypes do exist. It is enough to state that overall marketing efficiency may be realized through the utilization of new technology and techniques in the storing, handling, and distribution of products.

Promotion. Mass communication is an important adjunct to a mass production economy. Marketers reach their vast potential markets through various forms of communication, primarily advertising. Technological innovations in the communications area, therefore, have significant import for marketers.

Evidence that our society communicates more and faster is visible in Table 15.2. Television will continue to dominate as the most effective communications medium for reaching millions of people simultaneously and, as far as the viewer is concerned, almost effortlessly. Television on the wall, built into the wall, or hung like a picture, will dominate the homes of the future. The ultimate in television will be world television. Receiving signals bounced from circling satellites, it can someday bring programs from any city on the globe.

Another technological breakthrough, which promises to revolutionize the industry, is cable television. The technology is present; all that is needed is an effective marketing system to realize a potential market of one billion dollars.[26] The advent of cable TV will allow viewers to subscribe to a service for as little as $4 to $6 per month for the privilege of viewing a much greater variety of programs to be selected by the subscriber himself. Of greater import to advertisers, cable TV will in turn allow sponsors to reach prospects on a much more selective basis.

TABLE 15.2.
THE DYNAMICS OF
COMMUNICATION IN THE
UNITED STATES

	1950	1960	1970
Number of telephones per 1,000 people	281	408	583
Percentage of American homes with black-and-white television sets	46.7	89.9	98.7
Pieces of first-class mail (in millions)	25,353	34,591	50,174
Paid circulation of daily newspapers (in thousands)	53,829	58,882	62,108
Total motor-vehicle registration (in thousands)	49,300	73,869	108,977
Passenger-miles traveled by air (in millions)	10,072	33,958	111,000
Intercity passenger traffic (in millions of passenger miles)	508,472	783,626	1,129,000
Number of books published	11,022	15,012	36,071

SOURCE: U.S. Department of Commerce, Bureau of the Census, *Statistical Abstract of the United States*, 1971, pp. 481, 482, 490, 493, 525, 535, 677.

Radio Corporation of America has developed its "Sets of the Seventies." Included are a pocket-sized, battery-operated color receiver combined with stereo radio in a case not much larger than a present-day transistor set; a book-sized color timer housed in a hinged travel case; a color set in an attaché case equipped with a video-audio tape player to show preselected television programs and sales presentations; a home television system that does everything from minding the children to providing entertainment; a large screen television console less than five inches deep for home use; and another console that enables the user to record the television shows on tape and play them back later. The big change in radio will be the improvement in tone and reception, despite reduction in size of speakers and other components. In summary, overall improvements in programming, portability, reception, color, and tone in radio and television will increase significantly the attractiveness and value of these media for advertisers.

Opportunities to communicate individually will be enhanced by new telephone technologies. Merchants talk of a telephone service that will enable the customer to examine what is being ordered on a miniature television screen. Eventually, clerks will be able to demonstrate different models and styles of products to the customer at home. They will point out features of the merchandise and answer customer questions by showing them over the telephone how an appliance works or how a garment fits. Telephones of tomorrow will give the customer all the advantages of in-the-store shopping with none of the disadvantages of coping with crowds, traffic jams, and other shoppers.

Prime benefactors of this new technology will be salespersons, who will be able to more efficiently distribute their time. Technology will significantly affect the salesperson in other ways. The increasing complexity of products will require a salesperson to be conversant not only with marketing and sales techniques, but also with product technology. The role of the salesperson will increasingly become that of a technology transfer agent.

TECHNOLOGY'S IMPACT ON MARKETING INSTITUTIONS

In addition to its impact on marketing practice, technology has also played an important role in the development of marketing institutions. Consider, for example, the modern supermarket. This well-known and popular retail operation had its beginnings in the 1930s, and it has evolved as one of the most significant institutional developments in the United States as the direct result of technology.

In 1930, Michael Cullen was working for the Kroger Grocery and Baking Company as a store manager in Herrin, Illinois. He had a "vision," and wrote to the vice president of Kroger in Cincinnati with an idea for what he called a "super market." He felt that the concept of the corporate chain with limited volume and small stores was soon to be an anachronism. Therefore, his proposal was to open five stores of "monsterous" size. These stores, he envisioned, would have dimensions as great as forty feet by one hundred and thirty feet! In addition, he proposed to make these stores eighty percent self-service, and as a result, charge prices below those of the competition. "I would lead the public out of the high-priced house of bondage into the low prices of the house of the promised land."

Kroger termed the proposal radical and rebuffed Cullen, at which point he quit and moved to Jamaica, Long Island. There, he joined forces with Harry Socoloff, vice-president of Sweet Life Foods, in 1930 to open the first supermarket in the United States. This supermarket was housed in an abandoned warehouse. By this time, Michael Cullen had taken to calling himself King Cullen. As his unorthodox advertisements proclaimed, he was "King Cullen, the world's greatest price wrecker—how does he do it?" Unfortunately, Cullen had to close his doors the first day he opened. He completely sold out his inventory! Once he had restocked, he sold more merchandise in one week than the average Kroger store at that time sold in one year.[27]

Was the entrepreneurial spirit of Cullen the sole reason for the emergence of the supermarket at this point in history? It is probably more accurate to say that Cullen had an idea that was inspired, perhaps subliminally, by the changes he saw in his environment. Yet, without those changes, his innovation could not have succeeded. It was, of course, the Depression Era of the 1930s. Money was scarce, low prices were obviously attractive, and working wives needed a convenient shopping outlet in order to economize on time.

The automobile was becoming a more popular mode of transportation. Automobile transportation meant that individuals were able to travel to do their shopping; they were no longer bound to the neighborhood. This ability to generate large numbers of customers at a single location created certain economies of scale in terms of volume distribution, with a resultant decrease in the price of individual products. And the storage and transportation functions could be shifted to the consumer, which also permitted a reduction in cost.

More homes were enjoying electric refrigeration, so the storage of frozen foods became practical. The practicality of self-service was enhanced by a rising level of literacy; packaging materials permitted examination of the product; and products could be "pre-sold" through advertising in national magazines. In addition, during this period, techniques evolved to allow full-color reproduction of ads in mass circulation magazines. Throughout all these developments, a trend toward urbanization helped to generate the mass markets required for volume selling.

Two elements in this example stand out. The first is the emergence almost simultaneously of a variety of new, or relatively new, technologies. The second significant element is the entrepreneur, an individual with vision. Cullen himself perfected no technology; his contribution was his insight and his ability to bring a variety of technologies together to offer a genuine marketing service to the consumer. Today, his supermarket continues to play an instrumental role in the retail structure of the United States.

TECHNOLOGY AND THE FUTURE

Around the turn of last century, Thomas Huxley came to Baltimore to proclaim "the great issue about which hangs a true sublimity, and the terror of overhanging fate is—what are you going to do with all these things?"[28] Before one can logically ask what can be done with all "these things," there must be some understanding of what "these things" will be. What technology will be employed in the future? What are the opportunities for marketers?

It is predicted that technology's greatest contribution to industry in the next decade may be "cheap intelligence" in the form of the incredibly shrinking computer. By the 1980s, this development will bring automation to the office, and even the smallest production machine will have its own brain. Quantum Science Corporation, a leading New York market researcher, predicts that by 1984 microcomputers will control 50 percent of automated factory equipment, and large minicomputers will control an additional 26 percent.[29] Already computers are being tied to accounting and bookkeeping systems so that when an item is purchased, it is immediately registered in the credit office, the inventory control office, the production scheduling department, and the shipping office, thus smoothing the flow of goods from raw material to store owner. This type of system is illustrated in Figure 15.3

Computers will also help management simulate business problems

FIGURE 15.3.
COMPUTERIZED INFORMATION
SYSTEM

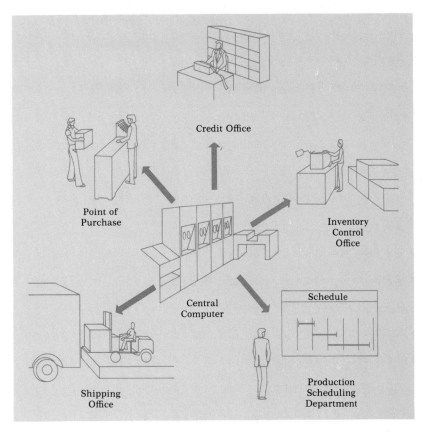

and propose various alternative solutions. They will further demonstrate which of the solutions have the greatest payoff potential. In government, computers will help plan for schools, roads, transportation, water needs, park land, sewage lines, etc. Officials will be able to more effectively schedule expenditures related to income, population, and community growth. Demographic data such as births, deaths, marriages, and migration will be stored in computers for ready access or analysis.

In the area of medicine, doctors will have complete health records available for broad segments of the population. Computers will be used in research to uncover secrets of body chemistry, the nervous system, and genetics. In another professional area, law, attorneys someday will have in their offices means for convening electronic connection to huge national central depositories of fact, rule, and procedures. In the field of travel, computers will assist as automatic reservation services to print tickets, debit accounts, and arrange schedules.

Another major area, the field of electronics, also promises significant technological breakthroughs. Molecular electronics will make possible miniature electrical machinery and equipment. In chemistry, the rearrangement of molecules has already made possible great strides in plastics, textiles, rubber, and drugs. Chemists foresee in the near future equally dramatic achievements in the creation of totally new building materials and possibly a reshuffling of food molecules to produce tastier and more healthful foods. Power for light and heat energy is undergoing revolutionary change also. Fuel cells, thermo-electricity, and thermionic generators are all believed to be future sources of energy.

Perhaps the most significant breakthrough is the advent of the microprocessor which contains thousands of microscopic transistors, diodes, capacitors, and the like all hooked together on a one-quarter inch integrated circuit. Its advent will make possible the introduction of such seemingly unrelated products as auto ignition and fuel mixture systems, home video recording discs, and miniaturized TV cameras.[30]

The housing industry represents a potentially fertile field for productivity increases. Engineers of the National Association of Home Builders are confident the day is near when a home builder will not have to buy lumber from one supplier, bricks from another, plumbing from a third, and wiring equipment from a fourth. Designers of tomorrow's home visualize blueprints based on a predetermined, modular scale. Everything will be measured in multiples of a single dimension. The modular concept, in turn, will determine the dimension of appliances, plumbing fixtures, and even the location of electrical outlets. The net result is that mass production will be brought to the housing industry.

What will be the energy sources of the future? The Federal Energy Commission predicts that by the year 2000, the United States might be able to derive 5 percent to 10 percent of its total electricity requirements from solar energy plants. Others feel that this prediction is far too pessimistic. The Deputy Director of the National Science Foundation's Division of Advanced Energy Research and Technology states that solar energy could be providing as much as 30 percent of the nation's electric power needs by the year 2000.[31]

Mining experts have known for years that certain parts of the ocean floor are littered with potato-sized nuggets called manganese nodules, rich in copper, nickel, manganese, and other minerals. Until recently, the notion of scooping up the nodules and refining metals from them seemed like science fiction. Now, however, a multinational race is underway to mine this underwater resource. At stake are ocean "mines" that contain fifty billion tons of these nodules potentially worth three trillion dollars. Such deposits would yield one and one-third times the world's land reserves of copper, thirteen times the land reserves of nickel, and ten times the land reserves of manganese. The value of the copper and nickel alone account for the $3 trillion estimate of worth.[32]

The above examples represent only a select few of the technological problems to be solved and opportunities to be exploited in the next several decades. It should be evident that business in the future will involve a constant adjustment to change. For marketing, this means that opportunities created by new technologies must not be lost and that new technologies must be utilized to make the marketing process more efficient. In conclusion:

> We find ourselves in the midst of a maelstrom which threatens to destroy age-old institutions, and a value system which took centuries to develop. Modern man is forced to live in a new social environment every five to ten years as technology imposes itself upon each and every person. . . . Some ask today if this exponential growth will level off or if it will continue its expansion for centuries to come. At times throughout history, it has been predicted that this growth would recede, but since 1950 technology has pushed forward like a tidal wave. The expansion of man-made material has become a pathological condition disrupting tradition, demanding new priorities, and creating many mutations in the age-old dream of the good life. . . .
>
> It is necessary to meet mechanical invention with social invention, and to prepare people to be flexible and adaptable to new environments. The attainability for man in the midst of this potential is beyond all expectations. But man must desire to determine his future, rather than allowing it to rule him or letting the system make irrational decisions based on profit, greed, ambivolence, or fear. . . . [33]

SUMMARY

It has been the purpose of this chapter to focus upon the technological environment and its impact on the social system in general and the marketing system in particular. Technology has been largely responsible for the growth of modern society. Yet, increasingly, man's ability to cope with rapid change is being called in to question. Values and social institutions, not to mention products and processes, are altered almost overnight through new technology. It has been noted throughout this chapter, however, that every new technology creates a corresponding marketing opportunity. Through its marketing activities, the business firm must adjust to change if it hopes to compete and survive in the future.

From this chapter it may be observed that the technological environment impinges on marketing in three distinct ways. First, technology creates new products and processes. Many of these have been discussed throughout this chapter. Second, technology must be marketed. Finally, new technology assists marketing in accomplishing its many tasks. The scope and importance of these latter two areas were treated in this chapter in the section on technology and marketing.

QUESTIONS FOR DISCUSSION

1. What is technology? Define in both a narrow and a broad sense. What is the distinction between invention and innovation?

2. What means have been used to measure the impact of technology on the economy? What has been the nature and extent of the impact of technology on the economy?

3. How does technology affect society at large? How is this impact reflected in changing values?

4. What is the role of government in the introduction of new technology? How prominent has the role of government been in generating new technology?

5. How has new technology affected marketing's ability to distribute goods and services and to communicate about those goods and services?

6. How will technology affect the role of marketing in the future? What sort of products and services might we anticipate? What means will be available to more efficiently market these goods and services?

NOTES

[1]J. Robert Oppenheimer, *The Open Mind* (New York: Simon and Schuster, 1955), pp. 140–141.

[2]Karl Manheim, *Ideology and Utopia* (New York: Harcourt Brace and World, 1936), p. 16.

[3]Melvin Kranzberg and Carroll W. Pursell, Jr., "The Importance of Technology in Human Affairs" in Melvin Kranzberg and Carroll W. Pursell, eds., *Technology in Western Civilization,* Vol. I: *The Emergence of Modern Industrial Society, Earliest Times to 1906* (New York: Oxford University Press, 1967), pp. 4–6.

[4]Richard A. Vaughan, "Technological Change: Its Impact on the Social and Economic Systems" (unpublished research report, College of Business Administration, Arizona State University, January, 1972).

[5]Paul W. Strassmann, *Risk and Technological Innovation: American Manufacturing Methods During the 19th Century* (Ithica, New York: Cornell University Press, 1959), p. 8.

[6]*Ibid.*

[7]John E. Jundt, *Final Report on the Ohio Technical and Business Services Program* (Columbus, Ohio: The Ohio State University, November, 1973), p. 50.

[8]Emmanuel G. Mesthene, *Technology and Social Change* (Indianapolis: Bobbs-Merrill Company, Inc., 1967), pp. 28–29.

[9]J. Jewkes, G. Sawers, and R. Stillerman, *The Sources of Invention* (New York: St. Martin's Press, 1959).

[10]D. Hamburg, "Invention in the Industrial Laboratory," *Journal of Political Economy* (April, 1963), pp. 96, 98.

[11]M. J. Peck, *Inventions in the Post-War Aluminum Industry, the Rate and Direction of Inventive Activity: Economic and Social Factors* (Princeton, New Jersey: National Bureau of Economic Research, 1962), pp. 279–292.

[12]Keith Davis and Robert L. Blomstrom, *Business, Society and Environment: Social Power and Social Responses* (2nd ed.; New York: McGraw-Hill, Inc., 1971), pp. 57–58.

[13]Earll B. Dunckel, William K. Reed, and Ian H. Wilson, *The Business Environment of the Seventies* (New York: McGraw-Hill, Inc., 1970), pp. 41–42.

[14]"Benefits Result from Moon Missions," *Tempe Daily News,* June 27, 1974, p. 12-A.

[15]*Ibid.*

[16]"Space Agency Research Offered for Industrial Use," *Arizona Republic,* October 7, 1974, p. 1.

[17]*Management and Technical Assistance,* GPO:1968, 0–311–356 (a pamphlet prepared by the Small Business Administration), p. 1.

[18]"MIT Hopes to Make Itself the Mother of Salable Inventions," *Wall Street Journal* (January 22, 1975), p. 1.

[19]"The ABC's of a High-Technology Business," *Business Week* (October 14, 1972), p. 55.

[20]Dunckel, *et al., The Business Environment of the Seventies,* p. 38.

[21]*Ibid.,* p. 39.

[22]"The SX-70 Camera Deglamourizes Polaroid," *Business Week* (November 30, 1974), p. 90.

[23]"A Minicomputer Tempest," *Business Week* (January 27, 1975), p. 79.

[24]*Ibid.*

[25]Alton F. Doody and William R. Davidson, "Next Revolution in Retailing," *Harvard Business Review* (May–June, 1967), pp. 4–5; and Seminars, The Ohio State University, 1968.

[26]"Cable-T.V. Dangles New Lures," *Business Week* (December 1, 1973), pp. 61–62.

[27]M. M. Zimmerman, *The Super Market* (Mass Distribution Publishers, Inc., 1955).

[28]Elting E. Morison, *Men, Machines and Modern Times* (Cambridge, Mass.: Massachusetts Institute of Technology Press, 1966), p. 208.

[29]"Answers from Technology," *Business Week* (September 14, 1974), p. 171.

[30]"Hello, Flash Gordon," *Forbes* (June 15, 1975), pp. 20–21.

[31]"Harnessing the Sun," *Forbes* (October 15, 1974), p. 23.

[32]"Tapping the Load on the Ocean Floor," *Business Week* (October 19, 1974), pp. 130–131.

[33]Epilogue, in Donald P. Lauda and Robert D. Ryan, *Advancing Technology, Its Impact on Society* (Dubuque, Iowa: William C. Brown, Co., 1971), pp. 533, 535.

SUGGESTED READINGS

Davis, Keith and Robert L. Blomstrom, *Business, Society, and Environment: Social Power and Social Responses* (2nd ed.; New York: McGraw-Hill, Inc., 1971).

Feldman, Laurence P. and Gary M. Armstrong, "Identifying Buyers of a Major Automotive Innovation," *Journal of Marketing* (January, 1975), pp. 47–53.

Hannavy, Anthony, "Can Engineering Cope with the Debris of Affluence?" in Lauda and Ryan, *op. cit.,* pp. 435–446.

Hlavacek, James D., "Toward More Successful Venture Management," *Journal of Marketing* (October, 1974), pp. 56–60.

Kransberg, Melvin and Carroll W. Pursell, Jr., "The Importance of Technology in Human Affairs" in Donald P. Lauda and Robert D. Ryan, *Advancing Technology: Its Impact on Society* (Dubuque, Iowa: Wm. C. Brown Co., 1971), pp. 51–59.

Mesthene, Emmanuel G., *Technological Change: Its Impact on Man and Society* (New York: New American Library-Mentor Books, 1970).

"M.I.T. Hopes to Make Itself the Mother of Salable Inventions," *Wall Street Journal* (January 22, 1975), p. 1.

Schoen, Donald R., "Managing Technological Innovations," *Harvard Business Review* (May–June, 1969), pp. 156–167.

Shallenberger, Frank K., "Management and the Challenge of Change," *Stanford Graduate School Business Bulletin* (Winter, 1966), pp. 2–7 and 27–30.

"The Breakdown of U.S. Innovation," *Business Week* (February 16, 1976), pp. 56–68.

Toffler, Alvin, *Future Shock* (New York: Random House, Inc., 1970).

FOUR

CONTEMPORARY
ISSUES IN MARKETING

Based on the presentation in Part IV, the reader should be able to:

- understand the scope and importance of marketing productivity and explain the difficulties that are encountered in measuring productivity

- evaluate the micro marketing system and explain several productivity improvement tools

- discuss marketing ethics and social responsibility in the context of a concept of ethical business

- define consumerism and discuss the contemporary consumer movement as an important area of consideration for the field of marketing

- define metamarketing and discuss the broadened concept of marketing in its application to the area of not-for-profit marketing

- take a crystal ball look at marketing in the future and recognize some important changes that are likely to take place between now and the year 2000

16
MARKETING
PRODUCTIVITY

16

MARKETING PRODUCTIVITY

From the preceding chapters dealing with the macro environment, it should now be apparent that marketing is more than a specific business function. In order to further emphasize this point of view, this final section is devoted to several contemporary issues in marketing, including marketing productivity, marketing ethics and social responsibility, consumerism, metamarketing, and marketing in the future. As the lead for the section, this chapter presents an analysis of marketing productivity, evaluated from the perspectives of both the individual firm and society. In the discussion, special attention is given to the difficulties encountered in the measurement of productivity, specific problems associated with the evaluation of marketing productivity, and an analysis of several selected areas where significant increases in marketing productivity are possible.

MEASURING PRODUCTIVITY

In the performance of most business activities, it is desirable to achieve the greatest output for the least amount of input. This may be identified as the desire for high productivity. Given scarce resources in terms of time, money, labor, materials, and equipment, productivity can be defined as the units of desirable output per unit of input. As an illustration of this definition, consider the field of advertising. One measure of the productivity of a television advertisement might be the number of viewing families reached per advertising dollar. In the context of an advertising campaign, the dollar expenditures represent the input; the number of viewing families reached identifies the output. This simple illustration, however, does not provide a true evaluation of the productivity of the campaign.

EFFECTIVENESS AND EFFICIENCY

When measuring and subsequently evaluating productivity, the accomplishments of an activity must be considered in light of two sets of criteria. The first of these, *effectiveness,* provides an evaluation of how nearly a set of actions accomplishes a given goal. For example, if a salesperson reaches or exceeds a goal of $1 million sales year, the salesperson would be considered effective. The same salesperson, however, may not have met the second criteria, efficiency. *Efficiency* may be defined as a measure of how well given inputs have been utilized. If the salesperson described above had to work twice as long as a second to accomplish the same sales level, the first salesperson might be viewed as inefficient. In a classic example contrasting these two criteria, Charles T. Horngren explains that "the killing of a housefly with a sledge hammer may be effective, but it is not efficient."[1]

443

DEFINING OBJECTIVES AND STANDARDS

If the productivity level associated with a given activity is to be evaluated, some benchmark against which operating results can be compared must be established. The development of objectives and standards facilitates evaluation. An *objective* is a desired level of attainment. The previously mentioned salesperson's goal of a $1 million sales year is an example of an objective. Broadly based objectives provide benchmarks against which to evaluate effectiveness. A *standard* also is a form of objective, but is narrower in scope and represents a desired level of attainment for utilization of resources. An example of a standard would be a predicted expense of $3.00 in transportation charges per delivered unit of product. This type of benchmark can be used to measure both efficiency and effectiveness.

It is often difficult to establish truly meaningful standards and objectives. In general, they should be established prior to the completion of the activity being evaluated, which requires some degree of planning. An absence of predetermined standards may reduce the objectivity with which performance is evaluated. Any "standards" and "objectives" established after the fact may be biased by a desire to place poor operating results in a more favorable light. For example, an automobile manufacturer, who lost money during the recession of the mid-1970s, might try to rationalize the results of operations based on prevailing economic conditions; results may be claimed to be "good," considering the "overall weakness of the economy." In such a situation, the purpose of developing standards has been defeated, since standards imply an "absolute" desirable level of attainment over a long period of time.

DIFFICULTIES IN SETTING OBJECTIVES

When establishing objectives, it is necessary to consider the potential behavior patterns the objectives will trigger from those expected to fulfill them. For instance, establishment of very high, practically unattainable, sales quotas may discourage salespersons from trying to achieve them to such a degree that the standards become meaningless: if a task is too hard, why try? Similarly, a sales quota that is set too low may produce undesired results because peak performance is unnecessary. This means that human behavior must be considered when setting standards.[2]

Besides establishing the desired level of attainment when setting objectives, it is necessary to consider the type of objectives. Similar objectives stated in slightly differing ways may result in very different types of behavior. A goal of profit maximization may achieve one kind of marketing effort, and a goal of revenue maximization may achieve another. In the former case, an effort will be made to move a high percentage of items with larger markups. In the latter case, goods will be moved irrespective of profit margins. The results of the two courses of action may not be compatible, since in the second case a nonoptimal marketing mix may result. Indeed, if the low margin item carries a bigger price tag, a disproportionate amount of sales effort may be

TABLE 16.1.
SALES PATTERNS USING
DIFFERENT SALES OBJECTIVES

	Product A	Product B
Price	$10.00 per unit	$8.00 per unit
Cost	8.00	5.00
Margin	$ 2.00 per unit	$3.00 per unit

If a salesman is able to sell a maximum of 100 items of product in a one month period, the following profits will result if:

(a) the salesman is a Profit Maximizer:

Sales — 100 units of Product B

Revenue	$ 800.00
Cost	500.00
Profit	$ 300.00

(b) the salesman is a Revenue Maximizer:

Sales — 100 units of Product A

Revenue	$1,000.00
Cost	800.00
Profit	$ 200.00

spent trying to sell that item to increase total revenues. Therefore, when management establishes objectives for marketing effort, care must be taken to develop objectives that will result in desirable behavior patterns that benefit the overall efforts of the firm. Table 16.1 illustrates the effects of the two types of action identified above.

A further example of setting objectives may help to clarify this point. For the amateur athlete, winning is an important, but not an overpowering, objective. Often it is just as important to the athlete to compete against the best possible competition, or to improve on a personal record. With the professional, the objective may change due to monetary incentive. As Ben Jipcho, the professional distance runner, has said, "Running for money doesn't make you run fast. It makes you run first."[3]

DIFFICULTIES IN EVALUATING PRODUCTIVITY

This section describes two areas that present difficulties in evaluating productivity: cost effectiveness and suboptimization. It also presents an example to demonstrate the types of problems that may be encountered.

Cost effectiveness. It is often difficult to evaluate the productivity of the marketing effort because direct cost-benefit relationships are hard to define. To illustrate, if a company introduces a multimedia advertising campaign at the same time one of its competitors introduces a large promotional campaign, the direct relationships between increases in the individual firm's sales level and its increased advertising expenditures may be significantly obscured. Stated another way:

> Since cost measures the use of resources, valid information on costs cannot be collected unless the underlying accounting data are structured in such a way that monetary information on the use of resources is available.[4]

To evaluate productivity, both the costs of inputs and the quantifiable costs of outputs not only must be available, they also must be compatible. One of the major problems encountered in evaluating marketing productivity is deciding which inputs and outputs are relative and to be measured, and how they are to be measured.[5] It is not too difficult to measure the costs of inputs, since invoices, billing statements, or wage reports will be generated as the expenses are incurred. But it is often difficult to measure outputs.

> Marketing is involved with the delivery of a bundle of functions or services. These shift over time ... So the output varies not only from changes in the volume of goods moving through the marketing system but also from the changing services performed by marketers in the discharge of their duties.[6]

In summary, the cost related problems of evaluating marketing productivity are twofold. There is the problem of identifying inputs and outputs and quantifying them. There is also the problem of defining input and output cause and effect relationships. These two problems must be resolved if useful evaluations are to be performed.

Suboptimization.   The second area of difficulty in evaluating marketing productivity arises from the interrelationships among the various parts of the marketing system of the individual firm. This is further complicated by the interrelationships between one firm's marketing activities and those of other firms in the same industry. Using the macro marketing system as a base, Moyer sees this problem as follows:

> What improves the efficiency for a firm may not add to macro-marketing efficiency. Take the case of the firm that increases its advertising budget. If effective, the increase might add to the firm's profits by lowering both per unit production and marketing costs. It might reduce the per unit advertising costs by increasing its effectiveness, but it might also reduce unit selling costs by reinforcing the selling effort and making it more effective. But what impact does this increased marketing efficiency have on rival firms? With rising demand, increased sales of one firm need not detract from another's; however, in stagnant or declining markets, losses in competitors' marketing effectiveness may offset the gains from the increased advertising.[7]

Within the firm, optimum performance by one segment may result in suboptimal performance by a second segment. This concept was discussed in Chapter 3. It is important that any reduction of efficiency in one area be necessary to efficient performance by the firm as a whole. Isolating the causes of inefficiencies based on such necessities

Participants	Payoffs Benefits	Costs
	Direct	
Producer	Product exposure, company image enhancement, specific information	Production costs of the advertisement, media time
	Indirect	
	Carryover effect to other products, goodwill derived from sponsoring a popular program, prestige of national name	Opportunity costs of a different campaign, damage to image from sponsoring unpopular program
	Direct	
Consumer	Product information, new or better uses for the product	Opportunity cost of time expended viewing the commercial
	Indirect	
	Entertainment or knowledge derived from the program	Advertising costs borne by products purchased, irritation with commercials and programs, misleading information
	Direct	
Society	Generation of jobs, incomes, taxes	Resources expended to produce and air commercial, time and energy consumed viewing
	Indirect	
	Increased expectations contributing to rising standards of living, entertainment, knowledge dissemination, contribution to social change	Inefficient allocation of resources, legal and economic consequences of deception, excess power over program content

SOURCE: Richard E. Homans and Ben M. Enis, "A Guide for Appraising Marketing Activities," *Business Horizons*, Vol. XVI, No. 5 (October, 1973), p. 26.

TABLE 16.2.
SUMMARY OF EVALUATION OF
A TELEVISION
ADVERTISEMENT

is exceedingly difficult. Such measurements will be relative, since absolute limits may not be quantifiable and since the precise level of reduction in efficiency required for each part of the overall system may not be defined.

Evaluation of a television advertisement. The following example gives some indication of the difficulties encountered in evaluating both marketing efficiency and effectiveness. The important elements in considering the evaluation of a television commercial are shown in Table 16.2. Although a quantitative judgment cannot be made from the information shown, it is important because it presents the types of relationships that must be considered. In particular, it demonstrates interrelationships between the benefits and costs of such commercials, as seen from the viewpoints of the seller, consumer, and society as a whole. These interrelationships further point up potential conflicts between marketing activities that may appear beneficial to one group, but are detrimental to another. These potential conflicts may result in uncertainty as to the overall value of the activity, uncertainty that can only be resolved by judgmental, subjective evaluation.

THE VALUE OF MARKETING

To determine the value of marketing, it is essential to look at it from both the macro and micro points of view, since the value of marketing for society as a whole may differ significantly from the value of marketing to the individual firm. This section focuses on the role of marketing in society, presenting an evaluation of how well that role is performed.

THE ROLE OF MARKETING

Earlier in this text, the role of marketing in an economy was described. In that discussion, it was shown that marketing plays a significant role in the development of an economy, thus contributing in a beneficial manner to society as a whole.[8] Marketing, through its order-getting and order-filling functions, performs two roles in society. First, it increases the availability of goods for the consumer, both in quantity and variety. Second, it encourages production efficiencies by facilitating large scale production activities that can incorporate production economies of scale.

In facilitating large-scale production activities, Adam Smith's description of the importance of geographic division of labor remains a key concept. This description specifies that the degree of specialization in a society is dependent upon the extent of the market for the particular goods to be produced. In the discussion, transportation was seen as a limiting factor. Today, this concept can be expanded to include both the sales and distribution (including transportation) functions of the marketing system. The sales function is necessary to obtain customers for products in adequate numbers to permit large-scale production. The distribution function is necessary to ensure that the product is distributed at a low enough cost to permit the firm to compete in a desired market.[9]

MACRO MARKETING PRODUCTIVITY

That marketing plays a significant role in economic growth is unquestioned. How effectively that role is performed is often questioned. Some aspects of the marketing role are discussed below.[10]

Promotional activities. As discussed in Chapter 7, one of the key accusations leveled at macro marketing is that advertising and promotional activities manipulate the public through the creation of false needs and wants. The creation of unnecessary wants then creates waste for society as a whole. The response to this charge is that although some waste may indeed exist through redirection of consumer demand, promotional activities cannot categorically change consumer needs. The recent shift of consumer preference toward smaller, more economical (although not necessarily cheaper) automobiles demonstrates this point. The automobile producers' efforts to maintain sales of high profit, big car lines did not prevent automobile buyers from turning away from bigger cars.

One problem inherent in any analysis of want redirection is the difficulty of defining consumer needs, and of deciding which of those needs should be filled. This problem is typified by the dilemma faced by producers in the tobacco industry. They must try to maintain sales and profits while displaying the Surgeon-General's warning that smoking may be hazardous to one's health.

Concentration of industry.   Another accusation made is that marketing concentrates industry by eliminating competition. This is a two-edged sword, however. Although effective marketing may eliminate competition, such actions are not a result of an "age of marketing." A desire for monopolistic operation and for development of large-scale production facilities, often requiring industrial concentration, predates the current heavy business interest in marketing.

In contrast, heavy marketing activity may open up new markets through encouragement of innovation. Also, abuse of monopoly power in most consumer product markets may be short-lived, since lower priced competitors, drawn by the success of the innovator, may soon enter the market with similar products. For example, the pocket-sized instamatic introduced by Kodak has been followed by the introduction of several similar products by Kodak's competitors.

Distribution costs.   Some analysts express concern over the magnitude of distribution costs as a percentage of aggregate product costs. They contend that product costs can be reduced through greater efficiency in distribution. However, improvements in distribution techniques may also result in increases in the proportion of total product costs devoted to distribution. Consider the situation presented in Figure 16.1.[11] The producer at supply point A has a production cost of $6.00 per finished unit. The producer at supply point B has a more efficient manufacturing operation with a production cost of $3.00 per unit. However, it is farther from B to the marketplace, M, than it is from A to M. This results in transportation charges of $2.00 for A and $6.00 for B. Ignoring profit, the total cost of A's product at point of delivery is $8.00, whereas the total cost for B's product at the same delivery point is $9.00. In this case, A will supply the market.

If some improvement in transportation techniques can be found that will reduce transportation costs by 50 percent along each route, A's total cost will drop to $7.00 per unit and B's total cost will drop to

FIGURE 16.1.
MARKET SUPPLIED BY TWO
PRODUCERS

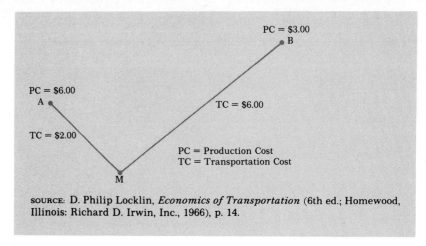

SOURCE: D. Philip Locklin, *Economics of Transportation* (6th ed.; Homewood, Illinois: Richard D. Irwin, Inc., 1966), p. 14.

$6.00 per unit. In this case, B will supply the market. From these examples, it may be observed that transportation (distribution) costs were 25 percent of the total product cost when A originally supplied the market, but 50 percent of the total product cost when B supplies the market.

Conclusions.   From the above discussion, it can be seen that any argument against the value of marketing to society as a whole can be countered by a convincing counter-argument that marketing is beneficial. McCarthy sums up the problem of measuring marketing effectiveness on the macro level as being one of measuring the degree of consumer satisfaction. Unfortunately, defining measures of satisfaction is difficult; it is necessary, therefore, to measure satisfaction in a subjective manner. The measurement of effectiveness for the firm must also be subjective, but it may be somewhat easier to determine if company profits are used as a surrogate measure of customer satisfaction.[12]

In making any analysis of the value of marketing, it is necessary to remember that analysis of the overall effectiveness of marketing requires the acceptance of a set of assumptions concerning the goals of the society within which the evaluation is being made. This results in a subjective analysis, since the standards for evaluation are subjective. With these restrictions in mind, it should be noted that marketing, overall, is viewed by most sources as providing benefits to society.

Example of macro marketing productivity.   That marketing for one segment of society is beneficial to society as a whole may be concluded from the experience of the toy industry in the United States. The benefits resulting from this industry's experience with television advertising, as reported by Robert Steiner, are presented below.[13]

Advertising

For a number of years, toy industry advertising appeared solely in print media and in radio broadcasting. Neither advertising medium could adequately reach the large number of children, ages 3- to 7-years (the primary audience), who either could not read printed ads, or were less than motivated by nonvisual advertising of radio broadcasting.

Prior to TV, "live" department store demonstrations of toys and other playthings had been the most efficient method of reaching the consumer. Such programs were feasible in only a few larger retail outlets, and thus only a fraction of the potential audience was exposed to the toy products demonstrated. Then, in the mid-1950s, the explosive growth of television and programs directed to children enabled toy makers to reach this primary target audience with an impact and an efficiency that was previously unthinkable.

As the number of TV homes increased in the 1960s, almost the entire child market could be reached through the television medium, at a cost per thousand that was considerably lower than the cost of store demonstrations. Furthermore, the small group of popular "old favorites" (e.g., "Monopoly"), which were prime candidates in the past for store newspaper ads, were now being joined by a multitude of playthings which were marketed each year to children by television advertising. Parents, too, were becoming involved, as their children described to them new toys and other playthings which were advertised on TV.

A substantial increase also occurred at this time in advertising to the secondary audience, parents. This advertising was largely run in local newspapers by major dealers handling toys. Discounters especially found that cut-price newspaper ads produced major results when they featured demanded TV toys.

Formerly, newspaper toy advertising had tended to require large amounts of space, because it carried the burden of explaining the toy's features to an uninformed parent. However, with the increased use of TV to advertise and educate consumers about toy products, newspaper ads placed by toy dealers only had to name the TV toy and the toy dealer's price. The manufacturer's name and a single copy sentence were optional extras. Hence, the post-TV newspaper ad required much less space, but sold far more merchandise.

Thus, toy industry advertising has developed along two avenues. It has utilized TV to reach children, and newspaper (print) to reach their parents. The result has been a marked increase of sales output produced from a dollar of advertising input—in short, a major increase in one kind of marketing productivity.

Manufacturing

The level of demand generated by the introduction of TV and the expansion of print ads was revolutionary. Where 50,000 units might have been the pre-TV forecast, 500,000 or even several million items of the same plaything could now be sold if the product had intrinsic merit and action features that permitted compelling presentation via the television commercial. Substantial economies of large-scale production were now achievable in toy manufacturing. In addition to savings in direct labor and raw materials achieved through larger purchases and longer production runs, major economies per unit also were obtained by the introduction of larger capacity molds and other tooling which now became efficient investments, considering the enormous increase in unit volume. *Thus an increase in the manufacturer's marketing productivity through advertising was directly responsible for an increase in his manufacturing productivity.*

While marketing budgets rose as a percentage of factory selling price, for heavy TV advertisers this increase could be partially offset by a decline in sales cost. Advertising made the factory salesman's job much easier. Now that he was offering an item that was in demand, due to heavy TV advertising, he could sell more dollars' worth of product per sales call. Consequently, his productivity increased, and the TV toy maker's sales cost as a percentage of his volume declined.

Distribution system

The surge of television advertising in the late 1950s coincided with two other momentous events in the American marketing system: the growth of discount stores that cut price on general merchandise, and the state-by-state demise of effective Fair Trade laws. Discount store sales rose from approximately $1.5 billion in 1958 to $26.6 billion in 1971. Such mass merchants became the largest retail outlet for toys, accounting for 28% of the industry's volume. Due to the intensive demand which TV advertising generated for specific toy items, toy sales climbed in mass merchandising outlets, and now toy departments rank eighth, just ahead of sporting goods and major appliances departments.

The larger volume and the quicker rate of turnover on TV-promoted toys increased the efficiency of both wholesalers and retailers. For instance, a jobber could now process and ship six one-dozen cases of a TV-promoted toy to a single retailer in less time than it once took to open one shipping case and repack its dozen toys and ship them to several dealers. For the retailer, increased turnover meant toys now yielded more profit per square foot of counter space, and his inventory investment turned over faster—again examples of productivity increments in the distribution of toys.

Mass merchants were quick to discover that a popular new TV-promoted toy with a $5.00 list price, which was selling for not less than $4.95 in the traditional retail outlets, sold exceptionally well when marked to sell for approximately $3.49. (Most toy makers soon discontinued the use of list price and sold their goods at a net dollar and cents cost price instead.) Discounters also found that if they took that same toy that was very much in demand (due to TV-advertising), and advertised it for sale in the newspaper at $2.97 during the height of the Christmas season, they would attract a spectacular traffic of bargain-hunting mothers whose children had been clamoring for that item. Moreover, by reading those newspaper ads and by making their own in-store price observations, consumers learned that toy retails were no longer frozen—that it paid to comparison shop. In turn, the practice of comparison shopping forced traditional retailers to reduce their prices almost to the level of discounters, or discontinue carrying TV toys entirely (a practice adopted by some department and specialty stores).

Indeed, discounting on leading advertised toy brands has often been so severe that margins at both wholesale and retail levels can be depressed below variable costs. Because initial investment per toy is typically high and product life cycles typically short, private label is relatively underdeveloped in the toy industry (the major exception is Sears Roebuck). Still, key chains and groups of wholesalers have taken vigorous action to protect their margins by encouraging smaller domestic makers and oriental factories to "knock off" last year's TV winners at such low cost that the imitations can be sold at retail below the advertised counterpart, yet earn the trade a high percentage markup. In addition, toy merchants frequently have protected their markups by limiting the number of heavily televised new items they carry in depth each season; and it has not been uncommon, either, for them purposely not to reorder a fast seller when the discounting gets too severe.

The reduction in margins did not stop with the leading advertised brands. It continued, in less severe form, to trim the markup and selling price of competing non-advertised merchandise. As successful advertising made its debut in a previously unadvertised category, the newly advertised toys enjoyed two advantages over the nonpromoted merchandise typically being vended from the same retail fixture. First, the promoted item turned over faster because of the advertising exposure. Furthermore, its retail price was slashed, so that for the consumer, it became a better buy than its non-promoted competitors in the same category. The retailer had to respond by trimming his historic markup on the non-advertised merchandise in that category to get it moving again.

The result was that, by 1970, strongly advertised merchandise enjoyed a distribution margin nearly 25 percentage points less than non-advertised goods, while non-advertised merchandise in heavily TV-advertised product categories went from factory to consumer for 5 to 7% less than other non-advertised goods. Furthermore, based on two separate markup studies conducted by the author, the overall toy distribution margin as a percentage of retail price fell by one-third, from 49% in 1958 to 33% in 1970.

The U.S. toy industry

The introduction of advertising by the American toy maker increased consumer demand which, in turn, led to a larger scale of factory operation and a growth in manufacturing productivity. Principally because toy life cycles are short, the manufacturing segment has remained quite competitive and savings tend to be passed on to the trade. The rise in advertising productivity combined with the efficiencies of mass retailing served to increase substantially the productivity of the distribution system. In the absence of Fair Trade laws, these productivity gains were reflected in lower distribution margins and reduced retail prices. Since the consumer demand for toys appears to be elastic, the public sharply increased its toy purchases, and the toy manufacturer received more orders, further enlarged his output, enjoyed additional gains in productivity, and so on.

Because of these interactions from 1958 to 1970, not only were distribution margins slashed, but it is estimated that toy makers enjoyed factory cost savings approximating 10%, and retail toy sales skyrocketed by nearly 80% in constant dollars.

EVALUATION OF THE
MICRO MARKETING SYSTEM

Although it has been concluded above that marketing, viewed in the aggregate, is effective and reasonably efficient, this conclusion cannot be generalized to apply to marketing within the individual firm. In this case, marketing is often neither effective nor efficient, recognizing as is stated earlier in this chapter, that effectiveness and efficiency are relative measures of performance. On the other hand, if areas of improvement are readily apparent for an individual firm, a value judgment concerning both effectiveness and efficiency of that firm may be formed.

This section looks at both the order-getting and order-filling functions of marketing in a micro context, and emphasizes the difficulties encountered in evaluating performance in each area. It will be shown that the order-getting function is most susceptible to analysis of effectiveness, with efficiency evaluation being restricted to comparison among firms. Once a sale has been made, the order-filling function may be more easily dealt with from the standpoint of efficiency. Before specific examples of order-getting and order-filling activities are considered, an overview describing both the importance of marketing costs and the difficulties encountered in isolating their effects on the overall performance of the firm is presented.

MARKETING COST ANALYSIS WITHIN THE FIRM

[Marketing] cost analysis is far more important than the scant attention it has received from accountants would seem to indicate and hardly deserves its present status as a stepchild to manufacturing costs. In the first place, [marketing] costs take up a large part of sales revenue, in many cases a greater portion than the manufacturing costs. In the second place, [marketing] costs offer a fertile field for cost reduction.[14]

A great deal of cost reduction effort recently has been centered on the marketing function. The very existence of this activity implies inefficiency in marketing at the micro level. As an illustration, consider the following statements:

The level of wastefulness in distribution is so high that *nearly any company* can slash away great hunks of excess marketing fat with an instrument no more delicate than a meat axe. Only a distressingly small number of companies have refined distribution to the point where fat removal is so delicate an operation as to require the use of a scalpel.[15]

Marketing costs.   Marketing costs can be roughly defined as fitting into one of ten separate cost categories.

1. *Financial costs* of carrying an inventory of finished goods, such as taxes and insurance;

2. *Warehousing costs,* such as building occupancy costs, materials handling costs, and stock record-keeping costs;

3. *Sales promotion costs,* such as advertising, publicity, and marketing research;

4. *Sales solicitation,* or *order getting, costs,* such as sales salaries and commissions, travel expenses, and entertainment expense;

5. *Order-assembly costs,* made up of the clerical costs of preparing and processing shipping orders and memoranda;

6. *Packing costs,* related to the preparation of the order for shipment;

7. *Transportation costs* and *delivery expenses;*

8. *Accounts receivable record-keeping costs,* such as billing, posting invoices, recording returns, and entering customers' payments;

9. *Credit and collection costs,* including the cost of maintaining a credit department, making credit investigations, legal fees, and bad debt losses;

10. *Administrative costs* such as general supervisory expenses, personnel services, payroll preparation, and the like.[16]

To measure the efficiency of the firm's operation, evaluation must be made of operations in each of the above areas. However, it is difficult to define meaningful objectives for each area because of two problems. The first is determining what will be measured; that is, the establishment of the pertinent marketing structure. The second deals with how the measurements will be taken. Both problems are considered below.

Marketing decision areas. In developing the marketing structure for the individual firm, a series of questions must be answered. These questions, presented below, help define the objectives of the firm against which both effectiveness and efficiency can be evaluated.

1. What products should be manufactured and sold?

2. At what prices should the output be sold?

3. To what groups of customers should the sales effort be directed?

4. In what geographical areas should the product be marketed?

5. What channels of distribution should be utilized?

6. On what terms should sales be made?

7. What means of sales promotion will best reach the potential market?[17]

In effect, the answers to these questions define a firm's marketing strategy. The evaluation of the results of this strategy will influence the formulation of future strategies.

Analysis permutations. If profitability has been chosen as a measure of satisfaction of customer needs, as was suggested earlier, it becomes necessary to decide how to measure profitability. Some of the ways this can be done are listed below:

1. By products or product lines;

2. By individual customers or groups of customers;

3. By order size;

4. By geographical areas or territories;

5. By salesmen;

6. By channels of distribution—distributors, direct retail, etc.;

7. By method of sales solicitation—salesman's call, telephone, mail, etc.;

8. By method of delivery;

9. By terms of sales—cash, regular credit, installment, etc.[18]

It is clear from the above list that there is no absolute measure of efficiency in marketing. To the contrary, efficiency is a matter of relative results. Indeed, it is probably better this way in that lack of "absolute" standards presents management with the freedom to gather the kind of information necessary to best meet the objectives of the individual firm, or segment of an individual firm, in terms of market share, profit, cost reduction, and so forth.

ORDER-GETTING ACTIVITIES   The problems involved in measuring the effectiveness, or efficiency, of some order-getting activities are described below. Areas included in the discussion are market research, advertising and promotion, and direct sales efforts.

Market research.   There has been a great deal of emphasis in recent years on market research activities. Generally, these activities are involved with gathering and analyzing data concerning marketing problems in the sale of goods and services. Information is collected on consumer needs and wants, on ways to better present products to consumers, on marketing channel effectiveness, and so on. Often the results of market research are long-run, making evaluation of effectiveness difficult. In addition, the established standards revolve around criteria such as "market research should be 10 percent of sales dollars." Such criteria are not standards. What is required is more understanding of the purpose of market research and of the value of the information gained through this process. Without a better understanding of the role market research plays in increasing sales, true ratings of effectiveness cannot be made. Comparisons with the research expenditures of others in the same industry may not be really useful because there is no guarantee that the firms studied have picked the proper level of expenditure for their individual operations.

That market research is beneficial is not at question here. The question is what degree of benefit it has. Until cause and effect relationships and until the value of market research in holding or increasing a firm's relative position can be defined, this question will remain essentially unanswerable.

Advertising and promotion.   Advertising and other promotional activities also play an important role in the overall sales effort. They are vital to the creation of consumer awareness and to the education of the consumer. Certain measures of both effectiveness and efficiency in this area can be made through analysis of exposure per dollar spent on advertising and promotion. In addition, market research may be used to evaluate the effectiveness of promotional campaigns in terms of added sales generated. But, again, a true measurement of effectiveness as a function of increased sales, or efficiency as a function of increased sales per dollar spent, may be difficult to determine. There is a timing factor to be considered since results may not be immediate, particularly in the area of durable goods marketing. In addition, there is always a question of the point at which decreasing returns set in, thereby decreasing productivity and making advertising expenditures less effective. Finally, in times such as those faced by business during the mid 1970's period of recession, it is difficult to discern the effect of advertising versus the general effects caused by major shifts in the economy.

Direct sales efforts. Productivity of direct sales effort is easier to analyze, but still may be complicated if a multiple promotional scheme of attack has been used. The efficiency of sales personnel, however, may be determined to some degree by looking at sales and profits generated by each individual.

In reality, profit is not the best criteria to use for evaluation. It is better to separate all product costs that have been allocated and make comparisons using contribution margin generated; i.e., the difference between revenue and all directly assignable costs. This removes erroneous results caused by arbitrary allocations of joint, or common, costs to individual products. In effect, this is the difference between the use of the direct costing and full-cost, or absorption costing, approaches to income accounting. The example shown in Table 16.3 demonstrates the importance of this cost separation.

Based on absorption costing information, the key figures are those representing net profit. Using these figures, a salesperson would be encouraged to push Product C, since it is the only one currently showing a profit. Indeed, the firm might be tempted to eliminate Product A altogether. Using a more sophisticated approach, however, it can be seen that all three products contribute to covering the allocated fixed costs. In reality, these costs should probably not have been allocated

TABLE 16.3.
INCOME STATEMENT BY
PRODUCT LINE

	Product A	Product B	Product C	Total
Units Sold	1,000	1,600	2,000	4,600
Revenue	$100,000	$200,000	$300,000	$600,000
Variable Costs	40,000	100,000	160,000	300,000
Contribution Margin	$ 60,000	$100,000	$140,000	$300,000
Discretionary Fixed Costs	10,000	20,000	30,000	60,000
Short-Run Profit Margin	$ 50,000	$ 80,000	$110,000	$240,000
Separable Committed Costs	25,000	50,000	60,000	135,000
Segment Margin	$ 25,000	$ 30,000	$ 50,000	$105,000
Allocated Fixed Costs	40,000	30,000	40,000	110,000
Profit (Loss)	($ 15,000)	$ 0	$ 10,000	($ 5,000)

at all, since their allocation was inevitably the result of a set of subjective judgments. Allocated fixed costs include general office expenses and the company president's salary. If Product A were dropped, the firm would be worse off, since it would lose $100,000 in revenue, while eliminating only the variable and discretionary fixed costs totaling $50,000. The overall loss for the firm would then be $55,000, since no revenue from A would be collected to cover the still present separable and allocated fixed costs. The short-run profit margin of $190,000 would be overbalanced by the remaining $245,000 in fixed costs.

In making a decision to encourage beneficial salesperson behavior, the firm in the example above would be better off to encourage sales of the item with the highest degree of contribution margin, in this case Product A, although additional sales of any item would improve the firm's overall profit picture.

ORDER-FILLING ACTIVITIES

The function providing business with the greatest short-term potential for improvement in efficiency is the order-filling or physical distribution management (PDM), function.[19] The distribution function contributes between 20 and 50 percent of gross sales, depending on the specific business activity.[20] The potential for cost savings to the firm lies in two concepts. The first concept deals with order cycle times and reliabilities that influence the effectiveness of the distribution system and, therefore, the potential sales of the company. The second considers PDM as part of the total cost concept. In the total cost concept, all aspects of distribution cost, such as packaging, transportation, and warehousing, are combined to obtain an optimum total cost for the entire firm's operations. This section discusses the elements of the order cycle, the total cost concept, and examples of potential cost savings in product packaging, warehousing, transportation, channel selection, and retail operations. It also discusses constraints within which the order-filling system must operate.

Order cycle time. One of the services offered by a company is product delivery. If the firm is to supply its products to other manufacturers, deliveries must be on time, since delays in delivery can hamper the customer's manufacturing abilities. In supplying retailers and wholesalers, deliveries must also be on time so that those customers' sales are not hurt by a lack of merchandise. This has become increasingly important as manufacturing firms have assumed the inventory control function for retailers and other manufacturers for whom the firm acts as a vendor. As supply times have decreased, reducing inventory requirements for receivers of goods, it has become essential for order cycle times to be reliable, since the impact of any delay will be magnified as reserves reach a lower level.

An *order cycle* consists of three major subcomponents: communication of orders, order processing by the shipper, and transportation of goods to the consignee.[21] The shorter the order cycle time, the fewer goods the receiver must keep on hand. For example, if it takes ten days to process an order completely, the firm placing the order must have at least a ten-day supply of product on hand at the time an order is placed, or face the likelihood of stockouts when new final customer orders are received. For an appliance dealer, this may amount to several thousand dollars worth of inventory. If the cycle can be shortened to three days, many dollars previously tied up in inventory may be freed for other uses.

Of perhaps more importance is the dependability of delivery times. The fact that delivery times will average three days may not provide a firm with savings in inventory carrying costs unless the variability in delivery times is small. A variability of one to ten days may leave the firm no better off than before, particularly if running out of inventory will have a significant effect on customer relations and future sales. Consequently, order cycles receive considerable attention, not because of their effect on efficiency, but because of the potential impact of being ineffective. In such instances, the need for effectiveness may override the need for efficiency.

As with other areas, efficiency and effectiveness may be difficult to measure when considering order cycle times. It may be that the process of handling orders can be changed to increase either efficiency or effectiveness. In this area, measurement of results is relatively simple. The problem lies in the development of meaningful objectives such as providing "adequate" service at the "lowest possible cost." What constitutes adequate service is the question; answering it requires a full understanding of customer needs, which are always difficult to measure.

Total cost concept.   The total cost concept is an extension of the techniques involved in determining economic order quantities, but it includes many more variables. This technique did not become sophisticated until the advent of operations research and the modern computer. The concept can be explained easily through the use of what Professors George Smerk and Joseph Hartley have referred to as the Dumbbell Model, shown in Figure 16.2. In this model, all aspects of the distribution process are considered in combination. As a result, the costs of performing each subfunction are integrated to provide the lowest total cost for the system as a whole. This is shown graphically in Figure 16.3, which applies to a transportation mode decision by a firm and reflects differences in costs implied by adoption of each mode. For example, packaging costs will be greater for transport by railroad than by motor carrier, since movement by rail is, in general, less gentle. Similarly, storage costs may be greater for rail movement, since it is typically slower than truck movement, requiring the carrying of larger inventories.

Operating constraints.   One problem encountered in improving efficiency or effectiveness in the order-filling portion of marketing involves the constraints within which this function must operate. Many

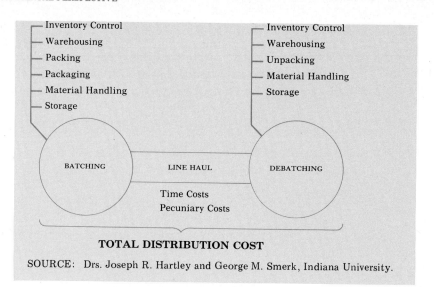

FIGURE 16.2.
DUMBBELL MODEL

SOURCE: Drs. Joseph R. Hartley and George M. Smerk, Indiana University.

FIGURE 16.3.
TOTAL COST ANALYSIS FOR A
TRANSPORTATION MODE
DECISION

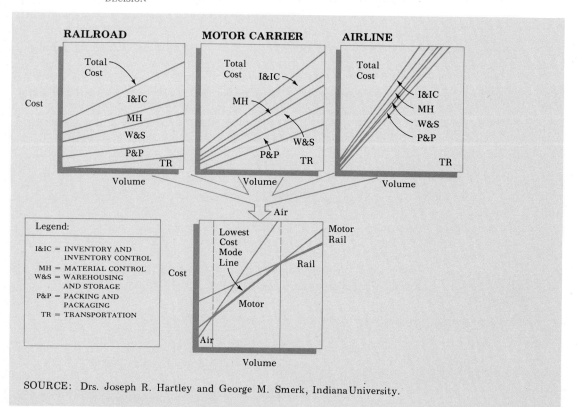

SOURCE: Drs. Joseph R. Hartley and George M. Smerk, Indiana University.

times, operating efficiency must be subjected to constraints prescribed by customer demand. If a major customer demands receipt of shipments within five days of placing an order, the supplier will have a limited number of ways of shipping an article. It may become necessary to ship by truck, or risk losing the customer, even though rail would better suit the manufacturer's overall distribution system. This lack of choice may make the supplier's operations much less efficient, so the supplier must strive for the maximum efficiency obtainable within this constraint.

Many additional areas could appear that would limit a firm's efficiency in carrying out its distribution function. For example, if a company does not have the money available to install a computer, it may not be possible to "streamline" the order handling function. Likewise, a firm may be saddled with antiquated and poorly located warehouse facilities, but lack the working capital to improve its situation. It is important to realize that efficiency must be related to the operating structure of the firm in terms of both organization and facilities; a truly optimum operating system may not be achievable. Given an existing operating structure, it is necessary to strive for as much improvement as is possible with an eye on potential changes in the structure as resources to facilitate such changes become available.

Examples of order-filling productivity.   To illustrate productivity in the order-filling function, examples from product packaging, warehousing, transportation, channel selection, and retail operations are discussed below.

1. *Product Packaging.* It is often possible to develop significant cost savings in product packaging, thus increasing marketing productivity. A good example of this is the stacking of paper cups for shipment. If paper cups had straight sides, most of what would be shipped would be air. The majority of the air can be eliminated, however, with tapered sides, as shown in Figure 16.4.

FIGURE 16.4.
PACKAGING OF PAPER CUPS

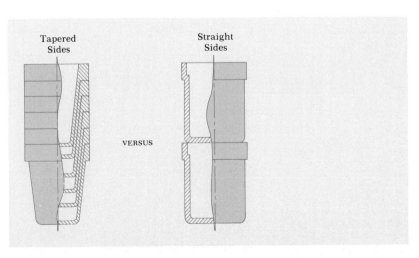

Tapered Sides

Straight Sides

VERSUS

With products such as china cups, where the value of the product is greater, this conservation of space is not as important.

It is interesting that packaging often has a reverse effect on marketing efficiency. For example, many small hardware parts are now packaged in small plastic boxes with volume capacity that greatly exceeds that required to hold the packaged items. This shows that packaging costs may have to be subjugated to other costs in the total cost concept. In this case, ease of handling by the retailer, a reduction in losses due to theft, and convenience may override a desire for lower packaging costs available in bulk packaging.

2. *Warehousing.* Efforts to improve marketing productivity in warehousing have occurred along several fronts, from layout of storage areas within a warehouse to facilitate efficient material handling to the location of new warehouses to minimize both order cycle times and transportation charges. Cost savings in these areas can often be accomplished through the use of techniques long used in production engineering projects.

3. *Transportation.* In improving marketing productivity, it is often necessary to analyze the transportation phase of the PDM process. Efficiency here must be analyzed within a framework of the need for effectiveness. Actual efficiency may be improved through the adoption of such things as containerization and the use of joint rail/truck movement in the form of trailer on flat-car, or piggyback movements. Again, transportation decisions, as was shown earlier, must be considered in light of the overall distribution cost structure. Efficiencies may be introduced, however, through the introduction of improved handling methods and better loading dock design.

4. *Channel Selection.* Various marketing channel mixes can provide the individual manufacturer with some added efficiencies in overall operations. The use of a regional warehouse system may provide improvement over the use of one central factory warehouse. Particular transportation savings may result because the regional warehouse may permit consolidation of shipments, allowing the use of carload or truckload rates that are lower than less-than-carload or less-than-truckload rates. This potential for consolidation is shown in Figure 16.5. In this case, without a regional warehouse, each

FIGURE 16.5.
REGIONAL WAREHOUSE PLAN

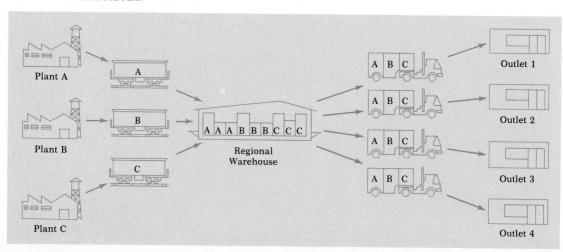

plant would be forced to ship four partial truckloads or carloads to each outlet, a total of twelve movements. With a regional warehouse, only seven movements are required. As with analysis of any part of the marketing organization, what is most efficient depends on what is best for the firm as a whole. Therefore, due to the interrelationships among the parts of the marketing function's operations, efficiency of any one area must be relative. Total efficiency can be measured only in the context of the total operation.

5. *Retail Operations*. Within the retail store, efficiencies may be accomplished in several ways. For example, an electronic cash register system may increase sales clerks' productivity by allowing them to process more customers in a given amount of time. Additionally, if the registers are hooked to a computer, it may be possible to automatically perform the inventory control function. Savings can also be made by modifying material handling methods to make them more efficient.

PRODUCTIVITY IMPROVEMENT TOOLS

This section looks at ways in which marketing productivity can be improved. In particular, it presents some factors necessary for implementation of improvements and provides one example of a firm's efforts to upgrade its distribution system.

MANAGEMENT INFORMATION SYSTEMS

As was stated earlier in this chapter, measurement of productivity is often extremely difficult, requiring development of data that will permit measurement in quantifiable, usable terms. A major trend in the development of such data has been the adoption of management information systems. These systems, which integrate the pertinent data available within a firm into a coordinated package, permit analysis and comparison of masses of data in a variety of ways without the expenditure of a great deal of energy.

The availability of a coordinated data base is necessary when analyzing marketing operations because of the numbers of interrelationships among the various functions of the marketing process. Without this data, a true total cost approach cannot even be attempted because of the complexity of these interrelationships. Therefore, a "total management information system" plays a dual role. First, it provides the data necessary for analysis. Second, it often provides the computer technology necessary to solve complex problems relating many interrelated variables.

COST REDUCTION PROGRAMS

Once an optimal set of operating characteristics for the firm have been developed, a set of characteristics that mesh the operation of the parts of the marketing system, it is desirable to make each function

Cost Sensitive Area	Questions to Ask
Clerical Costs	Does each administrative department have a plan for increasing productivity 5% to 7% per year and have goals been achieved?
	What is the magnitude of changes in administrative unit costs attributable to wage and salary expenses increases, work-load fluctuations, and efficiency and productivity changes?
Sales Force	Do you have detailed work-load planning procedures for classifying and segmenting accounts and assigning call frequency guidelines?
	Are sales territory assignments made on the basis of groups of accounts' potential profitability or sales volume?
Cash/ Accounts Receivable	What portion of their time are credit men spending on collection of receivables versus credit approval?
	How do your key cash management ratios, i.e., cash/sales, cash and M/S/sales, accounts receivable/sales, and accounts payable/sales, compare with the same ratios of the *best* performers among your competitors?
Pricing/Volume	What value have you added to your price structure for products' real engineering content and your technology self-image?
	Do you know the total volume per unit, unit margin, and total margin relationships among all industry segments and geographic areas to and in which you sell?
Direct/Indirect Labor	What percent and at what levels in the operating and marketing organizations are changes in operating schedules initiated?
Transportation/ Distribution	How much incremental money does your corporation spend annually to transport goods by other than the optimum transportation mode?
	Are the customer service levels you are maintaining really required, given the service levels your customers provide to their final distribution points?
	Are decisions to purchase proprietary vehicles based on proven productivity and efficiency numbers and are ROIs being achieved?
Materials Cost/ Inventory Control	Is an established, formal product evaluation process utilized for adding to, monitoring, and deleting from all product lines?
	What impact does fluctuating turnover rates have on reorder points and economic order quantities?
	Are the purchasing decisions of decentralized operations monitored to ensure the benefits of exercising purchasing leverage, e.g., buying in carload lots, are balanced against the costs of carrying large inventories?

SOURCE: Adapted from William D. King, "The Six Phases of Cost Reduction," *Business Horizons,* Vol. XVI, No. 4 (August, 1973), pp. 40–41.

TABLE 16.4.
SELECTED KEY QUESTIONS IN
COST SENSITIVE AREAS

operate as efficiently as possible. In doing this, since a true optimum is generally unachievable, cost reduction is the method employed to enhance productivity. Some questions relating to cost reduction in marketing areas are shown in Table 16.4. This illustration is intended to show relative improvement in efficiency, even if optimums are unknown.

CASE EXAMPLE   As an illustration of productivity improvement, the following case example describes the efforts of the Foxboro Company to improve the efficiency of its distribution system.[22]

Derby Day, dignified Kentucky Colonels and frosty mint juleps—until a few years ago, those were the images Louisville brought to mind. More recently, a fast-growing enterprise personified by mustachioed, ice cream-suited Colonel Sanders brought the city added fame as growing hordes of Americans licked their fingers over huge quantities of his Kentucky fried chicken. Better than 3,100 KFC Corp. franchisees, operating one or more retail outlets, plus some 1,000 company-owned stores supply consumers nationwide with this fresh fried chicken and an assortment of other fast food items.

Because this business expanded so rapidly, logistics operations initially followed the line of least resistance. In the spring of 1971, management recognized the need to improve services while concurrently reducing costs for franchisees, vendors and the company itself. Since then, KFC Corp., a division of the Heublein Corp., has followed a multi-phased distribution program that brought early benefits system-wide and built a new base to support the firm's rapid expansion. Added products, such as ribs, french fries and frozen desserts, as well as further consumer outlet expansion, make continuing logistics refinements essential.

Vice President of Food Services H. Richard McFarland has all of the logistics elements under his direct control. While the director of distribution carries the largest portion of these responsibilities, the directors of purchasing, sales and poultry procurement perform certain of the functions as parts of their overall duties. Because of perishability, for example, fresh chicken moves through 30 independent distributors and 14 of the 25 company commissary warehouse locations in a system apart from the basic distribution services' research and staff support.

Since 1971, the distribution services section itself has worked steadily at the installation and refinement of several major systems concerned largely with non-perishable foods, paper specialties and other materials that currently total some 200 line items. They tackled this activity in two overlapping phases:

1. *Distribution Service Program:* Initiation of 13 distribution centers that regionally consolidate inbound vendor deliveries and outbound store shipments brought early relief from service deficiencies and introduced an initial simple computer-oriented order processing system.

2. *Advanced Distribution System:* While an initial teletype-based order processing system brought immediate benefits to the service cycle, the distribution department used it as a stepping stone toward a more sophisticated procedure based upon intelligent computer terminals and decentralized order entry.

"We promised our franchisees an effective new distribution system within a year at the March, 1971 annual convention," states Vice President McFarland, "and we made it. By March 1, 1972, we had a five-center distribution network backing up faster, more reliable order fulfillment nationally with the assurance of more and better to come."

It was quite a change. The old system found mail or phone orders flowing into KFC-Louisville where they were coded by vendors who then received copies and forwarded the specified goods to the affected stores. Thereafter, the vendors invoiced KFC who, in turn, invoiced the stores individually for each separate vendor shipment. With typically seven or eight vendors represented on a single order, stores found themselves having their orders fulfilled with multiple LTL shipments typically in the costly 500 to 1,000-pound category. A one-month study in the spring of 1971 confirmed that deliveries under this procedure were irregular, expensive and slow. Normal order turn time was 17 days.

Management decided to seek a firm seven-day order turn, allowing two days for order receipt, one day for KFC processing and one day's warehouse processing with no later than third morning delivery to stores from new KFC distribution centers set up at public warehouses.

Those distribution centers were the key factor. Distribution Director Richard J. Fitz sought the cooperation of the many affected vendors in assembling needed stocks at strategic regional locations, thus lifting shipment weights over the 2,000-pound level, diminishing order cycle time and reducing paperwork.

At the March 1, 1972 annual convention, as promised a year earlier, the new system was inaugurated through five public warehouse distribution centers at Dallas, Atlanta, Columbus, Chicago and Charlotte with monthly additions planned to reach a total of 12. "After reaching this goal," notes Mr. Fitz, "we opened an additional center at Oakland. Others will be added when business levels require them."

Both ends of the pipeline benefited from the change. Vendors set up stores at the distribution centers that could be replenished with large shipments as needed, eliminating the multitude of direct LTL shipments formerly made to the stores. This shifted most outbound freight from vendor locations into lower rate categories. It also reduced paperwork and brought the handling economies that fewer, larger shipments make possible.

For the stores, merchandise delivered from a single source brought similar gains. With average shipments above 2,000 pounds, applicable LTL charges dropped sharply. (They have since moved on toward a 3,000 pound average.) A single delivery against an order in lieu of seven or eight, in addition to improving schedule reliability, meant a reduced handling and storage burden on necessarily restricted store facilities. Important, too, was the elimination of minimum order levels on several sources. Stores no longer must overstock marginal items because of freight requirements, so smaller inventories are possible, reducing investment and releasing storage space.

With the new system fully installed, KFC is now developing scheduled delivery procedures that will further increase store shipment sizes. "When the energy crunch began, we sought a means to combat freight cost increases while bringing still greater store service reliability," Mr. Fitz observes. "Scheduled deliveries give us both."

In a system that processes more than 1,000 weekly orders, the new plan offers important further gains through new handling and paperwork savings in addition to reduced freight costs. While stores under the plan may now order only once weekly or every second week on a specified day, they benefit from an order cycle reduced from seven days to five and assured delivery dates. "We've installed scheduled deliveries successfully from Seattle, Columbus, Charlotte and Dallas," asserts Service Manager James S. Kirkpatrick. "We're progressing steadily on a region-by-region basis."

SUMMARY

This chapter has shown that productivity measurement, in general, is difficult, requiring selection and quantification of pertinent input and output variables. Once productivity measures have been selected, they must be evaluated using criteria of either effectiveness or efficiency as a guide, depending upon the nature of the activity being analyzed. This evaluation is important in analyzing business activity because inefficiency and ineffectiveness can have detrimental results for the operations of the firm. Further difficulty is encountered at this stage in determining the standard against which to compare the results of operations.

In applying measures of productivity to marketing, it has been necessary to separate analysis of marketing on a macro level from marketing within the individual firm. Macro marketing effort has been judged generally efficient and of benefit to society. Within the context of the firm, however, marketing efforts are often inefficient and ineffective. It has been shown that it is necessary to split marketing activities into order-getting and order-filling activities for analysis within the firm. For order-getting activities, effectiveness may be the most important evaluation criteria. For order-filling activities, efficiency may be the most important criteria.

If marketing within individual firms is judged as less than satisfactory from the standpoint of productivity, there is room for improvement in that aspect of operations. Two areas are seen as providing the greatest boon to improving marketing productivity. These are the adoption of computer technology to aid both operations and evaluation, and the judicious application of cost reduction programs, instituted carefully to ensure no loss in operating effectiveness.

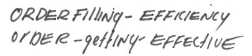

ORDER Filling - EFFICIENCY
OrDER - getting - EFFECTIVE

QUESTIONS FOR DISCUSSION

1. Distinguish between efficiency and effectiveness.

2. What is the total cost concept?

3. Define productivity as related to marketing. Why is marketing productivity often difficult to evaluate?

4. Is marketing productive in the macro sense? Is it productive in a micro sense?

5. Distinguish between order-getting and order-filling costs.

6. Why is it difficult to establish standards?

7. How may objectives and standards influence behavior?

8. How may marketing productivity be improved?

NOTES

[1]Charles T. Horngren, *Accounting for Management Control: An Introduction* (2nd ed.; Englewood Cliffs, New Jersey: Prentice-Hall, Inc., 1970), p. 260.

[2]Charles T. Horngren, *Cost Accounting: A Managerial Emphasis* (3rd ed.; Englewood Cliffs, New Jersey: Prentice-Hall, Inc., 1972), pp. 125–126, 151–161, and 187–189.

[3]"They Said It," *Sports Illustrated* (June 9, 1975), p. 16.

[4]Robert N. Anthony and Glenn A. Welsch, *Fundamentals of Management Accounting* (Homewood, Illinois: Richard D. Irwin, Inc., 1974), p. 108.

[5]Reed Moyer, *Macro Marketing: A Social Perspective* (New York: John Wiley & Sons, Inc., 1972), p. 78.

[6]*Ibid.*

[7]*Ibid.,* p. 79.

[8]For further information on the role of marketing in the economy see: Robert J. Holloway and Robert S. Hancock, *Marketing in a Changing Environment* (2nd ed.; New York: John Wiley & Sons, Inc., 1973), pp. 4–17; Harry A. Lipson and John R. Darling, *Introduction to Marketing: An Administrative Approach* (New York: John Wiley & Sons, Inc., 1971), pp. 11–23; E. Jerome McCarthy, *Basic Marketing* (5th ed.; Homewood, Illinois: Richard D. Irwin, Inc., 1975), Chapter 1; and Reed Moyer, *Macro Marketing,* Chapter I, among others.

[9]For an explanation of the relationship between distribution costs and economic activity see Roy J. Sampson and Martin T. Farris, *Domestic Transportation: Practice, Theory, and Policy* (3rd ed.; Boston: Houghton Mifflin Company, 1975), Chapters 14 and 15.

[10]This explanation incorporates in principle many of the factors presented in the evaluation of the marketing function by Holloway and Hancock, *Marketing in a Changing Environment,* pp. 638–645; Frederick D. Sturdivant, "Marketing and Society," in Frederick D. Sturdivant, *et al., Managerial Analysis in Marketing* (Glenview, Illinois: Scott, Foresman and Company, 1970), pp. 7–20 and 32–34; and, most importantly, McCarthy, *Basic Marketing,* pp. 603–610.

[11]D. Philip Locklin, *Economics of Transportation* (6th ed.; Homewood, Illinois: Richard D. Irwin, Inc., 1966), pp. 14–15.

[12]McCarthy, *Basic Marketing,* pp. 596–597.

[13]Robert L. Steiner, "Economic Theory and the Idea of Marketing Productivity," Marketing Science Institute Working Paper (December, 1974), pp. 5–12.

[14]Gerald R. Crowningshield and Kenneth A. Gorman, *Cost Accounting: Principles and Managerial Applications* (3rd ed.; Boston: Houghton Mifflin Company, 1974), p. 479. Copyright © 1974. Reprinted by permission of the publisher.

[15]Marvin Brower as quoted by Andre Parent, "Some Aspects and Applications of Distribution Costing," *Cost and Management,* the official journal of The Society of Industrial Accountants of Canada (January, 1956), p. 17.

[16]Crowningshield and Gorman, *Cost Accounting,* pp. 478–479.

[17]*Ibid.,* p. 481.

[18]*Ibid.,* p. 483.

[19]For a brief summary of the rise in importance of logistics or physical distribution management see Donald J. Bowersox, *Logistical Management* (New York: Macmillan Publishing Co., Inc., 1974), pp. 1–8.

[20]Donald J. Bowersox, Edward W. Smykay, and Bernard J. La Londe, *Physical Distribution Management: Logistics Problems of the Firm* (rev. ed.; New York: The Macmillan Company, 1968), p. 13.

[21]*Ibid.,* pp. 199–201.

[22]Jack W. Farrell, "Modern Logistics in 12 Months," *Traffic Management* (March, 1975), pp. 40–42.

SUGGESTED READINGS

Comer, James M., "The Computer, Personal Selling, and Sales Management," *Journal of Marketing* (July, 1975), pp. 27–33.

Corr, Arthur V., "A Cost Effectiveness Approach to Marketing Outlays," *Management Accounting* (January, 1976), pp. 33–36.

Hall, William P., "Improving Sales Force Productivity," *Business Horizons* (August, 1975), pp. 32–42.

Jackson, Donald W., Jr., and Ramon J. Aldag, "Managing the Sales Force by Objectives," *MSU Business Topics* (Spring, 1974), pp. 53–59.

Lambin, Jean-Jacques, "What Is the Real Impact of Advertising?" *Harvard Business Review* (May-June, 1975), pp. 139–147.

Libien, Gary L., *et al.,* "Industrial Advertising Effects and Budgeting Practices," *Journal of Marketing* (January, 1976), pp. 16–24.

Winer, Leon, "Putting the Computer to Work in Marketing," *Business Horizons* (December, 1974), pp. 71–79.

Wotruba, Thomas R. and Patricia L. Duncan, "Are Consumers Really Satisfied?" *Business Horizons* (February, 1975), pp. 85–90.

17

MARKETING ETHICS AND SOCIAL RESPONSIBILITY

17

MARKETING ETHICS AND SOCIAL RESPONSIBILITY

Fraud. Deceit. Trickery. Deception. Misrepresentation. Excess Profits. Conflict of Interest. Credibility Gap. Deceptive Business Practices. Bribery. Unresponsiveness. Public Be Damned! These explosive terms are quoted often in the press to describe the modern actions of business. Is that what business is really like? With accounts like these filling the reading and viewing times of millions of Americans, businessmen should not be surprised that the public scoffs when told that business is an honorable profession and that businessmen are honest and ethical. This chapter is concerned with one of the most important aspects of modern marketing—social responsibility and ethics and the new roles cast upon marketers in the last decade.

WHAT IS SOCIAL RESPONSIBILITY?

Social responsibility is a new dimension of marketing responsibility. It differs dramatically from the traditional view of business and marketing. Tradition holds that business exists solely to make a profit for itself and its stockholders. Private citizens are encouraged to participate in the profit by buying stock, or investing in partnerships and proprietorships. Proponents of this point of view contend the earning of profits is automatically beneficial to society and the country as a whole. The social needs of the community are fulfilled by private citizens, civic groups, the government, and philanthropists. Business accomodates the public by providing goods and services to be bought and by employing people whose wages can be taxed. Government also taps the till of business profits in the collection of taxes.

Times and perceptions about business are changing. The traditional concept of marketing and business is not broad enough to satisfy society in today's world. Contrasting the traditional viewpoint is the new social responsibility viewpoint: business exists to fulfill societal needs and wants, and, in doing so, it is able to make a profit for itself and its stockholders. The new concept, as shown in Figure 17.1, stresses the idea that business cannot seek profits and ignore public needs. The modern viewpoint identifies the necessity of focusing on both the needs of society and the profit goals of business.

Eilbirt and Parket have defined social responsibility this way: "A precise definition of social responsibility, especially of its contents or boundaries, is not easy to formulate. . . . Perhaps the best way to understand social responsibility is to think of it as 'good neighborliness.' "[1] In this definition, they divide "good neighborliness" into two categories: not doing things that spoil the neighborhood and voluntarily assuming the obligation to help solve neighborhood problems.

There is evidence of antisocial behavior by businessmen: antitrust problems, the treatment of labor, racial discrimination, pollution of the environment, discrimination against women, and inadequate consumer service and protection. During the past decade, the roster of

473

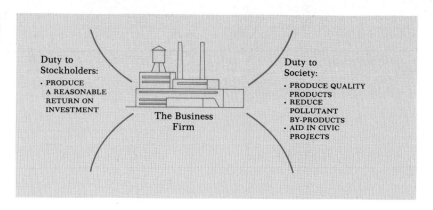

FIGURE 17.1.
SPLIT RESPONSIBILITY OF THE
MODERN BUSINESS FIRM

accusations seems to have been lengthening, and the intensity appears to be deepening in a number of industrial sectors.

CONCEPT OF ETHICAL BUSINESS

Business ethics can be defined as those principles, practices, and philosophies that are concerned with moral judgment and good conduct as they are applicable to business situations. In this context, the term "good conduct" contains overtones both for relationships among businesses and for those between business and society. In order for transactions to take place, firms must reflect confidence in each other—both in ability and in willingness to render acceptable service. If confidence is lacking, the transaction will be jeopardized. Furthermore, business needs the public's support and patronage to remain in business, and customers need businesses to satisfy their needs and wants.

Consider, for example, some of the issues that might reflect questionable conduct on the part of business. What if middlemen add mark-ups to the cost of products that are substantially in excess of the value added by the services that they perform? What if this information reaches the public? What if customers learn that final prices are extremely high in proportion to the true costs of providing products and services? What if customers learn that business owns or controls the mass media that communicates the language of business? What would be the consequence if this appears to be "political power" in the eyes of the public?

Business generates money to operate through sales to customers. If customers perceive the business philosophy as being a nonethical one, then not only is the image of business tarnished, but the survival of the free enterprise concept of business is in grave danger. The solution is not a simple one, but it should be noted here that marketing must play a vigorous role in the ethical conduct of business because of its external and highly visible position in society.

SOCIAL-ETHICAL RESPONSIBILITY

The central task of marketing is fulfilling the needs and wants of society. Society is constantly demanding and striving for the best life possible and expects business to listen to its demands and react accordingly. Along with informing business of what it wants, society also determines what quantity should be produced.

BUSINESS IMAGE AND SOCIAL ISSUES

The new "informed" or "consumerist" society has added one more requirement of business that deals with the quality of life.

Traditionally, business has been held responsible for quantities: for the supply of goods and of jobs, for costs, prices, wages, hours of work, and standards of living. Now business increasingly is being asked to take on responsibility for the quality of life in our society.[2]

There is little question that public expectations of business responsibility to society are increasing, comparatively. Past business practices, in many cases, would not be allowed to exist today. Citing automotive safety, Peter Drucker states:

In the late 1940s and early 1950s, the American automobile industry tried to make the American driving public safety-conscious. Yet when Ford introduced cars with seat belts, sales dropped so catastrophically that the company was forced to abandon the whole idea. But when 15 years later the American driving public suddenly became safety-conscious, the car manufacturers were sharply attacked for being "merchants of death."[3]

Concerning ecology, Drucker provides an interesting view of the efforts of business to curb air pollution:

A good many electric power companies tried for years to get the various state utility commissions to approve of their use of low-sulfur fuels and of cleaning devices in the smokestacks. The commissions refused again and again, with the argument that the public was entitled to power at the lowest possible cost, insisting that neither a more expensive fuel nor capital investment to clean the smoke would be permitted in the rate base. Yet when eventually air pollution became a matter of public concern, the power companies were roundly berated for "befouling the environment."[4]

In another illustration, Drucker comments on the problems of business in the field of medical care:

Ever since the advent of the "miracle drugs," which occurred in the 1940s, the medical profession has been urging the drug companies to respect the independence and knowledge of the physician and not, by word or deed, to interfere in his complete control of the relationship with public and patient. Similarly, the druggists have been demanding that the drug companies respect their "professional integrity" and continue to compensate them as if they, rather than the drug companies, were still the compounders of medicines. And yet the same physicians are now attacking the drug companies for making it possible for the slipshod physician to overprescribe highly potent drugs. And the public tends to hold the drug companies responsible for the "spiraling costs of medical care," even though drugs are the only component of medical bills the cost of which has risen less than the general level of prices.[5]

Finally, concerning defense contracts, Drucker identifies the problem that business has encountered in its dealings with government:

For 20 years, there has been a campaign to get private businesses to take part in defense production. Businesses that did not bid on defense work have been attacked in Congress, in the press, and in public as unpatriotic. Yet even though the profits on defense business are less than half what the same companies can earn on non-defense business, defense contractors are being criticized for "profiteering" on defense business. And companies that accepted defense contracts under great government pressure find their recruiters chased off college campuses and their offices picketed.[6]

From the above comments, it may be noted that Drucker has come to the defense of business in the area of social responsibility. Yet, Drucker carefully shows that the publics of business have, to a degree, restrained business action in the realm of social responsibility.

A multiplicity of problems arises in attempting to identify socially responsible corporate conduct. At one extreme, some would not permit profit until a company has met every conceivable social and environmental demand within its sphere of activity. This, of course, is a totally unrealistic position. Another viewpoint holds that a company's contributions to local charities are indirect purchases of publicity and that a company's insistence that its executives be "involved" in their communities is unfair compulsion. At the other end of the spectrum, and despite the progress of the past decade, too many companies still are dedicated to the utmost profit first, foremost, and always.

Momentarily, as the 1970s pass midpoint, the unfortunate fact is that government regulators, caught up in the consumerist movement, appear bent on over policing business and industry to the detriment of society in the form of costly regulation. This was noted in Chapter 13 on the legal environment. History shows that it would be safe to say that the movement will subside after doing some good and some harm. Only time will reveal the balance that will be achieved.

Impact of consumerism. Although some businesses have undertaken socially worthwhile activities, the wave of criticism aimed at American business is not entirely without basis. As discussed in Chapter 18, various movements of consumer protest, alternating with periods of consumer indifference, have occurred throughout the past century. Murmurings of dissatisfaction have grown stronger and stronger, and various groups of consumers have been able to reveal weaknesses to concerned audiences and revise abuses within the marketing structure.

The wave of consumer unrest, often referred to as consumerism, received a real impetus in this century during the Great Depression of the 1930s, when many consumers were unable to buy what they needed and wanted because they had little purchasing power. During the 1940s, consumers sacrificed many of their desires for goods because of the war effort. It wasn't until the late 1940s that consumers and businessmen alike had a chance to make the purchases they had postponed during the war years. Business and industry geared up to full production to satisfy the consumer wants, and many products never before dreamed of were created. The American society became "the affluent society," and consumers were finally able to have the luxuries they wanted. This affluence was especially pronounced in comparison to that enjoyed by consumers in previous decades.

With so much of the national industrial effort going toward the goal of satisfying the needs of a wide variety of consumers, selected discontent proved to be unavoidable. Business firms were enjoying new profit heights, and the prospects of even higher profits seemed strong. At the same time, consumers became accustomed to material comforts and leisure time. During this period, the public had the time to take a closer look at the activities and practices of big business.

As consumer activists became more and more vocal, they reached audiences in influential positions. As pointed out in Chapter 18, one person highly sympathetic to the consumerism movement was President John F. Kennedy. In a message to Congress in March 1962, he alluded to areas where legislation was necessary to protect the public:

The march of technology—affecting, for example, the foods we eat, the medicines we take, and the many appliances we use in our homes—has increased the difficulties of the consumer along with his opportunities; and it has outmoded many of the old laws and regulations and made new legislation necessary. ... Many of the new products used every day in the home are highly complex. The housewife is called upon to be an amateur electrician, mechanic, chemist, toxicologist, dietitian, and mathematician—but she is rarely furnished the information she needs to perform these tasks proficiently."[7]

President Kennedy was in a position to do something constructive to aid the consumerism movement. He appointed a Consumer Advisory Council (CAC) whose mission was to examine and provide advice to the government on issues of broad economic policy, on governmental programs protecting consumer needs, and on needed improvements in the flow of consumer research material to the public. Besides having a friend in the White House, consumer advocates had a place to air their discontent. The consumerist movement then had the necessary strength to accomplish something.

As noted in Chapter 18, one of the most prominent consumerism activists was a young lawyer, Ralph Nader. Nader fought one of his earliest campaigns against the use of DDT on the trees at Princeton University, his undergraduate alma mater. Later, he went on to investigate the human environment, particularly its commercial and technological aspects. Nader jumped into national prominence with the publication of his attack on General Motors. His book, *Unsafe at Any Speed,* exposed flaws in the Chevrolet Corvair. Nader's efforts were so successful that Chevrolet was forced to discontinue production of the Corvair.[8]

Since his exposé of the Corvair, Nader has investigated a wide number of other areas. His research assistants, dubbed "Nader's Raiders," have been responsible for uncovering numerous instances of improper behavior by both private corporations and governmental agencies.

Two women have made particular contributions to consumerism movements. Esther Peterson and Betty Furness have both served as special assistants for consumer affairs in the Executive Office of the President. They have been responsible for numerous pieces of legislation and voluntary reform by businesses. Their proximity to the power of the American presidency shows the importance and power of the consumerism movement.

An important aspect of the consumerism movement is that the wave of consumer unrest was there. Individuals like Nader, Peterson, and Furness merely echoed the desires of a vocal public. Without question, of course, this voice has had a tremendous impact on business practices and will continue to do so for years to come.

BUSINESS ETHICS AND MORALITIES

The consumerist movement has caused a number of business practices to be subjected to consumer assault. Some of those mounting pressures are justified, and some are unfounded. Many are exaggerated in some way. A word of caution, however, is in order. There usually is a difference between what is and what is perceived to be. Sometimes the gap is due to the human tendency to exaggerate, and sometimes it is caused by misleading information presented to the public. Some misleading information is given out inadvertently, and some is intentional on both sides. The intentionally misleading information has caused a credibility gap to develop between what business firms say about their operations and what the consumers believe actually exists. Business leaders must constantly be on guard against public criticism—whether it is founded on fact or fantasy.

Randall Meyer, president of Exxon Company, addressed himself to the problem of the decline in popularity of big business in a recent address at Florida State University. At that time, Meyer made the following observations:

In recent years, one of the most disturbing trends in American attitudes has been the decline of public confidence in virtually all the major institutions of society. Public opinion research confirms that confidence has declined in the federal government, the military, the news media, labor unions, the educational community, business, and a number of other institutions. For example, Opinion Research Corporation found in 1973 that of 13 major institutions, only two—the church and the medical profession—still retained a high level of trust and confidence from at least half the public. Large business companies ranked at the very bottom of that list. Fully 80 percent of the people had something less than high trust and confidence in big business firms generally. And the proportion of the public which views the petroleum industry favorably has declined from 73 percent in 1965 to 34 percent in 1973. Of course, the energy supply problems the nation has experienced in the past year or two partly explain public unhappiness with the oil industry. But this does not account for the general disenchantment with other institutions.[9]

Another recurring problem that permeates the community from time to time is determining what is fair. This is often the case when discussing corporate profits. Corporate leaders have been criticized for making excessive profits. Yet, the definition of what is excessive is still undecided. The question is philosophical in nature and may never be answered to the satisfaction of all sides.

Marketing has not escaped the criticism aimed at business in general. In fact, some of the most vocal arguments against business are really marketing problems. Again, however, the issue revolves around the question of what is and what is not immoral.

Marketing immoralities.   Marketing and advertising are particularly vulnerable to public scorn because of the very nature of the information they supply to the public about products and services offered in the marketplace. As discussed in Chapter 7, a major social responsibility criticism of marketing is the area of manipulation of demand caused by effective advertising. The criticism of manipulation of demand is closely tied to impulse buying and the issue of creating false needs within the buying public. The stated purpose of advertising is to persuade customers to buy "your" product and "your" brand. When that goal is reached, however, business is blamed for selling people items that they do not need or want. For the critics of advertising, this is a major issue. Consider, for example, the following household buying situation:

As the family purchasing agent, the housewife is confronted with a key buying decision in the area of family dental hygiene. In making the right decision, the housewife consults her dentist, reads printed advertisements, and views television commercials. Additionally, she critically analyzes packages of dental care products. To the critic, there is an element of manipulation in this process; to the marketer, the issue is one of creating awareness, providing information, and assisting the housewife in a difficult buying task.[10]

Basically, the question of social responsibility and business ethics is the difference between "manipulating" and "assisting" the customer in the purchase decision. Most people seek assistance—in fact, demand it to a degree—but shy away from manipulation at all costs. At what point does assistance become manipulation?

Kotler and Galbraith feel that advertising performs a necessary function in our society. Advertising—a major marketing task—completes the link in the cycle between production and consumption, which they call the "dependence effect."[11]

This lopsided interest in things is not seen as an unplanned consequence of American business but rather as an intrinsic feature that keeps both the production and consumption systems going. Business hires Madison Avenue to stimulate people's desires for goods. Madison Avenue uses the mass media to create materialistic models of the good life. Conspicuous consumption on the part of some then proceeds to create invidious desires by others. Person's self-concepts move toward congruency with this version of the good life. They work harder to earn the necessary money. This increases the output and productive capacity of the Industrial State. In turn, the Industrial State makes greater use of Madison Avenue to stimulate desire for the industrial output. Thus, people are seen as a manipulated link in the cycle between production and consumption.[12]

The public's attitude about this process depends on its concept of advertising, whether it is a public service or a public nuisance.

A similar argument can be made for other marketing functions, such as product packaging. Some espouse the point that an excessive amount of money goes into product packaging and that this spending raises the price without adding utility to the product. Furthermore, it is argued that packaging materials are discarded anyway. Others advocate the position that product packaging assists in giving satisfaction and that when that satisfaction is fulfilled, the product and its package are discarded for a positive reason.

Another area of criticism of business and marketing is obsolescence, which is illustrated in Figure 17.2. Of the four types of obsolescence, few criticize obsolescence caused entirely by new technological advancements. It is inconceivable that there should be a return to the old style of glass (brittle and easily broken) instead of using new safety glass that is harder to break and shatter-resistant. This axiom is also true for color television, automatic transmissions, and Teflon cooking surfaces. On the other hand, the three remaining types of obsolescence —style, postponed, and physical—have been targets of consumer groups for a long time.

Style obsolescence (also called fashion obsolescence) occurs when a useful product is made obsolete through advertising and promotion. Criticism revolves around efforts that make people feel out of date if they continue to use an old model. The two industries that have taken the brunt of this criticism are the automobile makers and the dress fashion designers.

Postponed obsolescence occurs when an innovation is held back so that a newer model may be introduced at a later time to make the

FIGURE 17.2.
EXAMPLES OF TYPES OF
OBSOLESENCE

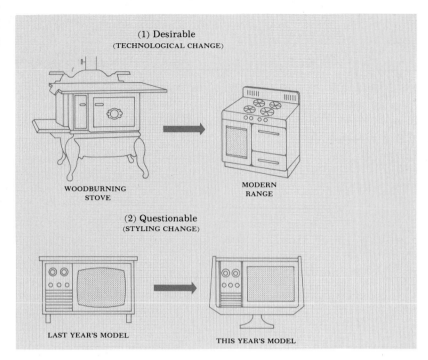

earlier model out of date. Auto makers are guilty of this, for instance, when they have new technological changes (such as a rotary engine) and hold off for awhile before putting it on the market.

Physical design obsolescence occurs when a product is planned and made to wear out within a relatively short period of time. This requires the user to purchase a newer model. Firms that use this technique soon earn a reputation for manufacturing shoddy merchandise.

Public outcries regarding these types of business practices are easily generated. Unfortunately, the damage to a reputation can be long-lived and even fatal to the firm. There is no doubt, however, that business has been guilty of various forms of socially unacceptable behavior. Publicity about alleged misconduct by business does not help the image either, even though some of the charges are never proved in court. It is the substantiated cases, of course, that cause the major problem.

> The public seems to be able to overlook an occasional stock swindle, an antitrust activity ... but when the pillars of capitalism—blue chips such as American Airlines, Goodyear Tire and Rubber, and Minnesota Mining and Manufacturing—get dragged into the courts, clearly something has gone wrong.[13]

When big business gets hauled into court, it is big news. Even if the claims are later proved false, the public image of business suffers. The snowballing effect of these activities causes heavy clouds to form over American business in general.

AN ETHICAL FRAMEWORK FOR MARKETING

Determining what is ethical in marketing is a complex task. Ethics are mainly an individual determination. Ethical behavior for one person may not be ethical for another, and individuals may even agree that a situation is ethical, but disagree over the extent of the ethics involved.

An individual's ethics are essentially a set of moral principles that guide his or her thoughts and actions. These principles are formed individually as the result of the environment, as shown in Figure 17.3. An ethical framework may be influenced by parental values, education, personal experience, religious training, group norms, personal introspection, culture, employer's policies, legal pronouncements, and industry trade practices.

It is conceivable that two individuals with identical environments could formulate differing ethical frameworks. Along with the environmental factors identified above, an individual's ethical framework will be determined by the relative weight or importance of each of the environmental factors.

A compounding problem in formulating an ethical framework is that there is no widely established set of guidelines in marketing ethics. The area of what is ethical in marketing is basically undefined. Consider, for example, how a marketing decision maker might react to each of the morally difficult situations presented in Table 17.1[14] Think of how one decision maker's views on marketing ethics might differ from those of others involved in marketing.

A diversity of interpretations is readily apparent in each case. One

FIGURE 17.3.
INFLUENCES ON INDIVIDUAL
BEHAVIOR

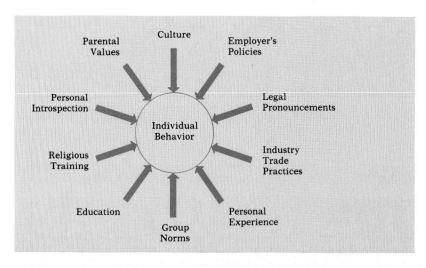

TABLE 17.1.
MORALLY DIFFICULT
SITUATIONS IN MARKETING

1. You work for a cigarette company and up to now have not been convinced that cigarettes cause cancer. A recent report has come across your desk that clearly establishes the connection between cigarette smoking and cancer. What would you do?

2. Your R&D department has modernized one of your products. It is not really "new and improved," but you know that putting this statement on the package and in the advertising will increase sales. What would you do?

3. You have been asked to add a stripped-down model to the low end of your line that could be advertised to attract customers. The product won't be very good, but the salesmen could be depended upon to persuade people to buy a better higher-priced unit. You are asked to give the green light for developing this stripped-down version. What would you do?

4. You are interviewing a former product manager who just left a competitor's company. You are thinking of hiring him. He would be more than happy to tell you all the competitor's plans for the coming year. What would you do?

5. One of your dealers in an important territory has had family troubles recently and is not producing the sales he used to. He was one of the company's top producers in the past. It is not clear how long it will take before his family trouble straightens out. In the meantime, many sales are being lost. There is a legal way to remove the dealer's franchise and replace him. What would you do?

6. You have a chance to win a big account that will mean a lot to you and your company. The purchasing agent hinted that he would be influenced by a "gift." Your assistant recommends sending a fine color television set to his home. What would you do?

7. You have heard that a competitor has a new product feature that will make a big difference in sales. He will have a hospitality suite at the annual trade show and unveil this feature at a party thrown for his dealers. You can easily send a snooper to this meeting to learn what the new feature is. What would you do?

8. You are eager to win a big contract, and during sales negotiations you learn that the buyer is looking for a better job. You have no intention of hiring him, but if you hinted that you might, he would probably give you the order. What would you do?

9. You have to make a choice between three ad campaigns outlined by your agency for your new product. The first (A) is a soft-sell, honest informational campaign. The second (B) uses sex-loaded emotional appeals and exaggerates the product's benefits. The third (C) involves a noisy, irritating commercial that is sure to gain audience attention. Preliminary tests show that the commercials are effective in the following order: C, B, and A. What would you do?

10. You are a marketing vice-president working for a beer company, and you have learned that a particularly lucrative state is planning to raise the minimum legal drinking age from 18 to 21. You have been asked to join other breweries in lobbying against this bill and to make contributions. What would you do?

11. You want to interview a sample of customers about their reactions to a competitive product. It has been suggested that you invent an innocuous name like the Marketing Research Institute and interview people. What would you do?

12. You produce an antidandruff shampoo that is effective with one application. Your assistant says that the product would turn over faster if the instructions on the label recommended two applications. What would you do?

13. You are interviewing a capable, personable black applicant for a job as salesman. He is better qualified than the other men just interviewed. At the same time, you suspect that some of your current salesmen will react negatively to his hiring, and you also know that some important customers will be ruffled. What would you do?

14. You are a sales manager in an encyclopedia company. A common way for company salesmen to get into homes is to pretend they are taking a survey. After they finish the survey, they switch to their sales pitch. This technique seems to be very effective and is used by most of your competitors. What would you do?

SOURCE: Excerpted from Philip Kotler, *Marketing Management: Analysis, Planning and Control* (2nd ed.; Englewood Cliffs: Prentice-Hall, Inc., 1972), p. 839, with permission of the publisher.

TABLE 17.2.
CODE OF ETHICS OF THE
AMERICAN MARKETING
ASSOCIATION

As a member of the American Marketing Association, I recognize the significance of my professional conduct and my responsibilities to society and to the other members of my profession:

1. By acknowledging my accountability to society as a whole as well as to the organization for which I work.
2. By pledging my efforts to assure that all presentations of goods, services and concepts be made honestly and clearly.
3. By striving to improve marketing knowledge and practice in order to better serve society.
4. By supporting free consumer choice in circumstances that are legal and are consistent with generally accepted community standards.
5. By pledging to use the highest professional standards in my work and in competitive activity.
6. By acknowledging the right of the American Marketing Association, through established procedure, to withdraw my membership if I am found to be in violation of ethical standards of professional conduct.

SOURCE: Reprinted by permission of the American Marketing Association.

viewpoint in marketing might argue that legal statutes and formal public policies provide an adequate guideline for solving ethical problems. In other words, if an action is not illegal, then it is morally acceptable. The opposition might argue that it was not intended that laws should govern all prohibited actions. Thus, individuals should exercise the spirit contained in the Golden Rule (Matthew 7:12). More likely, individuals will view ethical considerations somewhere between the two extreme viewpoints.

Marketing executives most likely will have company policies to consider when making ethical decisions, but company guidelines cannot be relied upon to solve all situations. The possibility exists that company guidelines may be in contradiction to the decision-maker's personal viewpoint. Naturally, the decision on an ethical question is easier to make if the company and the decision maker are in agreement on ethics.

Professional organizations, such as the American Medical Association, the American Bar Association, the American Institute of Certified Public Accountants, and the American Marketing Association, have established codes of ethics for their members. Enforcement of violations of any of the codes can mean expulsion from the association, which sometimes prohibits the violator from earning a living in that profession. The Code of Ethics of the American Marketing Association is presented in Table 17.2.[15]

COMPLEXITY OF ETHICAL DECISIONS

Marketing managers faced with problems requiring ethical decisions and actions have no simple course of action. Bartels identified three problems associated with ethical decisions:

First, not everyone is aware of or subscribes to a universal code of ethics. Therefore, decisions often necessitate superimposition of one's own standard, compromise of it, or surrender of it. These actions are not without some conflict and adjustment within one's frame of reference.

Second, in a pluralistic society not one but many expectations must be met. Therefore, resolution of what is right to do produces a balance of obligations and satisfactions. Ideally, full satisfaction of expectations of all parties would constitute the most ethical behavior. This is impossible, for expectations are often contradictory and sometimes exceed social sanction. Therefore skill and judgment must be used to guide one in determining the point at which his own integrity can best be maintained.

Third, because marketing obligations are of both a non-economic and economic nature, fulfillment of social expectations cannot be divorced from the economic limitations within which business decisions must be made. Thus, the complexity of determining what in a society are the standards of ethical behavior is compounded by the multiplicity of factors affecting application of the standard.[16]

EXPANDED VIEW OF THE FIRM

In formulating a conceptual framework for the marketing firm, why should the firm care about objectives other than earning a long-term profit? What has marketing to lose if it fails to broaden its perspectives to include social responsibility?

THE PRICE OF SOCIAL RESPONSIBILITY   Management has paid the price for past social errors. Business finds itself hemmed in by government regulations, limited at every turn by the power amassed by labor unions, and under assault by various consumer and community defenders. The price paid thus far has been substantial.

Today, the issue of socially responsible corporate behavior is linked to most government contracts. Washington has leverage to grant contracts to firms that exercise social responsibility. Murray L. Weidenbaum, a former Assistant Secretary of the Treasury, points out just how extensive this lever is:

The federal government can and does require that firms doing business with it maintain "fair" employment practices, provide "safe" and "healthful" working conditions, pay "prevailing" wages, refrain from pollution of the air and water, give preference to American products in their purchases, and promote the rehabilitation of prisoners and the severely handicapped.[17]

Government regulation of business has a strong grip on American business. Firms that choose not to accept government contracts are not exempt from government intervention. A number of statutes have been enacted that affect nearly every echelon of business. One example of such a statute is the Clean Air Act. Under this law, the federal government prohibits contracts to a company convicted of criminal violation of air-pollution standards.

The long-term effect of government intervention in behalf of social responsibility is the enactment of additional legislation. If business fails to regulate itself, then government will impose the will of the community. Rarely have these social provisions been eliminated or scaled down, even when the original conditions justifying them are no longer present. Rather, the trend has been to extend their application.

The attractions of using government contracts to promote basic social policies are quite obvious. Important national objectives can be fostered with no additional appropriations from the Treasury. To a Congressman, this may seem to be a painless and simple approach. Because restrictive procurement provisions appear on the surface to be costless, the government has been making intensified use of them. The disadvantages, being more indirect, receive less attention in the press and from aspiring politicians.

WHY SHOULD MARKETING BE RESPONSIVE TO SOCIAL GOALS?	Through its marketing activities, business should be responsive to broad social goals for one very important reason—business must be managed for the long run. The scope and importance of this very basic concept are summarized in the following statement:

> Successful capitalism means that business must profit from other's well-being, rather than from taking advantage of people. Business must conduct its affairs in a way that adds to the general good, making a mutually rewarding contribution to the achievement of worthwhile human goals. The measurement of business' success in doing this is profitability over time. . . . Corporations must act in a manner that will stand the light of examination over a considerable period of time.[18]

Unfortunately, businessmen ordinarily speak to the public in terms connoting the short term. References to "quarterly profits or dividends," "annual stockholder's meetings," "seasonal markets," and so forth tend to filter throughout the community. Seldom, if ever, do marketing decision makers promote their long-term goals to the public at large. It is no wonder, then, that businessmen are perceived to be interested only in short-term goals and profits. The realities of business force the manager to concentrate on long-term decisions as the focal point of survival. Given this situation, it should be apparent why businessmen are criticized for seeking short-term profits instead of fostering long-term commitments, such as socially oriented programs.

In spite of the above comments, it should be noted that business has not been completely negligent of social responsibility. A number of firms have contributed in one way or another to various social activities. Broader participation in response to mounting pressures, however, is still needed.

Research conducted by Eilbirt and Parket furnished valuable insight into what is, and is not, being done in the area of social responsibility. The results of this study showed that contributions to education were the most popular overt acts of business, followed by ecology and minority hiring. These activities are contributions to society as a whole, and are not specifically directed to company customers. It is interesting to note, therefore, that factors directly related to customers of the contributing firm did not appear until the tenth item on the list, with less than half of the respondents indicating that they were concerned about "consumer complaints." Table 17.3 contains the entire list of social responsibility activities engaged in by the firms surveyed.[19]

When the same executives were surveyed concerning which social responsibility activity they considered to be the most important, minority hiring and ecology were ranked the highest. Following closely were minority training, contributions to education, and consumer complaints. Rated least important was understandable accounting statements, which was preceded by guarantees and warranties and consumer oriented label changes. A comparison of the activities believed most important and the activities engaged in shows that the two lists do not go hand in hand. Most notably, contributions to education,

TABLE 17.3.
TYPES OF SOCIAL
RESPONSIBILITY ACTIVITIES

Activity	Percent Practicing
Contributions to education	86.0
Ecology	78.0
Minority hiring	78.0
Minority training	68.0
Contributions to the arts	68.0
Hard core hiring	58.0
Hard core training	55.0
Civil rights	53.0
Urban renewal	53.0
Consumer complaints	46.0
Understandable accounting statements	42.0
Truth in advertising	42.0
Product defects	36.0
Guarantees and warranties	32.0
Consumer-oriented label changes	24.0

SOURCE: Henry Eilbirt and I. Robert Parket, "The Current Status of Corporate Social Responsibility," *Business Horizons* (August, 1973), p. 9.

the most common practice, showed up as fourth in the importance rating. Conversely, dealing with consumer complaints was identified as tenth in practice, but rated fifth in importance. A problem of interpretation may explain why customer activities generally appear to be considered less important than the broader social activities. Consumer-connected activities are directly related to sales, profit, and market share. Broad social activities, of course, are not directly tied to sales and profits. Nothing in the Eilbirt and Parket study suggested the rationale behind this order, but it may be that the respondents excluded customer relations from their definition of social responsibility activities.

Additional findings clearly indicated that there is an association between sales volume and the extent of social responsibility exercised by the firm. Firms with sales over $1 billion were compared with firms with sales under $250 million. Figure 17.4 shows that the differences are marked and that the giant firms displayed far more participation than the smaller firms in all categories except one.[20]

It is difficult to know exactly why the larger firms participate more fully in social responsibilities than do the smaller firms, since profitability is not closely correlated with size itself. One conjecture is that giant firms may simply be, or perceive themselves to be, "targets" of public criticism, and thus find it necessary, because of their size and importance, to make visible efforts to establish social responsibility credentials. Further study is needed to determine if this is, in fact, the case.

APPLIED CONCEPTS

Two concepts related to marketing strategy are readily adaptable to determining what social activities need to be undertaken and implemented. These are market segmentation and the marketing information system. A marketing information system, marketing's data-gathering arm, is particularly practical when applied to social needs and goals, and marketing research may be easily applied to the social context.

Segmentation. Just as the marketer determines the composition of the target market for his product, so can market segmentation be used to determine social needs and goals appropriate to the marketing situation. Demographic and psychographic data will be as revealing about market reception of socially oriented activities as the research input is about product reactions.

Segmenting the marketing environment into identifiable areas will help determine desired social relationships in each area and indicate the appropriate strategies necessary to achieve them. Through segmentation, management can identify and understand the forces at play in each environment. In this manner, it can explain and predict forces for change to which it must adapt.

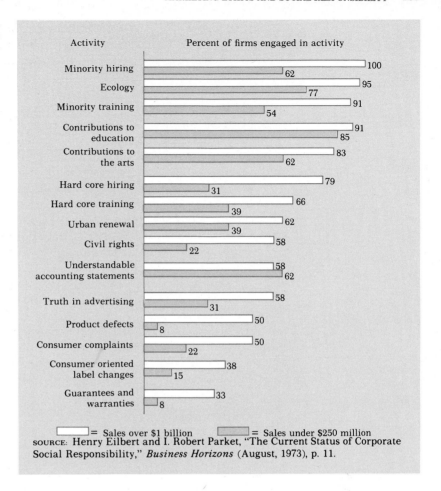

FIGURE 17.4.
SIZE COMPARISON OF SOCIAL
RESPONSIBILITY ACTIVITIES

SOURCE: Henry Eilbert and I. Robert Parket, "The Current Status of Corporate Social Responsibility," *Business Horizons* (August, 1973), p. 11.

Marketing information system.   After initial and basic market research is conducted in the social responsibility area, the information can be integrated into the company's established information system, or a separate social marketing information system can be instituted.

Successful marketing firms regularly employ marketing research and marketing information systems when making decisions. As noted in earlier chapters, most marketing information systems have four components: an accounting system, an intelligence system, a research system, and a decision making system. Marketing information systems compile information for internal use on a variety of subject areas. Demographics of the community are usually included in this first portion. The firm also has an intelligence system that acts as the firm's eyes and ears in the community to feed back informal information about needs and wants. A research team is composed of the surveyors, interviewers, and observers that compile the formal data for decision making.

The first two parts of the marketing information system can easily be used to determine areas of needed social change. Instead of hearing and ignoring information of a social nature, the marketing firm can actively incorporate these inputs into results. If new housing is needed in a section of town, entrepreneurs can determine ways that this need can be satisfied at an economic profit. Possibly, a new shopping center with prices geared for a low-income area needs to be constructed. With appropriate information and resources, business can assemble the needed establishments and provide the shopping center through which economic profits can be realized.

The marketing information system can also be used effectively to relate information about social responsibility to the development of new products. The public can be tested for its views in regard to a wide variety of social problems facing the marketing decision makers. In this manner, marketing research can be tailored to the social responsibility factor in business decision making.

If attitudinal surveys show that a company's image needs to be improved, this may be a reflection of a poor marketing mix. On the other hand, it may be a subtler reflection of the fact that the company has no social involvement image in its market areas.

Marketing information systems also can tell a company what socially responsible conduct would be appropriate. Involvement could range from sponsoring a little league team to contributing to the community symphony orchestra. The action taken in relation to a plumbing company would be different from that for a high-fashion shop, which further emphasizes that appropriate information is necessary in all processes of decision making.

Major companies have long included community relations functions in their marketing or public relations offices. More recently, companies like Dayton-Hudson Corporation of Minneapolis, a major retailer, have appointed vice presidents for cultural affairs. The responsibilities of these officials mainly involve determining the merit and quality of potential recipients of the company's charity contributions, one of the most direct and visible forms of social involvement.

The act of making charity organizations, civic or otherwise, prove their worth is as socially responsible a conduct as any company could perform. This is not to beg the question that marketing tools and methods can be, and are, used to determine what socially responsible conduct will best benefit the company. Cost-benefit analysis tends to destroy any concept of altruistic idealism about such conduct, but motive need not be faulted considering that the alternative is that nothing would be done.

Conversely, experience shows that many companies perform socially responsible acts regularly and work diligently to see that they never receive public credit for it. Some business executives consider it an embarrassing disadvantage to let customers, suppliers, or competitors know that they are doing anything voluntarily for the good of the community. These firms deliberately maintain a low profile on socially responsible activities.

SUMMARY

In this chapter, marketing ethics and corporate social responsibility have been discussed from the marketer's vantage point. The tradition that profit is the reason for business to exist and that any benefit to the community is naturally an afterthought is disappearing. The emerging concept is that business has a social responsibility; business exists to fulfill society's needs and wants in the economy in an efficient and effective manner. If it does so, profits will follow.

Business ethics are being influenced by changing mores. Ethics remain subjective, but instant communications today make the knowledge base so broad that the parameters of ethical conduct are becoming clearer, but more complicated. The consumerism movement and increasing government regulation of business have generated tremendous pressure on business to be socially responsible. Public expectations of business are increasing, in part as a result of the growing amount of leisure time that technological advances have made possible. One aspect of rising public expectations often overlooked is that business and industry have contributed to the education of the public to want "more and better." Advertising one product as "better," "more this," or "more that" than anything else has simultaneously numbed the consumer to superlatives and made him expect the best for the least, sometimes unrealistically. It might be said that business has brought consumerism on itself as much by educating the public as by shoddy production and merchandising practices.

Tracing the history of the consumer movement shows that it will abate eventually; the results of the movement will not be understood until some perspective can be developed. For marketing, this will mean, for some time to come, a vague never-never land of fuzzy ethical situations to be faced. This is due in part to the subjective nature of determining what is right or wrong in business conduct. In part, however, the fuzziness will continue to grow as long as new discoveries are being made about the consequences of man's acts on his physical, social, and economic environments.

QUESTIONS FOR DISCUSSION

1. "If behavior is legal, then it is ethical." Do you agree? State some arguments offered by both sides about this dilemma.

2. Describe several situations in the advertising area that involve ethics. Do the same for packaging and pricing.

3. Should the federal government create a cabinet-level position, "Department of Consumer Protection," to ensure that social responsibility and ethics are practiced in marketing? How effective would it be?

4. Define "social responsibility" and "ethics." Distinguish between the two. Give an example of a violation of each that was not given in the text.

5. Should the marketing vice president have a higher degree of social respon-

sibility and ethics than the vice president of production and the vice president of finance? Why or why not?

6. Should television advertising aimed primarily at children be expected to conform to a stricter code of ethics than that aimed at adults?

7. Has the consumerism movement developed because of failures of marketing to be socially responsible? Comment.

8. If a firm adopts a philosophy based on being socially responsible to the community's needs, would this philosophy be most likely to increase sales, reduce costs, both, or neither?

9. Make a list of marketing practices you consider unethical. Then propose a solution to each of the unethical practices. How difficult would each of these solutions be to implement?

10. If you were asked to prepare a code of ethics for retailers, what would it contain? Do the same thing for advertising.

11. A group of businessmen in your community has just appointed you chairman of the marketing ethics committee. The retailers have used this committee to hold hearings whenever a local merchant is accused of an unethical business practice. You, however, wish to make this committee *active* rather than *reactive*. What positive steps should you take to foster better ethical conduct among the local merchants?

NOTES

[1]Henry Eilbirt and I. Robert Parket, "The Current Status of Corporate Social Responsibility," *Business Horizons,* Vol. XVI, No. 4 (August, 1973), pp. 6–7.

[2]Peter F. Drucker, "Business and the Quality of Life," Sales Management, Vol. 102 (March 15, 1969), pp. 31–35. This article first appeared in Peter F. Drucker, *Preparing Tomorrow's Business Leaders Today,* © 1969. Reprinted by permission of Prentice-Hall, Inc., Englewood Cliffs, New Jersey.

[3]*Ibid.*

[4]*Ibid.*

[5]*Ibid.*

[6]*Ibid.*

[7]"A Special Message on Protecting the Consumer Interest," speech delivered to Congress, March 15, 1962.

[8]David J. Schwartz, *Marketing Today, A Basic Approach* (New York: Harcourt Brace Jovanovich, Inc., 1973), p. 605.

[9]Randall Meyer, "The Role of Big Business in Achieving National Goals," an address at the President's Lecture Series, Florida State University, Tallahassee, Florida, November 26, 1974.

[10]For the critics view, see Vance Packard, *The Hidden Persuaders* (New York: David McKay Co., Inc., 1957), p. 1. For the opposing view, see Alvin C. Achenbaum, "Advertising Doesn't Manipulate Consumers," *Journal of Advertising Research* (April, 1972), pp. 3–13.

[11]Philip Kotler, *Marketing Management: Analysis, Planning, and Control* (2nd ed.; Englewood Cliffs, New Jersey: Prentice-Hall, Inc., 1972), p. 806. See also

John Kenneth Galbraith, *The Affluent Society* (Boston: Houghton Mifflin Company, 1958), p. 158, and Galbraith's *The New Industrial State* (Boston: Houghton Mifflin Company, 1967), p. 200.

[12]Kotler, *ibid.*

[13]Andrew Mann, "The Ethics Puzzle," *The MBA Magazine* (September, 1974), p. 23.

[14]Kotler, *Marketing Management,* p. 839.

[15]Ben M. Enis, *Marketing Principles* (Pacific Palisades, California: Goodyear Publishing, Inc., 1974), p. 163.

[16]Reprinted from Robert Bartels, "A Model for Ethics in Marketing," *Journal of Marketing,* Vol. 31 (January, 1967), pp. 20–26. Published by the American Marketing Association.

[17]Murray L. Weidenbaum, "The Price of Social Responsibility," *Duns* (November, 1973), p. 11.

[18]Meyer, "The Role of Big Business . . . ," p. 10.

[19]Eilbirt and Parket, "The Current Status . . . ," p. 9.

[20]*Ibid.,* p. 11.

SUGGESTED READINGS

Donnelly, James H., Jr., "Marketing Intermediaries in Channels of Distribution for Services," *Journal of Marketing* (January, 1976), pp. 55–57.

Kotler, Philip, *Marketing for Non-profit Organizations* (Englewood Cliffs, New Jersey: Prentice-Hall, Inc., 1975).

Kotler, Philip and Sidney J. Levy, "Broadening the Concept of Marketing" in Howard A. Thompson, *The Great Writings in Marketing* (Plymouth, Michigan: The Commerce Press, 1976), pp. 59–71.

Mindak, William A. and H. Malcolm Bybee, "Marketing's Application to Fund Raising," *Journal of Marketing* (July, 1971), pp. 13–18.

Shapiro, Benson P., "Marketing for Non-profit Organizations," *Harvard Business Review* (September-October, 1973), pp. 123–132.

Stanton, William J., *Fundamentals of Marketing* (4th ed.; New York: McGraw-Hill, 1975), pp. 544–559.

Wilson, A., *The Marketing of Professional Services* (London: McGraw-Hill, 1972).

18
CONSUMERISM

18

CONSUMERISM

Along with the issues of marketing ethics and social responsibility that were considered in the previous chapter, the rise of consumerism in the United States is receiving increased attention by business. Although the scope of consumerism extends beyond the domain of marketing, most practitioners and academicians in the field have assumed the issue to be theirs. In this chapter, consumerism is defined, the rights of the buying public are examined, and the leaders of the consumer movement are identified. With this material as a base, the chapter further explores the responses to consumerism by government and business, the views of the critics of the movement, and the special problems of low income consumers. Finally, the chapter concludes with a discussion of consumer education as a solution to the problems in the consumer movement that are currently encountered by business.

MEANING OF CONSUMERISM

Recently a frustrated automobile owner stood in front of an auto show in New York City with a sign on his car saying: "For Sale. Please buy this car. It's a lemon and my dealer will not fix it." When a policeman asked him to move the car, the owner promised to try, but indicated that he wouldn't guarantee that the car would start. A group of Milwaukee consumers hired a Santa Claus one day during the Christmas season and marched with him in front of a furniture store carrying protest signs stating: "Santa doesn't shop at _____ because they don't give refunds." These isolated incidents are just two of many that have changed the marketer-consumer relationship over the last decade.

Although once viewed as a caprice, consumerism has endured under the guidance of Nader, other advocates, politicians, and the tacit support of millions of Americans. Over the last ten years, the movement has influenced marketing in the areas of advertising, personal selling, product safety, credit, and pricing. It should be noted, however, that the recent storms kicked up by an assortment of consumer advocates, politicians, professors, and housewives are not unique to the twentieth century. In addition to the present wave of consumerism, the United States experienced consumer activism in the early 1900s and the early 1930s. While each of these periods were somewhat different, to some extent each occurred during times of spiraling prices and eroded real incomes for certain sectors of society.

Around the turn of the century, rising prices made many people resentful of the prosperous trusts and growing labor union movement.[1] Consumer discontent with business, in particular, led to the formation of consumer organizations and the passage of a number of legislative acts. From 1879 to 1905 over one hundred bills to regulate marketing practices were introduced in Congress.[2] As noted in Chapter 13, the Food and Drug Administration was created in 1906, and the Federal Trade Commission came into being nine years later.

The Great Depression was characterized by extensive unemployment, declining incomes, and fluctuating prices. The impetus for consumer protection during this period was also fueled by the publication of *Your Money's Worth* in 1927 and *100,000,000 Guinea Pigs* in 1933. The second book was successful in stimulating the passage of food, drug, and cosmetic legislation. In his initial inaugural address, Franklin D. Roosevelt noted that the numerous consumer-business confrontations over the cost of living had served to illustrate the problems of the country's marketing system.

The current movement is different than its predecessors in that it is more widespread, more publicized, and more enduring. The beginnings of contemporary consumerism are often traced to the publication of the book *Unsafe At Any Speed* in 1965.[3] As noted in Chapter 17, the author of this book was a young, obscure Harvard Law School graduate. His book was an indictment of the unsafe nature of General Motors' Corvair. Almost overnight the author, Ralph Nader, received national attention and assumed the informal leadership of the movement.

CONSUMERISM DEFINED

From the above comments, it should be obvious that consumerism is a practical fact of modern business life. Yet, it is a very nebulous term. Furthermore, the dynamic character of the contemporary movement makes today's definition somewhat questionable tomorrow. This changeability has produced about as many definitions as there are writers on the subject. Consumerism, for example, has been described in the following ways:

The most common understanding of consumerism is in reference to the widening range of activities of government, business, and independent organizations that are designed to protect individuals from practices (of both business and government) that infringe upon their rights as consumers.[4]

The organized effort of consumers seeking redress, restitution and remedy for dissatisfactions they have accumulated in the acquisition of their standard of living.[5]

Consumerism means that the consumer looks upon the manufacturer as somebody who is interested but who really does not know what the consumers' realities are.[6]

Within the context of this book, consumerism is defined as "a force within the macro environment designed to aid and protect the consumer by exerting moral, economic, and political-legal pressures on business." Figure 18.1 illustrates the information and influence flows among the various groups involved in consumerism. The consumer interest groups, government, and marketplace (consumers) are all a part of the macro environment, and each has an interrelationship with one another and with the business firm.

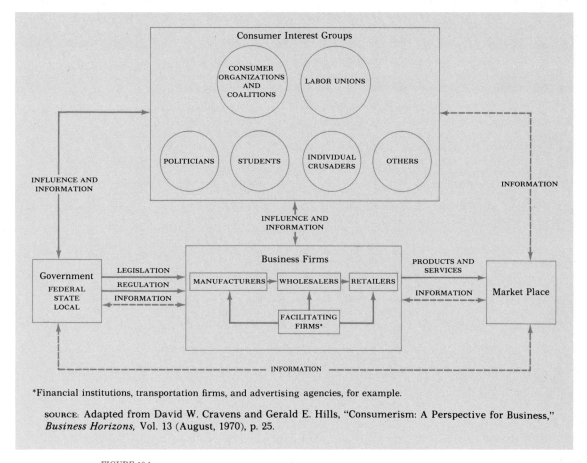

*Financial institutions, transportation firms, and advertising agencies, for example.

SOURCE: Adapted from David W. Cravens and Gerald E. Hills, "Consumerism: A Perspective for Business," *Business Horizons,* Vol. 13 (August, 1970), p. 25.

FIGURE 18.1.
THE CONSUMERISM
SYSTEM-GROUP AND
INFORMATION FLOWS

NATURE AND GOALS OF THE CONSUMER MOVEMENT

All consumers are not the same, and it is a known fact that only a small minority of people can be considered activists. Even though few individuals are willing to carry a picket sign, or write a letter of complaint to a manufacturer, a majority of Americans are sympathetic with the goals of the consumer movement. Thus, the leaders of consumerism have the implicit support of a vast number of people.

GOALS OF CONSUMERS

What are the goals of the consumer movement? First, consumerists say that the buyer needs help in coping with the complexities of the

TABLE 18.1.
SCHEMES FOR FLEECING
CONSUMERS

Special low price. Offering a consumer a deceptively low price in order to entice him into signing a contract.

Bait and switch advertising. Retailer advertises goods he has no intention of selling in order to switch the prospective buyer to another item, invariably higher priced and with a greater margin of profit.

Chain-referral selling. (Includes pyramid distributorships.) A person buys a distributorship from a company and then sells lesser distributorships and supposedly gets an override on business all of them do. Unfortunately, the company often goes defunct, leaving only the officers richer.

Free gimmick. Offering the enticement of a "free" product in order to sell another typically overpriced product.

Fear sell. The preying on people's fears in order to sell overpriced and sometimes worthless products.

SOURCE: Adapted from Warren G. Magnuson and Jean Carper, *The Dark Side of the Marketplace* (2nd ed.; Englewood Cliffs, New Jersey: Prentice-Hall, Inc., 1972), pp. 9–28.

marketplace. A supermarket, for example, now stocks over 6,000 items, and may change over 3,000 items a year. Despite advertising campaigns that portray the housewife purchasing agent as a computer, the average family does not have the specialized training in medicine, food chemistry, electronics, engineering, or textile manufacturing to enable it to make sophisticated decisions. New ways to provide customers with needed buying information through private companies, independent organizations (e.g., Consumers Union, publishers of *Consumer Reports*), or governmental agencies need to be found. Consumerists argue that merely drowning the buyer in volumes of data is not the answer. Instead, complete information should be presented in easy to understand messages and through appropriate media. There are, of course, situations where information is not the only solution, such as in matters of health and safety. Consumers, for example, need professional advice in selecting medications.

Second, the consumer needs protection from fraud, deceptive practices, and unfair methods of selling. Despite the efforts of responsible manufacturers and merchants, the work of Better Business Bureaus and trade groups, and the attention of government, practices such as small print in contracts and failure to deliver, install, or repair merchandise as ordered still exist. Table 18.1 describes some of the major schemes still used to deceive the unwary. Unfortunately, these practices and other schemes primarily affect low- and middle-income consumers who can affort it the least.

Third, the consumerists would like to have their interests better represented in government; the diffused interests of consumers need to be heard where decisions are made affecting buyers. Furthermore, the representation needs to be competent to offset the well organized and financed power blocs, such as business and the professions.

Fourth, consumerists stress the idea that unbalanced corporate power has made government an economic partner with business to the extent that competition has been eroded. They are particularly opposed to the concentration of a few firms in many major industries. Many consumer leaders support antitrust enforcement with the attitude that this will strengthen competition and ultimately benefit the public.

Fifth, the consumers' acknowledged rights to pure, safe, and unadulterated products are still said to be lacking. It is argued that the provision of these basic rights cannot be left to private enterprise and the professions alone, since they have not given adequate attention to these areas in the past. As a result, government action in ensuring health standards and safe products is advocated along with ensuring that all people have minimum medical and dental care.

Sixth, the existence of a substantial number of poor people within a prosperous society is upsetting to many consumers. Low-income individuals have less job opportunities, less education, and less mobility and may actually pay more for products than people with greater incomes. Consumerists often believe that the nation's business and political leaders fail to understand, or are not concerned about the atypical problems of poor consumers—high cost of credit, need for public transportation, poor diet because of low incomes, and so forth.

Seventh, consumerists argue that business, and more specifically marketing management, does not know its customers. Intentions notwithstanding, it is argued that the major decision levels of management have lost touch with the public. Nevertheless, many firms survive and prosper in spite of the fact that their workers may not do the work as they report, their products may cause harm and injury (lawn mower accidents, appliance short circuits, etc.) that go undetected by normal marketing research, or their companies tend to ignore consumer demand for new products or features. Consumerists feel that a more careful monitoring of the buyer will not only lead to the societal benefits, but will also enhance company profits.

ENVIRONMENTAL INFLUENCES

These seven concerns represent the thrust of the contemporary consumer movement. Consumerism, however, should not be viewed as an isolated area of socioeconomic concern. In the 1960s, the war in Vietnam, civil rights, pollution, and law and order made people more sensitive to all kinds of societal problems. Furthermore, during the 1970s inflation and morality are additional concerns that are interfacing with consumerism.

The economic, legal, and technological environments have also contributed to the continuation of the consumer movement. The inflationary aspects of the economic environment raised the prices for most products, and for many people increases in income were not sufficient to offset higher prices. The erosion of real income gains has caused consumers to become more concerned about product information and performance. In addition, the public has become more concerned with the utilitarian aspects of a product than with unnecessary frills. A good illustration of this point is society's attitude toward automobiles. In a short time, a product that represented a status symbol for many became a product valued primarily for its ability to transport people in an economical fashion.

In the 1960s, the politician came to the realization that the consumer was a huge, but underrecognized political bloc. The attention given to the consumer led to significant changes in the legal environment. The passage of laws such as truth-in-packaging and truth-in-lending helped further the goals of consumerism. Advances in the technological environment have been a mixed blessing for the consumer; the march of innovation has presented the buyer with a vast array of new and improved products, but it has now become more complicated to be a consumer.

SPECIFIC CONSUMER COMPLAINTS

As noted earlier, consumers are interested in a wide range of changes that would make the marketplace a more "favorable" institution. But what are some of the specific complaints? Holloway and Hancock have developed the following list of grievances:[7]

Deceptive advertising

Unfair tactics in selling

Proliferation in packaging

Unfair pricing practices

Merchandise tricks

Inflation economy

"Free goods"

Debt-collection deception

Refusal to make refunds

Used for new products

Promotion of superficial values

Planned obsolescence

Proliferation in products

Lack of competition

Exploitation of children

Lack of product information

Unsafe products

Junk products

Cheating of the poor

Impersonal selling

Poor service

High credit costs

Stress on quantity, not quality

Lack of communication with business

Complexity of technology

Misleading warranties

Bait and switch practices

Phony contests

Deceptive packaging

Substitution of merchandise

Although most of the listed items are still problem areas, it is interesting to note that considerable progress has been made in correcting many of these marketplace ills. In addition, these thirty complaints demonstrate the magnitude and diversity of consumerism.

Survey of consumers indicate that certain complaints are more significant than others. The following problems were most frequently mentioned: quality of medical care, auto safety, food shortages, dishonest advertising, consumer protection, adequate nutrition, and truth in packaging.

LEADERS OF THE MOVEMENT

The consumer movement has no formal unified organization to achieve its goals, but it does have some eloquent spokesmen. The most well known spokesman is Ralph Nader. Since challenging General Motors, he has attacked Congress, the Federal Trade Commission, the Food and Drug Administration, the Department of Transportation, and specific American industries in writings, speeches, and Congressional appearances. Typical of his campaign to educate the public is the following comment:

How many people realize, for example, that faulty heating devices injure 125,000 Americans a year or that poorly designed stoves, power mowers, and washing machines cause substantial injury to 300,000 people annually? Or that, as Rep. Benjamin Rosenthal recently revealed, the food rejected by Federal agencies as contaminated or rotting is often rerouted for sale in the market.[8]

In the past decade much of the consumer-oriented legislation and reorientation of Federal agencies can be attributed to the work of Nader and his "Raiders."

The efforts of consumer groups across the country have met with mixed success. In the early 1970s, there were over thirty statewide organizations and local groups in many major cities. These organizations are made up of diverse individuals who help achieve the goals of consumerism by issuing opinions on proposed legislation, testifying at hearings, and discussing consumer grievances with the business community. Public education is the broad but common objective of these state and local groups.

The Consumer Federation of America represents a group of organizations, including state and local bodies, labor unions, and the National Consumers League. The Federation was formed in the late 1960s to bring together the many individuals with interests in consumer affairs. The movement has also produced two communications-oriented organizations—Consumers Union and Consumers Research. Both nonprofit enterprises distribute objective product information and help develop the philosophy of the movement. Consumers Union publishes *Consumer Reports* to provide current consumer information to its nearly two million members. This respected monthly magazine covers such diverse topics as life insurance protection, toy safety, guarantees, automobile performance, and interest rates.

Leadership has also come from the political community. Senator Warren Magnuson of Washington, the coauthor of *The Dark Side of the Marketplace,* is probably the most respected and well-known consumer supporter in Congress. Magnuson has fought for many consumer rights and is a strong spokesman for the poor. Other Senators who have led a number of consumer causes include Wisconsin's Gaylord Nelson and William Proxmire, Minnesota's Walter Mondale, Michigan's Philip Hart, and Montana's Lee Metcalf. Benjamin Rosenthal (New York), Emanuel Celler (New York), and Wright Patman (Texas) have been prominent in the House. The activities and leaders of the Executive Branch are discussed in the next two sections.

THE RIGHTS OF CONSUMERS

The manifesto for the contemporary consumer movement was created by John F. Kennedy in a message to the House of Representatives in 1962. In this landmark statement, the President outlined the following "rights of consumers":

1. The right of safety—to be protected against the marketing of goods which are hazardous to health or life.

2. The right to be informed—to be protected against fraudulent, deceitful, or grossly misleading information, advertising, labeling, or other practices, and to be given the facts he needs to make an informed choice.

3. The right to choose—to be assured, wherever possible, access to a variety of products and services at competitive prices and in those industries in which competition is not workable and government regulation is substituted, to be assured satisfactory quality and service at fair prices.

4. The right to be heard—to be assured that consumer interests will receive full and sympathetic consideration in the formulation of Government policy, and fair and expeditious treatment in its administrative tribunals.[9]

These four rights have provided a theoretical framework for the evolvement of consumerism. The bipartisan endorsement and general acceptance of the rights of consumers is evidenced by a similar message delivered to Congress seven years later by President Richard M. Nixon. Although Kennedy provided a framework for consumerists, his level of direct activity was overshadowed by the individuals and groups discussed above.

RESPONSES TO CONSUMERISM

The strength of the movement is evidenced in its impact on the institutions of government and business. The responses of these two segments of society have, of course, been different. One survey revealed the varying views of consumerism among consumer, government, and business spokesmen. Table 18.2 highlights some of these findings.

GOVERNMENT
RESPONSES

Consumerism has caused some significant changes in government. On the federal level, recent presidents have assumed a more active consumer posture, agencies have taken on more responsibilities, and Congress has enacted numerous pieces of consumer legislation.

Presidents. As indicated earlier, President Kennedy provided a framework for the movement in his 1962 rights of consumers message. This historic speech also set the stage for the many consumer bills introduced to Congress in succeeding years. Kennedy recommended truth-in-packaging and truth-in-lending laws, more regulatory effectiveness from federal agencies, consumer research, and the establishment of a Consumers' Advisory Council. In terms of tangible accomplishments, however, the Kennedy years were overshadowed by the activities of succeeding administrations.

President Johnson continued the executive support of consumerism through several public statements, an appeal for legislation, and the signing of a number of bills. In addition, he appointed as his special consumer adviser, Esther Peterson, an outspoken and well-known

		Consumer	Government	Business
"Consumerism is an attempt to preserve the free enterprise economy by making the market work better."	Agree	82.0	76.0	12.0
	Disagree	6.0	16.0	68.0
	Uncertain	12.0	8.0	20.0
Opinions about the nature of consumerism: "Consumerism is primarily: . . ."	Political in nature	29.0	47.0	67.0
	Economic in nature	29.0	39.0	5.0
	Social in nature	21.0	0.0	14.0
	Other	21.0	14.0	14.0
Possible underlying causes	A feeling that business should assume greater social responsibilities	75.0	100.0	64.0
	A bandwagon effect	54.0	50.0	68.0
	Political appeal of consumer-protection legislation	67.0	77.0	88.0
	Widening consumer-information gap	74.0	85.0	25.0
	A deterioration of business ethics	61.0	0.0	9.0
	Lack of public awareness of the legislation which already exists	26.0	8.0	70.0

SOURCE: Adapted from Ralph M. Gaedeke, "What Business, Government and Consumer Spokesmen Think about Consumerism," *Journal of Consumer Affairs*, Vol. 4 (Summer, 1970), pp. 10–15.

TABLE 18.2.
OPINIONS REGARDING
CONSUMERISM FROM
DIFFERENT GROUPS (IN
PERCENTAGES)

consumer advocate. Building upon his extensive Congressional background, Johnson called for legislative activity in areas such as:

1. Truth-in-packaging

2. Truth-in-securities

3. Truth-in-lending

4. Greater warranty protection

5. Product warning labels

6. Product safety

7. Elimination of unfair trade practices

8. Assistance for the poor

9. Protection from fraud and deceptive selling practices

10. Consumer legal assistance

Although often thought of as a probusiness figure, President Nixon also furthered the cause of the American buyer. The first general use of the term "consumerism" by a president was by Nixon. In his October 30, 1969, message to Congress he began with the statement, "Consumerism—Upton Sinclair and Rachel Carson would be glad to know —is a healthy development that is here to stay."[10] In this same speech, Nixon outlined a consumers' bill of rights that bears a striking resemblance to Kennedy's rights of consumer's message (see Table 18.3). He also suggested programs in the areas of:

1. Product safety

2. Consumer legal assistance, including provisions for class action suits

3. Greater power for the Federal Trade Commission

4. Consumer finance

5. Stronger state and local programs

6. Office of Consumer Affairs in the Executive Office of the President

It should be noted, however, that during his concluding years, Nixon gave evidence of minimizing the consumer movement. A good example of this is the transfer of the Office of Consumer Affairs from the White House to the Department of Health, Education, and Welfare.

Following Nixon, President Ford was preoccupied with economic matters. After an attempt to curtail a spiraling inflation, executive attention shifted to the problems of recession and energy. Although it is hard to evaluate President Ford's position on consumerism because of these factors, his efforts were designed to produce a healthy eco-

TABLE 18.3.
THE CONSUMER'S BILL OF
RIGHTS

The Consumer's Bill of Rights
Consumerism—Upton Sinclair and Rachel Carson would be glad to know—is a healthy development that is here to stay.
Consumerism in the America of the seventies means that we have adopted the concept of "buyer's rights."
I believe that the buyer in America today has the right to make an intelligent choice among products and services.
The buyer has the right to accurate information on which to make his free choice.
The buyer has the right to expect that his health and safety is taken into account by those who seek his patronage.
The buyer has the right to register his dissatisfaction, and have his complaint heard and weighed, when his interests are badly served.
This "Buyer's Bill of Rights" will help provide greater personal freedom for individuals as well as better business for everyone engaged in trade.
SOURCE: President Richard M. Nixon, Special Message to Congress, October 30, 1969.

nomic climate for the benefit of both business and the consuming public.

Agencies.   Upwards of forty agencies of the federal government have been identified as having important consumer responsibilities. Most of these agencies have been made acutely aware of their duties by consumer advocates. The consumerists have criticized some of them for not carrying out their responsibilities, and have sought a broader role for others.

The Federal Trade Commission is probably the most important agency in the area of consumerism. As recently as the late 1960s, the FTC was often referred to as "the little old lady of Pennsylvania Avenue." In more recent years, however, the FTC's regulatory posture has strengthened in the areas of advertising claims, deceptive pricing, and warranties. The Commission, for example, has taken the position that an advertisement is deceptive if it falsely implies that a feature is unique to a product, even when the claim is literally true. Thus, a Wonder Bread message that it "builds bodies 12 ways" was labelled deceptive, not because the message was untrue, but because other breads could make the same claim. Once acceptable puffery such as "highest quality" and "best for the money" is now being challenged.

The new activism of the FTC is most evident in advertising enforcement. As noted in Chapter 13, the Commission's only legal right for prohibiting deceptive acts and practices is through a cease and desist order. Due to court delays, however, by the time the order is obtained, the advertisement has run its course, and the company has initiated a new campaign. To overcome this weakness, the corrective advertisement program was introduced. The first case requiring corrective advertising was that of the Continental Baking Company. In various advertising claims, Continental had communicated that Profile Bread was lower in calories than competing breads. In complying with the FTC corrective order, Continental advertised the following message:

I'd like to clear up any misunderstandings you may have about Profile Bread from its advertising or even its name. Does Profile have fewer calories than other breads? No, Profile has about the same per ounce as other breads. To be exact, Profile has 7 fewer calories per slice. That's because it's sliced thinner. But eating Profile will not cause you to lose weight. A reduction of 7 calories is insignificant. . . .[11]

The obvious goal of this and other corrective advertisements is to overcome past deception.

Other federal agencies have also become more consumer oriented in recent years. The Securities Exchange Commission has shown concern over the welfare of the individual investor. The harmful effects of cigarette smoking and television violence have been publicized by the Public Health Service. The Food and Drug Administration has been active in the areas of food and drug ingredients. A relatively new agency, the Consumer Product Safety Commission, has aggressively pursued its mission of protecting consumers from product hazards. The report that helped spawn the CPSC estimated that nearly fifteen million annual injuries were caused from the products investigated. Through product safety standards and consumer education, the Commission expects to reduce this figure.

Congress. As indicated earlier, Congress has also responded to the demands of consumers. A number of their significant legislative initiatives relate to the consumer's right to be informed. The consumer's ability to make astute purchase decisions has been aided by laws in areas such as truth-in-lending (true rate of interest), and truth-in-packaging. Various studies have shown that the availability of information does not ensure that a consumer will make comparisons. In a 1962 study, for example, a group of housewives were given a shopping list and asked to choose whichever package contained the largest quantity at the lowest price. The results showed that nearly 50 percent of the choices were incorrect. In 1969, after passage of the truth-in-packaging act, the study was replicated and this time just over 50 percent made wrong judgments.[12]

State and local levels. Government on the state and local levels has also responded to the consumer movement. These governments have established complaint offices, strengthened credit laws, beefed up attorney general responsibilities, and passed a host of specific laws ranging from prohibiting chain letters to restricting odometer tampering. The greatest activity has been in traditionally progressive states such as Wisconsin and Oregon, and affluent states such as Massachusetts, New York, and California. Many cities also have in operation various types of agencies, the most well known being the Office of Consumer Affairs in New York City.

BUSINESS RESPONSES The reaction of business to consumerism has been mixed and varied over the years. In the early days of Ralph Nader's crusade, for example, most firms (with the exception of a few, such as General Motors) ignored consumer advocates with the belief that consumerism was a passing fad. When it became apparent that the movement was growing and here to stay, the response became more vocal. Reactions have run the spectrum from "discredit the critics," "deny everything," "pass the buck," "appoint a committee," to "let's do something positive." Our attention in this chapter will focus on the creative efforts to respond to consumerism in a positive manner.

As noted in Chapter 17, there seems to be little question that the image of American business has diminished in the eyes of America's consumers. In comparing the public's confidence in business from 1966 to 1971, Opinion Research Corporation's survey work uncovered a significant decline in favorable opinions.[13] With the continued growth of self-service retailing, computerized communications, and anonymous chief executives, the prospects for improvement are not encouraging. Nevertheless, there are some bright spots among certain business groups and individual firms.

Organized groups. Collective business responses have come from trade associations, The Better Business Bureaus, and Chambers of Commerce. Traditionally, trade associations served their members through lobbying and other defensive, or protective, actions. The threat of government regulation and consumer unrest, however, have caused many associations to assume a leadership role for their members in the areas of (1) coordinating and disseminating research, (2) consumer and dealer education, (3) development of standards, and (4) complaint handling.[14] An example of the research activity is the Consumer Research Institute sponsored by the Grocery Manufacturers of America. The efforts of the Outdoor Power Equipment Institute to familiarize users on the safe use of power mowers is an illustration of the educational efforts of many trade groups. The development of standards usually manifests itself through self-regulation in the areas of product quality and safety. Certification is the common method of identifying whether a product meets acceptable standards. To encourage the buyer with a problem to turn to business rather than government, many industries have established their own complaint handling mechanism. The appliance industry, for example, with dealer cooperation has developed a consumer action panel to act as a "court of last resort" should the buyer be unable to resolve a grievance to his satisfaction.[15]

Better Business Bureaus have for many years been the consumers best source of information about firms. The strength of the contemporary consumer movement has forced the national, and many local bureaus, to step up their educational activities. The United States Chamber of Commerce and its local affiliates have also provided a group response to consumerism. Through its Consumer Issues Committee, the national organization has made suggestions to its members on ethics, product safety, sales training, and complaint systems. Table 18.4 illustrates the Chamber's Code for business-consumer relations.

Individual firms. Responses to consumerism by individual firms have been positively handled by corporate giants such as RCA-Whirlpool, Ford, and Sears, as well as by many lesser known companies. Individual firm efforts include such actions as decreasing the puffery in advertisements, introducing unit pricing, providing more useful product information, and revising product guarantees and warranties. In succeeding paragraphs, the following four positive responses to consumerism will be examined: (1) handling consumer grievances,

TABLE 18.4.
UNITED STATES CHAMBER OF
COMMERCE CODE FOR
BUSINESS-CONSUMER
RELATIONS

1. Protect the health and safety of consumers in the design and manufacture of products and the provision of consumer services. This includes action against harmful side effects on the quality of life and the environment arising from the technological progress.

2. Utilize advancing technology to produce goods that meet high standards of quality at the lowest reasonable price.

3. Seek out the informed views of consumers and other groups to help assure customer satisfaction from the earliest stages of product planning.

4. Simplify, clarify, and honor product warranties and guarantees.

5. Maximize the quality of product servicing and repairs and encourage their fair pricing.

6. Eliminate frauds and deceptions from the marketplace, setting as our goal not strict legality but honesty in all transactions.

7. Ensure that sales personnel are familiar with product capabilities and limitations and that they fully respond to consumer needs for such information.

8. Provide consumers with objective information about products, services, and the workings of the marketplace by utilizing appropriate channels of communication, including programs of consumer education.

9. Facilitate sound value comparisons across the widest possible range and choice of products.

10. Provide effective channels for receiving and acting on consumer complaints and suggestions, utilizing the resources of associations, chambers of commerce, better business bureaus, recognized consumer groups, individual companies, and other appropriate bodies.

SOURCE: United States Chamber of Commerce.

(2) using candid advertising, (3) establishing executive-consumer interfaces, and (4) reducing after-sale problems.

One of the major causes of a buyer's frustration is an inability to have his problem solved. When a product is not functioning properly, the consumer too often is confronted with an inaccessible manufacturer or retail sales person who doesn't have the authority to remedy the grievance. These situations frequently lead the consumer to believe that he is getting the "run around." A way to overcome this problem is for a firm to create an *action oriented contact point* where customers can express their problems. The most well-known example of this strategy is Whirlpool's "cool line" telephone service. Consumers with complaints are encouraged to call the company toll free, and in a substantial number of cases the problem is quickly corrected. It should be noted that to make any action contact point work, the program must be staffed with people who have the authority to take action.

A second positive response can be initiated through a firm's *advertising.* Instead of relying on puffery and gimmicks, more and more firms are moving to candid advertising of an informative nature. Lee Carpets, for example, has run advertisements answering typical questions of carpet buyers and offering an informative pamphlet. Ford Motor Company advertisements have instructed individuals on how to buy automobiles and offered them the free booklet, "Car Buying Made Easier." These kinds of communications are useful to the public, and also enhance the creditability of the sponsoring firm.

Establishing *executive-consumer interfaces* is a third creative response to consumerism. Unfortunately, the major decision makers of American industry are often insulated from the "real world." Top executives simply are not exposed to typical consumers on a regular basis. Instead, their monitoring of the buying public comes through feedback from friends and relatives of their own social strata, subordinates, and marketing research reports. Even though each of these sources can benefit the firm, none of them provide a "flesh and blood" exposure to the marketplace. Executive-consumer interfaces are one means for encouraging this type of communication. In attempting to create these important interfaces, some companies have set up Departments of Consumer Affairs within the firm. These departments are generally staffed by individuals who have experience and knowledge in consumer activities. If not simply created as window dressing, these kinds of departments can be a valuable input into the corporate decision process. Another vehicle for developing interfaces is the establishment of periodic small group sessions attended by a cross section of consumers and top executives. Within an informal, freewheeling environment, these sessions can focus on topics of major concern to the consumer.

Reducing after the sale frustration is a fourth technique for positively responding to the challenge of consumerism. It is not unusual for a buyer to have some reservations about a product following purchase. This real or imagined frustration is particularly evident when the product represents a significant purchase for the consumer, such as the buying of a home, car, or whole life insurance policy.

Too few firms recognize the significance of this common postsale apprehension. Although at the time of sale most buyers are convinced that they are making an astute investment, weeks or months after the sale frustration may arise unless the seller reinforces the purchase decision. In the case of an automobile dealer, this reinforcement might amount to a letter or phone call a few weeks after the purchase of a car to ascertain that the customer is satisfied. Although this procedure will surely lead to added demands on the dealer's service department, these costs should eventually be offset by the goodwill generated among buyers. This goodwill will increase the probability of repeat purchases and also create favorable word-of-mouth communications to potential customers. An example of this on the manufacturing level is American Motors' "Buyer Protection Plan" with its "hot line," understandable guarantee, and better service.

CRITICS OF CONSUMERISM

Although responses to the consumer movement have been quite positive, the movement has naturally created controversy and opposition in its development. While many criticisms have been made, none have seriously forestalled the movement. Nevertheless, some of the themes of the critics outlined in the following paragraphs have limited the effectiveness of consumerism.

First, some have argued that consumerism is destroying the free enterprise system. These individuals maintain that capitalism has brought a high standard of living to America and nothing should be done to interfere with the system. In a few cases, it has been alleged that consumer groups have socialist philosophies, or even communist infiltration.[16]

Second, it has been suggested that consumerism underestimates the sophistication of the buyer. According to this line of thinking, the turnover of brands and models in the market is evidence that consumers are not pawns under the clever influence of the advertiser or salesman. Furthermore, it is argued that the reforms recommended cost too much and are ultimately borne by consumers in the form of price increases; for example, that safety standards and requirements have raised automobile prices.

Third, it is said that leaders of the movement are negative rather than constructive in their approach. In preaching a theme of disaster from low quality, unsafe, and overpriced products and services, consumerists give the impression that the economic system is rotting. For example, the former chairman of General Motors, James M. Roche, has said that the leaders "jump from cause to cause, going wherever popularity or expediency lead, using whatever means are at hand, inflaming any issue that promises attention."[17]

Fourth, the competence and accountability of consumerists is attacked. The inexperience and lack of training of most consumer spokesmen in proposing production and marketing reforms is cited as an example. The movement's concentration on the tangible features of products while ignoring the complex sociopsychological aspects of consumption is also upsetting to many critics. Another criticism is directed toward the self-appointed position of the leaders; that is, they are generally not responsible to voters, elected boards of directors, or elected leaders.

LOW-INCOME CONSUMER PROBLEMS

The low-income consumer represents a special case of consumerism. The previous sections of this chapter have highlighted the situation of all consumers, but the disadvantaged sector of the marketing system has some unique problems. After presenting a profile of the poor, this section will examine the low-income marketing system, consumers with special problems, and the future of the low-income consumer.[18]

PROFILE OF THE POOR

The low-income consumer may be identified in terms of poverty thresholds as defined by the federal government. According to the Bureau of the Census, poverty levels are determined as follows:

> Families and unrelated individuals are classified as being above or below the low-income level, using the poverty index adopted by a Federal Interagency Committee in 1969. This index is based on a sliding scale of income, adjusted for such factors as family size, sex, and age of the family head, the number of children, and farm-nonfarm residence. In order to keep the poverty standard constant over time, the thresholds are updated annually based on changes in the Consumer Price Index.[19]

In 1970, there were nearly 26 million persons, or 13 percent of the nation's population, classified as poor by the federal government. When grouped by race and ethnic origin, whites accounted for the largest proportion (60 percent) of the poor population. However, whereas blacks were only 10 percent of the nation's population, they accounted for 30 per cent of the poor population. Also, persons of Spanish origin accounted for only 4 percent of the nation's population, but represented 9 percent of the poor population (see Figure 18.2).[20]

Some of the major socioeconomic characteristics of the poor are large families, low skills and education levels, lack of full-time employment, and poor health. Poor families, especially poor black families, are generally larger than nonpoor familes. While 60 percent of the nonpoor have completed twelve or more years of school, only 30 percent of the poor have done so. In regard to occupational status, it is significant that, contrary to popular opinion, the majority of the poor who are able to work do so. The discrepancy arises because a disproportionate share of poor persons are young, elderly, ill, or disabled.[21]

Given the characteristics of low-income individuals, it would seem probable that their goals and values would be vastly different from those of middle America. To the contrary, evidence indicates that low-income people seek and value the same things as the nonpoor. True, they are poor, but they are poor Americans. They are exposed to the same American dreams and wants as is everyone else, and thus, "have the same life aspirations and the same commitment to the work ethic as the middle-class people."[22] Unfortunately, a large majority of the disadvantaged fail in achieving most of these goals. As a result, these consumers often seek to fulfill their desires by purchasing costly durable goods. It is argued that the poor purchase these goods because such possessions can symbolize at least some progress toward achieve-

FIGURE 18.2.
RACIAL-ETHNIC BREAKDOWN
OF POOR AND TOTAL
POPULATION

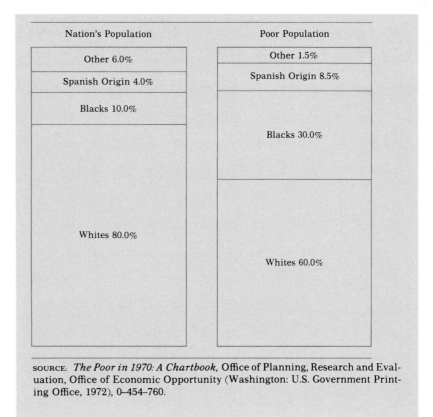

FIGURE 18.2.
RACIAL-ETHNIC BREAKDOWN
OF POOR AND TOTAL
POPULATION

SOURCE: *The Poor in 1970: A Chartbook,* Office of Planning, Research and Evaluation, Office of Economic Opportunity (Washington: U.S. Government Printing Office, 1972), 0–454–760.

ment of the "American dream"; appliances and automobiles may compensate for restricted socioeconomic mobility.[23]

MARKETING SYSTEM The consumption activities of the poor can be attributed to their incomes, generally limited shopping scope, and lack of education. Although the latter two factors are interrelated, they are each significant enough to deserve individual attention.

Even though the poor can and do shop a variety of retail institutions, evidence shows that they often frequent independent neighborhood stores.[24] This limited buying scope is in part the result of inadequate transportation, but there are other major reasons for the restricted scope.

Patronage of local stores is partially the result of the availability of credit from these retailers and the personalized environment provided by the neighborhood independent. The personalized environment contrasts sharply with the bureaucratic and impersonal nature of typical nonghetto retailers. In other words, the low-income consumer normally feels more at home in the neighborhood store. Since small independents typically charge more for products than chain and department stores, the individuals that patronize these establishments end up paying more for their products.[25]

Insufficient education also affects the low-income marketing system. The growing importance of education in consuming activities is a result of the variety and number of goods on the market, the complexity of many of these goods, and the intricacies of credit arrangements. Education is associated with the degree and kind of deliberations made when considering a purchase. Lower-educated poor families tend to use friends and relatives as major sources of information concerning durable goods, and make relatively little use of any kind of reading material, including advertisements. One expert has concluded that education induces a more critical attitude in the choice of consumer goods and less reliance on reference groups.[26]

Most stores in low-income areas are run inefficiently relative to larger stores. Such firms lack the managerial sophistication, capital, and capacity to serve their market efficiently and effectively. As a result, their customers generally pay more for goods and services, are forced to shop in deteriorated facilities, and must select from a limited variety and quality of goods.[27] These factors, which are often magnified by the high cost of credit, lead to higher prices.

Conspicuous by its absence in the low-income marketing system is the efficient national chain store. The large and efficient retailing systems of firms such as Montgomery Ward and National Foods are rarely found in poverty sectors of a community. Various explanations are given to justify the absence of these type of retailers; high costs, and the resultant need to charge high prices, is most frequently mentioned. One of the commonly mentioned costs is that of insurance. Retailers in ghetto areas have traditionally paid higher insurance rates, and these costs have soared in many areas since the riots of the 1960s. In addition to insurance premiums, large retailers also complain of the high costs associated with personnel problems, vandalism, and shoplifting.

A discussion of the marketing system catering to the poor would be incomplete without a brief mention of retailing practices. While many low-income merchants are ethical and responsible, a significant number utilize various schemes to trick and deceive consumers. According to the Federal Trade Commission, the five schemes that are most responsible for swindling American consumers (particularly the poor consumer) are "the special low price," bait and switch advertising, chain-referral selling, the free gimmick, and the fear-sell.[28] Although these practices are used in all sectors of American life, they are used more frequently in dealing with poor consumers. Furthermore, in many states, some of these activities are perfectly legal.

FOOD STUDIES　　　Following the riots of the 1960s, numerous studies were conducted on the food marketing practices in low-income areas. The impetus for most of this research was to determine if poor pay more. Unfortunately, the procedures and the findings of most of these studies have differed. Because of these differences, the various research conclusions must be viewed cautiously.

Many of the studies were restricted to one city, which obviously does not make them indicative of conditions in other areas. Another limitation is the difficulty in comparing foods, since some items are more or less likely to be purchased in poverty areas than in middle- and upper-income areas. Furthermore, the same two products at two or more stores may differ significantly in quality. Most observers agree that the poor typically have an inferior quality of produce and meat products from which to choose. Another problem arises in attempting to stratify stores by type. Supermarkets in poverty areas, for example, are typically fewer and smaller than those in suburbs. Poor sampling and statistical procedures are also a problem in some of the studies. Critics have even argued that food retailers are sometimes given advance warning before surveys are conducted.

Despite these problems and limitations, most of the research provides a consensus on a number of points. The poor pay more primarily because a majority of their shopping trips are made to small, higher-priced "mom and pop" grocery stores. Thus, the type of store patronized is an indicator of whether or not the poor will pay more.

The existence of quality discrimination in low-income areas has also been established. Relative to suburban stores, chain food stores located in ghetto areas are inclined to offer less fresh produce, are smaller, provide less service, and market relatively inferior meat and produce. This evidence leads to the conclusion that quality discrimination is practiced by chains and independents in the ghetto. Therefore, it is clear that the reasons the poor are paying more for food are too complex to be investigated in a mere price-comparison survey. As the *Monthly Labor Review* stated in the mid-1960s:

> The poor are not paying more because of price gouging by the chains, but because of the type of store they patronize and the small quantities they buy. To draw any more inferences it would be necessary to have information on volume and distribution of food sales, income areas, and family expenditure by type of store and geographic area within the city.[29]

CONSUMERS WITH SPECIAL SITUATIONS

Although this section has focused on the problems of low-income consumers, primary attention has been given to poor people residing in metropolitan areas. The justification for emphasizing this group is that it is the low-income group that has been most heavily researched. Nevertheless, there are other low-income groups that contribute significantly to the makeup of the low-income population. These other groups, which seem to have been overlooked by consumer researchers, are elderly, rural, American Indian, and Spanish-speaking consumers. While not all of the individuals composing these groups suffer from low incomes, the incidence of occurrence is high.

Elderly consumers. Senior citizens represent 10 percent of the total population of the United States and are primarily concentrated in urban areas. In 1971, older Americans were twice as likely to be impoverished as younger Americans, and 25 percent of all older persons were below the poverty threshold.

Three of the unique problems of elderly consumers relate to their source of income, cultural orientation, and health status. Senior citizens are generally retired and live on fixed social security and pension payments. These payments are typically drawn out of retirement funds established many years before, and are often insufficient to meet the inflated costs of the necessities required by the elderly consumer.

A second problem facing older consumers is the youth orientation of Western cultures, particularly the American culture. Elderly consumers very often feel out of place in a youth oriented society. They are constantly faced with negative and sometimes discriminatory attitudes toward aging and the aged.

Health status is a third problem facing most older consumers. Physical and mental impairment contribute to the consuming difficulties of this group. For example, the elderly often have trouble reading the fine print on labels due to faltering eyesight. Also, aged consumers are often confused by the proliferation of goods and services and related information that modern technology has provided.

Another difficulty facing elderly consumers is common among most low-income consumers; that is, a susceptibility to fraudulent and deceptive practices in the marketplace. Older consumers are particularly prone to the fraudulent practices of medical quackery. Their degenerative state of health makes the aged susceptible to the utopian promises of wonder drugs. Phony land sales, second career opportunities, and deceptive insurance policies also provide special marketplace problems for elderly consumers.

Rural consumers. Although rural consumers account for a relatively small percentage of the nation's total population, they make up nearly half of the poverty population. Several of the special problems that the rural consumer faces in the marketplace are associated with transportation, health, and consumer services. Transportation inadequacies reduce the consumer alternatives of rural residents; therefore, many become dependent upon door-to-door salesmen and mail-order houses for shopping.

The health care needs of rural consumers is a particularly troublesome problem. All Americans are faced with a shortage of doctors and rising medical expenses, but these problems are particularly acute in rural areas. As the nation has become more urbanized, doctors and medical facilities have concentrated in metropolitan areas. The consumer services found in many urban areas (legal aid and consumer-protection offices) are nonexistent in rural areas. Even if such services are available, they may be inaccessible due to transportation or distance problems.

American Indian consumers. The mean per capita income of Indians is about one-third of the nation's average, and 80 percent of all reservation Indians were below 1970 poverty thresholds. The employment opportunities on or around reservations are meager, and, as a result, the unemployment rate among Indians is extremely high.

Two of the special problems of Indian consumers are malnutrition and unfair marketing practices. Nutritional problems, prevalent among many Indians, are especially severe among children and women of childbearing age. As a result, there is a high incidence of certain diseases related to malnutrition. Indian consumers are, in essence, rural consumers, and share many of the same problems of limited consumption alternatives, including poor transportation, inadequate health facilities, and the absence of consumer services. The Indian also shares problems with low-income urban consumers. The retailing practices of merchants around reservations are often similar to the fraudulent and deceptive practices of ghetto retailers.

Spanish-speaking consumers. The majority of Spanish-speaking consumers are concentrated in twenty of the country's two hundred metropolitan areas. Three groups, the Mexican, Puerto Rican, and Cuban Americans make up this sector of the population.[30] While each of these groups differ in the nature and extent of their problems, a number of generalities hold for all three groups.[31] Many of these consumers do not speak, understand, or read English, and thus face special problems in an English-oriented marketplace. It is difficult for Spanish-speaking consumers to communicate their product needs to English-speaking sales personnel, and it is just as difficult to ask the questions that may be essential to wise purchasing. The language problem makes package contents and directions incomprehensible; it also makes these consumers vulnerable to deceptive and misleading contracts; and to schemes such as "learn English overnight" courses that cost hundreds of dollars.

THE FUTURE FOR LOW-INCOME CONSUMERS

What does the future hold for the low-income consumer? What solutions have been suggested to remedy the difficulties of this portion of the marketing system? Many government agencies have attempted to aid in the problem of consumer education of the poor. The Federal Housing Authority and Welare Departments both have numerous clients in low-income areas. They conduct courses on topics such as money management and clothing, but they reach only a small portion of the people that need help. Many voluntary and official groups have been established to assist these consumers. The Chicago Urban League, for example, has obtained legislation to protect installment buyers. The New York Commission on Human Rights investigates the exploitation of minority group consumers and conducts price checks in certain Harlem markets. Credit unions, labor unions, and schools are also attempting to aid in the problem.

Although many concerned individuals and groups have worked hard to change the low-income marketing system, so far the progress has been essentially restricted to certain geographical areas. A comprehensive program that will effectively alter the system on a national scale is needed. One expert contends that the problems can only be solved by extending into low-income areas the competitive and efficient marketing system that most Americans know. To accomplish this goal, the creation of a governmental program to provide incentives for business to locate in poverty areas is suggested.[32]

CONSUMER EDUCATION:
A PRESCRIPTIVE FRAMEWORK

Knowledgeable buyers are the key to making business more responsive to the needs of all consumers—poor and nonpoor. Individuals may become more sophisticated buyers through trial and error, or through programs of consumer education. Although the latter is generally the favored alternative, most educational efforts have fallen short of their intended goals.

This concluding section of Chapter 18 offers a prescriptive framework for developing effective consumer education programs. Although controversy surrounds the subject of possible solutions to the problems of consumerism, education is the one area about which all sides agree. Consumer advocates, business, government, and educators concur that the best approach to constructing a harmonious marketplace is through education. Therefore, it is appropriate to end the chapter with a look at this overlooked, but significant topic. Table 18.5 summarizes the sequence of steps recommended for establishing quality consumer education programs.[33]

MOTIVATION AND INFORMATION UTILIZATION

The first step, as shown in Table 18.5, is the determination of the motivations and kinds of information being used in decisions by all major categories or demographic segments of the consuming public; for example, senior citizens, young married couples, various ethnic groups, those living in poverty. Low-income consumers will be used as an illustrative category throughout the six steps.

The low-income consumer, as was stated in the previous section, is motivated by many of the same factors as other Americans. Nevertheless, because of his unique plight, the low-income consumer is also motivated by some different factors. For example, low levels of education and income cause the poor to view life differently from their more

TABLE 18.5.
STEPS FOR DEVELOPING
EFFECTIVE CONSUMER
EDUCATION PROGRAMS

1. Determine the motivations and kinds of information being used in decisions by all major categories or demographic segments of the consuming public.

2. Assess the degree of understanding and competency of each of these groups to deal with a series of business terms, situations, and problems involved in consumption activities.

3. Inventory the nature and content of the existing literature in consumer behavior in relation to information generated by steps one and two.

4. From an understanding of the consumers' behavior patterns, evaluate the most appropriate vehicles for communicating the necessary information to the individuals comprising those groupings found to be relevant.

5. Utilizing the appropriate professionals (at a minimum, representatives of government, business and education) develop programs tailored to meet the educational needs of the individual consumer.

6. Establish the necessary devices for feedback, or reinforce those presently existing, to private and governmental organizations.

SOURCE: Adapted from Stephen W. Brown and Parks B. Dimsdale, Jr., "Consumer Information: Toward an Approach for Effective Knowledge Dissemination," *Journal of Consumer Affairs*, Vol. 7, No. 1 (Summer, 1973), pp. 55-60.

affluent counterparts. Their view of life, of course, is reflected in their consumption behavior. One example of the poor's atypical consumption behavior is the type of information they use in making purchase decisions. Since low-income consumers shop heavily in their own neighborhoods, they rely on the information they receive in their face-to-face contact with these neighborhood merchants. Determining this kind of motivation and information utilization is the starting point for an effective educational program.

ASSESS CONSUMER SOPHISTICATION

After determining the motivations and information used by the relevant groups, it is necessary to assess the degree of understanding and competency of each of these groups to deal with a series of marketing terms, situations, and problems involved in consumption activities. For example, low-income consumers are often exploited by ghetto merchants in credit sales. The consumer needs the product, and is therefore forced to rely on costly credit as the only means of obtaining the product. As the result of little formal education, the poor consumer in many cases can neither read nor understand the contract to which he affixes his signature. Frequently, the result of such a signing is usurious interest rates over long payback periods.

LITERATURE SEARCH

The third step in developing meaningful consumer education programs involves assessing the nature and content of the existing literature in consumer behavior in relation to the information generated by steps one and two. Continuing with the example of the low-income consumer, a review of the literature indicates that marketers, sociologists, political scientists, historians, and other scholars have studied the poor in an effort to better understand their motivations and the types of information they use in making decisions. For example, "traditionalistic" values affect the consumption patterns of many low-income consumers. Because local merchants are able to personalize their services, low-income consumers are provided with an incentive to shop in their neighborhoods and avoid the impersonal atmosphere of stores in other areas.

EVALUATE EDUCATIONAL VEHICLES

After the literature about consumers has been studied and an understanding of the consumers' behavior patterns has been acquired, the next step in developing effective consumer education programs is to evaluate the most appropriate vehicles for communicating the necessary information to those groupings found to be relevant. For example, the federal government is in various stages of introducing consumer education programs into the existing educational system. The programs would attempt to shift some of the emphasis of the educational process from "producer education" (education in preparation for the work force) to "consumer education." Such a program may prove to be invaluable for the majority of Americans, but it may not be as effective for low-income consumers who generally have a lower level of educational attainment. At present, unfortunately, the poor seem to be the societal group with the greatest need for consumer education.

FORMULATING NEW PROGRAMS

The fifth step in developing an effective consumer education program involves utilizing the appropriate professionals (representatives of government, business, and education) to develop programs tailored to meet the educational needs of the individual consumer. These programs should provide the consumer with an understanding of relevant terminology and sufficient awareness of the buying environment to give him confidence and knowledge to ensure his satisfaction with his marketplace choices. The producer education idea mentioned in step four could be tailored to the educational needs of the individual consumer. Aside from implementing programs designed for the general needs of a given segment of the population, programs could also counsel consumers on an individual basis and help solve special problems they may have in the marketplace.

Traditional classroom consumer education, briefly discussed in step four, is another possible means of educating consumers on a somewhat individualized basis. Consumer oriented topics can be woven into much of the existing curricula. For example, mathematics courses could be designed that would utilize examples dealing with practical consumer problems, such as the computation of interest rates and payback periods and the utilization of unit prices in making price-quantity comparisons. In English courses, students could be taught to perceive advertisements objectively, and learn to rely on informative, rather than persuasive and emotional appeals.

The experiences of the State of Illinois illustrate how a classroom program can succeed. Consumer education has been a reality in Illinois since 1967. Smaller schools sponsor such activities as instructional media workshops and utilize slides and popular music to introduce students to consumer education. The larger schools of suburban Chicago are able to capitalize on the availability of television and video-taping facilities. Presentations by businessmen and consumer activists are filmed and placed in a consumer education resource library. Commercial advertisements and consumer related programs are also produced for classroom use. Other Illinois consumer education activities include Youth Conferences designed to provide students with an understanding of the many problems facing the consumer in the marketplace.[34]

UTILIZATION OF FEEDBACK

The final step in developing an effective consumer education program requires the establishment of the necessary devices for feedback to private and governmental organizations. Since good feedback is difficult to achieve and expensive to maintain, institutions frequently utilize some incomplete or ineffective measures of programs. Returning to the low-income consumer illustration, consider the existing methods of feedback used by local consumer protection agencies. These agencies attempt to protect consumers by informing them of the fraudulent practices of certain businesses. The agency may communicate the information to consumers in several ways. The message may be printed on flyers and distributed. Local radio and television stations and newspapers may also be used to inform the consumers. Still another method to disseminate information would be to communicate with neighborhood opinion leaders.

Although there are several alternatives available in communicating information, little is actually known about how effective the information distributed is in educating low-income consumers. How effective is information printed on flyers and randomly distributed in a neighborhood? How can a consumer agency assess the value of radio, television, and newspaper advertising designed to educate consumers? These are the same questions that marketers, particularly advertisers, have been asking for years. Thus, the establishment of an effective feedback system is vitally important in providing the necessary degree of control for maintaining viable consumer education programs.

SUMMARY

This chapter has focused on one of the biggest challenges faced by marketing in the twentieth century, namely consumerism. After highlighting the historical development of consumerism, various definitions of this complex term were reviewed. Within the context of this book, consumerism is defined as "a force within the macro environment designed to aid and protect the consumer by exerting moral, economic, and political-legal pressures on business."

The goals of consumers and the environmental influences affecting these goals were identified. President Kennedy's historical "rights of consumers" message provides an often used framework for the movement. According to this perspective, the consumer has the rights to safety, to be informed, to choose, and to be heard. Although Kennedy is credited with this historical message, the informal leader of the movement for over a decade has been Ralph Nader. Through research, writing, and speeches, this once obscure attorney has stimulated change on the part of business and government. Supplementing Nader's efforts are other private citizens and groups such as the Consumers Union, publishers of *Consumer Reports.*

The demand for change has sparked responses from government and business. Presidents Kennedy, Johnson, Nixon, and Ford have all offered various proposals to enhance the consumer's lot. Federal agencies have also become more active in watching out for the buyer's welfare. The legislative efforts of Congress in the last decade in the area of consumer protection have surpassed the combined activity of all preceding House and Senate bodies. At the same time, state and local responses have heightened.

Through group and individual firm efforts, the business community has also responded to the consumer movement. Trade associations, Chambers of Commerce, and Better Business Bureaus have led the collective retorts of firms with proposals for self-regulation and related private means of action. Individual companies have also formulated positive responses to consumerism, such as better handling of consumer grievances, candid advertising, executive-consumer interfaces, and reducing after-the-sale problems.

The low-income consumer represents a special case of consumerism. The profile of the poor includes atypical income, educational, life style, and consumption features. As would be expected, the marketing system serving the poor also differs from that of more affluent areas. The composition of the low-income population includes consumers under distinctive circumstances, such as the elderly, rural, Indian, and Spanish-speaking.

Consumer education represents perhaps the least controversial approach for helping solve the problems of consumerism. Unfortunately, most efforts in this direction have fallen short of their intended goals. Nevertheless, a prescriptive framework for developing effective consumer education was offered in the closing portion of the chapter. The proposal suggested represents a massive, but promising undertaking.

QUESTIONS FOR DISCUSSION

1. How many consumer movements has the United States experienced in this century? How does the current movement differ from its predecessors?

2. What is consumerism? How do you account for the different interpretations of the term?

3. Compare and contrast the goals of consumers with the comments of the critics of consumerism.

4. According to President Kennedy, what are the "rights of consumers"? Discuss.

5. Discuss the nature of the private leadership network in the consumer movement.

6. Trace the responses of the Kennedy, Johnson, Nixon, and Ford administrations to consumerism.

7. Which of the federal agencies has become particularly active in protecting consumers? What has this agency been doing in the area of advertising?

8. Discuss three ways that an individual firm can positively respond to the challenges of consumerism.

9. What are the major characteristics of low-income consumers?

10. Discuss the differences between the marketing system found in low-income areas and the system in more affluent areas.

11. What kind of consumer education program was suggested in the chapter as a relatively non-controversial but promising solution to the problems of consumerism?

NOTES

[1] Robert O. Herrmann, "Consumerism: Its Goals, Organization, and Future," *Journal of Marketing,* Vol. 34 (October, 1970), p. 56.

[2] Ralph M. Gaedeke, "The Movement for Consumer Protection: A Century of Mixed Accomplishments," *Business Review* (Spring, 1970), p. 32.

[3] Ralph Nader, *Unsafe at Any Speed* (New York: Grossman, 1965), p. 365.

[4] George S. Day and David Aaker, "A Guide to Consumerism," *Journal of Marketing,* Vol. 34 (July, 1970), p. 13.

[5] Reprinted from Richard H. Buskirk and James T. Rothe, "Consumerism—An Interpretation," *Journal of Marketing,* Vol. 34 (October, 1970), p. 62. Published by the American Marketing Association.

[6] Peter Drucker, "Consumerism in Marketing," a speech to the National Association of Manufacturers, New York, April, 1969.

[7] Robert J. Holloway and Robert S. Hancock, *Marketing in a Changing Environment* (2nd ed.; New York: John Wiley & Sons, Inc., 1973), pp. 564–565.

[8] Ralph Nader, "The Great American Gyp," *The New York Review of Books,* Vol. 2 (November 21, 1968), p. 29. Reprinted with permission from *The New York Review of Books.* Copyright © 1968, Nyrev, Inc.

[9] *Message from the President of the United States* Relative to Consumers Protection and Interest Program, Document No. 364, House of Representatives, 87th Congress, 2nd Session, March 15, 1962.

[10] President Richard M. Nixon in a special message to Congress, October 30, 1969.

[11] "Mea Culpa, Sort Of," *Newsweek* (September 27, 1971), p. 98.

[12] Holloway and Hancock, *Marketing in a Changing Environment,* p. 574.

[13] "America's Growing Antibusiness Mood," *Business Week* (June 17, 1972), pp. 100–103.

[14] David A. Aaker and George S. Day, "Corporate Responses to Consumerism Pressures," *Harvard Business Review,* Vol. 50, No. 6 (November–December, 1972), pp. 114–124.

[15] *Ibid.*

[16] Honorable John R. Rarick, "Consumerism and Consumerists," *Congressional Record,* November 20, 1971, page E12527. See also pages E8374 to E8379 in the *Congressional Record* of September 18, 1970, for extensive criticism of consumerism.

[17] James M. Roche in a speech before the Executive Club of Chicago; reported in the *Wall Street Journal* (March 26, 1971), p. 4.

[18] The content of this section has been adapted from Stephen W. Brown and Lee Richardson, *The Unique Problems of Low-Income Consumers* (Baton Rouge: Division of Research, College of Business Administration, Louisiana State University, 1973).

[19] U.S. Department of Commerce, Bureau of the Census, *Current Population Reports: Consumer Income,* Series P. 60, No. 77, "Poverty Increases by 1.2 Million in 1970" (Washington, D.C.: Government Printing Office, May 7, 1971).

[20] *The Poor in 1970: A Chartbook,* Office of Planning, Research, and Evaluation, Office of Economic Opportunity (Washington: U.S. Government Printing Office, 1972), 0-454-760.

[21] *Ibid.*

[22] Leonard Goodwin, "Environment and the Poor," *Current History,* Vol. 61, No. 363 (November, 1971), p. 296.

[23] David Caplovitz, *The Poor Pay More* (New York: The Free Press, 1967), p. 13.

[24] For an interesting discussion of the low income marketing system see: Leonard L. Berry, "The Low Income Marketing System: An Overview," *Journal of Retailing,* Vol. 48 (Summer, 1972), pp. 44–61.

[25] Most chains and department stores try to avoid being located in low-income areas. Those that are situated in these areas are usually planning for suburban expansion and phasing out their ghetto operations.

[26] Lola M. Ireland, *Low Income Life Styles* (Washington: United States Department of Health, Education, and Welfare, 1966), p. 76.

[27] Frederick D. Sturdivant, "Retailing in the Ghetto: Problems and Proposals," *Proceedings of the American Marketing Association* (Chicago: American Marketing Association, 1968), p. 532.

[28] Warren G. Magnuson and Jean Carper, *The Dark Side of the Marketplace* (2nd ed.; Englewood Cliffs, New Jersey: Prentice-Hall, Inc., 1972), p. 14.

[29] "Prices in the Poor Neighborhoods," *Monthly Labor Review,* Vol. 89, No. 10 (Washington: United States Department of Labor, October, 1966), p. 162.

[30]For two interesting articles on Mexican-American consumers see: Frederick D. Sturdivant, "Business and the Mexican-American Community," *California Management Review,* Vol. 2 (Spring, 1969), pp. 73–80; and Leonard L. Berry and Paul J. Solomon, "Generalizing About Low-Income Food Shoppers: A Word of Caution," *Journal of Retailing* (Summer, 1971), pp. 40–46.

[31]Cuban Americans, for example, have a relatively high standard of living and are concentrated in Miami, Florida. Mexican and Puerto Rican consumers are more prone to have low incomes, and are primarily situated in the southwest and northeast states, respectively.

[32]Sturdivant, "Retailing in the Ghetto."

[33]Adapted from: Stephen W. Brown and Parks B. Dimsdale, Jr., "Consumer Information: Toward an Approach for Effective Knowledge Dissemination," *Journal of Consumer Affairs,* Vol. 7, No. 1 (Summer, 1973), pp. 55–60.

[34]"New Direction in Consumer Education," *Consumer Education Forum,* Vol. 3 (Fall, 1972).

SUGGESTED READINGS

Aaker, David A. and George S. Day, eds., *Consumerism* (2nd ed.; New York: The Free Press, 1974).

Andreasen, Alan R., *The Disadvantaged Consumer* (New York: The Free Press, 1975).

Berry, Leonard L. and James S. Hensel, eds., *Marketing and the Social Environment: A Readings Text* (New York: Petrocelli Books, 1973).

Brown, Stephen W. and Parks B. Dimsdale, Jr., "Consumer Information: Toward an Approach for Effective Knowledge Dissemination," *Journal of Consumer Affairs* (Summer, 1973), pp. 55–60.

Cohen, Dorothy, "Remedies for Consumer Protection: Prevention, Restitution or Punishment," *Journal of Marketing* (October, 1975), pp. 24–31.

Cunningham, William H. and Isabella C. M. Cunningham, "Consumer Protection: More Information or More Regulation?" *Journal of Marketing* (April, 1976), pp. 63–68.

Diamond, Steven L., Scott Ward, and Ronald Faber, "Consumer Problems and Consumerism: Analysis of Calls to a Consumer Hot Line," *Journal of Marketing* (January, 1976), pp. 58–62.

Gazda, Gregory M. and David R. Gourley, "Attitudes of Businessmen, Consumers, and Consumerists Toward Consumerism," *Journal of Consumer Affairs* (Winter, 1975), pp. 176–186.

Grikscheit, Gary M. and Kent L. Granzin, "Who Are the Consumerists?" *Journal of Business Research* (January, 1975), pp. 1–12.

Warland, Rex H., Robert O. Herrmann, and Jane Willits, "Dissatisfied Consumers: Who Gets Upset and Who Takes Action?" *Journal of Consumer Affairs* (Winter, 1975), pp. 148–163.

Webster, Frederick E., Jr., *Social Aspects of Marketing* (Englewood Cliffs, New Jersey: Prentice-Hall, Inc., 1974).

19
METAMARKETING

METAMARKETING

Marketing's vital role in today's complicated, bustling economic world is validated constantly by its part in the success of growing and profitable companies. In an earlier chapter, corporate involvement in society was discussed from an "inside looking out" context. *Corporate social responsibility,* once an unknown phrase, has become a management catchword in today's environment of consumerism and extensive government regulation. Many of the concepts underlying corporate awareness of the world outside have their roots in marketing principles—particularly in the idea that marketing must begin with the consumer. In much the same sense, marketing theory, principles, and methods are spreading rapidly into applications in the non-business realm.

THE BROADENING CONCEPT OF MARKETING

The larger marketing arena looming on the near horizon is the subject of this chapter. The generally accepted macro and micro marketing concepts provide an excellent approach to begin this discussion. As noted in Chapter 1, macro marketing "is concerned with the creation and delivery of a desired standard of living for society through the effective and efficient distribution of an economy's goods and services under conditions of constraint imposed by the marketing environments." This suggests that companies exist in a specific environment, encountering consumers in markets, publics, and the society at large. The micro marketing approach recognizes the marketing manager's concern for the internal activities of his firm in relation to that environment.

One of the most important tools of the marketing manager, in his role of seeing that the customer is satisfied, is his communication with the marketplace—in both directions. Satisfying the customer (while making a profit) has replaced the traditional production oriented approach of "This is what we make best—now let's go convince the customer." Marketing today has been broadened greatly from those production oriented days. Marketers study the market to determine what is needed there, and then the needs and the company's ability and desire to produce are coordinated.

Just as the meaning of marketing has been going through transition, so are the applications and strategies of marketing being reexamined. As the definition of marketing has been expanded to focus on the consumer, the philosophy of marketing is gaining wider recognition. Business executives are the prime spreaders of the marketing philosophy. They are carrying its doctrine into their extracurricular activities, such as serving on boards of directors of civic and charitable organizations. These outside activities represent almost every area of human interaction. With the civic and the charitable activities go the political, the educational, the religious, the professional, the social special interest—all with the common element of not existing primarily for monetary profit. These managers of not-strictly-for-cash-profit organizations are beginning to see the advantages in the framework of total systems management. Understanding what good marketing can do in business, they are beginning to apply that knowledge to the nonbusiness organization, with modifications, for the benefits it may offer in the way of problem solving.

METAMARKETING DEFINED

The broader concept of marketing as applied to other than profit-seeking organizations has been referred to in the marketing literature as *metamarketing*—literally defined, the term means "changed marketing" or "beyond marketing." Philip Kotler, the most prolific author of note on the subject of marketing beyond the dollar marketplace, advanced the use of metamarketing as an innovation in the discipline in 1972 with this definition: metamarketing describes "the processes involved in attempting to develop or maintain exchange relations involving products, services, organizations, persons, places, or causes."[1] Kotler gave credit to Eugene J. Kelley for the first mention of the term metamarketing, in 1965, and pointed out that Robert Bartels later used it in a slightly different sense. Kotler, however, found both usages vague.[2]

Marketing formerly was conceptualized in the restrictive sense of being based in the buy-sell transaction relationship. Broader vision such as that of Kelley, Bartels, and Kotler has led to the understanding that marketing does not even begin in the buy-sell situation, although the discipline has its roots in that tradition. Clearly, marketing as a means of directing and accomplishing desired ends between persons or interests is valid in social, or noncommercial, transactions. The metamarketing concept then fits well into a definition used by Kotler in a later work. Marketing, he said, is "the effective management by an organization of its exchange relations with its various markets and publics."[3] This definition does not limit the use of marketing concepts to profit seeking, product oriented business enterprise. Rather, it expands their application not only to not-for-profit organizations but also to individuals.

This text has stressed the idea that the successful marketer of any product or service places great emphasis on determining the needs and desires of his target market. Information input from that target market is utilized to formulate and execute product development, pricing, promotion, and distribution strategies. Sophisticated marketing information systems have been designed to provide the marketing manager not only with continuing market condition awareness but also with continuous feedback on the failure or success of his decisions. Most organizations that might use metamarketing have similar information needs but often lack the tools to satisfy them.

NOT-FOR-PROFIT MARKETING

No tremendous imagination is required to see generally how commercial marketing can be applied readily to noncommercial operations. Two areas of social activity lend themselves most obviously to the metamarket concept, and it is in these areas that marketing already is being applied extensively.

The first of these is the political arena. As Theodore White and others have documented, Presidential candidate Richard M. Nixon was a "product" that was deliberately marketed as fully as any political candidate has ever been.[4] The discussion in the news media in the Nixon-Kennedy campaign of Nixon's "5 o'clock shadow" represented a marketing breakdown. This incident in the application of marketing techniques to politics serves to make an important point: the goals and objectives of the organization override marketing strategies; the latter must be exercised in the context of what the organization expects to accomplish.

The other area in which marketing has been applied extensively is fund raising. Through successful marketing techniques, this large societal activity has become so sophisticated in its methods, it now requires the guidance of professional fund raisers. In both the political and the charitable arenas, "products" are being offered, and a gain, although not entirely monetary, is being sought.

NONDOLLAR EXCHANGES

Although the nature of the transaction is sometimes difficult to analyze, there are a large number of potential "marketing areas" that do not involve a strict dollar-for-resource exchange. Kotler's definition of an organization, however, provides a good analytical framework. An organization, he said, is "a purposeful coalescence of persons, materials, and facilities seeking to accomplish some purpose in the outside world." That is, a marketing organization attracts resources, converts them into products, services, and ideas, and distributes these outputs to various consuming publics.[5]

A business is a "purposeful coalescence"—its elements work together to convert resources into a product and to distribute that product in exchange for more resources and profits. By the same token, a nonprofit organization exists as a coalescence of persons and facilities, perhaps not quite as tightly bound as a business firm, trying to accomplish some purpose. Thus, the metamarket organization faces the same requirements to raise resources, convert them into products, and distribute them. In both profit and non-profit organizations, marketing facilitates goal achievement. Although there may be differences in defining markets, products, and resources, the basic marketing principles are the same in both cases. In a commercial organization, the product most often is of greatest concern to the marketer. In a metamarket situation, raising the resources may receive more emphasis.

Regardless of the situation, exchange is an important element in the marketing process. Exchange requires two parties, each having something that might be valued by the other. It should be noted, however, that there are a number of different types of exchange transactions. The most common is the buyer-seller transaction involving an exchange of goods or services for money. The second is the employment transaction wherein an employer provides wages and fringe benefits in exchange for productive services. A third is the civic transaction in which protective services such as police or fire services are exchanged for taxes and cooperation. A fourth is the religious transaction in which the organization provides religious services and experiences in exchange for the members' contributions, service, and participation. The fifth is the charity transaction involving exchange between an organization and a donor of money or service.[6]

Given the above transactions, it is possible to establish categories of organization types. These are: business concerns, service organizations, mutual benefit associations, and commonweal organizations.[7] Metamarketing is concerned directly with the latter three. Service organizations include social welfare agencies, hospitals, schools, legal aid societies, mental health clinics, and the like. Mutual benefit associations include labor unions, professional and fraternal associations, political parties, religious groups, and others. Commonweal organizations involve every level of government where services are exchanged for taxes and cooperation.

In analyzing each of these organization types, it should be noted that a degree of overlap exists. A school, for example, is a service organization, but a public school district is a commonweal organization. Furthermore, some mutual benefit associations perform service organization functions. A good illustration here is the fraternal group that operates a crippled children's hospital.

METAMARKETING APPLICATIONS

The above categorization of organization types is a useful one, but a more descriptive view of metamarketing tasks will provide a better idea of how exchange relations are managed in not-for-profit marketing situations. For the most part, these tasks involve the marketing of organizations, the marketing of persons, the marketing of services, and the marketing of ideas, as shown in Figure 19.1. Each of these is discussed below.

Marketing of organizations. When monetary profit is not the motive of the organization, it is possible that the organization itself is what must be marketed. In some cases, the principal marketing mission may be to manage internal relationships, such as in a union or other mutual benefit group in which the true product is the organization and what it can accomplish for its members. Thus, the organization itself,

FIGURE 19.1.
APPLICATIONS FOR
METAMARKETING

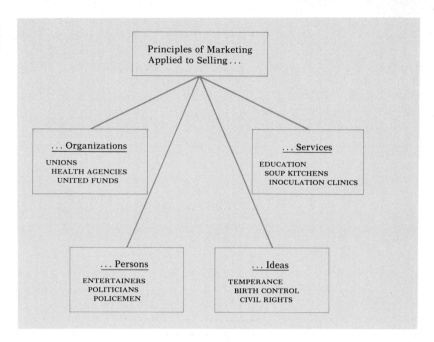

its reliability, its social role, or its community necessity may be the "real product." It should be noted, however, that the organization is not always marketable. For example, an organization may be socially vital but not openly marketable because of some societal bias. The venereal disease clinic cannot advertise its cure rate against that of another clinic. The same principle applies in many of the professions. As an illustration, the American Medical Association expressly prohibits a local medical society from promoting its physician members as the best in the state under existing AMA standards of ethical practice.

Marketing of persons.   The marketing of individuals, or groups of individuals, is a widespread practice today. This is precisely what occurs in professional political campaign management. Individuals and groups are also marketed outside of the political arena. Gospel music performers, the "man in blue" police officer, and religious crusaders are all examples of the marketing of persons. Star performers in the arts provide the most visible illustrations of "persons marketing" in the commercial world. In a noncommercial context, has the evangelist Reverend Billy Graham been marketed any less professionally?

In the gospel singer example, the singers provide a service (religious stimulation and entertainment) to their market, which in exchange provides the resources for the singers to continue performing their service. In addition, the singers serve another market. They help local religious organizations attract their publics. The local groups, in exchange, provide logistic and promotional support for the singers.

The "man in blue" is a clear case of marketing a group of individuals in an abstract sense. The exchange presumably involves heightened respect for the police, more community awareness and cooperation, and better pay and working conditions in return for more effective law enforcement at the basic level. The metamarketer may encounter some problems here, of course, if a good-guy community service image is suddenly lost in a labor-management wage dispute when the trusted "man in blue" threatens to go on strike.

Marketing of services.   In some instances, distinctions between marketing persons and marketing services are difficult to maintain. It should be noted, however, that marketing a service depends less on the specific persons involved. A school, for example, can market its services without emphasizing its individual teachers. In a political campaign, it is impossible to separate the candidate from the proposed service to society that the candidate is offering. Marketing of services covers most metamarket activities, since few metamarket organizations deal in physical, tangible products as a direct objective. This is true even in the case of social welfare agencies, such as Goodwill Industries and The Salvation Army thrift stores that salvage, repair, and resell used goods. Goods marketing is simply a means to accomplish the organization's real end—the rehabilitation of individuals. In this situation, the goods attract resources that are used in the performance of services.

Marketing of ideas.   Marketing of organizations, services, and persons is fairly straightforward. Although included in all three, the marketing of ideas can be a separate marketing activity. The idea that charity nursing is a valid social service is behind public support donations; the ideas of a politician are part of marketing the person; the ideas embodied in the objectives of a professional group are a part of marketing membership in the group. At the same time, some organizations offer an idea as their principal product. In such cases, the exchange involved is the most intangible: the organization markets the idea in exchange for resources in the form of support that permits the organization to continue to foster the idea. Planned parenthood, marijuana legalization campaigns, civil rights, antiwar movements, and the Women's Christian Temperance Union are all ideas that are marketed.

As one far-fetched, backhand example of marketing's applicability to ideological movements, consider capital punishment. The idea of capital punishment would be a much greater deterrent to crime, in all probability, if it were marketed effectively. Some organization, of course, would have to apply the principles and techniques of marketing and promote the idea that capital punishment is indeed a guaranteed deterrent. This is not to imply that capital punishment is endorsed here. The example is merely an illustration of how meta-marketing might be applied to an idea. This case does raise a question of concern to managers of not-for-profit organizations, however, for marketing ideas can sound like "propagandizing" in the worst possible sense. Unfortunately, marketing suffers from the bad name of "Madison Avenue" and "hard sell" advertising to the extent that some metamarket managers are suspicious of anything that resembles it.

A number of important concepts in marketing have evolved in recent years to offset the narrow view that marketing is synonymous with promotion and selling. One of these is the broadened view of *social marketing,* which may be defined as the "design, implementation, and control of programs seeking to increase the acceptability of a social idea or practice in a target group."[8] Deliberately designing and carrying out programs to convince the public of the need to provide emergency food and shelter for the needy, to drive safely, and to give to the United Fund are regular practices of metamarket organizations. There certainly is nothing sinister in these worthwhile endeavors.

Nonetheless, attempts to professionalize the marketing management of these types of activities often elicit cries of anguish from the social arbiters and critics who worry that the public is being swindled or is the dupe of a hoax. Social marketing, of course, is a common fact of life, even though such programs may not be recognized or acknowledged as marketing efforts. It may be argued, therefore, that a lack of acceptance of marketing management's utility has greatly hampered the efforts of many not-for-profit organizations.

THE METAMARKETING MIX

At this point, it should be clear that there is little difference between marketing and metamarketing other than the unit of measure; marketing transactions are measured normally in terms of dollars; metamarketing deals as often in non-monetary units. Following the concept of a marketing mix that was introduced in Chapter 4 and developed in Chapters 5 and 6, this section focuses on the metamarketing mix, which includes the same controllable variables of product, price, distribution, and promotion as applied to the metamarket. An example of the application of the marketing mix to metamarketing is illustrated in Figure 19.2.

THE PRODUCT VARIABLE When expanded to the metamarket, a product is "anything that can be offered to a market for attention, acquisition, or consumption."[9] This definition extends the traditional concept of a product or service well

FIGURE 19.2.
THE METAMARKETING MIX

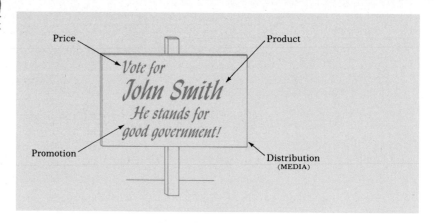

beyond the realm of the buy-sell relationship and into almost every area of social interaction. In this sense, a campaign to respect the rights of nonsmokers in public places through legislation is a "product" that is as real as a Winston "that tastes good like a cigarette should." This broader, more abstract, definition also means the conventional theory of a "product life cycle" is pertinent to metamarket organizations. In a political campaign, for example, the product is the candidate, and the product's life cycle ends if he loses and retires from politics. The cycle enters a new phase if he wins, or if he loses and decides to run again.

Metamarket products are more difficult to define than a manufacturer's products, since the former may range from the intangible to the sublime. A Chicago politician, for instance, is a much different sort of product than that offered by an organization whose purpose is to verify the existence of UFOs. The metamarket product, because of the broader theoretical base in metamarketing, is also more readily confused with some of the processes used to achieve the product. A private social welfare organization that holds an arts and crafts show, for example, does not offer the handicrafts as its product. To the contrary, the organization uses them to raise resources to produce its real product, which may be anything from an adoption service to a "save the buffalo" effort.

THE PRICE VARIABLE

Price, in the conventional situation, implies profit maximization, or at least cost recovery, and it serves as a market incentive or disincentive, depending on the marketing intention. Price presents one of the larger problems of transferring marketing techniques to metamarketing, since many intangibles are involved in the price variable. In commerce, price depends greatly on cost, demand, and competitive circumstances. To a degree, all are measurable and quantifiable in some fashion. In the metamarket, costs become nonmonetary. More importantly, near-barter conditions often prevail in metamarketing when one pure resource, such as labor, is exchanged for another.

The organization that tries to apply cost accounting principles to its efforts, assigning hourly dollar rates to its volunteers' work, will end up in theoretic chaos. Metamarket costs most often are best expressed in terms of relative demand for the group's service (to provide clients) and relative recognition by the group's publics (to provide resources). The corollary of profit is the degree of accomplishment of the group's objectives, its growth or improvement in quality, and its continued existence.

Competition opens a similar set of complications for the metamarketer, but the principles still apply. In most service organizations, for instance, there is little direct competition. One social welfare agency rarely vies with another for the same client. Public schools do not compete with each other directly for students. Their boundaries are fixed. At the same time, quality of education is an implicit competitive factor. When population is attracted to a school district because of its high academic reputation, for example, an increase in the tax base provides more resources for the district. There are other exceptions, such as the recruiting of athletes, where competition does enter. In that environment, the price a college pays to have a good football team is definitely part of the marketing mix considered best by that college's management. In this case, both dollar and intangible costs and rewards—prestige, public support, recognition—are involved.

For metamarketing in a mutual benefit association, price can have both tangible and intangible manifestations, depending on what services the organization seeks to provide. The exchange of values between dues and pension checks in a union is different from the price involved when union dues are spent on collective bargaining efforts. Commonweal organizations, relying as they do primarily on taxes for resources, also find themselves paying political or social costs and reaping benefits in kind. Community involvement and political support in response to a strong crime prevention campaign would be an example.

| THE DISTRIBUTION VARIABLE | In marketing terminology, distribution is concerned with getting the product to the consumer at the right place and the right time as effectively as possible. It involves factors such as transportation and storage. The metamarket distribution function strongly parallels distribution in the service company, since tangible goods rarely are a primary factor in metamarketing. Running a volunteer "hot line" telephone counseling service for women with problem pregnancies, for example, would not succeed if the "product" were not made readily accessible to the target market—if, say, anonymity were not guaran- |

teed to the client. Delivering an idea presents a great challenge to the metamarketer; the choice of medium becomes critical. Marketing a local bond issue on national television, for example, simply does not make sense. In metamarketing, therefore, the medium is the delivery system.

THE PROMOTION
VARIABLE

As the fourth variable in the metamarketing mix, promotion embodies communications; advertising, publicity, personal contact, incentives, and atmosphere play important roles in the metamarket. Promotion is the most visible element of marketing, and it is the factor that has been most often abused in the marketing mix. Not-for-profit organizations with legitimate aims and methods have been as much victimized by promotion abuses by unethical marketers, as legitimate businesses have been hurt by unethical hucksters. Many special interest groups with legitimate purposes and professional lobbyists suffer from the abuses of unethical lobbyists.

The information explosion, the ease and rapidity of communication today, and the technological revolutions of the past few years have made it inexpensive and uncomplicated for unscrupulous promoters to lie, exaggerate, and cheat the consumer. Their overindulgence in deceitful practices has indeed hurt marketing's image, but sound marketing knowledge suggests that for the most part such abuses are self-destructive. The promoter without scruples may deceive some people for awhile, but extremes of ulterior motives will usually be exposed before many are defrauded. Additionally, it should be noted that marketing is only the vehicle, not the fashioner, of the organization's objectives. Too often, marketing is unjustly blamed for bad motives.

In a positive vein, the metamarketer must understand the fundamental promotion tools, such as advertising and public relations. The metamarketer's selection of the means of communication clearly will vary from those of business, but the underlying principles pertain. Mass-media advertising most likely will not work as well for a group seeking funds for a museum of fine art as will a well-prepared direct-marketing campaign from a carefully drawn mailing list. Conversely, mass communications techniques can prove quite adaptable to more restricted markets. The national telethons to raise funds, for instance, have been applied on the local level with a high degree of success.

Promotion is another area in which it may be difficult to distinguish the organization's product from the means it chooses to raise resources. It may be, however, that the organization will want to encourage the confusion. In a commercial enterprise, both product and resource means are quite often the same. Although this is not necessarily the cause in a metamarketing situation, it may be desirable to equate the two. The familiar Salvation Army kettles at Christmas time is a good example.

SYSTEMS CONCEPT IN METAMARKETING

As pointed out in Chapter 3, the systems concept provides an appropriate framework of analysis for business. This concept may be used also in metamarketing to emphasize the need for an integrated approach to the problems presented by the metamarket. To illustrate the application of the systems concept in metamarketing, this section will present a brief analysis of a fairly common social organization project from a systems point of view. The situation is a communitywide rummage sale that is conducted annually to raise funds for local social service work.

In this situation, the immediate, visible product (rummage) is produced through appeals to the organization's members and to the community at large. Selection of the product may have included some rudimentary market research, such as determining how many other rummage sales might be around to compete, but it is probable that the product concept began with the experience of a member who participated in a rummage sale in another area.

Internally, accounting for the rummage sale is handled on a simplistic level by the organization's treasurer who keeps a checkbook ledger account. The success of the sale is gauged by how much is in the treasury when the sale is over and the bills are paid. The quality and quantity of the organization's final product—a social service—will depend on the single "bottom line" of how much is left to spend on the group's real work. Product research and development falls within the expertise of experience of organization members from previous sales. From past experience, they learned something about how to encourage the best kinds of donations, which, along with setting prices on the donated goods, is a fundamental marketing function.

The finance function for the rummage sale is marginal, since the treasury provides expense funds for the sale. Warehousing and purchasing also are minimal. Personnel depends on volunteers, although the organization may employ a paid executive director. (If employed, that person should have at least some basic marketing knowledge. One of his main marketing jobs would be seeing that enough volunteers of the right quality are found and maintained.) Shipping of the rummage depends greatly on the volume of the goods. If the sale is large, chances are that professional services and equipment will be purchased, or donated in part.

Externally, sales are geared to a short-term, highly intensive selling period of two or three days. Marketing experience has shown that longer sales reduce productivity. The metamarketer will see to it that prices are clearly posted, that goods are efficiently assorted and displayed, and that cashiering functions are convenient. Advertising and sales promotion will be one of the chief functions of the executive director, if there is one. If not, the promotion function may be handled by an organization member in those professions. The importance of promotion as a basic marketing task becomes vividly apparent in this analysis. The success of the sale depends to a large extent on the quality of the rummage, but, given the nature of the immediate product, it is clear that good advertising and publicity are critical to the success of the sale.

In the above illustration, there are several special factors that relate more to the metamarketer than to the commercial marketer. It should be noted, for example, that accounting and tax situations for not-for-profit organizations are quite different from normal business operations. Other rules, laws, and regulations also may be peculiar to certain types of metamarket organizations. CARE, for instance, certainly has to have management expertise in dealing with export laws, tariffs, and import regulations in every nation it enters. Likewise, a church organization seeking to establish a regular bingo game may encounter some restrictive city ordinances, or even state laws prohibiting gambling.

In this age of consumerism, including environmentalism, business is becoming more aware of the power of government regulation. Quite often in business management decision making, the discussion will include: "If we (business and industry) don't do it, government will." This awareness may be necessary also for the metamarket. As social accountability grows, so may it spread into the metamarketing environment. The metamarketer must not fail to consider the possibility.

APPLIED METAMARKETING

Thus far, the application of marketing principles to the nonbusiness world has been treated in general terms. This section focuses on some of the practical applications of metamarketing. Special attention, therefore, will be devoted to the use of accepted marketing techniques in the field of metamarketing.

TARGETS AND STRATEGY

The metamarketer, like the marketer, must first define his target market and then formulate his marketing strategy. For several reasons, however, defining a target market may be more difficult for the metamarketer. Consequently, it is important to note that special care and attention must be devoted to the metamarketing task.

In many instances, the resources for market research may not exist, or may be denied by the metamarketer's managers out of ignorance. Given that the resources are available and apparently cost-justifiable, the metamarketer's target market analysis can use the same methods of analysis as those used by the conventional marketer. By whatever means, however, the metamarketer must determine the needs, perceptions, preferences, and satisfaction levels of his publics. In some cases, this may have to be accomplished through intuition and educated judgment.

The organization's goals or objectives assume paramount importance for the metamarketer at this point, but they may present complications. The group seeking to sell the concept of trial marriages as an esthetic experience is going to be more of a challenge for the market analyst than the traditional political group. The political group trying to get its candidate elected will be able to call on some of the most sophisticated research techniques in the world to analyze its market. The trial marriage group might use some of this expertise, but its resources are probably much more limited than those of the political group.

With a broad market definition under the organization's objectives, the metamarketer can apply market segmentation in the determination of the geographic, demographic, and psychographic characteristics of the market. Census reports, door-to-door surveys, other public marketing surveys, and telephone samplings may be helpful in this task. The problem, of course, may be complicated when a variety of distinct markets exist.

Consider, for example, the local Young Men's Christian Association (YMCA) organization in a large urban area. The most obvious and largest market segment contains those persons who come into the "Y" to use its services. Therein lies the beginning of the market analysis complications. If the "Y" has athletic facilities, at a centrally located main branch, it will attract noontime businessmen athletes for handball, jogging, basketball, or badminton. These businessmen also may wish to use lockers, showers, and massage facilities. This market is probably upper middle class, male, and geographically close to the facility. But what about young persons who use the "Y"at other times, the mothers and infants who come for swimming lessons, and the high school-age weightlifters? What about the older person and others who are attracted to jewelry classes and rock-polishing, or travelogues, or language, or dance instruction? Consider also the youngsters who attend summer day camps. And the traveling men who find the "Y" an inexpensive place to get a bed and a decent meal at a reasonable price.

The above descriptions cover a variety of what might be termed consumer markets. These are not all-inclusive, by any means. The YMCA is structured as a community organization, and, as such, it draws on local leadership for its board of directors. Because it is a nonprofit organization depending in part on contributions for its continued operation, the board tends to rely heavily on the rich and the powerful in the business community. At the same time, the "Y" may have branch facilities, and they may lie in areas inhabited by publics at the other end of the economic spectrum. Meanwhile, the board knows the importance of neighborhood involvement and the need for contributions, so it finds that it must go to still another market—the public at large—for funds.

Undoubtedly, the YMCA is offering its programs and facilities to the markets that it can reach, and it has done so mostly on the evidence of informal reflection of demand from the community. Managerial awareness of the segments of the market exists, however, and one of its most effective manifestations is in the composition of the board of directors—the most influential segment of its total market.

MACRO ENVIRONMENTAL FACTORS

The metamarketer may find limitations other than those of resources in both defining markets and determining the proper mix for them. For example, macro environmental factors, which have been referred to throughout this book as the "uncontrollable variables," can interfere more with the metamarketer than with the conventional marketer. As identified in Chapter 2 and discussed in detail in Part III of this book, the macro environments most relevant for the metamarketer appear to be the market environment, the sociocultural environment, the legal environment, the economic environment, and the competitive environment. One might argue that the metamarketing organization is aimed, in some instances, at changing one or more of those environments. Marketing an idea like birth control, for example, would be an attempt to change the sociocultural environment. The following newspaper account of blood bank management provides a dramatic illustration of how the macro environments can impact on the metamarketer:

"Because Phoenix' blood bank is a nonprofit organization dependent on community support, its managers insist they must be above public reproach. Our believability must be immaculate," said David Graef, director of management services for Blood Services, which supplies blood to 22 cities across the country, including Phoenix. "All Blood Services facilities are under one corporate umbrella, which has its headquarters in Scottsdale. Blood Services is dependent upon the goodwill of the people it serves," Graef said, "since all blood is donated on a purely voluntary basis."

Blood Services stopped paying donors for blood last year after the U.S. Department of Health, Education and Welfare (HEW) strongly recommended that commercialism be eliminated from the blood banking business. "Because the voluntary concept involves community support, we have set up an advisory board composed of leading citizens in the community to act as a liaison between us and the public," Graef said. "Thus, we feel we must justify our (management's) salaries and pay scale to the board and to the public." Since Blood Services does not pay for blood, he noted, the public has a right to know where the company's money comes from and where it goes. "Our income is derived solely from the testing and processing charge on the blood we supply to hospitals and other facilities," Graef said. That charge comes to about $25 per unit (pint) of blood.

"The salary of the top executive position is between $46,000 and $67,000 a year," he said, adding that this pay range is "commensurate" with salaries in other companies of similar size. "Blood Services provides blood to hospitals that serve almost 14 million persons," Graef said. "The salary range for three vice presidents of Blood Services is $25,000 to $34,000, and for the 22 district managers, $17,000 to $25,000," he said.

"We are always trying to make our operation more efficient, and bring down the price of blood," Graef said, "and we have a good record at that. For example, the national average for the expiration of blood is about 25 per cent, while at Blood Services we have about 2 or 3 per cent expiration rate. By law, blood must be used before it is 21 days old. After that, it is considered expired. The reason Blood Services wastes so little blood," Graef said, "is because of constant shipping back and forth between cities served by the company. Whenever a city has a surplus of blood, which may expire before it can be used, that city transfers it to another city which is short of blood," he said. "Despite the efficiency of Blood Service's operation, it is in constant need of fresh blood to maintain a 12-day stockpile, about 2,000 pints, considered adequate to handle any emergencies," Graef said.[10]

From the above commentary, it may be noted that the blood bank's entire method of operation was upset by a federal agency's "suggestion" that commercialism be eliminated from the blood banking business. The Phoenix, Arizona, blood bank management was aware of the stigma of paying donors before HEW dropped its hints. The blood bank already had been running a careful counter-marketing campaign against the image that it bought blood from derelicts who were selling their blood to buy more wine. The image was not entirely true, but incidents elsewhere alleging transmittal of hepatitis and other infections through donor blood clearly harmed the Phoenix campaign.

From a metamarketing standpoint, this account represents a casebook capsule rarely found in such condensed form. A further investigation revealed that the article was prompted by a high-ranking executive of the newspaper publishing company who also happened to regularly donate blood as a part of his civic responsibility. He was aware that the blood bank had encountered a situation (basically marketing in nature) that was threatening the organization's existence. This case shows evidence that the "uncontrollable variables" are at work, posing a real challenge for the metamarketer.

THE METAMIX

The blood bank case also provides an excellent opportunity for an analysis of the metamarketing mix that was presented earlier in this chapter. In this illustration, the product is blood—a taboo subject, made less so by medical science's development of transfusion and storage technology. The price of $25 a pint is charged to the hospitals and other users for testing and processing, not for the blood itself. The distribution is difficult, because there are laws that require blood to be used within a relatively brief period of time. Further, its storage poses special problems. As indicated above, however, blood bank organizations have become very adept at handling the storage and transportation functions. Promotion, for the most part, is directed to donors and potential donors for the purpose of building a good image of the blood bank that will attract volunteers.

The social reluctance about blood-giving makes this a negative situation, presenting several obstacles for the metamarketer to overcome in the marketing area. The blood donation centers, for instance, are made as pleasant as possible, but the donor market previously dictated that the centers be located closest to the donors who wanted pay. These locations were not always in the best neighborhoods. The marketing aspects of relocating the centers poses yet another problem that is not considered here.

In other metamarketing situations, the need may be to maintain a strong organizational image without generating too much demand in one market. An organization offering volunteer "big brothers" to work with disadvantaged boys, for instance, needs to recruit volunteers. At the same time, it finds itself in a dilemma. On the one hand, the big brothers organization cannot popularize its services too greatly lest it attract too many boy-clients. On the other hand, it cannot make the need for volunteers seem so severe that the clients are scared away, thinking that no big brothers are available.

OTHER BORROWED ELEMENTS

Several other aspects of commercial marketing are finding their way into metamarketing. For example, not-for-profit organizations are developing accountability systems that permit professional marketing to be practiced. Without internal records, some system of market feedback, and some organized effort to conduct market research, the metamarket organization cannot expect to fully reach its goals.

Beyond this, it is clear that more specific marketing methods are carrying over into the metamarket. Many charity groups, for instance, are learning that the bank credit card may be a useful convenience for potential givers. On the other hand, they have found that the more conservative and most prepared to donate among the target market may object strenuously to this "seductive" sort of charity on credit. The organization then faces a task of calculating whether the volume of gifts added because of the charge card convenience will more than offset the flow of gifts from those who are offended. At the same time, the metamarketer must determine whether the credit-broadened base of donors will offer a gain in community support that can be traded off against the objections. Some organizations, such as churches, have compromised in this situation by offering an installment plan pledge system, including quarterly "bill reminders," in lieu of credit card payments.

The credit card situation described above provides a good illustration of changing environmental conditions. Public attitudes about credit and thrift are changing rapidly, and the organization must determine what point the transition has reached. Certainly to most metamarketing organizations, social factors will be almost as important as economic conditions. The veterans' organization that does not recognize that finding jobs for vets in economic hard times is going to be more difficult than it is in good times is not marketing wisely. Conversely, sound marketing will help overcome such a problem. By recognizing that some intangibles such as community pride, individual ego, altruism, patriotism, and the like may be as important as dollar values, the metamarketer can benefit greatly from the practical adaptation of conventional marketing techniques.

SUMMARY

Much of the sense of corporate responsibility to society has grown, so has awareness of marketing spread to the noncommercial arena. The definition of marketing, in the conventional sense, is more and more being focused on the consumer of the noncommercial organization's product.

With this concept expansion has come a proliferation of marketing ideas, techniques, and applications to the operations of organizations that do not exist strictly for profit. This chapter has identified this translation into the not-for-profit area as metamarketing. As the means of directing and accomplishing desired ends between persons or interests, it has been shown that metamarketing is valid in social as well as economic transactions. Metamarketing is being applied extensively in several areas of social interchange, ranging from politics to religion.

Adapting the definition of an organization as a "purposeful coalescence" seeking to accomplish something through exchange of resources, this chapter has explored the concept of applying conventional marketing to metamarketing. It has been noted, however, that metamarketing covers transactions outside of the buyer-seller relationship, including employment, civic, religious, and charity transactions. That is, metamarketing, in some ways differing from conventional marketing, involves marketing organizations, persons, services, and ideas. Metamarketing, in addition to its larger scope, is faced with problems of accountability and vagueness because it is not involved directly with tangible goods or well-defined services. It also suffers from what might be called the "volunteer" fixation—the mistaken notion that if something is nonprofit, it can not be done professionally.

In this chapter, it was suggested that the extension of conventional marketing concepts to metamarketing hinges on broadening the definition of the term product to include "anything that can be offered to a market for attention, acquisition, or consumption." The politician may be the product in an election campaign; the services of a social welfare organization may be its product, supported by a subproduct consisting of the arts and crafts offered at a benefit sale. As the analysis of a rummage sale shows, however, metamarketing presents some special problems in distinguishing between the organization's product and the means it chooses to raise resources in order to be able to produce.

The metamarketer has at his disposal all the tools, methods, and market resources available to his conventional counterpart, and the metamarketing specialist must define his target market or markets and then formulate his marketing strategy. One difference, however, may lie in the fact that the metamarket organization may have more goals and objectives than the conventional business with its profit-seeking nature. The same information sources (census reports, surveys, telephone samplings, and mailings) are available to the metamarketer to determine his markets. Those markets may be diverse and overlapping, as a discussion of a YMCA operation indicated, ranging from the users of its services to the businessmen on its board of directors.

Macro environmental factors often are more influential in the meta-market situation than in the conventional mode, in part because the metamarket organization may be bent on changing its environment, rather than existing harmoniously in it. The impact of such external factors was outlined forcefully in the case of a blood bank that changed its entire operation because of a government suggestion, and then found itself struggling for survival. The blood bank was used also as a further illustration of the metamarketing mix.

Although the metamarket may involve more intangibles than the conventional market, it faces the same problems and challenges. This chapter proposed the idea that the marketing discipline will continue to grow and expand into areas previously considered not in the realm of marketing. Further, the discussion presented here attests to the idea that modern marketing methods can be used to improve the efficiency of not-for-profit organizations.

QUESTIONS FOR DISCUSSION

1. This chapter has as an undercurrent the fact that many business organizations "build in" time for their executives to participate in what we have defined as *metamarketing* activities. Is this a part of the expanding concept of corporate social responsibility, or is it a throwback to earlier proprietary ways of doing business?

2. List as many metamarket organizations as you can. Briefly define their products.

3. Distinguish between the profit motive of a commercial organization and the goals of a not-for-profit organization.

4. Discuss the ethics of applying hard-sell techniques to a "moral" metamarket organization such as a religious denomination.

5. Metamarketing involves dealing in intangibles such as pity, community pride, and individual ego—all elements of the psychographics of a market. How would the metamarketer explain these factors to a cost accountant?

6. In the trends toward consumerism and a clean environment, business often has "done something" when faced with a government "or else" challenge. Apply this to metamarketing.

7. Discuss how someone responsible for the marketing function in a small metamarket organization could meet market research needs on a low budget.

8. What would you advise the management of the blood bank in the case cited to do about the bank's predicament?

NOTES

[1]Philip Kotler, *Marketing Management* (2nd ed.; Englewood Cliffs, New Jersey: Prentice-Hall, Inc., 1972), p. 868.

[2]See Eugene J. Kelley, "Ethics and Science in Marketing," in George Schwartz, ed., *Science in Marketing* (New York: John Wiley & Sons, Inc., 1965); Robert Bartels, *Marketing Theory and Metatheory* (Homewood, Illinois: Richard D. Irwin, Inc., 1970).

[3]Philip Kotler, *Marketing for Non-Profit Organizations* (Englewood Cliffs, New Jersey: Prentice-Hall, Inc., 1975), p. x.

[4]Theodore White, *The Making of the President 1960* (New York: Atheneum House, Inc., 1961).

[5]Kotler, *Marketing for Non-Profit Organizations,* p. 5.

[6]*Ibid.,* pp. 24–25.

[7]*Ibid.,* p. 21. [Table adapted from Peter M. Blau and Richard W. Scott, *Formal Organizations* (San Francisco: Chandler Publishing Company, 1962), pp. 45–58.]

[8]*Ibid.,* p. 283.

[9]*Ibid.,* p. 164.

[10]"Valley Blood Bank Needs Trust of Public, Director Says," *The Arizona Republic* (June 17, 1975), p. B-1.

SUGGESTED READINGS

Aldag, Ramon J. and Donald W. Jackson, Jr., "A Managerial Framework for Social Decision Making," *MSU Business Topics* (Spring, 1975), pp. 33–40.

Goodman, Stanley J., "Raising the Fallen Image of Business," *Marketing Management Perspectives and Applications* (Homewood, Illinois: Richard D. Irwin, Inc., 1976), pp. 50–59.

Kotler, Philip and Gerald Zaltman, "Social Marketing: An Approach to Planned Social Change," *Journal of Marketing* (July, 1971), pp. 3–12.

Lazer, William, "Marketing's Changing Social Relationships" in Howard A. Thompson, *The Great Writings in Marketing* (Plymouth, Michigan: The Commerce Press, 1976), pp. 564–576.

Parket, Robert and Henry Eilbirt, "Social Responsibility: The Underlying Factors," *Business Horizons* (August, 1975), pp. 5–10.

Patterson, James M., "What Are the Social and Ethical Responsibilities of Marketing Executives?" *Journal of Marketing* (July, 1966), pp. 12–15.

Steade, Richard D., *Business and Society in Transition: Issues and Concepts* (San Francisco: Canfield Press, 1975).

Steiner, George A., "Institutionalizing Corporate Social Decisions," *Business Horizons* (December, 1975), pp. 12–18.

Toward a New Environmental Ethic, a publication of the Environmental Protection Agency (Washington, D.C.: U.S. Government Printing Office, 1971).

Wyman, G. H., "Role of Industry in Social Change," *Advanced Management Journal* (April, 1968), pp. 70–74.

20
MARKETING AND
THE FUTURE

MARKETING AND THE FUTURE

In the opening paragraph of this book, a quotation from Alvin Toffler's *Future Shock* was used to dramatize the scope and importance of change on the field of marketing. This theme then became the focal point for ensuing chapters as the marketing environments were examined as the basis for an analysis of the problems and opportunities that exist for marketers. Since change is virtually synonymous with tomorrow in today's dynamic world, it is appropriate to devote this concluding chapter to the future and what it is likely to hold for the field of marketing. While an accurate prediction of the future is an overwhelming, if not impossible, task, a marketing futurist's *look at tomorrow* should concentrate on the realities of a postindustrial society and its impact on marketing practice.

THE EMERGING POSTINDUSTRIAL SOCIETY

For most experts in the field of economic development, the postindustrial society is more abstract than concrete. Yet, there are indications that pockets of postindustrial society now exist in parts of the United States, Sweden, and other Scandinavian countries. Characterized by a deemphasis on economic growth, an increase in leisure time, and an interest in the dignity of the individual, this form of society is the logical extension of industrial society. Although it is not now predominant in the United States, the emergence of postindustrial society in this country is suggested in the following discussion of some of the changes that are expected to occur over the last quarter of the twentieth century.

SHIFTING POPULATION AND INCOME PATTERNS

As indicated in Chapter 9, overall population growth will continue to level off in the United States. At present, the Census Bureau is forecasting an addition of 50 million Americans by the year 2000. This means that the U.S. population will increase from 214 million in 1975 to a total of 264 million over a twenty-five-year period. This represents an expected gain of 24 percent as compared to the 40 percent growth that occurred between 1950 and 1975. More importantly, however, there will be a dramatic aging of the American population. The number of children, teenagers, and young adults under 34 will increase by less than 10 percent. The younger middle-aged segment between 35 and 49 will expand by 76 percent, and the older middle-aged group in the 50 to 64 age category will grow by 23 percent. People 65 and over will increase by 30 percent. Thus, over 80 percent of all population growth in the last quarter of this century will occur among people 35 and older. A complete breakdown of U. S. Census Bureau projections of population is presented in Table 20.1.

With respect to regional distribution, there will be a shift in popula-

TABLE 20.1.
POPULATION PROJECTIONS BY
AGE GROUP, 1975–2000

Age Group	Population (thousands)		Percent Increase
	1975	2000	
Children and Teenagers	74,839	80,743	7.9
Young Adults, 20–34	50,169	54,925	9.5
Younger Middle-Aged, 35–49	34,655	60,855	75.6
Older Middle-Aged, 50–64	31,746	39,065	23.0
People 65 and Over	22,262	28,842	29.6

SOURCE: Adapted from U.S. Census Bureau data.

TABLE 20.2.
REGIONAL CHANGES IN
POPULATION, 1975–2000

Region	Population (thousands)		Percent Increase
	1975	2000	
New England	12,210	14,700	20.4
Mid-Atlantic	37,305	43,020	15.3
East North Central	40,995	48,270	17.7
West North Central	16,750	18,820	12.4
South Atlantic	33,760	47,320	40.2
East South Central	13,510	16,900	25.1
West South Central	20,860	26,050	24.9
Mountain	9,660	13,220	36.9
Pacific	28,100	35,600	26.7

SOURCE: Adapted from U.S. Census Bureau data.

tion from the Midwest and Northeast to the South and the West. As shown in Table 20.2, the slowest growth will occur in the West North Central region, and the South Atlantic sector will experience the largest increase in population.

In terms of income, Americans can expect a rise in median family income from $14,500 to approximately $25,000 in 1975 dollars during the last quarter of this century. Assuming an inflation rate of 5 percent a year, the average family will have a gross income of $85,000 in the year 2000. Based on recent trends, it is likely that this income level will increase the huge middle class that now contains approximately half of the population. In 1974, for example, over 52.0 percent of American families were earning between $10,000 and $25,000 a year. Furthermore, only 11.6 percent of Americans were living in poverty in 1974 as compared to 22.4 percent in 1959.

The middle class, of course, sets the tone for household buying with an estimated 75.0 percent of consumer purchases. Although the middle income ranks have been dominated by white-collar workers, it is significant to note that blue-collar families have been rapidly moving into the middle class. The result is a category of wage earners in the middle income group that now includes everyone from plumbers, mechanics, and truck drivers to engineers and professional managers. All of this has served to produce a new set of values and attitudes for a sizable portion of the American market.

CHANGING VALUES
AND ATTITUDES

According to most experts, the start of a long term change in middle class values and attitudes is now occurring. From the myriad of life-styles, age groups, and educational and professional backgrounds that make up the middle class, there will emerge a new ethic to replace or supplement traditional values. In the past, for example, growth meant progress and was synonymous with goodness. Today, growth means waste, congestion, and pollution of the environment. In the future, people will be more sensitive to their surroundings, and they will be more skeptical, involved, and inclined to contribute to finding solutions to societal ills.

One significant evidence of change in values and attitudes is America's movement away from the Protestant work ethic. Traditionally, Americans have been ambitious, hardworking, and conscientious. The trend today is away from these ideals and toward pleasure, as evidenced by the desire for immediate gratification, more sexual freedom, the declining interest in religion, and less worry about the future. As advances in technology continue to improve the quality of life, it is likely that the ideals of the Protestant ethic will play a smaller and smaller role in shaping the values and attitudes of Americans.

INCREASING
CONSUMER
DOMINANCE

The changes in values and attitudes in American society will also produce a new variety of consumers. According to today's marketing experts, tomorrow's consumer will be more enlightened, sophisticated, articulate, creative, impatient, suspicious, casual, and better educated. It is therefore expected that the consumer will revolutionize the traditional approaches of marketers throughout the remainder of the twentieth century as consumers exercise an increasing dominance over the goods and services that are produced. Concern for the environment, fair value, and quality will eradicate the planned obsolescence, product frills, and inefficiency in design that have existed for the past two or three decades. These will have to be replaced with reasonable and acceptable prices, good durability, and high quality.

A profile of tomorrow's consumer suggests a number of significant characteristics. Above all, he will demand a more *active* role in deciding the nature and quality of the goods and services he buys. His tastes will be *simpler* as he returns to more basic, natural, and functional products. He is likely to be more *creative* in home life, work, and recreation as he actively engages in crafts, home improvements, sewing, baking, and home canning. Tomorrow's consumer will be better *educated* with an estimated 40 cents of every dollar being spent by families with the head of the household having at least some college training. He will also project an element of *suspicion* as he exhibits distrust and skepticism toward government and industry in his complaints about faulty products and misleading advertising. He will be *casual* in dress, home care, and entertaining, and he will be *impatient* in his search for instant gratification as he demands product and service availability throughout the day and evening. Finally, tomorrow's consumer will be highly *conscious of the environment,* and ecological considerations will play an important role in his purchase decisions.

MOVEMENT TOWARD EQUALITY

Beyond population and income shifts and changes in values and attitudes, the emergence of postindustrial society in the United States is bringing forth an equality movement unparalleled in the history of mankind. As a result, Americans are experiencing an equalization program that is reshaping institutions, reordering industry and education, and affecting courts, athletics, prisons, mental institutions, and even the military. For many, the expected results are consistent and compatible with the American dream. Others fear that the pursuit for equality will lead to a nightmare of bureaucratic rule and national insolvency. One concerned government official, for example, has projected that over half of the country's gross national product will be spent on domestic social programs in the year 2000 if expenditures over the past two decades continue at the same pace.

In terms of existing programs, the equalization movement has provided for integration of the races, equality for women and racial minorities, welfare to the poor, medicare for the aged and disabled, and special education for the handicapped and disadvantaged. Future programs now being implemented or proposed provide for equal and fair treatment for homosexuals in government employment, equal opportunity for women in competitive athletics, a government-subsidized health insurance program for everyone, a guaranteed minimum income to all families below the poverty level, and wage subsidies that would bring the minimum wage earner up to the average hourly wage.

The ultimate success of the equality movement in both quantitative and qualitative terms will not be known for a number of years. Based on current trends, however, it is clear that current and future equalization programs will be costly to the American taxpayer. In effect, government will continue to use the tax system to shift income from middle and upper income classes to the poor. Referred to as transfer payments, this form of equalization is simply the transfer of income from one group to another through the tax system in the form of social security benefits, unemployment compensation, veterans benefits, medicare, and public assistance. In 1945, these payments amounted to $5.7 billion and represented 3 cents of every dollar of personal income. By 1975, transfer payments had risen to over $175 billion and accounted for $1 out of every $7 of personal income. How long this trend will continue into the future is uncertain, but it is safe to assume that government will remain a formidable force in the equality movement as American society approaches the year 2000.

RECURRING SHORTAGES

Whereas the pursuit of equality will remain a key government issue for most of the remainder of this century, many economists, business-men, and government officials express more concern over the possibility of a long-term trend of recurring shortages. The fear, of course, is that there will be a repeat of the epidemic that struck the economy in late 1972 and 1973. At that time, there were significant shortages in basic commodities such as cotton, lumber, steel, oil, paper, cement, and plastics. Within a matter of months, tight supplies developed in a wide number of manufactured goods as raw materials became un-available. Some economists attributed the problem to economic ex-pansion and population growth that finally pressed exploitable resources to the limit, but others viewed the situation as only a tempo-rary set of circumstances that are unlikely to be repeated on a regular basis.

Whether shortages will recur in the future is a speculative question, but there is now evidence that American industry is intensifying its search for substitutions that can replace commodities that are high priced and in short supply. If this trend continues, it is likely that industry will be devoting more attention to replacement and synthet-ics research in an effort to lower the costs of raw materials and ensure a steady source of supply.

EXPANDING TECHNOLOGY

From the above discussion, it should be obvious that technology must continue to expand in the future in order to meet the needs of postin-dustrial society. To date, the gloomy forecasts of those who predicted the end of civilization due to overpopulation and resource scarcity have not materialized as the direct result of new technology. Pessi-mism is unnecessary during the remainder of this century as scientific and engineering knowledge focus on the problems that will confront society. Even the conservative experts agree that American technol-ogy will add new dimensions to the well-being of mankind in the years ahead.

Based on futuristic projections, it is expected that researchers dur-ing the last quarter of this century will develop new sources of nutri-tion, discover ways to cure and prevent cancer and heart disease, create life in a test tube, make extensive use of robots, provide chemi-cal control of some mental illnesses, successfully generate solar en-ergy, and develop techniques for long-range weather forecasting. Although some of these developments may seem impossible, contem-porary scientists and engineers contend that the tools for generating

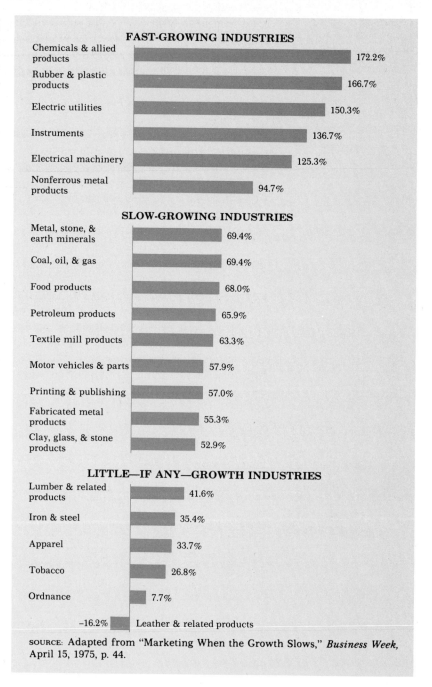

SOURCE: Adapted from "Marketing When the Growth Slows," *Business Week*, April 15, 1975, p. 44.

even more advanced new technologies are already available. The only thing missing at this point in time is the realization of their full potential. The computer, for example, is expected to be a most pervasive tool in shaping the future when the scientific community begins to fully exploit its total capability.

SLOWER GROWTH RATE

Even though expanding technology will serve to meet the pressing needs of postindustrial society, the American economy should experience a slower growth rate over most of the remainder of this century. Between 1950 and 1975, the U. S. gross national product averaged 3.9 percent a year in real growth. According to many economic forecasters, however, the growth rate is expected to be in the 3.2 percent range through the 1980s, and some anticipate that this rate may continue into the twenty-first century. The American economy will be fueled by a number of fast growing industries such as chemicals, rubber, and plastics, but the slow growth industries like foods, motor vehicles, and textiles will act as a drag on the total economy. Figure 20.1 provides a detailed picture of the projected growth patterns for key U. S. industries through 1988.

Economic recessions, of course, can play a significant role in slowing down the growth rate in the United States. Even assuming a relatively stable economy, however, it is likely that resource shortages and a leveling-off in population gains will dramatically impinge on future growth rates. In addition, the changing nature of the American consumer will materially affect the growth levels that are achieved during the latter part of this century. As implied above in this chapter, the conspicuous consumer of the 1950s and 1960s is being rapidly replaced by an ecology-oriented consumer who is driving his automobile for a few extra years, wearing his clothes longer, and avoiding the fads and conveniences that were so popular during the past couple of decades.

MARKETING IN POSTINDUSTRIAL SOCIETY

From the above discussion of some of the changes that are likely to take place in American society during the last quarter of this century, it should be apparent that there will be a need for significant changes in the field of marketing. As suggested throughout this chapter, tomorrow's world will be a different world. Accordingly, the marketing system that served the needs of a materialistic, acquisitive society will require adjustments and even some restructuring in order to satisfy the requirements of postindustrial society. This section, therefore, is devoted to a brief analysis of several key areas that relate to the practice of marketing in the future.

CUSTOMER ORIENTED MARKETING

The ideals and principles of the marketing philosophy of management have permeated the marketing literature for the past couple of decades, but the contemporary wave of consumerism suggests that some marketing practioners gave only lip service to the importance of a customer orientation. Furthermore, the high product failure rate of the 1960s and early 1970s is now a grim reminder that too many new product decisions were made without adequate consideration of the customer and his needs. As the new type of consumer moves into the marketplace of the future, a customer focus will be a mandatory pre-requisite to success in marketing. Tomorrow's enlightened consumer will play a dominant role in shaping marketing practice throughout the remainder of this century, and his needs will be satisfied by enlightened marketers. Some examples of responsive action now being taken to meet the challenges of the future are presented below.

Retailing: Prior to World War II, Sears, Roebuck and Company built a strong reputation by offering good value merchandise at competitive prices. In an effort to take advantage of Americans' growing affluence following the War, however, Sears moved aggressively to get their customers to trade-up to fancier, higher priced merchandise. In so doing, Sears abandoned the market base on which it built its business. The results proved to be quite disappointing. In 1964, for example, Sears enjoyed 56.0 percent of the total sales generated by the big four retailers in the United States (Sears, J. C. Penney Co., S. S. Kresge Co., and Montgomery Ward and Co.). By 1971, that figure had declined to 47.0 percent with most of the Sears loss going to Kresge's highly successful K-Mart Discount Stores. In response to a continuing position loss, Sears reevaluated its trade-up emphasis in 1975 and began a partial return to its original pattern of underselling the competition. While the company will not go back to its bargain-basement days, alterations in a thirty-year trade-up strategy indicate a keener awareness of the changing consumer market.

Automobiles: The automobile industry provides another dramatic illustration of response to consumer demands. When small automobiles accounted for over 50.0 percent of all new cars sold in the United States during the first half of 1975, Detroit finally conceded that "the little cars are here to stay." Most industry experts, in fact, were predicting that the compact of 1975 would be the standard-sized automobile of tomorrow. Without question, of course, Detroit's move to smaller car production was prompted by consumer resistance to high priced, large automobiles and a desire for better fuel economy to offset rising gasoline prices. In an effort to meet the needs of tomorrow's car buyer, it is now apparent that the U.S. automobile industry will be committed to smaller, lighter products in the years ahead.

Housing: The home building industry provides yet another example of the trend toward responsive marketing action. Many builders around the country are now offering smaller houses and variations of the row house. These homes are being built to attract the large number of Americans who cannot afford to buy the average 1,650-plus square-foot ranch house that dominated the market throughout the 1960s. Some builders, in fact, are predicting that the house of tomorrow may turn out to be the house of yesterday. They do not see a return to the 1,000 square-foot cracker box of the 1950s, but they do envision more functional, less luxurious housing. Living and dining rooms, for example, are being combined into an activity room, and the traditional garage and carport are being eliminated entirely. The result is that a number of key builders are moving out of the $50,000 price range into the $30,000 to $35,000 range.

The above examples illustrate the importance of a customer focus, and they also serve to show why conventional marketing strategies must adjust to meet the needs and wants of the new variety of consumer. As indicated in the early part of this chapter, traditional values and attitudes are being replaced by new norms of behavior and an entirely different set of expectations. Accordingly, tomorrow's customer focus will require a complete reexamination of many of the classical marketing truisms that have dominated the philosophy of marketing for the past several decades.

CONSERVATION MARKETING

The subject of demand creation presents one important example of the need to reexamine classical marketing thinking. Historically, marketing has been concerned with the task of expanding demand by selling more and more of an abundant supply of goods and services. In recognition of contemporary supply problems, however, many resource economists are now suggesting that marketing must play a more dominant role in the conservation of resources. This is certainly a broadened view of marketing, for it proposes the notion that marketers must become involved in *demand containment,* which means to restrain, or to check. Marketing's role in demand containment, therefore, would be the promotion of intelligent product use, rather than the stimulation of waste and overconsumption. Further, there would be an emphasis on customer satisfaction through the consumption of fewer products in place of gratification from a greater number of products.

To the businessman educated under the assumptions of abundance, the above proposal may raise some questions regarding long-term firm survival. There are indications, however, that demand containment may be the trend of the future. In product management, for example, scores of companies are now deleting and consolidating their product lines in an effort to provide more basic, frill-free, high quality product offerings. In addition, cost pressures are forcing marketing economies that are resulting in fewer customer options, and there is a return to the basics in a wide number of key consumer products industries. For a growing segment of the American population, this form of *functionalism* is a refreshing move that is consistent and compatible with the concerns now being expressed over the depletion of the world's resources.

From a marketing standpoint, this trend may not be as disastrous as it first appears. In the future, business will derive its profits by selling smaller quantities of higher priced products. Prices can be expected to rise due to lower supply and greater costs incurred in research and development devoted to making products perform more efficiently and effectively. The net result should be buildings that are built better and last longer, automobiles that go further on less gas and require fewer maintenance stops, and appliances that can be repaired periodically at reasonable costs instead of having to be replaced due to planned obsolescence.

If this trend does materialize, marketing will shift from a *demand expansion* function to a *demand containment* function. As companies devote more attention to increasing the efficiency of products, marketing will have to assume the task of increasing the efficiency of consumption. Instead of promoting the use of more products, marketing will promote the idea that greater satisfaction can be derived in the consumption of fewer products. The marketing job of the future, therefore, will involve selling the product, educating the consumer in its proper use, justifying its higher cost, and convincing the consumer that maintenance and repairs are reasonable expenditures.

As a contemporary illustration of conservation marketing, consider the recent developments in the tire, battery, and accessory (TBA) field. Top quality automobile tires once lasted for only 15,000 to 20,000 miles. Today, top of the line offerings are realistically guaranteed for 40,000 miles and can be expected to exceed this limit. Although prices are higher, the consumer is now being educated in proper tire use and the viable efficiency of high performance tires. Similar technologies have been applied in the production and marketing of automobile batteries. From an expected life of two or three years, this product is now engineered to last "the life of the car," and manufacturers are providing guarantees up to five years and longer. Even with higher prices, the consumer is realizing greater value and fewer problems. The net result in both of the above examples is increased consumer satisfaction and better utilization of society's scarce resources.

SOCIETAL MARKETING In addition to the issue of resource conservation, marketing in the future will become increasingly concerned with the pollution of our air, water, and land. As a result, a whole new field of business ecology will evolve to provide marketers with an opportunity to assist in the development of new techniques for preserving and improving the environment. Marketers have traditionally concentrated on consumer wants and company profits; now societal welfare will become an overriding consideration in the future. Automobiles that pollute the air, detergents that pollute the water, and packages that pollute the soil will not go unchallenged, and tomorrow's marketers will have to carefully weigh the societal ramifications of their product decisions and offer, where possible, those products that are the most societally desirable. The question of should it be sold may then become more important than the question can it be sold.

Figure 20.2 provides a comparison between tradition directed marketing priorities and society directed marketing priorities. In the traditional view, marketing is user oriented, placing individual and corporate needs above those of society and the environment. When conflicts developed, the former were satisfied first, even at the expense of the latter. In the societal view of marketing, the needs of society and the environment have the highest priority, and the needs of the individual and the corporation are relegated to a lower position. Under

FIGURE 20.2.
TRADITION DIRECTED VERSUS
SOCIETY DIRECTED
MARKETING PRIORITIES

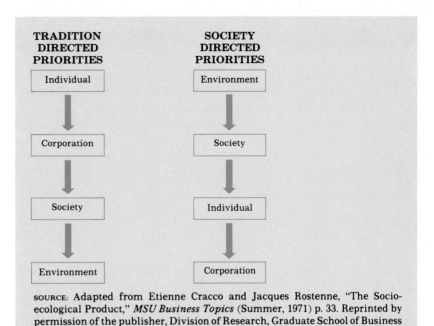

TRADITION DIRECTED PRIORITIES

Individual

Corporation

Society

Environment

SOCIETY DIRECTED PRIORITIES

Environment

Society

Individual

Corporation

SOURCE: Adapted from Etienne Cracco and Jacques Rostenne, "The Socio-ecological Product," *MSU Business Topics* (Summer, 1971) p. 33. Reprinted by permission of the publisher, Division of Research, Graduate School of Business Administration, Michigan State University.

this change, the user of a product will be able to buy that product only if society approves its positive benefits.

As society directs the marketing system of the future, however, the costs of a cleaner and safer environment will be high. The 1975 automobile, for example, carried approximately $500.00 worth of federally mandated equipment in the form of new bumpers, emission controls, and other safety gear. Estimated costs of the controversial air bag could add another $500.00. In 1974 alone, conservative estimates indicated that American industry spent $7.4 billion on air and water pollution controls and an additional $3 billion on occupational safety equipment. According to the Environmental Protection Agency, the cumulative pollution control expenditures by private industry during the 1973–1982 period will reach $43 billion. Industries such as paper, steel, nonferrous metals, petroleum, and chemicals will carry a major portion of the burden with much of the cost being passed on to the consumer in the form of higher prices. The end result is a tradeoff between costs and benefits. The real question, of course, is how far the nation will be willing to go in improving the quality of life.

The nation's developing mass-transit system provides one contemporary example of the debate over costs versus benefits. In an effort to get people out of their automobiles and into commuter vehicles, federal, state, and local governments are encouraging the building of new transportation systems and the upgrading of old ones. The question of who pays the costs, of course, will be the critical issue in the future. Although taxpayers are now paying out billions of dollars in the form of federal, state, and local government subsidies, most experts contend that the taxpayer's bill will grow larger. Mass transit is simply not expected to pay its own way, and it is generally conceded that subsidies will be required to supplement the fares paid by those who ride the nation's buses, subways, and commuter trains. The issue here, of course, is whether the benefits derived from resource conservation and cleaner air are worth the public costs in the form of higher taxes.

A LOOK AT MARKETING TOMORROW

How mass transit and other developments will affect life during the last quarter of the twentieth century is a matter for conjecture, but the mystery of tomorrow is now beginning to unfold through the happenings of today. Current trends, therefore, can be used to provide a fairly accurate "crystal ball" view of what marketing will be like in the more immediate future. In an effort to provide some idea of what marketers can look forward to in the years just ahead, this final section is devoted to a brief review of the more significant trends that are likely to continue throughout the decade of the 1970s and into the 1980s. In general, current signs point to a concentration on market share, better product positioning, more product functionalism, increased product-line simplification, a search for new markets, and an emphasis on distribution.

CONCENTRATION ON MARKET SHARE

Given the economic conditions of slower growth that are expected to prevail over the next decade or two, marketers will be concentrating on holding market share. Tomorrow's marketing success will be measured by sales performance relative to competitors, and intensive efforts will be made to achieve maximum share of the smaller markets that will exist for the low-growth industries. With limited growth, of course, significant gains by one company have to come from the market shares of other companies in the absence of expansion in the total market. Under the circumstances, it is likely that competitive rivalry in the near future will take the form of a battle for share-of-the-market.

The petroleum industry provides an excellent example of what can be expected. Brand loyalty has virtually disappeared with the advent of higher gasoline prices, and the consumer is now searching for the best value for his money. In addition, less driving and the rising costs of building and maintaining facilities has resulted in a dramatic decrease in the number of service stations. The number declined from 220,000 in the late 1960s to approximately 200,000 in 1974. Forecasts indicate that there will be only 125,000 stations in operation by 1980. In an effort to maintain market share, the major oil companies are now attempting to hold their customers by providing more value and service through retailing sidelines such as drive-in banking, dry cleaning services, film processing, bike repairing, garden shops, boating supplies, and even drug outlets.

BETTER PRODUCT POSITIONING

The lack of an expanding market will also place a great deal of emphasis on better product positioning. New products could generally find some place in the growing markets of the past; but it will become increasingly difficult for "look alike" products to make it in the future. Many experts in the field of marketing, therefore, are describing tomorrow as *the positioning era* in which all successful products will occupy a distinct position in the market. Distinctive products will possess certain differentiated attributes or appeals that will enable them to stand out when compared with competitive products.

Soft Drinks: A good example of product positioning can be found in the soft drink field. Coca-Cola enjoys the dominant position in the industry with Pepsi and Royal Crown a distant second and third. Coke's strength is indicated by the fact that its sales increases in prior years have often been more than Royal Crown's total volume. Competing with Coke's strong market position has posed a difficult challenge for both Pepsi and Royal Crown, and neither has been able to displace Coke in the cola soft drink area. Another product, however, has done well by not going "head-on" against the leader. Seven-Up used its "Un-Cola" theme to establish a position as an alternative to a cola drink. This, of course, is a real success story in an industry where two out of every three drinks consumed are colas.

Auto Rentals: Avis provides another example of a company that took an "against" position that proved to be quite successful. For over ten years, Avis attempted to battle Hertz for market position. The company's efforts were generally unsuccessful, and Hertz continued to dominate the market. Finally, Avis changed its entire theme and admitted through its advertising that "Avis is only Number 2, but we try harder." The campaign was a phenomenal success and established Avis firmly in its own market position with the ability to profitably compete with Hertz.

MORE PRODUCT FUNCTIONALISM

In addition to better product positioning, tomorrow's marketers will be offering simpler, more functional products. This trend is already in evidence, and it is expected to intensify in the future. Some of the airlines, for example, are now cutting out everything from meals and free coffee to a number of reservation conveniences in return for fare reductions up to 35 percent. Automobile manufacturers are beginning to do the same thing by "stripping down" selected models through the elimination of steel-belted tires, four-speed transmissions, and other product features from the list of standard equipment items. As previously discussed, similar patterns are developing in the building industry where there appears to be a trend back to basic, no-frills housing.

Although the move toward more functional products is a response to rising costs and an effort to hold down prices, there is strong evidence to support the view that marketers are also responding to a "new functionalism" in demand. The new breed of consumer, for example, appears to be more interested in product usage than in product ownership. Furthermore, he is highly value oriented, and he takes a dim view of costly and unnecessary features that do not add materially to his satisfaction. All of this is leading many marketing experts to believe that a "leased life style" may be the wave of the future as many items such as recreational equipment, automobiles, appliances, and furniture become popular short and long-term rentals.

Convertibles: America's declining love affair with the convertible automobile provides an excellent illustration of the move to more functional products. From a sales peak of 540,000 units in 1963, convertibles accounted for only a small fraction of 1 percent of Detroit's output in 1976. American Motors dropped the convertible in 1968, and Chrysler followed suit in 1971. Ford continued to produce some models through 1973, but declining sales took Ford out of the business at the end of that year. General Motors offered a soft top automobile in 1976 through its Cadillac division, but announced that convertible production would be phased out at the end of the model year. Today, this once popular vehicle is now almost as extinct as the dinosaur. In retrospect, it may be argued that the convertible *function* ceased to provide a desirable benefit for today's "back to the basics" consumers.

Spare tires: Another example of the new functionalism in product design and use is Detroit's search for a realistic substitute for the spare tire and the gear to repair it that motorists now haul around in their trunks. With the removal of the spare and jack equipment from American automobiles, it is estimated that a decrease of some sixty pounds in weight could save a million gallons of gasoline per day in the United States. With pressure from Detroit, the major tire firms are now working on the problem and have experimented with a number of alternatives with varying degrees of success. Although none of the new developments represent a really satisfactory solution, auto industry experts are hoping for an end to the spare tire in its present form. If a viable solution can be found, the improved function in automobile tires could produce considerable savings for American motorists.

INCREASED PRODUCT-LINE SIMPLIFICATION

As tomorrow's marketers begin to offer more functional products, they will also concentrate their efforts on fewer products in order to maintain profitability. Thus, product lines will be consolidated and marginal items will be eliminated entirely. The end result will produce fewer customer choices and a decline in the annual rate of new product introductions. Overall, however, these moves may prove to be highly desirable. Critics of marketing, for example, contend that the high new product failure rates of the 1960s and early 1970s could have been avoided if companies had used more restraint in the proliferation of their product lines. These critics further point out that far too many new product introductions were only imitations that unnecessarily confused the consumer without providing real benefits. The trend toward product-line simplification should satisfy these complaints and provide a more conservative approach to new product development in the future.

SEARCH FOR NEW MARKETS

With a decline in new products, there will be a more intensive search in the future for new markets for existing products. Referred to as *remarketing* by some marketers, this is a product strategy that is designed to find new applications for old products. When sales cannot be increased through new product development, a strategy of increasing existing product sales through market expansion is a logical and often economical alternative. In an effort to accomplish this task, tomorrow's marketers will be analyzing different market segments, exploring new geographical areas, and evaluating the opportunities in foreign markets.

The Church & Dwight Company presents one of the classical examples of success in remarketing. Founded over 125 years ago, this firm produces Arm & Hammer baking soda and is recognized as the leader in the field. When sales began to level off in 1971 as the result of a decline in home baking, the company started to look around for new markets. At that time, Church & Dwight started promoting their baking soda as a cleansing and deodorizing agent. Today, it is highly valued by the consumer as a bath additive, a kitchen cleaner, and a deodorizer for refrigerators, automobile ashtrays, and kitty litter boxes. Still searching for new applications, the company is now promoting Arm & Hammer for the control of acidity in swimming pools.

EMPHASIS ON DISTRIBUTION

As a further effort to improve profitability, there will also be a renewed interest in cost reductions and improved efficiency. Most marketing experts agree that this will result in an emphasis on distribution. Since the costs of physically moving goods from the factory to the market now account for nearly 20 percent of the nation's gross national product, there is an indication that distribution may be a fruitful area for achieving marketing economies. Those who see this as marketing's most critical problem area are advocating the establishment of better relationships with wholesalers and retailers as a move designed to improve efficiency and lower costs. Others are proposing direct distribution in an effort to increase margins and expand volume through aggressive selling programs.

In the future, the emphasis on distribution will produce a number of significant changes in both the distributive institutions and the manner in which goods are moved. For example, conventional channels of distribution are now being replaced by vertical marketing systems. Thus, instead of goods moving through a network of loosely aligned, relatively autonomous manufacturers, wholesalers, and retailers, they will move through a coordinated and vertically aligned network of establishments that are managed as a system. With the pressure on for more efficiency and a reduction of costs in distribution, there will also be an acceleration in the life cycles of distributive institutions. Accordingly, existing institutions will mature more rapidly and new institutions will be developed to replace those that can no longer serve a useful and efficient function. Such is the case with the convenience markets, which are rapidly replacing the old "mom and pop" stores.

SUMMARY

In this chapter, the future provided the major theme of discussion for a crystal ball view of what life, in general, and marketing, in particular, will be like in the years ahead as American society races toward the twenty-first century. In an effort to present a marketing futurist's look at tomorrow, the chapter concentrated on the emerging postindustrial society, its impact on marketing, and a review of current trends that are likely to affect the practice of marketing throughout the 1970s and into the 1980s.

The emergence of a postindustrial society in America is indicated by a number of expected changes that are likely to occur during the last quarter of the present century. The first section of this chapter focused on these changes with special emphasis on those that will affect the nature and quality of American life in the future. Attention, therefore, was given to shifts in population and income patterns, changes in values and attitudes, the increasing dominance of the consumer in the marketplace, and the equality movement that is reshaping life in American society. The latter part of the section was devoted to the economic considerations of recurring shortages, expansion in technology, and the realities of slower growth rates.

The second major section of this chapter provided a brief analysis of several key areas that relate to the practice of marketing in postindustrial society. Given the changes in society that can be expected during the remainder of this century, it was suggested that marketing will require a greater customer orientation, a new philosophy that will emphasize conservation of resources, and a societally directed approach that places the needs of the environment and society above those of the individual and the corporation.

In an effort to provide some idea of what marketers can look forward to in the years just ahead, the final section of this chapter was devoted to a brief review of the trends in marketing practices that are likely to evolve in the more immediate future. From this analysis, it was suggested that tomorrow's marketers will be concentrating on market share and better product positioning in a slower growing economy. Further, they will offer more basic, functional products, and they will greatly simplify their product lines through the deletion of marginal items and a deemphasis on new product development. Finally, tomorrow's marketers will look for profitability in new markets and improved efficiency in distribution.

QUESTIONS FOR DISCUSSION

1. Is postindustrial society now a reality in the United States? List and explain at least five general trends that suggest the emergence of postindustrial society in America.

2. What impact will a decline in the population growth rate have on the field of marketing? Is it possible that the decline could produce a zero growth rate by the year 2000?

3. Compare and contrast contemporary American values and attitudes with those that influenced the behavior of Americans throughout the history of this country. Explain why values and attitudes are changing in American society.

4. Through an analysis of contemporary society, explain why the consumer is assuming a more dominant role in the marketplace. How will this dominance influence marketing decision making in the future?

5. Trace the equality movement in the United States and evaluate the results that have been achieved in line with the goals that have been established. Do you feel that these goals are acceptable to society in general?

6. What impact will recurring shortages and slower growth rates in the economy have on the field of marketing in the future? Are these trends only temporary, or are they likely to continue over a long period of time? Why?

7. Explain how an expanding technology can be used to offset the projected economic problems of the future. In what ways can technology help in the solution of tomorrow's social problems?

8. What is conservation marketing? Will this approach actually work in a profit oriented economy and is it a practical solution to a better utilization of our scarce resources?

9. What is societal marketing? What changes in the thinking of marketers will be required in order to fully implement a program of societal marketing?

10. During the next ten years, what major changes can you anticipate in the field of marketing? How will these changes directly influence the practice of marketing?

SUGGESTED READINGS

Cravens, David W., "Marketing Management in an Era of Shortages," *Business Horizons* (February, 1974), pp. 79–85.

Crawford, C. Merle, *The Future Environment for Marketing* (Ann Arbor, Michigan: University of Michigan Press, 1969).

Cullwick, David, "Positioning Demarketing Strategy," *Journal of Marketing* (April, 1975), pp. 51–57.

"Marketing When the Growth Slows," *Business Week* (April 14, 1975), pp. 44–50.

Mee, John F., "Profiles of the Future: Speculation about Human Organization in the 21st Century," *Business Horizons* (February, 1971), pp. 5–16.

Nanus, Burt, "The Future Oriented Corporation," *Business Horizons* (February, 1975), pp. 5–12.

Rothe, James T. and Lissa Benson, "Intelligent Consumption: An Attractive Alternative to the Marketing Concept," *MSU Business Topics* (Winter, 1974), pp. 29–34.

Shipchandler, Zoher E., "Inflation and Life Styles: The Marketing Impact," *Business Horizons* (February, 1976), pp. 90–96.

Shuptrine, F. Kelly and Frank A. Osmanski, "Marketing's Changing Role: Expanding or Contracting," *Journal of Marketing* (April, 1975), pp. 58–66.

Toffler, Alvin, *Future Shock* (New York: Random House, Inc., 1970).

GLOSSARY OF SELECTED TERMS

Acculturation is the process of learning a new or second culture.

Advertising is the impersonal communication of ideas, goods, or services, to a mass audience by an identified paying sponsor.

Advertising Agencies are specialized firms that assist companies in the creative and technical aspects of advertising, including idea creation, copy and art work, media selection, and production.

Advertising Media are organizations providing facilities for the dissemination of advertising messages.

Agents and Brokers are middlemen whose role in marketing is to negotiate sales or purchases for the clients they represent. They are compensated in the form of commissions based on the dollar value of sales or purchases. In performing their function, they do not take title to the goods they buy and sell.

Aggregate Concentration is the percent of value added by manufacturers for the largest 50, 100, 150, and 200 firms. Another measure used is the percent of all manufacturing assets accounted for by the largest firms, although value added is preferred.

Allocation Process refers to the manner in which an economy's scarce resources are allocated to meet society's needs through the four stages of extraction and agriculture, fabrication and manufacturing, distribution, and consumption.

Allocative Efficiency is a macro concept which refers to the allocation of resources among industries in an economy.

Anthropology is the study of whole societies, or major segments of a society, such as culture, subculture, and symbolism.

Assemblers are marketing institutions which operate primarily in agricultural growing areas or in port areas where fishing fleets bring in their catches. They purchase relatively small quantities from numerous producers and concentrate large quantities for economical shipments to major market centers.

Atmospherics is a term that is used to identify other environmental factors.

Balance of Payments is the algebraic sum of all payments made by one nation to all other nations in the world and the payments made to that nation by all other nations.

Balance of Trade is part of the balance of payments. It shows the net figure for the value of all the goods imported and exported by one nation.

Barriers to Entry are those elements that determine the ease with which firms are able to enter an existing industry.

Barter is a term used to describe an exchange of goods for goods. This type of exchange exists in the absence of a money economy wherein goods are exchanged for money.

BBB is an abbreviation for Better Business Bureaus. These are local, business-supported organizations that provide consumers with information about firms. The local bureaus are loosely affiliated with a national bureau.

Behaviorists are those economists that believe market conduct and market structure are the primary determinants of market performance.

Bonded Warehouses are a special type of private warehouse used to store products on which a federal tax must be paid before they can be sold.

Brand is a word, mark, symbol, design, term, or a combination of these, both visual and oral, used for the purpose of identification of some product or service.

Breach of Contract refers to the breaking of an agreement or promise by one party to it. Herein, it is applied to mean the responsibility of the seller in insuring that the product is capable of doing what was communicated to the consumer.

Breakeven Analysis looks at cost and its effect on profit at different levels of output.

Breakeven Point is that volume of sales (in dollars or units) where revenues equal cost. At a breakeven point there is no profit and no loss.

Business Ethics can be defined as those principles, practices, and philosophies that are concerned with moral judgment and good conduct as they are applicable to business situations.

CBR is an abbreviation for crude birth rate. It is the actual number of new births expressed as a rate per 1,000 population.

CDR is an abbreviation for crude death rate. It is the actual number of deaths expressed as a rate per 1,000 population.

Cease and Desist refers to orders given by the Federal Trade Commission to firms to stop action alleged to be illegal.

Channel of Distribution is the structure of intra-company organization units and extra-company agents and dealers, wholesale and retail, through which a commodity, product, or service is marketed.

Closed Systems are self contained and their operations are not affected by their external environments.

Command System is a term used to identify the manner in which resources are allocated through the centralized decisions of government. This form of allocation is common in Communist countries.

Common Law represents the body of unwritten law based on custom, usage, and decisions of the court.

Common Markets attempt to reduce tariffs and other barriers to trade between member nations to zero while raising a common tariff barrier to all nonmember nations. They also attempt to effect common economic and political policies.

Commonweal Organizations exist in every level of government where services are exchanged for taxes and cooperation.

Comparative Advantage arises because of different natural factor endowments. Thus, Ecuador's climate permits that country to produce bananas at a lower cost than another country such as Norway.

Competitive Environment is a term used to identify those forces in the macro environment that relate to the nature, form, and conditions of rivalry in the marketplace.

Concentration Ratio is the share of an industry's shipments accounted for by an identified number of the largest firms.

Conglomerate Merger is a merger among firms which operate in separate and distinct markets.

Conservation Marketing is a term used to define a role for marketing in the conservation of resources. When engaged in this role, marketers shift from demand expansion to demand containment.

Consumer Education represents efforts to improve the sophistication of the buyer. Many experts believe that education is the only real solution to the problems presented by consumerism.

Consumer Federation of America represents a group of organizations, including state and local bodies, labor unions, and the National Consumers League, interested in consumer affairs.

Consumer Goods are those goods purchased by household consumers for final consumption and are not intended for resale or further use in the production of other products. They are classified as convenience, shopping, or specialty goods.

Consumer Product Safety Commission is a five-person board appointed to administer the 1972 Consumer Product Safety Act. The board has the power to force a firm to recall, repair, or replace any product it deems hazardous to a consumer.

Consumerism is a force within the macro environment designed to aid and protect the consumer by exerting moral, economic, and political-legal pressures on business.

Consumers Union is a nonprofit organization which distributes product information, primarily through its publication, *Consumer Reports.*

Control Mechanisms are used to insure direction and coordination of system activities.

Convenience Stores are those stores for which the consumer, before a need for some product arises, possesses a preference map that indicates a willingness to buy from the most accessible store.

Copy Strategy is an advertising decision involving the content, style, and design of an advertising message.

Cost Reduction Programs identify efforts by marketers to increase marketing productivity.

Cross Cultural Analysis is the assessment of the similarities and differences in the customs, values, and behavior among two or more societies.

Culture is the broad aggregate of values, norms, and customs that are imparted to individuals in a given society.

Demand Curves are graphical representations of demand schedules.

Demand Economies are those that enable a firm, because of its size, to increase demand for its products.

Demand Schedules show the quantity of a good that consumers will buy at given prices.

Derived Demand is the demand for goods that is derived from, or depends upon, the demand for final consumer goods.

Differentiated Oligopolies are industries that sell products that may differ in real or imaginary qualities. Examples are automobiles and soap.

Diffusion Theory is concerned with the spreading of an innovation throughout society. The diffusion process identifies the manner in which new products are adopted by the market.

Discretionary Income is the balance of disposable income remaining after spending units have provided for the basic necessities for their standard of living.

Disposable Personal Income is personal income minus taxes to all levels of government.

Distribution Strategy is concerned with getting the product to the customer at the right time and at the right place. Included are the areas of channels of distribution and physical distribution.

Domestic Market Environment is a term used to identify the market as a part of the macro marketing environment. It includes both household consumers and nonhousehold buyers.

Dumping is the practice of selling goods in foreign markets at prices lower than the selling price in the home market.

Ecological Niche is a position within the environment wherein an opportunity for survival exists. For the business system, this is a competitive position in the marketplace.

Ecology, derived from the Greek word *oikos,* which means "place to live," is the study of an organism within its environments.

Economic Environment is a term used to identify those forces in the macro marketing environment that pertain to economic structure, government policies, general economic conditions, and national resources.

Economies of Scale occur when increases in the size or scale of operations result in decreases in the per unit cost of production.

Effectiveness relates to an evaluation of how nearly a set of actions comes to accomplishing a given objective.

Efficiency is a measure of how well inputs are utilized.

Engineering is concerned with the application of knowledge from mathematics and the natural sciences to problems dealing with the economic utilization of the materials and forces of nature.

Enterprise Competition exists between firms selling similar products in an identifiable industry such as General Motors, Ford, and Chrysler. Here the firm can increase its sales by expanding the total demand for the product or by taking sales away from competitors.

Environmental Threat is a challenge created by a disturbance in the environment.

Equilibrium Price is the market clearing price for a good. It is that price at which the quantity of goods demanded by consumers exactly equals the quantity of goods that producers are willing to offer.

Exchange Process involves a buyer and a seller in the relationship that entails the offering of a product or service in exchange for a payment in fair value.

Family is the smallest sociocultural group whose members generally interact regularly on a face-to-face basis.

Family Life Cycle involves the various stages through which a family passes from bachelorhood to solitary survivor.

FTC is an abbreviation for the Federal Trade Commission. This government agency is one of the most important federal agencies in the regulation of business activities. It is especially significant in the area of consumer and business protection.

Feedback Loops are used to return information concerning system outputs for use as additional informational inputs.

Finance is concerned with the value of the assets of the business system and the acquisition and allocation of the financial resources of the system.

Fishy-backing is a term used in the field of transportation to identify the shipment of truck trailers in ships. The benefits of two transportation modes can be obtained by using this innovation.

Form Utility is created through production activities when the physical form of a raw material or fabricated part is changed.

Generic Competition represents a firm's effort to sell a total product based upon its role and importance in satisfying a basic need. Since each consumer has a variety of needs to be met, each firm is basically competing with all other firms.

Government Markets include the federal government and all of its agencies and bureaus, state and county governments, and township and city governments.

Gross Margin is the difference between the delivered net cost to the retailer or wholesaler and the asking price to the firm's customers.

Gross National Product is the sum of the final purchase prices paid for all goods and services produced in the nation in a given year including net exports.

Income Elasticity of Demand describes the relative change in demand for a good resulting from a unit change in income.

Individual Ethics are essentially a set of moral principles that guide thoughts and actions.

Industrial Goods are those goods that are purchased by nonhousehold buyers for nonhousehold use or for use in the production of other products. They are classified as installations, accessory equipment, fabricated parts and materials, raw materials, and industrial supplies.

Innovation is a term used in a technological context to identify all of the actions taken to bring an invention into commercial use.

Institutional Environment is a term used to identify that part of the macro marketing environment that includes all of the retailing, wholesaling, and service institutions engaged in the physical flow of goods and services and the movement of title between producers and final customers.

Institutional Markets include educational institutions, penal institutions, religious institutions, hospitals, and nonprofit and charitable organizations.

Integrated Marketing is a concept that recognizes the need for a coordinated effort by all functional areas in a firm oriented to the marketing philosophy of management.

International Market Environment is a term used to identify the international market as a part of the macro marketing environment. This market is separate and distinct from the domestic market.

Invention is a term used in a technological context to identify the application of scientific principles to the contrivance of a new device or process.

Joint Venture is one technique for entering the international scene. A foreign firm joins with a local firm to manufacture and/or market in the local country.

Laissez-faire expresses a political-economic philosophy of the government of allowing the marketplace to operate relatively free of restrictions and intervention.

Legal Environment is a term used to identify those forces in the macro marketing environment that relate to the laws governing the practice of marketing. These include all federal, state, and local regulations.

Licensing is the sale of a license permitting the use of patents, trademarks, or other technology to a foreign firm.

Low-income Consumers represent about 10 to 15 percent of the U.S. population and experience many special consumer problems.

Macro Marketing is concerned with the creation and delivery of a desired standard of living for society through the effective and efficient distribution of an economy's goods and services under conditions of constraint imposed by the marketing environments.

Macro Marketing Environment is a term used to identify the set of external forces surrounding the business system that represent both threats and opportunities for marketing. These are the institutional, domestic, and international markets, and the sociocultural, economic, legal, competitive, and technological environments.

Macro Marketing System refers to the total network of individuals, organizations, and customer groups that engage in marketing activities in an economic society.

Management Information Systems are used to integrate the pertinent cost data available within a firm into a coordinated package, permitting analysis and comparison of masses of data in a timely and useful manner.

Manufacturers and Processors operate in the macro marketing system to produce finished goods and components for use in further production.

Manufacturer's Sales Branches are separate, but integrated businesses operated by large manufacturers for the sale of their products and services at wholesale.

Market is a term used to identify people and organizations with needs to satisfy, and the ability and willingness to buy.

Market Concentration is the number and size distribution of the firms in an industry. A widely used measure for market concentration is the concentration ratio.

Market Conduct refers to the actual commercial behavior of the firms in an industry. From a marketing perspective, it is the combination of price and nonprice policies used by the seller in the marketplace.

Market Performance refers to the end results of market activity and the criteria by which results are evaluated. The criteria used in evaluating market performance are efficiency, profits, innovation, marketing costs, consumer benefits, and national economy benefits.

Market Segmentation is a product strategy that focuses on the offering of special products that will satisfy the particular requirements of specific market segments.

Market Share is the percentage of a market that is controlled by a firm. A 20 percent share of market means that the firm has captured 20 percent of the actual sales in the market.

Market Structure refers to the broad organizational characteristics of a market. The major characteristics are seller concentration, product differentiation, and barriers to entry.

Market System is a term used to identify the manner in which resources are allocated through the operation of a free market mechanism. This form of allocation is common in capitalistic countries.

Market Targets are selected segments of an overall potential market to which a firm wishes to appeal.

Marketing Control is a managerial activity that is concerned with the continuous evaluation and analysis of marketing plans. It is designed to react to deviations from plans and make corrective adjustments.

Marketing Execution involves the execution of marketing plans. This managerial activity is concerned with getting the right product or service to the right place at the right time at the right price.

Marketing Functions include buying, selling, transportation, storage, standardization and grading, market information, market risk, and market finance.

Marketing Institutions include all of the individuals, groups, or organizations that carry on the work of marketing, both directly and indirectly.

Marketing Intelligence is evaluated information generated through the business firm's marketing intelligence system.

Marketing Mix is a term used to identify the blend of product, price, promotion, and distribution that is developed by marketing management to appeal to selected market targets.

Marketing Opportunity is a challenge to purposeful marketing action that may be met by innovation, improvements in efficiency, the creation of a competitive differential, or carving out a new market niche.

Marketing Philosophy of Management is a term that identifies a philosophy of doing business that embraces four major elements. These are a customer orientation, a defined profit motivation, an integrated marketing effort, and a sense of social responsibility.

Marketing Planning is a managerial activity that is concerned with deciding in the present what to do in the future. It charts the course for a business system and involves the establishment of goals and objectives and the steps necessary to accomplish them.

Marketing Research is a part of the marketing intelligence system that is concerned with the task of gathering, analyzing, and interpreting marketing information from primary and secondary sources.

Marketing Research Agencies are business firms which generate research data for their clients and sell their specialized services for a fee.

Marketing Strategy is a plan of action. It is concerned with the development of a marketing mix that will satisfy the needs of selected market targets.

Materials Management involves the control of materials movement from supplier to the manufacturing firm, control of material inventory levels, and handling of materials during the manufacturing process.

Media Strategy is the choice of channels through which advertising messages flow.

Merchant Wholesalers are marketing intermediaries that purchase their inventories in large quantities and take title to the goods they buy. They normally store and physically handle the goods before reselling them in smaller quantities to retailers, smaller wholesalers, and industrial and business users.

Merger refers to the acquisition by a corporation of another's stock or assets wherein the acquired firm is controlled by the acquiring firm.

Metamarketing is a term used to describe the processes of developing and maintaining exchange relations involving products, services, organizations, persons, places, or causes.

Micro Marketing is concerned with the satisfaction of customer needs and the accomplishment of an organization's marketing objectives through the efficient and effective distribution of that organization's goods and services under conditions of constraint imposed by the marketing environments.

Micro Marketing Environment is a term used to identify the set of internal forces within the business system that influence and are influenced by marketing. These are the other functional areas of the firm such as research and development, engineering, production, and finance.

Micro Marketing System refers to the functional component of the business system that is responsible for the surveillance of market targets, the detection of change in the marketing environments, the establishment of marketing objectives, and the formulation, implementation, and control of marketing strategies.

Monopolistic Competition is a market setting characterized by a significant number of both large and small firms offering similar, but not identical products. Here, individual sellers protect themselves from competitive pressures through product differentiation.

Monopoly is a market setting where one firm produces the entire output of a given product for which there is no close substitute. Entry to the market is blocked and the firm has considerable power over the price it can demand for its product. The majority of monopolies that exist today are regulated by the government.

Mutual Benefit Associations include labor unions, professional and fraternal associations, political parties, religious groups, and others.

NASA is the abbreviation for the National Aeronautics and Space Administration. This Federal Government agency has been instrumental in the development of the by-products of space technology for commercial use.

National Income is GNP minus depreciation and other capital consumption, indirect business taxes, and the nontax liabilities of government.

Need may be defined as a lack of something requisite, desirable, or useful.

Negligence is the failure by a firm to use such reasonable care and caution in the production of a good or service as would be expected of a prudent firm.

New Product Development is a strategic product decision that is concerned with the process of developing new products. The six stages in the process are exploration, screening, business analysis, product development, test marketing, and commercialization.

NNI is an abbreviation for net natural increase in population. It is the difference between the crude birth rate (CBR) and the crude death rate (CDR).

Nolo Contendere refers to a plea of no contest by a defendant in a legal proceeding. As used herein it refers to price-fixing cases that are resolved by an agreement between the defendant and the government.

Nondollar Exchange is a term that refers to those marketing activities that do not involve a strict dollar-for-resource exchange.

Nonprice Effects on Demand refer to shifts in the entire demand curve generated by such non-price effects as changes in taste or changes in technology.

Nontariff Barriers to Trade include quotas, which limit the quantity of the good being traded, and other restrictions such as limiting or prohibiting trade for health reasons or national security.

Not-for-profit Marketing is the application of marketing principles and practices to non-profit organizations.

Objectives are desired levels of attainment.

Oligopoly is a market setting where there are a few large sellers and each has a market share sufficiently large so that its actions affect the other firms. Entry to the market is restricted and competition is usually based on marketing mix factors other than price.

Open Systems interact constantly with and have their actions modified by their external environments.

Order Cycle Time refers to the total time lapse between a customer's placement of an order and receipt of the desired products.

Order Filling is the process of getting an order, once received, to the customer and encompasses the firm's distribution activities.

Order Getting is the process of obtaining orders for a firm and includes such marketing activities as advertising, marketing research, and sales.

Organized Behavior System is a term used to identify an organism in which people are the interacting components. Therefore, a business firm is appropriately identified as an organized behavior system.

Per Se Violations is a term that implies that certain types of business agreements, such as price fixing, are considered inherently anticompetitive and injurious to the public without any need to determine if the agreement has actually injured market competition.

Personal Income is national income minus corporate profits and social security contributions, plus dividends, government transfer payments to individuals, net interest paid by government, money and imputed income received by individuals, unincorporated businesses, and nonprofit institutions.

Personal Selling is the oral presentation in a conversation with one or more prospective purchasers for the purpose of making a sale.

Petroleum Bulk Stations are specialized merchant wholesalers that handle a wide range of liquid petroleum products in bulk.

Physical Design Obsolescence occurs when a product is planned and made to wear out within a relatively short period of time.

Physical Distribution involves the determination of inventory levels and dispersion along with the selection of transportation modes.

Piggy-backing is a term used in the field of transportation to identify the shipment of truck trailers on railroad flat cars. The benefits of two transportation modes can be obtained by using this innovation.

Place Utility is created through marketing activities (transportation, for example) that make products available *where* customers wish to buy.

Possession Utility is created through marketing activities (selling, for example) that provide for the transfer of title or ownership of products.

Postindustrial Society may be characterized by a deemphasis on economic growth, an increase in leisure time, and an interest in the dignity of the individual. Although more abstract than concrete, pockets of postindustrial society exist in parts of the United States, Sweden, and other Scandinavian countries.

Postponed Obsolescence occurs when an innovation is held back so that a newer model may be introduced at a later time to make the earlier model out of date.

Price Discrimination exists when a buyer pays a price that is different from the price paid by another buyer for an identical product or service. Price discrimination is prohibited if the effect of this discrimination may be to substantially lessen or injure competition, except where it was implemented to dispose of perishable or obsolete goods, the result of differences in costs incurred, or given in good faith to meet an equally low price of a competitor.

Price Effects on Demand refer to movements along the demand curve generated by changes in price.

Price Elasticity of Demand for a good describes the relative change in quantity demanded of a good resulting from a unit change in price.

Price-fixing is the cooperative setting of price levels or ranges by competing firms.

Price Policies are established by management as a guide to the formulation of price strategy and the implementation of price tactics.

Price Strategies represent the actual pricing practices of firms. In formulating price strategies, marketers are influenced by costs, demand, and competition.

Price Tactics represent the moves followed by management in setting specific prices.

Pricing Objectives are the goals that a company wishes to accomplish in its price making decisions.

Private Foreign Direct Investment is defined for most purposes by the U.S. Government as any investment by a citizen, corporate or otherwise, that amounts to at least 10 percent control of a foreign firm.

Product Differentiation is a product strategy designed to attract demand through the offering of products with features, quality, style, or images that can be differentiated from rival product offerings.

Product Elimination is a strategic product decision that is concerned with the task of eliminating marginal items from a company's product line.

Product Liability refers to the legal liability of sellers to compensate buyers for damages suffered because of defects in goods purchased.

Product Life Cycle is a term used to identify the life span of a product. The four stages in the life cycle are introduction, growth, maturity, and decline.

Product Modification is a strategic product decision that is concerned with the task of improving existing products. This may be accomplished through quality, feature, and style changes.

Product Positioning refers to the marketers attempt to find a distinct position for a company's product in the competitive field. This may be accomplished through positioning strategy in the introduction of new products or through repositioning strategy designed to find a new position for an existing product.

Production is concerned with the problems of plant layout, materials handling, inventory control, quality control, and the administrative organization of the production function.

Productivity relates the level of desirable output to the level of inputs required to produce that output.

Products are tangible items with the capability of providing need satisfaction.

Promotion Strategy is the means of informing, persuading, and reminding consumers about the firm and its product(s) through optimal combinations of advertising, personal selling, sales promotion, packaging, branding, public relations, and publicity.

Psychographic Characteristics identify mental characteristics, or the mental behavior of individuals in the marketplace.

Psychology is the study of individual behavior through an analysis of learning, perception, personality, attitudes, and motivation.

Public Relations includes those activities of a corporation, union, government, or other organization in building and maintaining sound relations with special publics, and with the public at large.

Public Warehouses are privately owned storage facilities that profit by renting space and performing certain related services for others.

Publicity is the nonpersonal stimulation of demand for a product, service, or business unit through non-paid-for commercially significant news in a published medium or favorable presentation on radio, television, or stage.

Pure Competition refers to a market setting in which there exists such a large number of sellers and buyers that no one is capable of influencing price. Also included is a homogeneous product and easy access to the market. This setting is identified as the form of market that will lead to the most efficient allocation of resources, but it is doubtful if it exists.

Raw Materials Producers are those individuals and organizations in the macro marketing system that operate in the field of agriculture, forestry, commercial fishing, and mining.

Reference Groups are those individuals or groups to which a person looks for shaping personal attitudes or actions.

Remarketing refers to the implementation of product strategy that is designed to find new applications for old products. It is a strategy of increasing sales by finding new uses and new markets for existing products.

Resale Price Maintenance is an agreement between a manufacturer and retailer that the latter should not resell below a specified minimum price. The Federal laws which exempted this from antitrust action were repealed in 1976.

Research and Development is concerned primarily with the translation of technology into marketable products.

Retail Establishments operate in the macro marketing system to serve the household consumer, and the retailer is a type of middleman who buys and sells goods for final consumption.

Rights of Consumers include the right to safety, to be informed, to choose, and to be heard.

Rule of Reason refers to a criterion adopted by the courts in the 1911 Standard Oil and American Tobacco Company cases for applying the Sherman Act. The rule presumably requires an examination of the "effects" of an alleged violation in order to determine whether, in fact, a violation has occurred.

Sales Promotion is the activities other than personal selling, advertising, and other forms of promotion, that stimulate consumer purchasing and dealer effectiveness, such as displays, shows and exhibitions, demonstrations, and various nonrecurring selling efforts.

SBA is the abbreviation for the Small Business Administration. This Federal Government agency is an important interface between government and business in the development of commercially viable technology.

Segment Analysis is used to isolate marketing performance by product line, sales territory, or other logical division of sales activity.

Segmentation is the process of taking a large heterogeneous market for a product and dividing it into a number of submarkets or segments, each of which tends to be homogeneous in a number of important characteristics.

Service Establishments are commercial operations in the macro marketing system that provide services for both household and nonhousehold customers. These include management consulting companies, accounting firms, and barbershops.

Service Organizations in a metamarketing context include social welfare agencies, hospitals, schools, legal aid societies, mental health clinics, and the like.

Services are intangible items with the capability of providing need satisfaction.

Shopping Stores are those stores for which the consumer has not developed a complete preference map relative to the product to be purchased, thus requiring the consumer to undertake a search to construct such a map before purchase.

Social Classes are groupings of people whose socioeconomic status is objectively similar.

Social Marketing may be defined as the design, implementation, and control of programs seeking to increase the acceptability of a social idea or practice in a target group.

Social Responsibility may be defined as "good neighborliness." This refers to actions that do not spoil the neighborhood and voluntary acts that help solve neighborhood problems.

Socialization is the learning of one's culture.

Societal Marketing is a term used to identify the broader scope of marketing beyond the provision of a quantity of goods and services. This concept of marketing recognizes the qualitative aspects of life and suggests that marketers must be concerned with societal welfare.

Sociocultural Environment is a term used to identify those forces in the macro marketing environment that pertain to the values and institutions that shape the patterns of living in society.

Sociology is the study of social groupings such as social class, reference groups, and the family.

Sorting Process involves four distinct operations performed in the macro marketing system that are required in the movement of goods from production to consumption or use. These are sorting out, accumulation, allocation, and assorting.

Specialty Stores are those stores for which the consumer, before a need for some product arises, possesses a preference map that indicates a willingness to buy the item from a particular establishment, even though it may not be the most accessible.

Standards are forms of objectives, but are narrower in scope and represent desired levels of attainment for the utilization of resources.

Standard Metropolitan Statistical Area is an integrated economic and social unit with a total population of at least 100,000 people, including a central city or "twin cities" each with a minimum population of 50,000.

Strict Liability is a concept presently applied by the courts in product liability cases in which a seller is liable for any and all defective or hazardous products which unduly threaten a consumer's personal safety. This concept applies to all members involved in the manufacturing and selling of any facet of the product.

Structuralists are those economists who believe that market conduct is determined by market structure. A concentrated industry structure is assumed to be a major cause of inefficient competition.

Style Obsolescence, including fashion obsolescence, occurs when a useful product is made obsolete through advertising and promotion.

Subcultures are smaller groups of the total culture, such as nationality groups, geographic areas, and racial groups.

Suboptimization is the process of tuning a system to achieve an overall optimum level of output, even though this may force individual components of the system to operate at suboptimal levels.

Supply Curves are graphical representations of supply schedules.

Supply Schedules show the quantity of a good that producers are willing to supply at given prices.

System Inputs include information and material inputs used as a basis for decision making and to facilitate system operation.

System Outputs are the end products of system activity, including both informational and material outputs.

Systems are complex entities whose components must act in a coordinated manner to achieve desired outputs.

Systems Approach refers to the application of systems theory to the analysis of business activities and the operation of the firm.

Tariff Barriers to trade are essentially taxes on trade. Ad valorem tariffs charge a percentage of the value of the goods while specific tariffs charge a fixed amount per unit.

Technical Efficiency is a micro concept which refers primarily to the manner in which resources are allocated within a firm or industry.

Technological Environment is a term used to identify those forces in the macro environment that relate to the application of scientific knowledge in the field of business to the development of new products and functions, or the improvement of existing products and functions.

Test Marketing involves the selection of two or more cities or markets to serve as test areas for a marketing program on a small scale level. Results are evaluated as the basis for a decision to implement the marketing program in a larger market.

Third World Nations are developing economies not in the U.S.-Western European industrialized world nor in the Communist-influenced world.

Time Utility is created through marketing activities (storage, for example) that make products available *when* customers wish to buy.

Total Cost Concept refers to the total cost of product distribution, including transportation, warehousing, inventory control, and packaging.

Transfer Pricing is the pricing of goods sold from one plant of a corporation to another plant of the same corporation.

Transportation Modes include railroads, motor carriers, water carriers, pipelines, and airlines.

Trusts are legal devices for bringing a number of independent firms under a common control. They are formed by a majority of the voting stockholders of two or more independent firms turning over their voting stock to a common group of "trustees."

Undifferentiated Oligopolies are industries that sell products that are homogeneous in nature, such as steel, nylon, or bread.

Utility is the want-satisfaction power of a product or service.

Venture Teams are organizational arrangements that combine specialists from marketing, research and development, engineering, production, and finance to work on the development of new products. Linked directly to top management, the team normally functions separately from the regular organization structure and is dissolved at the end of the project.

Vertical Channel Systems represent an integration of individual distribution channel members into an organized entity through direct ownership, administration, or contract.

Wholesale Intermediaries are middlemen in the macro marketing system who perform marketing functions and facilitate exchange on the wholesale level of distribution.

Wholesaling involves marketing transactions in which the purchaser is actuated by a profit or business motive in making the purchase, whether the goods are purchased for resale in the same form or for use in the business or industrial process.

NAME INDEX

Aaker, David A., 312, 525, 526, 527
Adams, Corwin D., 407
Adams, W., 407
Adelman, M. A., 407
Adler, Lee, 105, 311, 341
Agodo, Orize, 377
Aldag, Ramon J., 469, 549
Alderson, Wroe, 30, 58, 222
Alexis, Marcus, 312
Alpert, Mark I., 140
Andersen, R. Clifton, 197, 223
Anderson, W. Thomas, Jr., 31, 59, 253
Andreasen, Alan R., 527
Anthony, Robert N., 83, 88, 468
Armstrong, Gary M., 436
Arpan, Jeffrey S., 285

Bagozzi, Richard P., 31, 341
Bain, Joe S., 408
Baker, James C., 285
Barksdale, Hiram C., 31
Bartels, Robert, 484–485, 493, 532, 549
Beckman, Thedore N., 30, 208, 222, 375, 407
Beik, L. L., 253
Bell, M. L., 253
Bell, Martin, 55–56, 59
Belli, David, 284
Beman, Lewis, 375, 376
Bentley, Catherine Carlisle, 31
Bernhard, R. C., 381, 406
Berry, Leonard L., 59, 170, 526, 527
Bessom, R. M., 223
Blackwell, Roger D., 311, 312, 313
Blau, Peter M., 549
Bleiberg, Robert M., 376
Blomstrom, Robert L., 197, 435, 436
Boewadt, Robert J., 59
Bott, Elizabeth, 312
Bowersox, Donald J., 113, 469
Brooks, John, 30
Brower, Marvin, 468
Brown, Stephen W., 170, 521, 526, 527
Brozen, Yale, 376
Bucklin, Louis P., 169, 170, 197, 205, 207, 222
Burck, Gilbert, 341
Burley, James R., 376

Burton, John, 113
Buskirk, Richard H., 170, 525
Buzby, S. L., 253
Buzzell, Robert D., 408
Bybee, H. Malcolm, 493

Caffyn, John, 284
Caplovitz, David, 526
Carper, Jean, 500, 526
Carruth, Eleanore, 408
Carson, Rachel, 507
Caves, Richard, 345–346, 374
Celler, Emanuel, 504
Churchill, G. A., Jr., 253
Churchman, C. West, 88, 89
Clark, J. M., 388, 407
Claycamp, Henry J., 141
Cleland, David I., 89, 113
Clewett, R. M., 222
Cohen, Dorothy, 527
Comer, James M., 469
Converse, Paul D., 243, 252
Cooper, Arnold C., 59
Cooper, P. D., 223
Copeland, Melvin T., 205, 222
Corr, Arthur V., 341, 469
Cox, Keith K., 113, 311–312
Cox, Steven R., 403–404, 408
Cracco, Etienne, 563
Cravens, David W., 140, 499, 569
Crawford, C. Merle, 569
Crowningshield, Gerald R., 468
Cullen, Michael, 429–430
Cullwick, David, 569
Cundiff, Edward W., 171
Cunningham, Isabella C. M., 376, 527
Cunningham, William H., 376, 527

Darden, Bill, 31
Darling, John R., 184, 468
Davidson, William R., 30, 208, 222, 375, 407, 435
Davis, Grant M., 170
Davis, Harry L., 312
Davis, Keith, 88, 89, 197, 435, 436

Davis, Kenneth R., 112, 113
Dawson, L. M., 253
Day, George S., 312, 525, 526, 527
Dean, Joel, 386, 407
Deardon, John, 83, 88
Dhalla, Nariman K., 113
Diamond, Steven L., 527
Dickinson, R. A., 223
Dickinson, Roger, 170
Dickson, Clyde H., 103
Dimsdale, Parks B., Jr., 170, 521, 527
Dommermuth, William P., 197, 223
Donnelly, James H., Jr., 223, 493
Doody, Alton F., 435
Downing, George D., 99, 112, 113, 170
Drucker, Peter F., 475–476, 492, 525
Duncan, Delbert J., 30
Duncan, Patricia L., 469
Dunckel, Earll B., 435

Eels, Kenneth, 312
Eilbirt, Henry, 473, 487, 489, 492, 493, 549
El-Ansary, Adel I., 170
Engel, Ernst, 238–239
Engel, James J., 311, 312, 313
Enis, Ben M., 112, 113, 169, 383, 407, 447, 493
Etzel, Michael J., 170, 223

Faber, Ronald, 527
Farrell, Jack W., 469
Farris, Martin T., 170, 222, 468
Feldman, Laurence P., 436
Firat, Fuat A., 377
Fisk, George, 30, 85–86, 88, 89
Ford, Gerald, 507–508, 524
Ford, Henry, 8, 109
Ford, N. M., 253
Forrester, Jay W., 81, 88, 89
Frank, Isaiah, 284
Frank, Ronald E., 112
Freidlin, Julius, 284
Fry, Albert Wesley, 169

585

SUBJECT INDEX